SECRECY AND THE MEDIA

Secrecy and the Media is the first book to examine the development of the D-Notice system, which regulates the UK media's publication of British national security secrets. It is based on official documents, many of which have not previously been available to a general audience, as well as on media sources.

From Victorian times, British governments have consistently seen the need, in the public interest, to prevent the media publishing secret information which would endanger national security. The UK media have meanwhile continuously resisted official attempts to impose any form of censorship, arguing that a free press is in the public interest. Both sides have normally seen the pitfalls of attempting to resolve this sometimes acrimonious conflict of interests by litigation, and have together evolved a system of editorial self-regulation, assisted by day-to-day independent expert advice, known colloquially as the D-Notice System.

This book traces the development of the system from nineteenth-century colonial campaigns, through two World Wars, to modern operations and counter-terrorism in the post-Cold War era, up to the beginning of the Labour government in 1997. Examples are drawn from media, political and official sources (some not yet open), and cover not only defence issues (including Special Forces), but also the activities of the secret intelligence services MI5, MI6 and GCHQ. These cases relate principally to the UK, but also to American and other allies' interests.

The story of how this sometimes controversial institution now operates in the modern world will be essential reading for those in the media and government departments, and for academics and students in the fields of security, defence and intelligence, as well as being an accessible exposé for the general reader.

Nicholas Wilkinson served in the Royal Navy 1959 to 1998, and from 1999 to 2004 he ran the independent Defence, Press and Broadcasting Advisory Committee. He was a Press Complaints Commissioner from 2005 to 2008, and is a Cabinet Office Historian.

WHITEHALL HISTORIES: GOVERNMENT OFFICIAL HISTORY SERIES

ISSN: 1474–8398

The Government Official History series began in 1919 with wartime histories, and the peacetime series was inaugurated in 1966 by Harold Wilson. The aim of the series is to produce major histories in their own right, compiled by historians eminent in the field, who are afforded free access to all relevant material in the official archives. The Histories also provide a trusted secondary source for other historians and researchers while the official records are not in the public domain. The main criteria for selection of topics are that the histories should record important episodes or themes of British history while the official records can still be supplemented by the recollections of key players; and that they should be of general interest, and, preferably, involve the records of more than one government department.

THE UNITED KINGDOM AND THE EUROPEAN COMMUNITY
Vol. I: The Rise and Fall of a National Strategy, 1945–1963
Alan S. Milward

SECRET FLOTILLAS
Vol. I: Clandestine Sea Operations to Brittany, 1940–1944
Vol. II: Clandestine Sea Operations in the Mediterranean, North Africa and the Adriatic, 1940–1944
Sir Brooks Richards

SOE IN FRANCE
M. R. D. Foot

THE OFFICIAL HISTORY OF THE FALKLANDS CAMPAIGN:
Vol. I: The Origins of the Falklands War
Vol. II: War and Diplomacy
Sir Lawrence Freedman

THE OFFICIAL HISTORY OF BRITAIN AND THE CHANNEL TUNNEL
Terry Gourvish

CHURCHILL'S MYSTERY MAN: DESMOND MORTON AND THE WORLD OF INTELLIGENCE
Gill Bennett

THE OFFICIAL HISTORY OF PRIVATISATION
Vol. I: The Formative Years 1970–1987
David Parker

SECRECY AND THE MEDIA: THE OFFICIAL HISTORY OF THE UNITED KINGDOM'S D-NOTICE SYSTEM
Nicholas Wilkinson

SECRECY AND THE MEDIA

The Official History of the United Kingdom's
D-Notice System

Nicholas Wilkinson

Routledge
Taylor & Francis Group

LONDON AND NEW YORK

First published 2009
by Routledge
2 Park Square, Milton Park, Abingdon, Oxon, OX14 4RN

Simultaneously published in the USA and Canada
by Routledge
270 Madison Avenue, New York, NY 10016

Routledge is an imprint of the Taylor & Francis Group, an informa business

© 2009 Crown Copyright

Typeset in Times New Roman PS by
Florence Production Ltd, Stoodleigh, Devon
Printed and bound in Great Britain by
TJ International Ltd, Padstow, Cornwall

British Library Cataloguing in Publication Data
A catalogue record for this book is available from the British Library

Library of Congress Cataloging in Publication Data
Wilkinson, Nicholas, 1941–.
Secrecy and the media: the official history of the United Kingdom's
D-notice system/Nicholas Wilkinson.
p. cm.
1. Freedom of the press – Great Britain.   2. Censorship – Great Britain.
3. Executive privilege (Government information) – Great Britain.
4. National security – Law and legislation – Great Britain.
5. Official secrets – Great Britain.   I. Title.
KD4114.W55 2009
342.4108′53 – dc22   2008051506

Published on behalf of the Whitehall History Publishing Consortium.
Applications to reproduce Crown copyright protected
material in this publication should be submitted in writing to:
HMSO, Copyright Unit, St Clements House, 2–16 Colegate,
Norwich NR3 1BQ. Fax: 01603 723000.
E-mail: copyright@hmso.gov.uk

ISBN10: 0–415–45375–5 (hbk)
ISBN10: 0–203–87645–8 (ebk)

ISBN13: 978–0–415–45375–2 (hbk)
ISBN13: 978–0–203–87645–9 (ebk)

To the sailors, marines, wrens, soldiers and airmen, dead and surviving, from whose courage, pragmatism and humour I have learnt so much during my long public service.

The author has been given full access to official documents. He alone is responsible for the statements made and the views expressed.

CONTENTS

FOREWORD

The 'D-Notice' system is a compact between the British Government and the British media to prevent inadvertent damage to national security through the public disclosure of highly sensitive information. A natural and quite correct tension exists between Government (charged to run the country) and the Media (their natural watchdogs). Yet uniquely in the closely-defined area of national security and alone in the World, Britain's Government and Media set to one side these tensions and work together formally in the public interest.

The system first came into being in 1912 and has evolved progressively ever since. The expression so common in the post-World War II era of 'slapping a D-Notice on it' became synonymous with a 'back-door' form of censorship. Yet, right from its inception, the system involved collective and widespread consent from the Media and compromise and restraint by the Government.

The advice offered was purely guidance, supported by no legal sanction, and could be rejected or accepted in whole or in part, an arrangement which was formalised in 1993 when D-Notices became Defence Advisory (DA) Notices. So they remain today, and in every case an editor is fully responsible for whatever national security information he or she publishes or broadcasts. The Notices (at one time closely-guarded and attracting the official security classification of 'Confidential') and the working arrangements of the Defence Press and Broadcasting Advisory Committee (the DPBAC: the body that oversees the System) have for some years been available to the world on the 'dnotice' website (http://www.dnotice.org.uk/). Moreover, although not subject to the Freedom of Information Acts, the system practices a policy of maximum transparency, consistent with the undertakings of strict confidentiality it gives to all those who deal with it. A history of anything which is still in existence can never be completely up to date. This account ends in 1997, when the Labour administration took power. But it would be wrong to infer that since then the DA Notice system has not continued to evolve and develop. The system has always 'moved with the times' and in recent years the pace of progress has, perhaps, been faster than ever before. As the technology of information collection, collation and dissemination has accelerated, so the development of the DA Notice System has had to keep pace.

Views on what information should – or should not – be considered to be widely available in the public domain have been (and continue to be) revolutionised by the internet, the growing impact of which is under constant and active debate by the DPBAC. A representative of Google has recently joined the committee. Of equal significance is the arrival of the 24-hour news cycle. The live transmission of news, enabled by satellites and other new technology, has put increased pressure on the Committee Secretary. In some cases he may have only minutes to intervene to try to prevent publication of something which could damage national security. But technology is by no means the only driver in the DA Notice system's development. The increase in the international terror threat in 2001, and Britain's involvement subsequently in large-scale combat operations, led the committee to review its role and its remit, and have shaped the development of the system.

All that said, the way the system now operates, and the possibilities for future evolution, cannot be properly understood without knowing its history. Why and how it came into being, the dynamics of the relationships between the main architects, 'trustees' and executives and the various trials and storms to which it has been subject over the years have been extremely important in making the system what it is today. Despite its obvious limitations and the existence of clear alternatives, the D/DA Notice system continues to exist and indeed prosper. Why this is so is traced in the pages of this book.

We, as its temporary guardians, sit on opposite sides in the committee room, and inevitably have our disagreements. But we are as one on this: the System remains the preferred choice of both Government and Media in the UK because, although clearly far from perfect, it is nevertheless well-suited to an imperfect world. As Churchill said of democracy, it's the worst system apart from all the others which have been tried. The enduring attractions of the DA-Notice system, and the lack of appeal of the possible alternatives, are 'secrets' that lie in the historical record. They can be found in the pages that follow.

Sir Bill Jeffrey, Chairman and
Simon Bucks, Vice-Chairman & Media-Side Chairman,
Defence Press and Broadcasting Advisory Committee,
September 2008

ABBREVIATIONS

1st Sea Lord	Head of Royal Navy (aka CNS)
ACPO	Association of Chief Police Officers
AEA	Atomic Energy Authority
AERE	Atomic Energy Research Establishment
AOC	Air Officer Commanding
AUS	Assistant Under Secretary (civil servant)
AWOAMPC	Admiralty, War Office, Air Ministry and Press Committee
AWOPC	Admiralty, War Office and Press Committee
AWRE	Atomic Weapons Research Establishment
BARRAS	Operations Sierra Leone 2002
BBC	British Broadcasting Company/Corporation
BEF	British Expeditionary Force
BLPES	British Library of Political and Economic Science
BoT	Board of Trade
BSkyB	British Sky Broadcasting
BST	British Summer Time
BUP	British United Press
C	Chief of Secret Intelligence Service (MI6)
C&AG	Comptroller and Auditor General
C(I)GS	Chief of the (Imperial) General Staff (head of British Army)
CAS	Chief of the Air Staff (head of the RAF)
CENTO	Central Treaty Organisation
CH	Companion of Honour
CIA	Central Intelligence Agency (US)
CID	Committee of Imperial Defence
CinC	Commander-in-Chief
CND	Campaign for Nuclear Disarmament
CNI	Critical National Infrastructure
CNS	Chief of Naval Staff (head of Royal Navy)
CNSC	Official Committee on Co-ordination of National Security Cases
CNZM	Companion of the New Zealand Order of Merit
CO	Commanding Officer

COI	Central Office of Information
CPGB	Communist Party of Great Britain
CPO	Chief Petty Officer or Chief Press Officer
CPR	Chief of Public Relations
CPU	Commonwealth Press Union
CSAR	Chief Superintendent Armament Research
CVA	Aircraft Carrier (fixed wing)
D(G)MI	Director General of Mobilisation and Intelligence
DA-Notice	Defence Advisory Notice
DAO&I	Director of Air Operations and Intelligence
DCI	Defence Council Instruction
DETERM	Operations Afghanistan 2001/2
DFC	Distinguished Flying Cross
DG	Director General
DGSS	Director General Security Service (MI5)
DIB	Delhi Intelligence Bureau
DIS	Defence Intelligence Staff
DMI	Director of Military Intelligence
DMO	Director of Military Operations
DNE	Director of Naval Education
DNI	Director of Naval Intelligence
DoE	Department of the Environment
DoRA	Defence of the Realm Act
DPA	Data Protection Act
DPBAC	Defence, Press and Broadcasting Advisory Committee
DPBC	Defence, Press and Broadcasting Committee
DPR	Director of Public Relations
DSC	Distinguished Service Cross
DSF	Director Special Forces
DSO	Distinguished Service Order
DUS	Deputy Under Secretary (civil servant)
EEC	European Economic Community
EOKA	Greek Cypriot Nationalist Independence organisation
EPU	Empire Press Union
EPU	European Press Union
ETA	Basque Terrorist Group
ETC	Exchange Telegraph Company
FANY	First Aid Nursing Yeomanry (and much more than nursing)
FCO	Foreign and Commonwealth Office
FM	Field Marshal
FO	Foreign Office
FoIA	Freedom of Information Act
FRU	Force Requirements Unit
GC&CS	Government Code and Cypher School
GC/GM	George Cross/Medal (for gallantry)
GCB,KCB,CB	Grades of Order of the Bath (military and civil service)

GCBE,KBE,OBE,MBE,BEM	Grades of Order of British Empire (anybody) (D = Dame)
GCHQ	Government Communications Headquarters
GCIE,GCSI etc	Defunct Indian Empire Orders
GCMG,KCMG,CMG	Grades of Order of Sts Michael and George (diplomats) (D = Dame)
GCVO,KCVO,CVO,LVO,MVO	Grades of the Royal Victorian Order (in Monarch's gift)
GEC	General Electric Company
GHQ	General Headquarters
GMTV	Good Morning TV
GOC	General Officer Commanding
GPO	General Post Office
GRANBY	Operations Iraq 1991
GRU	Soviet Military Intelligence Service
HCDC	House of Commons Defence Committee
HM	His/Her Majesty's
HMG	His/Her Majesty's Government
HMS	His/Her Majesty's Ship
HQ	Headquarters
IBA	Independent Broadcasting Authority
INLA	Irish National Liberation Army
IoJ	Institute of Journalists
IPC	International Publishing Corporation
IPI	International Press Institute
IRA	Irish Republican Army
ISPA	Internet Service Providers' Association
ITA	Independent Television Authority
ITN	Independent Television News
ITV	Independent Television
JIB	Joint Intelligence Board
JIB	Joint Intelligence Bureau
JIC	Joint Intelligence Committee
KC/QC	King's/Queen's Counsel
KG/LG, KT, KP	Knight/Lady of the Garter, Thistle (Scotland), St Patrick (Ireland)
KGB	Soviet Secret Intelligence/Security Service
LSE	London School of Economics
MAS	Military Advisory Service
MC	Military Cross
MD	Managing Director
Met	Metropolitan Police (London)
MI5	Security Service
MI6	Secret Intelligence Service
MI9	WWII Organisation for Escape and Evasion in Enemy Occupied Countries
MinTech	Ministry of Technology

MoD	Ministry of Defence
MoI	Ministry of Information
MoS	Mail on Sunday
MP	Member of Parliament
MRCA	Multi Role Combat Aircraft
MRT	Media Response team
NATO	North Atlantic Treaty Organisation
NCO	Non Commissioned Officer
NEC	National Emergency Council
NHS	National Health Service
NID	Naval Intelligence Division
NITAT	Northern Ireland Training and Advisory Team
No.10	No.10 Downing Street (Office/Residence of Prime Minister)
NPA	Newspaper Proprietors' Association
NPEC	Newspaper and Periodical Emergency Committee
NS	Newspaper Society
NSA	National Security Agency (US)
NUJ	National Union of Journalists
NZ	New Zealand
OCSE	Organisation for Security and Co-operation in Europe
OD(DIS)(O)	Governmental/Official Committees co-ordinating Secret Intelligence/Security administration
OM	Order of Merit
Op	Operation
OPEC	Organization of the Petroleum Exporting Countries
OSA	Official Secrets Act
P&B	Press and Broadcasting
P&C	Press and Censorship
PA	Press Association (usually) or Publishers' Association or Personal Assistant (see context)
PB	Press Bureau
PC	Privy Counsellor
PI	Public Information
PIRA	Provisional Irish Republican Army
PLO	Palestine Liberation Organisation
PPA	Periodical Proprietors' Association
PQ	Parliamentary Question
PR	Public Relations
PRO	Public Record Office
PSIS	Permanent Under Secretaries of Intelligence Services Committee
PTPWNPA	Periodicals, Trade Press, Weekly Newspaper Proprietors' Association (more often PPA)
PUS	Permanent Under-Secretary (senior civil servant)
PV	Positive Vetting
QC	Queen's Counsel

QGM	Queen's Gallantry Medal
QPM	Queen's Police Medal
RAF	Royal Air Force
RAFVR	RAF Volunteer Reserve
RARDE	Royal Armament Research and Development Establishment
RFC	Royal Flying Corps
RIC	Royal Irish Constabulary
RM	Royal Marines
RMA	Royal Mail Ship
RN	Royal Navy
RND	Royal Naval Division
RNVR	RN Volunteer Reserve
RUC	Royal Ulster Constabulary
RUSI	Royal United Services Institute for Defence Studies
S&I	Security and Intelligence
SALT	Strategic Arms Limitation Treaty
SAS	Special Air Service
SBS	Special Boat Service, Royal Marines
SDNS	Scottish Daily Newspaper Society
Sec	Secretary
SF	Special Forces
Sigint	Signals Intelligence
SIPO	Official Committee on Defence, Intelligence and Security public disclosure
SIS	Secret Intelligence Service
SOE	Special Operations Executive (WWII)
SofS	Secretary of State
SPBC	Services, Press and Broadcasting Committee
SS	Steam Ship
SSB	Secret Service Bureau
SSVC	Services Sounds and Vision Corporation
T Sol	Treasury Solicitor
TA	Territorial Army
TD	Territorial Decoration (medal)
TELIC	Operations Iraq from 2003
TNA	The National Archives
TNT	Trinitrotoluene (explosive)
TU	Trades Union
TUC	Trades Union Congress
UDA	Ulster Defence Association
UFF	Ulster Freedom Fighters
UKSF	United Kingdom Special Forces
UN	United Nations
USAF	US Air Force
USN	US Navy
USofS	Under Secretary of State

ABBREVIATIONS

USSR	Union of Soviet Socialist Republics
UTV	Ulster Television
UVF	Ulster Volunteer Force
VC	Victoria Cross (highest award for valour)
VJ	Victory over Japan
VSTOL	Vertical/Short Take-off Launch
WEU	Western European Union
WMD	Weapons of Mass Destruction
WO	War Office
WWI	First World War
WWII	Second World War
YMCA	Young Men's Christian Association

PREFACE

'And though all the winds of doctrine were let loose to play on earth, so Truth be in the field, we do injuriously by licensing and prohibiting misdoubt her strength. Let her and Falsehood grapple; who ever knew Truth put to the worse in a free and open encounter?' – John Milton, 'Areopagitica', November 1644, pamphlet in defence of the liberty of unlicensed printing, then under threat by the Parliament which otherwise he supported; referred to in a debate on D-Notices in the House of Commons April 1939.

'Secrecy is the essence of successful warfare. Publicity is the essence of successful journalism. How is a common ground to be found or manufactured between these abrupt opposites?' – Sydney Brooks, 'The Press in War-Time', *Fortnightly*, 1907.

'The main principle stands, and must stand, unshaken. Complete frankness on the one side; loyal discretion on the other; and mutual co-operation in the great and almost sacred task of educating and steadying the public, especially in times of national stress or crisis.' – Major General JH Beith (pen name as an author 'Ian Hay'), Public Relations Officer to the War Office, in a speech to the Institute of Journalists, April 1939.

'The task of the Secretary was an unenviable one and I doubted whether any man would be regarded as ideal at all times by all sides. He had to run with the hare and hunt with the hounds.' – Sir Martin Furnival Jones, Director General of the Security Service, about the D-Notice Secretary post, to Lord Radcliffe, 1967.

'Security also lies in the value of our free institutions. A cantankerous Press, an obstinate Press, a ubiquitous Press must be suffered by those in authority in order to preserve the even greater values of freedom of expression and the right of the People to know.' – United States Judge Murray Gurfein, in his Pentagon Papers Opinion, 1971.

'You can't have a free society without a free Press, Bernard.' – Prime Minister Mrs Thatcher to her Press Secretary Bernard Ingham during the early years of her Premiership; quoted with delight by him back to her whenever subsequently she took a less dispassionate view; and to this author 24 July 2007.

'The D Notice system is one of those quaintly British institutions which should be preserved as long as possible.' – Robert Edwards, Editor of the *Sunday Mirror*, to the House of Commons Defence Committee, 5 June 1980.

'We do not believe it would be right to attempt to introduce a formal censorship system at home in any future limited conflict. There would, however, be merit in providing an improved advisory service for editors and journalists who might be unsure whether the publication of certain information would be detrimental to military operations.' – 'The Beach Report', Study Group on Censorship, December 1983, after the Falklands Conflict, recommending the continued involvement of the D-Notice Committee.

The Two Sides of the Public Interest

The British 'D-Notice System' exists to provide advice, to the Media and to officials, about the publication of national security matters.

Although this is an *Official* History, it must however be rather different from most in that category, rather quirkier. For a start, it deals with a system which 'belongs' as much to the Media as it does to officials. It therefore represents two aspects of the public interest, by their nature often in opposition. They are, in simplistic terms, the public's right to know what is being done in its name, versus the governmental need to keep certain things secret for the time being in order to maintain the security of the public.

There are many other inherent dichotomies. The D-Notice System operates in a highly political area: national security. Politicians have responsibilities in both the above conflicting areas of public interest, and the right and duty from time to time to scrutinise and comment on the System. But the System is also necessarily apolitical, in the sense that the direct involvement of Party Politicians in its routine workings would jeopardise its delicately balanced nature – non-statutory, voluntary, independent, adversarial, pragmatic, semi-formal, yet accepted almost invariably, if not invariably happily, as representative both of the Media and of officials. And, as is recorded in this book, Political intervention has indeed occasionally jeopardised the workings and even the continuance of the D-Notice System.

It operates too in a predominantly grey area. In my research, I have found little evidence that the great institutions of our Nation (academe apart) have regularly been given to proactive, dispassionate, philosophical self-analysis, least of all about such vital but nebulous concepts as the public interest, and as freedom of expression and of the Media. We know approximately what we mean, and a pragmatic, often hasty, reaction to particular events is our norm, with full rein given to current special interests. National security is just such a generally understood term, and is mentioned in many Acts of Parliament, but it is nowhere defined. It is what governmental lawyers delightfully call 'an ambulatory concept', in other words something which, in the particular and unpredictable circumstances of each case, will be defined at the time for that case, by politicians, or by officials, or by courts, according to the circumstances.

Or by the D-Notice Committee (as it is colloquially known, despite several changes of official title since its inception[1]); or, even more commonly, day-to-day on the Committee's behalf by its only full-time post-holder, the D-Notice Secretary. In practice therefore there is scope for wide interpretation of what national security means in differing circumstances, to different people, at different times. Such differing interpretations are discussed where appropriate in this book. It would be highly unlikely today, for example, that (as happened during World War I) the D-Notice System would be applied to Rasputin and to The Queen of The Belgians – in separate communications, I hasten to add.

A further twist is that, although the System exists within a framework of the law, it has no direct connection with the law nor with the several Acts of Parliament dealing with national security, such as the Official Secrets Act(s) in force at the time. The D-Notice System interprets national security, as it applies to the Committee's work, in a much narrower sense than Government generally does. The Committee distinguishes between what might endanger the public (and its secret intelligence and security servants and their operations) and what might endanger wider (or narrower) Political interests. The Committee must take into account too what is already widely in the public domain. This is now a 'virtual' place, where the international and electronic dimensions of modern information dissemination make for nice and fluid judgements about what 'widely' means.

The D-Notice System in its current application is unique to the United Kingdom. It is imperfect, but a better system of self-regulation has not yet been devised, and generally it suits our particular national ways. It has evolved over about a hundred years, adapting to changing external circumstances, while retaining its fundamental characteristics. It remains relevant because the conflicting aspects of public interest outlined above are still relevant. And because at present both the governmental and the Media sides continue to prefer adversarial self-regulation, with agreed and informed advice, to the alternatives commonly used in other countries: legislation, litigation and/or varying degrees of direct and indirect intimidation of the Media by the Political apparatus.

The Audiences of This History

This History is directed at several very different audiences: professional historians, students of journalism, editors and others already in the Media coming for the first time into jobs which deal with national security, officials and military being appointed to posts which interact with the Media, parliamentarians, and, most importantly, the wider public in whose interest the D-Notice System exists. Furthermore, the number and international origins of the hundreds of thousands of hits on the D-Notice website (*www.dnotice.org.uk*) since it was revitalised in 2000, have brought home to me that those who read this book, including many who live in the United Kingdom, will *not* invariably have an intimate knowledge of the history of this country.

The chapters which follow therefore include much general background information which will be already well known to some, and conversely much detail which is of only passing interest to the general reader. Few will need to read every paragraph carefully, nor to absorb every one of the copious footnotes, in order nevertheless to acquire a good idea of the nature and development of the D-Notice System, and of the continuing conflict between the two aspects of public interest described above, as represented by the Official and the Media sides of the Committee.

Despite the background of significant historical events and of sometimes colourful characters involved, much of the actual work of the D-Notice Committee and Secretary has always been dry, detailed, and commonplace. It has dealt most often with media stories which, even when true, were the stuff of the next week's fish-and-chip wrapping or these days of the paper recycling bin or the 'Delete' key. The several ex-naval holders of the Secretary post have found the work not dissimilar to operations at sea: long periods of routine activity and of unseen threat to equilibrium, interspersed with short periods of intense excitement, caused sometimes by hostile elements or by the hazards of the environment, but more often by human failings.

Similarly, if I have dwelt sometimes on events and personalities which are unusual, resonant to modern minds, colourful, or significant to the principles of the public interests involved, the reader will I hope accept that the unmentioned routine advice of the Committee's Secretary, to officials and military and to editors and journalists and publishers, has meanwhile been continuing; in the same way that even when those directing a ship's operations are completely absorbed by the excitement of action, somewhere below a mechanic is routinely lubricating the machinery.

The Form of the Book

The form of the book is chronological, as this most clearly shows the evolutionary nature of the System, but certain recurring themes, principles and arguments are highlighted. Interspersed through various sections of the book, the nature and work of the D-Notice Committee is put in the context of its period, as regards both the general security situation and also the development and wider concerns of the Media. Those parts are a very potted and *non*-official history, intended to give the unfamiliar reader enough background to understand why things were happening, and the kinds of people who were involved; this has been done to a greater extent for the earlier years than for the better-known recent decades. Footnotes are likewise intended as much for the general reader who may not be knowledgeable about all the events and personalities referred to, as for scholars, for whom many research references are included.

Clearly, in covering governmental/media interaction from before the Boer War until post-Cold War, it would be impracticable and tedious to mention every case with which successive D-Notice Secretaries have dealt. Instead, where records still exist, sufficient detail has been given of formal meetings of the Committee (which are the buoys marking its passage through history), and of its modus operandi, illustrated briefly by examples, with a fuller description of selected individual cases. This is intended both to fulfil the role of record of an Official History, and also to give the wider public an understanding of how the System has worked at successive periods in the past, and how it has evolved to operate today, somewhat differently.

Whether the System is wholly representative of the wider public is another matter; in writing this book, I have become ever more conscious that, even in modern times, the interlocking circles of government, officials, military, and relevant parts of the media are notably white, male and middle-class (very upper to clerkly lower); all seethe rivalrously with testosterone. Yet, in studying the history of the D-Notice System, and the involvement of so many men once considered important, by themselves and often by others, we are spectators at a parade of imperial and post-imperial ghosts. It is too early to tell whether their successors, on an even more global and intercommunicable stage, will have different attitudes to the conflicting poles of public interest.

I have been very conscious while writing this book that Official Histories are concurrently being written of the Security Service, the Secret Intelligence Service, and the Joint Intelligence Committee; these will provide more detailed background to this book, which I have not therefore duplicated. This History is complementary to them, as it is to more mainstream national and international events barely covered here. One uncomfortable aspect for all Official Historians is that they are not permitted to include secret governmental matters which, although now in the public domain, have not so far been officially confirmed nor denied. This book has also been restricted to events before mid-1997. Finally, although this History is intended to contribute to Freedom of Information, those readers hoping for fresh revelations of highly secret matters will, I regret, be disappointed; one of the quaint aspects of Official Secrecy in Britain is that, despite the strenuous efforts of all those involved in preserving it, not much remains secret for ever, or usually even for very long.

Acknowledgements

I owe warm thanks to many who have assisted or advised in the research and writing of this History. These include: my late Deputy D-Notice Secretary Commander Francis Ponsonby, who was to have written this book 2001–3, but who most sadly died whilst still undertaking the research, leaving for me copious notes and photocopies; Glenys Evans MBE and Nicky Georghiou, loyal and assiduous Personal Assistants to the D-Notice Secretary, 1986–2004 and 2004-present respectively; my three predecessors as D-Notice Secretary and our Deputies; Tessa Stirling, Head of the Cabinet Office's Histories, Openness and Records Unit, and Sally Falk of that department; the courteous National Archives staff for Kew's excellent service; recent DPBAC Vice-Chairman Bob Hutchinson and his successor Simon Bucks; Nigel Roche of the St Bride's Institute; Professor Christopher Andrew; several Professors of Journalism; the Guildhall Library Keeper of Manuscripts, the BBC Written Archivist, the Librarians of the London School of Economics and Political Science, and British Library; Mr Harry Chapman Pincher; the heads and staffs of GCHQ, SIS and especially the Security Service; all those who have been willing to discuss past events with me; Tom Johnston, General Kay, Edward Hill, and the staffs of the *Daily Express*, the *Daily Telegraph*, Getty Images, the National Portrait Gallery, the Press Association and Reuters, and in particular the generous Associated Press Ltd and of News International Ltd, for their permission to use cuttings and material for illustrations; my photographer son Chev Wilkinson for the cover montage; and Juliet Wilkinson, who has not only helped in my labours, but tolerated the inherently undomesticated behaviour of an author. This book's imperfections are despite the best efforts of all of the above; any idiosyncratic opinions are mine alone; any necessary corrections communicated will be gratefully received.

Nicholas Wilkinson, London

Section 1

PRE-FORMATION
The Long Debate, 1880s–1912

It is wise to disclose what cannot be concealed.

JF Schiller, Poet and Dramatist (1759–1805)

1

VICTORIAN NATIONAL SECURITY
AND PRESS INTERACTION

This is the story of over a century of wrangling between on the one hand politicians and officials, and on the other all forms of the Media. It is sometimes about great principles, more often about deadly detail. The Media have commonly felt under threat from slings and arrows of outrageous government; Governments from those of outrageous reporting. The D-Notice System was not created suddenly, in reaction to some major historical event, nor to meet some new public demand. It evolved slowly, in response to a confluence of trends in the late nineteenth and early twentieth Centuries. These trends included changes in the pattern of rivalry between the major European powers, developments in technologies (particularly those of communications and of warfare), sociological changes within the United Kingdom, the increasing complexity and organisation of British institutions (including the Press), the gradual weakening of Britain's economic strength relative to that of other countries, and decreasing self-confidence in the country's predominance as the world's most powerful nation.

The D-Notice System was not the idea of one individual or of one group. It emerged amorphously, across three decades of increasing concern about Army and Navy operations being compromised by reports in the British (and sometimes foreign) Press, in ways which gave useful intelligence to the enemy of the day. Each time there was a war crisis, governmental minds were exercised by how to censor the Press. But, each time, such thoughts provoked a combination of Press and Parliamentary resistance and of consequent governmental nervousness, in particular about driving anything through which smacked of the erosion of the liberty of Britons. No censorship legislation was therefore introduced before that particular crisis passed. There was, however, de facto censorship in theatres of operations themselves, and there was a limited Official Secrets Act. The institutions directly concerned (including the Press) felt, in their different ways, that how to avoid the publication of matters which would endanger security was a lingering problem, to which no satisfactory solution had been found.

The following chapters trace the slow evolution, from the 1880s onwards, towards the adversarial system of assisted self-regulation eventually agreed, in lieu of the imposition of censorship legislation. The general security and press contexts cover some contemporary parliamentary action, but it is not for this History to detail all the tortuous development of successive Official Secrets (and other restrictive) Acts; while relevant background to the operation of the D-Notice System, they do not directly dictate its modus operandi. This section focuses on internal official discussion, press reaction and interaction, and the lead-up to the establishment of the first joint Committee in 1912.

The Security Context

Those involved with national security have long been vividly conscious of the importance of the Press, whether for perceived benefit to the public weal or for personal enhancement. After the 1797 Battle of St Vincent, the future Vice Admiral Viscount Nelson took care to ensure that his part became known to the Press, by privately sending home information additional to that in his Commander-in-Chief's official dispatch. After his death in 1805, the Government needed a British superhero for the public, and some good news to balance Napoleon's continued conquests elsewhere in Europe; it ensured therefore not only that Nelson's funeral in 1806 was a State occasion, but also that it received lavish coverage in the Press; the first use of illustration in *The Times* was of the funeral. From the 1870s to the 1890s, the four times Prime Minister William Gladstone assiduously used the Press Association to further his political publicity; he conveyed in his own coach his favourite journalist, the 20-stone Walter Hepburn (known by all as 'Mr Gladstone's Fat Reporter').[1]

The War Office subscribed to the major newspapers, and advertised in them.[2] At the 1895 Newspaper Society Annual Dinner, General Wood[3] talked more fondly than he privately thought about the many newspapermen he knew from campaigns. At the same event the following year Captain Beresford[4] was not shy about publicly thanking the Press for their support of his campaign, when an MP in the 1880s, in persuading the Treasury to agree to '£21M for the defences', and he used his after-dinner speech to push for an increase in naval manpower.[5] Beresford's more innovative naval rival, Admiral Fisher[6] courted the Press assiduously in his long campaigns to gain support for Naval reforms. Field Marshal Roberts[7], commenting on the pros and cons of 'telegraphic war reporting', acknowledged the benefits of articles on the 'glorious record of heroism and willing sacrifice'.[8] For the politico-military Establishment, such uses were positive aspects of the Press. Furthermore, until the mid-nineteenth century, news from distant parts travelled slowly, and, where warfare was concerned, governments and naval and military commanders normally had the advantage of faster communication to London than did the Press, and therefore largely of controlling when and how news was announced.

The negative aspects of the Press for governments and for commanders included the publication in newspapers and magazines of operational information useful to the enemy. The Duke of Wellington, from Celorico in August 1810, complained to the War Office about the publication of officers' 'private' letters which gave details of his batteries and fortifications at Cadiz.[9] This problem became ever more apparent from the time of the Crimean War; improvements in the European transport system, especially railways, and the linked nascent international telegraph network, not only made strategic military communications much swifter, but also enabled the Press to become more independent of official communications. From the Crimea between 1854 and 1856, *The Times*[10] and other newspapers reported the serious defects in the command and logistic performance there. Although this caused no threat to national security, such journalistic disclosures were not surprisingly unpopular with the Generals and War Office; just before the Peace was signed, the British Commander-in-Chief issued orders forbidding publication of details of value to the enemy, and making provision for expulsion of offending correspondents. The smouldering memory of press criticisms lingered through the remainder of that century, reignited by subsequent frictions (before Omdurman Kitchener addressed waiting journalists as 'you drunken swabs'). All contributed to habitually jaundiced views of the Press held by the military into the twentieth and twenty-first Centuries.[11]

Secret Intelligence Gathering

By the 1880s there was still no permanent secret intelligence service, nor a nationwide security service, nor an organisation for intercepting and decoding the secret communications of the enemies of the state. Even though France, then regarded as the principal adversary, had all three, such was the self-perceived superiority of Britain that the threat did not appear to merit such underhand institutions. There had indeed been a Secret Service Fund since the Restoration in the 1660s, and Secret Service funding had been voted annually by Parliament since 1797. The Fund was useful to successive administrations not so much for secret service work, however, as for other more nefarious activities, such as bribery at home and abroad. Lord Aberdeen commented: 'although there are many charges upon it that ought not to be there, they at least remain secret'.[12] The last newspaper to receive a Secret Service Fund grant was allegedly *The Observer* in 1840.[13] The Decyphering Branch, established in 1703 and run part-time and largely from home by successive generations of the Willes family, had meanwhile been abolished in 1844 without replacement.

Intelligence of a political and economic kind was routinely handled by diplomats, but British espionage was conducted, as and when required, by freelance amateurs, and it focused mainly on imperial rivalries in remote parts of the world. In the War Office, the lack of basic intelligence evident at the start of Crimean War in 1854 had caused a small intelligence section to be created, based on cartographers. Its role declined however after that War, and from 1856 the War Office and Admiralty relied for general intelligence on military and naval Attachés in Paris, Berlin, St Petersburg, Turin and Vienna. Subsequently, lack of prior intelligence about the Franco-Prussian War (1870) had caused the War Office's Topographical and Statistical (T & S) Department to be augmented, and given responsibility for limited semi-covert intelligence-gathering by army (and occasionally naval) officers in the margins of their mainstream duties, for example Robert Baden-Powell on the NW Frontier.[14]

The T & S Department had become the Intelligence Branch in 1873, with responsibility also for planning for war; a similar Indian Intelligence Branch was established in Simla in 1878.[15] These Branches were however viewed without enthusiasm by more traditional elements in the higher headquarters, in particular by Field Marshal the Duke of Cambridge, Commander-in-Chief of the Army.[16] The Navy too had needed external stimuli to set up an embryo intelligence organisation, in this case the Russo-Turkish conflict of 1877–8, and Captain John Colomb's[17] lobbying in 1881 about French naval threats to British trade. With the support of politicians such as Lord Salisbury,[18] further progress was then made in formalising the intelligence organisations. The al-Mahdi's successes in Sudan and the death of General Gordon[19] also led to re-energising the still small intelligence apparatus, and the first Directors of Naval and Military Intelligence were appointed in 1887. The Admiralty and War Office at the end of the nineteenth century were nevertheless still small and simply-organised departments; the principal parts of the War Office were contained within the Horse Guards building (now HQ of the Army's London District alone), and those of the Admiralty within the Ripley Building (now one small part of the distended Cabinet Office); the politico-military headquarters of the most powerful Navy in the world had only 32 civilian administrators.

Internal Security

The organisation for internal security meanwhile had developed initially in Dublin and the Royal Irish Constabulary to counter the Fenian threat, briefly and separately supplemented in Great Britain after the 1867 bombings in Manchester and London. After the 1882 Phoenix Park assassinations of the Chief Secretary for Ireland and his Permanent Secretary, there was a reinvigoration of the security organisation in Ireland and at the Home Office in London under Robert Anderson.[20] The Lord Lieutenant of Ireland[21] appointed his Private Secretary EG Jenkinson[22] as the Dublin head and link with Whitehall. The London organisation was augmented again by the Metropolitan Police's new but short-lived 'Special Irish Branch' in response to the Fenian campaign 1881–5 (including bombs in the House of Commons and Tower of London, and damage to the Special Irish Branch Headquarters itself). Despite the seemingly haphazard nature of these arrangements, the authorities were partially successful in infiltrating the Fenian movement and in suborning its Irish-American links.[23] In 1887, under another ex-Indian Civil Servant, James Monro[24], the Metropolitan Police established the Special Branch which survives to this day, then responsible direct to the Home Secretary for political surveillance (not just of Fenians, but also of anarchists and foreign 'commune-ists'), but the Branch remained very small until World War I.

The Press Context

The Press evolved to a form we would recognise today during the post-Napoleonic period. From the 1830s there was rapid expansion of the railway system; the companies involved were quick to realise that, not only did they need a matching telegraphic system for their own purposes, but that wires laid along their tracks to achieve this would have spare capacity profitably marketable to others, both as the means of transmission and also in the collation of information for transmission.[25] Telegraphy was further improved in 1840 by the ABC system, which could achieve 15 words per minute, and by the mid-1840s approximately two thousand miles of railway track/cable had been laid. Similar developments were taking place in Europe, North America and in other parts of the developing world where commercial interests then justified them; the Morse Code[26] was first regularly used for telegraphy in 1844.

Primitive fax machines were invented in 1850, and in the same year the first cross-Channel cable was laid, connecting Britain with major European centres, followed by a cable to Ireland two years later. At about the same time, the Newfoundland Electric Telegraph Company was formed to find a way of laying a submarine transatlantic cable, and advances in oceanography in the Atlantic[27] and in cable technology enabled a fully operational telegraphic service between London and New York from 1866. By 1870 a submarine cable also connected England via Portugal to Gibraltar, and Hong Kong was connected by 1881. By 1886, the strategic and commercial dependence on the worldwide international telegraphic system was so firmly established that the first Convention on the Protection of Submarine Cables was held.

In 1897, commercial development started of perforated tape ('tickertape') machines, soon in use by the Post Office. In late 1901 Guglielmo Marconi [28] made the first transatlantic wireless transmission, commercialised a few years later. By 1902, when the British Government set up the Imperial and International Communications Company,[29] Britain was linked from Cornwall to the rest of the world by 14 submarine cable systems, and 72% of all the world's cable systems were British-owned. In 1911 Asquith's Government approved a deal with Marconi to set up a chain of state-owned wireless stations throughout the Empire. The telephone was also slowly becoming established, Bell's company having been founded in the USA in 1877, and in Britain a year later, with the first very small British network operational by 1882; the Post Office acquired control of all British trunk lines ten years later. Thus by the early twentieth century, both the Government/military and the Press had access to extensive international communications networks, albeit still relatively slow and limited in their reach beyond major centres of prosperous population.

Within Britain, unlike other major European countries, the inland telegraphic system had no close connection with nor control by the military and security organisations, despite its key strategic role; it was driven by commercial interests. By 1869 there were five major telegraphy companies operating in the United Kingdom, handling between them about six and a half million messages a year. However, these companies operated as a cartel and were widely disliked, especially by Chambers of Commerce and the press, because of their unreliability, the small number of their offices, and their complex charges. The provincial press had a particular complaint, because of the telegraph companies' poorly carried out contractual secondary role in providing news to regional newspapers, an activity on which they employed few journalists.

In 1865, the cartel raised its basic price from one shilling for 20 words to one shilling and seven pence. This enormous increase, on top of existing dissatisfaction, sparked a public campaign for nationalisation of the whole system and for its transfer to the already nationalised Post Office management. In 1868, Parliament approved nationalisation, which came into effect in 1870. Many more telegraphic offices were opened throughout the country, the basic price being reduced to one shilling and one penny per 20 words. Nationalisation did not happen without controversy over the excessive compensation paid to the five companies. Railway companies too were given residual financial advantages, which caused increasing problems for the Post Office in subsequent years, as did high wage costs, parliamentary interference in pricing, and Treasury mistrust. The Newspaper Society Circulars of these decades contain regular complaints of inadequate and unreliable service, lack of commercial responsiveness, and under-investment.[30] The relevance of nationalisation to the Press was nevertheless that its landline usage, and that of the public, trebled in the first two years, and went on expanding rapidly until the end of the century, by when about 90 million messages a year were handled. This eruption of information flow and public communication was one of the several factors which changed the environment in which Press and officials interacted in the last part of the nineteenth century.

Demographic and Political Change

Other factors were demographic and political. The population grew rapidly from after the Napoleonic Wars, surging from 21 million in 1851 to 44 million by 1908, with the number of employed (excluding the large numbers doing part-time work, especially women) increasing from 9.4 million in 1851 to 16.4 million at the start of the new century. Education Acts of 1870 and 1876 led to the founding of five thousand extra schools and to education for almost all children below the age of 13, and the Fee Grant Act of 1891 ensured elementary education was free. Basic literacy grew from 69% of the population in 1850 to 97% in 1900. This was accompanied by significant growth in general public spending power, and together these factors helped provide for the Press a large new lower middle- and working-class readership, including women. This part of the public also increasingly had more leisure time and potentially more interest in political activity. Amongst other contributing factors, the 1867 and 1884 Reform Acts extended the franchise, the Independent Labour Party was founded in 1893, and by 1912 the suffragette movement was active.

The press response from the mid-nineteenth century was also aided by parliamentary reforming measures: Lord Campbell's Libel Act of 1843, which inter alia allowed a legitimate defence if a statement of truth were made in the public interest; repeal of Advertisement Duty in 1853; abolition of stamp duty on newspapers in 1855, and repeal of the excise duty on paper in 1861. Improved technology had sparked press growth even before this, with development of continuous newsprint rolls, steam-powered presses, lithographic and photographic negative processing all being in use by the 1830s. The first photograph in a newspaper was printed in 1842, and high-speed rotary presses functioned from the 1860s. Electrically powered presses replaced steam-powered; the September 1884 Newspaper Society Circular reported that the *Lawrance American* was boasting the first ever use of electricity for its print run, with the advantages of being able to start at the flick of a switch rather than having to wait for the boiler to raise sufficient steam pressure; the Circular added however that there might be some doubt about this in view of 'the North American tendency to exaggeration'. The number of London and provincial (excluding Irish) newspapers rose from 221 in 1836, to 2,064 in 1892; magazines increased from 557 to 2,097 between 1866 and 1896, spurred on by advertisers to specific interest groups. Many new journals had political affiliations, and ruling political parties placed government advertising shamelessly in their 'own' journals.

Organisation of the Press

This expansion was reflected in the evolving organisation of the press. The Associated Press agency was founded in 1848 in the USA to make use of the opportunities opened up by the advances in telegraphy. The first 'modern' press agency established in Britain was Reuter's in 1851, principally to handle foreign news,[31] followed by the Central News agency (later Central Press) in 1863. In anticipation of nationalisation of the telegraph system, and to meet the dissatisfaction of the provincial press with the supply of news to them, the Press Association (PA) was founded in 1868; the following year an agreement was reached with Reuter's, whereby the latter undertook to supply the PA with foreign telegrams for exclusive use in the British Isles outside London (which was served direct by Reuter's) and to disseminate PA news of Britain overseas.

Almost as soon as the Post Office took over the telegraph system in 1870, this arrangement was put to the test by the need to report the Franco-Prussian War; the agencies and newspaper associations were frustrated by the inability of the Post Office to work at the speed and accuracy required.[32] The agencies were constantly seeking new areas of business, for example the PA taking over dissemination of regular 'Wind and Weather Reports' from the Met Office in 1912 ('maximum 200 words'). The Empire Press Union was founded in 1909, to provide better coverage between the countries of the Empire. Generally, the agencies were regarded by the Press as essential and admirable, but not faultless – clerks who transcribed telegrams for distribution caused particular amusement, despite the dangers of libel: 'It was reported that Mr Gladstone had died at such a place' instead of 'dined', and 'Mr Campbell said that he had not more than a carnal knowledge of Mrs O'Shea', followed later by a correction to 'casual knowledge.'[33]

Within the Press, despite or because of the intense and increasing competition, organisations of mutual interest were established. The Provincial Newspaper Society (NS) was founded in 1836 to address the concerns and promote the interests of the provincial newspapers, although later it also had London members. The London newspapers set up their own organisation, the Newspaper Proprietors' Association (NPA), in 1906, and the Periodical Proprietors' Association (PPA) was established two years later.[34] A large part of the records of these organisations concerned the impact of the increasing legislation and competition of the period. For example, in July 1910 George Toulmin MP[35] of the NS led a delegation including PA and NPA representatives to see the Postmaster General, Herbert Samuel,[36] to complain about the National Telephone Company (state-owned from 1911); in the past two general elections it had not only transmitted the results to all-comers but had also collated them as they were announced, a role which the Press had made for itself in late Victorian times (in 1911, the Court of Chancery ruled in favour of the Press on this). Meanwhile, the employees of the Press sought in turn to protect themselves against the proprietors and editors by forming their own institutions, the Institute of Journalists (IoJ) in 1884, and the National Union of Journalists (NUJ) in 1907, with the printers and other blue-collar trades forming or joining their own numerous trades unions. A further reflection of the increasing organisation of the Press was the IoJ campaign in 1910 to establish a School of Journalism within London University.[37]

'New Journalism'

There is debate amongst media academics as to when 'New Journalism' started in the nineteenth century, and why. There is no disagreement however that even by the 1880s, the style of newspapers and magazines had changed significantly from the early Victorian news-sheets, and from the separate pamphleteers and cartoonists. Innovations in the late Victorian press were in subject matter, language, format, and general accessibility to the artisan and working classes. The influence of American newspaper styles was also felt: 'Columns were replaced with paragraphs, long sentences with short ones, and sober words with sensational ones. Headlines, sub-heads, and illustrations broke up the mid-Victorian rows of unbroken columns. Battlefield photography started in the Crimean War. The leading article, formerly the key site of a paper's editorial identity and moral authority, was swamped by the expansion of news. This news, moreover, became less serious, focusing not merely on parliamentary politics but on human interest stories or "features"'.[38] In 1890, even Reuter's found it necessary to alter the style of its reports to reflect the widespread use of 'New Journalism'. Alfred Harmsworth's[39] founding of the *Daily Mail* in 1896 gave further impetus to these trends, which continued up to the start of the First World War; for example, its front page on 5 August 1914 was one large illustrated advertisement (for Boot's the Chemists – 'A Reminder for the Holidays'), the paper cost a halfpenny, and it boasted its eight pages were 'six times as large as that of any Penny London Morning Journal except *THE TIMES*' [same proprietor]; the headline 'GREAT BRITAIN DECLARES WAR ON GERMANY' was on page 5, with North Sea map ('Where the Fleets will Meet'), and naval and military information/photographs already widely in the public domain.

Centralisation of Ownership

The large fall in the price of newsprint in the last quarter of the nineteenth century had been outweighed by the high cost of the new technologies, and by the overheads of maintaining high-circulation large-staff newspapers. Fierce competition led to halving the sale price of newspapers in the 1850s and 1860s, and subsequently to halfpenny newspapers, a price not covering production costs. Newspapers therefore depended increasingly on advertising to survive; by 1907 the total spent on press advertising had reached about £20 million. Editors and owners became more concerned not to offend advertisers; this in turn had a self-censoring impact on content and editorial policy, which simultaneously had nevertheless to seek to attract and hold new readership. Advertisers did indeed on occasion use their power, for example in boycotting the *Daily News* in 1886 when it campaigned for Irish Home Rule.

Support of social order therefore predominated in the mainstream press, an important element in the years leading to the First World War. Economics led to the ownership of the Press becoming more concentrated in the hands of those with capital, including industrialists from other fields, and the era of the "Press Barons" started in the late 1880s. The Press became gradually as much a business as a vehicle for political views, but conversely the political allegiances of the new press helped to consolidate the position of the Parties as political groupings, as opposed to factions of the wealthy, with liberalism rather than radicalism as the leftward edge of the mainstream press. The exception was the *Daily Sketch*, a socialist newspaper which originated in a strike in 1911, against the owner of the *Daily News* by print-workers over their demand for a 50-hour week.

Thus by the turn of the century, those responsible for national security were having to adjust to a press which well within living memory had changed significantly, and which in the new 'popular' parts was perceived to have (in today's parlance) 'dumbed down'. When the young proprietor CA Pearson[40] acquired the *Standard*, his accumulation of titles (*Evening Standard, St James Gazette, Daily Express*, and six Northern newspapers) and his connection with the more popular end of the market (*Tit-Bits*) was attacked by *The Spectator* and by the then Home Secretary Winston Churchill,[41] and a vigorous correspondence ensued.[42] Then as now, this trend of popularisation and exposé sometimes included legitimate intrusion into areas of activity which in former times had been conducted by government largely out of sight of the British public. It also exposed governmental policy-making more directly to newspaper campaigns which purported to represent public opinion; the newspaper(s) concerned had sometimes themselves led the formation of such opinion, or at least stoked it.

2

REGULATION OF THE PRESS, AND THE BOER WAR

While the intelligence and security organisations were slowly evolving in the last decades of the nineteenth Century, other parts of the War Office and Admiralty were periodically returning to the problem of how to respond to the presence of the Press in theatres of operations, and to the threat of espionage, in particular by the French. Clauses in the 1803 Act of Parliament passed to address the latter during the Napoleonic War had gradually been repealed since the Battle of Waterloo in 1815. In late 1887, at a time of a perceived increase in the French threat, and after some alleged breaches of security, the Admiralty initiated a new Act, and with the War Office attempted to stiffen the Treasury draft of a new 'Breach of Official Trust Bill'. This proposed severely penalising various aspects of espionage, and leaks by public servants.[43]

This Bill later transmogrified, with some political difficulty, into the Official Secrets Act (OSA) 1889, but when it reached the House of Commons there was little debate; before the Act was passed, only the intervention of one alert MP[44] secured an amendment which removed the general application of its Section 2 (treacherous disclosure of official information) to any departmental interests of any part of the government machine, as opposed only to its specific application to the wider security interests of the State. Even those Members of Parliament who were journalists or proprietors were acquiescent in the passing of OSA 1889.[45] The Press at the time was more concerned with other Bills which appeared more immediately threatening to their business, such as the Libel Bill,[46] and later the Copyright and Employment Bills.

Nevertheless OSA 1889 was still thought by the War Office and Admiralty to be inadequate as a deterrent to spying, because it did not apply to everyone, only to Crown employees and certain government contractors; and because an offence was committed only if it could be proved that information had been communicated to a person to whom it ought not to have been, and that the communication was not in the interests of the public. After a small number of unsatisfactory OSA 1889 prosecutions, the War Office staff therefore returned to the charge in 1895. It recommended strengthening the relatively lenient maximum punishment for passing information to a 'foreign State'.[47]

Parliamentary Counsel however recommended against this, because of foreseen further opposition, querying 'whether it is worth while to reopen the very difficult and delicate questions raised by the Official Secrets Act'. The Secretary of State (SofS) for War (Campbell-Bannerman) agreed, minuting: 'Let this sleeping (watch)dog lie. If we find burglars pass him, we may stir him up. My personal opinion has always been against amending the Act'.[48] This caution proved justified, for when a new draft Bill was discussed in Parliament in June 1896, which would have placed the burden of proof on the accused that he had obtained information for innocent purposes rather than for espionage, opposition caused the Bill to be withdrawn.

Planning for Control of the Press in Time of War

Experience in the recent Egyptian campaign had led in June 1889 to two areas of discussion within the War Office: reporting in the home Press on potential and actual operations, and relations with the Press in theatres of operations. The first emerged in due course as a proposal 'that no matters of military interest should be allowed to be published by any newspaper until it has been approved by press censors, appointed by the Secretary of State in every town where the newspaper is published'. For reasons of practicality and acceptability, this proposal was eventually not proceeded with.[49]

More was achieved in the second area, the problems of the relationship with the Press in a theatre of operations itself, or, as the Press saw it, the problems with the military there. For example, the Newspaper Society Circular of December 1884 reported: '[General] Sir Garnet Wolseley[50] appears to be acting the martinet towards newspaper correspondents representing the English Press with the Nile Expedition.' In addition to constraints on their movements, there had been delays in clearing and transmitting correspondents' telegrams; and the *Standard* complained that its reporter, having been forbidden by the General personally to take passage in government boats, had therefore had to proceed in the wake of the Army along the banks of the Nile very slowly by camel.

'Serious complaints' were again reported in the NS Circular four months later, this time about a delay of almost a day by the War Office in releasing news of the fall of Khartoum to the press: 'a finer example of bureaucratic dawdling has not been seen, even at the War Office, for years'. The *Saturday Review*, referring to the censorship exercised over the war correspondents accompanying the 'Soudan Expedition', expressed the opinion that 'it would really be better and more dignified for the newspapers to withdraw their correspondents altogether than to see them exposed to the daily humiliation which is their lot';[51] the Army might well have been very pleased by such a withdrawal of Press intrusion, but, to put things in perspective, three months later the NS Circular reported the awards of medals to the war correspondents of the *Daily Telegraph* and *Illustrated News*, for their parts respectively in the 1886 Campaign and at the Battle of Atbara.

The War Office responded robustly to the general unhappiness of the Press by the subsequent issue of 'Revised Rules for Newspaper Correspondents at the Seat of War'.[52] These applied to what today would be called 'embedded' journalists, and, although contained within just two pages of quarto, were even more stringent than before. In addition to strict licence application and revocation procedures, 'Licences will not be granted to those whom it is considered undesirable to have as correspondents in the field. Retired Officers will be preferred, and only one correspondent will be allowed to each newspaper.'

Tight rules applied to the movements and outward communications of correspondents (who were placed under the Army Act), and a supervisory Staff Officer was appointed as the sole channel of access to the command and as the vetter of dispatches. 'The Military Authorities will give as much information to correspondents as they may consider advisable and consistent with their duty. The above-mentioned Staff Officer will fix an hour when correspondents may call upon him daily for information, and he will be authorised to tell them everything that can be published with safety to the Army.'

The Realities of War

Things did not work out quite as neatly as the Army intended when the next major shocks to the politico-military establishment occurred. The perceived problems caused by the presence of the Press on the battlefield were tolerable to the military when things went well; for example at the Battle of Omdurman in 1898, when General Kitchener's[53] army and accompanying naval gunboats defeated the Sudanese dervishes, there were no complaints about, for example, the journalist Winston Churchill's presence in the charge by the 21st Lancers. However, political and military nervousness was exacerbated more widely at home by the Fashoda incident at about the same time.[54] The possibility of French attacks in Europe and other parts of the world seemed for several months credible, and the authorities again became concerned by the amount of information then published in the Press about military and naval dispositions.

The 2nd Boer War

Worse was to follow. The Second Boer War started badly in 1899. Although by then the Director of Military Intelligence Major General Ardagh[55] was well respected, had the support of Field Marshal Wolseley, now C-in-C of the Army, and of the Secretary of State for War, and had a room assigned to him in the Foreign and the Colonial Offices, his department nevertheless played a minor role. The small 'Secret Section' set up inside the War Office Intelligence Department was smartly abolished in 1903, even though the Royal Commission on the War in South Africa concluded inter alia that this Department had been 'undermanned for the work of preparation for a great war'. A historian later opined more pithily that the War Office attitude to its Intelligence Department during the Boer War had been like a man who 'kept a small brain for occasional use in his waistcoat pocket and ran his head by clockwork'.[56]

The War Office and the generals may not have been unduly concerned about their own intelligence-gathering capabilities, but in every crisis they did become agitated about those of their potential enemies. As the likelihood of war in South Africa had increased through late 1898 and early 1899, the General Officers Commanding the troops there and at home had become increasingly alarmed at the amount of information about military plans, strengths, movements and other logistics, which was available to the Boers from newspapers published in South Africa and in Britain. This added to existing perceptions about vulnerability elsewhere to French ambitions, and in particular to espionage, invasion and sabotage in Great Britain and Ireland.

1899 – Early Proposals for Control of the Press in War

On 1 March 1899, General Sir Evelyn Wood, now the Adjutant General[57] sent a file entitled 'Control of the Press in Time of War' to the Commander-in-Chief in the War Office, for endorsement and upward transmission. In a history in which many might claim the fatherhood of the D-Notice System, this file has as strong a claim as any to be the direct progenitor of what eventually emerged.

The submission started by alluding to 'certain indiscretions in the Press' some months previously (during the Fashoda crisis). These were later described more fully in a CID Paper of October 1904: 'Towards the end of 1898, when the country was believed to be on the eve

13

of war with France, the newspapers contained exhaustive information concerning our defences and preparations. The composition of the garrisons of all home defended ports was given, and the artillery and engineer units of the auxiliary forces allotted thereto were named. The existence of submarine defences at Portsmouth, Falmouth, the mouths of the Humber and the Mersey was mentioned, and details given of electric installations at Portsmouth, Falmouth and other points.' These perceived leaks had caused the DMI to recommend seeking the Law Officers' opinion 'as to the power of the Government to control the Press in such matters in time of an emergency or of war'.

The Secretary of State had decided however not to take this forward then, but the Adjutant General now raised the issue again more formally. A key paragraph, which could describe (with the addition of air forces and electronic media) the official position, avowed if not always practised, at any time since 1899, states:

> We are all proud of the freedom of the Press and recognise that the maintenance of that freedom is essential to our national vitality; yet without in the least diminishing or impairing the right of the Press to criticise without constraint Government administration, some control over the publication to the world of military and naval intelligence in time of war or expected war must be accepted as essential to national safety. It is unnecessary to quote historical examples to prove the advantages derived in past wars by military commanders from a study of the newspapers of the enemy. The possibility of so reaping advantage has been greatly enhanced in modern times by the multiplication and acceleration of the means of communication and the feverish competition of modern journalism to obtain news, which will interest the enormous reading public, for which it caters.

Wood went on to acknowledge the underlying patriotism of the British Press, but to explain the difficulties seen to be faced by editors of pressure and of lack of expert knowledge as to what was 'injurious' and what was not, an assessment with which he believed some editors agreed (the Editor of *TheTimes* was a friend). And he went on to suggest that, rather than wait until 'grave mischief had actually occurred' in a crisis, the matter should be dealt with then 'in a time of tranquillity' [perhaps, with the advantage of hindsight, a curious description of the immediate prelude to the Second Boer War].

He acknowledged, having talked to some 'managers and owners of Papers', that the difficulties of the 'most obvious remedy', the enforcement of a press censorship, would be insuperable 'in a country such as England . . . and that no workable machinery for the purpose could be devised'. However, he then went on to suggest an alternative and almost as censorious solution, namely the prohibition of the publication of 'any military or naval news, except what could be supplied to them daily by the W.O. and Admiralty' (reminding that a similar solution had been adopted by Germany since 1874). He ended by proposing that Parliament should be asked to pass enabling legislation to this effect, but suggested that firstly press and public support should be secured by a public enquiry, and that a committee should be set up to effect this.

The CinC, agreeing, immediately forwarded this submission to the senior civil servant in the War Office, the Permanent Under Secretary (PUS) Sir Ralph Knox.[58] Next day Knox however minuted his disagreement with the Generals: 'I much doubt whether an Act of this kind would be obtained, except under pressure of the actual emergency, when such a measure could be passed in a few days', and he suggested merely having a draft Bill prepared.

He went on furthermore to give a rather different view of recent events: '. . . no emergency was proclaimed and yet there was a desire to suppress some of the information that appeared in the press. I do not think that any statements appeared which were in any way injurious to public interests. On the contrary, altho some statements were exaggerated & theatrical, in the manner of the press of today, they made known the activity of the Govt and gave a reality to the words and arguments of the Govt'.

The junior politician in the War Office, the Parliamentary Under-Secretary of State George Wyndham[59] agreed with the PUS, adding however a suggestion which the passage of time has shown to be prescient: not only should there be a conference with the Press, but also 'the Press, generally, is not so anxious to give news as to see that some papers shall not give news which others suppress from patriotic motives. If we tabulated the classes of fact which might not be published in time of war, or expected war, & then invited the Press to send representatives to confer with us, I am inclined to think that they would accept such limitations, & that they wd be able to impose them on all journalists'. In other words, aided by expert advice, some form of self-regulation.

The Secretary of State, Lord Lansdowne,[60] agreeing in general with the previous two minutes, ordered the matter be discussed at the next War Office Council meeting. Afterwards, he minuted his decision: '. . . out of the question to attempt legislation at the present time, but I have no objection to a short Bill being drafted which might be carried through Parliament whenever the necessity arises'. He saw difficulty in legislating classification of facts which ought not to be published, and favoured a single clause forbidding the publication of any unauthorised news. But even this he felt would be problematical, and on balance he favoured 'an appeal to the leading representatives of the Press which would, I believe, loyally support the Government of the day in an attempt to prevent journalistic indiscretions'. And with this sphinx-like statement, he invited the Commander-in-Chief to have the Staff produce the proposed draft Bill.

The Director of Military Intelligence accordingly submitted a draft on 20 April 1899, still hoping for legislation immediately rather than when a crisis occurred, and suggesting that, if this were not acceptable, 'a small confidential committee' should be set up, with representatives of the Admiralty (belatedly brought into the drafting), the Home Office and the Press. Regarding the last, General Ardagh differentiated between the *'leading* representatives', in whom one could have confidence, and the 'smaller fry' over whom 'those gentlemen' had no control and 'from whose indiscretions we have most to fear'. He enclosed papers giving recent examples of such indiscretions. This draft did not find sufficient favour however with either his military or civilian superiors, and in mid-May Lansdowne minuted tersely 'bring up in the autumn'.

In late September, Wood therefore re-opened the submission process, writing 'Pressing' at the top, and enclosing cuttings from three newspapers of the previous day. These were from *The Globe*, which included details of regiments and strengths at Ladysmith and Dundee (North Natal), of troop movements in and from Cape Town and lightly defended Pietermaritzburg, and of the expected deployment that day of an armoured train to named front line destinations, with the thickness of its armour; from *The St James Gazette*, which reported current troop deployments in Natal, and details provided by Reuters in South Africa; and from an unidentified newspaper, details not only as above, but also of transport and supply companies being sent from England to South Africa 'for the movement of an army corps in the field'. All this useful intelligence was assumed by Wood to have been passed the previous night by the Boer Consul-General for the Transvaal back to his government.

He therefore urged 'that something should now be done, and while we are talking and discussing the matter, perhaps the Colonial Governments (ie in Natal and The Cape) might be induced to have a strict censorship'.

Wolseley passed this on immediately to the PUS, scribbling: 'We cannot make war as the country expects we should, whilst our enemy is kept informed by our press of everything we do and of every movement made by our troops & the number of guns then posted at various stations'; and hoping that telegrams could be sent without delay to the Governors of the Natal and Cape Colonies urging censorship, particularly of information being sent over the local telegraph lines. Once again, however, Civil Service minds thought differently. Knox considered it 'impossible to prevent the publication of facts known to many people', and pointed out that, even if the British Press were persuaded not to publish such details, there was no way of stopping the foreign press from doing so, and that, if thus discriminated against, 'the people of this country would cry out'.

He also queried how encoded press messages could be handled, and presumed that if 'hostilities' broke out, then wire communication to Transvaal would anyway be stopped. Wyndham was more sympathetic, but reiterated that it would be impossible to proceed by Act of Parliament ('not sitting for some little time'). He was less concerned about the foreign press 'who will have but few and indifferent correspondents' and their reports would not 'obtain the same credit on the part of the Boers as would news in our own organs'. He returned to his earlier ideas of making a list of the kinds of information that should not be published, and of 'submitting this in a friendly but formal conference to representatives of the News agencies & leading papers'.

Two days later, Lansdowne gave his decision. The General Officers Commanding Cape and Natal were to be instructed at once to supervise all telegrams sent from the offices which each could control, and should expel any correspondent 'detected in the revelation of secret information'. The Colonial Secretary should be invited to approach the Governors of the Cape and Natal Colonies, with a view to their introducing wider local censorship. At home a Bill remained 'out of the question'; he asked Wyndham however to take forward discussion with the Press, but 'I am not very sanguine as to the practical value of the result', because so much was known to so many, and information would therefore continue to be published by the 'less public spirited journals here', and transmitted thence to the Transvaal.[61]

Control of the Press in Theatre during the 2nd Boer War

Events however intruded before any of these initiatives could be pursued. As the Secretary of State was writing his minute, negotiations with President Kruger's South African Republic and the Orange Free State were reaching final breakdown. Within a week the British Army had been mobilised for the war which started four days later when the Boer ultimatum expired, and Boer forces invaded the Cape and Natal Colonies on 12 October 1899.

More immediate and practical press matters were already now occupying the members of the Army Board. The first was the issue of licences to correspondents, dealt with personally at Army Board level. General Buller[62] was formally appointed as CinC South Africa on 9 October, having minuted his views about correspondents to the Adjutant General eight days earlier, including: 'If it can be avoided I hope that licences will be refused to all foreign correspondents – they are only spies.' Wyndham hoped American journalists could be treated differently from other foreign correspondents, but Lansdowne ruled that, as it would be impossible to stop foreign journalists from coming to South Africa, there should be no attempt to license them, but they should be warned they were there at their own risk.[63]

A fortnight later, following further representation from Buller, Wolseley minuted the Adjutant General about the presence in theatre of correspondents of 'unknown' newspapers, who were mostly wealthy gentleman freelances.[64] Wood responded tartly that the current regulations for the Press were written by his predecessor (Buller himself), who had clearly not foreseen the presence of such people. Wood now suggested the number of licensed journalists in theatre should be limited to those representing journals with a circulation of at least 20,000 or illustrated magazines of at least 10,000, and whose expenses were guaranteed by their editor, who in turn must have signed the declaration in the 1889 'Rules for Newspaper Correspondents at the Seat of War'.[65]

The impact on the Press of these policies was quickly apparent. In November 1899, the Newspaper Society reported: 'Considerable dissatisfaction has arisen in consequence of the rigid military censorship which is being exercised over Press telegrams in South Africa. Allegations of partial treatment are also being freely made. Whether these are justified or no, it is indisputable that newspapers and agencies . . . have, up to the present, been unable to get more than a small fraction of their messages through.' *The Times* commented in measured terms on 3 November: 'A censorship has been very properly established at the Cape and other points . . . the Press in general, and we ourselves in particular, may have suffered perhaps more than was strictly necessary in the public interest from the censorship exercised over homeward telegrams from South Africa and, above all, from the delay which such censorship, exercised with an inadequate staff, must unavoidably involve. But that is of minor importance at the present juncture . . . But it is impossible to overlook, on the other hand, the evidence afforded by the Continental Press that the censorship has not yet succeeded in closing other channels through which information still passes between the Boer Republics and their sympathisers abroad.'

The *Daily Telegraph* (1 November) was more apoplectic:

> The arrangements at headquarters in Natal . . . are simply ridiculous. Those who have the control of men most truly representing public opinion [ie war correspondents] are childishly indulging in proclivities. Newspapers they approve of are liberally treated; those for whom they have a limited liking are muzzled. It is needless for us to assert that a special correspondent of the vast experience and tried ability of Mr Bennett Burleigh [a previous medal winner referred to above] is not likely, in his history of a battle, to divulge facts that would be useful to an enemy; the lifelong performance of such arduous and dangerous work would make a lapse from duty in his case impossible. Nevertheless, lengthy messages, full of point and interest, for which we have to pay more than four shillings a word, have been sent through in meaningless fragments days after they have been handed in. . . . Is the war in South Africa, we venture to ask, a private enterprise? Is it to be conducted out of sight and criticism of the English nation, whose heart is in it, and whose sons compose its fighting force? Or do these pipe-clayed wiseacres fear that men like Mr Bennett Burleigh and his colleagues can or will play the traitor, anticipating movements or divulging plans? Some of them are older in warlike experience than many in command; all of them have a code of honour and patriotism as high as any good soldiers. We declare it a monstrous and insane abuse of military authority . . . They [the correspondents] themselves have never objected , and never will, to

restrictions consistent with military circumstances and the reticencies indispensable to successful movements on the field. But to tell them they shall only send a few paltry words in the moment of action which it is their business to depict and transmit to an expectant country, that must be stamped and branded as an administrative betise which, though it will bring its own punishment upon the absurd people who decree it, is over and above that, an insult to the profession, and an impudent disregard of public opinion.[66]

Even a year later, when the campaign had begun to go more favourably for Britain, Press complaints were still being heard. In July 1900, Baron Herbert de Reuter wrote to the Press Association: 'The censor's action is nothing short of a scandal. The censor, undoubtedly acting under orders, suppresses everything which is not favourable. The way in which the British public are being continuously misled and the honesty of the correspondents frustrated is a disgrace to the authorities.'[67] The Newspaper Society did however feel that there was also an internal organisational problem for the Press, noting: 'The opinion prevails amongst provincial newspaper conductors that the experience of the past twelve months points to a simplification of the existing methods of war correspondence, should this country be involved in another great war.' The NS Secretary suggested 'an organised and compact corps of correspondents' (similar to what today is called 'pool reporting'), and was more sympathetic than most newspapers to the problems which had initially faced the military; because of the number of journalists in theatre: 'Telegrams had to be limited to the extreme point of brevity, the wires were congested with scores of practically identical messages . . . and alongside this journalistic chaos was the fact that the Commander-in-Chief [by then the more successful and popular Field Marshal Roberts] became also the Reporter-in-Chief, and, moreover, did the work extremely well.'[68]

Conclusions from the Boer War Experience

The Boer War was the first relatively modern British interaction between military and media in a major theatre of operations. The pace and quantity of press activity was such that the Press Association rented the upstairs rooms of a Whitehall tavern, the *Red Lion*, as its forward operating base, where its reporters processed the information received from the nearby ministries, and whence its uniformed messenger boys scurried to the London newspapers and to the PA headquarters near Fleet Street.[69] As the War progressed, and British forces gradually regained the upper hand, experiences with the Press caused the Army again to review the 'Rules for Newspaper Correspondents at the Seat of War'. In February 1901, by which time Transvaal had been annexed by the British and the Boer guerrilla campaign was starting, the former Principal Press Censor in Natal, Major Jones,[70] submitted his recommendations to the War Office. His summaries of the scale and nature of press activity during the first part of the War, and the military reaction, not only had resonances in more recent campaigns, but also had a direct bearing on how the evolution to the D-Notice System continued.[71]

Firstly, the centralised War Office system of licensing had not worked as intended because of the 'rapid succession of events' and the number of journalists already working in South Africa (who had had to be licensed locally). In London and South Africa, 108 licences had been issued by early 1901, and there were never less than 100 correspondents with the Army at any one time, some representing more than one journal. These included 22 morning and evening newspapers, 16 weekly and illustrated journals, 27 colonial newspapers (nine of them South African), three American newspapers, and six telegraphic agencies.

Jones divided correspondents into four categories: legitimate licensed journalists, free-lances (some there at their own expense and risk), those using their licence to get to private interests in Transvaal, and 'those who saw in a War Correspondent's position the possible means of successful speculation'. Many correspondents also employed 'dispatch-riders' and 'servants' (both categories included journalists' personal friends). Each correspondent was entitled to draw (from the Army) rations for himself and for a servant, and forage for a horse, and to be accompanied by his own transport and supply of stores. All this greatly affected 'the length of the column'; Jones therefore considered the number of correspondents allowed was 'unnecessarily large'. Furthermore, correspondents had been surprised by (and unsur-prisingly disliked) the priority given to military dispatches, especially because away from telegraph lines a single military wire/heliographs became the only means of communication back to base. Their editors meanwhile, then as now, were demanding 'something every day even when there was no news'.

Jones's recommendations included that there should be no more than 12 'qualified and experienced' correspondents allowed in any headquarters and even fewer in a column, excluding all foreign, financial, weekly, evening, colonial, independent and telegraphic correspondents, and with very few photographers/artists (because, with an unusual rationale, so many officers had cameras and sent their photographs back to the Press themselves). An authorised record of events would be issued to this small Press group each day by an Intelligence Officer, and use of army communications would be greatly tightened up. The advantages foreseen would include the 'public spared incorrect reports and consequent sensational headlines', and the army having fewer non-combatants to look after, and 'less extraneous work, and not so much irresponsible criticism'.

General Buller[72] agreed most of the report, except the proposal that the Press be confined to an authorised daily record; he thought this would throw extra responsibility on the Commander-in-Chief (CinC), and deprive the Press of 'the independence expected by the public'. He added ideas of his own: editors should guarantee to defray the expenses of their correspondent, no telegraphic press report should be sent until 24 hours after the military one, and his 'Natal rules' would be 'not undesirable in any future Campaign'. These had included: no reports by telegraph of dispositions nor of possible operations; and no censoring of press 'letters' but withdrawal of licences for publishing information which was 'mischievous, wilfully incorrect, or likely to be of injury to the Country'. He added that he had had to warn only three correspondents in his time as CinC, and that local (Natal) papers had indeed been censored before publication.

Forwarding the Jones report to the Adjutant General, the War Office Financial Secretary, Lord Stanley,[73] said he had already previously made a similar report to Lord Roberts, that he was keen on 'a uniform with distinctive badges for correspondents', and that while he agreed with Buller (in particular on no censorship of letters, the letters of officers and men not then being censored either), a hard and fast 24-hour rule on telegrams was unnecessarily rigid. Stanley further recommended the War Office keep three lists of correspondents for use at any time: those licensable and acceptable, acceptable freelances, and a 'Black List'. He would wish also to 'stop the practice which grew up, and which is a most pernicious one, of newspapers taking as their correspondents gentlemen whom they do not pay, and who simply wish to go out "to see the fun"'. Finally he recommended 'a conference with a few well-known correspondents'.

Meanwhile, the tetchy War Office relationship with the Press continued. A dispute arose in June 1901 between the new SofS for War, Brodrick,[74] and the *Daily Mail* over a report by one of its war correspondents, Edgar Wallace,[75] that the Boers had shot two of their wounded British prisoners. Brodrick, on advice from South Africa, told the House of Commons there was 'no foundation whatsoever for the report'; but four days later, when told there was now indeed evidence of the killings, the Government suppressed the telegram. Wallace however filed further substantiated reports confirming the story in early July, and the Government threatened him with severe punishment. The *Daily Mail* continued to publish similar stories, whereupon the Government decided the newspaper should be cut off from all War Office news, attempted to muzzle its correspondents in South Africa, and threatened the News Agencies with similar deprivation of official information if they supplied the miscreant newspaper. The *Daily Mail* fought back, accusing the Government of suppression of facts, and the Government retaliated by accusing the paper of 'offering pecuniary temptations' to War Office clerks to obtain early news.

Other newspapers, alarmed by the possibility that government action against the freedom of the Press might become more general, then began themselves to supply the *Daily Mail* with information which had been withheld. The paper denied it had ever published anything of assistance to an enemy, and challenged Brodrick to make the accusations outside Parliament, so that he could be taken to court on grounds of libel. As often happens in cases of intemperate Political behaviour, the Government had to back down. *The Times* (owned then by the same proprietor as the *Mail*, Northcliffe) commented: 'It is not wise to attempt punishment of a newspaper by withholding direct information concerning ordinary official matters when that information is being sent out broadcast to other newspapers and to news agencies. That kind of thing can only end in failure'.[76]

3

FACING THE GROWING
GERMAN THREAT

Early Preparations for a Control of the Press during
War in Europe

No further action on Control of the Press was taken however until well after the Boer War ended with the Treaty of Vereeniging in May 1902.[77] Meanwhile, wider forms of media activity had been stimulating public and political concern about the vulnerability of British interests to French and German activity. The *Daily Mail* had been warning about the German threat since before the Boer War, an almost lone and certainly unpopular voice, as generally France was still regarded the most likely threat. This perception was mutual; in early September 1899, for example, while Britain was completely preoccupied with events in South Africa, *La Patrie* published an article headed 'Too Many English on Our Coasts', alleging British officers were photographing/mapping parts of France near Le Havre, and criticising their authorities for allowing such espionage to continue unchecked. Journalists such as WT Stead[78] and authors such as William Le Queux[79] lectured and wrote well-publicised articles and books on this theme. Erskine Childers'[80] 'Riddle of the Sands' (1903), involving German espionage, indirectly led to the First Lord of the Admiralty, Earl Selborne[81] tasking the NID with a study into the feasibility of an invasion of the United Kingdom; this concluded that it was not possible for such an operation to succeed.[82]

The War Office meanwhile drafted a new Censorship Bill and rules for correspondents. The draft Bill 'for controlling the publication of news calculated to prejudice the success of British arms' was considered by the Committee of Imperial Defence in February 1904. The covering paper pointed out 'The urgent need for preventing publication of the strategical distribution of our forces in anticipation of war', and an early Bill was suggested for activation by Order in Council in the event of emergency. The CID agreed the draft be circulated to the full Cabinet, subject to the Opposition and directors of 'the principal newspapers' being sounded out.

On the regulations for correspondents, a new and tougher report was drafted, embodying the recommendations of Lord Stanley and Major Jones, and now entitled 'Censorship – General Rules'. It both increased censorship on the private communications of soldiers, and also widened the gamut of press reporting considered unacceptable. This included not only information useful to an enemy but also 'messages tending to cause despondency and alarm, or to excite political feeling.'[83] This draft acquired much red ink amendment, but the file degenerated into an internal War Office argument between the General Staff (operations and intelligence) and the Adjutant General's Staff (personnel), as to which should be responsible for censorship rules (the former eventually won the lead). The only other staff investigation was into the Japanese rules for controlling foreign press. Very restrictive, these politely but severely limited the activity of correspondents; the copious detail specified even that correspondents were to wear 'foreign costume with white badge on left shoulder, name of newspaper in red'. An unnamed War Office staff officer recommended the British army should take a similarly strict line, noting with approbation that 'the Japanese leave nothing to chance or the honour of the correspondent'.

The new SofS for War in November 1904, Arnold-Forster,[84] sympathetic to the Japanese system, queried with Wood whether the question of correspondents in time of war had been 'adjusted on a proper basis', and opined that journalists more often proved 'an embarrassment than an aid to the Army'. However, he thought it would be difficult to make a change 'because the idea that war is conducted for the benefit of the newspapers has taken a very firm root in this country'. Nevertheless, the War Office did indeed introduce the new tougher set of Rules by the end of that year, more helpfully listing five points which correspondents should refrain from mentioning: the existing state of the troops, their future movements, or any anticipation thereof; the strength of the army, names of regiments and their whereabouts, and the dates of their movements; the name of the place whence communications were despatched; mere suppositions or reports contrary to facts; and the arrival or departure of transports or ships of war.[85]

Wider Refocusing from Empire to Europe

While the problems of how to control the Press in contemporary warfare preoccupied some in Whitehall, others had meanwhile been looking at wider aspects of planning. Although the South African campaign had eventually been won, events there and rivalries with other European powers elsewhere in Africa had dented British feelings of imperial invincibility; perceptions of threats closer to home also again achieved greater prominence in government circles. As early as 1901, Ministers had considered papers on 'The Military Needs of the Empire in a War with France and Russia' and 'The Military Resources of France and Probable Method of Employment in a War between France and England'.[86] In December 1902, the CID commissioned papers on the military position on the North-West Frontier of India in the event of a Franco-Russian alliance, with special reference to the needs for reinforcement from Britain; and on the effect on Britain's strategic naval position in the Mediterranean in the event of Russian occupation of Constantinople.

The following February, a 'Statement' was commissioned on what would have been the smallest and most lightly equipped force with which 'an enemy' (clearly France) could have undertaken 'a landing in England with a view to the occupation of London at the time when this country was most denuded of its regular land forces during the greatest stress of the South African War in the beginning of 1900'; and 'a landing in Ireland with a view to incite an insurrection'. The Prime Minister Arthur Balfour[87] nevertheless commented in November 1903 that these studies revealed 'no new anxieties'.[88]

In the following three years, the War Office and Admiralty increasingly refocused their thinking from imperial to European operations. There was a crescendo of papers, minutes, reports, and meetings under the aegis of the CID, of such volume that the Director General of Mobilisation and Intelligence was given a considerable increase in staff (the Director of Naval Intelligence a smaller one) to cope with the extra load. Papers written covered, for example, substituting a cheaper new police force in India, thus releasing some British troops there for duties closer to home. There was debate as to who should pay for the 15,000 troops in South Africa who were there in part as possible reinforcements for India (the government in India declined to foot this bill).

Every aspect of Home Defence was considered in detail. Balfour had himself secretly sent his own 'spy' to Dover during one Easter holiday weekend, who had 'without any difficulty' compiled an accurate report on the 'chief works of that town'; this led to greater focus nationwide on secrecy around forts and ports. Plans were discussed about exactly where the defensive line should be drawn in Afghanistan in the event of Russian invasion. A paper was written (with the Committee on Colonial Defence – there were many committees and sub-committees at work) on the 'Military Needs of the Empire', including the defence of all colonies and protectorates, starting with Egypt; this left, for the defence of Britain, the very precise figures of a 'Field Force of 31,059 Regular troops, and 18,617 Regular troops for garrison purposes'.

Concern about costs led to discussion of substituting Reserve for Regular troops, of their relative merits, of the lack of modern equipment for the Reserves, and of the difficulty of obtaining 'competent' officers for the Volunteers. Although the Navy believed that, because of its overwhelming command of the seas, no significant invasion force could reach the shores of Great Britain or Ireland, the Prime Minister did not at first accept this assurance, and much work had to be done on the invasion threat. Some politicians agitated meanwhile for legislation to 'prevent private persons from using telegraphic stations in times of war.'[89]

The Changing Threat

In 1903, the potential 'enemy' in official papers began to change. In April, the Admiralty circulated the translation of an article in the German magazine *Marine-Rundschau* concerning 'The Feasibility of Oversea Invasion' [of Britain]. DGMI was now out of tune with change when he criticised to the CID a recent secret letter sent by Lansdowne (now Foreign Secretary) to his French opposite number, suggesting an Anglo-French Agreement 'for the settlement of various outstanding questions'. While the War Office considered that the effect of this Agreement might be 'to weaken seriously our strategical position in the Mediterranean' with no corresponding strategic advantages for Britain in Egypt, the Admiralty on the other hand 'did not consider those criticisms, which were mainly of a kind affecting naval rather than military interests, were of sufficient importance to outweigh the advantages which this country would derive from the adoption of the Agreement as a whole'.

Intensive diplomatic, political and royal activity in the months following led to the signing of the Entente Cordiale in April 1904. France became in government files no longer a potential enemy, but a potential ally. The War Office Intelligence Department produced papers on 'The Military Resources of Germany, and Probable Method of Employment in a War between Germany and England', speculating that Germany would invade while the British Fleet was occupied elsewhere. Sceptical comments on these papers were made by the Director of Naval Intelligence, His Serene Highness Captain Prince Louis Battenberg,[90] views which perhaps had something to do with Naval apprehension about the Army's likely bid for consequent increases in funding in competition with the Navy's bid, rather than with any pro-German sympathies.[91]

The Admiralty had indeed begun to warn the Prime Minister about the potential threat caused by the German naval build-up as early as 1901. In January 1904 the Naval Commander-in-Chief China Station had been instructed to watch German ships 'reported to contemplate survey operations'. Russia also remained a potential enemy. In February 1904 the Russo-Japanese war started; off England's east coast in October, the Russian Baltic Fleet en route to the Far East, believing itself about to be attacked by Japanese motor torpedo boats, shelled British trawlers fishing on the Dogger Bank, sinking one and damaging two others, killing four fishermen and injuring 85. The Royal Navy was stood to, and the Admiralty became concerned about the amount of information then published in the Press on the deployment of the British Fleet. However, the affront was resolved by an international commission in Paris.

1904 – Control of the Press in War, Again

This and other feverish activity were the background against which discussion of relations with the Press continued. A further CID paper on 'Control of the Press in Time of War or Threat of War' was tabled in October 1904.[92] The summary raised three much-discussed questions for decision: '1. Is a general control of the press, apart from all censorship on cable messages or correspondence from the seat of war, required in the national interests at the outset and during the course of hostilities? 2. Can such control be rendered effective in any other way than that proposed by the General Staff? [censorship] 3. If this proposal is accepted, the necessary action appears to resolve itself into the following alternatives, viz: (a) To prepare a draft Bill conferring the required powers, this Bill to be passed through Parliament when the need arises; or (b) To pass a Bill empowering the Government to take the necessary action under Orders in Council whenever an emergency presents itself.'

The supporting notes gave examples of the military tactical use of enemy press information during the Franco-Prussian (1870) and Spanish-American (1898) Wars, adding that 'In modern times, these advantages are enhanced by the multiplication and acceleration of means of communication, and by the increased enterprise of modern journalism.' The notes acknowledged the difficulties facing editors of the period: 'From paid correspondents and from press agencies they receive, often late at night, a mass of intelligence, more or less accurate, with respect to naval and military preparations, the disposition of troops and ships, the armament of works, &c. Some of this intelligence it might be possible to publish without danger; other items, apparently trivial in themselves, it may be vital to withhold. Having insufficient expert knowledge to distinguish between these two classes, they must either publish the whole, or, at great financial sacrifice, suppress the whole. In the latter case, they may find that another editor has published what they have suppressed.'

The War Office therefore submitted that 'the only effective remedy is to prohibit the publication of any intelligence of naval or military interest, except such as is supplied officially by His Majesty's Government; and there is reason to believe that this course would find most favour with the editors of the better class of London newspapers. By this means, it is anticipated that the supply of information from other sources would at once cease; for if an editor is not permitted to publish any independent information on naval or military subjects, he will not go to the expense of appointing correspondents to keep him informed on these subjects'. Such remoteness of distinguished official minds from the realities of Press and public interests is not unique to the early twentieth century.

The final memorandum appended for CID consideration listed the four major areas of security concern, of which, in the opinion of the War Office, only Control of the Press remained unaddressed: '1. The detection and prevention of espionage' – 'a matter for the War Office in communication with the police'; 2. 'The censorship of posts and telegraphs' – 'The censorship of suspected correspondence can be authorised by a warrant from a

Secretary of State'; 3. 'The censorship of submarine cables' – 'separately considered and provided for' [The Admiralty had recently and secretly been given responsibility for the censorship of wireless telegraph messages, the War Office for those transmitted by submarine cable. In 1912 these responsibilities were refined to include a Chief Censor for each, working 'side by side']; 4. 'The control of the Press.'

After discussion, a revised CID paper was produced in December 1904, now entitled 'Control of the Press in Time of War'. It once again concluded that 'A draft Bill should be prepared at once and kept in readiness for submission to Parliament when an emergency arises', proposed activation by Order in Council, and added that 'it appears desirable that the leaders of the Opposition and the Directors of the principal newspapers should be sounded in regard to the proposed policy'. When the CID met in December 1904, chaired by the Prime Minister himself, and attended by amongst others the Foreign Secretary, the First Lord of the Admiralty, the Chancellor, the Secretaries of State for India and the Colonies, Lord Roberts, the First Sea Lord and the Chief of the General Staff, they agreed that the work should be taken forward as recommended.[93]

In a January 1905 note to the CID Secretary, Sir George Clarke,[94] the Treasury Solicitor's drafter said he had kept the Bill 'quite Confidential, as it would be inconvenient if the intention to legislate on the subject was known. I do not think there would be any chance of passing such a Bill in cold blood; i.e. you would have to wait until we were within measurable distance of a war . . . Can you insert any form of words which would prevent the publication of really mischievous news, and yet allow such a notice that Midshipman X has been posted to HMS PINAFORE? . . . When the form of the Bill has been settled, it will, I suppose, be pigeon-holed somewhere ready for introduction when the emergency arises'. Battenberg said however that he shared the views of the Japanese General Staffs, 'which means that our measures cannot be stringent enough. I am quite aware of our limitations in this country. How far we can go is for the Parliament-men to say . . . What I like least is the idea that nothing can be done until war is upon us . . . My impression is that any Government would hesitate to bring in this bill before the reserves were called out and the bill cast. The whole of our, what the Germans call "Strategischer Aufmarsch' would by then be common knowledge.'[95]

In the War Office, staff officers discussed the inadvisability of making the danger caused by publication the essence of an offence; this would throw the onus on the Crown to prove it, which would both sometimes be difficult legally and also might involve having to disclose matters which would in themselves add to the public danger. War Office comment also favoured including news vendors amongst those liable to prosecution because 'if the big newspaper firms such as W H Smith & Sons incur liability by selling newspapers containing matters the publication of which is an offence, it will cause them to keep a sharp eye on the papers they sell, and might easily lead to their boycotting a paper which sailed near the wind'. This suggestion that Smith's might become a de facto arm of censorship is not as bizarre as it might seem, since newspaper editors already considered the Company to be far from benign. The NS Circulars of these decades contain frequent complaints about Smith's near monopoly of railway station bookstalls, and of the unfair competition which this caused for not only local newsagents, but also (when Smith's extended their range of merchandise) for local stationers, drapers, etc.[96]

Having suggested Smith's as a potential de facto arm of censorship, the War Office minute continued: 'Perhaps the chance of being boycotted might have greater terrors to an editor than the possibility of conviction. It may safely be assumed that the Attorney-General would not permit the prosecution of a newsboy.' A short manuscript note refers to Clarke's view that, as the Act would be brought into force at a time when public opinion was 'thoroughly aroused', the ground would be prepared for passing 'much stronger measures'. Seizure of an offending publication was ruled out as being not particularly useful, but powers of search and confiscation of equipment, or even of closure of a newspaper in the case of persistent and wilful offending, were recommended. 'The mere imprisonment of an Editor will not stop a paper from publishing information if money is to be made by doing so . . . It is unfortunately the case that a certain class of newspaper exists which would face the risk of fine and imprisonment for the sake of the enormous sale likely to follow the publication of sensational secret intelligence in a time of great public sentiment.' That accurately describes a timeless view of the media held by governments and officials.

When however the printed two-page draft 'Publication of Naval and Military Information Act, 1905' was circulated later, it omitted some of the more draconian recommendations. The Act, for introduction by Order in Council as required 'in the event of an emergency', would nevertheless have permitted no such information to be published unless it had been issued by or passed by the Admiralty or War Office censors, and would have made anyone, in any part of the media responsible for contravening publication, liable to punishment by a fine up to a thousand pounds, or to imprisonment up to twelve months, with or without hard labour. Prosecution was only to be with the consent of the Attorney-General, although an optional clause in the draft added 'except by order of the Admiralty or Army Council.'[97]

In Parliament in March, the First Lord of the Admiralty (Selborne), emphasised the importance of finding a solution; but political attention became preoccupied by more pressing events in 1905 and in early 1906, including the First Moroccan Crisis. Pro-Moroccan independence comments made by the Kaiser in Tangier in March challenged the internationally agreed predominant French and Spanish influence in that country, and led to the threat of war; France and Germany moved troops to their mutual border at the end of 1905, before the matter was resolved mainly in favour of the status quo at the Algeciras Conference of 1906. There was also concurrent internal dissension within the ruling Conservative Party over tariffs, which ultimately led to the resignation of the Balfour Government.

The Campaigns for Increases in Defences

In November 1905, Field Marshal Lord Roberts,[98] feeling he had failed in the CID to gain support for a larger army for service at home, submitted a paper suggesting 'Universal Training' for all fit British males aged 17/18, followed by conscription. Balfour, who had already shown his lack of enthusiasm for this project, wrote to Roberts that it was 'alien to our national sentiments'. Although Roberts would not give up, and ensured his sentiments became widely known, Balfour was equally convinced Britain could only fight in continental Europe as an ally, with reserves which were properly trained and equipped (and therefore limited in size by finance), and that India could survive without reinforcement for at least a year, something with which he believed the CinC there (Kitchener) agreed.[99]

Nevertheless, Roberts was supported by some of the Press, in particular the *Daily Mail*. In 1905 the paper commissioned from Le Queux a series of articles on 'The [German] Invasion of 1910',[100] which in book form were translated into 27 languages and sold over a million copies. The new Prime Minister, Campbell-Bannerman, made disparaging remarks in the House of Commons about the book and series, saying he was surprised to see such material 'even in newspapers of which a few years ago we were all proud'; the newspaper chided him for having thus 'at a stroke given the book European fame.'[101]

4

WRANGLING WITH THE PRESS

At the annual meeting of the Newspaper Society in May 1905, the 'War News' question had been considered 'perhaps the most important clause in the Annual Report'. By autumn 1905, the authorities were ready to consult the Press informally about the draft Bill on the 'Publication of Naval and Military Information', and the chosen messenger was a prominent freelance journalist, Sydney Brooks.[102] With official support, between October and January he wrote similar letters to about 110 editors (some of whom edited more than one journal) of London and provincial newspapers and periodicals. He quoted from March speeches in the House of Lords about the dangers (despite the patriotism of journalists) of inadvertent disclosure of sensitive information, the problem which would be caused by waiting until war was imminent before introducing legislation, and the need therefore to address the problem in time of peace.

Brooks continued: 'With the object of carrying out the wishes of the Committee of Imperial Defence, I beg to invite your most earnest consideration to the following questions and to request the favour of an early reply:

1   Are you prepared to support a Bill making the early publication of all news of naval and military movements, not authorised by the responsible authorities, penal?
2   Are you prepared to accept and advocate the principle that such a Bill should be passed with powers to make it operative by Order in Council when the Government of the day so decides?
3   Are you willing to attend a Conference of the leading Editors of the United Kingdom at the offices of the Committee of Imperial Defence, should such a Conference be thought advisable for the further discussion of the details of the Bill in question?'

Brooks ended by attempting to reassure editors such a bill would leave the Press free to criticise, comment on and expose any campaign, would not include dispatches from the Front if passed by the censors there, and 'would involve, as an almost inevitable corollary, a fuller and more adequate supply of official news'. This somewhat optimistic supposition was seemingly his own thought, since research reveals no official thinking of such a quid pro quo. He signed off with the equally over-optimistic statement that, from informal conversations he had had with some editors, 'I am persuaded that a Bill along these lines would be welcomed by the Press.'[103]

By late January 1906, Brooks had received replies from most editors. There were indeed many who, in principle at least, were prepared to consider some such Bill. Of the 25 London editors, only the *Telegraph* implied serious doubts, but agreed nevertheless to attend a conference, but even *The Times* viewed 'with apprehension any system which made penal the publication of all military and naval news except as authorised by the government'. Of the provincial editors, however, only 47 of the 84 who replied approved generally; some, led by Charles Clifford of the *Sheffield Daily Telegraph*, felt that their professional body, the Newspaper Society (of which he was then President) should come to a collective view rather than that they should respond individually; others were against agreement, the *Manchester Guardian* for example asserting 'such power in the hands of government would be a very dangerous weapon'.

Representative of those strongly against was CP Redmond of the *Waterford Evening News*: 'My answer to your first two questions is an emphatic *NO*. I protest in the strongest possible manner at any movement calculated to retard the liberty of the Press. In Ireland we pressmen have suffered enough from the tyranny of Parliament. We do not wish to see the tyranny extended to our brothers of the Press in England, Scotland or Wales. The South African war indicated very clearly that the British can muzzle the Press and examples shown in the recent war between Japan and Russia will no doubt be forced upon England in case of a great international war. Why should members of the Press endeavour to tie their own hands? It is their duty to 'Hold the mirror up to nature' if possible, irrespective of the desires of any particular government. Should I have an opportunity of attending your conference, I shall oppose with all my strength your attempt to impose restrictions on the Great World's Power, a free and unfettered Press.' This letter accurately describes a timeless Media view of the threat from governments and officials.

In the light of the mixed response, the CID Secretary himself wrote in February to the NS President, along similar lines to the Brooks letter, ending 'It would be a national service of the highest order if the Newspaper Society would endorse the principle of the Bill as here outlined and would appoint an individual member or a small committee to confer with me as to details.' A few days later, the NS Secretary replied to Clarke that the Society's Committee had met and unanimously agreed to a resolution expressing 'sympathy with the objects which the Imperial Defence Committee desire', and stating that a Sub-Committee would be appointed by them to consider any Bill that might be drafted. The Society then informed its members of this resolution, and Brooks wrote a supportive letter to Clifford, suggesting, as though they were his own independent ideas, what the Bill should include, which was almost exactly what the secret printed draft Bill did indeed include; it must be concluded that Brooks had privately seen the draft Bill, even though others in the Press were unaware that work within Whitehall was so advanced.[104]

The NS duly formed a Sub-Committee, whose members were Clifford, Sir Douglas Straight (*Pall Mall Gazette*), F Carruthers Gould (*Westminster Gazette*) and the Society's solicitor, J Soames.[105] The Sub-Committee met many times from February 1906, including sometimes with Clarke, but ultimately informed their members at the end of May that it had come 'to the conclusion that the matter was not one with which the Society has power to deal definitely, or to commit the Press generally to approval or disapproval of any measure that might be drafted'. Their Report nevertheless restated broad principles of their discussion with Clarke:

1   Prohibited Action. Publication of all news with regard to Naval and Military matters, or to movements of ships and troops;
2   Exception. No restriction as regards the publication of news supplied by the Admiralty or the War Office, or sent from the seat of war;

3   Comment. No restriction on comment or criticism based upon information furnished as in Clause 2, or upon facts which were common knowledge;

4   Persons liable to Prosecution. Those liable under Lord Campbell's Act or to process by way of Criminal Information;

5   Penalty. Such as Parliament might sanction to be recovered in the High Courts;

6   Prosecution. No prosecution to be instituted except by leave of the Court, on motion made by one of the Law Officers of the Crown;

7   Costs in Case of Acquittal. The Judge before whom the case was tried to have the power to direct the Crown should pay the defence costs;

8   Power to Put in Force. The Act might be put in force by Order in Council, and should remain in force until revoked by a further such Order.

The Sub-Committee nevertheless continued to make a sympathetic interpretation of the Government's intentions, and they therefore invited all their members to a conference at the Royal United Service Institute three weeks later (21 June), to be presided over by Arthur Walter,[106] Chairman of *The Times*. The printed letter of explanation and invitation ended: 'We may state that the Prime Minister [Campbell-Bannerman] is greatly interested in the steps which have been taken to ascertain the opinion of the directors of the Press, and he trusts that general unanimity will be attained in regard to a question which is of extreme importance to national interests.'

A new standard-bearer of resistance now emerged. Sir John Leng,[107] not a recipient of the original Brooks consultation, wrote to the new NS President, explaining what he would have said had he been able to attend the conference, and, 'as one of the oldest members of the Scottish Press', expressing his 'strong objections to the proposals for placing the Newspaper Press of this country under State control, and Government Editorship of news in time of war'. His main objections were, firstly and based on an optimistic assessment of the international situation: 'Who is threatening us with war?'; having listed inter alia the friendly relations with European States ('Thanks to our Royal and Imperial Peacemaker'), Britain's Treaty with Japan, and the desire of the President of the USA [Theodore Roosevelt] 'for the displacement of war by arbitration', his view was that 'Any uneasiness with respect to Germany is being diminished rapidly by the exchange of courtesies between influential representatives of the Municipalities and the Press of the two countries, and if a few bellicose London journals would cease their mischievous provocations good feeling would be unbroken and undisturbed between two peoples largely of the same race and equally interested in the avoidance of war.' He concluded therefore that 'The Movement [censorship Bill] is altogether premature', and, based on doubts about 'the wisdom of Governments and the judgement of Government officials', that the extent of the proposed prohibitive action concerning the Press was excessive. He also alluded to 'the stupid military censorship of news despatches and correspondence during the South African War'.

1906 – Government/Press Stalemate

At the conference, attended by about 50 editors (but not by Waterford's redoubtable Redmond), similar dissenting opinions and reservations were voiced. The NS resolution proposed by the Chairman was to approve the work of the Sub-Committee, fully endorse the eight principles (above) as the basis for any legislation, and authorise the Sub-Committee to continue its work with officials on any Bill drafted. However, this resolution was opposed and amended from the floor. Fabian Ware (*Morning Post*) proposed that full endorsement of the Sub-Committee's principles should be omitted, that it should be enlarged to incorporate some members with wider views, and that it should only then continue to consider any Bill which might be drafted. This amendment was carried, as was a second resolution requiring any such further work by the Sub-Committee to be submitted to a future conference before the Bill was introduced into Parliament.

There was strong support for this course in newspaper editorials in the following days.[108] This was a clear disappointment to the Government; replying to a House of Commons question on 27 June, the Prime Minister could only say '. . . restricting the dissemination of news in time of war is being considered by the Committee of Imperial Defence. His Majesty's Government hope to deal with it early next year', a similar answer being given in the Upper House by the First Lord of the Admiralty, Tweedmouth.[109] Despite this setback, the CID continued working on the draft Bill, adding an extra clause enabling police to search and seize if they had 'reasonable cause to believe that an offence under this Act is about to be or has been committed'. Although the undisclosed printed draft Bill had not otherwise been changed, the working title had moved from 'in War' to 'in Cases of Emergency.'[110]

Meanwhile, Sir John Leng published his pre-conference letter as an 'Open Letter to the Press of the United Kingdom', and also sent a copy to the Prime Minister. Clarke replied on the latter's behalf, politely reiterating the official arguments, and pointing out that security crises could emerge very suddenly and unexpectedly (he quoted the Dogger Bank incident as an example, and reminded of the potentially 'injurious' information which the Press had published at that time). Leng suggested consultation should be extended beyond just newspapers, in particular to the news agencies who 'are becoming more and more the swift, trustworthy and trusted distributors of news'. Referring to the poor standard of censorship during the Boer War, he made a plea that in future 'such a responsible duty shall be discharged by men of intelligence and good commonsense', and suggested that 'an experienced journalist' should be attached to any censorship organisation. Clarke replied inter alia that he feared that 'it would be practically impossible for the Admiralty or War Office to ask the Press to withhold information on a particular subject, although I am sure that, as you say, Editors – if so asked – would be careful in complying.'[111]

With the wind temporarily out of official sails, the Bill continued to be discussed in Press circles, both within the NS Sub-Committee, and at its annual conferences and those of the Institute of Journalists (IoJ). The latter tabled the subject at its 1906 and 1907 conferences, at the second of which a resolution was proposed by AF Robbins,[112] laying down some markers, namely that there should be no restriction placed on comment or criticism based on facts which were common knowledge, that no penalty should be inflicted on anyone in the Press unless it could be proved that he had published a matter covered in the Act 'wilfully and knowingly', and that there should be a right of appeal to the High Court of Justice.[113]

In November 1906, Sydney Brooks wrote six closely-reasoned foolscap pages to the First Lord of the Admiralty (Tweedmouth), making it clear that the Bill in its current form had very little chance of being accepted by the Newspaper Society, which was about to hold another conference to discuss it, nor by the IoJ. He suggested more precise definition of which naval/military information should not be published, the addition of a clause that no restriction would be placed on comment or criticism based on 'facts of common knowledge or on news that had already been published in foreign journals',[114] and that the power proposed for judges to be able to have someone confined 'for the safe custody of that person' should be omitted. He ended by admitting his opinions were 'in no sense official', and suggesting that if his amendments were agreed by the government side, 'the best way of getting them incorporated into the Bill would be to allow the Sub-Committee of the Newspaper Society to themselves bring them forward. The Government in that case would be able to create an excellent impression of magnanimity by simply agreeing to them – an impression that would undoubtedly carry great weight when the amended Bill came to be submitted to the full Conference'. Whether this Machiavellian proposal was Brooks' own, or had been concocted by members of the NS Sub-Committee for internal reasons, is not now possible to establish. At a 13 November 1906 CID meeting, 'Control of the Press During or in Anticipation of War' was on the agenda, but after the Prime Minister (Campbell-Bannerman) had spoken, there was little discussion prior to agreement that governmental powers of preventing dissemination of naval and military information were essential, and should not be delayed until the outbreak of war, when they should be enacted by Order-in-Council; but the decision was left to the whole Cabinet.[115]

In the House of Lords, Tweedmouth announced his intention of having a further draft submitted to the Law Officers and then to the NS Sub-Committee; 'I have no reason to think that the Press will not be with us.'[116] Work on the Bill continued within Whitehall, and the printed 1908 version was sent by the Admiralty to the NS in October 1907. Its Sub-Committee was reconvened with the further additions of Baron de Reuter[117] and Edmund Robbins, Manager of the Press Association.[118] The draft does indeed show some adjustment had been made to meet press concerns. Clarke himself had also previously removed clauses concerning search and seizure by the police ('a rather Russian flavour about them which is bound to cause bitter resentment').

Nevertheless, at the further NS conference in February 1908 ('Strictly confined to Newspaper Proprietors, Managers, Editors, Reporters, War Correspondents, and News Agencies'; 27 attended), the Secretary of the (London) Newspaper Proprietors' Association, Ernest Parke,[119] unexpectedly read a paper strongly condemning the co-operative resolution. The final part of the statement read: 'we consider that no good cause has been shown for suspecting the patriotism and discretion of those who conduct the newspapers of this country, and that there is no occasion for the proposed legislation. When the emergency actually arises Parliament can make such provisions as are required to meet the special exigencies of the situation. In short, we prefer to leave the control of the dissemination of naval and military information in the hands of Parliamentary representatives of the people, instead of empowering Government departments, who are proverbially averse to criticism, to set in motion a secret legislative authority armed with extraordinary and penal powers'.

Unsurprisingly, this surprise attack caused bad feeling between Newspaper Society and the Newspaper Proprietors' Association, reflected three months later in an angry letter to *The Times* from the President of the former, blaming the NPA and its 'non-possumus attitude' for the lack of progress. Although the condemnatory counter-resolution was easily defeated, the only resolution which could be passed was merely 'That this Meeting does now adjourn in order that communication may be opened with the Newspaper Proprietors Association'. In effect, the Newspaper Society therefore suspended all further action. In consequence, nothing further was done pro tem in Whitehall.

5

GOVERNMENT ATTEMPTS TO LITIGATE

1908 – A Further Attempt to Amend the OSA

Action in Whitehall switched back to amending OSA 1889, and to tightening up internal security. In Parliament, the Lord Chancellor, Loreburn,[120] gave his opinion on the lack of protection afforded by the existing OSA to the secret correspondence of Ministers, the Viceroy of India, and HM Ambassadors.[121] A new draft OSA was introduced in March 1908. It aimed not only to strengthen the law on espionage, but also to prohibit the unauthorised publication by any person of official information unless in the interests of the State, and to extend the application of the Bill beyond government employees and contractors to any member of the public. Despite assurances from the Lord Chancellor that 'anyone in the Press conducting his duties honourably would be quite safe', neither the press nor Parliament were convinced that reporting of governmental business would not be adversely affected by such amendments. In May 1908, the Second Reading of the Bill was abandoned, although the Government made clear it had no intention of dropping the subject.

Gearing Up For Future War

Departments of State were anyway meanwhile much preoccupied with further adjustment of plans to meet the perceived threats to post-Victorian security, and to redirect/cut spending accordingly. For example, having concluded that major invasion of Britain was not feasible, the old forts and military warehouses of London were closed. The Haldane[122] reforms of the Army began, including reorganisation to be able to mount an expeditionary force of 5,546 officers and 150,740 men, including 30,000 Militiamen, and establishment of the Territorial Army in April 1908. The reduction of overseas garrisons was continued. The defences of Ireland were scaled down to those necessary for defended ports, with any 'insurrection' to be coped with by auxiliary reinforcement of the Royal Irish Constabulary from Great Britain. The CID considered possible future operations in the Dardanelles, and concluded 'the operation of landing an expeditionary force on or near the Gallipoli Peninsula would involve great risk, and should not be undertaken if other means of bringing pressure to bear on Turkey were available'; the Admiralty considered it could force the passage through the Dardanelles, but only with heavy losses, because modern (German-made, -maintained and -controlled) shore batteries had the advantage over ships in those confined waters.

In June 1908, the Government was asked in the Lords whether it intended 'to allow the session of 1908, like that of 1907, to slip away without bringing in a Bill dealing with the dissemination of news in war time', and also whether, as the subjects were akin, it would discuss with members of the Press the wording of the Official Secrets Bill. The replies by Granard[123] and the Lord Chancellor indicated the continuing desire for a Bill but not for action to bring it forward then. The NS commented tartly: 'It is to be feared that the prospects of an ultimate agreement with the press are not improved by the association of the original proposition with the Lord Chancellor's Official Secrets Bill, the tenor and scope of which have been generally condemned.'[124] This distinction in the minds of the Media, between the principles of a system of self-regulation and the content of Acts of Parliament, has been a constant through the years since. The End of Session list of Parliamentary Bills of interest to the press did not contain one on Control of the Press.[125]

In October 1908, the CID again considered major invasion; again it concluded (in mid-1909) that, as long as Britain maintained naval supremacy, invasion was not possible; if on the other hand Britain lost command of the sea, subjection of the country would be inevitable, however strong the Home Force; the latter should therefore be maintained only at a size sufficient to deter raids, and thus to cause any enemy to bring a detectably large force. Discussion also began of Japan as a potential enemy, and comparison was made of the combined German and Japanese naval strength with that of the Royal Navy.[126] By 1910 there was much discussion too of the implications for defence of the new 'Aerial Navigation.'[127]

The Media and the Threat

The media campaign about the growing German threat meanwhile also continued apace, inducing in politicians and the public occasional somewhat over-alarmed reactions. From 1906, when the Royal Navy's first *DREADNOUGHT* battleship was launched, much publicity was given to the German threat to British supremacy, even more so after the November 1907 announcement of the accelerated German shipbuilding programme. Questions were asked in the Houses of Lords and Commons about the number of German spies and soldiers believed to be in the United Kingdom, mentioning figures of between 66 and 80,000. In 1908, Baden-Powell was the recipient of a bogus German invasion plan from a source in Brussels. It had been pressure from such journalists as Colonel Repington and Herbert Wilson,[128] which had led to fresh consideration by the CID of the threat of invasion. Northcliffe suggested to Haldane that training of military censors should start.

Le Queux continued his output, with a claim in mid-1908 that he had the text of a speech by the Kaiser to a secret German council of war about invasion, a text subsequently found to be false, but believed by a number of senior political and military figures at the time, and even by the officer in charge of the War Office's small department responsible for counter-intelligence and 'secret service', Lieutenant Colonel Edmonds.[129] In 1909 Le Queux added to his lobbying a new book: 'Spies of the Kaiser. Plotting the Downfall of England'. In January that year, 'Empire of the North', a play about invasion[130] opened in London, leading to an upsurge in military recruiting there (a recruiting office was even opened in the theatre foyer). The public increasingly reported suspicious aliens (the number of such reports received by Edmonds had risen from 5 in 1907 to 47 a year later). The founder of the naval/military publishing house, Fred Jane,[131] having encountered a suspicious German in Portsmouth, persuaded him to accompany him to Woburn, where he locked the 'spy' in the Duke of Bedford's animal park. This curious incident and others led to the War Office compiling a list of various categories of suspicious aliens.

1908/9 – The Official Reaction

Inside the Admiralty and War Office, there was a two-fold response to the public mood and to their own intelligence concerns. The first was organisational. The DNI, now Rear Admiral Slade[132] and his opposite number in the War Office, Major General Ewart,[133] concerned about the lack of an organised secret service, set up an embryo intelligence network in Hamburg in 1908. Their second response was political. Ewart gave evidence to the CID that year about the lack of a satisfactory intelligence organisation for acquiring secret information on Germany and other continental powers, and he and Slade began to lobby in Whitehall for such an organisation. In March 1909 another high-level CID Sub-Committee, chaired by Haldane, was formed to consider 'The Question of Foreign Espionage in the United Kingdom'.

This Sub-Committee produced its report in late July 1909. It mentioned Admiralty evidence of attempts by a foreign agent in Brussels to acquire secret information about British naval gunnery, and it discussed a map of the United Kingdom which showed marked in red the various places where alleged agents had been reported, as an indication of Germany 'having in contemplation the invasion of this country'. All this left no doubt in their minds that 'an extensive system of German espionage' existed, and that there was no organisation to watch it. Similarly it had been represented to them that Britain had no organisation of its own for acquiring information, in particular about German ports and dockyards; and that the Admiralty and War Office were 'in a difficult position when dealing with foreign spies who may have information to sell, since their dealings have to be direct and not through intermediaries' and they 'are therefore compelled to exercise precautions in order to prevent the Government from becoming involved'.

The Sub-Committee therefore recommended that a 'Secret Service Bureau' should be formed, to 'serve as a screen between the Admiralty and War Office and foreign spies', to 'keep in touch through the Home Office' with police forces and if necessary to send agents to various parts of the countries 'to ascertain the nature and scope of espionage'. These recommendations were regarded as being so secret that only a single typed copy was made, given to the Director of Military Operations, who it recommended should undertake the organisation of the Bureau 'without delay', in conjunction with the Admiralty and the Commissioner of Police.

The Sub-Committee then went on to comment on the inadequacies of the Official Secrets Act 1889, and the 'great need' to amend the Act to make it 'an efficient weapon in dealing with espionage'. The First Lord of the Admiralty, McKenna[134] had drawn attention to secret information recently published in a newspaper [the *Daily Mail*], where the Act did not currently enable the Editor to be prosecuted. The Sub-Committee, while recommending the Act should be amended accordingly, did however add it should only apply to actual espionage and not contain clauses which would have a tendency to restrict the freedom of the Press; it quoted the Press resistance to the draft 1908 Bill, which had not therefore been proceeded with.

It was recommended however that an early Bill to introduce these measures should be introduced by the SofS for War rather than by the Home Office, because the plea of its being a measure of precaution of great importance to national defence 'would excite less opposition'. A separate Bill for 'the prevention of the publication of certain documents or information' should also be introduced after negotiations with representatives of the Press. At the Sub-Committee's meeting on 24 April, Haldane referred to the abortive 1908 Bill, and said that 'At the present time public opinion was much more sympathetic towards a Bill of the nature proposed, and this attitude of the public should be taken advantage of'. Finally, the Sub-Committee recommended that communication on secret matters between the Post Office and the Admiralty, War Office and Secret Service Bureau should not be through normal channels, but between 'particular members' of the Post Office and SSB; and that an enquiry should be held into the guarding of 'magazines, dockyards, large oil-stores, cable landing stations, wireless stations, private shipbuilding yards, railway bridges, tunnels', and other points vulnerable to pre-hostility sabotage 'by two or three determined men.'[135]

Establishment of Embryo Secret Intelligence and Security Services

The Secret Service Bureau was established accordingly shortly afterwards, in 1909. Initially it had Naval and Military sections, but within a year these were reorganised into a Home Department, responsible for counter-espionage (the ancestor of the Security Service, aka MI5) and a Foreign Department, responsible for espionage (ancestor of the Secret Intelligence Service, aka MI6). The first Head of the Military/Home department was Captain Vernon Kell, a CID Assistant Secretary, proposed by his former superior, Colonel Edmonds; he started work in August 1909 with a staff of one clerk, and by 1914 still had only three officers, a barrister, and seven clerks. In 1910, the Home Secretary Winston Churchill gave permission for Kell to collaborate with Chief Constables of Police Forces throughout Britain on certain security matters. Kell devised a 'Return of Aliens Form', which, with the assistance of local police, enabled him to build up a quite comprehensive database. In 1911 Churchill further authorised general warrants to be issued to Kell to intercept and secretly examine the correspondence of those on his database suspected of subversive activity, and the first prosecution for espionage under the OSA 1889 took place in 1911. Nevertheless Kell and the police thought OSA 1889 inadequate, because it required the proof of intent to obtain information illegally; they pushed for an increase in powers.

The first Head of the Naval/Foreign department was Commander Mansfield Smith-Cumming, a retired officer who had been invalided from the Navy and was employed on Boom Defence duties at Southampton. Again suggested by a former superior, he started his new appointment in October 1909, operating in the early days from a flat in the roof of Whitehall Court. He too began with a very small staff, enhanced in due course by recruitment of an individualistic kind. Initially the interests of his department were imperially wide, but they became more focused on Europe as war approached. Both Kell and Cumming,[136] although not previously earmarked for distinction within the conventional branches of their respective Armed Services, had singularly unusual personalities and qualities, spent many years as Chief of his new department (Kell rather longer than Cumming), and built it up to be an institution of some renown.[137]

6

EVENTS BRING MATTERS
TO A HEAD

1909/11 – Further Attempts to Amend the OSA
and Press Control Bills

The long-awaited propitious moment for a new OSA to be brought to Parliament seemed at last to have arrived. The attempt to draft the separate Bill on the publication of naval and military information, in a form which would meet both official and political concerns and yet be acceptable to the Press, was also restarted. In March 1910, the Prime Minister invited Winston Churchill to chair the CID Standing Sub-Committee in considering the matter anew. At a June meeting, amendments were agreed to meet known press concerns, and there was discussion of a War Office proposal that a joint Naval and Military Bureau should be established 'to deal with the issue of information to the Press in time of war'. There were now four major areas of CID study affecting the Press:

- Amendment of the OSA.
- Control of the Press in Time of Crisis.
- Regulation of War Correspondents.
- A Press Bureau.[138]

It was decided Churchill should see Sydney Brooks, still volunteering his services as an intermediary, to ask him to ascertain the attitude of the Press to the revised draft Bill on its control. In late October, having interviewed seventeen leading newspaper editors, Brooks met the CID Secretary, now Admiral Ottley,[139] but reported the reception was still not favourable. Furthermore, 'all the various societies were now affiliated and they would act together'. There were therefore two courses open, either 'to be quite firm' and to tell the Press that legislation along these lines was a necessity and that the Government were determined to carry it through, but would be prepared to meet a small committee to consider points of detail; or 'to get hold of Lord Northcliffe, whose influence in the Press was great. This *might* succeed'. Meanwhile he would make 'further enquiries'; but Churchill's Sub-Committee did not in fact meet again to consider the matter until November 1912, by when other arrangements had been made.

While awaiting this further press sounding, Ottley had pressed ahead with co-ordinating the establishment of a Joint Bureau, contacting the Director of Military Operations, now Brigadier-General Wilson[140] and the Director of Naval Intelligence, now Rear Admiral Bethell,[141] and reminded them that 'Mr Churchill is evidently strongly of the opinion that some organisation for the dissemination of naval and military intelligence of a harmless kind is desirable, and it might be considered by the press as some slight compensation for being muzzled'. Wilson commented that in time of crisis there were many other Government Departments whose work was intimately connected with defence, and he suggested therefore that at least the Foreign and Colonial Offices ought to be part of the scheme. The Foreign Office rejected this idea, however; a manuscript note made clear the view of the Foreign Secretary Sir Edward Grey[142] that 'the Admiralty and War Office are concerned with their own news (and leakage), the FO deals with news from abroad'.

Ottley considered a Press Bureau would need to be operative not just in time of war, but in the preceding period of strained relations; apart from the risk of war plans being disclosed, precautionary measures might prejudice diplomatic measures, or precautionary measures might have to be delayed for fear of themselves causing 'disastrous consequences'. It would therefore be necessary for the flow of information to be filtered rather than stopped (as intended by the Act), and it was for this that a Bureau was needed. Its effectiveness would 'depend largely on the degree of intimacy with the Press' which it had been able to achieve beforehand and the degree of confidence inspired thereby. The Admiralty and War Office staffs decided however that firmer plans for a Bureau should await the passing of the hoped-for Act, even though they agreed it was desirable: 'If the Bureau adopted a sympathetic attitude towards the Press from the outset and supplied the Press liberally with information and without charge, it is probable that many of the existing paid sources of [Press] intelligence, some of them undesirable and all of them more or less inaccurate, would tend to dry up, so that the Press would come to lean more and more on the Bureau for Naval and Military information.'[143] Alas, in the following hundred years, such a Utopian relationship between governmental press offices and the Media has rarely been achieved, and never for long.

While staff officers considered longer-term plans, once again events elsewhere intervened. In what were already difficult times for the British Government, at home with railway and dock strikes, the Irish Home Rule problems, the Parliament Bill (to reduce the power of the House of Lords), and abroad with concerns over Russian intentions in Persia, and politico-military instability in the Mediterranean area, now a new crisis occurred in Morocco. In July 1911, as French forces consolidated their hold on the country, Germany sent the gunboat *Panther* to Agadir, ostensibly to protect German citizens and interests from local insurrection, but in reality as part of wider Franco-German rivalry in Africa.[144]

Although it was to France and Germany which this almost brought war, the potential ramifications were wider (some in Britain believed that Germany was seeking to establish a naval base in Morocco), and although Britain never felt it necessary formally to declare the existence of a 'precautionary period', she secretly took certain precautionary measures. These were then promptly and widely reported in the British Press in articles 'purporting to give correct information concerning the naval movements, the movement of coal, measures of precaution on board ships of war, the steps taken for strengthening the guards on magazines, and many other matters of importance'; a *Morning Post* report on 'The Guardianship of British Forts' caused particular umbrage.[145] The concern caused in official circles, coupled with the aroused state of public alarm, finally gave the Government the confidence to bring forward for action two initiatives, the amendment of the OSA, and measures to control the Press.

OSA 1911

The draft OSA was given its first reading in Parliament in mid-July. Haldane steered the Bill through the House of Lords shortly afterwards, where the limited discussion focused mainly on the currently perceived threat of espionage; the Government's line was that the Bill was nothing very new except in the procedures. It then passed through all the House of Commons stages in one day (18 August 1911), the only strong resistance coming from Sir William Byles,[146] who feared it might undo Magna Carta. Only at the Committee stage was there a Division, and the Bill was passed without amendment by 107 votes to 10 (the latter including future Labour Ministers who contentedly used OSAs 1911 and 1920 against the Press). Even the USofS for War, Colonel Seely,[147] who steered it through the readings in under an hour, was surprised by how little discussion there was; he noted in his memoirs that, when Members got up to speak, they had been 'forcibly pulled down by their neighbours'. He later considered the 'striking success' of the secret Agencies in WWI could not have been achieved without this OSA.[148]

The House seemed to have accepted the assurances of the Attorney-General, Sir Rufus Isaacs[149] that the Bill was merely a remodelling of the 1889 Act to deal with certain points then unforeseen: 'There is nothing novel in the Bill which the House is being asked to accept now.' In fact the OSA 1911 did many other things: inter alia, it extended the provisions beyond government employees and contractors, it altered the burden of proof on the prosecution so that it no longer had to prove that the accused's purpose was prejudicial to the interest or safety of the State, and introduced new offences and penalties under its Section 2 of wrongful communication or retention of official information, of receiving such information in contravention of the Act, and of harbouring suspects. It also gave additional powers of search and arrest to local Justices of the Peace and police. Despite these changes, there was relatively little comment from those responsible for co-ordinating the interests of the Press, who at the time were again more concerned about the implications of the Libel and Copyright Bills, and by strikes and 'riots' by newsboys.[150]

1911 – An Agreement with the Press

Meanwhile, also in the wake of the Agadir crisis, and against a background of continuing press reports of naval and military precautionary measures being taken, and continuing governmental unhappiness therewith, Seely had reopened discussions with the Press, but using a different channel. He had instructed the Assistant Secretary of the War Office, Mr Brade[151] to re-enter into informal negotiations, this time not with the editors nor their organisations, but with the 'dominant press interests', namely the proprietors, 'with the view of arriving at some friendly arrangement for regulating the publication of naval and military news which might be contrary to public interest'.[152] Brade went first however to the parliamentary correspondent of *The Times*, Arthur Nicholson,[153] 'of whose interest in the matter I was assured privately, and whose influence with Lord Northcliffe seemed to give a special value to any support that we could secure from him.'[154] In initial discussion, Nicholson seemed considerably more extreme in his support of total censorship than did the civil servant, who pointed out the political realities and the dangers of it doing 'more harm than good by giving occasion for the dissemination of wild and fantastic rumours based on leakages of scraps of information and on malicious perversions of the truth'.

The two then went on to debate the possibility of setting up 'some body representative of the important press interests with whom the Admiralty and the War Office could agree, from time to time, as to the suppression of news the publication of which would be detrimental to the public interest'. Brade later discussed the same idea with the ex-*Times* staff

MP Leopold Amery,[155] from whom, as a former war correspondent, he had previously been authorised to seek comments on the revised regulations for correspondents with the Army in the field. Brade also consulted Reginald Nicholson, Manager of *The Times*.[156] All agreed the Newspaper Society should not be brought into the discussion because it 'existed rather for other purposes' and was not entirely representative,[157] and advised indeed that it was the proprietors not the editors and journalists whom Brade should seek to influence, both because the former were better organised and because they had 'more complete control' of the Press. It was also suggested Brade should get in touch with the Empire Press Union, which was 'a comparatively young and therefore vigorous body.'[158]

While Brade's discussions were in progress, the NS did however show that it too could act co-operatively and reasonably effectively. When the Admiralty had been about to conduct secret gunnery trials, it had asked the Society to use its good offices to suggest to its members that, in the public interest, these trials should not be publicised, and its request had been effective. Later, when a combined exercise was about to be held at Southampton in January 1912 to test measures for the embarkation of an expeditionary force, Brade himself and the Admiralty's PUS (Sir Graham Greene, see Section 2) had made a similar request; the Society had on that occasion forwarded their letter to 400–500 journals throughout the United Kingdom, and the subsequent thanks from the Army Council referred to all newspaper and agencies 'having, without exception complied with the request.'[159]

Even these successful ad hoc arrangements were not liked by all: a letter to *The Times* of 10 August from a 'Correspondent for Naval Affairs' complained of the 'futility of excluding correspondents from manoeuvres'; he observed there had been sufficient leaks nevertheless to have enabled at least one newspaper to publish 'authentic narratives' from both sides in the exercise, and suggested that if such leaks could not be prevented, it would be better to allow 'honourable correspondents' onboard. Officials too thought ad hoc contacts were unsatisfactory, because the Press owed the Newspaper Society no more than goodwill.

In July 1912, the Prime Minister (Asquith), recounting in the House of Commons the many CID activities, mentioned it had paid particular attention to control of the Press in time of war, which he described as 'a very serious matter that has never received adequate attention'. This inaccurate assessment drew a furious response in the *Pall Mall Gazette* a few days later from 'a Journalist' (in fact Sydney Brooks), who alluded to the discussions of recent years between the press and successive governments, put the blame for lack of progress on the 'indifference or timidity' of the Cabinet, and described the constructive actions of the Press in terms as partial as those used by the Prime Minister about the governmental side: 'It is not often that a profession or a trade, on its own initiative and from motives of patriotism alone, approaches the Ministry and asks to be shorn of privileges and of a liberty, the unrestricted exercise of which it has come to recognise as detrimental to the national interests. Yet that is precisely what a large element in the Press did some six or seven years ago; and it is altogether the fault of the Government if its self-denying endeavours failed to culminate in legislation.'[160]

Brooks nevertheless went on to remake the case for some such legislation being approved in the current time of peace for use when war came. 'The real "liberty of the Press", it is worth remembering, is not the liberty to publish news, but to express opinion; and the only liberty that such a Bill would abridge would be the liberty to jeopardise the security of the nation.' A few days later, Brooks followed up by writing to Haldane, offering his services again in persuading the Press to back the introduction of a Bill. The new CID Secretary,

Captain Maurice Hankey[161] politely but firmly replied on behalf of Haldane, saying the latter did 'not consider the present moment a very favourable one for you to set to work with the newspaper proprietors'; and that he anyway did not see any reasonable prospect of introducing let alone passing such a Bill in the current Session 'owing to the immense pressure on Parliamentary time'. It is perhaps unsurprising that the independent views of Brooks, not entirely pleasing to either side in the debate, ensured that henceforth he appears to have played no significant further part in the discussions.[162] Nevertheless, there had been an undertone perceived by some in the Press in Asquith's statement, implying that the patience of the Government was running out.[163]

Brade meanwhile had approached the Empire Press Union (EPU) as suggested, only to be told it could not help in its current early state of organisation; on the one hand, the Press in some colonies was not itself well organised, and on the other, 'in India, the Press is entirely under the control of the [Indian] Government'. The EPU did however suggest Brade should attend a meeting of yet another press body, the Joint Committee of the Federations of Newspaper Owners of the United Kingdom. There he once more expounded the problem and the possible solution, and was favourably received, 'the only points on which hesitation was expressed being the possibility that an agreement on the part of the Press to co-operate for the purpose indicated might lead to interference in cases where the need for silence was not really important, and might involve them in undertakings to accept the repression of Press criticisms of policy in regard to our relations with foreign powers, and might favour the revival of a press Bill such as had been rejected in the past'. However, Brade subsequently received the suggestion which that Committee now made: the formation of two linked standing representative committees, one of officials (proposed to include not only the Admiralty and War Office but possibly also the Home Office, Foreign Office, Board of Trade, and Government of India) and one of newspapermen, who 'should co-operate with a view to preventing the publication of naval and military intelligence, when such publication would be likely to prove prejudicial to the interests of the country'.

In Whitehall meanwhile, Churchill's Sub-Committee not having re-met because of his 'pre-occupation with other matters' as the First Lord of the Admiralty,[164] informal discussion had continued about the formation of a joint Naval and Military Press Bureau. The decision of the newspaper owners to co-operate in joint discussions now moved this aspect of relations with the Press to the forefront, and the Admiralty and War Office decided to arrange for an early meeting with the proposed press committee, but pro tem not to involve representatives of other Government Departments 'until superior authority was obtained'. Indeed, other departments were still not then much interested in a formalised relationship with the Press; for example, the Foreign Secretary (Grey) told Parliament at the end of 1911, when asked about a premature publication of Foreign Office matters: 'There is no regular organisation in connection with the Foreign Office for inspiring any Press agency or newspaper in order to put forward, either officially or semi-officially, the views of His Majesty's Government with regard to foreign affairs.'[165]

The Admiralty therefore convened the first meeting of the Press and Official sides in August 1912. Thus, after many years of debate, within Whitehall, within the Press, and within Parliament, a modus vivendi was about to be achieved. During these years of debate, Britain and its place in the world had been changing fast, as had the social, financial and technological environment of both. These changes had sharpened the already jagged edges between Government Departments and the Press where national security was concerned, edges which time and the D-Notice System have done a little to smooth, but have not removed. The principle of assisted self-regulation by the Press had now been established. Some of the themes which have distinguished the subsequent arguments within, and activities of, the D-Notice Committee had already been exposed in the long period of debate. Britain and much of the rest of the world were about to undergo further rapid and violent change. There was now only a short interval in which to establish this new System, to set it to work, and to refine it, in a way acceptable both to the Press and to Government, before much more serious tests of the relationship were made by impending events.

Section 2

FORMATION AND EARLY MODUS OPERANDI OF THE COMMITTEE, 1912–14

7

ESTABLISHING THE COMMITTEE

Sir Graham Greene,[1] the Admiralty Permanent Secretary, convened a 'conference' there on 13 August 1912, 'to consider the establishment of a Joint Committee of Official and Press Representatives to deal with the publication of Naval and Military news in times of emergency'. The War Office was represented by Brade, Brigadier-General Wilson, and Lieutenant Colonel GMW Macdonogh.[2] The Press were represented by Sir George Toulmin MP (Newspaper Society), Ragland Phillips[3] (Federation of Northern Newspaper Owners), David Duncan[4] (Federation of Southern Newspaper Owners), Robert Baird[5] (Irish Newspaper Society) and Ernest Parke, Secretary of the (London) Newspaper Proprietors Association.[6] This meeting and subsequent ones, and the records thereof, were 'Secret', although the content very rarely contained any detail which would have endangered naval or military activities. Considering the number of people in both governmental and press circles who had participated in the establishment of the system, who would be consulted in the coming months, and who subsequently were involved in the production and receipt of Notices from the Committee, it was in general the British public alone who remained for some years ignorant of what was being done in their interest.

At the initial meeting, Greene explained that the Admiralty and War Office were 'seeking some body representing the interests of the Press with whom a standing agreement could be arranged' in time of war or of emergency. This first meeting was held to discuss not the sort of news to be forbidden or withheld, nor the machinery for effecting this, but how the Press might best be represented. Assurances were given by the official side that all parts of the Press would be treated alike, that when the Press were given initial warning of a subject they would also be given an 'indication as to the state of affairs necessitating the desired reticence', and that they would only be asked 'to restrict the publication of news in really important cases where national interests were at stake'. As an example of such a matter, 'it might be said that at times of tension the Press would be asked to print no reports, except when supplied officially, of moves of naval or military units'.

Parke had most to say about the composition of the standing press representation. He thought it best initially to deal only with the UK Press (ie excluding the EPU), and suggested a small press committee of three to deal with the Admiralty and War Office. The newspapermen present agreed, and there was also some discussion of the possible role of the Press Association. The press representatives undertook to consult their parent bodies and report back to Brade through Parke 'their proposal as to the formal constitution of the committee'.

This consultation took two months, a reflection of the several press fingers in the pie, some of them scrabbling after the same morsels. Having received the record of the initial meeting written by Brade, Duncan wrote to Parke stating firmly 'I do not know when or how it is proposed to nominate the small committee of three, but it must be clearly understood that the provincial press is represented on that committee, and probably the best way to do so would be to appoint Mr Robbins, the Manager of the Press Association, one of the committee'. Duncan also wrote to Robbins the same day, enclosing copies of the Brade record and his letter to Parke, 'so that you may know what is going on', pointing out that it had been his suggestion that the PA and other news agencies should be consulted, but 'of course you will treat the whole matter as confidential, at any rate for the present'.[7]

Robbins[8] was away at the time, but his son and deputy HC Robbins noted that this was 'the first intimation we have had of the conference'. On his return, Edmund Robbins agreed with Duncan's suggestion. He consulted the PA Chairman, Ragland Phillips, who had anyway been at the first meeting and who complained that Parke had said the agencies should not be directly represented but should merely 'assist the committee'. Robbins consulted the other press agencies (Central News, the Exchange Telegraph Company, and Reuter's Telegram Company), and all accepted him as their representative.

Armed with this support, Robbins went to see Parke, and then wrote a full report to his Chairman in Yorkshire.[9] The meeting had begun badly, he wrote. 'You will be interested to know that at first our friend was a little "standoffish", and wanted me to state my case before he would say anything. Even then he refused to admit that the News Agencies had any right to claim representation on the small committee, as he was of the opinion that the responsibility rested solely with the Newspaper Proprietors.' Robbins was however a determined and persuasive personality. Parke softened, explaining the reason why the agencies had not been included at the Conference (i.e. press bureaucracy), and admitting he had 'thrown out the suggestion that the PA should be asked to co-operate', because he had thought the agencies were 'at daggers drawn'. He was surprised when Robbins assured him that, whatever the competitive nature of their relationship, there was no personal ill-will; he also persuaded Parke the Agencies had the right of direct representation rather than merely of 'co-operation'.

Before Parke had conveyed any press decision back to Brade, Robbins had an invigorating and unusual experience, namely a summons to a private audience with Admiral of the Fleet Lord Fisher, now heading the Royal Commission on Fuel and Oil.[10] Fisher had evidently been told of the 13 August meeting at the Admiralty, and that the PA had not been invited. He said Robbins should have been there for wider representation and for the avoidance of 'jealousy' amongst editors, and he supported Robbins' view that the PA should be a full member of the committee. He also thought the authorities should issue news items for the Press through the PA (rather than directly to individual newspapers).

In reviewing the current international security situation, Fisher 'said that the constant talk about war very often led to war; two parties at last felt that they were compelled to bring about what they had been so long talking about. Eve would not have wanted the apple in the Garden of Eden if she had not gazed at it continually and convinced herself that it looked good'. What Robbins thought of this oracular assessment he did not record. He explained to Fisher the pivotal position of the PA (with Reuter's) in the dissemination of news not just in the United Kingdom but worldwide. Fisher ended by advising Robbins to talk to the CID Secretary, his protégé Hankey,[11] and, with the typical Fisher taste for intrigue, suggested that such a meeting should be at his Royal Commission offices in Winchester House rather than at one of the 'Government Offices'. Such a meeting turned out to be unnecessary, and whether Fisher himself contacted Hankey privately in support of Robbins can now only be conjecture.

Robbins was subsequently approached by Sir George Toulmin, who told him he 'thought all parties would agree to the selection of the Press Association as the medium for carrying out the wishes of the Admiralty and War Office in times of crisis'. The PA Committee itself then reiterated its view that the 'press committee' should adopt machinery 'whereby cypher telegrams might be sent by the Press Association to the various newspapers should either the Admiralty or the War Office desire that important Naval or Military movements should not be published'. This apparent press willingness to submit to some degree of censorship must be seen against the background of continuing widespread public concern about German intentions, 'spy fever' and trials, and the concurrent fighting by other nations in the strategically sensitive Balkans.

Knowing of the progress being made in the discussions with the Press, Hankey now reminded Churchill that his Sub-Committee on Postal and Press Censorship in Time of War was overdue for a meeting, but suggested that because Churchill as the First Lord of the Admiralty was 'so pressed with matters more closely connected with your present office', the Chairmanship might pass to someone else. This it duly did in mid-October, when Seely as now SofS for War took over; Greene and Brade also joined the Censorship Sub-Committee.

The Admiralty convened a further meeting of officials and press representatives on 16 October 1912. Those present were as at the first meeting, except that John Scott[12] had replaced Phillips for the Northern Owners, and, most importantly, Robbins had been added to the Committee. Parke reported press consultation on membership was complete, and those present had the authority collectively to be representative of all UK Press interests. 'They were empowered to agree from time to time, as might be decided by that committee, to withhold from publication in the Press information which at times of emergency it might be against the public interest to make known.'

Toulmin added that Robbins would also act as secretary to the press representatives, and 'would work the machinery for giving effect to any decisions' of the Committee. In the event of urgent action being required, Robbins would be authorised to act on behalf of the press members until they could be gathered. The latter would be nominated and replaced as necessary by their constituent federations, and might send deputies if unable to attend. Greene thought 'these arrangements would meet the requirements perfectly', not only in war, but also in peace in cases like the recent gunnery trials and embarkation exercises.

Scott hoped the Committee would not be used for the dissemination of 'false news', because such deception of the public would destroy 'confidential relations between the Press and the departments'. After brief discussion this was agreed. Brade was appointed the official 'medium of communication', and he and Robbins were tasked with working out how the Committee would interact with the Press. Greene and Brade agreed any expense incurred in circulating official decisions of the Committee to the Press would be defrayed by the State, and a joint brief report to Ministers was put in hand. From this time until the First World War had started, Robbins became the pivotal Press figure in the work of the Committee, and the Press Association which he managed therefore became the pivotal press institution. Parke (NPA) remained involved, and the Newspaper Society Council continued to be briefed on the arrangements, but their role became subsidiary.

Brade now also submitted an internal report to his Secretary of State.[13] Having summarised events and agreements to date, he explained the official tactics:

We have thus succeeded in launching an organisation which will at least provide considerable support to the scheme of precautionary measures which forms part of our system of military preparation, and which will be equally useful in the event of a pre-precautionary period being declared. It may be remarked that in the record of the negotiations above, there is no closely drawn definition of the new committee's powers and functions. This is not unintentional. So far as my observation goes, the Press interests have been suspicious all along, and I am given to understand, privately, that there has not been complete unanimity amongst these interests as to which [functions] they could safely pledge themselves. I have accordingly confined myself, when explaining our objects, to pointing out the need for the organisation in the cases of resort to the precautionary measures of defence, and of experimental work such as the embarkation exercises at Southampton. The great point to secure seemed to be to induce the Press to work together and to work in conjunction with us. This has been secured, and it is left to the future to develop occasions of usefulness for the committee outside the classes of cases named. So far, however, nothing has been done or said which will limit the functions of the committee, except that we have promised not to use the machinery for the dissemination of false news, or in cases where there is not real national necessity, or for the purposes of stifling criticism of policy.

Brade referred to the new OSA, on which he considered 'the power of the department is really not so meagre as would appear' in dealing with an editor who had published information damaging to security. At the time of the Agadir crisis, the War Office had not only drawn editors' attention to their damaging articles, but had also subsequently referred cases to the Treasury Solicitor, and thence to the Director of Public Prosecutions, for hypothetical comment; the contention was that publication had been 'prejudicial to the safety and interests of the State', and that therefore proceedings could have been taken under Section I.c of the new Act, the editor having by publication 'communicated to another person information which might be useful to an enemy'.

After deliberation, government lawyers had agreed that, 'on certain assumptions as to the correctness of the information communicated by the newspapers then in question, that information was or might be directly or indirectly useful to an enemy within the section of the Act quoted'. From this opinion, the War Office inferred that, in certain circumstances, the Act could indeed be used against a newspaper. The Admiralty had subsequently summoned an allegedly offending editor (the files do not reveal which) for a private warning by the Director of Public Prosecutions that the OSA could have been used against him.

There was however one inconvenient point about the new Act, but Brade swiftly brushed this under the ministerial carpet. 'We have a note on our official papers [apparently no longer extant] to the effect that the speedy passage of the Act through the House of Commons was due to a general understanding that the new measure was not directed against any new class, but against that at which the former Act was aimed, viz, the spy class,[14] and that to use it against a newspaper merely for publishing news useful to an enemy would amount to a breach of faith with Parliament. But there is no record to this effect in the official version of the debates.'

Brade explained to his Minister that Departmental interpretation of the possible use of the OSA had a bearing on the continuing 'hesitancy and perturbation' about the introduction of a Press Bill amongst the Press, but from whom he had now received 'valuable help' in setting up the new Joint Committee. He reminded that the Press Bill was still being considered by the CID Sub-Committee on Press Censorship, and he attempted to steer his

Minister (who was now chairing the Censorship Sub-Committee) away from such a course: 'If, however, the Official Secrets Act can be used it seems doubtful whether any further consideration need be given to the terms of a Press Bill.'

A Hiccough

Even before the communication machinery of the new Joint Committee could be discussed between Brade, Robbins and the Post Office, the authorities attempted to use the embryo system. Not surprisingly things did not go smoothly. Robbins received a telephone call from Greene early on 9 November, asking him to attend a meeting that day; being a weekend, besides Robbins only Parke of the Press side was in London. At the Admiralty, Greene explained certain orders had been given the previous evening, and that 'the First Lord [Churchill] desired that instructions might, if possible, be given to prevent the newspapers from making a scare, as was done on Saturday last in connection with the mobilisation orders telegraphed to Portsmouth and Devonport'. The latest orders concerned accelerating the construction of certain ships, which might require 'men working overtime, and also possible Sunday labour'. The Admiralty hoped the Press would not mention these instructions.

Apparently without argument, Robbins and Parke agreed to this. The former telephoned the leading evening papers, and wrote to all morning and weekly papers: 'Very Private and Confidential. Immediate and Important. You are probably aware that an arrangement has recently been agreed between the Admiralty and War Office authorities and the Press for the purpose of preventing alarmist statements being published'; and, having briefly explained the request, he ended 'I trust that, acting upon the arrangement entered into, you will accede to the suggestion made today by the Admiralty Authorities.' This was neither precisely the kind of thing which had in fact been agreed, nor, as it quickly transpired, were most editors aware of the as yet unformed arrangement. The following Monday, Robbins had a larger than normal postbag. Several editors complained that, although they had complied, the *Daily Telegraph* had not. It contained reports of Sunday working at Portsmouth, Devonport and Barrow-in-Furness, and of rumours during the weekend that Army reservists had been ordered to join their regiments, albeit adding: 'On inquiry last night we were assured by the War Office that there was no foundation for the report'.

Robbins also heard that morning from the Managing Editor of the *Daily Telegraph*, John Le Sage,[15] acknowledging Robbins' Saturday letter, but adding just: 'I am much obliged to you for your courtesy, but if the Admiralty or War Office wish to communicate with the *Daily Telegraph*, doubtless they have not forgotten that we have an office in Fleet Street.' Parke, consulted by Robbins about this NPA member's response, could only say there appeared to have been 'some misunderstanding' between Le Sage and his proprietor, Harry Lawson, who had attended the NPA meeting at which the committee arrangement was discussed; evidently first use of the new system had been rather more rapid than internal communication within the newspaper. The Editor of the *Daily Mirror*, Alexander Kenealy,[16] also wrote: 'On Sunday I received a mysterious letter from you asking me to leave some Admiralty information out of the paper at the request of a mysterious committee. As you did not say which committee you were acting for, I did not know whether it was a committee of the Institute of Journalists, the Press Club, the Cheshire Cheese, or the Press Association, so that I was compelled to ignore your request.'

From the provinces too, the Secretary of the Federation of Northern Newspaper Owners Association telegraphed 'Our members asking why *Telegraph* published Monday banned news with big headline'; and its President (Scott) also wrote, expressing surprise that as a member of the new Committee, he had not been contacted, making it clear he expected the provincial members to be informed in future, 'as the matter might some day be of first rate importance'. Robbins did his best to explain this half-cock start, referring to work in hand on the communication machinery. To Scott, he privately regretted he and Parke appeared to have exceeded their authority, but explained the urgency of the consultation: 'From what I can see, the matters to be dealt with will nearly always be of an urgent nature.' Experience in the intervening years has shown this to be an unduly pessimistic forecast; both media and officials have tight deadlines, but they are rarely so urgent that the D-Notice Secretary has insufficient time to consult, if necessary.

That same busy Monday, Robbins, Parke and Brade met at the Press Association to consider another urgent request, this time from the War Office, which that evening was to issue orders that staff at the Ordnance Survey Department at Southampton were to spend three or four nights working overtime on producing maps. The authorities 'suggested' that no mention should be made of this in the Press, 'as, with the electrical state of the European atmosphere, it may cause unfavourable or alarming comment.'[17] Robbins considered it would be unnecessary to send this request to the whole Press, and that 'it would be sufficient to stop the supply of news at source', namely by telegraphing a letter to the editors of the Southampton *Southern Echo* and the *Portsmouth Evening News*, and to his own representative in the area. This was done, with apparent effectiveness, and this time no comebacks.

In the midst of this flurry of new activity (a significant addition to his already onerous role as PA Manager), Robbins received a sharp letter from his former Chairman. Phillips pointed out there were still many editors unaware of the recently agreed arrangements, told him a notice should be sent out at once, and gave him some unnecessarily detailed suggestions as to how this should be done. Robbins wisely decided to wait a few days, until he had worked out more details of the methods of communication with Brade and the Post Office, before sending out such a circular. He told Phillips: 'I have to walk on a two-edged sword, in order not to offend the susceptibilities of certain very thin-skinned individuals.' He stated firmly that, in an emergency, it would be necessary for those in the provinces to have confidence in their London representatives, as, if the Admiralty and War Office had to wait for all the press representatives to convene from distant parts of the country, officials would take other and unpalatable steps.

8

ESTABLISHING MACHINERY AND PROCEDURES

The CID Sub-Committee on Press Censorship and on Postal Censorship met in late November 1912, to consider voluminous documentation provided by Hankey.[18] The conclusions which emerged were that the Joint Committee arrangements should be given a 'fair trial', and that an annual report should be made on the general working of the scheme; but nevertheless that the Bill for Control of the Press should be introduced on the outbreak of war, 'or at such time as the Cabinet may think desirable', and meanwhile kept on the Statute Book for operation as required by Order in Council.[19]

Officials were meanwhile considering what other types of topic the Joint Committee might deal with. In late November, Brade wrote to Robbins asking for press reaction to a new idea: so far they had discussed suppression of information from official sources 'not known beyond Whitehall'; but they realised there was also important and sensitive information which the Press acquired from their own sources, which an editor might wonder whether it would be against the public interest to publish. Phillips had indeed raised this type of case at one of the early meetings, but had been told merely that in such cases an editor should seek advice from the relevant Ministry. Now however Greene and Brade believed a better system could be devised, using the Committee as authority for advice about such enquiries.

An early meeting to discuss this duly took place on 9 December 1912.[20] Greene explained what officials had in mind, illustrated by recent examples: the *Sunday Chronicle* had published specifications of certain armaments of new ships, stating quite openly these were 'known only to a few', and the *Sphere* had published, with illustrations, details of 'a new system of gun firing which had been the subject of experiment and investigation by an official committee and was still under consideration'. In both cases, he said, the editors must have been aware that secret information was involved; officials hoped that in such cases in future the Press should consult the Department concerned as to what could and could not safely be published.

In agreeing to this, the Press representatives sought certain undertakings. Toulmin said every reference by an editor must be dealt with promptly, and a named person in each Department should be appointed as "referee" in such matters. He also asked for official reaffirmation that only really secret information would be kept from publication, and that editors should not be denied the liberty to criticise policy. These points were agreed by the officials. Scott emphasised it was unreasonable to expect the Press to co-operate if the Government did not treat all newspapers equally in official communications. Brade said he had raised this point with Departments, who had all undertaken to observe impartial practice. However, it 'was of course impossible for official representatives present to make a definite pledge in regard to information communicated extra-departmentally [ie by politicians], but they would endorse very strongly the opinion expressed by their Press colleagues'.

The problems for usually well-intentioned officials caused by politicians who comment/publicise/leak sensitive information through their own channels, is another recurring theme in the discussions of the Committee through the years; and it has never been only politicians who leak information. At the end of this discussion, JR Scott 'alluded to what he described as a matter of some notoriety, viz, that there was constant leakage of information from Government departments, and he asked whether this could not be stopped'. This suggestion, unusual in an editor, was followed by an even more curious and still (almost a century later) as yet unfulfilled expectation: 'The official representatives admitted that this leakage might occur, but they agreed with Mr Parke who pointed out that when the undertakings of the Committee got into full working order the market for that class of information would practically cease.'

The Committee now felt the time had come for Brade and Robbins to produce a letter which each press representative could send editors of his federation, explaining what had so far been agreed. Scott reiterated his unhappiness at a meeting not having been called to discuss the request about acceleration of shipbuilding, and it was agreed that normally a Department would await such a meeting before taking action. Robbins suggested it would be a great advantage if a brief explanatory note were added to each request, so that the Press understood the rationale. On illustrated weekly papers (such as the aforementioned *Sphere*) and of magazines (such as *Strand*), which did not belong to the organisations represented and were therefore not covered by the new arrangements, it was agreed that the Secretaries and Parke should investigate. These and other minor details below are indicative of the empirical way in which the Committee was set up, and in which it felt its way towards a modus operandi, establishing quite quickly at first and then more gradually the principles, coverage and general methodologies which have evolved to present times.

The day after this meeting, Brade published the results of his work with Robbins and the Post Office. A Department wishing non-publication would communicate immediately with Robbins. If there were time, the Committee would be assembled. If it were extremely urgent, Robbins and Parke would decide on the spot whether to accede to the Ministry's request. The London Press would be contacted by letter or telephone. The provincial press would normally be contacted by letter, but in some cases by telephone or telegraph. The difficulty of ensuring that in provincial newspaper offices only a 'responsible official' received the telegraphed message, and that there was no violation of secrecy or serious loss of time, had caused much discussion between the Joint Secretaries and Post Office officials. Robbins' suggestion of some form of code was ruled out as too complex on the advice of the latter; they suggested instead a telegram from Robbins to the Clerk-in-Waiting at the GPO Central Telegraph Office, who would arrange, before the telegram was sent on, that for each newspaper 'a responsible official' at the local Post Office (ie the Postmaster) was at hand to receive it and pass it personally to the editor addressed.[21] Brade's secret report on the agreed machinery of communication included lists, approved by the Admiralty and War Office, of those newspapers needing to be thus addressed in order to give full coverage of their requests, although Robbins was allowed discretion as to whether to send every request to all of them.[22]

A few days later, on 16 December 1912, again before these procedures could be transmitted to the Press, a further request from the War Office was received by Robbins, but there was time to convene at least three from each side of the Committee. The request, to withhold publication of anything concerning the imminent strengthening of the armament of, and number of troops guarding, the naval magazines at Chattenden, near Chatham Dockyard, was agreed; but with only the London, Chatham and Portsmouth newspapers being contacted (the troops were being transferred from Portsmouth's neighbour Gosport). The case led to discussion of Services' newspapers, not covered by the new arrangements; it was agreed that they should be brought 'into line' by means of a meeting with the Committee, and that meanwhile the War Office would write to them semi-officially. Robbins reported that, since the internal circulation of Brade's memorandum about the machinery of communication, the Post Office had discovered a problem on the distribution of telegrams in the provinces through local postmasters: a number of smaller towns did not have a postmaster. It was agreed that the journals of such places would generally be of minor importance, and a letter from Robbins would therefore suffice.

At the final meeting of the year, on 19 December 1912, Greene, Brade and Robbins met the editors of seven Service journals/newspapers.[23] Brade explained the two types of cases which were involved: officially issued information, and information from the Press's own sources; Robbins outlined the measures and machinery now agreed. Discussion raised the same press concerns previously debated within the Committee itself, and similar assurances were given by the officials; but two new, more specialist questions were also asked: how might an editor decide whether, for example, the perceived move of a flotilla from one station to another was "in the ordinary course" or otherwise? And how should one deal with details of design, potentially secret, but disclosed in technical/scientific papers, and which editors then republished in more popular form? Greene said that in the first case, if the matter were not in the ordinary course, the Admiralty would issue a warning notice. On the second question, he could only admit that 'special reference to the technical papers was necessary'. As Brade had foretold, the Services' journals editors, who included two retired Lieutenant Colonels and whose readership was largely serving and retired officers, agreed quite readily 'to fall in with the wishes of the Admiralty and War Office, and to respect any notifications received via the Press Association.'

Confirmation but Further Teething Problems

The year 1913 opened with the despatch to the Press Association of Brade's letter, still classified 'Secret', presenting the outline agreement and describing the machinery of communication. The enclosure covered the Constitution of the Committee, and Procedures in Cases (a) (information issued by the Admiralty and War Office) and (b) (Information acquired otherwise by the Press).[24] In (b), the Committee would play no part in the discussion of particular cases; the editor was to contact the Clerk-in-Waiting at the appropriate department (this title was used within the Admiralty and War Office solely for such AWOPC business), where a 'responsible official' had been appointed to oversee such referrals (the response to Toulmin's request for a "referee"). Contact was to be by letter or telegram; 'The use of the telephone should be avoided as much as possible, owing to the risk of mis-understanding. In giving this undertaking, however, the Departments feel that they must ask that Editors will as far as possible refrain from making references of this nature during the night or at times when it would be reasonable to expect that an official of the limited class to whom secrets are entrusted would not be readily available.'

Brade also wrote a lengthy progress report to CID Sub-Committee on Censorship.[25] He considered that 'there would be nothing more to require us to regard the negotiations as still in progress' and the results so far were 'satisfactory to the two Departments'. He reported too his recent discussions with the Secretary of the Royal United Services Institute and its *Journal*'s editor, and those that he and Greene had had with the editors of the technical magazines *The Engineer* and *Engineering*. All had given assurances of compliance with the agreed arrangements. Robbins and Parke were conducting similar discussions with other weekly and monthly journals, with similar results. Brade reminded the Sub-Committee of two matters which the Press still regarded as 'difficulties', namely 'any departure from an attitude of severe impartiality on the part of authorities', and 'the existence of numerous channels through which official information leaks, irregularly, to the Press ... but if the Editors act up to their recent undertakings the market for contraband of this sort – of at least the really important kind – will gradually be closed.'[26]

A few days later, from the Press Association office in New Bridge Street, under the new 'Admiralty, War Office and Press Committee' heading, Brade's 7 January letter was distributed over the signatures of its press members.[27] They said: 'A careful study of the document will show that the machinery is simple and effective, and the Committee feel assured of your cordial co-operation in their patriotic aim.' In the years since this initial request to the Press, the machinery of the system has evolved, but has remained simple and usually effective; co-operation, if not invariably cordial, has been intelligently pragmatic; patriotism has probably been less in the minds of editors than (wisely) "fear of something worse", and officials have usually been similarly wise in their prevailing desire to avoid the political and administrative pitfalls of legislation and of litigation.

The CID discussed Press Censorship in Time of War again on 6 February 1913.[28] The tabled paper reminded of press leaks about defences and troop dispositions in 1898 and 1911, and cited the part censorship had played in successful German, Japanese and Bulgarian campaigns. Because the 'chief weakness' was the lack of penalties, it recommended any press transgressor (from owner to printer) should be liable on each offence for a fine of up to £1,000 or imprisonment (with or without hard labour) for up to 12 months. Seely said that, while the arrangements now in place were a great improvement, he still felt the Government should have statutory powers in grave emergency to enforce censorship. Churchill[29] however praised the new arrangements, saying they had been effective recently when the Royal Navy's 3rd Battle Squadron had been deployed to the Mediterranean 'to increase our margin of safety', 'no excitement had been caused' by the preparations for the deployment, and 'he doubted whether any foreign power had had its suspicions aroused'. The Committee therefore decided to give the new system a fair trial, and to postpone introduction of any legislation until the outbreak of war.[30]

The initial arrangements having been promulgated, casework continued, with ad hoc meetings as necessary, attended sometimes only by Robbins and one other press member, for example on 3 February 1913 when a request was agreed from the Captain of HMS *VERNON*[31] that certain experimental work being carried out onboard should not be reported in the Press. Greene (not present) had suggested that, because of the secret nature of almost all *VERNON*'s work, the Press might be asked to agree that nothing about it should ever be published, and Toulmin and Robbins thought this might be done (it was not in fact followed up). Brade also mentioned recent press reports about measures taken to sweep a minefield in order to ensure safe passage out of Portland for a battle squadron, and to repel submarine attack on a squadron in Lyme Bay, about the new gunnery control system in the Dreadnought *HMS THUNDERER*, and about defence works at Cromarty and Rosyth.

Because of all this, the Admiralty thought a further letter to the Press would be advisable, spelling out in detail the kinds of information on which editors should consult officials before publication. In agreeing, Toulmin suggested in each case the involvement of the Committee should also be mentioned, with a veiled allusion to the possibility in future of the Committee formulating a scheme 'for ensuring a disclosure in such cases of the source of the information'. It was thought better however that such a threatening point be left to each press representative to put across in his own way when distributing the Admiralty examples to his federation.[32]

Brade's very short supplementary letter to editors accepted that much information did not appear on the face of it to be harmful to publish, but suggested that, 'in the stress of journalistic work', it was difficult for them to be sure without expert advice whether publication was 'not departing from the spirit of the agreements of the Joint Committee'. The only specific additional guidance given was: 'Generally speaking, information relating to *plans* or *proposals* of the naval or military authorities dealing with new ships or armaments, new defences or new methods of employing in warfare the armed forces of the Crown, will always be found to have a bearing on secret matters . . . In all cases details of these matters are secret in the initial stages, and in some they are necessarily always secret.' By way of illustration, Brade listed recent matters which should not have been reported: not only cases discussed in Committee, but also the location of new oil fuel tanks at Invergordon, experiments with 'air-fighting guns', and what is described as the 'super-submarine' (probably *NAUTILUS* or *SWORDFISH*). 'Experience has shown that newspaper references to such matters serve to focus the attention of foreign professional experts.'

Because AWOPC communications were marked 'Secret' and 'Private and Confidential', dissemination and security in newspaper offices was problematical. It can have been only a slight surprise when Brade learned that a New York Irish newspaper, the *Gaelic American*, had on 15 February published his letter of 7 January and the press representatives' covering note. He supposed it had been leaked by an Irish newspaper, but had no proof of this and did not wish 'to stigmatise any particular portion of the Kingdom'. Robbins nevertheless wrote to Baird, who (from his albeit Unionist *Belfast Evening Telegraph* office) subsequently 'repudiated the possibility' of any Irish newspaper being responsible. He believed personal promises from all Irish managers that faith had not been broken. He said 'Irishmen in London were more embittered against the British Government for the alleged down-trodden state of Ireland than Irishmen living in Ireland, and that he was certain it was from London that the disclosures were made', and he had 'met some very rampant and ultra Nationalists amongst the pressmen in London'. Obviously still riled, he continued his investigation, and reported a further theory from the *Irish News*: 'The Civil Service in Ireland contains a very large number of extraordinary Irishmen . . . most probably some of these men who are engaged in connection with the War Office or Admiralty may have had an opportunity of obtaining copies of the printed documents, and forwarding them to the *Gaelic American*.'

Brade was not surprised Baird had failed to track down a culprit, and was not unduly concerned that the existence and details of the Committee had been leaked; 'I don't myself see how we can expect that through some channel or other the facts would not become known by people outside our organisation and those whom it represents.' He was however concerned that in the future, in giving the Press certain information in order to achieve non-publication, some secret plan or movement might leak out. He was meanwhile certain that on this occasion a leak had not occurred from inside the Civil Service; apart from those on the Committee, only one other in each of the two defence Departments had seen the letter, and 'Both are in high positions and neither is Irish.' Nor, he felt, could it have been a leak through the printers who did all War Office secret work, as they had too much to lose. Robbins felt likewise that, based on the secrecy so far achieved in cases concerning London and the south of England, it cannot have been a leak from London. And there the matter rested, as with so many other inquiries into leaks since that time, most of them indeed emanating from London.[33]

At about this time, Scotland too became involved. Robbins had received a letter from a Dundee editor, suggesting Scotland should also be represented on the Committee. After over a month's cogitation, he forwarded the letter to the Northern representative on the Committee, Scott, who placed it before his own Federation, where 'nothing definite' arose, because other matters had been of more concern to them. Robbins did nevertheless show the letter to his PA Scottish Member, Robert Wilson of the *Edinburgh Evening News*, who said he did not think there was any real basis for the demand that Scotland should be directly represented on the AWOPC. The idea was effectively dropped, for several years.

The other matters which *had* concerned the Northern Federation much more stemmed from press dissatisfaction with the way in which Ministries had been using the new system. Scott reported the general feeling that the Committee had been 'too exacting in their endeavour to suppress news which was public property'. The example of the new Invergordon oil tanks was quoted, as being something widely known in the district, as well as having been referred to by the Chairman of the Highland Railway in his latest Company Report, as 'likely to increase the Traffic Receipts on their system'. Scott was therefore in favour of limiting the support of the Press just to non-publication of secret information from official sources, not from journalistic sources. Anything beyond that could be dealt with by 'private remonstrance'. He emphasised again his concerns about governmental 'leakage', which 'might lead to disclosure of secret matters more prematurely than if nothing had been done'. Robbins does not however appear to have passed on this dissenting and inconvenient attempt to undo part of the recent agreement.

Press unhappiness with officials nevertheless continued. In early April 1913, the editor of the *Daily Mail*, Thomas Marlowe[34] wrote to Brade and Robbins, complaining that when, as instructed, his reporter had called the previous night at the Admiralty for advice, on telegrams which the newspaper had received from its own sources about a trial mobilisation, the Resident Clerk had replied he had no information to give about it, nor about publication. 'If this is the kind of assistance which your department proposes to give to Editors, under the new scheme, I must be permitted to say that it is not likely to be of much value to them. They might just as well be left to act, as before, at their own discretion.' Greene (whose was the Department at fault) subsequently saw Marlowe, and cleared the matter up as having been due to a 'misunderstanding' between the reporter and the Clerk; Brade told Robbins privately it had been the fault of the reporter, who 'did not seem able to make clear what he had come about'. This cannot have been the last time in this history that nocturnal (and possibly postprandial) journalistic contact with a lone and sleepy duty official has led to 'misunderstanding'.

Other minor problems cropped up that first year. The official side was upset when informed that Toulmin was to be replaced on the Committee by the new NS President, Colonel AR Holbrook.[35] Brade complained: 'at the inception of the scheme we [officials] rather thought that the composition of the Committee would not be liable to frequent changes of personnel. The matter is, of course, entirely one for the Press to settle, but I cannot help thinking that some inconvenience is likely to be the result if membership is of short duration.' Robbins responded that in principle the Press held a similar view, and in practice only NS representation was liable to annual change. Nevertheless, Robbins regretted the departure of Sir George on secretarially practical grounds because 'he had been a very strong member of the Committee, and his position as a member of the House of Commons gave him opportunities of attending suddenly-called meetings, which rendered his loss the greater'.

At the next full AWOPC meeting on 28 July 1913, Holbrook worried that small east coast newspapers might 'by inadvertence' publish information about Royal Navy ships seen passing. Robbins raised continuing Press unhappiness with Admiralty policy on manoeuvres, and suggested an official statement should be issued by the Admiralty every night of their duration; Greene said the First Lord and the First Sea Lord were 'sympathetic, but so far had been unable to see their way to make a change',[36] but a committee had been appointed, which he hoped would lead to a reduction in 'illegitimate information' from other sources. Robbins agreed 'the more official information that was issued the less would be received from "liners" [free-lances] and others who seek to make money by the supply of information.' To demonstrate the Admiralty was not entirely anti-press, Greene said the daily orders of the CinC Portsmouth were now posted on a board, the Press asked not to report certain passages, and this had worked well.

The *Gaelic American* leak was discussed; it was agreed no further action was worthwhile. On Brade's wider security concerns, press members pointed out it was impossible in newspaper offices to comply with requests without a few besides the editor seeing them. Rejection of the Scottish request for representation was confirmed, but every editor in Scotland would be visited by the Northern Newspaper Owners' representative. Strong press objections to the draft Regulations for Press Correspondents in the Field were mentioned, and a sub-committee of Brade, Robbins and the War Office's Macdonogh was tasked to review them in detail. Finally, Holbrook explained the NS policy on representation (the need also to be a member of the NS Executive Committee), and suggested the annual injection of new blood might indeed be a good thing. This prompted Greene to remind press members that while the administrative aspects of the AWOPC might be discussed with internal press committees, the relevant Department's reasons for a request should not, unless authorised; this was accepted by the Press side.[37]

Robbins later reported to the PA Committee that Brade had confided that the CID appeared to be satisfied with what had already been done by the AWOPC, believing it 'had led to more circumspection being shown in the publication of paragraphs than before'. Brade also told him 'the King takes a personal interest in the observance of the policy which led to the formation of the Committee.'[38] On wider preparations for hostilities, the CID was now focusing for example on 'The Treatment of Aliens in Time of War'. In 1911, Churchill as Home Secretary had approved two draft Bills on Aliens, but neither had been approved; nor did OSA 1911 meet War Office concerns. In 1913 therefore a further draft Bill was introduced for enactment by Order in Council, which allowed exclusion of aliens, restrictions at ports of entry, registration and identity cards, expulsion of aliens already resident from certain areas, restrictions on movements, and prohibition of ownership by aliens of firearms, explosives, signalling equipment, and 'carrier or homing pigeons'. A Bill was also approved to enable full postal censorship to be introduced at the outbreak of war.[39]

9

ESTABLISHING A MODUS
OPERANDI PRE-WAR

Dissent in the Press

In early September 1913, Robbins was summoned with Brade by Greene's deputy, OAR Murray,[40] to be told of an imminent announcement by the First Lord of a reshuffle, between private and public yards, of Torpedo Boat Destroyer construction work. Churchill did not however want these changes reported by the Press in such a way as to imply an acceleration of the building programme, 'which might cause misunderstanding abroad'. A paragraph to the Press had been prepared accordingly, and Robbins was asked whether he would be prepared to issue it on behalf of the Committee. He agreed to do so, suggesting only that it should be sent out 24 hours before the Ministerial announcement.

The press reaction to Robbins' confidential letter about the shipyard reshuffle was not as he had expected. Firstly, Baird immediately reported that the *Irish News* had published it: 'It seems to be hopeless to get any Nationalist paper in Ireland to favourably consider anything English; their only motto seems to be 'England's extremity is Ireland's opportunity'. The better way to deal with these people is to give them no information whatever.'[41] 'Greatly surprised', Robbins asked Baird to let him know by the next post what steps he had taken. Next, and perhaps even more surprising to Robbins, was a sharp letter from Scott, who regretted the Admiralty letter had been issued without AWOPC sanction. 'We have considerable difficulty already in getting our members to act on the spirit of the agreement . . . the circular seems to me to go very much beyond anything which we have contemplated. It is a distinct attempt to influence the Press on the question of public policy of the greatest importance. We ourselves [*Manchester Guardian*] have taken a strong line from time to time in criticising the acceleration of the Admiralty programme without the public being fully informed as to precisely what was being done.' Although his letter was marked 'Private', 'you are at liberty to show it to any member of the Committee. Indeed I would be glad if you would do so'.

Robbins did not do so, but responded robustly, justifying his decision: the Admiralty was taking the Press more into its confidence, as suggested by the Committee; it had wished to avoid causing alarm abroad, 'especially in Germany'; and had the Admiralty actually been accelerating the programme rather than 'merely reshuffling the cards between the public and private yards', or 'determined a change in policy', he would 'of course, have advised that a Meeting of the Committee should be instantly summoned'. Scott was not satisfied, retorting that, while he appreciated the need for the Admiralty to help the Press from making errors of judgement in commenting on naval matters, this did not fall into that category. There was no confidential information in the circular, just 'an exhortation to the Press to put a certain interpretation on those facts'. He suggested that the only acceptable circular, which would have been 'valuable and quite in the Spirit of our arrangement', would have been one on the lines of 'The Admiralty have decided to take over certain Destroyers now being built for stock by certain firms. To this extent the programme is being accelerated, but the Admiralty state that the purchase is not an augmentation of their programme. . . . We ought to avoid assiduously anything which may be construed as an attempt to influence the opinion which may be formed on the facts.'

Robbins replied: 'In my opinion a great deal depends on the bona fides or otherwise of Government Departments . . . As I understand the meaning of the circular issued yesterday week, it was not so much that the Admiralty desired the Press to put a certain interpretation on the facts (to be subsequently announced) as to ask the Press not to put a wrong interpretation on what might appear to be a possible acceleration of the Naval Programme.'

This correspondence was tabled by Scott at the next meeting of the Northern Federation's Committee, where opinions were mixed but generally supported Scott. Scott nevertheless took the Admiralty's side later in that meeting when its complaint about a *Glasgow Herald* article on German espionage around HM Dockyard Rosyth (near Edinburgh) was discussed, on the grounds that it would have alerted any such spies that the Navy, Police and Post Office [and presumably the Press] were all watching them. The Northern editors were certainly not insensitive to security concerns, as shown by their allusion to a recent entry into the Tyne, during nearby Royal Navy manoeuvres, of a German destroyer wishing to coal, a reason established by the local editor to be spurious.

All this was reported privately to Robbins by his former PA Chairman, Phillips, who commented that the distinction between security concerns and political views was sometimes 'very indefinite'. Phillips had reminded the Northern meeting of Asquith's July 1912 speech in the House of Commons, and its implication that unless the Press censored such news for itself, 'we shall have the Government do it for us'. Robbins wondered, if he were going to be subject to such severe criticism for sending out a request from a Liberal First Lord, what would be the reaction of the Liberal Press (which included the *Guardian*) if he had to do so in future when the Unionists were in power; he would invariably have to convene the Committee, whatever the urgency. Meanwhile his position had become 'far from being an enviable one'. The official side seems to have remained unaware of this press dissension.

Greene asked Robbins' advice on whether to issue a circular on imminent secret gunnery experiments on a hulk target, the *Empress of India*. Robbins agreed this came within the procedures, but thought that, if the Admiralty really could keep the trial secret, sending a circular out would give more publicity than it would otherwise receive. A few days later, however, he changed his advice, following 'indiscreet publication by some papers yesterday of the experiment in firing explosives at distance by means of "F" Rays'; he issued a letter about the *Empress of India*, asking for exclusion of particulars of firing ships and distances from target, of hits obtained, and of information on damage inflicted. Again, this message was immediately leaked by an Irish newspaper (*Sinn Fein*), and again Baird's opinion was that the culprit was 'some extreme Irishman in a London newspaper office'.

This leak was discussed at the 20 November 1913 AWOPC meeting; Robbins confirmed he had not sent *Sinn Fein* the circular, and mentioned Baird had suggested 'somewhat drastically' that certain Irish newspapers should anyway not be on the circulation list. This caused an exchange on how many saw the circulars in all press offices, where practices clearly differed; press members undertook to consult each other separately on this. The main topic was however the destroyer building programme circular so disliked by Scott and others. The contrary arguments previously used by him and Robbins between themselves were re-stated.

Greene confirmed Robbins' interpretation of the Admiralty's benign intentions, but agreed that in future care must be taken to avoid even the appearance of 'controlling comment'. Greene was displeased that some London newspapers, in reporting the *Empress of India* trial (without infringing the security aspects) had incorrectly alleged 'live animals had been put on board so as to ascertain the effect of shock'; the papers had not contacted the Admiralty before publication to check the accuracy of the report. It was agreed he should write to the editor who had first run the story, and that in such cases it would be acceptable to mention that the matter had been 'laid before' the Committee.[42]

In early December, the CID Oversea [sic] Sub-Committee reviewed AWOPC progress, and thought it satisfactory. Their report added: 'Nothing is, however, known publicly of the agreement; and it is desirable that its existence should not be communicated more widely than may be necessary for the purpose of framing similar schemes' throughout 'all parts of His Majesty's oversea dominions.'[43]

At a very reduced attendance AWOPC meeting on 3 February 1914, Greene consulted just Brade, Robbins, and Parke[44] about gunnery trials the following week involving *HMS HOOD* (an obsolete 1891 battleship, sunk as blockship 1914), to ascertain the effects of explosions in compartments hitherto filled with coal but in future to be filled with oil in some classes of ship. That some trial involving *HOOD* was taking place would be known locally, but the Admiralty did not wish it to be brought to the attention of 'foreign Powers'. A message was accordingly drafted for Robbins to issue during the weekend, but on Friday he learned his own Portsmouth correspondent had filed about the trial. He quashed any further dissemination by the PA, telephoned other press agencies to cancel it, and sent out the agreed circular rather earlier than intended.

The Bournemouth Postmaster discovered however, when he delivered the PA telegram to the local *Echo*, that the newspaper had already published the news, as had the *Portsmouth Evening News*, both having received it from the rival Exchange Telegraph Company agency before the cancellation. An acrimonious exchange of correspondence followed between Robbins and the ETC, whose Managing Director pointed out with some justification that if the circular had been sent out earlier in the week when first agreed at the Admiralty, the error would not have occurred. The *Portsmouth Evening News* editor also wrote, suggesting the Admiralty and War Office ought to be asked to give far more notice of such trials. In the case of *HOOD*, it had been common knowledge locally 'for weeks past' that the ship was to be used for important experiments, and yet nothing had been heard from the Committee (nor from the Navy locally) restricting publication. 'Not until the ship was towed out of harbour in broad daylight and in view of hundreds of interested and talkative spectators does the Admiralty communicate with you'. Robbins passed on these sensible and pragmatic points to the two Ministries.[45]

There were also still internal organisational problems within the Ministries themselves. In March, Robbins went to see Greene to complain about the Admiralty Resident Clerk's lack of response, when approached by a PA sub-editor for advice on its Dover correspondent's story about deployment thence to Belfast of a Destroyer Flotilla. Greene explained the Clerk had not replied because he had not been advised on the subject and because he (Greene) was away. Robbins emphasised that his subordinate had sought advice because of 'the electrical condition of the political atmosphere', on which Greene's comment was 'the Resident Clerk would know nothing about politics'.

There was an *HMS HOOD*/Ireland problem in May. Robbins issued a circular about new secret trials, and heard from the Post Office that, when the telegrams had been delivered to

Dublin editors, six had given assurances nothing would be published, but *Sinn Fein* had declined to do so, the *Irish Times* pretended it knew nothing of any such arrangement, and another newspaper said it would use its own judgement. The Post Office pointed out that on the previous occasion in February, not all the Irish papers had been sent the telegram by Robbins (although of course a copy was leaked to *Sinn Fein* anyway). Robbins now came round to Baird's view that some or all Irish newspapers should be deleted from the list, and earmarked the topic for the next AWOPC meeting.

The Rush to War

More serious events in Europe however intervened. Through the spring and summer, many in both government and press had been preoccupied with the unstable situation in the Balkans, the perceived German challenge, and the implications for peace. On 28 June, Archduke Franz Ferdinand of Austria was assassinated in Sarajevo; on 23 July, Austria (supported by Germany) presented an ultimatum to Serbia (supported by Russia); on 25/26 July Austria, Serbia and Montenegro all mobilised. On 27 July 1914 an emergency AWOPC meeting was called at the Admiralty, attended by those who could be rapidly convened – Brade, Riddell, Macdonogh, and (in his father's absence on holiday) Harold Robbins. 'Those who were there presented marked contrasts', wrote Riddell later,[46] 'Graham Greene, carelessly dressed, thin, wrinkled and immobile; Brade, smart and debonair; Macdonogh, soldierly and imperturbable; Robbins, like an alert bird, eager for information' [and Riddell himself, already a bustling Press panjandrum]. 'Greene was an able, courteous official, with a sense of humour, but eloquence was not his strong point. In a few halting words', he referred to the 'critical state of foreign politics' and said that the Admiralty had 'found it necessary to make certain arrangements about the fleet' which it did not want published without prior consultation.[47] Riddell pointed out the public was avid for news, and asked if more precise guidance could be given than that agreed in the peacetime deliberations of the Committee at the beginning of the previous year; Robbins Junior suggested a circular. Both hoped that, in return for the Press refraining from publishing much of which it would become aware, the authorities would issue as much information as they safely could.

Riddell and Robbins drafted the agreed letter to editors 'on a stray sheet of paper I [Riddell] found on the table', and it was sent out by Robbins over his father's signature block that afternoon:

Private and Confidential

The Crisis in the Near East

At a meeting of the Admiralty, War Office, and Press Committee, held this afternoon, it was resolved that as, in view of the present situation, the authorities may have to take exceptional measures, the Press should be asked to refrain from publishing any information relative to movements of British warships, troops, and aircraft, or to war material, fortifications, and naval and military defences, without first communicating with the Admiralty or War Office respectively in accordance with the arrangement which was notified to you by me in January of last year.

Having regard to the nature of the case, it was found impossible to further indicate the character of the information the publication of which is undesirable in the national interests. The request does not affect the dissemination of news concerning ordinary routine movements or training on the part of the Navy or the Army; its object is to prevent the appearance of anything concerning steps of an exceptional kind which may be rendered necessary by the existing state of affairs.

I may add that the authorities from time to time will continue to issue such information as may be made public.

The following day Austria declared war on Serbia; in the next few days Harold Robbins was involved in a flurry of AWOPC (29 and 30 July 1914) and other meetings and circulars. Requests to the Press included not to refer to the 'exceptional measures' put in place by the authorities on 29 July, nor to any details of them of which the Press learnt; not to publish details of arsenals, dockyards, oil depots, ammunition stores, and 'electric light installations', without referring first to one of the two Ministries; not to mention, 'in any report which you may think it necessary to publish of the special meeting of the South Wales Miners' Federation at Cardiff today', any reference to the Admiralty contracts for coal, nor anything which might suggest that the Naval Authorities were short of coal; and to refrain from reporting that some Territorials from London had been sent to guard parts of the southern railways.[48]

Despite the thinness of this guidance, with in some cases borderline naval/military (as distinct from political) justification, and the temptation which there must have been to publish information/comment on known matters, editors in these hectic few days made no significant complaint about requests issued through the AWOPC, and generally abided by their spirit. Indeed, on 3 August the authorities, through the Committee, thanked the Press 'for the restrained manner in which the newspapers have dealt with the publication of all information affecting the Navy and the Army during the crisis'. Nevertheless, the 'unexampled situation' caused the Committee to remind again of 'the vital importance in the interests of the community of suppressing all information of the character described in the recent circular'.

Events were however once again about to overtake peacetime thinking and machinery of communication. Germany had declared war on Russia on 1 August, and in rapid succession then invaded Luxembourg, France, Poland, and, on 4 August, 'plucky little Belgium'; this brought Britain into the War later that day. The barely commissioned AWOPC now entered further uncharted and even more difficult waters.

Section 3

WORLD WAR I, 1914–18

10

THE SECURITY CONTEXT

The Course of the War

Despite all the pre-war planning orchestrated by the Committee of Imperial Defence, the governmental machine was unevenly prepared when hostilities started, and continued thereafter to be poorly co-ordinated. It had foreseen neither that war would last so long, nor the 'total war' nature of the conflict, directly involving a large proportion of the population; but the disorganisation continued because of lack of a department charged with a wider overview, and with overall direction beyond the military. There was nothing akin to the modern Cabinet Office until David Lloyd George[1] established his War Cabinet after he became Prime Minister in late 1916. Its Secretariat was created out of the CID, and Hankey was from then until well into the interwar years the leader and developer of the nascent department.

Similarly there were many organisational deficiencies within the Admiralty and the War Office, not least in those for handling tactical intelligence, and an insignificant capability for the gathering, analysis and dissemination of secret intelligence. Nor was there a Security Service in more than embryonic form. The British aptitude for improvisation was therefore once more called into play, out of urgent necessity rather than out of preference, and with the usual eccentricities of personalities and actions which characterise such rapid and un-pre-planned expansion.[2]

The Armed Forces were also only partially prepared for the 'modern' warfare which they now experienced during four years of heavy losses of manpower, equipment and merchant shipping, although significant improvements were eventually achieved. The Royal Navy had to adapt to the greater than expected effectiveness of mines and submarines, and to the less than expected effectiveness of its gunnery. The Army was only partially ready to mount and sustain an Expeditionary Force, and certainly not prepared for the scale of mass mobilisation and prolonged trench warfare which it experienced on the Western Front. The scale of the part required to be played by the forces of the Dominions and of India had also been underestimated. At the beginning of the War, air warfare (indeed aviation generally) was in an untried state, and few had foreseen the emergence of a third Service to specialise in this arena.

For the AWOPC there were two specific under-prepared areas of Admiralty and of War Office activity which were directly relevant to what could and could not be published: secret intelligence and security operations, and censorship. This had relevance to how the AWOPC system was used during the War; and some aspects of its WWI role (see Appendix 1) contributed to the permanent evolution of the young system.

Secret Intelligence and Security – Codebreaking

It is almost incredible to the modern mind that, despite advances made in civil and military wireless and cable communication by 1914, there was no interception and codebreaking capability whatsoever in the Admiralty or War Office when the War started, nor anywhere else in the British governmental structure. On 5 August, Britain began cutting the enemy's underwater cables, thus forcing Germany to rely heavily on wireless communication. The DNI, Rear Admiral Henry Oliver[3] almost immediately started to receive, from Admiralty Wireless Stations, Marconi and the Post Office, copies of encoded German wireless messages, but he had no way of finding out what they said.

In mid-August, on the way to their club for lunch, he met the Director of Naval Education, Sir Alfred Ewing,[4] temporarily underemployed because the Admiralty had closed the Naval Colleges and sent even the youngest midshipmen off to war at sea. Oliver invited Ewing, an engineer rather than cryptologist or mathematician, to set up an organisation to decode German signal traffic. Ewing initially established his small department with a few mathematics and German language schoolmasters from the Naval Colleges and elsewhere,[5] none of whom initially knew anything about cryptology. Early progress depended on German naval code documents captured by Russians, Australians and a British trawler skipper, and on painstaking trial and error work by Fleet Paymaster Charles Rotter.[6]

The support of Churchill and the new DNI, Captain Hall,[7] led to the gradual development of the codebreaking section and its liaison with the NID. It eventually controlled 14 GPO-manned wireless interception stations in UK and three abroad, but its core was in Admiralty Room 40, where a small group of brilliant minds was brought together, mainly from disparate parts of civil life.[8] From the end of 1914, almost no significant movement of the German High Seas Fleet took place without being detected by this team. It gave warning of German operations against the east coast in December 1914, around the Dogger Bank in January 1915, off Jutland in May 1916, and detected Admiral Scheer's intended final death or glory breakout for his Fleet in November 1918 (foiled by the mutiny of his sailors). Nevertheless, linkage between this intelligence and its use by operational staffs and the Grand Fleet remained inadequate until 1917.

Room 40's most famous achievement occurred in 1917, when it decoded the Zimmermann telegram, intercepted between the German Foreign Minister and his ambassadors in Washington and Mexico. In the telegram Germany attempted to persuade Mexico to join it against the USA, should the Americans as expected abandon neutrality when Germany launched its campaign of unrestricted submarine warfare in February 1917. In return for Mexico invading the southern USA, Germany would agree to Mexico recovering territory it had lost 70 years earlier in Texas, New Mexico and Arizona. Germany also suggested Mexico should persuade Japan to join a German/Mexican alliance. The British Foreign Secretary (Balfour) showed the decrypted telegram to the American Ambassador in London, Hall satisfied American experts it was genuine, and when the telegram was published in the USA in March 1917, it played a major part in persuading public opinion there to support entry into the War against Germany.[9]

The War Office similarly set up a codebreaking section from scratch, under Brigadier F.J. Anderson[10] who at least had some previous experience of communications intelligence in the Boer War. He too recruited bright young men, but it was the French who first cracked the main German military code at the beginning of October 1914, and passed it to the British. Naval and military decryption staffs at first worked jointly, but inter-Service rivalry brought this to an end by mid-October 1914, the final blow to Army amour-propre being when

Churchill (First Lord of the Admiralty) was able to tell Kitchener (SofS for War) some army intelligence decrypted by the naval team; co-operation did not start again until early 1917. In April 1917 alone German submarines sank 835,000 tons of Allied shipping, and the unrestricted German U-boat campaign was the greatest direct threat faced by Britain during the War; Lloyd George thereafter settled internal Admiralty debate about the best counter, by insisting on convoying. This led to belatedly bringing together Admiralty decryption, intelligence and operations staffs, in support of a rapidly successful Convoy Section.

Field Intelligence

Although an intention had existed in the War Office as far back as 1904 to establish a new regiment dedicated to collection and handling of tactical intelligence in the field, by 1914 it had still not been done. Colonel Macdonogh,[11] meeting his relative Captain TGJ Torrie,[12] home on leave from Lucknow, appointed him Commandant of the new regiment on 5 August 1914, despite Torrie's lack of any previous intelligence background. From this nepotistic beginning, they built up the Intelligence Corps from a handful of randomly recruited volunteer officers to, by late 1918, an ubiquity so unwelcome to line regimental officers that it was doomed to rapid reduction thereafter.

Despite this significant development in tactical intelligence capability, co-ordination with operational staffs in higher formations remained generally sub-optimal. Aerial reconnaissance in primitive, unarmed biplanes of the new Royal Flying Corps began two weeks after the declaration of war and was initially effective, when the weather permitted, particularly in detecting enemy movements towards and at the Front. As the Front stabilised, the Germans used trains rather than roads to move troops up, which made it harder to estimate accurately from the air the scale of reinforcement. Once aerial photography became more refined in 1915, the RFC again achieved remarkable results, and the Intelligence Corps was able to produce very accurate maps of German-occupied areas and order-of-battle. Air reconnaissance was disrupted briefly in 1916 between the first appearance of the German machinegun-armed Fokkers and the subsequent introduction of improved British Farman and de Havilland aircraft. Spotting for artillery proved less effective until attachment of specially trained Intelligence Corps sections to each RFC Squadron during the long Battle of the Somme. Until mobile warfare restarted in spring 1918, human intelligence (spies, informers, captured soldiers) remained the best source, easily surpassing electronic military intelligence-gathering. The Germans, once established in their trenches, made little use of wireless, preferring landlines, and had better equipment for listening to indiscreet discussion of plans in opposing trenches than did the British.

Secret Intelligence-Gathering

Commander Cumming now reoriented his small overseas intelligence section away from maritime and invasion preoccupations towards support for the BEF, in particular focusing on German reinforcement. His section, now known as 'the Secret Service', was responsible to the War Office, and from August to October 1914 he continued to respond to General Macdonogh when the latter transferred to the BEF; but when Cumming was en route to Paris in October, in a Rolls-Royce driven by his son (one of the young officers recruited into the Intelligence Corps), they hit a tree, killing his son, and for several months incapacitating him (he lost a foot).

BEF meanwhile set up its own espionage organisation, so on his return to duty Cumming found he had competition in running agent networks. The British GHQ in St-Omer ran two, and also behind the German lines (with the reluctant co-operation of the RFC) a force of courier-pigeons, replaced later when portable radio sets became available.[13] Attempts were made to rationalise all networks by a geographical split of responsibility; they continued to attract operatives of varying degrees of eccentricity and effectiveness, including the authors Compton Mackenzie and Somerset Maugham, advantageous at least to the quality of future espionage novels. The organisational fragmentation and rivalry made it easier for Germany to take countermeasures against British networks; a revised system had therefore to be established in mid-1917. The most successful (in Belgium, known as 'La Dame Blanche') was under Cumming's control. Previous tensions between War Office and GHQ intelligence staffs were resolved when Macdonogh returned to London as DMI in late 1915. Nevertheless, the use made by British Commanders and their operational staffs of this more plentiful and accurate intelligence remained spasmodic on the Western Front until near the end of the War.

On the Eastern Front, intelligence gathering in conjunction with tsarist Russia was bedevilled by the War Office's separate strands of representation. The flow of accurate intelligence was erratic, but useful information was obtained about redeployment of German units from Eastern to Western Fronts. In other theatres, such secret intelligence-gathering as there was remained largely in the hands of volunteers temporarily released from normal operational duties there, only partly in very small Intelligence Corps detachments. 'Dear Mother' wrote Captain Loder from Port Said's Casino Palace Hotel in December 1916, 'Life is really quite like a page out of a novel . . . the air vibrates with hushed whispers, the stairs leading to the office resound with the stealthy tread of stage villains, corpulent Egyptians with tarbooshes, down-at-heel Greeks, Syrian refugees, and terrified enemy aliens.'[14]

Home Security and Counter-Espionage

Despite its small size and over-estimation of the threat, the internal security section under Captain Kell had become quite successful by August 1914. In conjunction with the Special Branch, it had destroyed the only potentially effective German spy network, and put together records of many aliens and other suspects.[15] During the War it grew from 19 to 844 staff, being renamed MI5 in the War Office reorganisation of January 1916. It gained its information principally from police reports, surveillance by its operatives, intercepts through cable and postal censorship, and, less accurately, numerous reports from the public.

Well before hostilities started, the War Office made plans and earmarked staff to fulfil its responsibilities for cable censorship; but no such preparations had been made for postal censorship, partly because the CID and GPO had concluded such censorship would be impracticable, and partly because the Home and Foreign Offices resisted any mass censorship of civilian mail. However, realisation quickly dawned in September 1914 that valuable intelligence was being lost because of this, and DNI and DMI began secretly to censor mail. This was discovered, much to the Home Secretary's horror, three weeks later, but Hall managed to persuade Asquith that it was essential, and by the end of the War there were 4,861 censors (mostly women) working in the War Office section concerned.

The overlapping responsibilities of MI5 and of the Special Branch headed by Basil Thomson[16] caused inevitable rivalries between them in the search for spies; both were also concerned with rounding up aliens. The Aliens Restriction Act, in draft before the War began, was pushed through Parliament ahead even of the Defence of the Realm Act in early

September 1914, requiring all 'enemy' aliens to register with the police, and restricting where they could live and work. The pre-war spy mania increased so much that in May 1915 the Government ordered the internment of about 32,000 aliens of military age who could not prove themselves 'harmless'; about 20,000 other men, women and children were repatriated. Throughout the War there were trials and occasionally executions of spies; twelve were shot (in the Tower of London) or hanged between November 1914 and September 1917, including Sir Roger Casement,[17] and others imprisoned.[18]

In the latter stages of the War, Irish and Bolshevik subversion became a greater concern. Kell helped the Ministry of Munitions to set up its own internal security apparatus; Thomson disapproved and, when this Ministry consulted him about the ineffectiveness of its security, assumed responsibility for it. Other Ministries followed in setting up security departments (including those of Labour and National Service, the Board of Trade, and various industrial parts of the Admiralty and War Office), and from spring 1917 their reports were collated to help the Government deal in a conciliatory manner with widespread industrial unrest in 1917. Coinciding with the Russian Revolution, there were some who saw Bolshevik hands behind this, but Thomson considered it more the result of war weariness and genuine workplace grievances. By the end of the War, Kell had nevertheless wrested back the lead on Bolshevik subversion.[19]

11

CENSORSHIP

Before Lloyd George's War Cabinet was established in 1917, censorship was an area where lack of a central co-ordinating body sparked many ad hoc organisations, hastily established in reaction to events and to lacunae in responsibility. Consequent overlaps and confusion led to further organisational adaptations and less than ideal inter-departmental relationships.[20] Even press censorship, despite having been much discussed pre-1914, and already with a basis of organisation in the AWOPC, suffered many problems throughout the War, albeit to a declining degree.

As the War continued its lengthy development, governmental desire to control information more widely also increased, and with it the wish to use propaganda. Censoring factual and fictional film intended for viewing in UK was delegated to the British Board of Film Censors. Cross-departmental publicity and 'propaganda' aimed at Britain became the responsibility of a National War Aims Committee. Overseas publicity and propaganda were shared by several departments, including the War Office, the Foreign Office News Department, the War Propaganda Bureau, and the Neutral Press Committee.

The War Propaganda Bureau, commonly known as 'Wellington House', under Charles Masterman,[21] was set up almost as soon as the War started, with strong support from the Chancellor of the Exchequer (Lloyd George). Its task was to counter an existing and similar German bureau, by disseminating disinformation about Germany, for example by giving credence to reports of German atrocities. In early September 1914, Masterman gathered 25 leading British authors to discuss how best to implement its work; sworn to secrecy (the Bureau's wartime existence did not become public until 1935), many wrote propaganda pamphlets.[22] John Buchan[23] edited a monthly history of the war for the Bureau, which also employed many leading British illustrators in its propaganda publications. The Neutral Press Committee, also established in September 1914 to counter German propaganda in neutral countries, incorporated press representatives and the Home Secretary, Press Censor and Masterman; an executive unit (including agencies in Greece and Sweden) was formed to do its work. In early 1917, the News Department, War Propaganda Department and the Neutral Press unit were merged into a new Department of Information under Buchan (given Lieutenant Colonel's rank), while Masterman retained responsibility for books, pamphlets, photographs and war paintings.

The Department of Information was initially responsible direct to the War Cabinet, but was soon added to the responsibilities of Sir Edward Carson,[24] who already had charge of home publicity. The Department's tasks included propaganda distribution, use of literature and art therefor, political intelligence, and, as agent for the War Office, the dissemination of military news to non-military and non-Dominion authorities. The Department (later Ministry) of Information maintained outstations, including those in New York, Chicago and San Francisco, its Spanish Bureau (dealing with propaganda aimed at predominantly Catholic countries), and until the October Revolution an Anglo-Russian Commission in Petrograd. Early in 1918, Lord Beaverbrook[25] was appointed Minister of Information, with responsibility too for propaganda concerning the Near and Middle East theatres of operations, intelligence (including cable and wireless), and public relations. Beaverbrook also established, under Arnold Bennett,[26] the British War Memorial Committee, not as a propaganda department but as an organisation of record, employing well-known artists such as John Sargent, Augustus John, Wyndham Lewis, and Stanley Spencer.

The Political Intelligence Bureau was however transferred to the Foreign Office, and the [Central Powers] Propaganda Branch to a newly named Department of Propaganda in Enemy Countries, headed by Northcliffe.[27] Northcliffe's influence on public affairs before and during the War is more than tangentially connected with the AWOPC; he was an active proponent in his newspapers (and behind the scenes with politicians), of both censorship (of what was genuinely endangering) and of openness (on everything else). He was also an early champion of air forces, a campaigner against the Dardanelles campaign, and unafraid of criticising the national hero Kitchener over the shortfall of high explosive shells; he knew it would lose his papers many tens of thousands of readers – he regained them later when proved right.[28]

The department dealing with propaganda in neutral countries was now headed by Robert Donald, Managing Editor of the *Daily Chronicle*.[29] Donald had campaigned in his columns for Lloyd George to replace Asquith as Prime Minister, as had Beaverbrook and Northcliffe, ultimately successfully. When all these appointments of senior newspapermen were announced in February 1918, Lloyd George was attacked in the House of Commons for having thereby obtained de facto control of the Press.

In practice this criticism was only partly justified; the subsequent attitude of the Press generally to the Government and to Lloyd George was not invariably subservient. Even in 1918, for example, after he had addressed the House of Commons on 9 April on the strength of the British Army, the Director of Military Operations General Maurice[30] wrote to the CIGS, now Field Marshal Wilson, complaining the Prime Minister had knowingly misled Parliament. His letter was leaked, and he had to resign, but he was swiftly offered employment by Donald, as Military Correspondent of the *Daily Chronicle*; Lloyd George later had his revenge, arranging in October 1918 for a consortium of friends to buy the *Chronicle*, whereupon Donald resigned as its managing editor.[31] Beaverbrook resigned in October 1918, having lost a demarcation tussle with the Foreign Office, and was not replaced before the end of War the following month, when the Ministry of Information was dissolved, some residual functions transferring to the Foreign Office. Bringing so many senior press people into key governmental positions has not since been repeated; it is hard to imagine so many media hands ever again being allowed a direct grasp on political levers.

Throughout the War, there was in addition another kind of censorship, namely political manipulation of domestic news for reasons of perceived national interest, particularly concerning pacifism, industrial relations, and Ireland. Nervousness about these, which also had links with concerns about (conscientious and political) objectors to the War and to service in the Armed Forces, caused Ministers to seek to use any means available to reduce concomitant publicity and tension while the War was in progress. Industrial problems were ever there, and as War casualties mounted, so did the profile of pacifists; but the Irish controversy became largely dormant in the public mind in Great Britain until the Easter Rising in Dublin in 1916. The relationship of the Press Bureau with the Irish Press was, for reasons of political sensitivity, somewhat less direct than with that in Great Britain. Ireland had its own Censor, for much of the War Lord Decies;[32] his censorship, although taking into account Press Bureau requests, was more concerned with the internal political/security situation there. Censors deleted such matters as references to Nationalist calls for independence, manifestations of support therefor however peaceful and local, and repressive measures by the authorities.[33]

In Great Britain and Ireland, the multi-headed censorship machine was used in conjunction with vigorous application of the Defence of the Realm Act (DoRA). This Act, drafted by the CID before the War as one dormant precautionary measure, was passed in Parliament with only perfunctory debate on 8 August 1914. The first version was brief but wide-ranging in executive powers given to the authorities, including imprisonment without trial, control of labour, commandeering economic resources, and suppression of publication of criticism. The aim of the last regulation was to 'prevent the spread of false reports or reports likely to cause disaffection to His Majesty or to interfere with the success of His Majesty's forces by land or sea or to prejudice His Majesty's relations with foreign powers'.

The Act was amended and extended ('consolidated') six times during the War. Although the initial intention was undoubtedly to protect national security, its numerous additional Regulations strayed into many other areas of national life; the effects of some survived not only the War but into more modern times. A Central Control Board (Liquor Traffic) was established in June 1915, and concern about alcohol damaging productivity and industrial safety led to restrictions on beer strength, on purchase of spirits, on licensing hours (reduced from 0500–0030 pre-war, to 1200–1430 and 1630–2130), and a No Treating Order forbade buying drinks for others; British Summer Time was introduced to make more productive use of daylight; there were prohibitions on binocular sales, ringing church bells, bonfires and fireworks; powers were given to requisition utilities, land and other resources; restrictions were placed on the public's use of postal and other communications; there were orders to control food supplies (actual rationing was not introduced until January 1918, usually to ensure availability rather than restrict overall consumption); and power was given to prohibit 'persons convicted of offences against morality, decency, etc from frequenting the vicinity of camps.'[34] The DoRA was also used in industrial relations; in 1916, for example, the Minister for Labour John Hodge,[35] although himself a Trades Unionist, said he would be willing to use the Act against strikers.

It was, however, the threat of prosecution for expressing opinions unacceptable to the Government which was the major concern of editors, particularly as the authorities did occasionally make DoRA prosecutions under Regulation 27 ('false reports likely to cause disaffection'). They indulged in de facto harassment under Regulation 51 (which enabled the police to enter premises suspected of being used for publishing or distributing dissident literature); for example, in October 1915 the Marxist John Maclean was charged with sedition and fined (he chose prison rather than payment, and lost his schoolteacher job); and in November 1915 the *Globe* was suppressed when, having already upset the Government by attacking the First Sea Lord (Battenberg) for alleged pro-German sympathies, it further threatened the delicate political harmony inside Cabinet and Parliament by reporting (wrongly) the imminent resignation of Lord Kitchener. In 1916, the joint editors of the Clyde Workers' Committee's journal *The Worker* were sentenced respectively to 6 and 12 months' imprisonment for publishing an article (about the War) considered seditious by the Government, and members of that Committee were arrested, court-martialled and exiled from

Glasgow.[36] Other journals against which DoRA action was taken included the *Morning Post*, the *Jewish Times*, the *North London Guardian*, and *Glasgow Forward*. Action was also taken against books; for example, an anti-War book, *Despised and Rejected* by AT Fitzroy, was banned in April 1914, and its publisher prosecuted.

Nevertheless, politicians were more reluctant to take action against those who were purely pacifist rather than seditious. Herbert Samuel, Home Secretary in 1916, considered that 'prosecutions, which would have to be numerous if a policy of repression was once decided upon, would cause more harm than good. [They would] have the effect of advertising speeches and publications which are now for the most part left in obscurity'. The Government was also concerned about losing the backing of supportive parts of the Press (fearing a perceived mutual professional bond between otherwise disparate journals), and about its image abroad, where it did not want to give the impression, particularly in the United States, that it was abusing its powers in order to prevent freedom of speech. Even the Director of Public Prosecutions felt the power to enter premises was 'of so drastic a character as too closely to approach the application of martial law at a time when the civil law had not been suspended'.

In June 1916, the Home Office therefore sent a circular to all police forces discouraging their hitherto not infrequent and vigorous raids against offending journals; and in December 1916, when prosecution of the leading pacifist and socialist newspaper *Labour Leader* was being considered, it was dropped at the urging of the leader of the Labour Party, Arthur Henderson,[37] who had just been invited by Lloyd George to join his new Government. Instead of draconian use of their powers, the authorities used instead the various forms of harassment enabled by the Regulations, including seizure of publications, incidental damage to printing equipment during searches, and the requirement that all publications from November 1917 should bear the name and address of author and printer. Anti-War meetings were more difficult for the authorities to prevent, but were often spontaneously disrupted by pro-War groups or members of the public.

By late 1917, however, the Cabinet realised the national mood was changing, that pacifist arguments for a negotiated peace were gaining ground, and that the Government needed to put across more clearly to British and foreign publics its intentions and rationale on bringing the War to an end. This was one reason for setting up the Ministry of Information under Beaverbrook.[38] It was not just at home that the Press, commerce and public were riled by some aspects of censorship; by the end of the War, the Foreign Office had accumulated a thick dossier of complaints from foreign governments, firms, newspapers and individuals.[39]

12

THE PRESS BUREAU

Establishment

Private and Confidential [to all Editors]

ADMIRALTY, WAR OFFICE, AND PRESS COMMITTEE

URGENT AND IMPORTANT   August 8, 1914

Dear Sir,

As officially announced in the newspapers this morning, the Admiralty and War Office have decided to organise a Bureau for the co-ordination and distribution of official news, relating to naval and military matters concerning the progress of the War, which can be made public. The Right Hon F. E. Smith, M.P., has agreed to undertake the supervision of the Bureau, which will be staffed by naval and military officers.

Accommodation will be provided at the Bureau for the representatives of the News Agencies and such newspapers as are prepared to bear the expense of special representation.

As soon as practicable, such News Agencies and newspapers will be entitled to install direct telephonic communication between the Bureau and their respective offices.

For the present, the Bureau will remain open permanently, and it has been arranged that all news shall be issued without delay.

On behalf of the Press members of the Admiralty, War Office, and Press Committee, I would remind you of the circular which was issued on January 7, 1913. It is essential that the suggestions contained therein shall be most carefully observed.

Inquiries respecting the advisability of publishing any information directly or indirectly connected with the War should be made to the Bureau.

It is most important that the names of the ships which may bring in enemy merchant vessels, or may perform duties on the coast, should not be reported; nor (as intimated in mine of July 30) should any mention be made regarding (a) Movements of Ships, Troops, Aircraft, or War Material; (b) Fortifications, Defence Works, Arsenals, Dockyards, Oil Depots, Ammunition Stores, and Electric Light Installations, without first obtaining the sanction of the Admiralty or War Office respectively. In fact no information should be given bearing on naval or military movements, as such information – however remote it might appear to be – would probably be of advantage to the enemy, and, therefore, prejudicial to the national interests.

You will have read the testimony given by the First Lord of the Admiralty to the assistance which the Press has already rendered to the Admiralty and War Office. At the same time the Authorities have confidentially intimated that certain information has undoubtedly been publicised which would have been better suppressed, and it is hoped that every precaution will be taken to prevent such publication in the future.

If the Press continue to act in this spirit, there will be no necessity for the officials to alter the present voluntary arrangements.

Yours faithfully, E Robbins

This letter was crafted by the AWOPC to imply a large measure of continuity of existing arrangements, but what was effectively being introduced was a new and largely undiscussed (with the Press) control organisation, with wider prohibitions on areas of reporting; the threat of something more draconian if the Press did not co-operate was only skimpily veiled. That this was nevertheless generally accepted by the Press in principle, as was the very varied use made in the coming years of the Bureau and the machinery of the AWOPC, on subjects far beyond the originally agreed limits of prohibition, must be seen in the context of the times.[40]

The Press did occasionally complain about particular prohibitions and about the censorship machinery, and was certainly not cowed by politicians; but it was constrained by the need to reflect popular patriotism and support for the Armed Forces, and by genuine concern not to endanger British/Allied lives, and achievement of victory. The immediacy of events removed political hesitations about public and press opinion, and swept aside previous institutional lethargy in establishing new organisations. Indeed there was no parliamentary authority for the establishment and operation of a Press Bureau, and, apart from the announcement above to the Press, it was not until 27 August that the Prime Minister revealed its existence to the House of Commons. At first it was not even decided which Minister was responsible for the new Bureau, but on 8 September the Home Secretary announced he would be. No statutory powers were given to the Bureau, but in practice the Law Officers did usually consider any action against offending elements in the Press which the Bureau recommended. After Sir John Simon[41] became Home Secretary, he had drafted a Bill which would have regularised the Bureau as a statutory Government Department, but it was never proceeded with. The only statutory acknowledgement of the Bureau's existence was eventually a mention in revised DoRA Regulation 27A.[42]

Of differing accounts of how the first head of the Press Bureau was appointed, the most colourful is Lord Riddell's,[43] in which he records having dined on 6 August with the 'Other Club', founded a few years earlier by Churchill and FE Smith.[44] Those present, in addition to Churchill, Smith, Riddell and Kitchener (in the chair), included the Leader of the Opposition in the House of Commons (Bonar Law), the King's Private Secretary (Lord Stamfordham), Admiral Beresford, Lloyd George, the then MP (later Viscount) Waldorf Astoria, Colonel Seely, and the architect Edwin Lutyens, a reflection of the then interlocking establishment circles. As new Secretary of State for War, Kitchener told the gathering he was going to appoint a 'Press Censor' and pointed to FE Smith as his choice, inviting Riddell to come and talk about it next day.

At the War Office, asked by Riddell what Smith's role would be, Kitchener replied 'He will see that nothing dangerous goes into the newspapers. Go away with Brade and settle the matter.' This Riddell did; the greatest difficulty was finding premises for the Bureau close to the Admiralty and War Office: 'Ultimately we arranged to install FE Smith with a scratch staff in a disused, rat-infested building' [40 Charing Cross Road]. Unsurprisingly this was not a successful start. Not only were the premises unsuitable, but Smith and the small number of naval and military Officers selected as the initial censors knew little about the Press, and had no training in nor clear directions as to censorship. Smith spent most of his time in discussion with Riddell and other senior London newspapermen, and trying to find more suitable facilities.

After some weeks, having at least achieved his organisation's move to the Royal United Services Institute in Whitehall, he had had enough, and left on 30 September to join the frontline Services [one is struck by how many Ministers, MPs and their sons went to war in both WWI and WWII, and how many suffered family losses, e.g. Bonar Law, Asquith]. He was replaced at the Bureau by Sir Sydney Buckmaster,[45] who himself remained only until 26 May 1915, having been appointed Lord Chancellor. At that stage, Sir Frank Swettenham and Sir Edward Cook,[46] both of whom were by then already working in the Bureau, were appointed as Joint Directors, remaining until the Bureau was disbanded after the War. In his War Diary, Riddell later paid tribute: 'Sir Frank Swettenham and Sir Edward Cook worked like galley-slaves, and no two men were subject to more vituperation. There is no doubt that the War killed Cook – a gentle, kindly, sensitive creature – although I believe it only fair to say that he suffered more from his encounters with the military authorities than he did from the criticism he received at the hands of the Press. Swettenham was made of tougher fibre – a genial, witty cynic, with the gift of mordant sayings.'

Development

Gradually the organisation, staffing and responsibilities of the Press Bureau were brought under control. Military and naval censors moved to the Royal United Service Institute, linked by tube to the Telegraph Office, and soon became responsible to the Press Bureau. As ever more D-Notices were issued through the AWOPC system, those of lasting import were incorporated in pamphlets, which eventually became the text book of Press Censorship. As an increasing number of books about the War were written, the Bureau approached the Publishers' Association in December 1915, offering to vet manuscripts; 'most of the more important publishers' thereafter submitted manuscripts accordingly. The Bureau's duties included the selection (with the AWOPC) of journalists for 'special missions', the distribution to the Press of their reports and of the work of Official Photographers, and the sale of some of the photographs to the public. The Directors calculated that if they had been allowed by the disapproving Treasury to make wider commercial use of photographic work (including 'kinematograph films'), 'the profits, after payment of all expenses, would more than meet the cost of the whole establishment of Press Censors.'[47]

The broad rule with which the Press Bureau started was similar to that already in use by the AWOPC: self-censorship was requested only 'to prevent the publication of anything likely to help the enemy or to damage the interests of the Allies'. Initially, only naval and military matters were covered, but very quickly the Bureau's net widened at the request of other Government Departments. The Directors reported in 1917 that, 'to make the censorship at all effective, it has been necessary to protect the interests of ourselves and our Allies in other respects, viz., Foreign Affairs, Finance, Supplies, and in other directions'. In 1915, however, the Parliamentary Under-Secretary for Foreign Affairs, Lord Robert Cecil[48] decided the Foreign Office would no longer use the PB system, but instead when essential would deal direct with editors.

This decision was not only anathema to the Bureau, but did not in practice happen; a large number of articles submitted by the Press clearly had foreign affairs components and were dealt with routinely by the Bureau. When the Foreign Office did want to communicate with the Press in general about matters it deemed detrimental to the national interest, it had to do so through the Bureau/AWOPC machinery anyway, by secret/confidential letter or by D-Notice. This remained a source of friction between the Foreign Office and the Bureau for the remainder of the War. The Foreign Office apart, other Government Departments used the Bureau to disseminate information about their activities, the principal reason why all the leading newspapers maintained a representative in its office day and night. This role also ensured the Bureau was de facto kept up to date about business across government. Nevertheless, not all Departments used the system *consistently*; the Joint Directors felt this placed them at such a disadvantage in their censorship duties that in mid-July 1916 they issued a circular to all Government Departments asking for the invariable and immediate supply of such information; they later reported 'It is to be regretted that this circular was, for all practical purposes, ignored.'

Other imperfections perceived by the Directors included that the Neutral Press Committee was amongst 'several large establishments' with overlaps of function, duplication of effort and waste of resources, leading to a sub-optimal service to the Press and others, at home and abroad. 'The Press Bureau has often been able to prevent a Department making a mistake, and a good many other blunders would have been prevented if Departments had referred to the Press Bureau before taking action.' In contrast to un-cooperative departments, the King's Private Secretary was singled out by the Directors in a Report in mid-March 1917 as an example of always keeping the Directors informed about the Monarch's public engagements.[49]

Wider Thoughts of the Joint Directors

Looking ahead to a future war, the Directors made suggestions for a similar organisation. The DoRA should be retained or an equivalent kept on the Statute Book ready for use; the Bureau should be constituted as the only authority for permission to publish, in a statutory rather than voluntary system; the future Act should be tightened up to cover 'false or misleading forecast' of the contents of confidential documents, and the publication of 'unduly alarmist articles or posters'; all dealings with the Press by all Departments should be conducted through the Bureau, as should transmission of press matter by post; the (single) Director should have the power to dismiss the incompetent in the Bureau (in WWI they had no power to remove those seconded from other departments); a nucleus of experienced censor and administrative staff, and the premises and text book of the existing Bureau, should be earmarked to start up the next Bureau, which thus 'might be got to work within 24 hours'; and the Bureau should issue Notices and Letters direct to the Press rather than through the machinery of the AWOPC – after its useful work during the early years of the War, the Directors felt by 1917 that 'the Committee's raison d'etre seems to have gone' [in war time].

Looking back on the pre-March 1917 performance of the Press itself, the Directors summarised, a little contentiously:

On the whole the Press have behaved with great forbearance and loyalty and by far the most friction has been caused by the fact that, as submission to censorship is voluntary, the most careful papers are always suffering by reason of the 'enterprise' of the less scrupulous. We do not think that this is a sufficient reason to make reference compulsory, but we do think that the remedy is to be found in prosecuting where there is any chance of success. Our opinion is supported by the fact that some Scotch newspapers gave a great deal of trouble up to a time when the Lord Advocate began to prosecute them whenever the Press Bureau submitted a case.[50]

The Swettenham/Cook general recommendations were indeed used in the establishment of the Ministry of Information for the next World War. In their views on the imperfections across the then governmental machinery, they were correct. But in their view of the performance of their own Bureau, the Press of the day did not entirely share their satisfaction.

13

EARLY INTERACTION BETWEEN AWOPC, PRESS AND PRESS BUREAU

The sometimes tetchy relationship between the Press Bureau, the AWOPC and the Press had many causes. The course of the War itself did not run smoothly until near its end. The AWOPC, still new itself, had to adjust to rapid improvisation and innovation (of which the unplanned Press Bureau was part), to confusion and disorganisation (in the press as well as in government), to expansion in almost every field except the Press, to continuous tension between government and press, and, after the initial optimism and patriotic fervour, to strong public apprehension about the progress of the War. Although the public was generally not aware of the AWOPC, its existence and role were openly reported within the internal organs of the Press, such as the house journals of the NPA and NS.[51]

As the War progressed, the focus of interaction became increasingly the Press Bureau, but Ministers, their Departments and the plethora of Committees continued also to talk direct to editors and journalists. Political rivalries, especially between individuals rather than parties, were at least as intense during the War as in peacetime, and the Press joined in enthusiastically, lobbying for and against Ministers. On the Press side of the interaction too, there was de facto multi-headed activity, partly by individual proprietors, and partly in the rivalry between the London press and the provincial press. In this interaction, Sir George Riddell was the key figure for the former, and Edmund Robbins for the latter. Their own relationship, although professionally harmonious in seeking normally common goals, was made uncomfortable by the ever-resented assumption of superiority by the London Press, and by differences in the two men's personae: Riddell the wealthy metropolitan pantopragmatic and friend of Lloyd George and other Greats of the day, Robbins of relatively humble Cornish stock and an ink-stained working journalist and manager.

Early Adjustments

In the unexpectedly rapid rush to War, Robbins hastened back from summer holiday in Switzerland on 7 August. That afternoon he attended an ad hoc meeting to discuss establishment of a Press Bureau. Officials suggested access to the Bureau should be allowed only to Press Agencies and to the principal London newspapers, but Robbins persuaded them this would be unacceptably inadequate, and that any of the principal provincial papers which cared to bear the expense of keeping a representative at the Bureau should also be accepted. He had too, as PA Manager, to make swift supplementary adjustments to his own staff: the Bureau immediately decided news would be issued 'whenever received', so the PA had suddenly to provide costly 24/7 shift-workers. His problems were exacerbated by a diminution in the supply of foreign and defence news, causing newspapers supplied under contract by the PA to demand rebates (eventually given); and by some of his key younger staff volunteering for the Services.

In the following days Robbins received numerous complaints from newspapers that, while they obediently abided by promulgated prohibitions, rival newspapers did not. This resulted sometimes from different editorial stances, sometimes from different censors giving different guidance. He attempted at first to deal with these complaints himself, but quickly realised both that this was an unacceptable extra load, and above all that the authority now responsible for finding consistency in the administration of censorship was the Press Bureau, whose Secretary he rapidly persuaded to deal with such complaints there.

Reuters too was frequently to complain to the authorities, initially about the cutting of submarine cables to Europe and the Empire, upon which it had depended for its direct news service, now filtered by the Press Bureau. At the end of August, Reuters was unable to receive reports when the Germans routed the Russians at Tannenberg, because the Russian agency's cable was mislaid in the Bureau; and soon afterwards the Bureau deliberately withheld a telegram to Reuters reporting the fall of Maubeuge because 'if Reuters published the news, it would be believed, and the public is already discouraged enough.'[52]

On 18 August, Robbins accompanied the NPA Chairman and Vice Chairman, Harry Lawson[53] and Riddell, to a meeting with Smith, where all three made complaints on behalf of the Press. The PA Board was particularly aggrieved that the Bureau, in its own issues of information, was 'milking the Press Despatches'; Smith replied, to Robbins' discomfiture, that the Bureau had in fact 'not sent out a single word beyond what had been received from the British and Foreign Governments'; furthermore, when the War Office had suggested foreign official telegrams should be issued exclusively through the Bureau and not through the Press Agencies, Smith had rejected this. Lawson was particularly concerned about the ban on war correspondents at the Front, but Smith explained that was at the request of the French (who were following the Japanese practice, something of which Kitchener's War Office did not entirely disapprove).[54]

A 20 August 1914 AWOPC meeting was convened to consider the position of the Committee vis-à-vis the Press Bureau; besides Greene, Brade, Riddell and Robbins, the only representative of the wider Press who could attend was Scott. Significantly perhaps, it was not the two senior civil servants but Riddell who reported on meetings which the London representatives had had with Smith. The latter had explained to them his three-fold capacity: as distributor of news, as adviser of the Press, and as initiator of any proceedings against the Press. Under the new DoRA, he did not have full responsibility, 'but he had the assurance of the Government that any action he advised would be taken'.

It was feared the AWOPC might be 'abolished'; the Press members advised therefore that Churchill and Kitchener be consulted about its continuation, and suggested Smith should be invited to the next meeting. Scott raised the desirability of co-ordinating the duties of the Director of the Bureau, as the Press Censor, with those of the Cable and Post Office Censors who dealt with press messages, an area of confusion and delay, and therefore of immediate concern to the Press. Greene and Brade undertook to consider this.

Four days later (24 August 1914), the Committee reassembled, this time with three more press representatives and with Smith in attendance, who, it was agreed, should also become a member of the Committee. The most urgent press concern continued to be duplication between the Press Bureau and the General Post Office over censorship of press cablegrams; they recommended the solution eventually reached: collocation in and under the Bureau. It was also pointed out that in some parts of UK local censorship of press telegrams was being applied, even of material which would go to the Bureau; Brade undertook to resolve that too.

Finally Smith reiterated his role. On reporting newspapers which infringed the DoRA, he thought (wrongly as the coming years showed) that 'the necessity of having recourse to the drastic powers conferred by these rules would be unnecessary'. He also acknowledged that with his current small staff, it would be impossible to answer all press queries as to news, but that the Admiralty and War Office had undertaken that casualty lists and reports of engagements which did not contain information useful to the enemy 'would not be withheld from prompt publication'. This too turned out to be an over-optimistic hope.

On about 27 August, Riddell recorded in his diary: 'The Press is furious regarding the censorship arrangements. The Cable Censor's department is chiefly responsible. It has been created hastily and is officered by half-pay officers, many being of an antiquated type. I am carrying on a campaign for reform and hope to get fresh arrangements made.[55] There has been a great row in the Cabinet, so I am told, regarding suppression of news and delay in publication. Kitchener cannot understand that he is working in a democratic country. He rather thinks that he is in Egypt where the Press is represented by a dozen mangy correspondents whom he can throw in the Nile if they object to the way in which they are treated. This is FE Smith's statement, not mine.' Kitchener had indeed had 'unauthorised' British journalists in Flanders tracked down and sent home.

The next problem faced by the Committee was an internal press matter. Brade told an NPA meeting he attended that the French Government had invited the British Press to nominate one representative to the French forces in the field, an attractive option because at this stage there were no journalists allowed at the British parts of the Front (Belgium soon made a similar offer). The proprietors decided the invitation should be delegated to the Press Association, 'as being the Press Agency most representative of British interests'. However, this put the PA in a dilemma, because the basis of its contract with Reuters was that the latter provided foreign news to the London Press, the PA only to the provincial press. H Robbins was despatched to the Old Jewry to see Baron de Reuter, who, in an emotional interview, said he would rather resign than accept an arrangement which cut Reuters out. For contractual reasons, Robbins had therefore to explain to the London proprietors that the PA could not accept the invitation, much though it would have liked to.

In response to a compromise suggestion that the PA and Reuters might act jointly, as they had done successfully in previous situations, the proprietors' view was that a British representative ought to come only from a British organisation, and that Reuters was an international agency (despite the Baron pointing out it was international only in its coverage, was based in London and financed by British capital). There was considerable resentment amongst the PA Management Board and amongst the provincial press more widely at the veto by the London Proprietors of the PA/Reuters proposal. An alternative of offering one completely independent British Press representative was subsequently discussed by the PA, but rejected on the grounds that one reporter could not adequately cover the then 200 miles of the Allied Front. Later that year however, Robbins opined to the PA Committee that, in the absence of journalists at the British part of the Front, official reports being provided by 'Eye Witness',[56] although personally censored by Kitchener, were filling the gap adequately pro tem.

Robbins meanwhile had to tell Brade the French invitation could not be taken up, unless each of the agencies and leading newspapers were allowed to send a representative. Brade replied it was up to the French; neither the War Office nor the Foreign Office pushed this request with France, but later it was discovered that, without further formal consultation, its London Embassy had taken discreetly to inviting selected British newspapers to send a journalist to visit the French sector of the Front. A further press problem concerned news from Germany itself, which was now available only through the official German press agency, Wolff, with whom (unknown to Reuters) the French agency Havas had therefore made an agreement. Reuters however considered it politic not to do so.

At the 16 September 1914 AWOPC meeting, Greene announced that the Home Secretary himself (Simon) had intended to chair it.[57] Robbins was asked to suggest some journalists to be attached to the GPO censorship department to give advice on press matters, 'the kind of men whom he would choose as Sub-Editors for the Press Association.' The first he subsequently suggested was none other than one of his own sons, CE Robbins (then his Chief Sub-Editor); Robbins 'had every confidence in his judgement, and believed he would be the right man in the right place'; nepotism and paternal pride aside, his son did indeed prove to be a most suitable choice, and was soon joined by two other journalists and three barristers, whose collective function was to 'advise the Military Officers as to what should or should not be allowed to pass'. Smith wrote a personal note to Robbins: 'Greatly appreciate your patriotic decision to place your son's great experience at the disposal of the Government'.

Even Robbins Senior must have been moved by this arrangement to over-optimism; he told the worried PA Management Board that these arrangements and assurances from Smith would ensure that 'very shortly such an improvement in the system may be effected as will minimise, if not prevent altogether, the uncertainty and delay which are the subject of complaint'. He also claimed, with more justification, that the AWOPC was being effective in pressurising the Bureau into improving its responsiveness to the Press, even though this was a new system of censorship for Britain, 'therefore the experience was strange and irksome. There had also been some feeling between various Government Departments'.

The 16 September meeting also discussed, at Scott's behest, how to simplify the cable censorship of commercial news, because unless market quotations appeared at once in the Press they were of no value commercially. Robbins was tasked to produce a limited list of approved addressees of guaranteed bona fides, to which commercial press cablegrams could be sent direct without censorship. Brade and Robbins were also asked to consider some form of 'passed by censor' codeword being affixed to messages to the United States and Dominions. Finally, it was agreed the GPO should be persuaded to forego charges on telegrams handed to them for transmission elsewhere by a cable company, and also 'to secure that the words "excised by the Censor" from outgoing messages should not be charged for.' Little of this was to do with protection of national security, but the sinews of war and the sinews of finance are interdependent; the AWOPC was in this instance where they joined.

At the 28 September 1914 AWOPC meeting, attended by Buckmaster as new Director of the Press Bureau, the Committee agreed that censorship once applied should if possible be final, and that there should be early resolution over commercial press cables, as arranged by Robbins and the new War Office military representative, Colonel Cockerill.[58] Cockerill, as head of the War Office Military Operations Section 5, had very wide responsibilities, including press and legal matters, submarine cable and wireless telegraphy policy, censorship, and the sections MO5(d) under Major Kell (subsequently MI5) and MO5(e) under Brigadier-General Anderson (the forerunner with its naval equivalent of GCHQ).

Attendance at the 13 October 1914 meeting was typical of this period: the regulars were Greene, Brade, the PB Director, a War Office military representative, and on the Press side Riddell, Holbrook and Robbins; the regional press members attended when they could get to London. On this occasion there was an embarrassing first agenda item: on the day of his handover to Buckmaster, Smith had appointed, as third sub-editor attached to the GPO cable censors, a Mr Woods of the *Morning Post*. Not mentioned in the minutes, but in his manuscript PA Memoranda, Robbins recorded not only his irritation that Smith had done this without consulting him (he having been tasked to find sub-editors), but also that Woods worked for the Conservative Party of which Smith was then the Chairman; furthermore, Smith alleged this appointment had been agreed with Riddell, which the latter indignantly denied, saying it was 'very likely a political job'. At the AWOPC meeting, officials were at first supportive of Woods but, faced with press hostility, gave way; it was decided that 'in the circumstances the services of Mr Woods could not be utilised, but that the Home Secretary be recommended to make him some adequate pecuniary compensation for the work already done'. It was Robbins who was given 'the unpleasant duty of informing him of the decision'.

The other business that day included agreement to circulate revised regulations for guidance of the Press compiled by Buckmaster; he wanted to issue these direct from the Bureau, but the Press members of the Committee insisted they went through AWOPC channels. Robbins duly issued 1,600 numbered (and therefore traceable) copies on 16 October 1914, to all newspapers except the Irish weeklies. He also enquired at the meeting whether the War Office thought it possible for the football results to be telegraphed by the PA on Saturdays to British Headquarters, for dissemination to the Army in the field, and Cockerill said he would find out.[59]

When Robbins met Cockerill two days later, the Colonel was in complimentary mood about the Press. At his first AWOPC meeting he had been 'struck by the attitude of the Press members'. Instead of being, as anticipated, 'up' against the officials of the two Departments, he had found them to his surprise most reasonable. They had actually suggested restrictions 'beyond those which the authorities had proposed'. Cockerill also told Robbins he had had difficulties in persuading some officials of the need for change, particularly the 'conservative' Admiralty, which, 'being charged with the defence of the country', was currently uneasy because of a 'recrudence of disclosures in the North' [mainly in the Scottish Press].

In his time-consuming part-time AWOPC role, Robbins continued to act out of committee on behalf of individual members, improving co-ordination of censorship staffs and with other Press Agencies, arranging 'private wires' between them, and representing the many Press complaints to the Bureau. One example of a 'stupidity' was prohibition of photographs of the Naval Brigade in Belgium, even after two days fighting, when its 'presence was perfectly well-known to the enemy'. Robbins sent this (and many other) complaints to Buckmaster, who replied that Field Marshal French[60] refused to send twice daily reports from his BEF Headquarters. On disregard of prohibitions by some newspapers and magazines, he pleaded that although there were powers under Statute and Order in Council 'to bring offending newspapers before a Court Martial . . . it is quite evident that a power so tremendous would not be put into operation excepting in a case of grave and continued disregard of the injunctions of this office'. Furthermore breaches were nearly always 'due to obvious stupidity or negligence . . . not due to a malicious or contumacious breach of rules'; a letter to the editor was a more effective remedy. Commenting later to the PA Committee, Robbins felt Buckmaster's reply was 'a reasonable one'.

There were many such AWOPC/Press complaints about the Bureau then and later, but Buckmaster suffered many disadvantages: in addition to building up an unplanned organisation, he was an administrative cog between two large and incompatible wheels. He told

Riddell in October 'It is an awful job. How would you like to control an office staffed by men whom you have not appointed, whom you cannot dismiss, and most of whom have been appointed in order to find them jobs at £300 to £400 per annum?'[61] The initial staff provided by the War Office and the Admiralty were indeed mostly undistinguished and untrained officers brought out of retirement, known in the Army as 'dug-outs'. Buckmaster had powerful enemies in the Press too: in November he told Riddell he was heading for a row with Northcliffe, 'who is becoming more and more impertinent', and that he could 'prove that Northcliffe induced the American papers to attack the Censor so that he (N) may quote their comments in The Times'.

Buckmaster also had to contend with the foibles of Ministers. In the week before Antwerp fell to the Germans, the Admiralty asked that no press reference be made to the movements of the First Lord, Churchill, about to visit the beleaguered city; a Notice was issued accordingly, cancelled after his return four days later, but keeping a retrospective prohibition in place. Four days after Antwerp fell (9 October), the Central News Agency asked Churchill direct to comment on a very critical recent article in the *Morning Post* about the unsuccessful defence of Antwerp. A consequent D-Notice requested by Churchill's office, which would have stopped any criticism of his decision to send a Naval Brigade there, had been cancelled by Buckmaster, on the grounds that it exceeded agreed prohibitions. Buckmaster did not attend the meeting between Churchill and the *Morning Post*, but later that day received a note from Churchill's Private Secretary asking the Bureau not to let through any 'lurid accounts . . . which would lead the public to suppose that the services of the [Naval] Division had not been of great use'. Buckmaster this time did not stop the request, but did give guidance to his staff that discretion was to be used, and 'the broad lines of our policy, which consists of only censoring what may be of value to the enemy, are to be adhered to'.

The next day he also wrote to the *Morning Post* editor, about a further leading article critical of Churchill in the paper that day, and mildly rebuked this attack on a Minister 'who could not reveal all'. The editor, HA Gwynne,[62] immediately thundered back that it had been 'a very grave military blunder' sending untrained and inexperienced officers and men to defend Antwerp, that Churchill's own visits to Antwerp, France and Denmark, were ill-judged when he should have been at the helm of his Department in London, that the article gave no help to the enemy, and that it was his duty as an editor to criticise politicians when necessary. Buckmaster went to see Churchill that evening, to explain why it was not his role to stop criticism, adding that in a previous case of bad news,[63] it had not been stopped, and the Prime Minister and Home Secretary had confirmed this was the correct decision. Churchill sent him a note soon afterwards, saying that on reflection he would 'rather you took no action'.

Next day however Buckmaster heard Churchill had summoned the Foreign Editor of the Central News Agency; Buckmaster declined to attend, since he had a critical view of the Agency, whose 'action . . . throughout my management of this office has been reprehensible to the extreme degree'. Next day the Agency submitted to the Bureau an article particularly eulogistic about the First Lord's position over Antwerp and his visits there. The Bureau, with what must have been some pleasure, stopped the article, on the grounds that the First Lord's retrospective prohibition about reporting his movements were still in force; however, Buckmaster told Churchill's Private Secretary that further concealment of the visit 'will render us ridiculous' because Antwerp had been 'filled with journalists'. The latter immediately suggested lifting the prohibition, adding that perhaps it would be a good thing at the same time to release 'any compliments that may be forthcoming'.

One of the first compliments which appeared, in the *Daily Chronicle*, did not praise Churchill however, but the Government's support of Belgium, the gallantry of the British marines, sailors and troops, and the bravery of Colonel Seely, the former SofS for War (now back in the Army), for having personally risked his life taking a message to the front line with the order to withdraw. A few days later, Buckmaster received a further note from Churchill's Private Secretary, saying that if he thought a great deal might still be published about Churchill and Antwerp, 'it will be better to let the matter sleep after all – so will you please continue the embargo'. Lloyd George told Riddell (Diaries 1908–1923) that Churchill was so annoyed with Buckmaster that he wanted to abolish the Bureau and revert to the practice of the Admiralty and War Office censoring their own news. Buckmaster conversely complained about lack of Cabinet support, and that Kitchener and Churchill were afraid to court-martial Northcliffe. Or so Riddell alleged.[64]

At a further brief AWOPC meeting on 28 October 1914, although not fully recorded in the minutes, Greene asked for opinions on 'an unfortunate matter which had happened the previous day', when a British battleship [*HMS AUDACIOUS*] had been sunk by a mine (fortunately with only one killed) off Ireland, something which the Government wished to keep from the Germans for a few days. The more important reason for temporary prohibition of this information was that, with the possibility that Turkey might imminently decide to declare war on Germany's side, 'news of any serious incident, such as the loss of an important naval unit, which did not call for publication for other reasons, should not be published in the Press for the present.'

This request for blanket censorship caused some dissent. Riddell's much later recollection of the debate differs from that written immediately by Robbins; the former claimed he opposed suppressing the news, because the crew had been landed, the disaster must therefore be well known, and the public would 'be rendered suspicious and unduly apprehensive when the news was disclosed' later. Whether or not so, Buckmaster eventually suggested, and Riddell and Robbins agreed, that the Press should be taken into confidence and asked not to publish. Scott, while not disagreeing, 'feared that the position of the English Press was being weakened by a policy of too much secrecy being observed by the Government'. Riddell later recollected that he too reported 'the Press is in an irritable and dissatisfied state . . . This statement seemed to cause some surprise [to the official members of the Committee]', except on the part of Buckmaster, who agreed'.

Greene countered by mentioning attacks on the Admiralty in the *Globe* and *Morning Post*, and asked advice on the latter's editor being talked to; press members were lukewarm, so Robbins suggested as a compromise that Riddell not Buckmaster should speak to the editor, and 'in a private capacity – not as conveying an intimation from the Committee'. This was agreed, as was that a 'Parker' telegram should be sent to all except the Irish weeklies on the battleship damage/Turkish problem.[65] None of the Press infringed this prohibition, but Turkey anyway sided with Germany next day. In his customary post-Cabinet handwritten note to the King on 30 October, Asquith assured him that the publicity policy remained one of prompt disclosure, especially where there were casualties, but that in this case politico-military considerations had been over-riding for the time being.[66]

Dissatisfaction with the Press Bureau was raised in the House of Commons on 12 November, where Buckmaster was attacked by Members from both main Parties. Sir William Bull[67] complained of the lack of information on matters of public interest, and described the Bureau's attitude as like that of the little girl who said 'Whatever the baby is doing, tell it not to'. It had refused to permit publication of criticism of transport of the wounded, of delays in payment, of references to the foreign policy of neutral countries, of an announcement by Asquith of the landing of Indian troops at Marseilles, and of official French despatches, and had made veiled threats against newspapers. Colonel Yate[68] complained the censorship had harmed recruiting, and Mr Sherwell[69] felt that individual members of the Government were taking powers too freely, adding 'if the Country finds certain minor Napoleons claiming arbitrary powers without consulting the House, the Solicitor-General will be made to realise that they have miscalculated the temper, spirit, and traditions of their countrymen'.

Buckmaster's response was robust; he spoke 'with considerable warmth', saying he would have liked to have exercised an even more severe and exact control over some newspapers on aspects of foreign policy. Some French despatches, for example, had disclosed important movements of our troops, and 'I grieve to say, I was too late effectually to strike it out'; and the Prime Minister's reported statement about Indian troops had not been accurate. The powers to back his actions existed, and he claimed the Bureau stood between the Press and the penalties that might otherwise be inflicted on them for their transgressions.

The following week (23 August), Bonar Law[70] also protested in the House, criticising Buckmaster's comments, and reaffirming that 'it is the right of every newspaper in this country . . . if [it] honestly believes that a member of the Government is incompetent or not doing his work properly, to try to get rid of that Minister'. Such parliamentary exchanges were widely reported in the Press, and editorials continued to inveigh against the degree of censorship. On 19 November for example, one paper used the occasion of Lord Roberts' funeral in St Paul's Cathedral to complain: 'We pay public and fitting honour to the dead; we veil the achievements of the living. Officialdom has even seemed to take a perverse delight in waging this war in the dark, anonymously, as though it were a thing apart from the lives and emotions of our people . . . It is a profound mistake . . .'.[71]

It would be wrong however for a modern reader to assume from the barrage of complaints that the newspapers were bereft of any War news. The day of Bonar Law's intervention, many pages in the Press included coverage of the ramming of a German submarine by a Royal Navy patrol vessel, of naval pilots' feats against a Zeppelin base, of exploits of British troops at Ypres, and of British artillery at Zeebrugge, amongst other stories. What came from the Press Bureau was at this stage well supplemented by reports and letters from individuals involved, often passed on to the Press by proud families and colleagues.

14

SETTLING DOWN TO A LONG WAR

Press complaints about the Bureau continued, albeit at a reducing rate as the system settled down. Robbins continued to be a pivotal figure in attempting to improve relationships between the two sides, and in handling representations from the Government side and from public figures. In early December 1914, for example, he received a request from Admiral of the Fleet Lord Fisher to discourage the press from mentioning the repatriation by the Germans of British invalids in occupied Europe, for fear of retaliation by the Germans against those still to be returned if press reports were adverse (Fisher's daughter and invalid son-in-law had just been so returned). Robbins received fulsome thanks from Buckmaster for the visit he organised for the latter to talk to the PA Committee. Buckmaster was also Solicitor General,[72] but he had found time too to visit the GPO, to resolve another complaint from the evening papers about the 'archaic' arrangements there for sending out official French and British communiqués (the GPO's afternoon transmission was often delayed until 5.15 p.m., too late for the evening papers' deadline).

Robbins also acted as link between the PA Committee and the War Office in the selection of a candidate to be the PA/Reuters correspondent, should one be allowed in due course at the British Front. The journalist provisionally engaged was a Captain Clarence Wiener (the Germanic surname did not rule out *this* selection). He had fought in the British Army during the Boer War, but Robbins now noticed he had not received a campaign medal; not knowing the reason, he deduced it 'must have been something very bad'. His own enquiries and discreet conversation with Brade elicited that Wiener 'apparently had means . . . had a place in Norfolk where he . . . entertained chorus girls . . . suspicion he was mixed up in the White Slave Traffic'. Because of this colourful journalistic CV, the two Press Agencies decided Wiener was not after all the right candidate, but Reuters wished it to be the War Office who said so, for fear he would take legal action against the Agencies for breach of contract. Robbins persuaded Brade to oblige, and Wiener was ruled by the War Office to be 'unacceptable' as a war correspondent.

This may have been a quid pro quo for a request from Brade to the PA to assist with rebutting unfavourable reports in the German Press about the conditions of those interned in concentration camps in Britain. He asked if the PA could arrange unannounced visits to the camps, and distribute its reports afterwards. The PA Committee immediately agreed to do this (at its own expense, as Robbins pointed out managerially but proudly), thus putting out of joint the noses of the London Press (who had until then taken little interest in the concentration camps).

Riddell at this time was more concerned about the 'consolidation' of the Defence of the Realm Act: 'The drastic and unique provisions of this legislation have not attracted the attention they deserve. The legislation has taken place so rapidly that the measures have not been properly discussed. The Press have been singularly ill-informed and lacking in criticism regarding a law which wipes out Magna Carta, the Bill of Rights, etc, in a few lines. We have got some alterations made, but trial by Court Martial still stands. A very dangerous innovation.' The amendments he sought included one giving those not subject to the Naval Discipline or Army Acts the right to apply for a civil trial rather than court martial, something about which many editors had strong feelings, tinged perhaps with personal apprehension.[73] The NPA Secretary also wrote formally to the Home Office in December 1914, complaining of the all-embracing nature of Clause 27, dealing with anyone who might 'spread reports or make statements likely to prejudice the recruiting, training, discipline or administration of His Majesty's Forces. If construed literally, this would prejudice all reports of fact or criticism.'[74]

On 30 November 1914, Robbins received a telegram from the *Nautical Magazine* in Glasgow, telling him the editor had received a copy of the *New York Shipping Illustrated*, which included photographic information about 'HM Battleship sunk North coast Ireland October 27. May interest you'. Robbins replied he had already heard that the American Press had the information, so the telegram was 'not altogether a surprise. At the same time, so long as the Admiralty decides not to have anything published in this country about the matter, any statements which may be circulated abroad can only be regarded as rumour'. However, obviously concerned about this *Alice in Wonderland* situation, Robbins contacted the Admiralty, which meanwhile was attacked in *The Times*, *Globe* and *Morning Post* for suppression of important news of a disaster.

On 4 December the Bureau asked Robbins to issue the following letter to the Press by telegram:

> The Board of Admiralty are satisfied that up to the present the enemy do not know with certainty whether the *AUDACIOUS* has been lost or not. They are not sure whether she is a total wreck or whether she is under repair. This fact justifies, at any rate for the present, a continuance of the reticence which for nearly a month was successful in preventing even a rumour from reaching the enemy. In these circumstances they are unable to make any official statement. Their Lordships consider that this is a matter on which their judgement should prevail, even with those who do not agree with it, and a grave responsibility rests upon any person who attempts to force their hands ... their Lordships desire most earnestly to emphasise the importance of shrouding in mystery and secrecy at all times and by all means the number of *DREADNOUGHTS* available ... This must be accepted as the settled policy of the Board ... it is the duty of loyal subjects and friends of the country to do their utmost on all occasion to further it.

It may be no coincidence that parts of this lofty message have a Churchillian tone. The flaw, as Robbins pointed out privately to the PA Committee, was that the American Press had not only carried the full story, but that it had been accompanied by photographs taken by the international passengers and crew of *SS Olympic*, who had rescued the ship's company of the *AUDACIOUS*. With officials, however, Robbins loyally supported their line, writing next day to Buckmaster that he was glad the Admiralty had taken the Press into its confidence in explaining its position. He reported that in the previous three weeks he had visited the principal daily newspaper offices in Ireland, West England and South Wales, and that he had

had few queries about the *AUDACIOUS* story, which he had passed off (as with whispers about Dominion troops arriving in England) as rumours. Nevertheless, he did suggest that messages such as the one above should if possible be passed in future by post rather than by telegraph, because in more than one town he had visited he had been assured that the locals knew of the existence of matters which the authorities were trying to keep secret, Post Office clerks being the alleged source of leaks. Scott for example had told him 'the loss of the vessel was generally known in the tram and on the street at Manchester'.

At the 18 December 1914 AWOPC meeting, the main topic was how to respond to a new French invitation for ten British Press representatives to visit the 'zone of military operations in France'. There was discussion significantly as to whether to allocate one of these to a United States Press representative, but this was decided against; the allocation was one each to Reuters/PA and to the other Press Agencies, five to London newspapers and three to provincial 'groups' (with a fourth to the provincials if the French could be persuaded by Brade to increase their offer). Robbins was asked to co-ordinate the selection of names accordingly.

Other matters discussed were arrangements for the Christmas Day shutdown (of the London newspapers and of the Bureau), the absence of a system of censorship of local stories obtained by the provincial press ('This question required further consideration'), and the lack of effective steps taken by the Government against newspapers which disregarded Bureau prohibitions to the disadvantage of the 'loyal Press'. Once again it was press representatives who felt most strongly that firm action should be taken, Scott complaining of the 'many evasions'; and once again Sir Frank Swettenham assured them there was 'no favouritism' and that breaches were indeed reported by the Bureau to the legal authorities.

Robbins referred to a German Press report that two British destroyers had been sunk, and suggested that in such cases the Admiralty ought to issue a statement admitting or denying it [the Admiralty did indeed eventually agree to this, allowing a delay in each case, for intelligence and next-of-kin reasons]. Robbins also sought guidance on a confidential Bureau notice he had seen about a proposed discussion between the Scandinavian States of their position as neutrals; Swettenham explained it had been sent to a limited number of newspapers, but the Foreign Office did not wish it to be more widely circulated as a 'Parker'. This was an early indication that the Foreign Office had a different concept of how to interact with the Press.

Dissension Within The Press

Over the Christmas and New Year period, Robbins struggled to achieve agreement, amongst the provincial press in particular, as to who the nominations should be to take up the French invitation. He reported the infighting to the PA Committee (the 'project was in state of hotch-potch'), but to no avail. At the 8 January 1915 AWOPC meeting, he had to explain why no agreement had been reached. It was decided that a further meeting should be convened of the 16 newspapers principally concerned, but at proprietor level. The Press side were forcefully unanimous meanwhile in rejecting a proposal that the Press Bureau might close each day between 1 a.m. and 8 a.m. as so little was submitted by the Press during the night.

Robbins raised again local censorship of the provincial press, reading a letter from Buckmaster which, 'while admitting the serious disadvantages under which the Provincial Press laboured in comparison with the London Press in the matter of censorship, deprecated the appointment of local censors', on the grounds principally of maintaining uniformity of censorship. Robbins explained that in practice the provincial press often rang enquiries and/or copy through to the Press Association, which it then transmitted to the Bureau, whereas the Bureau itself was not allowed to receive copy by telephone. The Committee agreed with Riddell's views that local censorship was 'undesirable in Great Britain except in the case of invasion or threatened invasion', and that Ireland and the Channel Islands should be 'linked in some way' with the Press Bureau.

Colonel Cockerill pointed out that King's Regulations forbade officers and soldiers from communicating with the Press without permission, and held them responsible too for anything published in the Press from letters to friends and family. He suggested it was therefore 'scarcely proper' for newspapers to advertise for such letters to be sent in for publication; a Notice was agreed reminding editors that just because letters had been passed by local unit censors, it did not mean publication was justified. Riddell reported he and Brade had corresponded about the right of access to the Court of Criminal Appeal being granted to any newspaper or journalist court-martialled for a breach of the DoRA, pending amendment of the Act.

Finally at this meeting, Robbins complained about the Press Bureau delaying telegrams which had 'little apparent connection with military operations', and about the Bureau 'issuing important communications to certain sections of the Press direct, instead of through him'. He gave as an example a public speech by Sir Edward Carson in Bangor, which had reached the Press so late that 'it was useless to all newspapers' [Swettenham later explained to him that the blame lay with politicians, who did not understand the system, and who anyway did not have to use the Bureau]. Robbins was told to discuss this with the Director, and to report back if the problems were not resolved. Insofar as they could be, they were, but these tensions in the at least four-cornered relationship (Government, Bureau, AWOPC, Press) remained to varying degrees throughout the War.

Within a week, Robbins attempted again to achieve provincial press agreement on the French invitation to visit the Front. Thirteen representatives answered his summons to the PA offices, including his brother Alfred Robbins of the *Birmingham Daily Post*. Some newspapers insisted on their own man being chosen, and when told that this was not feasible, walked out. Others showed more willingness to compromise and accept Robbins' proposal of representation by region; but ultimately no agreement was possible.

Robbins meanwhile complained that the Army was trying to prevent publication of the CinC's commendations of individual BEF battalions, on grounds of security. Although some reports did get through, commendations being recorded for example in the *Evening News* on 12 January (1st Coldstreams, 1st Northamptons, East Surreys) and the *Daily Mail* on 14 January (Gordon Highlanders), Brade explained that usually such information did not reach the War Office until a month later; as for Field Marshal French's speeches to the troops, 'he never prepares anything, no notes are taken, and what the Press gets must be drawn from the recollections of people who have heard him'. Robbins felt Brade was 'on our side' in his promise to try to have 'eulogies' passed to the Press Bureau for distribution. Brade also told Robbins a few days later he had obtained permission for up to five journalists at a time to visit the British lines in France and Belgium for short periods, with similar arrangements to those of the French, and under the rules agreed pre-war.

Robbins had a less smooth relationship with Greene, who complained about a story arising from a telephone interview given to the PA by a Commander Hewlett, the 'aviator concerned in the Christmas Day raid'. The PA's resultant strong piece was quashed by the Admiralty, which complained the PA reporter had obtained it by subterfuge, namely by falsely claiming the approach had been cleared with its Air Department, something the reporter denied [the story in fact went out by another route, after PB clearance]. Robbins took the opportunity to list to Greene other Admiralty delays and inconsistencies, to point out that often the Press had information before the Admiralty (for example the *Belfast News Letter* knew of actions in the Irish Channel before the news reached Whitehall), to opine that the more 'loyal' a newspaper was, the worse they were treated, and to suggest that Greene had a word with Lord Fisher (recalled as First Sea Lord) about the Admiralty's performance in this area; but Greene 'did not think any good would be gained'. Instead, Robbins went to see the Naval Censor, Lieutenant Commander Chichester,[75] ran through the litany with him, and received an apology for some of the Admiralty's faults.

On 19 January Robbins was summoned by Buckmaster and Swettenham to hear a complaint that the Bureau was being treated by the Press as an "Aunt Sally". They did not mind being attacked about their own faults, but not for the shortcomings of the Government Departments concerned. Robbins agreed the latter were often at fault, and as an example reported his recent interview with Greene, characterising the Admiralty's censorship as 'great delays, apparently no effective co-ordination, and no uniformity in treatment'. He also however reminded Buckmaster and Swettenham that the Bureau had been set up as the Government's means of communication with the Press; he referred to the speech the former had made in Parliament the previous 26 November, explaining the workings of the Bureau, and asserting that, although what was published would be the decision of the Departments not of the Bureau, 'it has been and will be the policy of publishing everything that can be made public without danger to the State.'[76]

Some days later, Swettenham complained the Press Association itself had 'flagrantly disregarded' a prohibition on reporting the movements of Lord Kitchener. It had not in fact done so; the *Evening News* had acquired a report about an inspection of troops at Epsom by Kitchener and the French War Minister, and submitted it direct to the Bureau (where left-hand/right-hand mix-ups still frequently occurred between different censors). Robbins countered that there were instances where the PA did not carry a report because of a known prohibition, only to find that a newspaper had submitted something direct to the Bureau and been allowed to publish. Robbins reported all this sometimes acrimonious activity to the PA Committee in March 1915. He told of continuing problems with timely delivery of communiqués to the Press, and that some of Field Marshal French's early ones had been issued through the *London Gazette*, causing *The Times* to complain that the *Gazette* received preferential treatment because it was a 'Government organ'; that there had been false claims by correspondents of Zeppelin raids on Cromer, Dover and Deal; in passing he commented to his Board on the limitations of the use of the telephone for PA business: it did not have 'universal transmission', and was expensive in some parts of the United Kingdom.[77]

Robbins opened the 5 March 1915 AWOPC meeting by reading a letter from the Colonel stationed in the GPO, about the Central Telegraph Office practice of intercepting certain Inland Press telegrams which contained matter whose publication might seem 'injudicious'. There appeared to be no authority for them to do this, and anyway 'it appeared wrong in principle to expect the Post Office to discriminate in such matters'. Moreover, because no such check existed outside London, provincial newspapers might gain an unfair advantage. The Colonel proposed therefore the practice should cease, and that it should be left to newspapers to have regard to the DoRA and to use the Press Bureau. Robbins confirmed that, from the Press point of view, the system 'operated in a partial, irregular and inefficient manner', but, rather than stop it immediately, the Committee decided to make enquiries 'regarding the genesis of the practice' prior to it next meeting.

A much longer discussion then took place about newspapers which 'systematically disregarded' DoRA Regulations. The running was again made by the Press side: Duncan proposed a Resolution, seconded by Baird and carried unanimously, that 'the authorities should take legal proceedings in a test case or cases for the purpose of securing a decision or decisions as to the infringement of Regulations 18 and 27.'[78] Other matters discussed included a further letter from the French about places at their Front, the need for more copies of casualty lists, and that these should be listed by Regiment [Brade was sympathetic, but he knew Kitchener objected because of high casualties in particular Regiments; Brade prevailed; from 24 March the lists were issued by post on Mondays for publication on Wednesdays, 'to reduce the burden on the wives'].

The minutes of this meeting were drafted by Colonel Cockerill, and included the sensitive discussion of the Press side's wish for test prosecutions of newspapers which regularly ignored the Bureau's prohibitions; all agreed his draft except Riddell, who suggested it might not be advisable to include this because 'we do not . . . know who might get hold of the document in years to come'. Robbins was 'inclined to agree' with Sir George, and went to see Brade, who however remarked subtly that 'no doubt the Bureau would be very pleased to have the discussion recorded, as they would think it made a point not against the Press, but against the War Office'. Brade asked for time to consider the matter, and it does not seem to have been raised again; the record of the discussion remained in the minutes, and the document is indeed in The National Archives for Riddell's posterity unknowns to 'get hold of.'[79]

There were anyway other bones of contention. A Notice issued by the Bureau at the behest of the DMO, Major-General Callwell,[80] complaining about 'the exaggerated accounts of success printed daily in the Press and especially by exhibiting posters [on news-stands] framed to catch the eye and magnify comparatively unimportant actions into great victories. Reported reverses to the enemy are reported as crushing defeats, Germany is represented as within measurable distance of starvation, bankruptcy, and revolution, and, only yesterday, a poster was issued in London declaring that half the Hungarian Army had been annihilated. All sense of proportion is thus lost, and with these daily, and often hourly, statements of great Allied gains and immense enemy losses, the public can have no true appreciation of the facts and of the gigantic task and heavy sacrifices before them'. After more in the same vein, he asked for press restraint.

This greatly offended the London Press in particular, at whom it was principally aimed. Riddell replied on 26 March, copy to the Prime Minister and other Ministers, indignantly claiming the Notice had 'no adequate justification': the Press had faithfully reported news issued by the naval and military authorities, and he blamed the Government for any public misconceptions. He quoted optimistic statements of Asquith and French, and those in official 'Eye-Witness' reports, and said it was unreasonable to expect the 'industrial population' to display the energy and self-sacrifice being asked of them by the Government unless they had the facts. 'It is futile to endeavour to disregard the long-established habits and customs of the people.' The upshot was a meeting at No.10 Downing Street, at which Ministers and London proprietors agreed Riddell should hold discussions with Kitchener and Churchill every week. The meetings were not in practice so regular, but it did give Riddell unique access on behalf of the Press to the War Minister and the First Lord.

Another bitter controversy almost immediately arose within the Press, over representation in the Dardanelles campaign, then in its build-up phase. On 13 March Churchill minuted that Kitchener was leaving decisions on this to him, and he instructed Greene to arrange 'with your Press Committee for the selection of three Gentlemen, representing the whole Press of this Country, who are to be allowed to go as War Correspondents for the combined Naval and Military Operations in the Dardanelles. An Officer at present serving on the Staff of the RND [Royal Naval Division] is to be allowed to report as 'Eye Witness' for the British Forces . . . Let me see your proposals'.

Brade asked Robbins to convene an AWOPC meeting to make the selections, but even before this could be done the commercial and contractual concerns of the Press again came to the fore. Robbins consulted Riddell and the NPA Secretary, who agreed one place should go to Reuters/PA for the provincial press, one to the NPA for the London Press, and one to the Empire Press Union for the remainder of the Empire, the latter to be dropped if (as the Admiralty were now reconsidering) the allocation were reduced to two places, since Reuters already covered the Empire. The other press representatives on the Committee agreed, but, in doing so, Scott added 'provided that no single London newspaper has any special advantage and that the NPA service will come through to such provincial papers as buy war services from London papers'.

What he had in mind was that the two War Correspondents were likely to be in two different places, and that while Reuters already contractually supplied the London Press with international news, the provincial press only received news from NPA members if they paid for 'Special Articles' under contract. If Scott's proviso were not agreed, the London Press would therefore have the advantage over the provincials of news from two places rather than from just the place where the Reuters/PA man was. This proviso was communicated to the NPA, and meanwhile nominations went forward to Greene, with the EPU selection to be made later if the third invitation was confirmed.

This seemingly fair and agreed arrangement immediately fell apart. On 17 March Riddell had to tell Robbins that the NPA Council were not in fact in favour of supplying their articles to provincial papers; the London papers would all be carrying the same articles and not writing 'Special Articles', so existing contracts did not apply. Scott said he could only agree to this if his local rivals, the Manchester editions of the *Daily Mail* and *Daily News*, would also not carry the NPA reports. Robbins suggested to Scott that, as the matter was between his paper and the *Daily Telegraph* (the NPA nominee's employer), he should take it up direct with Lawson; Scott (not alone in his view) quickly bounced the ball back to Robbins, telling him to do this himself; Robbins, with Riddell's support, declined to do so, on the grounds that he had no locus standi.

The London Press members of the AWOPC proceeded nevertheless. Riddell wrote to Greene on 19 March, informing him of the NPA's selection, undertaking to distribute his dispatches after Press Bureau clearance to named morning newspapers,[81] and asking that these should not have to seek further clearance before publication. He explained to Greene that, while London evening and weekly newspapers and linked foreign and colonial journals were then free to copy these dispatches, those London newspapers currently under contract to supply certain provincial newspapers were in this case 'not at liberty to include this particular service'; but neither he nor Greene informed other officials that the provincial press were not at all content with this arrangement. The London representatives also agreed that any photographs/illustrations from the Dardanelles would be issued through the Press Bureau, in the same way as official dispatches and 'Eye Witness' reports.

The Admiralty agreed the two correspondents should make their own way to Malta, and there 'make themselves known' to the Vice Admiral Commanding the East Mediterranean Squadron, who would arrange warship transport to the Dardanelles. Robbins summoned his man for a final interview, telling him that 'as the operations in the Dardanelles were of such extreme importance, he need not practise economy so far as the length of his cables was concerned, ie he need not have the fear of Mr Robbins before his eyes when he wanted to cable in full a good story'. Robbins had meanwhile discovered the Empire Press Union did not want to take up the third place still on offer; he and Riddell suggested it should be given to the provincial press, thus giving them too a second source of reports, but it was too late; the place had already been given locally to an Australian journalist with his Army in Egypt.[82]

On the Western Front there were also tensions. In his father's absence, Harold Robbins was summoned by Northcliffe to *The Times* offices in mid-April, to be shown a long despatch on the Battle of Neuve Chapelle, written by Valentine Williams,[83] one of the by now authorised five special correspondents near the British lines. Northcliffe, just returned from visiting Field Marshal French in Belgium, alleged the CinC was, unlike Kitchener and the War Office, very much in favour of having correspondents on the Front, and had given Williams 'every facility'. Northcliffe was lunching the Field Marshal in London next day, and wanted to know whether, if French wanted the despatch 'published exactly as it is, are you [the PA] prepared to fight the Press Bureau?' The younger Robbins replied he hardly felt the PA could act like that with the Bureau. The upshot was that *The Times* sent the despatch instead to the rival London News Agency [who did submit it to the Press Bureau, but marked 'Read and approved by the Commander-in-Chief, sgnd Brigadier-General Mcdonogh [sic], Chief of the Intelligence Department']. Although wise to keep out of an internal Army battle between Kitchener and French,[84] and to support Press Bureau procedures, Robbins senior rightly remarked 'the PA has not been treated well in the matter'.

Robbins was still 'frequently making representations at the Bureau, personally and by letter, with a view to keeping the Censors up to the mark'. He complained to Cook, for example about 'liners' [i.e. freelance journalists] who did not submit their material to the Bureau before selling it to newspapers and who therefore had an advantage over the PA, which did submit; Cook replied the Bureau had no powers to compel. Such was the volume of D-Notices now being sent out as 'Parkers', that the PA was also becoming concerned about the cost it was bearing;[85] Swettenham agreed to discuss with the Postmaster General the PA proposal that the envelopes should be stamped 'On His Majesty's Service' and go free of charge. There were frequent delays in GPO handling of telegrams because so many of its staff had gone off to war. The PA also had to make further financial concessions to newspapers, because many matters on which it had contracted to report were no longer available; Parliament was sitting only three days a week, first class cricket and football had been stopped because so many players had joined up, and disruption of the telephones and cables meant the flow of news from local reporters was often impeded. Furthermore 16-inch deep flooding of the PA offices caused not only disruption to business, but also 'a most unpleasant odour.'[86] On a personal level, Robbins was distressed when, a few days after being thanked by Julius de Reuter for his support in the wrangle over supplying Dardanelles reports, the Baron committed suicide (in mid-April, a few days after the death of his wife).

There were even more fundamental complications to the orderly flow of information between governmental sources and the Press. Further 'tours' to the British lines had now been authorised for journalists, and all four places had, under Riddell's influence, been allocated to the London Press. The London papers had also arranged a secret briefing meeting with the Prime Minister, Kitchener, Churchill and Buckmaster; the PA's West End correspondent had however got to hear about it, and informed Robbins, who even as AWOPC Secretary had known nothing about it. Robbins complained to his Board that the Committee was in danger of being marginalised and 'knocked out of time' because 'Sir George Riddell is a great "pusher", and a close personal friend of Mr Lloyd George'. Through the latter, he had frequently interviewed Kitchener and Churchill 'over the heads of the Permanent Under Secretaries', and then written articles for selected parts of the Press. At about this time, Kitchener nevertheless complained to Riddell about Lloyd George misrepresenting the number of troops in France, and also commented on what he called 'newspaper embroidery' and criticisms of conflicting statements between Kitchener and the Prime Minister about the efficiency of munitions output, adding 'The Times has been the most virulent critic, I am told, but I never read it.'[87]

Within the AWOPC too, Scott and Phillips had initiated correspondence about the Dardanelles direct with officials, without keeping Robbins informed, thus weakening his ability to exert influence on behalf of the Press. Indeed, not even his own Board was completely sympathetic. Robert Wilson, the Scottish representative, defended Riddell, saying he sent the provincial editors all that he sent the London ones and 'it is extremely interesting, much more so than the dry instructions and suggestions of the Press Bureau'. Robbins angrily pointed out that the Riddell letters were not sent to all the provincial press, who therefore ought to raise it in the AWOPC: 'Sir George has a motor car, enjoys a big income, and can pass his time at the Government Offices'.

At the 27 April 1915 AWOPC meeting, the first press concern raised by Robbins was once again the Post Office interception of Inland Press telegrams, on which he now suggested withdrawal of all censorship, leaving editors responsible for what was published; in this he was supported in particular by Baird of the Irish Newspaper Society, who felt Editors were by now sufficiently acquainted with DoRA Regulations to do this. Cockerill objected, arguing any breaches would lead to demand for something even worse for the Press, namely local censorship. Long discussion produced a compromise agreement: the current system would continue, but the three leading Agencies (PA, Central News, and Exchange Telegraph Company) could apply for exemption, as long as they also undertook to submit all messages to the Bureau before publication, which all three duly did.

The Committee discussed Scott's complaint: 'a very strong feeling that the Admiralty had placed the London Press in a privileged position' over the Dardanelles. A pained Greene explained that his Department had intended equal treatment and been unaware of the press disagreement until after the two correspondents had left England. Riddell suggested permitting the provincial press to send out an extra correspondent. This did not satisfy Scott, who said it was now too late to select and send out a suitable man; with land as well as sea operations imminent, one of the correspondents would be at sea and one on land, and this could mean that 'Important events might then take place, regarding which the Provincial Press would find themselves entirely without information.' He therefore suggested the AWOPC should write to the NPA, pointing out it was never the intention of the authorities to create a situation preferential to the London Press, and asking them to 'accede to the request of those provincial papers who wish to share the services of [the NPA reporter] on an equal basis. This was agreed to, Sir George Riddell dissenting'.

Smarting perhaps as business moved on, Riddell now read a letter 'of considerable importance' received from the First Lord [still Churchill], on the responsibilities of editors concerning news supplied by the Admiralty,[88] referring to the 'contradiction [by the Admiralty] of fake paragraphs submitted by the Press' [i.e. false information included in articles submitted to the Bureau for clearance]. The First Lord said 'the Admiralty could not undertake the responsibility of appending notes stating that allegations were untrue', on the grounds that, because the Department received the first news of all important events and released it immediately, in the absence of 'an intimation from the Admiralty, the Press may assume the news is untrue'. Although Riddell queried this over-simplification of how news reached the Press, and suggested the Press Bureau should try to prevent dissemination of false information, which the Press too 'would be anxious to suppress if they knew it to be false' [another oversimplification of reality], 'Winston would not have this' and wrote the letter accordingly. It attracted little discussion however in the AWOPC.[89]

Scott referred to further correspondents being allowed to visit the British Front, and asked that the War Office lay down principles of selection which would avoid another Dardanelles-type situation. Riddell proposed a grouping system allowing representation of both London and provincial press, but when Robbins tartly observed that such arrangements for the previous visit to the Western Front had not been 'so successful as they had hoped' and requested a Reuters/PA correspondent in the group, Riddell made conciliatory remarks, and Scott's suggestion was adopted. The timing of casualty reports was criticised; Greene and Brade said their only concern was that relatives should know of casualties before they appeared in the Press, and when asked for a vote by press members on suggested changes, three out of five (with Robbins abstaining) favoured retaining the existing system.

Robbins later attended an NPA Committee meeting about the Dardanelles. Riddell said Churchill was now so pleased with the reporting that he considered it 'rather a condemnation of the conservative policy hitherto adopted by the Admiralty, and two or three correspondents could be allowed'. However, a Coalition Government was now being formed in which Churchill was no longer First Lord,[90] and because the new First Lord (Balfour) knew nothing about an increase in correspondents, further action was not taken until later. Meanwhile, at sea the PA correspondent was complaining of excessive censorship and transmission delays, and Ashmead-Bartlett, who had survived the sinking of *HMS MAJESTIC*,[91] had not been allowed to report it, perhaps the ultimate injury to an eye-witness survivor journalist.

15

APPROACHING THE STEADY STATE

The 17 June 1915 AWOPC meeting was more placid than its predecessors. Three extra Dardanelles correspondents were agreed for the provincial press and the press agencies; Riddell (in his PPA hat) asked if an Illustrated Press artist could also be accommodated, and Brade undertook to investigate. It was agreed that Friday casualty lists could be published on Saturday evening as well as on Sunday and Monday morning [the Army remained uneasy about security aspects of casualty list publication, and decided later to omit the theatre of operations]. Swettenham agreed to Riddell's request that the Bureau be manned by a 'responsible official' until 2 a.m., for the 'convenience' of the Press. Scott, supported by Baird and Riddell, gained agreement that a Scottish representative now be appointed to the AWOPC.

Cockerill said steps needed to be taken 'to prevent the use by spies and their agents of the advertisement columns of the Press for communication of information to the enemy'; he, Riddell, Scott, and Baird were delegated to meet subsequently and draft a note to editors, instructing them to seek police advice if in doubt about any advertisement.[92] Holbrook suggested the DoRA Regulations be amended to exclude journalists from the prohibition on collecting information, subject to it being submitted to the PB; the difficulties of administering such an exemption led however to this suggestion being dropped. Although not then discussed, the Committee did not meet again for seven months, an indication of a Press/Official modus operandi having been achieved, whatever its continuing imperfections, and whatever the political, military and naval turmoil elsewhere.

Air raids by German Zeppelins now became a major concern. On the night of 31 May 1915, there was a major attack on the East End of London, long forecast by the Admiralty's Air Department (which in 1914 had assumed responsibility for UK Air Defence when the Army decided it could not allocate sufficient assets, in addition to Western Front air warfare). Next day the Press Bureau issued a Notice (but not as a D-Serial):

> The Press are specially reminded that no statement whatever must be published dealing with the places in the neighbourhood of London reached by aircraft or the course supposed to be taken by them, or any statement or diagrams which might indicate the ground or route covered by them. The Admiralty communiqué gives all the news that can properly be published. These instructions are given in order to secure public safety and the present intimation may itself be published by the Press explaining the absence of more detailed reports.

This Notice was given by the Bureau to the Press Association night staff for distribution as an open message, but with the instruction they should do so as a 'Parker' (i.e. as a telegram to the provinces also). The PA staff beyond Robbins' immediate assistants did not however know what a 'Parker' was, because the secrecy required by Government about the AWOPC meant Robbins handled these matters personally. The night staff therefore gave the Notice the much wider full PA circulation, including to many who did not receive D-Notices, and shortly afterwards similarly distributed the Bureau's sensitive details of the air raid.

Amongst these unaccustomed recipients was the *Jewish Times*, a Yiddish-language Whitechapel newspaper, which published full details in ignorance of prohibitions placed by previous D-Notices. The authorities immediately seized that issue, and prohibited further publication for several days. The editor considered he had a legal grievance against the PA for not having sent him 'Parkers'; a solicitor's letter and claim for compensation rapidly followed. Robbins told his Board he and the Bureau had some months previously discussed whether the *Jewish Times* should receive 'Parkers' and 'it was considered that a Yiddish publication in Whitechapel ought not to receive these very private and confidential documents'. Robbins deflected the solicitor's letter by placing responsibility on the Bureau, and litigation ceased.

Nevertheless, this was not the only reason why the authorities realised they needed to extend the reach of their Zeppelin prohibitions beyond the bigger newspapers. The Vicar of St Jude's, Mildmay Park (North London) wrote to the 'Press Censor', presumably having seen the gist of the open Note to the Press: 'If I am troubling you needlessly pray pardon my making this suggestion. It is possible that the *religious press* will report the effects of last night's air attack upon places of worship + by putting claims together confirmation as to aircraft cd be gathered'; he patriotically suggesting communicating inter alia with the *Church Times*, the *Life of Faith*, the *Christian*, and the *Church Family Newspaper*. The Bureau tasked Robbins accordingly to ensure that air raid Notes reached newspapers 'likely to offend by inadvertence', including small London local papers such as the *Shoreditch Gazette* and the *Islington News*.

Otherwise the second half of 1915 saw a more settled pattern of press and official interaction. That was so for Riddell and Robbins too, with the former attending to wheeling and dealing aspects, the latter to day-to-day administration of the System, on which he was much consulted by the sympathetic Brade. Robbins continued to be immersed too in the detail of the commercial and administrative aspects of press activity. Because of the dearth of office boys caused by recruitment to the Forces, the PA started employing office girls from August 1915.[93] In arguing with the Minister of Recruitment (Lord Derby) for Reserved Occupation status [exemption from military service for some of his staff], Robbins pointed out that he 'could not employ female labour on night work'. In selecting two extra correspondents to go to the Fronts, he instructed they should not look too young or soldiers would think they should be in the Army.

On Press 'discipline', when the *World* published news of an alleged secret decision, at an Anglo-French military meeting at Calais, that both Armies should 'trench themselves for the Winter and remain on the defensive, instead of attempting a forward movement, which would entail very heavy losses', the authorities considered prosecuting the editor, because of the effect of the report on French morale. The Press representatives however suggested such prosecution would merely give additional publicity to the report, and it was agreed the War Office should instead give him 'a very serious warning'. Robbins did complain that censorship was becoming more severe every week, and he continued to take up with the Bureau the provincial press concerns about unfair treatment and lack of action against newspapers flouting prohibitions.

When the authorities did prosecute, it was sometimes with mixed results. The *Southampton Pictorial* for example was taken to court for publishing photographs likely to provide the enemy with useful information, namely some taken at a Red Cross fund-raising fete at which wounded soldiers assisted. The jury concluded these pictures were unlikely greatly to aid the enemy, but even so the newspaper was fined for having committed a technical offence, in an attempt discourage others.[94]

In August Robbins himself raised examples of inconsistency, where the PA had submitted stories (one concerning correspondence between the Navy League and the First Lord, the other a 'souvenir bomb' accident in Liverpool), only to see the information published in the London Press before the Bureau had actioned the PA submission. Cook replied that, even were it possible to introduce total censorship, there would still in the grey areas be different human interpretations. From Western Front correspondents came complaints about Macdonogh as Chief Field Censor tightening up on reporting beyond official communiqués from Field Marshal French: no current events, only general mention of fighting, no praise or censure, nothing about formations, just articles confined to 'topographical descriptions and generalities'. Some editors considered withdrawing their correspondents because of this censorship, but Robbins advised a policy of wait and see.

Editors continued nevertheless to highlight the degree of censorship in their columns. A leading article on 20 September 1915, entitled 'A Confused Public – Why Not a Plain Statement', started 'Slowly and unwillingly the Hide-the-Truth newspapers, politicians, military experts, and lecturers are being obliged to reveal what readers of the *Daily Mail* have known, as far as we have been allowed to tell them, for many long months. They now know that much of the official information and most of the merry prattle of the late unlamented "Eye-Witness" concealed from us all matters that we ought to have known and many matters which the Germans did know.' It criticised 'some of our public mis-Leaders' for thinking the Public could not cope with depressing news, and cited the calm attitude of Londoners 'under the recent air bombardment'. It acknowledged the censors had done some good things, and that Lloyd George and Churchill had lately been more frank, but contrasted the propaganda that 'the Germans have almost shot their bolt' with the actual progress their Army had made, and asked how the man in the street, of whom much was being asked in sacrifice and increased production, was to understand the situation and the need for his support.

In Parliament too, there were many questions asked about the degree of censorship. On 30 September 1915, the Home Secretary (Simon) was asked whether the principle laid down by a predecessor (Buckmaster, 26 November 1914), that no information should be withheld from the public 'which would not be of service to the enemy', had been strictly adhered to. Simon replied affirmatively, but acknowledged the rules had to be applied in a general way because of the load, and because the Press had to be asked to publish only official statements about certain matters, for example the Zeppelin raids. Simon followed up with an open letter in the *Daily Telegraph* on 12 October in defence of the censors, but the same day *The Times* carried a critical comment on the Bureau's handling of an article by Buchan, which had been cut by two separate Censors 'contrary to the express desire of the generals in the field'.[95]

Reuters too were having problems with the Bureau, in particular because it was silently deleting unfavourable parts of German communiqués before passing them to the Agency. This was soon spotted by the Press at home and abroad, and in early October Reuters felt it necessary to tell London editors that it was not responsible for this 'mutilation'. It had previously had to send a similar message to the dissatisfied South African Press, explaining how much Reuters' Dardanelles despatches were adversely affected by censorship. The official Reuters/PA correspondent there had to file from Malta his first despatches on the Gallipoli landings, based on interviews with the wounded. By the time he was allowed to do so from Gallipoli, unofficial correspondents in the area had already managed to send first-hand reports.[96]

Another argument between Government and Press was the cost of telegrams, which the Post Office and Treasury threatened to increase markedly. The cost of telegrams was calculated furthermore not on what was usable after censorship, but on what was paid for and often then cut; it was calculated that in the first 18 months of the War cable text costing more than £1,000 had been thus blocked (the equivalent of about £50,000 today). In October 1915, a press delegation led by Sir George Toulmin went to see the Postmaster General (Herbert Samuel) and a heavyweight team of officials. The meeting was inconclusive; Robbins appears to have made much of the running (he said afterwards he felt Toulmin had been too easy on the Government), pointing out that the War had much reduced press revenues, and countering the official claim, that the GPO was effectively subsidising the Press by favourable discounts agreed in 1869, by reminding that it was the press which publicised the statements of Ministers and Departments.

Soon afterwards Robbins was summoned one evening to Samuel's Porchester Terrace residence for a one-on-one discussion. The Minister relayed an offer from the Chancellor of the Exchequer of a reduced increase, which to his surprise Robbins rejected outright. Samuel similarly rejected Robbins' proposal that any rise in telegram charges should be left until the War ended. Next day Robbins convened a meeting of press representatives, and a compromise position was agreed that some increase would be accepted but not until the end of the War, or at least from the end of 1916; meanwhile the Post Office should provide some new 'high-speed apparatus'. This formed the basis of eventual agreement with the Government.[97]

Despite many improvements in over a year's AWOPC/Press Bureau interaction, there were still those on the governmental side dissatisfied with the arrangements. In October, Riddell was summoned to tea at the Home Office, where Simon outlined new censorship proposals which he was considering. These included: disobedience of a D Notice would ipso facto constitute a DoRA offence; a committee of civil servants from various Departments should be formed to manage the Bureau; and the Government should have the power to punish disobedience by suspension of the offending newspaper. Riddell assured Simon he was mistaken in his apparent belief that these proposals would meet with the approval of most of the Press, and that, although the Press might quarrel amongst themselves, they would all unite against any attempt to impose restraints or punishments. He suggested instead employing more trained sub-editors at the Bureau, strengthening the AWOPC role instead of creating a new body, and having a Secretary who was authorised to keep in direct touch with the various Departments.

When Riddell saw Simon the following month at the House of Commons, he was able to hand the Minister a recent Newspaper Conference Resolution, submitting that no change should be made without prior consultation with the Press. Riddell subsequently had similar conversations with the Prime Minister's Private Secretary and with Greene, deducing from their interest in the matter that 'the subject has evidently been much discussed' in Government at the time.[98]

This press resistance did eventually achieve Government concessions. In a second debate on censorship in as many weeks in the House of Lords (8 November 1915), the Lord Privy Seal (Curzon)[99] announced: 'It is to be represented to the military authorities in dealing with war news that there are other considerations than their direct point of view – ie the effect upon public opinion, the stimulation of recruiting, and the comforting of the relatives of the fallen; the Press is to be encouraged to provide more news (for example about submarines) and suppress less'; and the Government's action in suppressing the *Globe* was explained on the ground that it had persisted in 'publishing false statements after due warning that they are false.'[100] A long debate followed, listened to by many Members of the House of Commons, about the unsatisfactory nature of the censorship. Much of the criticism came from 'Elder Statesmen' such as Lords Morley, Loreburn, Milner, Courtney and Parmoor.[101]

Morley led by reminding that 'No Government can prosper in this Country unless it has public opinion behind it. That is what enables us to get recruits and get our loans subscribed, and prevails against agitators in the industrial world.' He complained not only about excessive censorship of the Press, but also about 'misadventures' on which Parliament had been inadequately informed; he listed the Antwerp and Dardanelles expeditions and shortage of munitions amongst other examples. Milner criticised recent comments by Buckmaster in defence of the PB, and gave examples of even German reports being censored. Courtney spoke mainly against the conduct of the War, pointing out that although the Prime Minister had said in June that the Germans had not advanced one foot on the Western Front in the past seven months, he had not mentioned the lack of advance by the Allies. The constitutional lawyer Parmoor asked rhetorically 'Have we had information fairly and truthfully given which enables us neither as optimists nor as pessimists to form a true view for ourselves as regards the perils and dangers on the one side and, on the other hand, our victories and triumphs'. Buckmaster countered that the Bureau was merely the conduit for Departments, and Curzon and Lansdowne defended the Government's record. Although the debate ended with no particular conclusion, concerns reflected in AWOPC work had been well aired.

Robbins opened 1916 by firing further press criticism to the PB about continuing censorship delays. He told his PA Committee he had kept the AWOPC alive, and that as yet there was no need to give it 'as Mr Scott of Manchester said – a decent burial'. Brade had recently asked him to arrange an AWOPC meeting, for which Swettenham had provided a discussion paper on press complaints about those newspapers which ignored prohibitions. In outline, the four-paragraph paper said such complaints were received 'continually' by the Bureau, especially from the provincial press 'where there is keen competition between rival interests'; that although three pamphlets of instructions had been issued since August 1914 and the rules were now well understood, breaches were frequent; that, in a voluntary system, particular news might be submitted by one paper but not another; that the offence might not be serious enough to warrant prosecution under the DoRA, unfair though that was to those who complied; that the Directors of the Bureau felt they could not ignore the very strong press complaints and urging of punishment of offenders; but that before taking such action the Directors wished to consult the AWOPC.

The Committee duly met on 14 January 1916, and grappled at length with Swettenham's paper, which he supported with many examples. He suggested withholding official information from those journals which offended regularly. Riddell supposed there were 'only three suggestions for equalizing the conditions of censorship': that put forward by Swettenham, or to arrange for the offenders to be dealt with by their own Newspaper Association, or to insist on newspapers submitting all copy for censorship. The first would be ineffective, because the newspaper would obtain the information in some other way, the last was impracticable, but the second might be successful. Colonel Holbrook considered all the cases should be dealt with under the DoRA, but the Committee agreed the degree of offences under consideration did not merit the involvement of the Director of Public Prosecutions. Swettenham suggested the response to a first minor offence should merely be admonition, but that if such offences continued, official news should be withheld and any agency or newspaper which furnished the offender with such information should be placed on a Black List; but it was really for the Press to decide, since the offences were not so much against the State as against 'those who tried loyally to observe the instructions'.

This clearly irritated the Press members, and, in the 'prolonged discussion' which followed, Duncan, Scott and Baird all attacked the 'mass of instructions' issued by the Bureau and the 'numerous' and 'superfluous' prohibitive notices. It was unthinkable, Scott said, that the Press should be asked to give the Bureau further powers against the Press. Riddell pointed out the unfairness of Swettenham's Black List proposal, in that prosecution under the DoRA for a serious offence might incur a fine of only £50 or £100, while blacklisting might mean ruin for the paper, and the loss of up to ten thousand pounds. Even bringing a newspaper before its own Association had problems, because the Press would not care for the triple role of 'Prosecutor, Judge and Executioner'. Swettenham replied plaintively that all he was trying to do was to meet the Press's own complaints about some of its members. Cockerill reminded that the slightest indiscretion on the part of the Press might be useful to the enemy; *de minimis non curat lex* could not be applied to military information, since what appeared an unimportant detail to the public 'might be the one missing link in a chain of evidence accumulated by the enemy's Intelligence Department'.

Ultimately all the Press members present except Holbrook agreed that no disciplinary measures should be taken against the Press, other than for serious DoRA offences. Eventually two resolutions were adopted by the whole Committee: the first stating this opinion, and the second that in view of the frequent complaints, 'the Committee consider it very desirable in the interests of the Press as a whole that the instructions of the Press Bureau should be carefully observed, so as to obviate similar causes of complaint in the future'. Robbins subsequently sent these resolutions to all the Newspaper Federations and Associations, who in turn passed them to all their members, so that ignorance of them could not be pleaded by future transgressors.

With a final gripe from Robbins about the interception by the telegraph authorities of reports of speeches made by public figures in the provinces, which Swettenham undertook to investigate and later rectified, the meeting ended. It had encapsulated one of the insoluble and eternal problems of self-regulation, namely that a voluntary system is open to abuse, inadvertent or otherwise, which threatens the commercial interests of the Media on the one hand, and the security interests of the State on the other.[102]

16

CONTINUING TENSIONS

Eight months were to pass before there was another formal meeting of the Committee, partly because Robbins recommended against such gatherings if he thought he could resolve problems himself. Minor spats continued. In early February 1916, he went to see the PB Directors about their delays in clearing articles on a recent air raid. Swettenham complained he had been severely attacked by the *Daily Mail* and others about a D Notice prohibiting publication of photographs of the raid until the next day.[103] The Directors had made this ruling in the belief they were thereby helping the provincial press, who they mistakenly thought were unable to prepare printing blocks in under 24 hours; Robbins was able to explain it took only 3–4 hours.

The Provincial Press again tired of the perceived disadvantages to them of Riddell's selectively passing confidential government information to the Press, and asked that in future it all came through the PA rather than the NPA; although Robbins agreed with their sentiment, the informal NPA route did not greatly change. The Newspaper Society passed a resolution proposing that official information should be withheld from newspapers ignoring official prohibitions, but Robbins pointed out that this had already been rejected by the AWOPC, including the Society's representatives.

In mid-February, the War Office and Field Marshal French (now CinC Home Forces) asked that prohibitions on reporting air raids be reduced, so that local Press Association reporters might inform the authorities as early as possible of the whereabouts and courses of German Zeppelins. Robbins sent a note accordingly to his men, only to be carpeted by Greene for 'having gone too far'; Robbins showed him the War Office letter, as proof of another left-hand right-hand official muddle. Phillips of the *Yorkshire Post* wrote a scathing letter to Robbins in April about another recent French-inspired Notice, suggesting the Press in future refrain from reporting breakdowns in utilities caused by very severe weather: 'I know that Lord French has done remarkable things in France, but . . .'. The Press meanwhile reorganised representation at the Bureau, there being now too many journalists there with too little to do.

Robbins complained the GPO was sitting on the PA's application to have its own 'wireless receiving station' [he was in dispute with the Admiralty and Marconi's over the distribution and cost of news received by wireless]. From France, the Reuters/PA correspondent complained again about reporting restrictions. After the Easter Rising in Dublin and the attack on its Post Office, Robbins was asked for a rebate by Irish newspapers because of the consequent disruption to the telegram service. After Jutland, he acted on behalf of the Bureau in distributing the embargoed post-battle reports by Jellicoe; the *Daily Telegraph* complained there was not the usual 24 hours delay in publishing the casualty lists, something which had been introduced for the benefit of the provincial press against the wishes of the

London newspapers, as Robbins reminded, while explaining that the Battle was public knowledge and relatives were anxious. Journalists were also irritated by censorship of transcripts of German wireless broadcasts, and in February the Bureau turned down a request from Riddell that editors should be allowed to see the uncensored transcripts.[104]

In late April 1916, the Government introduced by Order in Council new regulations potentially imposing heavy penalties on anyone who disclosed information about Cabinet discussions, and effectively on those who published and criticised the doings of any Government Department. In the House of Lords on 2 May, Parmoor emphasised that our institutions had been built up 'on a basis of free discussion', and complained that freedom of the Press was at the 'will and beck and call of the Government for the time being'. Burnham spoke of how policemen were de facto being used by the Government as local censors of newspapers, how Cabinet Ministers themselves had always been the source of leaks to the Press, and how, if the new regulations were adopted literally, editors would find it impossible to comment on the work of government. Replying, Buckmaster claimed that the Order in Council, apart from reference to the Cabinet, merely applied the existing powers of OSA 1911. 'Why have the proclamation then?' interjected Parmoor, to which the reply was because of the Government's desire also to use the 'machinery of the Defence of the Realm Act'. On 8 May the House of Commons inconclusively debated the 'Hushing-Up' Order in Council, defended by the Home Secretary (Samuel), with similar points being made by angry Members of Parliament.

After the Battle of Jutland, there was criticism of the Admiralty's dissemination of information; it was slow, partial and much less full than that published around the world by Germany, who immediately presented the Battle as a victory, causing alarm to Allies and even a sharp drop on Wall Street. On 3 June, the day after the clash of the two main fleets, the leading article in the *Daily Mail*, headed 'The Great Sea Battle', included: 'The public will be somewhat surprised by the tone of the first British report which purports to give an account of the battle. After relating our losses it becomes curiously vague, and it contains what we have never become accustomed to see in British naval reports – namely, excuses. We are told, for example, that the enemy's battle fleet, "aided by low visibility, avoided prolonged action with our main forces". The fact appears, however, from this involved and obscure narrative, that the enemy engaged a part of our Fleet with his whole strength, and delivered a violent blow before our battleships were able to come into action.' The whole truth was of course more complex, and the Admiralty was still reeling from the shock of the scale of the losses of battle-cruisers; but an eternal lesson of British information policy is that any obfuscation is seen by the Press as cover-up, and the perceived cover-up quickly becomes the story.

Admiral Lord Beresford, never slow to criticise other admirals who had earlier been supporters of Admiral of the Fleet Lord Fisher, followed up with trenchant criticism of the tardiness, inadequacy and apologetic tone of the initial announcements to the press, and indeed to Parliament. 'How was it that men who came home with the light of pride and victory [which strategically it subsequently proved to be] in their eyes were fated to find a hesitant and anxious public ready to condole but quite unprepared to congratulate? The reason is simply that the Admiralty does not appear to possess an official capable of using the King's English so as to put together incomplete items of news and place them before the public in their just proportions.' To balance this, the newspapers began to publish their own interpretation of the reality of the battle, which after their initial propaganda the Germans too considered as unfavourable.

The authorities in 1916 nevertheless had ways of getting their wishes across to provincial journalists. Early that year in Glasgow, the police had seized all copies of an edition of the socialist *Worker* and its presses, and prosecuted three journalists for causing disaffection amongst the civilian population and impeding war production. Even more heavy-handed was police action in the summer against the *Poole and East Dorset Herald*, whose editor published a humorous article in local dialect in which fishermen complained about minesweepers being unfair competition; he was charged with prejudicing recruiting to His Majesty's Navy and publishing comments prejudicial to its administration. The local mayor presided over the police court, and felt obliged to return a guilty verdict, but having attested to the editor's complete loyalty, merely fined him £5.[105]

Matters discussed at the 29 September 1916 AWOPC meeting included the replacement of the recently nominated but dying first Scottish representative by his brother George Wilson.[106] There was a general wish that the Committee should again meet more regularly; the second Friday in January, April, July and October being agreed. Robbins mentioned an impression, which he did not share, that the Admiralty kept back its announcements to give to the morning papers. Greene denied this was done on purpose, and reminded that Admiralty announcements were 'much more infrequent than those issued by the War Office'. Riddell referred to the undesirability of issuing information to the Press with restrictions as to which parts of it could be published; it was agreed it was better generally to issue information which could be published in full or not at all.

Robbins reluctantly raised three NS items on behalf of Colonel Holbrook: firstly, the recent relaxation in some aspects of reporting air raids, complaining this gave unfair advantage to the London Press because of their close proximity to the Bureau – he asked that steps be taken to put matters on an equal footing, but as Holbrook had not suggested how this might be done, and as the feeling was against any provincial censorship, the item was adjourned sine die. Secondly he requested more equitable distribution amongst the Press of official advertisements, which the Committee decided was not a matter for them; and thirdly, on distribution of official photographs, he asked that the date of permitted publication always be given, in order that simultaneous publication could be achieved in the provinces and London – a delaying formula was agreed by the Committee.

Robbins reported a GPO complaint that time-consuming telegraphed transmission of long 'Parker' Notices caused delays to governmental and other messages; officials conceded that most of the examples produced by Robbins (one of them containing 250 words) had not been urgent, and it was agreed that, except in cases of urgency, Notices could in future be despatched by post. Finally, Riddell referred to secret memoranda originating from the War Office, and noted 'a tendency to indicate to the Press the policy which should be adopted', citing as an example one which 'pointed out the danger of making too much of air raids'; he asked on what authority such memoranda were issued. Cockerill explained they were all approved by the Directors of Military Intelligence and of Military Operations, with the authority of the CIGS, now General Sir William Robertson.[107]

Riddell, having made the London proprietors' disapproval sufficiently clear by asking the question, did not comment further. Not mentioned in the minutes, but recorded by Robbins in his own meticulously kept manuscript PA Manager's Memoranda, was a bid by Swettenham for the Bureau to take over the distribution of D Notices direct to the press. The Press Members took the view however that it was desirable to maintain the AWOPC as the direct link between the authorities and the press. In this they were supported by Greene from the Chair; the existing system was maintained.

The decision that the Committee should meet more frequently was subsequently not long sustained, because it continued to do as much business as possible out of Committee for pragmatic reasons, and because the need for meetings diminished as hostilities drew to a close (and during the early inter-War years). The Press during the period 1914–18 also had their own weekly 'Newspaper Conference' at the NPA offices, attended by Robbins and the NS Secretary, and chaired by Harry Lawson. Riddell, the NPA Vice-Chairman at the time, paid tribute in his War Diaries to the future Lord Burnham's chairmanship (he succeeded to the Barony when his father died in January 1916): '. . . an admirable Chairman, owing to his genial personality, wide knowledge, and experience of affairs . . . we all regarded him with feelings of affection'; Burnham in turn paid tribute to the AWOPC, opining it was a 'very valuable organisation from which he expected great things after the War when the Press Bureau . . . was disestablished'.

The Northern Federation meanwhile complained the War Office was attempting to introduce provincial censorship by stealth; it had acquired a War Office letter which asked for Volunteers around the country not only to monitor the local press for 'tendencies and general tone', but also 'on an emergency . . .[to] form a censorship staff'. Robbins went to the War Office and was reassured that monitoring was for information only; but he was also warned 'in a friendly manner' under the OSA about the unauthorised possession of a classified document. He retorted that as AWOPC Secretary he came by many sensitive documents, and he was then told 'under great secrecy' that the reference to provincial censorship staff would apply only in the case of foreign invasion of the UK. Robbins reassured the Northern Federation in guarded terms, but they reported to him shortly afterwards that the GOC Humber Garrison had sinisterly asked for lists/details of northern newspapers and their personnel.

At a weekly Newspaper Conference, Northcliffe again suggested American correspondents should be given some of the places at the British Headquarters; this was swiftly rejected by the others, who still felt the number of British places allocated by the War Office was inadequate.[108] Concurrently, Robbins asked the Irish Office for advance sight of the Blue Book (official report) on the Courts Martial following the Irish uprising, so that he might prepare press handling, but this was turned down. The Irish Censor complained that matters which he had prohibited in the Irish Press were published in Great Britain, then reaching Ireland immediately from West Coast towns; the AWOPC agreed that requests from the Irish Censor would be passed on to newspapers in Great Britain, but there was no Bureau censorship of Irish matters unless it came from the Government.

On 24 November, Robbins was summoned by Greene on behalf of the First Lord (now Balfour), to complain about disclosures that day in *The Times* as to changes in senior Naval posts [these included Jellicoe turning over command of the Grand Fleet to Beatty, and becoming First Sea Lord], as they did not want the enemy to know of the changes until they had taken place. Robbins suggested a 'Parker' to prevent further reporting, and, when Greene worried about whether the Press would accept a prohibition on such a matter, he reassured him as to the loyalty of the Press in responding to specific requests, and published a D Notice accordingly that day.

On 12 December 1916, in response to the increased activity and success rate of German submarines, a conference was held in the Admiralty to discuss the advisability of suppressing publication of movements of 'Merchant Steamers'. Chaired by Greene, it was attended by all AWOPC members except Brade, by the Chief Naval Censor Rear Admiral Sir Douglas Brownrigg,[109] the President of the UK Chamber of Shipping, and senior representatives of shipping companies, Lloyds, and the Boards of Trade and Customs and Excise. The Admiralty Trade Division explained that when the submarine menace first became acute in March 1915, the Admiralty and shipping industry had agreed 'certain rough rules', which had formed the basis of the prohibitions on publication currently in force. The Admiralty suggested no change, but did propose loading lists should in future be excluded from the Lloyds List, and that a 'fake' date of sailing should be maintained. The shipping representatives had considerable doubts as to whether the Admiralty plan was commercially and practicably workable, but were prepared to adopt it, as were other Government representatives. Riddell said the Press would suppress information about the movements of merchant vessels, including dockings, but pointed out the considerable financial loss which would be entailed. The resolution, unanimously carried, was that 'the publication of all shipping intelligence, with the exception of losses, should cease from midnight on 23 December 1916'.

The AWOPC members then adjourned to a short meeting of their own to discuss one item only, namely a protest by the London and Provincial Newsagents' Association against the issue of special editions of newspapers on Sunday evenings. With that in mind, the newsagents asked that the Press Bureau issue no news between 4 a.m. on Sunday and the time when Monday morning's papers were being prepared. The Newsagents argued that the 'existing conditions were becoming a menace to bona fide newsagents, and that the cries of newsvendors in the streets on Sunday evenings constituted a disturbance of religious services'. Robbins reported that his Association regarded the newsagents' request as 'an unwarrantable interference with the liberty of the Press, and an endeavour to dictate to managers of newspapers when special editions should be published'. The Newsagents' request therefore met with the 'unanimous disapproval' of the Press members, Riddell summarising: 'the entire Press were, in the public interest, anxious to receive official information at the earliest possible moment'. A unanimous resolution supporting these views was passed by the Committee. And so the work of the AWOPC for 1916, a low point in the War,[110] ended on statements of religious and press high principle – devoid, posterity must hope, of any subconscious commercial interests.

17

THE STEADY STATE

The arrival of Lloyd George as Prime Minister, with his reorganisation of government machinery for running the War, and his greater ruthlessness in using powers available to him, coincided with a more settled working routine between the Press, the Government, and the AWOPC. Relationships did still however sometimes become strained by events and organisational defects. Dissatisfactions and disagreements unavoidable between groups with different motivations continued to fester under the pressure of a most damaging War. It was unsurprising, for example, that newspapers should ask Robbins at the beginning of February 1917 to obtain for them very early communiqués when the expected 'Big Push' came, and equally unsurprising that the War Office and Press Bureau should give no such guarantees [the next major campaigns, the battles of Arras and of the Aisne did not in fact start until April].

The Press continued to complain about censorship stupidities; for example, the naval censors struck out the whole of a constituency speech by a former Civil Lord of the Admiralty instead of asking just for the possibly justifiable excision of certain references to Fisher and Jellicoe. The Bureau stopped the PA from putting out reports of the inquest following the loss of the *SS Laurentic*,[111] but allowed others to report it. Robbins received 'a demi-semi apology' from Cook for the Bureau's complete suppression of reports on another inquest, into the death of a lighthouse keeper at Shields killed by friendly fire from a shore battery aiming at an incoming enemy vessel.

In March Robbins asked the Bureau if it would allow the Press to play a part in quashing 'wild rumours' about an imminent invasion of UK, but he received no immediate reply. As the Western Front lengthened, the War Office asked the Press to extend the pooling system; the Press therefore asked for an increase in the number of British correspondents there instead, but this was vetoed by Field Marshal Haig[112] in May. George Wilson reported from Scotland that the *Edinburgh Evening News* had been tried in camera over an article on the potential effects a threatened Zeppelin raid might have on munitions factories, but that the case had been dropped after two days.

Reuters had continuing problems with the Bureau, exemplified by an exchange of increasingly sharp letters from January to April. At the beginning of March, for example, a telegram from New York about 'German intrigues in Mexico' [the Zimmermann telegram affair] was delayed so much that a rival agency in London received the cleared Reuters despatch before Reuters did (the error this time was blamed by the Bureau not on its own internal handling, but on the need to refer it to the Foreign Office). Reuters may have become a little too paranoid about their receiving less favourable treatment than others, as many others complained equally about similar problems; and the Bureau may have become a little too weary and under-resourced ever to provide consistently good service to the Press, but this environment was the background noise to AWOPC work throughout the War.[113]

On internal administrative matters, the Press complained that the 'Wireless Press' [i.e. broadcasters] still effectively had a monopoly over the product of the Admiralty/Marconi system. Captain Wiener, the allegedly shady character turned down as a Reuters/PA correspondent by the War Office just before hostilities started (because he was 'an alien officer', he now claimed) popped up again, applying to be appointed a correspondent with the American forces about to arrive;[114] this time Reuters and PA turned him down themselves, on the grounds he was unlikely to be accredited. Closer to home, Robbins told the PA Board that, as he reached the age of 70 in April, he wished to retire as its Manager in June, when his contract (which had already been extended a further three years in 1914) expired. His son and deputy, Harry Robbins[115] was appointed to succeed him. When the announcement was seen in the newspapers, Greene immediately wrote to Edmund Robbins, asking if this meant they would be losing him as AWOPC Secretary, and hoping not; Robbins Senior quickly accepted the unanimously supported indication that he should stay on in this post, to which the PA also agreed.

At the 20 April 1917 AWOPC meeting, Riddell immediately brought up an urgent matter not on the agenda, namely the shortage of paper-making materials. He referred to a recent meeting between the Press and the Prime Minister, who had said newspapers were essential to the successful prosecution of the War; but unless the supply of pulp from Scandinavia were increased from its current level of more than 50% below the previous year's total, paper mills would shortly be obliged to shut down. He referred to the 'Gyp',[116] recently taken over by the Admiralty, and asked that pulp might be placed on the approved list of essential import materials. The Admiralty said it was up to the Ministry of Blockade, and the meeting asked the NPA to provide the Admiralty with details of the Press requirement for negotiation with that Ministry and shippers.

Cockerill raised again the suspicion that enemy agents were using advertisements for communicating intelligence (a concern shared by the French, Belgians and Italians, he suggested). Riddell, while assuring of press co-operation, pointed out that scrutiny of the bona fides of all advertisers would not only cause much extra work for newspaper staffs, but also annoy the public. After lengthy discussion it was agreed that anyone wishing to insert a newspaper advertisement must include his name and address for publication, or give a reference as to his bona fides, unless personally known to the advertisement manager.[117]

Swettenham complained that certain Private and Confidential letters and Notices issued to the Press had been disclosed in newspapers, and that certain editors had disclosed they received such letters to staff not authorised to know about the System. Brade asked if the Press wished to continue to receive such Secret letters [a politely veiled threat?], and was told they were much appreciated and should continue; it was agreed the War Office would write formally to the NPA, so that Secret letters breaches could be raised at a weekly Newspaper Conference, and to Robbins, so that he could promulgate that 'it was most undesirable that "D" Notices issued through the Press Bureau should be alluded to in any form' [this is the first time they are called D Notices in a formal AWOPC document – see Appendix 1].

Robbins then returned to his suggestion that the Press should be used to deny rumours, referring to two days in late March when 'newspaper offices were inundated with telegraphic and telephonic enquiries as to the truth of certain rumours' [invasion imminent]; he had been refused permission by the Bureau to quash the rumours. He proposed that in any future such circumstances the Press Bureau 'should be empowered to issue the necessary dementi, or allow the newspapers to publish a contradiction'. Swettenham explained he had indeed asked permission, but it had been turned down by the War Office; the Committee nevertheless unanimously approved of its reasons [not included however in the minutes, nor in Robbins' Memoranda, nor in War Office archives]. The final agenda item, 'Prosecution of Newspapers under the Defence of the Realm Act', had been withdrawn [again for reasons unrecorded].

In mid-May, Burnham led a press delegation to Buckingham Palace to see the King's Private Secretary, Lord Stamfordham,[118] about the confusion caused by conflicting messages on publication of information about Royal visits. This was sparked by a recent D-Notice (D558), which differed markedly from one sent out the previous August. The intention was good, to enable the public to know more about the King's and Queen's programme of visits around the country, but execution by both Palace and Bureau had been poor. Stamfordham explained the difficulties which the Palace had in meeting the War Office's security wishes. A suggestion was made, seemingly by Robbins, that the Palace might benefit from including an ex-journalist on its staff.

Robbins' worthiness as a source of good practical advice bore fruit shortly afterwards in rumour-quashing; the War Office changed its mind and allowed the Press to publish reports denying a rumoured devastating Zeppelin raid on South London. Also, again at his suggestion, it allowed publication of the location (Folkestone) of an actual devastating air raid, linking it, as a contrast between British and German behaviour, with the concurrent 39th anniversary of the burial there with full honours of 150 German sailors after their ship had been sunk in a collision. As Robbins stood down from the Press Association, another welcome sign of improvement for the Press: in part because of his work, was that Haig chose the PA/Reuters correspondent for an exclusive interview for a scoop about his commendation of General Plumer.[119] Less welcome was the personal news that his censor sub-editor son, CE Robbins, now in the Army, was in hospital in Malta with malaria and dysentery.[120]

As the new Manager of the PA, HC Robbins had something of a baptism of fire, dealing with the crisis caused by the Zeppelin bomb strike on the Central Post Office on 7 July, and the disruption to national communications caused thereby. His first Newspaper Conference in his new role involved a complaint to the Press Bureau about the behaviour of the Chief of the Imperial General Staff, General Robertson. When heckled at a meeting of engineers at Plumstead whom he had been sent to exhort, alongside the Minister of Munitions, Robertson had lost his temper and stormed out; then when back at the War Office, he had given instructions to the Bureau that his presence at the meeting was not to be mentioned; the Bureau lamely said it had to do what it was told. The Conference was also unhappy that the new Foreign Office Director of Information, Colonel Buchan, was being used instead of the Bureau as the link between that Department and the Press; Buchan subsequently agreed he would only act in that way with the foreign and dominions Press, with whom the Bureau did not deal.

On 13 July 1917, the AWOPC met to discuss inter alia industrial relations matters, for which they were joined by the PUS of the Home Office, Thomson of the Scotland Yard Special Branch, and those responsible for security at the Ministries of Munitions and Labour. First however the meeting addressed again the Army's obsession with advertisements. Riddell pointed out that it was almost impossible to monitor small prepaid newspaper advertisements, and that there was no real evidence of danger of the enemy using them. Cockerill reiterated foreign concerns, and quoted the case of 'Monsignor Gerlach, the Austrian spy at the Vatican', who had used advertisements in the Italian Press, and of the

German Consul at Rotterdam who had used an adapted manuscript code in advertisements; the General also alleged harmless code messages were often inserted in advertisements by members of the public to communicate with friends in neutral and enemy countries.

The Home Office and police view however was that there was no evidence from the hundreds of advertisements studied in the past two years by the Special Branch that the enemy was using them. Swettenham agreed and believed the enemy was anyway more likely to use cables. Press members considered small prepaid advertisements were innocuous and that no fresh regulations could possibly be enforced; they also pointed out that the current delays in communications between the UK and neutral European countries were so great that it would be a most ineffective means for spies to convey information. Unsupported in particular by Thomson, Cockerill conceded.

Riddell raised the difficulties faced by reporters in gaining access to restricted areas, and asked that a general pass be issued to 'reputable journalists in the eyes of all naval and military authorities' [which then and now, if taken literally, would be a very small band indeed]. After detailed discussion, it was agreed that a limited number of passes (certificates of identity without any entitlement to special facilities) would be issued, not as Riddell at one stage proposed to national papers of 'established reputation and large circulation' alone, but to individuals selected by the Newspaper Conference. Cockerill was tasked to arrange this with the Home Office and Scotland Yard.

The meeting then focused on Press mentions of strikes. Swettenham said nine relevant prohibitory Notices had so far been issued 'at the instance of various departments'. Of these the Bureau wished to retain only one (D273), which said inter alia that the Press 'should refrain from seeking interviews with, or giving publicity to, the views of leaders in strike or lock-out movements . . . the result of which might, and probably would, interfere with the success of His Majesty's Forces by land and sea'. The Ministries' Security Officers said however they were in favour of all possible publicity regarding strikes, so long as no useful information was conveyed to the enemy; they also gave statistics to show the number of strikes in munitions establishments 'had decreased to a remarkable extent in the last two years'. Riddell reported he and Burnham had recently been to see the Munitions Minister, whom they had persuaded to withdraw all the prohibitory Notices, on the grounds that suppression did more harm than good, and gave rise to 'the suspicion among workmen that the Government and Press are united in a conspiracy to suppress the truth'.

The Home Office nevertheless considered D273 should stand, and was supported by Swettenham, who said that it was 'dangerous to publish rumours of impending strikes, as strikes were often thereby precipitated'. All the Press members except Holbrook were equally strongly of the contrary view that interviews with strike leaders should be published, Scott arguing 'publication of misstatements produced public denial, whereas suppression merely led to underground agitation by pamphlet and word of mouth'. After a long debate, it was agreed that all the existing Notices should be cancelled, and replaced by a revised version of D273, to be approved by the Committee. Most agreed that 'the reporting of strikes should be left as far as is possible to the discretion of editors'. This had been one of the more worthwhile and significant discussions held by the AWOPC during its short life, and, although little directly to do with national security, probably could not then have taken place in the same frank, informal yet effective way in any other forum.

Riddell was not yet done however. He launched a strong attack on the Naval Censor, with whom 'he had more than one passage of arms', particularly over a letter Brownrigg had written to him several months before, but which, as a result of Balfour's intervention [still

First Lord], he subsequently withdrew. Riddell suggested Brownrigg should be replaced (which was not supported by other Press members, Scott commenting it went beyond the functions of the Committee). Greene loyally would not admit there had been anything improper in the Brownrigg letter. Riddell was somewhat mollified by what he described as 'an excellent speech' by Robbins, whose point was that 'it was not what the Admiralty were doing, it was what they had not done . . .the Nation wanted to know what our gallant sailors were doing'. The Riddell diatribe was not reported in full in the minutes, but it was in Robbins' own Memoranda, and indeed Riddell made another 'frontal attack' on Brownrigg at the Newspaper Conference five days later.[121]

In August, Edmund Robbins was awarded a knighthood in the new Order of the British Empire (his younger brother Alfred (qv) was also knighted in 1917). Greene was moved to be PUS at the Ministry of Munitions, but before he handed over to his deputy, Sir Oswyn Murray, he saw Riddell, saying he wished to reconcile the Press with the Chief Naval Censor, and that the new First Lord, Sir Eric Geddes[122] also intended that there should be an improvement in the relationship between his Department and the Press.[123] In another contretemps Brownrigg complained strongly that an article on secret new Admiralty 'smoke boxes' had been cleared by the Press Bureau; this time he was not only right, but the article on Press Association headed paper turned out to have been concocted by a journalist no longer employed by the PA. Complaints about wider censorship continued, for example in the *Yorkshire Herald* about Post Office interception of a telegram to the PA, in contravention of the exemption granted when the PA had undertaken to seek the necessary clearances. More positively, it was agreed by the War Office that the Society of Women Journalists could send a representative in the autumn to visit the Women's Army Auxiliary Corps.

At the 12 October 1917 AWOPC meeting, Brade was elected Chairman in Greene's place, and they were joined by representatives from the Home Forces Headquarters, the Metropolitan Police, and the City of London Police (all three had military ranks). The Press wished the new DoRA Permit Books for journalists and photographers to be signed by the Commissioners of the Metropolitan Police and of the City Police, respectively Sir Edward Henry[124] and Sir William Nott-Bower.[125] Henry had agreed, but Nott-Bower objected on the grounds it would 'afford too complete a guarantee of the character of the bearers', and might be misused or fall into 'dangerous hands'. Riddell argued the signed passes 'would entitle the bearer to facilities and slight extra courtesies on the part of the Police'. After discussion, the City representative said his Commissioner, having made his point, would accept the decision to issue signed passes under conditions now agreed.

Cockerill then drew attention to a recent communiqué from Field Marshal French explaining the need for reticence in describing air raids on the UK, and clarified the reasoning behind it. Robbins proposed a D Notice, to be periodically reissued, which was approved. Brade observed that General Headquarters Home Forces had offered post-air raid briefings there to the Press, and at the Press Bureau, but these briefings had not been 'appreciated' by the Press [better and more informative stories could be achieved at the site of the damage], and it was agreed not to attempt to revive them.

Riddell raised the rumoured possibility of changes in censorship arrangements because of imminent establishment of a Ministry of Information, and because of Sir Edward Carson taking responsibility for propaganda, which might lead to mergers between the Press Bureau and the new Departments. He had seen Carson, who had denied such mergers. After discussion, the AWOPC agreed a resolution that no changes should be made to the arrangements for censorship without reference to the Press.

Riddell next raised press complaints about being 'occasionally flooded with official documents for publication on one day, when the issue might apparently be distributed equally well over a period of several days'; he had approached the Stationery Office about this, giving as an example the recent exhaustive report of the Parliamentary Boundary Commission. Swettenham had found this a problem for the Bureau too, especially parliamentary documents, but Murray warned that any attempt to interfere with these might be a breach of parliamentary procedure. Swettenham thought it almost impossible to regulate announcements from the Food Controller's Office, as implementation of its regulations was date-dependent, and it needed to be sure therefore of publication on a certain day. Discussion led eventually to the Press side asking Swettenham just to do his best.

Riddell next complained that, although Foreign Office censorship had theoretically been abolished and matters left to editorial discretion, in practice telegrams to editors on these matters were still being intercepted and censored. He gave as an example a report from Paris containing criticism by a French general about British co-operation in France. Swettenham pointed out that censorship of military information had never been suspended, and that this was a case of military not foreign information. This caused debate about problems of differentiation; Swettenham suggested the best definition was that given by the Foreign Office, namely 'that "foreign affairs" are material which if censorship were not suspended would be referred to the Foreign Office'. Not surprisingly this 360-degree circular definition did not satisfy the Press side, who demanded to see what had been cut out of the telegrams. Scott suggested a small committee of editors should be allowed to see past examples at the Bureau, and because of Brade's support, Swettenham had to agree to consult the Home Office.

Finally, Robbins raised the quotation from a secret Press Bureau document, a War Office commentary as background for editors on the current military situation, in a public speech by Charles Buxton;[126] he suggested action should be taken against Buxton. Scott did not think it a matter for the AWOPC, and Cockerill revealed the War Office had decided not to take any action, because it did not intend to issue information to the Press in this way again, the particular passages quoted by Buxton did not constitute an offence, and it would gain him the notoriety he was seeking.

18

THE FINAL PUSH

Public press criticism of the Bureau was by now less vitriolic. In mid-November, the *Daily Mail* carried a wry article about 'Our Comic Censor – Stupid Cuts in a Brilliant War Book'. This was a then much-praised American book about Italy's part in the War, of which the Bureau excised large chunks; the publisher decided to publish it with many blank pages to show how much had had to be omitted. Reviewers pointed out the book had been censored "idiotically", because the full version had been published six months previously in the United States and was therefore already available to the 'sleuths of the Kaiser's American intelligence service'; most of what had been censored was anyway public knowledge, eg that Spezia 'is an Italian Naval base of the first importance'. Alas, similar blue-pencilling of books, articles and programmes, so conscientious and so logical purely from a security point of view, but so isolated from the realities of the wider world of information, is a propensity which junior officials to this day find hard to avoid.

An AWOPC Special Meeting on 4 December 1917 discussed 'the dissemination of publications specially designed for what was called Peace propaganda', which Brade preferred he said to call 'interference with the successful prosecution of the War.'[127] He referred to a new DoRA Regulation 27c, which dealt with leaflets/pamphlets considered subversive, in a way which did not impede the mainstream Press, and which targeted propagandists were circumventing by producing ad hoc newspapers rather than pamphlets. He asked the Press side for their opinion as to how the DoRA Regulation could be further amended to protect against this practice. Press members considered the current Regulation sufficient to deal with the problem, but Cockerill and Swettenham disagreed, quoting cases where Law Officers had advised against prosecution 'when a conviction seemed not only appropriate but certain'. Moreover, magistrates hesitated to convict or gave only light sentences, and the Army authorities were unable to prevent propaganda which seemed designed to undermine the confidence and loyalty of the troops. Riddell and Robbins eventually proposed, to unanimous agreement, an all-purpose compromise Resolution which said both that the Committee believed the current Regulation was adequate to secure the conviction of persons interfering with the successful prosecution of the War or trying to cause disaffection in the Forces, but also that, if the Law Officers thought that the Regulation was inadequate, additional words or Regulations should be introduced to deal with the problem.

Riddell relayed a complaint from Northcliffe about the censoring of American cables passed from foreign countries via London to the United States, which 'had caused irritation in America', and referred as an example to a recent message from Elihu Root[128] to his government. Although not within AWOPC responsibility, Cockerill explained that such censoring had been agreed between the British, French and Italians and 'adhered to' by the Americans. He agreed however that prima facie the telegram quoted should not have been censored and undertook to look into it. Riddell thanked the Home Secretary (now Sir George Cave)[129] for the courteous way in which a small press sub-committee had now been allowed to inspect censored Inward Press Messages, as requested at the previous meeting.

Scott however complained that so far they had seen only messages which had been entirely stopped, and they now needed to see the parts of other messages excised by censorship. Swettenham explained this would be difficult because the words cut out were not kept, and 'the preserving of cuttings for inspection would entail a great deal of labour'. He ended the meeting by making a complaint of his own, not against the Press, but against those Government Departments which occasionally communicated with the Press direct without informing the Bureau. The result was that some consequent articles, if then submitted by the Press to the Bureau for censorship, might be stopped, because the Bureau knew nothing about them. 'The Bureau had more to do with the Press and could prevent the Departments making mistakes'. The AWOPC agreed.

Records of AWOPC activity between then and the next meeting, and indeed for most of 1918, are thin. Edmund Robbins was now effectively in retirement.[130] The last quarterly AWOPC meeting of the War was held on 12 April 1918, in the Admiralty with Murray in the Chair because Brade was at 'another important meeting.'[131] On behalf of the Newspaper Conference, Riddell and Robbins opened by complimenting the Admiralty, and Murray and Brownrigg in particular, on their changes to the information and censorship arrangements; 'a great deal of the matter which had been published had been excellent, and if the new system which had been inaugurated were continued there would be very little cause for complaint.'

The only item on the agenda of the meeting was 'the Photographic Arrangements on the Western Front and generally'. Riddell said that they had been 'of a very nebulous character', with photographers apparently having been employed by Military Charities, the salaries being paid out of the proceeds of the photographs sold, and the profits going to the Charities; the efficiency of this system was questionable. Cockerill too wished to seek the guidance of the Committee, because it had been suggested from France that, if the current regulation that nobody in the Army was allowed to use a camera without a permit could be relaxed, it would be much appreciated by the troops. Security considerations would require some control system if this were to be allowed, but he wondered whether it would be to the advantage of the Press if some such photographs could be submitted to them, for clearance with the Bureau if use was desired. It would have benefits both to publicity and to morale. Riddell however cautioned that many such worthwhile photographs 'would be mixtures of heroism and probably of the most ghastly sights which one could see – so gruesome, in fact, that they would increase the sufferings of the women or anyone who had a son in the War'.

Cockerill said he understood that the Ministry of Information was anyway about to take over the photographic arrangements in France, and eventually everywhere, whereas the official photographers with the Forces were there only to take technical pictures, not for propaganda. Riddell hoped the negatives were being kept 'in a fireproof and bomb-proof building' for posterity, and also that they could in due course be bought by relatives of soldiers. Scott thought that, if the troops were allowed to take photographs, there would be too many to be dealt with, and Wilson suggested there would be an even greater shortage of photographic material. The agreed Resolution was that it was desirable that photographic arrangements on the Western Front should be reorganised, and that any new arrangements should provide an improved service for newspapers, proper care of the negatives for historical purposes, and the establishment of a Bureau for the sale of photographs to relatives and others.

The progress and wider concerns of the remainder of the War are reflected in Appendix 1. The day-to-day frustrations continued. Correspondents in Mesopotamia complained of excessive censorship there, where there was now a better story to tell the public. Delays continued at the Central Post Office on telegrams, in communiqués from France, and in trunk telephone calls; HC Robbins was told privately by an insider that the 'Telephone Department was on the verge of breaking down . . . they were in a terrible state and did not know what to do'; this was because of a 'flu' epidemic, the 'inability to get girls' due to other better paid jobs being easily available, and the great increase in governmental use of the telephone.

The relatively new Ministry of Information wanted to take over from the War Office the responsibility for the 'Correspondents' Chateau' in France and for the jobs of the by then tolerated military Press Control Officers; Sir George Toulmin, still a leading PA figure, opined that the 'Ministry of Information is going to be a very great political danger . . . the Press should fight it from the beginning'; the Newspaper Conference agreed with him, seeing the new Ministry (headed of course by a newspaperman whom they all knew well, Lord Beaverbrook) as little more than a department for propaganda; they (and the War Office) successfully resisted the Ministry's takeover in France. An earlier idea from Sir Edmund Robbins now came to fruition, when Buckingham Palace told the Press (but not the public) that the courtier known as the 'Court Newsman' was to be replaced by an ex-journalist Press Secretary, SJ Pryor,[132] and the PA immediately agreed to his suggestion that they should distribute his new Court Circulars free.

Improved though the Admiralty's performance was in the eyes of the Press, Geddes still felt the Royal Navy was not getting the coverage it deserved. When consulted, Riddell continued to blame Brownrigg for any remaining deficiencies; Geddes pointed out the Admiral was reflecting the views of the Fleet's Commander-in-Chief, who had criticised a recent report which he regarded as endangering security; Riddell countered by citing a report of a German submarine 'outrage' (when the crew of a Lowestoft trawler had been placed on the deck of a U-boat which then submerged, causing them to drown), which had had to be cleared at such a high level that it had been too late for the Sunday papers.

The thrice-daily Military Conferences (press briefings) given by the Duke of Northumberland were also criticised for being confusing, and Cockerill undertook to provide written handout notes which indicated clearly what could and could not be published. There was press unhappiness that Sir Roderick Jones,[133] managing director of Reuters, was also now Assistant Director of Propaganda in the Ministry of Information, and paying large sums to his own firm for official communications carried by it. He resigned the Ministry post (but not from Reuters) a few days later, on the grounds of ill health (heart strain and dental poisoning, not 'diplomatic', HC Robbins informed his Board). Northcliffe, now heading the Department of Propaganda in Enemy Countries, privately suggested one of his own reporters, HW Nevinson,[134] to the War Office as a correspondent in France, and the Department then offered publicly to increase the numbers to accommodate this; but the rest of the Press quickly realised what was behind the offer, and resisted it in the Newspaper Conference.

In October the now publicity-conscious Admiralty separated information from censorship, and appointed Rear Admiral Gaunt[135] as Director of Naval Publicity, with a new department under him, manned by ex-journalists amongst others, such as Commander Beer, previous

News Editor of *The Times*. The Press reported 'the usual crop of difficulties' with the Press Bureau right up to the last month of the War; for example, the news which Notice D710 attempted to stop (the US Department of Information story of links between Germany and the Bolsheviks) had already been published in the *Times* two days previously. As late in the War as November, the *Dublin Evening Herald* was suspended for three days for having published prematurely news of the torpedoing of *SS Leinster*.[136] However, by now, with victory in sight, the Press was focusing not just on security, but also on Departmental obfuscation. 'Why Not Explain. The Vice of Official Secrecy. Secrecy is one of the besetting faults of our modern bureaucracy. The Civil Servant considers himself bound by rule and tradition to maintain an attitude of austere aloofness towards the Press and the public', and much more.[137] Such continuity in British public life, from Victorian times to this day, is in some ways reassuring.

At the last gasp of the War, it was ironically HC Robbins and the cautious and correct Press Association who unwittingly infringed the DoRA. Late on 7 November, they disseminated a Reuters message, mistakenly assuming it had previously been cleared as usual with the Press Bureau, which claimed prematurely an armistice had already been signed. Seventeen minutes late the PA had to issue an urgent message, telling papers to kill the story immediately. The Director of Public Prosecutions decided that prima facie an offence had been committed; although allegedly tempted to prosecute, the Attorney-General decided however that, because the Agency had taken immediate action, because the error had been based on a genuine misunderstanding, and because the Armistice was in fact signed only 84 hours later, no further action should be taken.[138]

On 14 November 1918, three days after the Armistice, a Newspaper Conference delegation of Riddell, HC Robbins and a representative of the technical press went to see the Home Secretary, 'to urge a considerable relaxation of Censorship', pending the signing of the Peace. The Minister 'gave them half an hour before proceeding to the House of Lords to take his seat as Viscount Cave.' They urged cancellation of the more draconian part of DoRA Regulation 18 (prohibition on obtaining and communicating naval and military information), and complete cancellation of Regulations 19 (prohibition of possession of documents or other articles that might be useful to the enemy) and 27 (prohibition of reporting secret sessions of Parliament, of publishing confidential information, and of spreading of false or prejudicial reports and reports of prejudicial performances or exhibitions).

The Press delegation also urged on Cave the cancellation of almost all the D-Notices and the cessation of the censorship of home telegrams. Swettenham claimed such censorship hardly now occurred, but Robbins was able to give examples, particularly of those concerning Ireland, and Sir Frank had to concede the point. Cave promised to abolish interception of inland telegrams, and to review continued censorship of incoming and outgoing overseas cables; he said the Germans were still continuing propaganda work, and there were therefore still reasons why this censorship should continue until Peace had been formally signed, but meanwhile he would consider what modifications could be made. Overall, he and Swettenham said they were in favour of abolishing censorship at the earliest possible moment.

However, although an Inter-Departmental Committee to consider cancelling the wartime DoRA Regulations was set up under Cave in late 1918, and the War Cabinet did approve that many minor Regulations which affected the normal day-to-day lives of the public should gradually be cancelled or suspended, it also decided that consideration of many others should be postponed until after the Armistice was finally signed in late June the following year.[139] Even after that, Cave's Committee kept many Regulations in force until mid-1920,[140] including those of which the Press here complained. The post-War British Government was not unique in this tardiness; administrations are habitually more eager to introduce restrictive legislation in a time of perceived crisis than they are to cancel it when the moment of crisis has passed.

Lessons for Post-War Activity

Thus ended the First World War for the AWOPC.[141] Barely established in August 1914, it had immediately become an essential link between Government and Press in setting up and addressing the teething troubles of the Press Bureau. It had provided, particularly in the early years, the main forum in which the Press aired its grievances to officials about the principles and methodology of censorship, and in which generally constructive dialogue and negotiation with senior officials took place, leading to better understanding of each other's positions and to the necessary working compromises. The Committee had also provided a forum in which the disparate parts of the Press, especially those of London and of the provinces, completed the ironing out of their own differences, with officials acting if not as arbiters, then at least as dispassionate voices.

It had also improved, especially through the work of its indefatigable Secretary Robbins and his Press Association, the machinery of distribution and consultation, and the lubrication of the interlocking smaller cogs of Press, officialdom, Post Office and other players. Although the Newspaper Conference and Sir George Riddell had become the predominant players at the higher level of politicking, the AWOPC throughout remained the place where, for all its imperfections and tensions, agreements were ultimately made which enabled responsible publication and responsible censorship to co-exist through to the successful conclusion of the War.

For the AWOPC itself, some 'lessons' which it took forward into the inter-war period included:

- The principles of the limits of official censorship which would normally be accepted by the Press (even though the spectrum in this War far exceeded that acceptable in peacetime, or that considered acceptable at any time since then, even in World War II; after the initial shock of the sudden outbreak of War, the Press side of the Committee queried vigorously most widenings of the spectrum, and generally made it clear what was acceptable only pro tem).
- The principle and habit accepted by both sides that, although there were laws which enabled censorship and other restrictions to be placed on the Press, the use of litigation even in time of crisis was generally avoidable, and preferably so, if there was a system of advised self-censorship in place for normal day-to-day activity.
- The habit of mind amongst the Press that such avoidance of draconian litigation and its implementation depended ultimately on them making self-regulation work effectively.
- The acceptance of the Committee as the only place where senior members of the Press and of officialdom met regularly, and at the same time both informally and semi-formally, to discuss robustly but sensibly items of mutual interest concerning national security and secret intelligence, with a view to finding binding solutions voluntarily acceptable to both sides.
- The comparative confidence amongst officials that the Press would not normally deliberately flout agreed prohibitions, even though concerns remained about inadvertent disclosure by, and rogue elements in, certain parts of the Press.

- The establishment of flexible systems for the distribution of confidential security warnings to various parts of the Press, based on the Press Association resources.
- The acceptance that the advice/prohibitions could apply to media beyond the Press, in this War to books.
- A systematic and numbered collection of such warnings, with the nomenclature 'D-Notices', the significance of which was known to most editors.[142]

Nevertheless, there were those, both in the Press and in Government Departments, who thought that a system which had been set up to resolve a particular problem in the run-up to the War, and which had done its job in making editors well aware of which remaining areas of naval and military activity were sensitive, was no longer needed now that the War to end all wars had itself ended. There was also a backlash over the degree of censorship which had been imposed, and the degree of self-censorship which patriotic editors had self-imposed, both keeping the public relatively unaware of the scale of losses; as Lloyd George had acknowledged to CP Scott of the *Guardian* in late 1917, if the full truth had been known, there might have been an irresistible demand for immediate peace. The financial and sociological problems facing the weakened and changed country in late 1918 now pushed security and intelligence concerns far down the list of national priorities, and the future of the AWOPC seemed then far from certain.

Section 4

BETWEEN THE WORLD WARS, 1918–39

19

SECURITY CONTEXT

For the AWOPC, the end of the First World War was followed by gentle taking stock, then by a long period of low activity, and eventually by increasing activity as another Great War became rapidly more likely. This pattern reflected the large-scale post-WWI demilitarisation, and the long-lasting perception of a low immediacy of external threats to British security interests. There was national and imperial preoccupation with more pressing problems, including those of Ireland, of the Depression, of the evolution of the United States as the predominant world economic power, and of adjustment to post-World War I social realities in Britain.

During the interwar years, the Committee's mechanisms were in place, and lightly used, but until the late 1930s there was little active consideration of its role, either by the media or by officials. Indeed, because of the hidden, specialist military and predominantly technological nature of its work, and the lack of openness about its role, very few people beyond those directly involved were even aware of its continuing existence. This section reflects the sparse and sketchily recorded activity of the Committee from 1918 to 1939, again starting with a brief résumé of security and media contexts.

Ireland

An immediate post-war concern of the Lloyd George Government was the situation in Ireland. After Sinn Fein's sweeping electoral success in December 1918, its declaration of an independent Irish Republic was not agreed by the London Government, leading to new Irish security problems. These were made more complex by poor co-ordination between the several security organisations involved, which included the Dublin Metropolitan Police, the separate Royal Irish Constabulary (RIC), the military intelligence branch in Ireland, MI5 in London, the Metropolitan Police Director of Security, and even the Naval Intelligence Division; much of their collective effort until the end of the War had been focused on actual and perceived German intrigues with Irish Nationalists.

The switch to the Nationalists as the primary intelligence target was slow, and within the ranks of the Nationalists there were anyway many variations of allegiance and activism. The Inspector-General of the RIC, Brigadier-General Joseph Byrne[1] favoured negotiation with Sinn Fein, to separate the moderates from the violent elements, but he was effectively dismissed by the Lord Lieutenant of Ireland (Field Marshal French) in late 1919. The vicious Anglo-Irish 'war' started in January 1919 and lasted until the de facto truce in July 1921, both sides realising they could not win by force alone. By then the security services in Ireland had been infiltrated by the Nationalists as effectively as the Nationalists had been infiltrated by the security services. The Anglo-Irish Treaty, dividing Ireland into the present two parts, was signed in December 1921. It was followed by the equally vicious Irish Civil War, but while the British Government could to a large extent walk away from Irish problems, British journalists in the Republic continued initially to lead a dangerous life.

Military Intelligence

The Allied Military Forces in Russia which had landed in 1918 ceased to have a real purpose after the ceasefire was agreed by the Germans. None of the Allies had the will, nor the means, to continue fighting against the Bolsheviks with sufficient strength to defeat them; intelligence-gathering was similarly unfocussed and semi-effective. In the UK, the Directorate of Military Intelligence, which at the end of the War had 11 sections and over 6000 personnel, was rapidly reduced after the Armistice,[2] similarly the much smaller Naval Intelligence Division. Nevertheless the Secret Supplement to the 'Manual of Military Intelligence in the Field' was updated in 1923, including regulations for censorship (acknowledging the new problem of growing civil telephone networks), and detailed advice on 'Secret Service in the Field.'[3] The Intelligence Corps had grown to over 1,300 by the end of the War, but was quickly run down, and when the British Army ceased to occupy the Rhine area in 1929, was effectively disbanded. The Treasury would not initially allow the new Air Ministry to have an Intelligence Department at all, ruling that such matters could be covered adequately by their naval and military colleagues. Needless to say, they were not, and the Royal Air Force therefore soon by subterfuge set up its own small intelligence cell.

Secret Communications

Out of the remnants of the Admiralty and War Office codebreaking departments, a permanent secret communications monitoring organisation did however emerge for the first time. In early 1919, the Secret Service Committee chaired by Curzon gained War Cabinet acceptance of its recommendation of a peacetime cryptographic unit. When cable censorship ended in August 1919, there was discussion between Room 40 staff and others about whether this organisation could legally acquire (surreptitiously) copies of telegrams, whether the OSA would need amendment so to do, and whether there was some way of tapping submarine cables (observing that unfortunately the cable between France and the USA did not pass through the UK). Law Officers' opinion was that the desired action was allowed under the Telegraph Act 1863, and that the Home Secretary could authorise, for one week at a time, the requirement on cable companies to hand over copies of telegrams.[4] That somewhat ad hoc procedure was regularised when the Official Secrets Act was revised in 1920. The new Section 4 empowered the Home Secretary by warrant to require of transmitting companies the production as directed of originals or copies of all outward and inward telegrams. From then on, a small proportion of all telegrams was thus examined regularly, selected because of their perceived relevance to security and secret intelligence.

After protracted interdepartmental negotiation, the new DNI Captain Hugh Sinclair[5] established the Government Code and Cypher School (GC&CS) later in 1919, with a staff of 25, mostly veterans of Room 40 and MI1b, headed by Alastair Denniston. The preponderance of the peacetime traffic intercepted and decrypted was diplomatic, and in 1922 the Foreign Office became wholly responsible for GC&CS. Denniston remained until early in WWII to establish Bletchley Park, which Sinclair purchased with his own money shortly before his death. Interwar, the GC&CS was only intermittently successful in reading the encrypted traffic of the Germans, even before they introduced their 'Enigma' machines in the late 1920s. It was however particularly successful in breaking the codes of Allies (many of whom also broke the British codes), and initially of the Bolsheviks.

Secret Intelligence

After WWI the responsibilities of the Directorate of Military Intelligence were partially redistributed, and overseas matters were transferred in 1921 to Cumming's Secret Intelligence Service, as it was now increasingly known in Whitehall, thus giving him for the first time responsibility for all espionage and counter-intelligence work outside the United Kingdom and the Empire. The Services Departments soon began to regret the removal of secret activities from their supervision, and in early 1923 their three Directors of Intelligence protested in particular about the paucity of decrypted information which they were now receiving from the Foreign Office's GC&CS and their lack of input on its targeting. This led to an organisational compromise, whereby after the death of Cumming in June 1923 the GC&CS was brigaded with SIS under Sinclair. Although both organisations now belonged to the Foreign Office, 'C' was able to ensure that the interests of the Services were in future covered to the best of the ability of the still small staff and resources allocated. The SIS continued to develop and expand, focusing on the Soviet Union and later on Nazi Germany.

Internal Security

Internal security in the early post-WWI years was divided between the Metropolitan Police Directorate of Intelligence under Thomson, for civil matters including industrial subversion, and MI5 under Kell for the military aspects. There was overlap and intense rivalry, and they had different views on the Bolshevik threat; Thomson had primacy; yet he was less concerned than Kell that Soviet attempts at subversion would succeed, probably because he understood the British civil populace better. The individuals who distributed pamphlets to, or tried to form cells within, the Armed Services made no general impact, and when there was significant disaffection, as in the Invergordon Mutiny of 1931, the cause was not political doctrine but politicians cutting naval ratings' pay.

Similarly amongst the civilian workforce, where there were indeed some widespread manifestations of discontent, the causes were usually immediate: pay and working conditions, not communist doctrine as peddled by the Soviets. In India too, where the Bolshevik threat was seen as a continuation of the traditional Russian threat to the North West Frontier, the Delhi Intelligence Bureau was assiduous in infiltrating the small Indian Communist Party, but in due course became realistic about the latter's lack of effectiveness, and about the inability of the Red Army to mount a campaign in that region at that time.[6]

As a result of some dissatisfaction about the accuracy of intelligence being provided to Curzon in particular about the Bolshevik threat to Ireland, a small committee of senior civil servants led by Hankey was tasked in 1921 to examine 'Secret Service expenditure', in effect the activities of the various branches. They were especially critical of Thomson, whose enemies also included his nominal superior, the Commissioner of the Metropolitan Police, General Horwood.[7] The Commissioner considered the independence of his Special Branch as 'a standing menace to the good discipline of the force'.

Thomson refused to accept his Department being placed fully under the Commissioner's direct control, and was forced to resign, much to the fury of his own allies, notably the ex-DNI and now Conservative MP, Admiral Hall, who raised the matter in Parliament, claiming it was the result of Thomson's anti-Bolshevik activities and a secret plot. The Directorate of Intelligence as such disappeared, but the outcry over Thomson was such that his chosen successor, the ex-RIC Sir Joseph Byrne, was prevented from taking up the post (partly because he was a devout Catholic and therefore unacceptable at that time to the Right). Thomson himself turned to writing novels and reminiscences; he was differently discredited in December 1925 when arrested by police in Hyde Park and charged with committing an act in violation of public decency with a Miss de Lava, remarkable considering his age and the climate. In 1931, MI5 was incorporated into the Security Service, and the latter continued the use of the War Office as the cover for its existence and activities.

Censorship

The censorship organisations were gradually run down after the War.[8] The large military department for postal censorship (MI9), numbering 10,554 in London and Liverpool by 1918, was similarly disbanded after ratification of the Peace Agreement in 1919; a very small rump left to record lessons for posterity included, pathetically, a description of their own eventual situation 'in a cold, ill-lighted and unventilated segment of the structure known as Cornwall House, and its [MI9's] history written to the sound of relentless hammering and the cries of children and the quarrels of their parents in the squalid street below.'[9]

Nevertheless, censorship lingered on to some degree well after WWI. In late 1918, an Interdepartmental Committee was set up under Brade to consider the suspension of those DoRA regulations 'no longer necessary in the national interest'. Some were quickly approved for cancellation or suspension by the War Cabinet (which also lingered on), but others had to await the Peace Agreement. In late January 1919 a delegation from the Newspaper Conference, including AWOPC members, appealed again to the Home Secretary to abolish political censorship, particularly as it was being used to prevent reporting fully on the situation in Ireland. This approach was unsuccessful; the proprietors therefore complained directly to other members of the War Cabinet, but again without success, although the Wartime Irish Censor was stood down at the end of August 1919.

Indeed relevant DoRA prohibitions had still not been revoked by mid-1920, when it was quite obvious that many of the Regulations, and not just those being used for directly political purposes, were no longer meaningful. Officials based in London's Hotel Windsor charged with taking the work forward in 1919–20 had the quaint title of the 'Liquidation Committee'; in May 1920, they listed about 50 Regulations which all agreed could be revoked immediately, but still another 40 or so which the Admiralty, War Office, Air Ministry and other Departments wished to keep in force, in addition to other Regulations in the new War Emergency Laws (Continuance) Act.[10]

Those in the category to be abolished immediately included 'Directions as to priority in supply of coal or coke' (2D), 'Power to take possession of any factory or plant' (8), 'Power to prohibit drilling except of H.M.'s Forces, etc' (9E), 'Power to close licensed premises, and to prohibit treating' (10), 'Restrictions on or internment of persons of hostile origin or associations' (14B), 'Prohibition on possession of wireless telegraph apparatus, etc' (22), 'Prohibition on reports of proceedings of secret session of Parliament or Cabinet Meeting, and publishing confidential information' (27A), and 'Power to stop and search vehicles' (52).

Those in the category to be retained pro tem included: 'Power to take possession of land, etc' (2), 'Prohibition on obtaining and communicating naval and military information' (18), 'Prohibition on possession of carrier pigeons' (21), 'Prohibition on spreading of false or prejudicial reports and against prejudicial performances or exhibitions' (27), 'Printing and circulation of leaflets' (27C), 'Duty of complying with navigation regulations in harbours' (36), 'Prohibition of supplying intoxicants to H.M.'s Forces' (40), and 'Powers of questioning' (54). Some, for example Regulations 18 and 27, were particularly disliked by the Press, for obvious reasons.

Because useful DoRA provisions were nevertheless obviously going gradually to be revoked, the War Office Emergency Legislation Committee considered drafting a National Security Bill, but this was set aside by the outcome of a post-war OSA case. In 1919, the Official Secrets Act 1911 was used to prosecute a War Office clothing clerk and the director of a tailoring company over the alleged passing of contractual information between the two ('communicating official information to an unauthorised person'). Although the magistrate ruled the OSA was intended not for this kind of case but for security matters which should be kept secret, the Attorney-General, Sir Gordon Hewart[11] obtained a judicial ruling that Section 2 could apply to any official information obtained by someone as a result of their employment by the Crown – much to the anger of those in the Press watching the principles at stake.

Afterwards, the Attorney-General and the Home Secretary, Mr Shortt,[12] raised a number of amendments to the Act, which were rushed through Parliament as OSA 1920, once again with more debate on espionage-related justifications than on the increase in powers taken to deal with offences under Section 2, and with misleading assertions by the Law Officer. It now became possible to be charged with making a false statement 'for any purpose prejudicial to the safety or interest of the State', or with retaining an official document without authority for such a purpose, with the onus on the accused to prove that he or she did not have that purpose. The Bill also introduced other new offences, and removed the right of an accused to remain silent in certain circumstances. Because of the stressed link with espionage, there was little opposition even in the House of Lords. Burnham did protest strongly however that the retention clause would mean no editor 'would be safe if the Bill were passed in its present form', and Parmoor regretted it would 'seriously interfere with our ordinary freedom in various directions'. This clause was therefore modified.

The mood in the House of Commons during the second reading was not conducive to further querying its clauses, coming as it did shortly after 12 British intelligence officers had been killed in Dublin on 'Bloody Sunday', 21 November 1920. Hewart again explained the necessity for the changes as being to deal with espionage, and the only fierce opposition came from Sir Donald Maclean,[13] who complained the Act would hit at legitimate functions of the Press, and would impinge most harmfully on the liberty of the individual. He referred to it as the 'complete abrogation of any semblance of justice' and as 'another attempt to clamp the powers of war on to the liberties of the citizen in peace'. Clause 6, which made it an offence for anyone not to give the Police or Armed Forces 'any information in his power relating to an offence or a suspected offence under the OSA', was seen as a particular threat to the Press. Nevertheless, the Bill was passed easily at 4 a.m. on 17 December 1920.[14] Even after this, however, the effects of the DoRA lingered on in practice: as late as September 1921, Scotland Yard was querying with the Home Office whether it could still use the Act to prosecute someone under the Lights (Vehicles) Order, one reason for the introduction of which had been to avoid confusion with farmers using vehicle lights to signal a hostile landing.[15]

The Government used the new OSA several times in the interwar years to prosecute in non-national security cases, for example the Governor of Pentonville Prison for passing information about executions to the *Evening News*, and an Air Ministry clerk for attempting to sell contractual information to an interested company. The Act was also used to threaten, for example, the author of a book about Casement, and to authorise police action such as the raid on the premises of the Russian Trade Delegation in 1927. In May 1930 it was used to justify a police raid on the offices of the *Daily Sketch*, *Daily Telegraph* and *News Chronicle*, after a leak about the imminent arrest of Gandhi in India; the newspapers were subsequently cleared of withholding their sources when they showed they had merely drawn correct inferences from a speech by the Home Secretary. In 1932 a temporary clerk at Somerset House was prosecuted for leaking to a reporter the contents of certain wills, and both were imprisoned under the Act, even though, as the Press pointed out, this had nothing to do with national security.

The author Compton Mackenzie was prosecuted the same year over inclusion in his new book *Greek Memories* of information acquired during his time as a low-grade WWI intelligence officer in Greece; he had used similar material in two previous volumes of memoirs, without official complaint, but this volume was written in part in criticism of inaccuracies in a contemporary book by the ex-Director of Intelligence, Thomson. The trial, most of which was held in camera not because of the sensitivity of the material but because of the presence in court of MI5 and MI6 witnesses, became an embarrassment to the Government, and resulted in only a token fine; Mackenzie later had his revenge by satirising the Intelligence and Security Services in his novel *Water on the Brain*. The trial did have one beneficial side effect for guardians of official secrecy: Churchill later admitted to Mackenzie that, as a result of the prosecution, he had rapidly destroyed some official papers he had kept, something he subsequently regretted.

One unpopular section of the OSA was eventually amended at the end of the interwar period, namely Section 6 (failure to give information to the authorities about an actual or suspected offence). It was another media prosecution which started the process. The Stockport *Daily Dispatch* published a report in June 1937 about a conman who preyed on the poor, based on a police circular which had been leaked to it. The paper's managing editor revealed the provenance to the police, but the journalist concerned refused to reveal who had passed him the circular, was prosecuted accordingly and fined £5 by local magistrates. Supported by the National Union of Journalists, the journalist appealed to the High Court, where unfortunately the presiding judge was the now Lord Hewart, the former Attorney-General who had assured the House of Commons in 1920 that Section 6 would not be used against the Press in this way; the Court dismissed the appeal. The further furore which this caused led to the Home Secretary, Samuel Hoare,[16] promising the Section would in future be used only in cases of 'serious public importance'.

This case in itself would not however have been enough to cause the OSA to be amended, but the following June, the Attorney-General considered using it against a Member of Parliament, Duncan Sandys.[17] He had been the recipient of leaks from within the Air Ministry correcting misleading information about the strength of the Luftwaffe which the Government had been providing publicly in its attempts to play down the German threat. The Government's apparent threat to use the OSA in this way was immediately seen both as an attack on parliamentary privilege and also as a misuse of the Act (although the former upset MPs more than the latter). The Government backed off, and as a result of this and the

Stockport cases, put in hand amendment of Section 6, limiting its use to espionage cases; this became law in OSA 1939 soon after the start of WWII.[18]

In September 1938, the Metropolitan Police refused official passes to the Progressive Film Institute, because of its adversely selective footage of Police action against the 1932 Hunger March. This led to complaints from the MPs Major Clement Atlee[19] and Ellen Wilkinson.[20] In due course the Home Secretary had to admonish the Police Commissioner, Sir Philip Game:[21] 'Unfortunately there is no method of preventing newspapers or newsreels misrepresenting facts without a system of control which is inconsistent with freedom'; he was ordered to reverse his decision.[22]

The final element of preparation for censorship in war was its machinery of implementation. The CID started work on this as early as 1922, when a Standing Inter-Departmental Committee on Censorship was established, with a plethora of sub-committees, and regular annual progress reports. From the start, the views of the Joint Directors of the WWI Press Bureau were the basis of work, including their preference, never achieved in WWI, that they should issue Notices directly to the Press rather than through the AWOPC. Almost all officials agreed with this, even strong supporters of the Committee such as Murray, who had hinted in the post-war Committee meetings that, well though it had done, its role was fundamentally one for peacetime. Nevertheless, all also agreed from the start that D-Notices should continue to be the vehicles of requests to the Press.[23]

The result of years of deliberation and redrafting appeared eventually as 'Regulations for Censorship, 1938'.[24] These dealt, in broad concept and in fine detail, with all forms of censorship. They started by defining governments' rights to censor, i.e. to examine and modify 'in the interests of national defence or public safety', qualified only by international law and conventions and by constitutional restrictions, if any [none were defined nor listed]. The Main Objective was to stop all communications/publications injurious to the national cause, and especially communications to and from the enemy. The detailed chapters listed types of information to be protected, including obvious military ones, and also utilities, morale (British and the enemy's), civil and industrial unrest, food shortages, etc; in effect the whole gamut of matters covered in WWI. Further chapters were devoted to the 'principles' and practices of censorship, including peacetime preparations (in which the AWOPC did have a role), and the establishment of a Ministry of Information. It was a masterpiece of methodical committee work. All it needed were the enormous resources involved, and rehearsal. As we see below, it received neither before it was first activated in a false alarm; resources trickled in only when WWII was well under way.

Politics and Security

Quite apart from OSA activity, the authorities between the Wars were also not above manipulating the Press for their own purposes, in security and intelligence matters with a strong political content. The first notorious case occurred in 1920. On 18 August, officials unattributably leaked to the Central News Agency eight secretly intercepted and decrypted telegrams between the Soviet Government and the *Daily Herald*. The background was the newspaper's desperate search for financial backing. Although the Soviets certainly wished to encourage industrial unrest in Britain, the content was fairly innocuous; but this link, as the Government desired, was widely and unfavourably reported by the other papers – *The Times* headline was 'Lansbury's Orders from Moscow' (Lansbury was the *Herald*'s editor).[25] The Director of Intelligence, Thomson, denied he was the source of the leak. The Manager of the Central News Agency did not reveal his source even privately to the Press, but he did confirm to Robbins that copies of the messages had been sent to him with the caveat that 'no intimation should be given that they were from an official source', and to imply that they had come from a neutral source.[26]

To Lloyd George's fury however, *The Times* article included 'The following wireless messages have been intercepted by the British Government'; Northcliffe had his own private governmental sources who had told him this, perhaps uncaveated. The Government's de facto admission that Russian telegram traffic was not only being intercepted, but also that Britain could decrypt it, was therefore from a purely security position a gamble which did not quite come off. Fortunately the affair did not cause the Bolshevik authorities on this occasion to change their code system; they were then still in a precarious position at home, and needed to keep financial and diplomatic bridges to the West open.

Later that year the Soviets did introduce a new code system which it took GC&CS a few months to break, but the Government at first decided, on the advice of Hankey about not compromising this ability, to refrain from publicly using evidence therefrom of anti-British activity. In 1923, however, concerned about the revived Russian threat to India, the Cabinet agreed the Foreign Secretary (Curzon) should deliberately quote verbatim from intercepted Soviet messages. The source of the information was not disclosed, but must have been obvious to the Soviets, if not to many in Parliament and the public, unaware of the GC&CS and its role.

When the CID was in 1923 considering some limited form of press control in 'minor [political] emergencies' such as major industrial disputes, it looked at the D-Notice System as a possible model. Murray pointed out the impracticality of the idea since, if this were to happen, 'it would, for example, be necessary to convey to such newspapers as the *Daily Herald* and other extreme Communist journals, requests for the suppression of objectionable material connected with industrial questions'. The Lord President of the Council (Salisbury) objected strongly to the Service Departments being thus drawn into political matters; in March he persuaded the CID to drop the idea, because it would prejudice the favour the D-Notice Committee had found with the Press.

The Zinoviev Letters case of 1924 also involved the Press and the intelligence and security services, but had a different cause and effect. During the October election campaign, when the Labour Government was attempting inter alia to persuade voters it was not soft on Bolshevism, the Prime Minister Ramsay MacDonald[27] wrote a firm letter to the Soviet Chargé d'Affaires in London about an intercepted (albeit now considered forged) letter from Grigori Zinoviev, President of the Comintern, which advocated action to foment unrest in Britain, including in the Armed Forces. The Prime Minister's letter was leaked, possibly by pro-Conservative past and/or present members of the British intelligence community, to the Editor of the *Daily Mail* (Marlowe), who used it to claim the Government was concealing vital information from the Country about Communist subversion. The ensuing Press uproar contributed to the Conservative landslide election victory a few days later.

In 1927, with the previous year's General Strike still a recent event and with much fresh evidence of Soviet attempts to foment unrest in Britain and the Empire (especially India), the Conservative Government[28] decided to bring matters to a head and to find a reason to break off diplomatic relations with the Soviet Union. They authorised a police raid on the offices of the Russian Trade Delegation, but this failed to find the expected documentary evidence. It was decided therefore to use the contents of decrypted telegrams as justification for breaking off diplomatic relations. In House of Commons debates on 24 and 26 May, the

Prime Minister Stanley Baldwin[29] and others quoted from intercepted and decoded telegrams. The effect was seriously to compromise the work of the GC&CS, by causing the Soviets again to change their diplomatic code arrangements to a system which it was rarely able to break before WWII started. Political action not press indiscretion was the cause of the significant weakening of this aspect of national security.

One other sensitive censorship problem was that concerning the Irish Free State, whose independence but geographical proximity and societal interchange caused particular worry to the British security authorities. A pragmatic solution was sought which did not offend Irish sensibilities yet gave some degree of reassurance to Britain on its own security. This was drafted by Major 'Pug' Ismay of the CID,[30] and in July 1928 a British delegation led by Lord Lovat of the Dominions Office[31] met an Irish delegation (including the Irish General Staff's Director of Defence Plans) to negotiate a modus vivendi. An informal channel of diplomatic contact on security matters was amicably agreed, as was the suggestion that Ireland's own Censor, when appointed, might beneficially attend the British Army Staff Course at Camberley.[32]

20

MEDIA CONTEXT

Internal Media Relationships

Although it took some years after WWI to reduce prohibitions on publication to former peacetime levels, the Press was generally more concerned with reverting rapidly to their own normal preoccupations. These included rivalry and sometimes even hostility between the London and the provincial Press; inadequate but increasingly costly telegram and telephone services provided by the GPO; post-war increases in the charges of the Agencies to each other, to newspapers and to advertisers, because of the Post Office monopoly and the more militant stance now taken by unions, in particular the National Union of Journalists; coverage of continuing imperial military campaigns, for example appointing a Reuters/PA correspondent in 1920 to accompany the 'Indian Frontier Punitive Operations' against the 'Wazir and Mahsud' tribes; and resuming normal services such as the PA contract with the Telegraphic Cricket Service in March 1920, prior to the first full season since 1914 with three-day County matches,[33] the Press sharing the cost (£45) of the GPO wires at Chelsea Football Ground for the April 1920 Cup Final, and complex agreements between the British and American Agencies over the 1920 America's Cup.[34]

Post-War Press disputes between London and the provinces first came to a head in mid-October 1920, when the latter's representatives at the weekly Newspaper Conference were told by Northcliffe this would be its last meeting. He had an aversion to committees, but he had also recently been heavily criticised by the provincial Press: contrary to a gentlemen's agreement, he had flooded the Lancashire market in particular with additional copies of his papers when the local journals were temporarily in dispute with their unions and unable to produce normal editions. The provincial Press decided to set up their own weekly Newspaper Conference. Its effectiveness was soon called into question, however, because the Government tended still to communicate more frequently with its familiars in the London Press, such as Riddell and other press 'barons' (Lords Northcliffe, Rothermere, Beaverbrook, Kemsley, and Camrose).

There had also been difficulties for the Press with the trades unions. In October 1919, the National Union of Railwaymen called a national strike at short notice. This action was so heavily criticised in all the London newspapers (except the *Daily Herald*) that the Press unions then threatened action against the proprietors. This was seen by them, by the public and by politicians (even many socialists) as a threat to press freedom, and for a few days the atmosphere in Fleet Street became very volatile; printworkers stopped the presses temporarily at the *Daily Mail*, *Daily Express* and *Daily Sketch*, and owners received anonymous threatening letters, for example: 'Lord Northcliffe, – Don't worry about stopping the publication of your different journals, because long before that occurs – very likely at the beginning of next week – your workers will have taken control and will run the *Daily*

Mail for themselves. Likewise, all your other London papers. Arrangements are being rapidly completed. A Press Worker'.[35]

This dispute ended when the Government settled with railwaymen later that month. In 1923, NPA proprietors signed an anti-union agreement with each other which would enable lockout of staffs of all newspapers simultaneously. Indirectly linked was the postponement of a decision on serial applications by the communist *Daily Worker* to join the NPA (the last in February 1938), although they were allowed to use NPA facilities and trains.[36] During the General Strike of 1926, the publication of most newspapers was suspended, but on 5 May the Government brought out the first issue of its own newspaper the *British Gazette*, and the Trades Union Congress published the first issue of the *British Worker*, both of which ceased publication when the workforce returned.

Ireland

Until July 1921, journalists working for London-based journals and agencies during the Anglo-Irish War suffered ill-treatment from both sides. In November 1920, the local PA correspondent in Ballinasloe (County Galway) was hauled from his bed by soldiers, severely beaten, put against a wall and threatened with shooting if he again filed a report unfavourable to the security forces. Robbins wrote complaining to the Chief Secretary of Ireland, whose office gave assurances such treatment was not authorised and would not be tolerated, but Robbins raised it too with the AWOAMPC. Journalists were similarly threatened by Nationalists, and in December 1920 eleven Special Correspondents from Great Britain wrote a joint letter seeking financial compensation for the danger they were in, pointing out that they received protection from neither side, and were 'under suspicion from both'. During the Irish Civil War (June 1922-May1923) the IRA ordered British newspaper representatives in Dublin to submit all copy about its activities to its 'Publicity Department'. The Irish people themselves were physical victims of the conflict, and in April 1922 there was a general strike in the Irish Free State against the 'gunmen'. Furthermore, censorship was imposed by the Irish Free State Government in July 1922, ironic in a country whose Press had played a leading part in resisting London's attempts at censorship of the whole British Press in the previous four decades.[37]

Impact of Technology and Press Organisation

After the War, the technology available to the Press continued to improve, in their own equipment for printing and transmission, and in that belonging to those they worked with. In early 1925 Harold Robbins witnessed a demonstration of transmission of pictures by telegraph, and was impressed by its ease. An even more significant socio-technological trend, during and particularly after WWI, was ever greater telephone use; the pattern of communication by press and public quickly changed. For example, in 1914 the number of telegrams sent was about 69 million, whereas by 1935 the use of long-distance telephone had caused this to fall to 35 million.

The Press Association became the majority shareholder in Reuters from late 1925, as a step in the structural 'Anglicisation' of the Company which had started in 1916; the NPA, for reasons of internal dissension, declined to join in purchasing Reuters shares at that time. Unknown to the PA, in November 1937 the Reuters Chairman Sir Roderick Jones secretly approached the Prime Minister Neville Chamberlain[38] about acquiring a government subsidy. His argument was that rival agencies, particularly the German and the French, received such governmental subsidies, which inclined foreign newspapers to obtain their inputs from them because they were cheaper or free, even though they were less accurate; but they were also often anti-British. After eight months of secret negotiation with the Treasury (opposed by the Foreign Office, for whom Reuters was not sufficiently supportive of the Government), and when Hitler invaded the Sudetenland, a clandestine subsidy was agreed.[39]

The growth in large newspaper chains which had started in the 1890s continued through and after the First World War. By 1921 the three Harmsworth brothers (Northcliffe, Rothermere and Sir Leicester Harmsworth)[40] controlled journals with a combined circulation of over six million; the percentages of morning and evening titles owned by the five big chains rose between 1921 and 1929 respectively from 12 to 44 and from 8 to 40. This trend also eliminated much competition, and in the same decades the number of towns with a choice of local morning and evening papers fell respectively from 15 to 7 and from 24 to 10. The circulation of national dailies overtook that of the provincial papers for the first time, rising from 5.4 to 10.6 million. The public's habit of reading a Sunday paper increased, and by 1934 more Sunday newspapers were bought than there were households in the country.

The position of the 'Press Barons', although significant in providing a platform for their personal views, was not however monolithic, and even within a group there was often a diversity of editorial agendas. Collectively nevertheless, they and their readers reflected an unradical view of Britain's leading place in the world and a gradualist attitude to changes in social conditions. The style of newspapers changed only gradually, the more upmarket papers continuing to start with several pages of small classified advertisements (the *Daily Telegraph* did not put news on the front page until 1939, *The Times* not until post-WWII), followed by lengthy and straight reports from the Courts, with news tucked well inside, followed by polite social gossip about the upper middle class. The more popular papers were also more staid in format than today's equivalents, but increasingly covered 'lots of celebrity gossip, lots of disaster, mixed with endless competitions, the new-fangled crosswords and 'what is the world coming to?' complaints.'[41] The intense competition between journals for readers and advertising led to further closures, takeovers and amalgamations. Price wars also occurred; when the *Daily Telegraph* reduced its price from twopence to three-halfpence in March 1922, *The Times* immediately followed suit.

The rapidly increasing importance of broadcasting was reflected in 1923 in the first publication of *Radio Times*, which eventually achieved the largest magazine circulation in Britain. The growth in advertising in the Press almost trebled between the beginnings of the First and Second World Wars, as the spending power of the wider public increased. This enabled a trend in content of less politics and more entertainment, and also made the cost of ownership generally too great for Party Political syndicates. In 1928 the Liberals had to relinquish their control of the *Westminster Gazette* and the *Daily Chronicle*, and the Tory *Daily Graphic* and *Morning Post* disappeared as separate titles for similar reasons.

The leading newspaper of the Left, the *Daily Herald* under the editorship of George Lansbury, had continued to pursue pro-striker, pro-Irish, pro-suffragette, pro-Bolshevik and anti-war policies, not hesitating to attack less radical Labour politicians and trades unionists. It built up a readership by 1920 of about 250,000, but it failed to attract sufficient advertising, despite Lansbury latterly toning down the radicalism, and was therefore unable to continue without subsidy. To achieve this, Lansbury reluctantly sold in 1922 to the Labour Party and the Trades Union Congress jointly. Readership rose to about a million, but by 1929 the Labour Party was unable to sustain its share of the costs, leaving the TUC as the minority subsidiser.

The majority business partner and producer was now Odhams Press, managed by J.S. Elias,[42] which ran it on a mainly commercial rather than ideological basis, becoming only moderately left of centre in its views. The circulation quadrupled rapidly to a million (compared to the 1.85, 1.69 and 1.45 million of the *Mail*, *Express* and *Chronicle* respectively), but because readers were mostly on low incomes, advertising revenues remained inadequate. When the *Daily Mirror* and the *Sunday Pictorial* remodelled as popular papers in the years 1933–37, under Cecil King and Hugh Cudlipp,[43] they did so initially not so much as left-of-centre newspapers, but to attract female and younger readers. In general the Press became more the criticisers of Government than the uncritical supporters of a political party, and more the advocates of particular policies (for example, Anti-Waste, Imperial Free Trade, Pro- or Anti-Industrial Action (especially around the time of the 1926 General Strike), for or against Appeasement and Pro- or Anti-Fascism, than of a particular political manifesto.[44]

Broadcasting

In the years after the War there was a lengthy but hopeless battle by the Press against the growth of 'broadcasting by wireless telephony', especially of news and of advertising. The impetus of broadcasting was irresistible and international, in demand by the more technologically aware members of the public, and with advantages immediately obvious to Ministers, so long as they retained some control over it. Despite press protests, on idealistic grounds which attempted to veil their commercial concerns, and in the face of forecasts by some that it would mean the end of the Press, the Postmaster-General in 1922 decided to allow experimental broadcasting to begin. The Press institutions did their utmost in 1923/4 to restrict the experiment, by such ways as negotiating with the BBC that it would limit broadcasts after 7 p.m. on events 'by microphone' (ie outside broadcasts) and 'studio narratives' on current events.

The broadcasters kept coming back and eventually the proprietors, steered by Riddell, decided that a 'non possumus' attitude on their part was going to be less profitable than some co-operation with the broadcasters. The Press initially supplied the information to the BBC for its news broadcasts, and the Company itself was not then always driven by the feeling that news was paramount; in early 1926, it asked Reuters not to supply quite so much information for the early news broadcast, which it wished to reduce from 12 to 9 minutes in order to allow 'more time for piano recitals'. By the end of 1924 the Government had already issued about a million wireless receiver set licences to members of the public. It was the obvious need for some system of control over this new medium that persuaded the Government to tell the applicants that they must all invest jointly, at least initially, in one experimental station, the British Broadcasting Company, under its Managing Director John Reith.[45]

The Sykes Committee in 1923 rejected advertising as the major source of revenue and proposed a licence fee from users; the Crawford Committee in 1926 accepted broadcasting as a monopoly and proposed the replacement of the Company by 'a Public Commission operating in the national Interest'. In 1926 the BBC became the British Broadcasting *Corporation*, operating however under Royal Charter rather than as a Department of State, with Reith as its Director-General.[46] It had broadcast its first news bulletin in December 1922, started weather forecasts 1923, programmes for schools 1924, and between 1926 and 1930 it established its own news-gathering department.

One reason why the resistance of the Press to broadcasting had declined arose out of the General Strike of May 1926. This caused Press proprietors to realise even more clearly that publicity given to events by broadcasting also increased the public's appetite for news, and thus increased newspaper circulation; the PA even started to listen to wireless news in its offices.[47] By the end of 1926 too, the number of wireless licences issued to the public had risen to two million, a 100% increase in two years. The first live sports broadcast (England v Wales Rugby) was made in 1927. For those overseas, the BBC Empire Service (later the World Service) was founded in 1932.

As with radio broadcasting in other developed countries, by the mid-1930s the Corporation had achieved a position at the forefront of the British media, and to some extent in the international arena, with a much-debated but established concept of political balance, of a cultural ethos which was admired although very much that of the middle-class intelligentsia, and outwardly of independence from political accountability. The political independence was in reality constrained by dependence on Government for the licence fee; if Ministers really wanted to persuade the Corporation towards or from a particular course of action they had ways of surreptitiously doing so. When in 1935 it was proposed to broadcast talks by a communist and a fascist, government pressure that it would not be in the national interest led to them being quietly dropped, without the reason being stated. There was a similar outcome in 1939 when the Foreign Office vetoed the BBC broadcasting direct messages to the German people by distinguished British socialists.[48]

John Logie Baird[49] invented one of the first forms of television, demonstrated it in 1926, and founded Baird Television Ltd in 1928. The BBC (and the German Post Office) first trialled limited use of his system in 1929, and in 1936 started experimental transmissions from Alexandra Palace. The Press resisted television broadcasting too. Proprietors feared that 'Assuming reasonably rapid progress is made, the newspapers might be confronted with wealthy stores televising with descriptive talk, mannequins displaying millinery and dresses, demonstrations of cookery, etc, which could be viewed by parties of ladies in drawing rooms.' As a compromise, the NPA therefore favoured the (non-commercial) BBC being the sole television company. The NPA Secretary shared a common apprehension with his opposite number at the Printing and Kindred Trades Federation about the 'pernicious effect on newspapers and consequent unemployment in the printing industry, if revenue from advertising which is the main factor in newspaper production is seriously curtailed by commercial and monopolistic trading bodies.'[50]

Nevertheless, although the official opening of the television service took place in November 1936, and its programmes reached about 35,000 homes within range of Crystal Palace by 1939, the BBC's development of television was still rudimentary by the start of the Second World War. Partly for security reasons and partly because the expert personnel were urgently required for war work (on for example the development and operation of radar), the service was suspended for the duration. Baird's company went into receivership in 1939, and although he demonstrated his full colour television, which he had first attempted in 1928, in late 1941, he died in relative poverty soon after WWII.[51]

At the other end of the scale of public recognition, honours continued to be awarded to newspapermen: amongst others, Sir George Riddell became Lord Riddell in 1920, the owner of the *Daily Telegraph* William Berry became Lord Camrose in 1928,[52] and his younger brother James became Lord Kemsley in 1936,[53] and J.B. Elias of the Odhams Press became Lord Southwood in 1937. Honours went to certain journalists too, for example a knighthood in 1920 to the Reuters/PA war correspondent.[54] Such is the background to the state of the media in the interwar years, more consistently concerned with competition between each other than with matters of national security and the work of the D-Notice Committee, yet still at times returning with vehemence to its work.

21

EARLY WORK OF THE COMMITTEE

The Press Bureau had eventually closed at the end of April 1919, unlamented by the Press, but Government Departments quickly realised it had been very useful to them as the vehicle for issuing information. They had done this pre-war through the News Agencies, but now saw there was more to the interface with the Press than just handing out official communiqués. The India Office suggested keeping something like the Bureau as 'some small office . . . to act as a channel between the Government Departments and the newspapers.'[55] When the Government had sounded out the Press about what might best replace the PB, Burnham thought there should be a special Ministry charged with such matters, but other proprietors were very much against what they saw would inevitably become not just a department for disseminating what the Government did want to appear, but also for concealing what it did not. The Government decided ultimately to deal with the London newspapers individually and direct, and with the rest of the Press through the PA.[56]

The first post-war meeting of the Committee was not held until 22 July 1919. Unsurprisingly, the mood was mellow and unpressured. Those present had all now been awarded knighthoods (Brade in the Chair, Murray, Riddell, Robbins (E), Duncan, Holbrook), except for Baird (who received one two years later); Messrs Scott and Wilson were in the USA, and there were no longer any serving officers on the Committee. The purpose of the meeting was to discuss the 'organization for peace times'. All agreed the Committee had performed a very useful function pre-war, and that it should continue. Brade talked about adapting to any new conditions, and that therefore the Committee would exist for the same purposes as before but also 'perhaps for others'.

Robbins gave examples of the services the Committee had rendered, in particular in late July 1914, claiming 'that had it not been for the fact that the Committee existed there would have been no means of acquainting the Press with the serious nature of the situation, and of requesting the newspapers to abstain from the publication of details which if published would have done incalculable injury'. He suggested that certain documents which he had issued on behalf of the Committee had historical importance and should be recorded in the minutes, which they duly were.

Of the 749 D-Notices which had been issued during the War, 'representing over a million single copies', on an addressee list which had increased from 500 to 1,500, Robbins singled out one as a particular example of how they had been handled, and of the success in preventing sensitive operational details being published.[57] Riddell asked how the nickname 'Parkers' had arisen, and it was agreed to consult the Post Office. Robbins reported that 'practically none' of the Notices had been disregarded 'except by one or two publications of a certain kind. The Press as a whole had loyally observed the warnings'. The only critical note in the discussion was struck by Riddell, who commented that it was 'a very great pity that the Committee were not consulted before the Censorship was set up'. He also felt that, had the authorities made greater use of the Committee in the later stages of the War, 'many errors might have been avoided', and that, 'although they trusted there would not be any other wars', the Committee should be maintained if there were.

Supported by others, he complimented Brade on 'the honour of being the father and mother and midwife of the Committee, and he was entitled to congratulate himself upon having conceived a very happy idea'; Duncan also mentioned Churchill's early support. Brade recalled the Committee's pre-war role in establishing 'the sort of atmosphere that was much more congenial to the growth of friendly relations between the Departments and the Press'. It was agreed that the Admiralty and the War Office should make public some appreciation of the 'valuable services rendered by the Press during the War', and of the AWOPC's 'very useful' war role; and that the Committee should be maintained, and should meet routinely every six months, in May and November, and otherwise as required. It was also decided that the Weekly Newspaper and Periodical Proprietors' Association, and the Air Ministry (but not other Government Departments) should be invited to be represented on the Committee. Murray enquired of Brade (they had apparently not consulted beforehand) whether the War Office was going to follow the Admiralty's example and appoint 'a liaison officer to communicate with the Press'; Brade replied it had already done so, and both undertook to pass Riddell the liaison officers' details for dissemination.[58]

Although the next meeting of the Committee had not been intended until November, there was a 'hastily-summoned meeting' on 31 July 1919, attended only by Brade and Riddell, as Robbins and others were unavailable at almost no notice. Brade explained the Government intended shortly to send three or four battalions to North Russia 'to make the withdrawal [of British Forces already there] successful'. The SofS for War and Air (Churchill) asked the Press to recognise this deployment as 'just as much a military operation as any during the war and that details should be kept from the knowledge of the enemy [the Bolsheviks]'. Riddell said he did not think 'the papers would receive the proposal with much enthusiasm', but agreed they would not wish to endanger the lives of those concerned. They drafted a Notice explaining the position, covering both military and naval forces involved, and ending that 'Sir Henry Rawlinson[59] is to take charge, as it is thought desirable to send a thoroughly experienced General.'[60]

When the AWOPC convened on 28 November 1919, it included for the first time an Air Ministry representative, Sir Arthur Robinson,[61] and one from the Weekly Newspaper and Periodical Proprietors' Association, G.J. Maddick.[62] Robbins reported the results of his investigation into the origin of the D-Notice nickname, 'Parker'. The GPO's Mr Kidner[63] had explained that, when the system of advising editors through the Post Office was first set up in 1912, it had been considered undesirable to include in the telegram an en clair instruction to postmasters to communicate only with editors. A code word was therefore required, and, according to Kidner's 'recollection, the word "Parker" was selected because Mr Parke is named in the printed War Office Memorandum, dated 3rd December, 1912. After the system was adopted for the regular distribution of urgent messages of the Press Bureau, the word "Parker" continued to be used both here and at the Press Association as a convenient means of referring to the system'.[64] The meeting agreed that from July 1918 ten guineas a year should be paid to Robbins' PA confidential clerk, Mr Boulter, responsible for directing and posting all 'Parkers' issued by the Press Bureau during the War, and for keeping AWOPC past and future records.[65] Not raised, although still contentious with the Press, was the continuing government practice of placing embargoes on the date of publication of official communiqués, but these were now almost always about civil rather than military subjects.[66]

In January 1920, the CIGS (Wilson), supported by Churchill, complained vehemently about reports in several newspapers that an Army spokesman at the mid-January Military Conference [the routine Press briefing] had said there was a strong possibility of 'heavy' British military intervention in the Caucasus and Asia Minor, which was both untrue and politically embarrassing. There was disagreement between journalists present and the War Office as to whether the hapless junior officer concerned had given the qualifications in his script, which made clear it was just contingency planning for a very remote possibility. Despite much correspondence between Riddell, Churchill, the PA and the War Office, the argument ended inconclusively. It did highlight, however, a difference in understanding between Department and Press over whether what was said at the Conferences was, like the printed handouts, able to be used by the Press publicly. Such disputes, in modern parlance about what is on or off the record, about what is attributable, and about what is for the background information of the media only and not for publication, are just as common today, and are sometimes of relevance to D-Notice advice about what is or is not already in the public domain.[67]

The 14 May 1920 meeting was the first whose minutes used the revised title: 'Admiralty, War Office, Air Ministry, and Press Committee' ('AWOAMPC' hereafter in this book). The agenda and press attendance were thin – Maddick for example explaining 'he had to be at his paper mills in Lancashire that day'. Robbins read his exchange of valedictory letters with Brade, who had retired in December because of ill health. Murray, as longest serving Permanent Secretary, was now in the Chair, and present for the first time was Brade's successor, Sir Herbert Creedy.[68]

Murray explained at length the Admiralty's revised procedures 'for dealing with the Press': it no longer had a 'Publicity' Department, 'because they were anxious to get rid of that word which had a suspicious flavour about it, as if they were going to try and influence the Press in some way'. Instead, the Admiralty had centralised the arrangements for the issue of news, downgraded the head of the section to Commander's rank, and placed it under the Director of Naval Intelligence; although not said, this was in fact a reversion to similar responsibilities pre-war, and made as the Admiralty reduced its size and expenditure post-war. Murray apologised for a recent 'unfortunate breakdown of that system' over the issue of the First Lord's Statement on the Navy Estimates, which was 'due to a most unfortunate series of accidents in which quite a large number of people had not done quite what they ought to have done without anyone being seriously to blame' [again it is warming to observe continuity in British public life, in this case non-attribution of personal responsibility].

Murray explained there were two categories of interaction: when a newspaper had acquired from its own sources 'what appeared to be important and confidential naval information', it could go to the new section for advice on whether publication would be 'proper or patriotic'; and where the Admiralty needed to inform the Press confidentially of some matter which it would be 'undesirable in the public interest' to publish, it would continue to use the machinery of the AWOAMPC to do this. On the first point, Robbins enquired what kind of information should be submitted by the Press 'now that there was no longer war', and Murray gave as examples 'details of construction, designs of naval guns, ships, etc'.

Holbrook expressed complete satisfaction with the Admiralty's arrangements and hoped the War Office and Air Ministry would initiate similar schemes. The new Air Ministry representative, WF Nicholson,[69] said that under the Controller-General of Civil Aviation there was a 'so-called' Controller of Information (General Swinton, the former 'Eye-Witness'), who, like the Ministry itself, covered both civil and military matters, the former being at that time where most publicity was called for. It covered not only equipment matters but also events such as air accidents, and Nicholson thought (to Robbins' evident apprehension) that most of its work with the Press was done by telephone.[70] Creedy said 'the War Office had a sort of publicity section in the Secretary's Department . . . and he had never heard any complaints'. Holbrook also reminisced about the 'olden days' when 'it was almost a crime for an officer to communicate any information to a newspaper man', and hoped restrictions could now be relaxed so that matters reflecting well on a unit could be publicised, and that officers 'could always place reliance upon the discretion of the journalist'. Neither officials nor other Press members present appear to have supported this Elysian memory and aspiration.

On behalf of the absent Riddell and the Newspaper Conference, Robbins queried the recent discontinuance of the War Office's 'weekly military lectures'. No doubt the recent argument with the Press, referred to above, had contributed to the War Office decision, but Creedy claimed it had been made mainly because 'we are not engaged in any warlike operations', because newspapers now had correspondents on the spot where there was fighting in any part of the world, and because the lectures would therefore be out of date; but that a written 'military appreciation' would still when appropriate be issued to the Press 'as a sort of guide to them on the military expert side'. Holbrook genially summed up the meeting: 'although their business might not appear to be of very great importance that afternoon, they had got a lot of useful information.'[71]

At a fuller meeting on 26 November 1920, Edmund Robbins was too ill to attend, and was represented by his son Harry. Murray referred to the imminent issue of official papers on the Battle of Jutland, which the Press had suggested should be given to them 24 hours before publication so that editors, leader-writers and naval experts would have adequate time to consider them before publication; the Admiralty was sympathetic. Robbins pointed out 24 hours might not be long enough for the Scottish and Irish papers because of the mailing distances, and Murray agreed a 36-hour advance issue; although not mentioned in the minutes, the background to this item was the London Press having sought advantage over the provincial Press in pushing for minimal time between issue and permitted publication. Murray said he had no other matters to raise, except to forewarn that he might later have to ask for discretion over Admiralty trials of some German naval material. Creedy mentioned a new manual of Military Intelligence (including revised regulations for war correspondents) and requested advice from Press Members.

Robbins raised the treatment of representatives in Ireland by 'Forces of the Crown', citing four instances of interference with journalists and one of ill-treatment. He had written to the Chief Secretary for Ireland Sir Hamar Greenwood,[72] complaining about the beating and threatening of the Press Association correspondent. He and Riddell had agreed the liberty of the Press was of such importance that the Committee should pass a resolution urging the authorities to do all they could to protect journalists. Baird, representing Irish newspaper proprietors, thought however the authorities in Ireland were showing every consideration to the Press; what had happened to the PA correspondent was 'common to a great many people, because, in the great turmoil, the innocent suffered with the guilty. He himself had had a narrow escape of being shot. He deprecated any resolution about the military authorities, who had their hands full and were doing their best'. Duncan suggested there was a very great difference between a special representative of a newspaper/agency and a local correspondent, and thought it inadvisable to do anything, and Holbrook too was strongly against the Committee intervening. Murray summed up that the Irish Office assurances were 'perfectly satisfactory'; to call attention only to certain cases would suggest there was something in them, and official members agreed there was not enough information to do that. Without the weight of Riddell or of the also absent and combative Scott, the younger Robbins said he was satisfied 'to have ventilated the question' and the matter was dropped.[73]

The work of the Committee now entered a period where what little there was devolved on the Secretary, without the need for formal meetings. The steady beat of the bureaucratic heart continued however, and in November 1921 Creedy wrote to the Treasury to tidy up the accounting for the Committee's costs. 'I do not know whether you have ever heard of the Admiralty, War Office, Air Ministry, and Press Committee' he started, going on to explain that 'As it was desirable to keep the existence of the Committee a secret it was decided to charge the expenditure against Secret Service Votes'; these in turn were hidden in the War Office, which then recovered 50% from the Admiralty. However during the War the First Lord had objected to this, so the War Office paid all. Now it had been agreed the Committee should continue, Creedy suggested the three Service Departments should take it in turn to pay the costs, but Murray disagreed, wishing each should pay one third every year. Creedy thought this 'cumbrous', so the War Office continued to bear the whole cost.

A junior civil servant in the Cabinet Office meanwhile wrote to his opposite number in the Treasury: 'I have had some difficulty in discovering anything about this Committee . . . we should be most reluctant to assume financial responsibility for it as we have never had or are likely to have any connection with it'; which showed not only the inherent reluctance of any Department to accept an additional charge, but also an ignorance of institutional history not uncommon in any period amongst young officials (and young journalists). The Treasury therefore agreed the War Office should bear the whole cost, in practice only then about £100 per annum,[74] but that Creedy should not show this as a separate item, and instead should 'tuck away' the sum under Miscellaneous Expenditure or Sundry Charges.

The length of time since the previous meeting, and the dearth of Press Members at the 7 July 1922 AWOAMPC meeting,[75] caused Sir Oswyn Murray to emphasise that Departments considered the Committee 'should not fall into any sort of suspended animation', as it could be needed at any time. He appreciated that some Press Members had to come from a distance, but said it was very desirable that Press and officials continued to meet, if the former still wished to do so. Riddell agreed the reasons for the Committee 'still existed in full force', and grumbled he 'did not think that it was asking very much of the Press Members of the Committee to spare two hours a year for the purpose of keeping on foot such a valuable organisation as that had proved to be through the War'. It was again agreed to meet twice a year, in January and July, another resolution not destined to be sustained in the following years.

The Committee should then have discussed press comments on the revised regulations for war correspondents, but Creedy had himself been too busy to consider them; it was agreed merely that they should be recirculated and 'not passed without reference to the Press'. Discussion returned to Ireland, now partitioned. The statutory position of the Irish Free State, independent but still then part of the British Empire, was not entirely clear, and the debate within the Committee about the practicalities of the relationship with the Press in Ireland as a whole was therefore similarly confused. Riddell and Holbrook disagreed about the comparability of the Free State with the Dominions, the former pointing out the Committee's reach had not extended to the Dominions even during the War.

Murray said that there was an 'important practical point' about whether Notices should continue to be sent to newspapers in Ireland, namely that 'owing to distance and other things, the question of the Irish Free State was much more important than the question of the Dominions'. Robbins reminded that hitherto for each 'Parker' the Department concerned decided whether it should be sent out generally, or not to Irish papers at all, or just to Northern Ireland [and Great Britain] papers only; he suggested this procedure should continue. Duncan proposed leaving the decision to the next meeting 'when Ireland would be more settled'; it was decided that meanwhile no 'Parkers' should be sent to Ireland, but that an issuing Department could if so desired consult with Robbins about his sending 'a special letter to some of the North of Ireland papers'.

Finally at this meeting, Riddell mentioned some recent 'Parkers' on subjects in his view inappropriate to the Committee, which 'was intended to deal merely with warlike operations'. Duncan cited a Notice about the movements of 'a foreign Royal personage', and Creedy admitted the War Office had issued this 'to oblige Buckingham Palace'. Riddell pointed out press sensitivities, and that such Notices 'might impede the usefulness of the Committee'. This led to discussion about which Departments might now use the machinery of the Committee. Robbins mooted that the Foreign Office, for example, might on occasion wish to issue something, but Riddell, Duncan and the three Permanent Secretaries were all against such an extension of the Committee's functions, 'except by special arrangement in time of war or strained relations.'[76]

In reality, there had recently been no shortage of war and of strained relations of serious concern to the Government. In the Near East, the remains of the Ottoman Empire had continued to fracture, and Greece and Turkey were involved not only in fighting but also in large-scale and sometimes bloody transfers of population; Palestine was unstable, and in Iraq there had been insurrection against the occupying British. On 16 October 1922, the Cabinet Secretary (Hankey) met with official members of the AWOAMPC (Murray, Creedy and Nicholson) to discuss an urgent request from the CID's War Book (Near East) Sub-Committee on Censorship. This Sub-Committee had met a fortnight earlier to discuss 'the best way of ensuring that no undesirable matter is published in the Press in Great Britain', but had rejected pro tem setting up a Special Press Committee for this purpose. Instead they asked that the AWOAMPC be convened to consider this, for both 'the present time' and for 'on mobilisation', and to advise also on how this might be achieved in the foreign and colonial Press. They also asked that, at all AWOAMPC meetings, 'steps should be taken, by liaison or otherwise, to ensure that the views of other Government Departments not represented on the Committee, regarding publications in the Press, are fully considered', and that these Departments be kept fully informed of the information policy of the 'fighting Services'.

Because 'undesirable' matters were predominantly political rather than military, Hankey had however thought it unwise immediately to convene the full AWOAMPC for such a sensitive discussion, at least until he had consulted the official members. The three Permanent Secretaries reiterated the Committee dealt solely with matters of naval, military and air interest, 'such as the design of a new pattern of tank or a new aeroplane', and that such requests to the Press on grounds of public interest were 'invariably respected'. They reminded that at the July 1922 Committee meeting, the Press representatives had been strongly of the view that 'matters of political interest . . . were not within the legitimate sphere of action of the Committee'. They agreed that, had the Government wished recently to keep military information out of the Press, any requests made through the Committee would have been respected; but that if any requests concerning political information had been made, not only might they not have been respected, but the 'usefulness of the Committee' in handling future military requests might have been 'seriously impaired'.

Officials still hankered however after some organisation 'by means of which political information which might during a crisis have a deleterious effect on portions of the oversea population of the Empire could be kept out of the Press' (a particular concern of the India Office). They recommended therefore to the CID that in any future similar crisis, the Governors/High Commissioner might be invited to consider some form of local censorship; that Hankey should inform the Prime Minister's Private Secretary about the AWOAMPC, 'so as to ensure that the information given by the Secretariat to the Press was in accord with the information supplied to the Press by the Department concerned'; that the AWOAMPC should keep the Secretariat informed of any notifications to the Press and vice versa; that when in doubt about publication of matters of military importance, the Cabinet should be consulted; and that the AWOAMPC should meet at an early date 'to consider whether some method of preventing the publication of information of a political nature which might have an adverse effect on portions of the oversea population of the Empire might not be devised', along lines similar to the AWOAMPC.[77] Not surprisingly, in view of the Press representatives' known opinions on the subject, the latter point was not formally followed up.

The 9 February 1923 AWOAMPC meeting opened with tributes to Sir Edmund Robbins, who had died in December, from Murray as Chairman, and from Riddell on behalf of the Press speaking at length of his 'very close friend' and of the great amount of work that he had done for the Committee, including that 'of a more or less private character'. They immediately appointed HC Robbins as their new Secretary. Creedy thanked Press Members for their comments on the Manual of Military Intelligence, nearly all of which the War Office had been able to accept; those points outstanding had been resolved between the War Office, Robbins and Riddell the previous day, 'in a liberal and modern spirit', as the latter commented. It was agreed that the Press Members would also assist Creedy in the imminent updating of the 1914 'Regulations for Press Correspondents accompanying Forces in the Field'.

The Committee debated again whether other Government Departments might use the Committee machinery. Although still agreed generally it would be inadvisable to extend the Committee's role, on further reflection it was decided to offer coverage to the Foreign, Home, Colonial and India Offices, stating that if, 'in times of public danger and difficulty', they wished to 'issue to the Press any secret notice regarding matters of vital importance concerning the safety of the Nation, or which may involve directly or indirectly naval or military operations,[78] such a notice can be issued through this Committee. It must be sent to the Chairman, and the departments concerned must understand that any notice which is issued is sent to all papers irrespective of opinions'. Murray undertook to communicate this offer to other Departments, adding nevertheless that officials were 'anxious not to impair the authority of the Committee by issuing through it requests that might be resented by the Press'.

Nicholson raised Air Ministry concerns about 'leakage' in reports in the daily and technical Press about new types of aeroplanes and air material. Concerning Royal Air Force aircraft, there was 'considerable temptation to this, as firms were very interested in booming their own designs', particularly as certain characteristics of fighter aircraft might be suitable 'for racing also or for passenger-carrying machines', and firms wanted to 'get their wares advertised in the Press'. It was feasible to issue a Notice where only one or two new types were involved, as with ships, but he wondered whether it would be preferable to issue a longer list of a dozen or even more types of experimental equipment. Maddick, the magazine proprietors' representative, pointed out that information normally came from manufacturers; Nicholson replied that for the future 'the idea of the Air Ministry was to have an arrangement with a firm who had designed a war specification to regard it as secret while it was under trial, and even for twelve months after they had given a production order. That would enable the Air Ministry to get two or three years ahead of competitors'. It was agreed Nicholson would draft a letter to the Press accordingly for discussion with Robbins.[79]

In the days after this meeting, the three Permanent Secretaries again met Hankey, to discuss whether the offer of use of the AWOAMPC machinery by other Departments should be taken forward. They decided not to do so, ostensibly because it would risk the System being drawn into attempts to stop the publication of political information, as had happened during the War. Afterwards Hankey wrote to Murray saying he had not even put the report of their meeting formally before the CID, but he thought the reason for the decision should be recorded in the next AWOAMPC minutes. He added that it would be useful if Murray were to have informal discussion with the Press Members, to confirm that they would indeed resent any political use of the Committee, 'as it would be deplorable if anything were done to weaken your admirable organisation.'[80]

At the 12 October 1923 AWOAMPC meeting, Murray accordingly reported this decision, and that the Government 'would prefer not to make it the channel for other purposes, and they would think out some other means of dealing with those Departments' requirements'. This seems to have drawn no comment from the Press Members (Riddell, Duncan, Holbrook and Baird were all absent, although Scott was present for the first time since the War). Robbins mentioned a routine D-Notice which had been issued in August requesting non-publication of details of new capital ships; that he did so at all is an indication of how few Notices were by then being issued. Creedy spoke about the revised 'Regulations for Press Correspondents accompanying Forces in the Field', of which they already had copies. Robbins proposed a small revision of the Preface to reflect 'the spirit which existed now between the Authorities and the Press', and all was agreed.

Nicholson explained the draft letter to the Press which he had forwarded to Robbins after the last meeting, on the publication of aircraft designs. The proposal was to issue two lists every six months, one of equipment whose general design but not details might be published, and the other of designs 'which had been new recently, but which might now be referred to fully'. Anything not in either list would need to be referred to the Air Ministry. In discussion, the practical difficulties for the Press were raised: specialist correspondents obtaining information from manufacturers would send in copy to journals, where the 'ordinary subeditor' would not know whether it referred to a military or civil machine, nor even necessarily which machines would have a certain piece of equipment, and they would not have the expertise to cross-refer to the Air Ministry lists.

The Press Members wished to be helpful, but said the system proposed was too elaborate and restrictive, so could they not adopt a system of referring to the Ministry in the case of all machines which were obviously of importance? Nicholson undertook to revise the draft, to lay greater stress on the vital interests involved (the manufacturers were already 'pledged to secrecy'), on the fact that foreign countries were maintaining greater secrecy as to their methods, 'to strike the patriotic note very strongly', and to say that when in any doubt the paragraphs in question should be referred to the Air Ministry. Robbins would recirculate the draft if he thought it was necessary.[81] As they left the meeting, those there would not have known that this was the last formal meeting of the Committee which would take place for almost eleven years.

22

MIDDLE YEARS LULL

During this period, news events involving the three Services appear normally to have been handled with a notable lack of friction between the Press and officials, perhaps because there was minimal official centralisation and politicisation, allowing interaction on the spot between journalists and local authorities. Thus in January 1924, when the submarine L24 was lost with her crew off Portland, every assistance was given by local naval commanders to correspondents sent to report the disaster. And so too at the end of the following year when the submarine M1 sank; a shortage of telephones apart, the PA correspondent was well pleased with access given, even to German diving equipment onboard the search vessel. The imperial operations of the three Services were similarly reported sympathetically; Reuters was complimented on its despatch from Hong Kong on firefighting by Servicemen in a serious conflagration at a local hotel, in which Prince George played a prominent part.

In London too, relationships were unusually harmonious; when the *Daily Express* published a report in August 1924 that, because of 'trouble brewing in Romania', Beatty's Mediterranean Fleet had been ordered there from Venice, it was the Press Association which not only quickly established from its own sources that this was untrue, but also immediately published the Admiralty denial. Similarly in March 1927, when British United Press issued an entirely fictitious story about *HMS VINDICTIVE* being in action off Shanghai, Reuters was quick to scotch the story and carry the official denial, no doubt with some schadenfreude in denting the reputation of the rival agency. For the Security Service and Special Branch too, there seems to have been a good working relationship with the Press; in late 1927 the Press Association carried a scoop about 'Alleged Spying', with details of the arrest of two suspects, obtained by 'our night Scotland Yard man.'[82]

Conversely, when the Government decided very occasionally to take action against the Press, the AWOAMPC steered clear of involvement, even though several of those who did get involved were members of the Committee. For example, in March/April 1927 the Government sought to use the OSA to authorise police 'visits' to the offices of newspapers which had published leaked stories about Scotland Yard's 'Flying Squad' vehicles. A Press delegation went to see the Home Secretary, Sir William Joynson-Hicks,[83] to complain about this use of the Act; the group included Lords Riddell and Burnham, and other representatives of the NPA, NS, SDNS, and of the Press Agencies, as well as the legal adviser to the *Daily Mail*, one of the papers raided (the others being *The Times*, *Telegraph* and *Sunday News*). They reminded the Home Secretary that one of his predecessors (Simon) had given specific assurances in 1920 that the OSA would not be used in this way.

Joynson-Hicks was unrepentant, saying that in recent years only four prosecutions had been brought under this part of the Act, three of which had been against government employees; and that in this case the action had been taken in order to stop journalists bribing police officers to supply information, something on which one editor had confided he spent a four-figure sum each year. Joynson-Hicks said he thought nobody could object to the Act being used for this purpose. Later, in return for the Minister's assurance the Government would not in the future use the Act against the Press beyond such reasons, he suggested they discuss further how to stop payments being made for such information. The proprietors decided not to take up this offer; unsurprisingly such payments have continued to this day, albeit involving a very small number of police, officials and military, usually in a minor way.[84]

Officials continued in a desultory way to discuss censorship. The CID Standing Departmental Sub-Committee on Censorship (on which Swettenham sat as Director designate of the War Press Bureau) in its 2nd Annual Report (August 1926) summarised outstanding matters as incomplete allocation of wartime cable and postal interception staff, and the unresolved relationship with the Irish Free State; there was no mention whatsoever of an AWOAMPC role. A sub-sub-committee on 'the Effect of Developments in Wireless Telegraphy' recommended closing down all broadcasting stations during war in the UK and the Empire, revoking all wireless licences, and setting up an organisation to detect those who did broadcast; the Post Office minority view was that doing this would lose the Government the best means of internal 'propaganda' amongst the public, and anyway be impracticable to police amongst two million licence-holders.[85]

The low visibility of AWOAMPC work during these years,[86] and the restriction of its use almost entirely to the new technologies of the three Services, meant the Committee gradually became unknown to many officials, even to those in departments dealing with intelligence, information and the media. In September and October 1931, the *Daily Telegraph*'s Aviation Correspondent wrote articles about 'R.A.F. Bombers in Secret Test. 80 Per Cent Hits on Battleship. H.M.S. CENTURION as Target' and 'Secret Apparatus in New Method'. Other papers picked up the story and followed suit. In mid-November the *Evening Standard* gave more details, headlined 'Dropping Torpedoes and Bombs on a Scrapped Battleship. Experiments to Find Out Damage by "Hits"', and mentioned further secret trials using *HMS MARLBOROUGH*, due to take place in January.

Following these articles, the Director of Air Operations and Intelligence, Air Vice-Marshal Burnett[87] wrote a secret letter to his opposite number at the Admiralty, Rear Admiral Usborne,[88] complaining about the Press revealing 'every item of information' about the secret new equipment used, proposing concerted action on an agreed statement to foreign Naval and Air Attachés 'who inevitably, I feel, will ask questions', and suggesting the two Departments should in future concert action *before* such trials 'and enlist the help of the Press in preventing reference to details in which secrecy is desired'.

The NID staffing of this letter revealed equal ignorance of the existence and role of the AWOAMPC, but did agree the Press should be taken into Departments' confidence, although acknowledging that habitually the Admiralty would be 'averse to issue any statement about anything until so badgered by the Press that they are forced to do so'. Usborne replied to Burnett, agreeing 'the behaviour of the Press with regard to these trials is abominable, particularly the *Daily Telegraph*, whose [Aviation] Correspondent is a great nuisance, though he has his uses at times'. He agreed with Burnett's proposals, suggesting they tell the Attachés just that the matter was confidential and that they did not intend to say anything more about it, and that the Press would probably not say anything more about it either.

The file meanwhile found its way to his PUS, still Sir Oswyn Murray, who in late December reminded all of the existence of the AWOAMPC. 'It has worked well on the infrequent occasions on which it has been utilised since the War.' He criticised his own Department for not having used the Committee before the *CENTURION* trial, and suggested an internal Confidential Acquaint to Departments, reminding however that the Committee dealt only with 'questions connected in some way with our materiel. It is no use going to it to prevent publication of general matters, past or future'. The minute reached the Controller of the Navy, the Board Member responsible for equipment, who confessed that he was previously ignorant of the System, and in January (and every January thereafter in the Admiralty at least) the Confidential Acquaint was issued, reminding the staffs about the AWOAMPC and encouraging its use when appropriate.

Meanwhile, Robbins had issued a D-Notice about the *MARLBOROUGH* trial, which was respected by the Press, and Usborne had written to Burnett, sharing enlightenment about the Committee. Burnett's apparent ignorance of the system is all the more surprising, because the technical departments of the Air Ministry had become the major users of D-Notices. In this case, Burnett queried whether it was realistic to demand complete secrecy about the trial, of which unavoidably many were aware, as opposed to about the secret details of the equipment being trialled; and, justifiably miffed, he suggested that before a D-Notice about a joint trial were arranged in future, the Admiralty might consult the Air Ministry first about the wording.[89] When the wheel is rediscovered, the carthorses have to be retrained too.

In July 1932, Robbins was approached by the GPO Director of Telegraphs and Telephones about 'Parker' telegrams, 'the organization in connection with which had fallen into desuetude though still maintained by the Department' [telegrams had not been used for 10 years or so, post having been found quite adequate in peacetime]. Robbins reminded editors of the system, promised the Post Office at least 12 hours' notice before first bringing the system back into use, and consulted the Committee's Irish representative, still Sir Robert Baird in Belfast, about which Irish journals should continue on the list; Baird suggested reinstating the pre-partition-excluded *Northern Whig*, but excluding three Londonderry papers and the Nationalist daily *Irish News*. Agreed by the Permanent Secretaries, Robbins in September produced a new Provincial distribution list for emergency telegrams, which now included just 45 morning papers, 86 evening papers, and eight Sunday papers.

In mid-September 1932, the Air Ministry Permanent Secretary, now Sir Christopher Bullock,[90] wrote to Murray with a different concern. The Ministry had recently issued a pass for the Air Force Display to a 'reputable paper', whose designated correspondent turned out however to be 'suspected of being in undesirable relations with the Soviet'. Bullock had discovered that D-Notices were now distributed to about two thousand press and film addressees, and Kell had given him the MI5 view: 'There are also many other persons connected with the Press, either as journalists or printers, who are known to me as members of the Communist Party of Great Britain.' Kell suggested therefore more restricted distribution of Notices, and that he should discuss this with the three Permanent Secretaries before taking Robbins into their confidence. Their respective Directors of Intelligence requested they too might attend such a meeting, but there is no record it ever took place.

Kell's concern was not unjustified. In 1967 an American journalist found a collection of German Intelligence papers in the Washington National Archives. Among them was reference to a pre-WWII agent (Fritz Block), who allegedly used the D-Notices, acquired through an unnamed friend in Fleet Street, to list, locate and photograph classified installations in Britain.[91] Because many interwar Notices have been destroyed, it is difficult to establish precisely which were involved, and how much information thus obtained was in practice already in the public domain. 'Fortifications and ammunition depots' are mentioned, for example, but these largely dated from WWI or before and were well known; such secrecy did not become more relevant until the rapid expansion of WWII infrastructure.

Murray's reminder to his Department about the AWOAMPC had sparked the new Director of Naval Intelligence, Rear Admiral Dickens,[92] also to query what the boundary was between the Committee and his Press Section, hinting there might be a confusing overlap. A long reply in October 1932 from Murray started testily: 'I think that if you will read again the papers, which I reattach, you will see that . . .', and went on to describe the two categories of cases which might be involved: where the Department wished to take the initiative, and where the Press sought advice about information obtained from its own sources. The AWOAMPC had been set up to deal with the first, while the Department itself was supposed to have the machinery for responding to the second, and Murray quoted at length what DNI's responsibilities were. He did not see any overlap between the two, especially as the Press Section of each of the three Services had never been in a position to deal with the Press en bloc in the way in which the Committee could [broadcasting was still not covered by the Committee].[93]

Meanwhile at the Air Ministry, the Head of the Press Section had in mid-October 1932 prepared a long brief for his own Permanent Secretary, suggesting some changes. He recorded that in the 14 years since the War only 48 Notices had been issued, while the number of addressees had grown to about 1,660. He listed the current categories: Regular Notices (Quarterly Lists of new, still secret RN and RAF aircraft, engines, etc), Occasional Notices (a maximum of 3 or 4 a year, for example on the movements of aircraft to Constantinople during the Near East crisis of 1922, equipment policy outlines, guidance as to what should not be published about the air defence of Britain, restrictions on publishing certain details of aircraft for the Schneider Trophy Contests), and Joint Notices with the Admiralty (bomb trials against warships and radio-controlled aircraft tests).

The Air Ministry Press Officer recommended review of the distribution by the AWOAMPC, Departments, and Robbins (and possibly MI5), including whether Notices should be targeted according to content; and reconsideration of the position of foreign/Dominion newspapers and foreign-owned companies and subsidiaries (Press, agencies and commercial). Murray discussed this with Robbins; the Secretary's view included that 'an editor or sub-editor is in a very responsible position and had his journalistic career and reputation at stake if he acts dishonourably. Even supposing, therefore, that a man in such a position has strong anti-military or even communistic sympathies, it is probable that he will keep them in check where his professional duty is concerned'. This (by today's standards) remarkably gentlemanly view of media professional and political probity seems to have been accepted.

Murray had further discussion with his official colleagues. He reminded that the system was voluntary, and that distribution excluded those few journals which did not belong to the represented press institutions, and Irish Free State journals whom it had been decided in 1922 to omit. He supported Robbins' view that press institutions would not favour selective distribution to their members, but Robbins had agreed a reminder about security be issued. On D-Notices 'falling into the hands of Communists &c on the staffs of newspapers resulting in confidential information being conveyed instead of safeguarded', Murray agreed with Robbins that putting personal responsibility for security on an editor, irrespective of his personal politics, was the best way of safeguarding the content of the Notices. They both pointed out that omission from the distribution could result in an editor publishing something sensitive that, had he known of the restriction, he would not have published.

They concluded that in the last resort the Service Departments must decide whether the value of the scheme, in normally preventing publication of confidential information, outweighed the risk (which could never be entirely eliminated) that a 'clue' in a Notice might be put to improper use. Murray's Permanent Secretary colleagues and Kell agreed, and Robbins issued D-Notice 799 in January 1933, thanking editors for past co-operation, and asking them, in view of the 'highly confidential nature of the Notices and the great importance of the interests involved . . . to take steps to ensure that the contents are not divulged to more members of their staffs than really necessary.'[94]

Those surviving D-Notices of this period show the focus on equipment. For example, D800 (January 1933) referred to trials of 'Queen Bee' aircraft (wireless-controlled aircraft targets) on which the degree of secrecy was relaxed by the Admiralty and Air Ministry for catapulting trials in *HMS ORION* a year later; D819 (July 1934) concerned materiel for the Air Defence of the United Kingdom; there were Quarterly Notices about Service aircraft, divided into the Secret List (no mention to be made of new equipment not otherwise mentioned below), the Part Publication List (older types of aircraft and engines) and the Open List (types which could now be mentioned); in 1935 the Admiralty transferred the 2-pounder "M" pom-pom Mk VII mounting (4-barrelled) from Class A to Class B, meaning the Press could now refer to the system, albeit still not to the fire control equipment, rate of fire and calibre; and in August 1939 the Admiralty and Air Ministry had a disagreement about a contravention of D934 (the Quarterly List of the previous month) in the Society of British Aircraft Constructors newsletter, in mentioning details of the Skua's folding wings.[95]

There were occasionally other disagreements between Departments about D-Notices. The Admiralty in mid-1934 became concerned that the Canadian British United Press agency, which it believed to be a subsidiary of a foreign agency (United Press of America), was receiving D-Notices. It considered it acceptable for BUP to receive routine departmental information but not Notices, because it was 'closely connected with foreign powers'. Murray complained accordingly to Robbins, who swiftly responded that the BUP had received Notices since March 1933 at the express request of the Air Ministry. The DNI was even more offended to learn this decision had been made by a mere Air Ministry Press Officer, and without consulting its Permanent Secretary. Bullock stood by his man however, suggesting the decision should stand because the BUP was not in fact American-owned and because it had shown itself to be 'loyal'. Murray agreed, opining it was better to have the link than for BUP unwittingly to publish restricted matters. DNI (now Rear Admiral Troup[96]) grudgingly accepted this, on condition that secret information would in future be omitted from the Notices; but although Murray wrote to Bullock and Creedy accordingly, there is no indication that anything in fact changed.[97]

At this time, the use made of the D-Notice System by MI5 and MI6 was effective but infrequent. When in June 1934 the *News Chronicle* considered writing a story about the secret Agencies' interception of foreign cables,[98] Colonel Vivian (SIS)[99] initiated an 'Urgent' note to Creedy requesting him: 'at once to use the Departmental Press Committee [sic] for the purpose of calling on the 'News Chronicle' and restraining them from publishing anything on the subject, or, at least, anything undesirable. We cannot possibly say what damaging rubbish might not appear as the result of the 'News Chronicle' snooping around by themselves . . . the Departmental Press Committee is, I understand from [Brigadier] Harker [also SIS], an organisation which deals with this sort of affair in the interests of the War Office and other Armed Services Departments. Colonel Kell enlisted their assistance in preventing undesirable publicity about M.I.5's move from Cromwell Road to [a previous] Thames House'.

The AWOAMPC met on 27 July 1934, for the first time in almost 11 years. There were some new faces: James Owen,[100] for example, had long represented the southern proprietors, but was attending the first meeting in his tenure; but many of the older Members were still there, presenting a collectively venerable interface between officialdom and the Press: Murray, Creedy, Riddell (aged 69), Holbrook (aged 84), Scott, Wilson, and Robbins (Baird was absent ill).[101] Riddell opened by recalling this was the twentieth anniversary of the 1914 meeting at which Sir Graham Greene informed them 'there was a likelihood of this country being involved in war, and that the advice and assistance of the Press Members was desired in regard to the dissemination and suppression of news about naval and military movements, &c'.

Murray explained the meeting had been called at the request of officials following a *Daily Herald* article on 19 July. This not only referred to certain secret aviation experiments being conducted currently, but also described the D-Notice System. It suggested the system was 'worse than useless' because the Air Ministry circular concerned had been distributed to over 200 journals. Murray referred to previous unintentional leakages due to oversights, which had been resolved by Robbins and Riddell out of committee and apologies made, but it appeared this breach could not have been made 'without some consideration on the part of the *Daily Herald* editorial staff'. At Riddell's suggestion, Robbins had rung not the editor but the chairman, Elias, who had not previously seen the article, was displeased by it, and undertook to obtain an explanation from the acting editor.

Next day, Elias had rung back and with deep regret explained it had not been understood that the existence of D-Notices should not be mentioned, only that their contents were secret. When Robbins informed Elias the AWOAMPC was to meet to discuss the breach, he wrote to tell the Committee 'very categorically that the assurance given [that there would be no repeat of the error] would be fully carried out'. Riddell suggested, and Murray agreed, no further action by the Committee was necessary, other than impressing on the newspaper 'the serious light in which the Committee regarded the breach, not only of the honourable understanding between the three Departments and the Press, but of a legal duty'.

This led to wider discussion of the Committee's status. The sharp-eyed Scott drew attention to the labelling of the Committee in the article as 'the Admiralty, War Office, Air Ministry Press Committee', which gave the impression that the Committee was a publicity body. Riddell thought the writer was 'perhaps a boy of about fourteen when the Committee was formed and did not understand its purpose', Scott suggested it would be 'well more frequently to call attention' to the role of the Committee, and a general Notice explaining the reasons for its existence was agreed. Press members suggested Robbins should also remind how Notices should be handled in newspaper offices when received, emphasising they were for the editor personally and should be kept by him 'under lock and key'.

Particular Air Ministry concerns were raised 'in view of the rapid developments of aircraft and their equipment', and it was suggested a list be published of all Notices still in force. Riddell reminded it was not the purpose of the system to put 'fetters on the Press'; Murray agreed that, despite the case under discussion, they should recognise 'the voluntary and cordial co-operation of the Press, which alone made this system workable'. The Air Ministry had, for example, recently initiated a D-Notice[102] which had had the specific aim of accelerating, in the interests of the Press, the stages at which information of new types could be made available. It was nevertheless agreed the distribution lists should again be reviewed.

Finally, Robbins asked about the desired pattern of future meetings, several members having said they should convene more regularly. Riddell thought 'the state of Europe' might require the Committee to become more active, and suggested twice a year, but others thought that once a year was sufficient, 'unless something special occurred', and it was agreed the Committee should meet each June.[103] Once again however this good intention was not put into effect, and in practice it was again left to Robbins junior [Riddell died in December 1934], when sparked by the officials, to do the business of the Committee, as and when required, until the outbreak of the Second World War.

Meanwhile in the War Office there was concern about the Press coverage it was receiving. An internal committee was formed at the behest of the military, chaired by an Assistant Under-Secretary, with six generals and a more junior civil servant. In its (secret) January 1935 report there was agreement amongst the generals as to the problem: 'We are concerned about the present attitude of the Press towards the Army'; and about its effect on public opinion and on support in Parliament. They had taken evidence from the Air Ministry's civilian Press Officer (who unusually was himself 'a trained journalist'). The generals' recommended solution, however, namely adding such a person and a senior military officer to the War Office Information Section, caused a split report. The AUS, with the prudent agreement of his subordinate, rejected the generals' plan on the grounds of cost.[104] A constant in the Media/Defence relationship has been the view of ministers and officials that Public Relations (as it became known later, and Corporate Communications even more recently) are a political matter which should therefore be under the control of senior officials, assisted by some military to give expert Services input; the overruled preference of the military (of all colours) and of the Media, for reasons of differing but convergent interest, has been that it should be the other way round. This has sometimes complicated D-Notice activity.

Early Preparations for a Ministry of Information

The Committee of Imperial Defence was also soon to start dusting off preparations for possible further major war. The intention had existed amongst officials since before the end of WWI that, were there another such conflict, there would be tighter control from the start, building on the experience and systems ultimately developed by 1918. At the CID's 271st Meeting on 14 October 1935, it was agreed to set up a new sub-committee to study 'Plans for the Establishment of a Ministry of Information'. It was chaired by the Minister of Information (Designate), then the Parliamentary Under-Secretary of State for Scotland, Lieutenant Colonel John Colville,[105] although the designated Minister was to change many times before WWII started, when the post existed at all. The eminence of this Sub-Committee was not reflected in its eventual output.[106]

Its remit was 'To prepare plans for the establishment on the outbreak of war of a Ministry of Information, taking into consideration all forms of propaganda, including broadcasting, and the arrangements already made for censorship'. They reported first in late July 1936, and suggested the Ministry's activation should not be automatic on declaration of the Precautionary Stage provided for in the Government War Book, but should be a separate decision required of the Government of the day. They foresaw a Ministry of five Divisions, to be established in two stages, Stage 1 including the immediate formation of the News, Control (ie Censorship), and Administration Divisions, and Stage 2 the later formation of those for Publicity and for Collecting Information.

They commented on the need to involve the BBC, the Press and the Film Companies, to produce 'a system of censorship which is not unnecessarily irksome' to them. The War Office would remain responsible for the Postal and Telegraph Censorship. They suggested the early appointment of a civil servant as Deputy Director-General, and recommended Sir Stephen Tallents,[107] the BBC's then Controller (Public Relations), and that he should work to the Home Office and Director-General designate in the detailed planning, setting up the Ministry when necessary.

The Sub-Committee did much outline theoretical thinking on how things would work, going into minute detail on organograms and numbers. Other recommendations included that the Ministry should have an Advisory Council, consisting of representatives of NPA, NS, EPU, BBC, Film Industry, 'a literary publicist' and 'at least one woman of wide public experience, together with such others as experience might suggest'; that personnel requirements should be referred to the Mobilization (Civil Departments) Committee; and that the experience of survivors of the WWI Ministry of Information should be 'codified'. All these recommendations were quickly approved by the CID a few days later; but as has often to be re-learnt, unless sufficient resources and dedicated experts are allocated to wished-for action, not much happens.

Eighteen months later (late 1937), the retired officer given the part-time task of taking the Control Division action forward, Rear Admiral Dannreuther,[108] wrote plaintively to Tallents, reporting the two meetings so far had 'opened our eyes to the fact that a great deal of further preparation is required, some of which can only be done effectively by experts'. He listed some of the unknowns which needed to be clarified before he could proceed, one of which was updating the instructions issued by the WWI Press Bureau, and he asked for an additional wider sub-committee to progress the detailed work, including representatives of the Censorship Committee, the Press Officers, and the AWOAMPC.[109]

23

THINKING ABOUT WAR AGAIN

It was not only in governmental circles that further war was now once again perceived as a possibility for which contingency plans were needed. Reuters and the Press Association had in 1934 commissioned for themselves a new shared building in Fleet Street, designed by Lutyens, of which the estimated cost was exceeded more than three-fold, and occupation not achieved until just before WWII started. One major reason for overruns was the late additional requirement for air raid shelters; in January 1936 Lutyens explained that meeting this requirement in full would be too expensive. In the years following, despite financial losses suffered covering the 2nd Italo-Abyssinian and the Spanish Civil Wars,[110] the Agencies did provide the resources to protect their staff in London (at £10 per head) and at their joint service centres and Creed (teleprinter) hubs in the provinces; but in case of bomb damage they chose to use their Manchester Centre rather than provide a new Emergency Base in the London suburbs.[111]

The First Review of the D-Notice System

As the likelihood of war increased, officials did indeed return to considering the workings of the D-Notice System too in time of tension. The Service Press Officers Committee[112] was tasked to consider afresh 'the principles which should govern the preparation and distribution of D-Notices, and to make recommendations thereon'. The 'Heads for Consideration' they were given included the general principles on which distribution should be based, the position of photographic agencies and topical film companies, whether and how Notices might be Department-specific and/or general in their distribution, how to inform those newspapers not in receipt of D-Notices about their responsibilities concerning defence secrets, whether it was possible to reduce the risk of leakage through D-Notices by taking greater care in the drafting, and 'any other matters which might be germane'.

Their January 1937 Report was the first major review of the D-Notice System, and is therefore outlined here in some detail. It started by recapitulating the history and current organisation of the Committee. The Chairmanship was still held by the longest-serving Permanent Secretary (then Creedy), and the only other officials were still his opposite numbers at the Admiralty and Air Ministry. There was still one NPA representative, then Esmond Harmsworth,[113] one from the Newspaper Society, still Colonel Holbrook, two from the English regions (albeit from now differently-organised federations), one from the Period-ical, Trade Press and Weekly Newspaper Proprietors' Association, and one from the News Agencies, still HC Robbins. The latter was also still the Secretary, and the Report saw no reason for changing this arrangement, which was 'efficient, speedy, and commands the confidence of the Press' because the Notices had clearly therefore had the endorsement of the Press side of the Committee.

The arrangements for distribution of D-Notices were also considered satisfactory (i.e. by messenger within London, and by post elsewhere), as was that for telegrams. Only half-a-dozen telegrams had been sent during the past 18 months, mainly in connection with special defence measures decided on early in the Italo-Abyssinian crisis. Although these Notices have apparently not survived, they had been reinforced by diplomatic and political correspondents being summoned to discreet Whitehall briefings, where the British Government's concerns were explained; for example, they were asked not to report the overflying of Abyssinia by British aircraft during the conflict, for fear that Italian awareness this was happening would impede the delicate (and ultimately unsuccessful) British diplomatic efforts to resolve the crisis.[114]

On the preparation of Notices, the Report criticised the lack of consultation between Departments, and suggested that 'in view of the closely linked interests of the Defence Ministries today' the potential interests of other Departments should be considered, if necessary by telephone, before the Notice was sent to the Secretary. Although the Committee's Press members did not need to consider Notices before despatch 'except in the case of matters of policy involving a marked departure from existing practice', a need was highlighted for newspapers staffs to have a better understanding of the work and activities of the Committee. The postal distribution list of Notices ('largely influenced by the views of the late Lord Riddell'), had been reduced by Robbins since the 1934 AWOAMPC meeting to about 1,120. The number of Notices issued since the Press Bureau had closed in 1919 had now increased to 123, and there had been an upward trend in recent times due partly to the Italo-Abyssinian crisis and partly to 'the present armament expansion'.

The Service Press Officers Committee considered it was not possible to issue Notices meaningful to the Press without including at least some secret or confidential information, but recommended keeping this to the essential. Each Department should issue a 'general warning D.Notice, clearly outlining, in as brief a form as possible, the various questions which [it] normally desires to be treated by the Press as secret'. The Press Officers also proposed issuing a long Notice, reminding the Press of the role and procedures of the AWOAMPC. They thought this would not only provide a basis for briefing the frequently changing personnel in newspapers, but also minimise the need 'for special Notices on individual matters'.

The Report's greatest departure from existing practice was a proposal to have two categories of Notice: 'A' Notices would be those referring to questions of defence policy, including national or international emergencies, and 'B' Notices would be those referring to 'technical matters of material importance'. They thought the need for the former would be rare, but should go to all publications which dealt with 'public affairs or defence matters'. The latter kinds of Notices, they said, were already frequently used by the Admiralty and Air Ministry, while the Army had instead relied on 'other matters of preventing leakage, eg hiding a new type of tank amongst standard types'. The proposed "B" Notices should be more specifically targeted, but should still include the daily papers, the agencies 'and certain other approved journals and organisations'. The Press Officers Committee recommended it was neither advisable nor safe to eliminate any class of recipients from existing lists, but did suggest ways of reducing the numbers, the technical "B" Lists going down to between 200 and 300, thus 'materially decreasing the risk of leakage'. Those thus omitted, 'with the exception of sporting journals', should be consulted annually, reminded of their editorial responsibilities on security, and asked whether they thought they should be reinstated.

The Press Officers Committee recommended changes for 'photographic agencies and topical film companies'. Several were British subsidiaries of American companies, who received passes for 'naval cruises' and Army and Air Force events, but did not receive D-Notices; this was considered acceptable, because 'in practice effective steps are taken to guard secret matters during the visits of all photographers'. However, it was suggested that the head of these companies should in future receive "A" Notices, in return for a 'personal guarantee' from those who were foreigners not to divulge, with an understanding that facilities would be refused to firms who offended. The representatives in Britain of Indian, Dominion and Colonial newspapers should be brought into the system; on the anomalous position of Irish Free State newspapers, many of which were on sale in Britain: 'we recognise that this is primarily a political question'.

The Press Officers also wished British editors to be reminded about not disclosing the contents of D-Notices to correspondents of foreign newspapers working in their offices. They had discussed this aspect and others with the Head of News at the Foreign Office, in view of his known concern in 1935 about the leakage of the contents of certain D-Notices to Germany [the aim then was not to offend Germany by implying concern about its rearmament]; he had thought it 'impolitic, however, for the Foreign Office staff to raise with foreign correspondents the question of disclosing information respecting our confidential defence measures or of the issue or contents of Notices, partly on the ground that they should not be aware of such matters'. The Press Officers accepted this curious interpretation of the realities of foreign journalism.

The Report recommended a return to a WWI practice that the D-Notice scheme should apply to 'Books Relating to Defence'. The consultation by publishers during WWI had largely lapsed when the Press Bureau had been closed down, and they did not now receive D-Notices. It was suggested the Publishers Association should be 'advised of the existence of D.Notice procedure and the co-operation of their members sought'. If this was forthcoming, they could receive the general warning Notices. A suggestion that a similar approach might also be made to the Incorporated Society of Authors was not apparently followed up, possibly because authors are ultimately at the disposal of publishers.

On the 'Integrity of Newspaper Staffs', the Press Officers Committee noted the frequent changes of personnel in newspaper offices; they had had informal conversations with MI5, who opined that 'no satisfactory method exists for ensuring regularly that suspected persons are not employed in British newspaper offices which receive D.Notices', although it did offer to check the integrity of personal recipients on the lists [integrity in a security sense only we must assume]. The Press Officers considered the position of sub-editors was just as important, and that each editor should therefore ensure these were briefed about the system and were 'loyal and trustworthy', and that sub-editors could then 'assist materially in preventing leakage by questioning and stopping reports which are contrary to official requests'.

The Report also referred to journalists' organisations, in particular recalling that, at the last Annual Delegate meeting of the NUJ (then having about 6,000 members), there had been discussion about D-Notices (although not mentioned by name) prohibiting the publication of political or semi-political information on an international emergency. The Press Officers suggested the principal officers of that Union and the IoJ should be 'confidentially advised' about the System, so that they understood it would not be used for this purpose, because otherwise 'serious harm may well result to the work of the Committee'. On trades union journals, particularly those whose members were employed in the armaments industry, they recommended their publications 'should be carefully examined for a time to ascertain whether there is any marked tendency to publish matter of a confidential nature'.

Turning next to nomenclature, their Report suggested the chance WWI Press Bureau designation of security-related Notices as the 'D' Series should be turned to advantage ('it might have a useful psychological effect amongst newspaper staffs') by associating the 'D' in future with 'Defence' and referring to them as 'Defence Notices'. On retention of Notices in newspaper and other offices, the Press Officers recommended the issue of a 'loose-leaf portfolio of foolscap size', the burning of Notices with no 'permanent value', and the issue of a list of extant Notices every January and July. They also recommended that similar steps be taken to keep officials up to date about the system, but that the editors of In-Service journals need not receive Notices since they were already subject to sufficient regulation.

Finally, the Report dealt with the preparation of a 'Manual of Press Instructions for Use on Outbreak of War'. It assumed that, although the Government had decided a Ministry of Information would be established on the outbreak of war, this new Department would wish to continue to use D-Notices as the means of communicating with the Press. It suggested it would be highly desirable to have ready a Manual containing 'the various points relating to defence and other matters on which it will be essential to request the Press to maintain full or partial secrecy or reticence from the outset of hostilities'. This would draw on the Great War experience and would complement the rules for the guidance of censors. Notices on matters not covered in the Manual would still be required, but its advance preparation would 'add materially to the efficiency of the censorship'.

They referred to 'secret documents courteously placed in our hands by the Home Office', which revealed that during the latter half of WWI, because of the number of D-Notices by then issued, it had become necessary to incorporate the essential matter in a pamphlet (revised several times) entitled 'Official Press Bureau Instructions'. They suggested that, after consultation with the Press members of the AWOAMPC, yet another sub-committee of the CID should be set up to draft such a Manual.[115] The Press Officers of the Admiralty, War Office and Air Ministry ended by saying that they had benefited so greatly from the [clearly non-habitual] contact necessitated by this work that perhaps their Committee ought to be maintained in existence 'for general purposes'.

The AWOAMPC was subsequently shown an expurgated version of the Press Officers' Report, but apparently did not convene to discuss it. In June 1938, the Permanent Secretaries of the Defence Departments met with Captain Guy Liddell[116] of the Security Service to discuss the recommendations. The latter still had reservations about the amount of sensitive information included in D-Notices, about the size of the distribution list, and about the potential access which this gave to foreigners and those of suspect loyalty in newspaper offices. He suggested the Notices should therefore be abolished, and replaced by a general list of sensitive topics on which the Press should seek advice. After mulling over this suggestion for a month, Creedy informed his colleagues that Notices would continue, but that he would talk to Jones about security at Reuters (a particular concern of Liddell's), that less sensitive detail would however be included in Notices, and that they would in future be addressed to editors by name. This compromise lasted, partially implemented, until the start of WWII.[117]

Slow Progress on the Ministry of Information

In mid-May 1938, the CID's Ministry of Information Sub-Committee met to consider its First Annual Report.[118] Colville was still in the Chair, and Tallents was now present too. Some progress had been made on consultation, Tallents having recently been authorised to take selected AWOAMPC Press representatives into his confidence; and on responsibilities, in particular that the Ministry of Information should take over from the Postmaster-General the control of the BBC. The Sub-Committee also anticipated that, in time of war, the BBC's Board of Governors 'might go out of commission since, for one reason, the members would be anxious to take up other work more immediately concerned with the nation's war effort' [that might not have been so tactfully put in modern times].

A major delay on the BBC's wartime role, however, was the lack of a Cabinet decision on whether broadcasting would continue at all; the Corporation, the Air Ministry and the CID Sub-Committee on the Control of Radio Transmission were deadlocked over whether radio and particularly television emissions could be used by German aircraft to home in on strategic targets in UK. Tallents had also inserted a strongly-worded warning in the Report: 'The foregoing . . . must not, however, disguise the fact that no such 'blue print' of a Ministry has yet been produced as would enable even those three of its Divisions which would be required immediately, to spring into existence . . . an examination of . . . the developments that have taken place since 1918 in physical methods of communication and in the employment of mass propaganda, suggests that in any future war on a large scale the efficient conduct of those activities for which the Ministry of Information is designed might prove to be scarcely less important than those of the fighting services.' He contrasted the large amount of expert work by then being done in the Defence Departments with the handful of part-timers employed on planning his Ministry.

Progress continued to be patchy. Tallents did have discussions with some members of the AWOAMPC, and a designate Press Advisory Council was nominated. It was agreed the BBC should retain as much independence as was 'compatible' with the needs of wartime censorship, and that Tallents should be given the authority to plan a nucleus staff of the dormant Ministry (but only for the Control Division).[119] Civil servants in the Home Office debated with each other whether to include, as an Appendix to Tallents' revised draft Press Instructions, the proposed new DoRA Instructions 12 (Safeguarding Information) and 38 (Propaganda). They noted this would be the first time that anyone outside Government Service had seen the Regulations (they had even been refused recently to MPs on the Evacuation Committee); they thought that, although it would be 'safe' to do so, it would be inadvisable 'as a matter of expediency. The Regulations are drastic, and . . . to let them [newspapermen] have them now would probably result in their making attempts to have them whittled down – especially in view of the present agitation for an amendment to the Official Secrets Acts.'[120]

24

RETURN TOWARDS A WAR
FOOTING

On 5 September 1938, in the midst of the crisis caused by the German threat to Czechoslovakia, a press delegation led by Colonel Lawson[121] of the NPA called on the Home Secretary (Hoare) to discuss 'War Preparations'. They talked in particular about 'the production of newspapers under air raid conditions', and mooted that in such an emergency there might be only partial or perhaps no use of the wireless for news distribution [a piece of special pleading which future events proved to be entirely wrong]. The Government-assisted rustication of the Press from central London was also raised as a matter for further study. This meeting was followed up by a written request that the Government make a public statement that it was essential the Press should continue to function fully in War, that a senior official should be appointed to ensure raw materials, utilities, staff and communications necessary for this, and that the system for censorship and information should be promulgated (they were aware that the undisclosed, dormant and skeletal Ministry of Information had been stood to during the current crisis). The Home Office replied at the end of September, 'now that the crisis has passed', that they would pursue these matters, albeit with less urgency.

In Parliament, the recent crisis led on 7 December to a debate on censorship and restrictions on liberty. Geoffrey Mander[122] put down a Motion that 'This House would greatly deplore any form of political censorship', referring to traditions of free speech. He criticised Ministers for giving secret interviews to some amenable newspapers, and for putting pressure on film censors. There were strong views on both sides of the debate, with some MPs defending the OSA and praising its recent amendments; the Motion was ultimately passed but only after amending it to end 'but is fully satisfied that His Majesty's Government have maintained these traditions unimpaired.'[123]

Desultory Diligence

Also after the crisis, Tallents reported again on the incipient Ministry of Information,[124] this time in response to a wider CID request to all Departments to review and report 'defects' revealed in measures taken during the crisis. Enough progress had been made at least to activate many of the Stage 1 measures when called on to do so by a Council of Ministers on 26 September. Office accommodation in the Board of Education building had been cleared that night, the teleprinters, telephones and 40 kiosks for the Press (provisionally ordered a fortnight before) had been delivered promptly by the Post Office, the AWOAMPC Secretary had provided back-up and expertise on D-Notices, and some of its Press members had been available as advisors, as had ad hoc interpreters and other improvised staff; the temporarily redundant HM Inspectors of Schools had been co-opted as emergency censors. Nevertheless, this ad hoc, partial and not in the event used activation had also revealed significant shortcomings.

Tallents' recommendations included that at least some of the Publicity and Collecting Divisions needed to be there at the start, not in Stage 2; the Ministry's existence (which was now de facto widely known to the Press and others) should be officially announced so that better planning with outsiders could take place; funds for adequate staff should be found, and the nucleus should be available during the days before a decision on peace or war was made; more accommodation was needed for the media; the circumstances in which compulsory censorship might be ordered should be defined; foreign affairs censorship/ announcements should be handled through the Ministry of Information not separately by the Foreign Office; a decision should be made whether information about parliamentary proceedings was to be handled by the Ministry; definition should be approved of the relationship between the Ministry and the BBC (who were to have an embedded censorship team for programme monitoring but refer policy to the Minister); the needs of Departments for monitoring by the BBC of foreign broadcasts should be ascertained; and the decision to discontinue completely radio-telephony to overseas during war should be modified to allow, for example, American and Commonwealth broadcasters to continue to do so (there had been evidence that during the crisis American journalists broadcasting from London had had a significant impact in moving American public opinion towards a less neutral view).

When the Sub-Committee met to discuss this detailed but crisply-written Report in mid-December 1938, the Treasury's Permanent Secretary, Sir Horace Wilson,[125] was in the Chair, and three other Treasury knights accompanied him. Such a strong Treasury team could only mean one thing, and indeed Tallents found many of his recommendations had already been quashed by them. It was 'a matter of principle' for them to turn down the Ministry of Information planning nucleus rather than each Department being responsible for working out 'publicity and Press requirements' in the period before and immediately after the outbreak of hostilities. They 'had doubts about its wisdom' on a (separate) nucleus Ministry of Information staff being in position in the critical period before hostilities, even though Tallents argued that the lack of it would alter the whole basis of setting up the Ministry and quoted the recent crisis experience; their response was that, although that might have been the case in September, 'as it had now been decided that all Departmental war preparations were to be carried out by the Department concerned, the position would be different should the occasion recur'. The Treasury 'was in favour of letting existing Departments function until it became clear where the Ministry would function under war conditions'. Tallents pointed out that the plan called for some staff to transfer from existing Departments from the start of the activation; the Treasury knights doubted this would be necessary in practice.

Tallents explained again the advantages of making a public announcement about the plans for the Ministry, especially as a description had already appeared in the *World's Press News* and the *New York Times* on 6 and 7 October. The Treasury opposed this as contrary to public policy, liable to lead to questions about propaganda in enemy countries, and putting the Prime Minister in the embarrassing position of having to answer questions about the Ministry of Information in the House of Commons. No financial provision had been made so far for the electronic systems needed by the Ministry; the Treasury would 'keep this requirement in mind'. Minor matters were then agreed, at least for further study, including that films too should be treated under a voluntary censorship scheme, and that foreign affairs should be treated the same way as other information, i.e. through the Ministry of Information (MoI);

the FO Permanent Secretary Vansittart had sent a Deputy to the meeting, who had to acknowledge that during the crisis there had been some dissatisfaction with the Foreign Office's performance.

There was also inconclusive discussion about how best to deliver propaganda to enemy countries, assuming that radio broadcasts would not reach the populations; the Air Ministry and the Foreign Office representatives disagreed as to whether leaflets which were to be dropped from the air could be produced quickly enough if the latter had not already prepared them in a running draft; there were hints that the Secret Intelligence Service was investigating alternative means of delivery; a sub-sub-committee was set up to study this further.[126]

The victim of a classic stitch-up, Tallents must have left this meeting a perplexed man. A week later, having received the draft minutes, he wrote a personal letter from his office in Broadcasting House to the Treasury PUS. 'I feel that I should put certain points on record ... I know you will not mistake the spirit in which it is written.' He argued that those planning the MoI had been working on the assumption that war, 'if it came, would be against at least one totalitarian state, i.e. against a state which, by possession of a fully equipped Ministry of Propaganda, developed in peace but organised ready for war, would enter a war against us with a long start in preparedness. In that respect we should begin with a serious mechanical handicap. On the other hand, the weapon of 'information', we felt, was one which this country could employ with a notable intrinsic advantage, since it would be largely a one-sided weapon'. He enlarged on the benefits of this contrast in being able to 'make a powerful impression on the minds of other nations' and thus 'exploit the intrinsic advantage'.

He explained that the plans and his recommendations were based on this assumption, but that there was 'very little of the expertise required to be found in the Government Service, and the mere herding together of a number of scattered schemes will never produce an efficient Ministry of Information'. He criticised the decisions of the previous week's meeting, in this respect and on those of leaving matters to individual Departments. 'They tend to delay, rather than to advance, the first stage of the Ministry's establishment.' He summarised the need for 'the weapon of "information"' to be used by any British Government at home and abroad 'by every channel of modern communication that war may leave available or wartime ingenuity devise'. He ended: 'The lessons of last September, my knowledge of the specialised ability which is to be found outside the Government service, and the work which I have put in on the plans for this Ministry, convince me that some of the decisions taken last week will make it impossible for such a machine to be available if war should come.'[127]

The Treasury did indeed receive this letter 'in the spirit in which it [was] written'. Such disagreement with the collective received wisdom of senior officials could not be tolerated, and Tallents was immediately replaced as Director-General (designate) by one of the Treasury's own, the Public Trustee Sir Ernest Fass.[128] The word was put around officially that this was because the BBC were reluctant to let their Controller (PR) continue indefinitely to give his services to the Government in this appointment, and that anyway Tallents, 'despite his great abilities, ... is inclined to get across certain of the people, including the Foreign Office.'[129] News of this change did not in fact immediately reach the media, nor did anything else concerning the Ministry with which they would have to deal when war came later that year.

In early March 1939, the Treasury knights saw the Home Secretary (still Hoare) to discuss both the Ministry of Information and also the arrangements for helping the Press prepare for war. Hoare told them the Prime Minister had decided not to appoint a Minister of Information (designate) for the time being, and had asked the Home Secretary to be responsible meanwhile.

On the Press, Hoare reported the proprietors' feeling that they lacked one person responsible for war planning with whom they could negotiate. The Government realised it could not ignore this dissatisfaction. 'The newspaper industry stands on a different footing from other industries, because it can cause so much trouble if it has any sense of grievance, and it was thought desirable to make special arrangements for helping the newspaper industry.'[130]

The follow-up meeting between the Home Secretary and the Press was held later that month, the latter led by the NPA Chairman Esmond Harmsworth himself. Hoare explained his responsibility for the again dormant Ministry, and its role. The Press would only be moved from central London if the Government so moved, and would be provided with adjacent facilities. The Press delegation explained they had started to stockpile supplies and to negotiate with the Ministry of Labour about exemptions from conscription for editorial and other staff, such as van drivers and packers, but they complained about the lack of war planning by Government Departments. It was agreed to continue discussion with the Home Office, using the AWOAMPC as the conduit for circulating discreet information about press aspects, because 'it is the general experience that those D-Notices are respected'.

The Government did make an announcement about the essential nature of the Press, but at a meeting of the Newspaper and Periodical Emergency Council in late May it was reported that 'although the Heads of Departments did take note of the speech [by Hoare] and in some cases said the newspapers must have priority, in other cases it seems to have been completely valueless'. Some progress was made in allocating fuel and reserved occupation status, but civil servants had more difficulty in allocating less obvious priorities, for example on the supply of 'carbon black' used in both newspaper printing and also in the Army's 'motor tyres.'[131]

In early April 1939, the D-Notice system became embroiled in a political fracas. A group of journalists had been invited onboard the aircraft carrier *HMS ARK ROYAL* in Portsmouth for a film evening. This was intended merely to publicise the work of the RN Film Corporation, the charity which enabled ships' companies to view films when away at sea, a brainchild of Captain Lord Louis Mountbatten,[132] who was there, as was the First Lord of the Admiralty, Lord Stanhope.[133] The latter, known as a normally unstimulating speaker, made the introductory address, but ad-libbed at the end: 'Unfortunately, there are others who are not with us tonight, because shortly before I left the Admiralty, it became necessary to give orders to man the anti-aircraft guns of the Fleet.' This was a dramatic statement, made at a time when the situation in Europe was highly tense and the Government was making every effort to avoid doing anything which might increase tension. The PA reporter there managed to find an unengaged shore telephone line and to file the story, which Mountbatten confirmed the Minister had no objection to being published.

After the George Formby film, the PA reporter also managed to speak to the Minister, who confirmed his words, explaining he wanted to show the Royal Navy was always on the alert. As these additional words were phoned through to the Press Association, it was told that the Admiralty, on instructions from the Prime Minister (Neville Chamberlain), had issued a D-Notice asking the media not to publish the Minister's words about the Fleet stand-to, on grounds of national security. However, the Press Association had to explain to the Admiralty that by then it was too late – the story had already gone out. Nevertheless, except the *Daily Sketch*, all newspapers initially withdrew the story from subsequent editions as soon as they received the D-Notice.

Questioned next day in the House of Commons about the reason for the issue of the D-Notice, Chamberlain replied: 'It was because I thought the words as reported would give a wrong impression', an explanation seen as implying the PA had misreported what Stanhope had said. The furious Editor-in-Chief of the Press Association, Henry Martin,[134] issued a detailed account of the background to the story, repeated by most papers next day. The *Daily Mail* also published an explanation of the self-censorship system, and of D-Notices ('It is desirable that the public should understand clearly the exact nature of a "D" Notice'). It also explained that the full story was now published because the Admiralty and Air Ministry had both confirmed that no special anti-aircraft precautions were in fact in place. The Press more generally now angrily made it clear the Prime Minister's attempt to use a D-Notice for political purposes was wrong.

In a Commons adjournment debate on 6 April, Chamberlain faced further criticism about misuse of the D-Notice System. Dingle Foot[135] complained such use of a Notice other than for reasons of national security was near censorship, and would lead the Press in future to ignore D-Notices. Arthur Henderson[136] suggested it would give 'our friends in the United States' the impression the UK Press was under government control, and complained of other recent misuses of the system for political purposes, for example during the Hoare-Laval plan affair,[137] and on another occasion when publication of troop movements from Lichfield to London was first suppressed, and then announced at 'a City luncheon'. Other Members however reminded that there was an equal responsibility on the Press not to publish tendentious headlines and articles. William Gallacher[138] asked if the Notice had been sent to the *Daily Worker*, adding that that newspaper would 'never under any circumstances accept such an instruction' [which was one reason why it did not then receive Notices].

Chamberlain expressed regret about the incident, said he had not ordered use of a D-Notice per se, agreed they were intended for 'matters of secrecy in connection with military or arms questions', and claimed that by 'as reported' he had meant as reported to him at the Foreign Office dinner he was attending when he heard the news of Stanhope's words, not 'as reported by the reporter'. He reminded the House that 'we are in a condition of affairs where a certain tension does exist', and explained he had been trying to prevent the public thinking some surprise attack was expected. Few in Parliament or Press were convinced. It was a reminder of another perpetual truth: attempted direct use by politicians of the delicately-balanced machinery of the D-Notice System involves dangers, for them as much as for the Press. The Stanhope affair also had one other significance: media coverage, including reports of the parliamentary debates, was the most detailed and high visibility public allusion to the D-Notice System since its inception.[139]

Four days later, D-Notices were again in the news. The War Office requested a Notice about the manning of Malta's coastal and air defences, and then had to withdraw it when it realised the news had already been issued openly in Malta and promulgated worldwide. On 18 April Mander asked in the House of Commons about this, and next day about the Stanhope affair and the number of D-Notices recently issued, to which the Prime Minister replied there had been 28 in the previous six months, none of which had been disregarded by the Press 'though in a few cases it has been inadvertently overlooked. (Laughter)'.

Another indication of the edginess of the time was the thrust of a talk given by the War Office's Public Relations Officer, General Beith,[140] to the Institute of Journalists. While mainly about the Army's relationship with the Press in WWI [with an eye on an imminent WWII], he digressed to talk at some length about the D-Notice System. He emphasised its voluntary nature, reassured disregard of a Notice would not bring about prosecution under the OSA, and said that in his experience where one had been partially disregarded it had been because the editor had felt that 'a Departmental indiscretion', rather than the public interest, was involved. 'The main principle stands, and must stand, unshaken. Complete frankness on the one side; loyal discretion on the other; and mutual co-operation in the great and almost sacred task of educating and steadying public opinion, especially in times of national stress or crisis.'[141] In very broad moral theory, that is indeed how it has been over the years; in practice both sides have been more venal.

Later that month news broke about the changes in the planning for the Ministry of Information. The front page of the *World's Press News* of 20 April 1939 led with 'Information Ministry: Startling News'. It revealed 'drastic changes' which 'illustrate vividly the extraordinary attitude of the average Whitehall mind where matters of propaganda are concerned' [the term propaganda did not then have quite the same exclusive connotations of 'spin' directed at a hostile group as it does now, but more one of official information, although this often was and is the same thing]. It reported that the Information Minister designated the previous September, Lord Stanhope ('hero of the "D" Notice comedy of a fortnight ago') was no longer acting in that role, and that Tallents had been replaced by Cass, who – 'as shown in "Who's Who" – gives no indication of any experience or particular ability in matters of propaganda'. The article pointed out that recent events indicated that such a Ministry might not be far from activation, and that it would therefore be no surprise if the Government took the step of doing so. 'Did the Government seek the advice and comment of responsible Press quarters before making this [Fass] appointment? Or is it yet another example of the type of outlook which has made certain Whitehall departments the despair of every newspaperman?'

Following this, the AWOAMPC met for the first time for almost five years on 19 May 1939. Creedy was elected Chairman in place of Murray, who had died in July 1936; survivors included JR Scott and Colonel Holbrook (now aged 89) from the provincial Press, and HC Robbins as the Secretary and as the Agencies' representative. Newcomers included Sir Arthur Street[142] from the Air Ministry, and Harmsworth from the NPA. Because of the number of changes and the de facto reorganisation of the provincial Press institutions, Robbins suggested that Press representation on the Committee should be reconsidered. After 'brief discussion' it was agreed that it should in future be two each from the NPA and NS, and one each from the SDNS, the PTPWNPA, and the News Agencies.

Discussing the Stanhope Affair, it was explained that 'the Officials of the Admiralty who knew the purpose of the D.Notice system were not immediately available when reports of the speech reached London – otherwise . . . the trouble would not have arisen'. The Press pointed out the impossible position in which they had been placed in having to suppress a speech which had already been 'circulated to the Press of the World, as well as broadcast in the [BBC] Empire Bulletin' [the first allusion in the Committee to the impact of broadcasting]. The Committee noted, without recorded comment, the explanations given by the Prime Minister in the House and his expressions of regret at the D-Notice machinery having been misused.

Robbins then reminded the Committee that, in the event of War, the shadow Ministry of Information would come into 'active existence' and take over the work of the AWOAMPC, 'the latter, presumably, remaining in a state of suspended animation throughout the period of conflict'. Tallents, before he had been replaced as Deputy Director-General (designate), had appointed a Press Advisory Council, and during the crisis of the previous year had asked Robbins to assist one of the Ministry's committees with information on distribution to the Press 'if war had then resulted'. Colonel Lawson complained that no progress appeared to have been made with the Press Advisory Council since the previous September's crisis, that

Fass too had now 'severed his connection' with the Ministry, and nobody seemed to know who had taken his place or what was happening. Others agreed with him the whole thing needed to be speeded up, and that the Press Members of the AWOAMPC ought to be incorporated in the Press Advisory Council. The Official Members undertook to represent these views 'in the proper quarter'.

The Press Officers of the three Defence Departments then joined the meeting to discuss the recommendations of their January 1937 Report on the D-Notice System. The AWOAMPC agreed Official Members would approach the Dominions Office about the possibility of requesting journals of those countries not to publish certain information 'contrary to National interests' [not apparently each Dominion's interests, and seemingly no similar approach was to be made on India or the Colonies]. Lawson said foreign correspondents working in the offices of British newspapers would not see D-Notices 'unless they were left lying about', and that there was no need therefore to write to editors about this. Scott and Lawson 'thought it would be better not' to bring the D-Notice System to the attention of publishers and authors, and the Committee 'resolved to take no action'.

On informing the IoJ and NUJ about the workings of the System 'so as to secure their goodwill', Scott felt many of their members would already be conversant with it, and Lawson and Marshall cautioned against doing anything 'that might detract from the responsibility of the Editor'; it was agreed not to adopt the idea. It was also decided Notices should continue to be called D-Notices not Defence Notices (except [for reasons not explained] by the Ministry of Information when in existence), and that the proposed two lists of addressees (for general and for departmental technical Notices) would be adopted.[143] On a separate procedural point, Creedy mentioned he was due to retire in October, and that the three Permanent Secretaries had agreed they would replace the custom of the longest-serving taking the Chair by, instead, its rotation between Departments; the Air Ministry would therefore then for the first time provide the Chairman [because of AWOAMPC suspension during the War, Street did not become Chairman until, briefly, 1945].

Finally the letter to be sent to editors 'explaining the objects of the Committee' was discussed. Lawson suggested it should start by reiterating that Notices were issued for the guidance of editors, and that even though they had no legal authority and depended on the voluntary co-operation of the Press, 'that very fact should make the system thoroughly effective'. Other points of detail were sent for redraft by officials and further discussion in Committee before circulation by Robbins to the Press. This led to Robbins again raising the frequency of meetings, and once more the AWOAMPC resolved to meet regularly, this time once a year in May 'as well as whenever thought advisable' by either side of the Committee. But once again resolve was to be edged aside by more pressing matters, this time the resurgent crisis in Europe.

On 31 August 1939 there was a short and unminuted AWOAMPC meeting, attended by a Ministry of Information representative, at which the arrangements for accreditation were discussed. In addition to BBC correspondents, up to 19 journalists would initially be attached to the Army and Air Force in each theatre overseas, to be selected by the NPA and NS, to be controlled by the new Ministry, and the selections approved by the two Departments. The licensed journalists would conform with the 'Regulations for Press Correspondents Accompanying Forces in the Field'. Occasional arrangements for visits overseas would be made for (unlicensed) 'technical correspondents', and the Ministry of Information would make similar arrangements for the Dominion, Colonial, Indian and Foreign Press. All photographs of overseas operations would be provided by Ministry of Information employees, who would be selected in consultation with the Press. The Admiralty would arrange 'periodical visits' to certain Naval Commands, and the War Office would do so for its Commands at home. The Air Force's plans for information on operations carried out from home air stations would follow. Two days later Robbins accordingly issued D-Notice 940 to the Press, 'which is highly secret and is *not* for publication', giving editors early warning of what was intended, subject to ministerial approval.

An indication of the relative 'desuetude' of the system between the Wars is the scribble on the Reuters copy of this Notice by its Managing Director: 'Who *are* the *Press* members of the Comte [sic]? Who represents Reuters on it?' To which the Secretary of Reuters, after three days' research, replied that his opposite number at the NPA was 'not very clear on the subject' [and he was certainly not accurate on the names of the NPA and NS representatives], that he 'rather thought that Robbins represented the Agencies', that he would check with the current Press Association Manager, and let the PA know that 'we are taking an interest in the Committee'.

Thus ended the strangely mixed interwar period for the Admiralty, War Office, Air Ministry, and Press Committee. It had been a period of transition, during which its principles had been re-established after WWI and maintained, it had been useful albeit normally in a narrowly technological field, and its limited use had reflected the confused tenor of the times. Nevertheless, when the spotlight did occasionally shine in its direction, the common feeling of both the Press and the Government sides was that the System had a place, and that its voluntary, non-statutory and informal nature was worth upholding. It also continued to provide a semi-formal forum in which senior officials and leading representatives of the Press could discuss concerns frankly when required.

The August 1939 meeting of the AWOAMPC was the last until after WWII. Following six years of total war, it re-emerged into a rather different environment. Nevertheless a spectral thread of continuity stretched through the first half of the twentieth century, in several respects: in the principles of voluntary co-operation and self-censorship, however diffused they had been by the light airs of peacetime neglect, and however buffeted they then were by the strong winds of wartime Government compulsion; in the continued issue of D-Notices; in the eternal tensions between Government and Press; and in the presence at either end of and during WWII of some of the same participants in the peacetime system, both Press and official.

Section 5

WORLD WAR II
Suspended Animation, 1939–45

25

THE PRESS AND CENSORSHIP BUREAU

The AWOAMPC having been suspended during WWII, this section has no Committee activity to cover, nor does it attempt to summarise events referred to in D-Notices issued by the Ministry of Information. It does however allude briefly to those aspects of wartime activity, regulations, procedures, developments and personalities, which are relevant to the work and ethos of the Committee before and after the War. Censorship categories covered in Britain's last major conventional war are outlined in Appendix 2;[1] those WWII Notices connected with the military and with secret intelligence are similar in coverage to Notices used since then in smaller wars and other operations covered by D-Notices.

Security Context

The Secret Intelligence and Security Services were greatly expanded and further institutionalised during WWII. Despite some shortcomings, both achieved successes under their new Heads, respectively Sir Stewart Menzies[2] and Sir David Petrie.[3] Scientific Intelligence achieved, for six years at least, the prominence it deserves with Reginald Jones (Air Ministry) becoming the SIS Scientific Adviser; on joining he was given its files to read, and later commented: 'These were not inspiring, for they were very weak on matters concerning science and technology, since (in common with most Ministers of the Crown and their Permanent Secretaries) the average SIS agent was a scientific analphabet.'[4] Several new organisations were formed, including the Special Operations Executive (principally to support resistance movements in Europe); MI9 (to aid escape and evasion of Allied servicemen in occupied countries); and the Armed Services Special Forces (to operate behind enemy lines). The Whitehall Committee system was expanded under the War Cabinet to provide co-ordination of other secret activities, for example Home Security. Some of these were publicly known, and therefore covered to a small degree in the Media. Others were not mentioned publicly.

One in particular was known only to those directly involved with its operation and, at very senior level, with its product, namely the GC&CS at Bletchley Park,[5] its many home and worldwide listening stations, and 'Y' stations of the three Services. Their now best-known achievements were breaking the Enigma machine codes (with initial leads from the Poles and French, and subsequently from the Royal Navy, which captured code documentation from several German submarines/ships), and the Lorenz codes used by Hitler and his senior military. The world's first significant computer, Colossus, was developed there.

Commander Denniston had begun to recruit outstanding mathematicians to his staff before the War began, having realised that the future success of code-breaking depended on machines being available to help the human mind. In 1942 the GC&CS was divided between Civil, under Denniston, and Service, under Commander EWH Travis,[6] and in early 1942 a new department dealing with communications security was established. The Bletchley product, crucial to eventual Allied success, was distributed to military and civilian intelligence officers throughout every theatre, but even most senior formation commanders did not know its provenance. That this secret was so well and universally guarded, even for about thirty years after the War ended, without the intervention of the Censor being needed, is one of the more remarkable aspects of WWII.

Media Context

The media were affected by the War in similar ways to during WWI, but more immediately and more widely. Call-up of staff for the Services started more rapidly;[7] extra wartime financial charges by Agencies to the Press were higher, reflecting the larger number of correspondents involved; contingency planning with the Post Office was more necessary (for example to use smaller exchanges if the London Central Telephone Exchange was disrupted by bombing); the increasing demands of the BBC were a new element both of competition and of co-operation with the Press; the system for reporting air raids was more widespread because of the greater Luftwaffe range/sophistication; war was more "total" and involved the civil population more widely in the dangers and the defences – the Press Association stored Home Guard boxes of ammunition on its premises,[8] and the NPA offices in Bouverie Street were destroyed in September 1940.

An early Ministry of Information decision in 1939 was to continue Reuters' secret subsidy, because 'a world service of news, collected and edited in this country, was a very important British interest for all purposes of overseas publicity', and because it saw no easy alternative way of discreetly achieving this.[9] In the militarily dark early war years, the Government's now increased secret subsidy became briefly of major concern to Press and Government. An August 1939 private letter referring to the subsidy, to the Reuters Chairman Sir Roderick Jones from Lord Perth[10] as briefly one of the succession of Ministers of Information Designate, came to the attention of the hitherto unaware Reuters Board members. Jones tried to pretend the deal had never been finalised; when challenged by one of his non-executive Directors William Haley,[11] he effectively admitted the deception and had to resign, the reasons being unspecified publicly. Media antipathy included concern about the degree to which subsidy facilitated governmental control over what Reuters disseminated.

Jones' resignation in turn led to an acrimonious tussle between the NPA and the provincial Press over ownership of Reuters, the former now demanding a half share, and many of the latter fearing this would give the NPA an unfair advantage in use of the Agency. Beaverbrook, previously against the NPA having a share, now joined Northcliffe in driving a deal through. The Government was inevitably drawn in, causing a debate in the House of Commons on 22 October 1941. Churchill's new Minister of Information Brendan Bracken[12] scorned nationalising Reuters, but, conscious it had been losing ground to the American Associated Press, later helped broker an agreement which provided a non-profit-making Trust, with equal ownership shares for NPA and NS, but with a non-Press independent Chairman to be nominated by the Lord Chief Justice.[13] Even so, in 1942 Haley had to make a long visit to the USA to reassure unsubsidised American Agencies that Reuters' subsidies were limited in scope and decreasing.

170

Other initiatives were necessary to compete with the major American agencies, able until the USA entered the war in December 1941 to file directly from enemy and occupied countries. Reuters therefore found British censorship irksome, particularly at home, its own official history commenting on the 'irritation' caused by Chief Press Censor Admiral Thomson (see below) sending out a 'stream of Defence Notices giving sometimes oracular advice on what could not be published and on what should be submitted. The censor enjoyed power without responsibility, stating: "the fact that the matter is passed for publication by the censorship does not mean that it is guaranteed as accurate or that publication is desired".'[14] In his own memoirs, Thomson however recorded that, where he could, he did tell the Press if he knew a story to be untrue.[15]

Thomson's own recollection of the censor/Reuters relationship contains some timeless wisdom about government/media interaction: 'In the end we came to see what we should have seen earlier on, that the business of an international news agency, which works under great pressure and to split seconds of timing, cannot be conducted efficiently under any system of remote control. If you wish a news agency to succeed in the highly competitive world market you must help it to get the best talent it can attract to its editorial desk and give its editors as much and as rapid assistance in the way of background news and information as they have time to ask for, but beyond that you cannot go. News has its own laws which determine whether it is a saleable or an unsaleable commodity among the world's purchasers, and to expect the agency to adapt to or modify its product to suit political requirements is both to outrage the traditions of good news men themselves and seriously to hamper the efficiency of the agency's service. In the end, therefore, we came to the conclusion that what our payments to Reuters entitled us to expect was the furtherance and development of the best news service that they could provide, taken with all faults, and not the conduct by them on our behalf of a service of propaganda news material composed to suit the purposes of H.M.G. . . . It became therefore a matter of long-term policy on the Ministry's part to find some way of withdrawing ourselves from this subsidy relationship with Reuters without wrecking the business of the Agency in the process.'[16]

Although this affair revealed again mutual suspicions between London and provincial press, whenever enemy bombing put a newspaper temporarily out of action, other parts of the Press rallied round to help. For practical reasons, this was normally done by region; when for example there was widespread fire damage in Plymouth after a raid, the *Western Morning News* was produced at the offices of an Exeter evening paper, and when similarly Belfast was ablaze after particularly heavy raids, two morning papers were still produced on the presses of an unscathed rival.[17]

Censorship and the Ministry of Information

The Ministry of Information was formally established on 5 September 1939.[18] As pre-planned, this was done not with direct approval by Parliament but by statutory order under the Ministers of the Crown (Emergency Appointments) Act 1939, and followed by issue of Defence (General) Regulations 1939, of which No.3 was of particular relevance to the media:

Subject to the provisions of this paragraph, no person shall –

(1) obtain,

(2) record, communicate to any other person or publish, or

(3) have in his possession any document containing, or any other record whatsoever of, any information being, or purporting to be, information with respect to any of the following matters, that is to say:

    (a) the number, description, armament, equipment, disposition, movement or condition of any of His Majesty's forces, vessels or aircraft;

    (b) any operations or projected operations of any of His Majesty's forces, vessels or aircraft;

    (c) any measures for the defence or fortification of any place on behalf of His Majesty;

    (d) the number, description or location of any prisoners of war;

    (e) munitions of war;

    (f) any other matter whatsoever information as to which would or might be directly or indirectly useful to an enemy.[19]

Even more directly relevant to the media was Defence Regulation No.38, entitled 'Propaganda', which included:

(1) No person shall –

    (a) endeavour, whether orally or otherwise, to influence public opinion, whether in the United Kingdom or elsewhere, in a manner likely to be prejudicial to the defence of the realm or the efficient prosecution of war, or

    (b) do any act, or have any article in his possession, with a view to making, or facilitating the making of, any such endeavour.

    A prosecution in respect of a contravention of this paragraph shall not be instituted except with the consent of the Attorney-General.

(2) The Secretary of State may make provision by order for preventing or restricting the publication in the United Kingdom of matters as to which he is satisfied that the publication, or, as the case may be, the unrestricted publication, thereof would be or might be prejudicial to the defence of the realm or the efficient prosecution of the war ... including ... documents, pictorial representations, photographs or cinematograph films [which] shall, before publication, be submitted or exhibited to such authority or person as may be specified in the order.

(3) Where any person is convicted on indictment of an offence against this Regulation by reason of his having published a newspaper, the court may by order direct that, during such period as may be specified in the order, that person shall not publish any newspaper in the United Kingdom.[20]

Some Order out of Much Chaos

Necessary statutory backing being swiftly in place for, in official eyes, a more effective system of control of the media than at the start of WWI, the Ministry of Information started work.[20] However, Treasury-led obstruction in the previous year meant the planned organisation could not function; it was neither all in place when war started, nor adequately manned in the weeks thereafter for the volume of work involved in censorship and in home and overseas information/publicity, nor was it trained. An early Minister of Information was briefly Sir Findlater Stewart;[21] by 28 September, failure to cope with the load caused him to ask the War Cabinet that his Information Officers should return to their parent Departments, that a Press and Censorship Bureau be established under some different Ministry, and that steps be taken to ensure the public should not believe that he was still responsible for the 'amount and character of the news issued . . . I am unwilling to accept any plan that does not secure this.'[22] On 9 October each Department therefore took back responsibility for censorship and for purely departmental information, while the Ministry of Information retained responsibility only for censorship *policy* and for provision of common information and distribution services. Under the guidance of Lord Camrose,[23] a separate Press and Censorship Bureau was then established (initially there was disagreement even over this title), with a News Division staffed by journalists, for issue of news to Agencies, Press and BBC.

The Press still found this unsatisfactory. Looking back, the PA Chairman Herbert Staines[24] summed up media feelings about the way in which the Ministry had been set up. 'In the negotiations with the officials of the shadow Ministry of Information, there was disclosed a tendency, born of a complete lack of knowledge of Press methods, to cabin and confine Press facilities; and the [newspaper] agencies found it necessary to carve a polite but insistent way through a jungle of red tape as well as to dispel an atmosphere that the Press must be content with small concessions. If, from the first, a wider view of the world-wide responsibilities of the Press had been adopted; if it had been appreciated that the facilities asked for were essential in the national interests; the storm that later blew up over the newly born Ministry might have been considerably moderated.'

Later, PA concerns differed, its Editor-in-Chief Martin becoming suspicious the Ministry was beginning to act as a de facto subsidised newspaper agency itself, controlling foreign sources and issuing reports about non-official matters too. This stopped only when Martin confronted the Minister (Bracken) himself.[25] Others too were unhappy with the censorship practices; from September 1939 until the later years of the War, the Treasury regularly received complaints about censorship delays in transactions from the Bank of England and other British and foreign financial institutions (as did the Board of Trade from businesses), and the matter was raised in Parliament.[26]

The Director-General of the new Press and Censorship Bureau was Sir Walter Monckton.[27] The Ministry of Information de-integration caused him both censorship and administrative problems. The War Office installed its News Division in the Whitehall building of the Royal United Services Institute (RUSI), where there was no room for News Departments of other Ministries, who remained therefore with Monckton at Senate House, although he had to communicate with them through the Directors of Intelligence in Whitehall.

The Army then decided it wanted its censors collocated at the RUSI too, but Monckton 'reserved his opinion' on that while he tried to establish the distinction between the respective responsibilities of the Ministry, the Bureau and the Service Departments. Their compromise was that, while the Bureau would run cross-departmental briefing of the Press, 'all Departments will continue to be at liberty to make their own arrangements in their own offices for special Press conferences'. It was made clear moreover that no Army censors would remain with Monckton, despite the obvious impracticality of having separate censorship staffs; the best division of labour which could be defined was that 'hot news' for the British Press would be handled by the Service Departments, and that for dissemination abroad by the Bureau.

The Security Service had similarly to expand on its responsibilities for advising on censorship. An internal minute at the end of the War records: 'In September 1939, the

Security Service found that it had no record of the operations of the Press censorship in the 1914–18 war – with the exception of a brief and inaccurate reference to the censorship of advertisements in the daily papers – and it was not possible to obtain such a record from any Government Department'. The casework practice which rapidly evolved during the War was for the Security Service to work through the Military Advisers to the Censorship Bureau; on policy matters MI5 went direct to the Minister of Information or the Chief Press Censor.[28]

Meanwhile Home Office and Services Press Officers (still led by CP Robertson), in response to an instruction to resolve the office accommodation problem in Whitehall, also attempted to bring some order to 'the dualism which has already caused the shipwreck of the original plan' (Monckton's description), recommending in a report in early October 1939 that the only practical solution was collocation with the MoI at Senate House, with the separate single Service Censorship and News sections being brigaded into a new 'Press Bureau'. The Air Ministry objected to this, suggesting further interdepartmental talks on the 'delimitation of functions,' and also recommending revival of the AWOAMPC (probably a sensible idea but not pursued by other civil servants). The Chief Press Censor had meanwhile started to issue the new Defence Notices direct to the Press, while the volume of message traffic and the congestion of lines were already overwhelming the muddled system. On 13 October Monckton wrote to Horace Wilson (as Head of the Civil Service), describing his problems, and summarising 'I am getting more of a Press flavour . . . seeking an absolutely first-rate lawyer . . . what is needed here is fresh air and more brains . . . and synthesis in what I am learning to call "hot news".'[29]

The first-rate lawyer he quickly recruited as his assistant was Cyril Radcliffe.[30] Rarely can a British Department have contained simultaneously two such outstanding practical legal minds. The Chief Press Censor, Vice Admiral Usborne (the former DNI recalled from retirement) moved quickly to his real area of expertise, technological innovation, and was replaced by Radcliffe, until Radcliffe in turn was promoted in December 1940 to be Controller of the Press and Censorship Division of the MoI (the Bureau having been abolished again in May 1940), still under Monckton, who became Director-General of the Ministry.

The two lawyers established a different underlying rationale for the way censorship was conducted, basing it on the legal powers which existed to enforce censorship if required; this was not in order to persuade the Media, but in order to overcome the excessively stringent requests for censorship from Government Departments; in simplistic terms, if an article or broadcast was not the kind of thing for which an editor could in theory be prosecuted under the relevant Acts or Regulations, it was not the kind of thing which should be censored.

A list was therefore compiled of specific subjects covered by Defence Regulations on which censorship should be based. The Security Service's first priority was censorship of reports of arrests and trials, not just those concerned with espionage and the OSAs but also with over 20 Defence Regulations. In January 1940, Monckton sent out his 'formula' for censorship, the first principle of which was that 'Decisions based on Censorship questions are to be based on security alone. This means that no news submitted to censorship will be held, altered or stopped except in so far as its publication would be likely to give the enemy information of value.' On these grounds alone he excluded from censorship: matters which would affect public morale, unless of 'real gravity' (leaving Departments to decide when this was so), material which might be used by the Germans for propaganda, criticism of Government Departments, inaccurate articles and those 'obtained contrary to rules of discipline.'[31]

The NID was concerned this formula did nothing to discourage reporters from collecting news about naval and military affairs and submitting it to their newsdesk. It gave as an unwelcome example the *Daily Express* man in Inverness who had asked locals to send him information about the Fleet's movements, and who was taking out 'girls employed by the Inverness censor . . . to make them talk'. The Security Service decided however that, in such cases, it would prefer merely to continue to listen covertly to the telephone calls of the reporter concerned, and to read mail passing through the postal censors, and only to intervene if such journalistic initiatives led to leakages of sensitive information, which to date they had not.[32] The Monckton formula was therefore largely accepted as the basis for censorship during the remainder of the War, the devil as always being in the detail of application to each case. He thus moved censored subjects away from the very wide WWI interpretation, his principles being similar to those applied by the AWOAMPC pre-war and to those used ever since.

This all took time to settle down, and meanwhile the relationship between Press and censors continued to be unsatisfactory to both. A Newspaper and Periodical Emergency Committee had now been established by the industry itself, chaired by William Will,[33] but it did not initially have the same locus as the AWOAMPC, with officials or with the Press. Its role was however much wider than security, and it set up many sub-committees, for example those dealing with editorial matters generally, with advertising (advertisements were also censored), and with newsprint (shortages, as in WWI). It also had to reflect press resentment of the BBC's apparently favoured position with Government and its increase in the broadcasting of news.[34]

As in WWI, those journals which sought and followed advice complained about the unfair advantage gained by those who did not. Another of Monckton's initial problems had been that his Bureau lacked a parent Department, the necessary source of funding and the essential provider of political direction and top cover. No Minister was keen, however, to take on what was already perceived as a political and practical minefield. Monckton therefore wrote to the Head of the Civil Service about this: 'I shall be known . . . as the unwanted child'. He was also beginning to realise other difficulties ahead: 'I have now had several talks with the Press and begun to understand the difficulties. I have learnt, for instance, that the war between the United Kingdom and Germany is nothing compared to the war between the Press and the BBC. I see signs also that those who have brought part of the Ministry of Information crashing down are a little apprehensive of the consequences which flow from the return to the Departments in loss of co-ordination and other ways.'[35]

Further correspondence between Monckton and Wilson followed, in which, as potential owners, the relative workloads of the Home Secretary and the Lord Privy Seal were discussed, but by 17 October the Prime Ministerial choice had fallen on the reluctant Home Secretary, Sir John Anderson.[36] He sent a paper to his War Cabinet colleagues, asking plaintively whether they really did agree that, while Departments were responsible for their own publicity and censorship, he should be solely responsible for how publicity and censorship were to be organised (including co-ordination between Departments, the relationship with press proprietors, censorship of films, etc). It did not of course make organisational sense, and it did not therefore last, but all his War Cabinet colleagues were predictably content to approve that someone else should grasp the unexploded mine.[37]

Delays and lack of uniformity in censorship caused most problems for the Press, especially in the early days of the War, while organisations and their personnel changed and re-changed for over a year. An incident in the first weeks of the War illustrated the extent of the problem. The War Office did not wish the news of the landing of the British Army in France to be reported immediately, even after the bulk of the forces had been successfully landed there, but by 12 September French radio was reporting their presence. At 9pm that evening, the Department therefore conceded that mention could be made, but *only* that the BEF had been transported to France. However, media articles then submitted to the Censor by the Press unsurprisingly contained far more information than this, and at 11.30pm the overwhelmed War Office censors suddenly withdrew all permission to mention even the Army's presence in France.

The Press and the MoI now protested that press telegrams to overseas, and early editions at home, had already been despatched, but the War Office was adamant. The Home Office had to instruct Police Forces throughout Britain to occupy newspaper offices and stop further printing, to intercept vans and trains carrying the early editions, even to stop private cars in the streets and confiscate early editions, and to stop further cables being sent. Some hours of fury followed, with editors ringing Ministers at home during the night, and American correspondents swearing at the Censors, until, at 2.30am, the War Office was ordered to rescind the instruction. The public initially remained unaware of this night of comedic activity, but consequent angry exchanges in Parliament led to a somewhat more realistic approach to what could not long be concealed.[38]

Monckton wrote again to Wilson on 3 November: 'I have been here a month . . . and have been driven by experience to the conclusion that the Press and Censorship Bureau cannot survive much longer without radical changes'. He said the Press was getting impatient and his staff demoralised. There was a need for speed of service, because only 'hot' news was good news, for the Press and for Departments. He gave as an example of inadequacy a case two days previously when an Admiralty communiqué about the successful beating off of a German air attack had been held up for five hours by the Air Ministry. Monckton's requested solution was for information and censorship to be brought together again under one Director-General, assisted by a small policy staff.[39]

These kinds of muddles persisted in the following weeks. After a series of media-angering incidents, Monckton wrote to the Home Secretary: 'my position has now become untenable'. A strong exchange of correspondence lasted until the following January. He reminded Anderson that 'the position was difficult enough in the present lull [the 'phoney war'] and would . . . involve a breakdown when active operations took place'. He said 'the great delay and dissatisfaction' was because everything had to be referred to the Service Departments and their ruling had to be accepted. He suggested that in all but matters of 'vital importance' to a Service, the decision ought to rest with him, as Director-General of the Bureau. He foresaw some matter would shortly affect all three Services and the Ministry of Home Security (the Home Office), and the current decision-making process would become untenable.

He gave examples in which he had been 'compelled to act in a manner which I consider wholly wrong and wholly unreasonable; and I am not prepared to continue in this course': a major fire in Middlesborough caused by a crashing aircraft, about which publication of both the incident and the inquest had been suppressed, even though the locals were well aware of it – 'buses pass throughout the day . . . Parties have been taken to see the place', and suppression was indeed causing suspicions amongst the populace that even more disastrous incidents were also being 'kept from public knowledge'; and an official communiqué from the Admiralty after the sinking of 'one of HM Destroyers', including the casualty list [the next-of-kin having already been informed], had been delayed so much it was too late for the evening papers, and the sinking was therefore first announced publicly by the BBC without a casualty list.

He ended: 'In these circumstances, bearing in mind that the illustrations I have given are merely illustrations of the general proposition which I put before you based upon my experience here for more than six weeks, I am sure you will forgive me when I say that I cannot let the matter stand over for a fortnight. If major operations begin in that time I should feel ashamed that I had allowed things to go on as though I were satisfied that the organisation for which I am responsible could be made to function, whereas in fact I am satisfied that it cannot.' Anderson replied next day that he agreed that the position was 'intolerable', and that, 'after a word with the P.M.', he was arranging to approach each Service Minister individually in order to get their agreement to the changes Monckton wanted.

Monckton wrote again to Anderson, in preparation for the latter's talks with Service Ministers, enclosing seven 'Essential Features in a Workable Scheme for the Press and Censorship Bureau'. He added that these suggestions were not novel, but reproduced in effect the advice given by the AWOAMPC and CID Censorship Sub-Committee before the War, which had been approved by the Cabinet before the planning had been undone by officials. In the covering letter, he also denied the political 'opinions and ambitions' sometimes attributed to him in the Press. 'I realise that the Government will probably not feel able to deal with the problem on anything like the lines I am suggesting. In that event it is no doubt desirable that, in the policemen's phrase, I should "go quietly".'

This threat by such a well-regarded public servant, at a time when there had already been an excessive number of changes of post-holders, and in the face of such dissatisfaction by the Press, caused Anderson immediately to ask Wilson to see Monckton. Wilson produced a compromise plan (a more senior representative of each Service at the Bureau), still unacceptable to Monckton, who made it even plainer that he wanted the reinstatement of a Ministry of Information, combining its 'publicity' functions with centralised censorship and press relations, while still allowing some co-ordinated direct press/departmental activity. He did not immediately wrest what he wanted from other Departments, but agreed to carry on for the present.

On 4 December 1939, the Admiralty sent Monckton a long-requested but very short three paragraph statement of its policy on reporting losses of and damage to HM ships: losses would be published as soon as next-of-kin had been informed, but damage should not be reported unless it was already widely known (and for certain to the enemy), and the Admiralty would not deny enemy claims unless it was in its interests to do so. Monckton immediately complained to Anderson about the practical inadequacy of this policy, ending: 'the problem is none the less urgent and I am sure that you will not allow me to remain here with the position unaltered, having regard to my letters on the subject last month'.

The Prime Minister now summoned Wilson to find a solution satisfactory to both Monckton and the Service Departments. The Cabinet Secretary went clutching a new Home Office compromise plan: a body of principles could be built up as a guide to all involved in censorship. To achieve this, each Service Department should produce a statement of general principles, and perhaps weekly a Cabinet Minister should chair a meeting of senior Bureau and Service representatives, to discuss any conflicts which had arisen and the way of handling such cases. Thus, Anderson hoped, not only would 'case law' be built up, but the balance between security and advantageous publicity would be discussed and achieved.

The situation was not improved by these theoretical discussions. In mid-January 1940, Monckton wrote angrily to the Admiralty about its censorship, following the sinking of the *SS Dunbar Castle* the previous week. Fifty-five articles had been held up by the Admiralty, ostensibly on humanitarian grounds (i.e. until all next-of-kin had been informed), but so widespread was the news of the disaster that the Press threatened en masse to ignore the censors' prohibitions.[40] Monckton did eventually get his way on departmental responsibilities, before he handed over to Radcliffe and moved on. The practical routines of censorship did also build up and gradually obtain unenthusiastic acceptance, from the censorship of school magazines (allowed to publish without permission only the name, rank and regiment of Old Boys), to the appointment by the Publishers' Association of two advisers to the Press and Censorship Bureau, to whom all manuscripts on war subjects now had to be submitted.[41]

Attention was also paid to the censorship of communication systems between the UK and Eire, after the Security Service reported in November 1939 it had evidence that Germany was acquiring intelligence from telephone intercepts, and using illicit wireless stations in Eire to transmit intelligence to Berlin. A discreet modus vivendi was established between Britain and Eire.[42] The censors occasionally became involved in protecting Irish sensitivities; for example in May 1940, when the *Daily Mirror* published an article headlined 'Britain Buys Bases in Eire', Monckton wrote to Kell undertaking to brief the Press confidentially at the conferences held with them by the Ministry, and to write to any provincial editor who might offend in this area. He ended his letter: 'As you know, I am most anxious to do all I can to meet Mr Dulanty's wishes.'[43] Nevertheless, as the Chief Press Censor pointed out in June 1940, strictly speaking the only matters in which D-Notices were applicable specifically to Ireland were planning against the invasion of Northern Ireland, and certain details of British Forces stationed in Northern Ireland.[44]

Of almost equal concern to the Security Service at this time was the distribution of Defence Notices themselves. The Chief Press Censor was asked to provide Kell with a list of all those to whom Notices were sent. The MI5 officer who received it declared he was 'frankly horrified at the results'. A quick 'look-up' by the MI5 Registry revealed inter alia an obscure agency used (according to MI6) by Italian fascists; a naturalised German; a publishing company with two German directors who regularly sent photographs of guns, searchlights, etc to Germany; the American-Hungarian-owned Keystone Press Agency whose European Branch was run by a known Belgian agent of the Germans; and the International Graphic Press run by a pro-Nazi Mr Silver (then currently in correspondence with Hitler's personal press photographer Herr Hoffmann, who had just asked him to supply 'pictures of British ships').

At a Security Service/MoI meeting to discuss the list, the former's preference for discontinuing the Notices altogether was not accepted, but it was agreed to be more selective in distribution. So that suspect addressees would not themselves become suspicious, they would thenceforth receive only a decreasing number of innocuous Notices. The revised list of recipients of Notices was all-British and now excluded the representatives in the UK of the Empire, American, and Irish Press, the communist *Daily Worker*, all news agencies except the large ones, photographic agencies, most periodicals, all book publishers, and most suburban papers. It was the most limited list for Notice addressees that there had been since 1912, and much more limited than any used since 1945.[45]

Monckton and later Radcliffe did try to avoid the use of legislation (there were only four prosecutions during the War as a result of Ministry of Information recommendations), but occasionally they tactically threatened to do so. In March 1940, Monckton wrote to the

Admiralty Press Division seeking blanket agreement to prosecute papers continually careless in observing 'stops' on sensitive subjects. The Admiralty did not reply, but a minute in its file shows the Naval Staff understood the real and subtle purpose of the request: 'As a matter of fact I feel fairly certain that the object of [the relevant paragraph] of Sir Walter Monckton's letter is not to secure for himself a free hand to prosecute, but rather to impress upon the Admiralty that "Stop" should only be used in cases of such gravity that there would be a prima facie case for a prosecution if the Press did not observe the "Stop".'[46]

Looking back at the highly unsatisfactory situation between the Bureau and the other Government Departments, and therefore between the Bureau and the Press, in the first 18 months of WWII, one cannot help speculating that much confusion, conflict and reinvention of practices and ethos might have been avoided, had there been in existence, as in WWI, a ready and practised Committee, perhaps a marginally enlarged AWOAMPC. The WWII Bureau did have its own shifting cast of Press advisers on the sidelines, but there was no forum, semi-formal or otherwise, in which all the representative players from both sides talked regularly about the optimal machinery to achieve the correct balance between information and security. Monckton's views about the optimal organisation would have been supported by the Press side through the Committee, and this additional weight might have reduced considerably, or even prevented altogether, the interdepartmental wrangling described above, which continued until well after Churchill became Prime Minister in May 1940.

26

THE PRACTICE OF CENSORSHIP

When Radcliffe was moved up to be Controller of the Press and Censorship Division in December 1940, he was replaced as Chief Press Censor by Admiral Thomson,[47] whom Churchill (as First Lord) had summoned in early September 1939 from holiday in France when Poland was invaded, and sent across to the MoI as the Admiralty's representative. Thomson remained as Chief Press Censor for the remainder of the War, and, with Radcliffe replacing Monckton as Director-General of the Ministry in 1941, a considerable measure of stability was at last brought to the Government/Media interface. Another regular feature was continuing correspondence with the Security Service about the degree of censorship thought by the latter to be required, and the potential for subversion from within parts of the Media.[48]

Having wrested back censorship from the other government departments, the MoI also gradually centralised other functions too. In April 1940, it absorbed Postal and Telegraph Censorship sections previously under the War Office,[49] and the Post Office Film Unit. Censorship of BBC broadcasting, the powers for which had been transferred from Postmaster-General to MoI as soon as war was declared, was exercised within the BBC by collocated censors. The Ministry's Home Intelligence Division took over the Social Survey Organisation and monitoring civilian morale. For overseas matters, the Ministry absorbed the recently formed Foreign Publicity Department of the Foreign Office, which retained nevertheless some news functions and responsibility for propaganda overseas. The Ministry was also responsible for co-ordinating morale-boosting activities, such as the BBC Publicity Programme in celebration of Empire Day in May 1940, and the regular BBC 'Naval Log' and its Army and Air Force equivalents.

In general the voluntary censorship system did eventually work. Casework based on precedent was gradually built up between censors and journalists, co-ordination between censors then improved, and a kind of wobbly equilibrium was achieved between what could be published and what could not. In the latter category came suppression of (false) rumours of imminent German invasion in mid-1941 (because articles would have revealed the paucity of the then defences); details of new technology such as 'petroleum weapons', radiolocation devices, radar, magnetic and acoustic mine countermeasures, jets (until early 1944, and even after that their role in countering flying bombs remained secret until the end of the War); the vast preparations for D-Day; and suppression from June 1944 of the news that 'flying bombs' were reaching London and further afield. Much attention was indeed devoted throughout the War, as in WWI, to how air raids were reported, particularly from the beginning of the German night bombing raids in late 1940 until after the last major blitz on London in mid-May 1941; major disasters, such as the 240 sheltering civilian casualties in Bethnal Green Tube Station when it was hit, were not immediately reported.

As the War started, all editors had received a booklet entitled 'Defence Notices', giving advance warning in general terms of what would be considered 'dangerous subjects' requiring advice from the censors.[50] It had been prepared by the Intelligence Divisions without reference to the AWOAMPC, and was immediately seen by the Press, and indeed by the censors, as inadequate and confusing. After rapid amendment, by discussion between the Ministry and its Press Advisory Committee, a revised pamphlet was issued in early 1940, and this formed the basis of dialogue which ensued while the system settled slowly down. This helped the Press too to accept the system as 'voluntary', and they were anyway not bound to use it invariably (except for photographs and newsreel films of war interest, where censorship was indeed compulsory, and carried out by the censors either at the Agencies or in the Ministry's own cinema).

After that initial revision, through the War the MoI issued amendments to these Secret quarto booklets of about 50 pages, containing all the subject matter of extant Defence Notices and other guidance. These were compiled with the help of press advice (including now BBC and book publisher input). Also sent to editors from time to time were 'Private and Confidential' communications, but the Media advisers were not consulted before their issue. Comparison of the booklets republished in April 1941, November 1942 and April 1945 (the latter 'Relating to the War in the Far East'), show the basics were well in place by 1941, that later nuanced amendments reflected experience (or relearning of lessons, such as that foreign affairs needed to be included), that the instructions actually shortened slightly as editors became accustomed to them, and that the contents had been drawn up in consultation with the representatives of the media.

The final Far East issue omitted such 'Home' categories as Air Raids, Defence of the UK, Finance, and Transport, and did include an additional heading of Casualties, but otherwise as before went alphabetically through Air, Government, Military, Naval and Shipping, Neutrals and Foreign Affairs, Prisoners of War and Internees, Production and Supply, and Spies.[51] The Notices were divided into those matters (the majority) which should not be published without prior reference to the censors, and (underlined) those which should not be published at all: 'The subjects so designated are regarded as being intrinsically secret in time of war and the Censorship practice will be to stop all references to them.'

The latter category included that no information was to be published on: plans for future or prospective operations; weather forecasts and cause of cancellation or postponement of 'outdoor events'; proclamations about future conscription; airfield defence, defence research, air raid warning systems, special lighting; locations or methods of BBC transmitting stations, navigational use of transmissions by enemy aircraft (and British countermeasures); interception/identification devices; methods of acquiring information about enemy air movements and signals; systems of passing information/orders to own forces; RAF radio signalling systems; details of warship types, armament, equipment, performance, or fuel consumption, other than those contained in *Jane's Fighting Ships*, and loss of, damage to, or attack on ships, until officially announced; warning regulations on danger zones and wrecks caused by mines, methods of searching for and destroying magnetic or acoustic mines; use of television and telegraphy for reconnaissance and defence; details of Services radio stations, call signs and messages; balloon barrage heights and equipment details; links between enemy projects/intentions and military and governmental actions; secret intelligence sources; British Cyphers and Codes; enemy codes captured; Secret Service and Secret Service personnel; future movements/whereabouts of King and Queen; Civil Defence assembly and communications points; shipments of bullion and securities; locality, output, and other details of factories and arsenals; Key Points, control points for utilities and other services, new or extended power stations and supply lines, and new/widened railway bridges.

The progress and problems of censorship throughout the War are lucidly described in Thomson's own memoirs.[52] He also broadcast a series of short talks on the BBC after the War ended.[53] He did not believe in draconian censorship. As an example he cited a munitions factory strike as a dilemma the early censors faced: 'The enemy would welcome the news that our supplies of ammunition, small as they then were, were to be still further reduced by the strike. On the other hand, if the strikers had a genuine grievance it was right that it should be ventilated and so be rectified. In a democratic country such as ours, publicity is the surest, indeed the only, method of getting wrong things put right.' Some changes since WWI were identified by Thomson, such as the speed of news circulation. When, for example, the *Graf Spee* was scuttled off Montevideo in December 1939, watching American correspondents telephoned the news to Buenos Aires, whence the news was sent by 'beam radio' to New York, and thence by radiotelephone to London, where within minutes of the scuttling it was reported on the UK news agency tape machines.

One area of media disgruntlement, this time amongst the journalists representing the Empire and Allies, was that all their reports back to their own country passed through the hands of the censors, whether or not they concerned the War. 'They felt, quite justifiably, that they had been placed on a lower footing than that of their United Kingdom colleagues whose material was submitted at the Editor's discretion.'[54] The censors considered, however, that this difference in treatment was unavoidable, because thousands of daily telegrams about multifarious subjects were censored at the offices of the Cable Companies, whose staff were unable for practical and cost reasons to separate those addressed to foreign press addressees from others. The Government was also able to impose such compulsory censorship without parliamentary approval, since it then either owned or controlled all the cable and the wireless transmitters. Nevertheless, as the War progressed, compromise arrangements were made with foreign correspondents, and special permission was given to authorised news and photographic agencies and selected newsagents to use radio and telephone facilities denied to the public.

In addition to military matters covered more routinely under the Defence Notices, in 1940 the censors received a number inspired by the concerned Security Service. For example, in February, without consulting the censors, the *Daily Mirror*, *Daily Herald* and *Daily Express* reported details about the broadcasts by 'Lord Haw Haw', unfortunately just as the Security Service was closing in on an illegal transmitter. In the same month, reports of IRA activity were censored. In October, Radcliffe was asked to prohibit publication of anything about known or potential enemy agents (although when he asked the Security Service for examples of the Press having done so, he was told that none had in fact occurred as yet).[55] Obeying the censors, unreported by the media was the enormous effort which the Security Service (with the War Office, Ministries of Food and Health, and Railway Companies) put into monitoring the security of utilities/companies, covering 2,390 firms and 3,517 factories which had defence contracts and/or were in Vulnerable Points.[56]

The Security Service was normally consulted by the censors on prosecutions under the Defence Regulations or OSAs; although court proceedings were open, the Service sometimes requested the judge to hear sensitive evidence in camera (and conversely sometimes told the MoI it wanted the case to be widely publicised). Other Security Service interest in censorship included morale-damaging false rumours, some originating in Germany; adverse/sensitive news from foreign countries (especially Sweden), which again the Press were asked to play down and not to comment on its veracity; escapes of foreign nationals and Allied Servicemen and agents from enemy-occupied countries, especially details of helpers and routes; internment and prisoner-of-war camps in the UK, where the authorities did allow names to be published; and suspicious personal advertisements, on which 'the newspapers were always ready to give us an advertiser's name in confidence.'[57]

Reporting on parliamentary matters posed particular problems for the censors. When the German night bombing campaign started in 1940, the House decided to rise before dark, and therefore to start its sittings in the mornings, but, in order to conceal the times and (after the Houses of Parliament were bombed) the alternative locations of sittings, and to give the impression of normality, the Media were instructed by the censors to delay by several hours the publication of parliamentary business. In addition, the fondness of Churchill and occasionally other Ministers for making speeches outside Parliament on prohibited matters, caused problems for censors who were unaware of the speeches until the press reports came in, and then rapidly had to adjust the Defence Notices.

Conversely, there were sometimes political constraints and delays which the censors found hard to explain to the media. When Rudolf Hess landed in Scotland in May 1941, nothing was allowed to be published in the British Media for two days, while the Germans meanwhile admitted his flight and said he was mad. Thomson justified the (in fact, political) delay by using the air raid regulation that details of night crashes by German aircraft could not be published. When the Cabinet did eventually authorise information being released, nothing was said about the reasons Hess claimed for coming to Britain, so that the Germans could not know what he had been telling his interrogators. As for German spies, because their trials were held in camera, and the authorities made no announcements of other than the sentences, the Press found out more from reports emanating from neutral countries.[58]

The Threat of Compulsory Censorship

Reorganisation and centralisation of Information and Censorship responsibilities were never in themselves enough to satisfy the desire of the re-formed Government led by Churchill to control the publication of information, especially at the low points in the War such as after the German occupation of Norway, the Low Countries and France. On 14 June 1940, the War Cabinet agreed to study proposals made by the new Minister of Information Anthony Duff Cooper[59] that compulsory censorship should be introduced. A committee was rapidly set up, chaired by the Lord President of the Council (Chamberlain), and the War Cabinet Secretariat circulated an MoI paper, written to political direction. This started by expressing the desire for a scheme, impossible under the then censorship system, for ensuring that nothing would be published in the UK Press on military matters (including indirectly related information on such as trade and industry, technology, and weather) until after it had been passed by the censor. It made clear this was in part in response to French wishes, while acknowledging that 'the different public reactions' might still cause 'substantial divergence' between the two countries in the practice of censorship.

The Paper reported 'no serious defects of security'; despite the lack of prosecutions and the provisos which made use of Defence Regulation 3 difficult ('It has been allowed to become a dead letter'), 'the newspapers have, on the whole, co-operated in making the system of voluntary submission moderately successful'. It nevertheless outlined two possible means of achieving a compulsory regime: Compulsory Censorship, or Compulsory Sources. The first would require an increase of five or six times the current staff, regional censorship centres, appropriate training, and some form of increased Service advice (necessarily regional and impeding). Of the calibre of the existing Services advice, the Ministry had a low opinion: 'Service advisers who are not in constant touch with their Departments are not much better informed than censors as to what is the safe or the dangerous in news.'

The MoI Paper therefore favoured Compulsory Sources, requiring no extra censors, and not being liable to interruption by impaired communications. This would allow publication only of subjects on a defined list, and official communiqués, and authorised news from the Agencies and the BBC. It did point out the disadvantages, principally: loss of press individuality and informed explanation and discussion, and creating in the public 'a feeling of mystification and panic' (the latter was the view of the Press who had been consulted). Finally the Paper suggested these disadvantages might be mitigated by setting up instead a Censorship Board, to give binding directions to the Press, based on a frequently updated list of forbidden matters. It acknowledged this was not that different from the current arrangements, but they would be legally binding and would be backed by 'effective and rapid penalties, ranging from fine to suspension'. However, 'the power of the Board to give directions with regard to such matters as criticism must be expressly negatived.'[60]

When the Compulsory Censorship Committee met on 17 June, Monckton pointed out that, although the Censorship Board would be less severe for the Press than the other options, it would still mean the Press could not publish anything until it had formally been approved by the Board. Discussion favoured the Board over the other options, but several imperfections were nevertheless perceived in its practical operation, and the Service Departments still wished to retain the ultimate control over what was published. Duff Cooper was invited to work out a Censorship Board scheme in more detail, and to discuss the idea with the principal newspaper proprietors. Chamberlain thought it would be undesirable to empower the Board to impose fines, and that the power to suppress a newspaper, for a period 'commensurate with the gravity of the offence', would be more effective, as it would not only affect circulation but would be publicly known.

The consequence of consultation with the proprietors about some form of compulsory censorship led unsurprisingly to both rejection and to adverse comment about such an idea in the Press, although the *Observer* did concede on 14 July 1940: 'What no-one could object to would be a punitive discipline for any journals that did make culpable errors' [i.e. persistent or deliberate violations]. Other ideas mooted but merely noted within the Home Office included compulsory censorship for a limited time for transgressors, but, as is often voiced as a concern about compulsion, it was conceded that *anything* said by a newspaper would then be perceived by the public as having government approval, a far more worrying thought to officials. The MoI, which had only recently negotiated improved arrangements with the Media, was itself actually against compulsory censorship; the idea was shelved.[61]

Through the War, press activities nevertheless continued to be gravel in the shoes of Ministers. At the War Cabinet meeting on 9 October 1941 it was decided to review what measures might be taken 'to prevent the publication by the Press of articles likely to react unfavourably on this country's relations with foreign Powers'. Accordingly, in mid-November the Foreign Secretary, Anthony Eden,[62] Home Secretary, Herbert Morrison,[63] and Minister of Information (Bracken) produced a Joint Memorandum. It conceded that the Press generally followed Foreign Office advice, and that there were matters on which there could be differences of opinion as to what the national interest was, for example the *Daily Mirror* considered that 'restraint and moderation in connection with [Franco's] Spain are symptoms of a mistaken policy of "appeasement"'.

The Memorandum also acknowledged 'the indiscretions of a controlled press are more embarrassing than those of a free press', citing frequent protests from foreign governments about BBC programmes, requesting the Corporation be admonished or restrained; also 'The influence abroad of a controlled press is far less than that of a press renowned for its freedom.' Having considered the legislative options, it reminded that when in October 1940 the *Daily Mirror* and the *Sunday Pictorial* had published 'objectionable articles', the Lord Privy Seal and the Minister of Aircraft Production (then Lord Beaverbrook) had put the Government's view to the NPA, after which 'the tone of these newspapers showed for some time a marked improvement'. The three Ministers therefore recommended against 'the introduction of new methods of coercion' (the War Cabinet agreed this on 17 November), but that the Prime Minister should in serious cases make some statement in Parliament stigmatising the offending newspaper for not acting in the national interest.[64]

A Steadier State

As the war progressed, the extent of censorship and the needs of the Provincial Press led to regional censorship units being established in Belfast, Birmingham, Bristol, Cardiff, Glasgow, Leeds and Manchester. By mid-1941, the number of censors had increased to about 200, and this was further increased by 50% in the build-up to D-Day in June 1944. There were branches of the Postal and Telegraph Censorship at all major ports, so that all mail leaving the country could be inspected and deletions from letters made if necessary. Another area not previously planned in detail, but which evolved successfully, was censorship of trade and technical journals; all the censors were recruited from amongst those who had worked on such magazines before the War, Editors readily submitted copy, and there were very few complaints; the only delays occurred occasionally when especially sensitive stories had to be discussed with experts in Defence Departments or the Board of Scientific Research.

Censorship also dealt with books for publication, although sometimes the Security Service took a close interest. When for example an officer (a Major Gribble) who had escaped at Dunkirk produced the manuscript of 'Diary of a Staff Officer', Captain Guy Liddell personally led the negotiation with the publisher Methuen, instructing them however not to reveal the MI5 interest. A similar caveat was placed on his instruction that copies of this book posted 'to all censorable countries' should be intercepted at ports and in Bermuda (for the American edition); all three thousand copies of the second edition (it was a best seller, and was also serialised by the *Saturday Weekend Post* and the *Manchester Evening News*) were bought by the War Office at the behest of the Security Service to stop further dissemination.[65]

Through the War, efforts were also made by the Ministry to brief the public about censorship. For example, while he was still Controller of the Press and Censorship Division, Radcliffe made a BBC broadcast late on New Year's Eve 1940 about 'How Censorship Works'. Having explained the principles of why censorship was needed (German use of British news in their operational planning), he went on to explain how the Press and Censors interacted in practice inside the Division, and between it and the newspapers and agencies (he did not specifically refer to the BBC's embedded censors): 'Each side at heart genuinely wants to help the other: though hearts are not always worn on sleeves. It is for the Press Censors to reconcile the right of the Press to produce their newspapers with the common duty of the Press and Government to hold back information from the enemy.' The sentiments were less noble in practice, and he went on to plead that censorship was not a science but an art, and to acknowledge that, because there were many newspapers and several censors, there could on occasion be an unevenness of treatment on the same story, 'a very high misdemeanour in the eyes of the suffering paper'.

Lord Hankey too was used to justify censorship to the public, writing in the *Sunday Times* of 19 April 1942: 'criticism . . . is always admissible, but must be attuned to the realities, which are very hard to judge when so much is hidden in the fog of war'. He emphasised the inadvertent help which might be given to the enemy, even by reporting the careless talk of politicians. Sometimes, however, the Press criticised the Government for not being careful enough about security. On 7 July 1942, the *Daily Mail* reported the Government was about to announce details of a 'new powerful anti-aircraft device'; 'But WHY tell the Germans?' it asked, alleging similar mistakes had been made in the past in prematurely revealing details of radio-location devices and the heavy anti-tank gun, thus allowing the Germans an opportunity to think of countermeasures.[66]

When the USA entered the War, arrangements had rapidly to be made to co-ordinate information and censorship policies. This was made easier by the commonality of much thinking on specifics, such as that nothing should be published about the escape and evasion methods of Allied prisoners and aircrew. It was further eased when Byron Price of Associated Press led a 12-strong delegation to the UK in early 1942, discussed the British experience, Regulations and Notices, and then initiated the issue of a US Government Code of Wartime Practices.[67] These were similar to Defence Notices but much less detailed. However, the US categorised the UK as a 'zone of military operations', and its correspondents were therefore subject to the much more stringent US Army censorship rules. Their censors in the UK were collocated with the British censors in the MoI, and anything that concerned US Forces, from whichever nationality of media, was in practice referred to the former.[68]

Attempts to Control the Press

In other difficult times in the War, the Government returned periodically to its relationship with the Press. In the spring of 1942, with the *Scharnhorst* and the *Prinz Eugen* having broken out into the Atlantic, Luftwaffe bombing of historic British cities, Singapore having surrendered to the Japanese, and Darwin having been bombed by them, the Committee on Press Restrictions raised the imposition of compulsory censorship in the event of invasion, a matter which had been studied but then placed in pending trays in the summer of 1940. The Home Office considered that, in the case of invasion, D-Notices should be given legal sanction (so proof that the information was of value to an enemy would not be necessary), and the MoI should have the power to impose administrative sanctions (suspension of publication, or compulsory submission of all copy) without necessity of legal proceedings.

Morrison approved, and Radcliffe (who favoured merely an extension of the 'voluntary practice') could only suggest that some of the threatening language used about measures intended against editors be removed as counterproductive. Fortunately, as the threat of invasion faded, so did the staffing of this compulsion. In June 1943 Morrison did submit a draft Regulation for further study: it included giving the Minister of Information (and each Regional Commissioner if communication with central government was no longer possible) the power to suspend publication, for a period at his discretion, of any newspaper which failed to consult the censors and published information which should not have been disclosed.[69]

Another serious crisis of confidence in March 1942 induced Government threats to suspend publication of journals which criticised it. Since becoming Prime Minister, Churchill had been increasingly irritated by any attacks on his conduct of the war and his selection of Ministers. The War Office also complained about the *Daily Mirror* in particular (which had become the most popular paper with the Forces) constantly sniping at the 'brass hats'. The governmental dissatisfaction with the Press came to a head at a time when national morale was fragile after the fall of Singapore; the newspaper published a cartoon of an exhausted sailor adrift on a raft, over the caption 'The price of petrol has been increased by one penny – Official', which most, including the Government, saw as an attack on petrol profiteering.

The Minister of Labour, angry at the impact on recruiting for the Merchant Navy if its heavy losses were perceived as contributing merely to higher profits for the fuel company owners, asked the Home Secretary to intervene with the Press. Cecil King[70] was summoned to be rebuked, but sent one of his senior editorial staff, whom Morrison threatened with prolonged closure as had happened with the *Daily Worker*. Later he made a statement in Parliament clarifying the threat to use Defence Regulation 2D, which authorised 'the suppression of a newspaper that systematically publishes matter calculated to foment opposition to the successful prosecution of the war'. The strong feelings aroused by this threat, within the Press but also in Parliament, caused both sides publicly to back down.

In March 1942, Morrison also became embroiled with the journalists' unions. This followed the temporary but prolonged suspension by the authorities of the *Daily Worker* and the *Week* (in January to August 1941) for 'systematically publishing matter calculated to foment opposition to the War',[71] and the threat of similar Defence Regulation 2D proceedings against the *Daily Mirror*, after the cartoon referred to above and articles hostile to the Government's handling of Army administration. These sparked a Parliamentary Question from Sir Percy Hurd;[72] he was also spokesman for the Institute of Journalists, which pre-war had proposed a Bill for a register of journalists, with a view amongst other things to enforcing a code of conduct; the National Union of Journalists had however opposed this idea. He now resurrected the proposal. In responding to the PQ on 26 March, Morrison was careful not to appear to support the IoJ, nor (as Hurd had done) to equate journalists with other professions which already had a self-enforced code of conduct (such as architects, lawyers and doctors), because these did not have a reason, such as the freedom of the Press, which obliged them to admit 'heretics'. But Morrison and his Home Office advisers did privately see this as an opportunity to support in principle the idea of an organisation which represented the whole Press, in this case as a means of exercising some influence over what was or was not published, to protect 'the country in war time against irresponsible journalistic policy or conduct'.

Less publicly too, Morrison's supplementary argument to the NUJ (who immediately saw what was behind it) was that such a body could also protect journalists against their own proprietors. The relationship of the Government at the time with the proprietors does indeed seem to have been at low ebb. A briefing note to the Home Secretary reported: 'There is in existence a National Emergency Council (NEC) representing the two bodies of proprietors, namely [those] of the London papers and [those] of the provincial papers, but I understand from the Ministry of Information that in practice this body is found to be ineffective. It does not exercise any control or any real influence'. This was a very different reputation to that of the AWOPC in the early years of WWI, although somewhat unfair to the NEC's Chairman William Will and members; they were indeed consulted throughout the War, and on post-war planning, but they lacked perhaps personalities of significant political and professional influence such as Riddell and Robbins.[73]

In the event, the idea of a statutory register and code got no further. At the 1942 Annual NUJ Conference, the adopted resolution stated that the Union 'emphatically rejects the proposal, and declares its inability to take part in meetings or talks for the purpose of forming such an organisation'. It saw it as potentially 'a most dangerous agency for the suppression of legitimate criticism, and must inevitably lead to a still further invasion of the freedom of the Press'. Morrison was referred to as 'an ersatz Hitler in the Home Office'. There were also resolutions calling on the action against the two newspapers to be withdrawn. Six weeks later, the Home Office was again involved in matters journalistic, this time however protectively of the Press. The Department reminded Petrie of MI5 and Game of the Metropolitan Police (who both readily took the point) that their powers to interrogate, under Defence Regulation 80A, had been specifically limited by an amendment to the OSA in 1939, which ensured 'journalists should not be questioned about leakages of official information resulting in publication or impending publication.'[74]

Behind the scenes however, Morrison continued to consider schemes for restraining press criticism. He followed up an MP's suggestion of ways to (in modern parlance) 'name and shame' the proprietors of journals which published matters which the Government considered contrary to the public interest. This would be by making a new Defence Regulation enabling Ministers to publish details of 'the beneficial ownership of shares in newspapers'. The First Parliamentary Counsel (on legal grounds) and the Board of Trade (on the practical grounds that many shares were held not by controlling proprietors but by banks, trustees, and companies) advised that this was a non-starter. With apparent regret, senior civil servants advised Morrison accordingly.

The Home Secretary was not pleased; he referred to the minute summarising the case against thus proceeding as 'perhaps the greatest triumph of official negation I have ever seen'. He accepted the advice might be right, but decided to consult Lord Beaverbrook, whose *Sunday Express* had initially backed the idea. Having outlined the practical difficulties and possible ways around them, Morrison asked Beaverbrook[75] whether he thought there would be 'strong opposition to it by newspaper interests, if only because it might have some effect on the attractiveness of newspaper shares as an investment? What would you think of the proposal to require newspapers to publish in each issue the name of the Editor and the names of the Board of Management?'

Beaverbrook replied from his Leatherhead home two days later that he thought the 'plan to disclose the beneficial ownership of all shares in a newspaper property, especially if it were followed through to investment trusts, would be altogether too vast an undertaking for too small a purpose. It seems to me that the object should be to ascertain where the controlling interest in a newspaper lies. It is not beneficial ownership but power to influence policy that matters.' He pointed out the key identities required were those of the owners of blocks of shares, and that a precedent had been set under the Defence (Finance) Regulations and Trading with the Enemy Act, in that (on the Stock Exchange) the true owner behind a nominee had to be disclosed.

On Morrison's final question, he explained that requiring publication of names would gain nothing, and gave himself as an example: 'I am neither the Editor of the Express, nor a Director, yet I own just short of three-quarters of the shares.' He ended that what was here involved was 'a passing phase of opinion', the pressure coming not from the newspapers but from politicians. Three weeks later Morrison decided, 'in view of the difficulties in the way of devising a practical scheme, not to take any further steps in the matter, for the present at any rate.'[76]

A more curious exchange between the Home Office and the MoI also took place in May 1942. The former became concerned that certain imminent events secretly briefed to editors by Churchill after a visit to the USA had subsequently appeared amongst astrologers' predictions in a few newspapers; officials saw this channel as a clever means of circumventing censorship, of passing information to Germany, and of undermining public morale. The author and MP AP Herbert[77] fanned the flames by writing to the Home Secretary making similar observations.

Radcliffe applied withering lawyerly logic when approached. 'It seems to me that Mr Herbert must be arguing for either of two possibilities. Either he thinks that the astrologers are on the whole so accurate in their forecasts that they are worth studying by the German Intelligence Service for their own sake; or he thinks that one or more of the authors of these columns is deliberately trying to sell the secrets of his country to the German Intelligence Service. As to the first alternative, I think it is misleading to concentrate one's attention on one or two accurate forecasts about events which are already the subject of widespread discussion and speculation and to ignore the far more frequent occasions when these prophecies are not justified by events'; and he referred to a recent newspaper analysis of the forecasts of 'Sunday astrologers': 'Disproof of their predictions was almost devastating'. As to the suggestion that he should tell certain editors that they had German spies lurking in their offices, he required 'something much more positive' as evidence.

The Home Office came back immediately, suggesting that informed editors might themselves be leaking news thus, or that the Germans might plant stories 'upon an innocent but insufficiently alert astrologer'. Radcliffe apologised for being 'so unaccommodating', but dismissed these suggestions with similar wit: 'What I cannot get beyond is the known fact that astrologers' predictions are habitually wrong. If that is so I cannot see why the German Intelligence Staff should be supposed to get any benefit from the occasional prediction which is subsequently found to have been right, unless they have some means of detecting right from wrong. If they have, they do not need an astrologer!'[78]

On 20 April 1943, the Stockholm correspondent of the *Daily Telegraph* filed a report (incorrectly) that Admiral Canaris, the Head of German Military Intelligence, had been dismissed. SIS and the Foreign Office wished to play down such rumours, knowing of Canaris' doubts about the War, and of the strained relations between him and Himmler. The FO wrote to 'C': 'As you probably know, it is always possible to prevent the publication of any piece of news by the expedient of circulating what is known as a "D" notice, but it has been calculated that such notices are seen by a minimum of some 500 people, which usually means that the news spreads like wildfire even though it may not be published or reproduced'. They therefore decided that it was better to do nothing proactively, but to get the Foreign Office News Department to tell any journalist who inquired about the rumour 'to lay off and not give the rumours any public circulation.'[79]

Inadvertent Leaks

In December 1943 the Government received a 'Most Secret' complaint from the US Government, about an item published in the *Daily Sketch* on 14 December. This reported in its 'Inside Information' column: 'Professor Niels Bohr,[80] world-famous physicist who reached London recently after escaping the Nazis in Denmark, has gone to the U.S. on a special mission after consultations with Lord Cherwell,[81] Mr Churchill's personal assistant.

Professor Bohr is, amongst other things, an expert on explosives. We understand that this subject is connected with his visit, and that he is taking some new ideas which are being shared between the two Allies.'

Germany had indeed seized his former workplace, the Institute of Theoretical Physics in Copenhagen, with the assumed intention of furthering its research in atomic physics for the development of atomic weapons (secret intelligence out of Germany through Lisbon had alerted the Allies to this work). Although Bohr had told the Allies no such research had been or could be done there, the Americans were concerned the Germans would connect Bohr's visit with their own atomic programme. Until the censors talked to him subsequently, the editor of the *Sketch* was no doubt unaware of any of these programmes and of just what kind of 'explosives' were involved, nor of Bohr's relevance.[82]

In March 1944, *The Observer* published information about confidential negotiations between the Soviet and Polish Governments, and in May 1944 it carried a story about Soviet proposals to use the German Army when it was defeated (if it fought 'to the bitter end') as prisoner-labour with which to rebuild Europe. Both articles caused protests from Britain's Allies about the leaks, and the Government therefore considered whether to attempt to make the editor reveal his sources under Defence Regulation 80A. On the first occasion it was eventually decided to take no legal or informal action, but on 11 May Churchill raised the matter in the War Cabinet, and it was agreed the Foreign Secretary and the Minister of Information should see the editor and ask him voluntarily to disclose his source, threatening him with using 'all the powers at their disposal' if he did not (the Police and Security Service meanwhile were making discreet but inconclusive checks on 'aliens' employed by the paper).

This interview took place next day, and the editor, Ivor Brown,[83] declined to name his sources, but thought the originator was a Russian third party "C"; however he wrote next day saying that source "B" had obtained all the information not from "C" but from the American Press, before passing it to contributor "A". The disappointed Eden asked for proof of this story, and Brown responded regretfully but firmly that, although his known contributor "A" was willing to be named himself, he was not willing to name the unknown (to the editor) "B", who anyway alleged he could not now remember where in the American Press he had seen the details; Brown could only say he would not use material from the assumed foreigner "B" again. Ministers concluded there was little likely to be gained from pursuing this tissue of vagueness further; they merely reiterated the harm it had done to Britain's relations with Allies, while Brown himself hoped there would be 'no further occasion for objection in our pages'.

The WWII Press/Government interaction included other examples of how, then as before and since, editors may misjudge the impact of publishing apparently harmless information at the wrong time, and Ministers may misjudge their ability to coerce editors into revealing sources. Nevertheless in WWII in general, again as before and since, Ministers more often than not ultimately held back from full use of legislation when national security was not genuinely endangered.[84] They also relied on the media to publish morale-boosting news, for example 'Britain Has Fighter With No Propeller' [the prototype jet aircraft].[85]

On 22 May 1945 the Washington authorities again remonstrated with the British Government about an article in the *Daily Express* the previous day about atomic matters. This discussed the relationship of heavy water to atomic bombs, and earlier operations in Norway to prevent Germany obtaining access to such heavy water. There were other complaints too to the British Security Council in Washington in the last months of the War about the British Censors' inability to prevent reports from outside the UK about such matters, and about linkage to reports in the Canadian Press.[86] The Media were however not entirely unhelpful to the secret Agencies during the War; 'almost all British Editors told their foreign correspondents informally that if we picked up some information useful to the British war effort, we should pass it on to the local spook.'[87]

27

TOWARDS PEACE

As early as October 1944, the MoI had been making proposals for amendment of Defence Notices when there was a ceasefire in Europe. The Ministry had already consulted the Security Executive and the Security Service in August, the latter wishing Notices No 78 and 80 to remain unchanged.[88] The Home Office however thought it would be hard to justify to the public the retention of detailed prohibitions on mentioning such matters as 'fifth columnists', wartime security committees, malicious damage, interference with essential services, making false statements, causing obstruction, and alteration of permits. On 'malicious damage' for example, the Home Office considered 'It can hardly be necessary after cease fire in Europe that the Press should submit for censorship every story about anyone who sets fire to his neighbour's tool shed or digs a pit in a bowling green or chips pieces off the statue of Abraham Lincoln' [the choice of examples is an interesting reflection of that Department's forecast of post-war crime].[89] The Security Service, represented by Lieutenant Colonel Cussen,[90] wished however to retain rigorous blanket censorship on counter-espionage in order to prevent an enemy knowing when and how one of their agents had been discovered.[91]

The Press, whose representatives had also been consulted, felt equally strongly that after the European cease fire, where mention of OSA use was concerned, they should only have to submit articles when the case was connected with the War. This was considered by most officials to be an impractical distinction, and anyway not to address the major press concern: 'what the Press have a right to fear is the use of the extraordinary powers provided by the Official Secrets Act in cases not connected with National Security.'[92] However, as undertakings (albeit not invariably honoured) had been given by successive governments that these powers would not be used against the Press, some officials felt the Defence Notices could be left unchanged.

Other officials however disagreed, the Home Office Press Officer even referring to 'this obnoxious D.N. . . . . It is most undesirable that a sharp difference of opinion between Whitehall and Fleet Street on an issue concerning the Official Secrets Act should be allowed to develop. Fleet Street regards these Acts as an anti-press law, and views with suspicion any proposal to strengthen the position of the executive in using or misusing the Acts against journalists'. A compromise was therefore sought, and bigger guns were brought into action: the Home Office DUS Sir Frank Newsam,[93] the Controller of News and Censorship at the Ministry of Information Francis Williams[94] and Brigadier 'Jasper' Harker of the Security Service. Their solution was to put the onus on anyone in the Press who discovered some matter concerning espionage, to check with the censors whether or not the case was covered by Section 1 of OSA 1911, before reporting. The Newspaper and Periodical Emergency Council did indeed subsequently agree in March to the continuance of this censorship requirement after the ceasefire in Europe, but only 'so long as the war with Japan lasts.'[95]

In every age, officials believe that if the Media are conceded a centimetre, they will come back and ask for a metre. They may indeed try, but officials can and do say 'sorry, that's it'; conversely, sometimes the Media are, in the public interest, right to ask for more. In this case, the Press came back in May 1945 and asked the Chief Press Censor whether, even if they could not report every new case of espionage, they could nevertheless now report cases from earlier in the War. Long discussion followed between lawyers as to whether, when the Emergency Powers Act expired at the end of the War, the Official Secrets or other Acts would be sufficient to preserve the current powers, in particular those to obtain proof that a particular piece of information could only have come from an official source. Newsam said 'there was no prospect of amending the Official Secrets Acts to enforce the disclosure of the source of information'; and it was pointed out that even if a conviction could be obtained under the OSAs it was open to the author to go abroad and publish his book or article outside the jurisdiction. Newsam in the end decided to postpone a decision on the post-war arrangements until after Japan had been defeated, and meanwhile to stick to current powers and conduct further studies into the problem.

The day after the USA dropped an atomic bomb (6 August 1945) on Hiroshima, Admiral Thomson reopened the debate. While legislation faced deadlock, he reminded: 'in point of fact, these legal considerations can safely be relegated to the background. Experience both in peace and war shows that Editors can be relied on to suppress any information if reasonable security grounds can be shown for keeping it secret. All that is needed is efficient machinery to facilitate consultation between the Government and the Press whenever desirable, and to enable the Government to tender advice to Editors by communications issued when the need arises. As has been mentioned, before the war the Admiralty, War Office, Air Ministry, and Press Committee was maintained to answer these purposes'.

He described, with examples from the 1930s, how the System had worked, and explained the option open to the Press to challenge any Notice 'by bringing it before the Joint Committee ... The system appears to have worked efficiently and to have answered satisfactorily a national requirement, and a preliminary discussion with a view to the revival of this necessary system has now become a matter of urgency'.

He persuaded others. The Security Service recommended that, in view of their probably wide distribution, the new Notices should not contain secret information about what was to be protected, and that it should lead on producing a revised list of subjects to be protected. It was also agreed that interim advice should be sent to the Media, but without discussing Section 2 of the OSA; Will insisted on the latter point, on which, although they were by now good friends, Thomson disagreed.[96]

By mid-August,[97] all Departments had now agreed the AWOAMPC should immediately be revived, and Will, as the Newspaper and Periodical Emergency Committee Chairman, asked government departments as an interim measure to let him have lists of those matters on which they should be consulted before publication. Cussen also recorded that Will had again resisted any letter sent to Editors starting with reference to the Official Secrets Acts; 'It was clear that Mr Will was already rejoicing at the prospective demise of Press censorship and that any reminder that the Official Secrets Acts were alive and well was distasteful to him. I think I can say, however, that the general tone of the meeting was hopeful so far as co-operation between the Press and the Services was concerned'.

Home Office reaction was also favourable, since it now considered the AWOAMPC in practice gave better protection than Court Orders, around which the Press would find ways. At the end of the month, Newsam chaired a further meeting of all departments concerned, merely to decide what to do about the extant Section 6 Orders (Espionage); opinion was now that these would only remain enforceable by contempt of court proceedings. It was quickly decided to give exemptions from the Orders, on condition the revived AWOAMPC was consulted about details before publication. The Lord Chief Justice, when consulted subsequently, assented. Thus, curiously, the AWOAMPC was revived very promptly after WWII on account initially of matters to do with the Secret Intelligence and Security Services, which pre-war had been only tangentially concerned with the Committee.[98] One other tail note: prior to the end of the War in the Far East, Thomson had not been forewarned specifically about the imminent use of atomic weapons. He was merely told to 'Hang on . . . something's going to happen in Japan very soon.'[99]

'Peace'

On 2 September 1945, Admiral Thomson wrote a final Private and Confidential letter as the Chief Press Censor to all editors:

> The Government has directed that the machinery of Press Censorship is to be wound up as from 0900 B.S.T. to-day, Sunday Sept. 2nd, 1945, following the signing of the surrender terms in Tokyo Bay.
>
> Even in peace time there are obviously some subjects about which information should be kept secret on security grounds. This matter is now under consideration by representatives of the Press and of the Fighting Service Departments, and the necessary advice will be communicated to you at an early date.
>
> Meanwhile the Minister has asked me to express to you his appreciation of the help and co-operation which you have extended to the Press censorship throughout these war years.
>
> May I also take this opportunity of conveying to you my personal thanks for your unfailing support and goodwill which have done so much to lighten the somewhat unenviable task of the censors? The success of the voluntary system has in my opinion been entirely due to the unremitting care you have all taken to avoid disclosing information of value to the enemy, and I shall always look back with the warmest pleasure on the cordial relations which have consistently been maintained between the Press and the Censors.[100]

These benign sentiments were responded to by the Press, whose reporting of the closure of the Censorship Division was almost affectionate, similar in tone to that used on the passing of a fearsome old aunt. Typical was the *Daily Express*: 'The Last Word – on 200,000,000 words' was the headline, and the article ended: 'Thus, for the first time by day or by night for six years, every censor's desk was empty, 500 telephones were mute, the teleprinter machines were silent and only a fading shadow of secrecy remained behind. On the 20th of this month the contracts of all the Press censors come to an end. These censors included elderly Army and Navy officers who will now be retired, authors, business men, farmers, country gentlemen. The only qualification was absolute integrity and ability to keep secrets. Not one of the Allies' major war secrets, the censorship claims, ever leaked out.'[101]

Thus ended the suspended animation of the AWOAMPC. The practices, lessons and ethos which the WWII experience carried forward into the early part of the returning Committee's Cold War period included:

- The need for any advisory system in support of self-censorship to be fully in place when an operation starts, manned and equipped qualitatively and quantitatively, and having been trialled realistically.
- The need for such arrangements, and the legislation relevant to media activity in reporting national security matters, to have been made with prior media advice and acceptance.
- The high desirability of some intermediary organisation between officials and the Media to be available, on which both sides are represented, and which is used to working together to resolve differences.
- Acceptance that governments may be able to use, but cannot fully control, the Media in a democracy.
- Advice about areas for self-censorship must be based on agreed principles which allow reporting of non-endangering information and comment, while protecting personal and operational security.
- Experience that, although censorship legislation must be available to governments should established intermediary measures occasionally be considered inadequate in crises, in practice their use has inherent difficulties; and that discussion, and use of public, parliamentary and private pressures, are often more effective in preserving security.
- Routine inclusion, in distribution of advice on publication of national security matters, of broadcast media, film news companies, and book publishers.
- Regular inclusion of Security and Secret Intelligence Services interests in the system's coverage.
- Inclusion of atomic matters.
- Increased speed of the transmission and handling of information by the Media, and the need of the System to be able to respond accordingly.
- Increased 'globalisation' of information; the need to take into account not just national but also allied security considerations; and the ability of those who wish to avoid legal prohibition to publish in other countries.
- 'Total war' involvement of the public in security matters.
- The need to balance the security of D-Notices with maximising their distribution.
- The need for advice in support of self-censorship to be independent of any official and media special interests, consistent across departments, and applied even-handedly across the Media.

The World War II experiences also raise some more fundamental thoughts. There were many areas of security activity in which thousands were involved, yet which were never mentioned in the Media until much later. The history of the Enigma code-breaking, and its enormous contribution to the success of the Allies, is now largely public; the fact that something known to so many remained unpublished so long after censorship was abolished, despite over 12,000 men and (mostly) women having worked at Bletchley Park and its outstations, was not due to the censors nor to the self-censorship of the Media; it was because those involved did not speak about it beyond their own circle; they self-censored at source. Even better known now is the history of the build-up to the Normandy Landings, including prior construction of mobile harbours, of pipelines and of massive amphibious capability, in all of which the wider public were involved, and yet sufficient secrecy was maintained to achieve surprise and mal-deployment of German defences; here censorship and media self-censorship did have a major part to play, but it was the self-censorship beyond their own circle of almost all of those involved which was the key factor.

Clearly, therefore, the best security is achieved when those in the public involved (including here the Media) have been convinced that revealing something really would be against the security interests of their community (in both the most immediate and the wider sense). This conviction can only be inculcated by sufficiently open, truthful and intelligent persuasion, and it can last only as long as the relevant and specific threat appears to remain valid. As seen in this History, disagreements between the governmental side and the Media, over what really matters to security, have occurred when persuasion has been insufficiently open, truthful and/or intelligent to be convincing; and usually it has been some of the government's own employees (or indeed members of the 'political class') who have activated the Media.

Section 6

EARLY YEARS OF THE
COLD WAR, 1945–67

28

SECURITY CONTEXT

Politics and Operations

Post-WWII governmental/media interaction on national security was dominated by rapidly increasing hostility between the Soviet Union and its recent Allies, and by Britain's residual problems as an ex-superpower. From 1945–48 these included violent action by both Arabs and Jews against the British Mandate in Palestine, and against each other; followed by the new State of Israel's successful defence of its then territory against Arab forces, in a region where Britain still maintained a substantial military presence, especially along the Suez Canal. Despite the wartime collaboration with the UK on atom bombs, the US McMahon Act of 1946 prohibited further exchanges of such information. In 1946 talks between the USA and USSR over the divided Korea broke down. In 1947 the Truman Doctrine on the post-war world was enunciated, followed by the Marshall Plan for rebuilding war-damaged economies, which the USSR (and therefore European countries under its control) opposed; in September 1947 Cominform was founded. The Berlin Airlift, resupplying the West-controlled part of the beleaguered city, lasted from June 1948 to May 1949.

Britain and the USA agreed an informal modus vivendi on intelligence/atomic matters in 1948.[1] The Malayan Emergency lasted from 1948 until 1960, when Communist insurgents were finally defeated. In 1949, the Soviet Union confirmed it had atomic bombs, NATO was founded (April), the Federal Republic of Germany was formally established in West Germany (September), and the People's Republic of China founded (October). In December 1949 the United Nations (but not the USSR) recognised the Seoul Government as the only legitimate government in Korea; in January 1950 the USSR declared its support for North Korea, in June North Korea invaded South Korea and was condemned by the UN, with the USA, UK and other nations intervening militarily on South Korea's side; China entered the war on the side of the North in October/November. In early 1951 UN forces under General Ridgway began to turn the tide, and a July 1953 settlement eventually ended the fighting (killed included a million Koreans of both sides, over 54,000 Americans, about 700 Turks and 670 British). In Kenya the Mau-Mau campaign against British rule lasted from 1952 until 1960. In October 1952, Britain tested its first atomic bomb in the Australian Monte Bello islands,[2] and another in 1956. Iran severed diplomatic relations with Britain in October 1952. In January 1953, Churchill forecast Central and Eastern Europe would be free of Communist rule in about thirty years. The British campaign in the Aden Protectorate lasted from 1953 until withdrawal in 1967, and successful operations in Oman in support of the Sultan lasted from 1957 to the early 60s.

In July 1953 French forces in Vietnam surrendered at Dien Bien Phu, leading to formal partition in 1954. In August 1953 the Head of Government in Iran, Mossadegh, was overthrown with American and British assistance, and the pro-West Shah reinstalled. The same month the USSR tested the first hydrogen bomb, followed by the USA in March the next year (Britain decided the following year to develop its own H-Bomb, tested late 1957). The South East Asia Treaty Organisation was founded in September 1954 (Australia, France, New Zealand, Pakistan, Philippines, Thailand, UK, USA). In October 1954, after three years of anti-West violence, UK Forces began to leave the Suez Canal Zone. The Middle East Treaty Organisation (the 'Baghdad Pact', later CENTO) was founded in February 1955 (Iran, Iraq, Pakistan, Turkey, UK – with US support, but not initially with US participation because of Arab sensibilities at the time). In May 1955, West Germany joined NATO, and the Warsaw Pact was subsequently founded by the USSR. The increasingly violent EOKA campaign against British rule in Cyprus lasted from 1953 until 1960.

In June 1956 the Polish Army suppressed an internal revolt. The Soviet Union suppressed the Hungarian Uprising in October/November (causing many to quit the Communist Party of Great Britain), at the same time as Britain, France and Israel were combining to retake the Suez Canal, following Nasser's nationalisation of it; there was no follow-through plan, and, having thus aroused US political opposition, these allies withdrew the following spring (adding to belated reassessment of Britain's place in the world). In 1957 too there was revolution in Iraq, civil war in Lebanon, war against France in Algeria, and Egypt and Syria came together politically as the United Arab Republic; Britain deployed a Parachute Brigade to Jordan in support of King Hussein. The European Economic Community was founded, without Britain. The 1957 Sandys Defence White Paper led to the abolition of National Service and to basing Britain's defence on nuclear deterrence (the Campaign for Nuclear Disarmament started the following year). In June 1958 those parts of the McMahon Act affecting nuclear collaboration with the UK were repealed. The USSR and China parted political company in 1959. The late '50s and early '60s were also a period of intensive development of nuclear weapons by the Soviet Union and United States, of their missile delivery systems (including submarine), and of build-up of massive nuclear weapon stockpiles.

The year 1961 included the failed US-backed 'Bay of Pigs' operation in Cuba in April, the British intervention against Iraq in Kuwait in June/July, and the building of the Berlin Wall in August. The Cuban Missile Crisis dominated Autumn 1962, when the USA and USSR were seemingly on the brink of nuclear war until the Soviets recalled their missile-transporting ships. The British-backed Malaysian campaign in defence of Borneo against Indonesia lasted from 1962 until 1966. In 1962 the USA agreed to supply Britain with Polaris nuclear missiles. In July 1963, the USA, USSR, and UK signed a Nuclear Test Ban Treaty, criticised by China. The US military build-up in support of South Vietnam started in 1963, and the Tet offensive by the Viet Cong took place in February 1967. The UK's MoD in 1964 incorporated the Single Service Departments. India and Pakistan went to war in 1965. In April 1967, after long hostilities between Israel and Arab countries, the former achieved a crushing victory in the Six-Day War, occupying Palestine and Sinai. Throughout this period, British forces and intelligence services were also involved in extrication from the colonies, usually but not always peacefully, and sometimes, as with Rhodesia, leaving residual problems. It was also a period of continuous underlying economic difficulty for Britain, despite improvements in standards of living, and of great social change.

The Secret Agencies

The organisation at Bletchley Park was rapidly run down when the War ended. The GC&CS moved to Eastcote in North West London in 1946, and was renamed the Government Communications Headquarters (GCHQ). In order that the new threat, the Soviet Union, should not learn from Bletchley's wartime successes, Churchill ordered equipment should be destroyed, apart from two Colossus computers and 50 Bombes (the smaller electro-magnetic code-breaking machines). GCHQ moved to two ex-War Office sites in Cheltenham in 1952–54, and from 1956 its Director-General reported direct to the Foreign Office. Although a cover story about its diplomatic communications function was now used, its cryptographic role was still not acknowledged publicly.[3] It maintained its close wartime links with its United States equivalent, despite the occasional political hiatus between the two countries, for example over the Suez invasion.

Menzies remained Chief of the SIS until 1951, by which time it had subsumed SOE and MI9 responsibilities for covert operations and support of escape routes in enemy countries. Close working links with the CIA continued, based in wartime collaboration, despite the buffeting caused by the unmasking of British insider spies and Suez. The SIS relationship with the Security Service was sometimes less harmonious, and there was then no Intelligence Co-ordinator in the Cabinet Office, although the Joint Intelligence Committee continued to meet. The term of office of the next Head of the SIS, Major-General 'Sinbad' Sinclair[4] was one of mixed success, with public allegations of involvement in controversial operations in Persia, Syria and Egypt damaging to the reputation of MI6. There was also publicity over a badly-organised attempt to inspect the underwater hull of a Soviet cruiser, unusually making a goodwill visit to Portsmouth at a time of attempted rapprochement with the post-Stalin USSR; this ended with the death of the out-of-condition semi-retired diver, Commander Crabb.[5] Sinclair was succeeded by Sir Dick White,[6] the former Director-General of the Security Service, who suspected Philby, and also directed the successful handling of the important Soviet informer Colonel Oleg Penkovsky.

In the Security Service, Petrie was succeeded in 1946, by another Police Officer, Sir Percy Sillitoe,[7] but although the Service still employed many ex-Armed Forces officers, most senior subordinates were now university graduates of other backgrounds, and one of them, White, succeeded him. Preoccupation with the communist threat, begun in the latter stages of WWII and increased by events in Malaya, was reflected in the heavy counter-espionage load. The British trades union movement was closely monitored, but even its communist members were not seen collectively by the Security Service as a great threat.

The identities of several Britons who spied for the USSR were revealed during this period, and there was speculation about others. These included the atomic scientist Klaus Fuchs, jailed in 1950; diplomats Guy Burgess and Donald Maclean, who fled to the Soviet Union in 1951; the Foreign Office radio-operator William Marshall, prosecuted in 1952; the engineer Brian Linney, jailed in 1958 for leaking information about a new RAF missile to the Czechs; two Oxford undergraduates (ex-National Service secret communications operators) were jailed in 1958 for publishing a story of a secret operation in the University magazine *Isis*; the intelligence officer George Blake was jailed for 42 years in 1961, escaped in 1966 and fled to the Soviet Union; the Portland Spies (Harry Houghton, Ethel Gee, Gordon Lonsdale, Peter and Helen Kroger)[8] were jailed in 1961, and the Admiralty clerk John Vassall sentenced to 18 years in 1962; the same year the civil servant Barbara Fell was imprisoned for passing official information to her Yugoslav lover; the SIS officer and journalist Kim Philby fled from Lebanon to the Soviet Union in 1963; and the Ministry of Aviation official Frank Bossard was sentenced to 21 years' imprisonment in 1965. There was also the as yet unpublished governmental knowledge that John Cairncross and Anthony Blunt had been spies for Russia. Almost all these cases involved information from defectors to the West, and/or information received from US authorities. The Security Service, so successful against Germany, did not at first achieve similar results against the Soviet bloc.

At the end of the War, intelligence about nuclear matters was separated from other scientific intelligence, in accordance with American practice, but against the advice of RV Jones, effectively the wartime co-ordinator of Scientific and Technical Intelligence; also contrary to his advice, a Committee under Professor PMS Blackett[9] established separate Scientific and Technological Intelligence sections for each fighting Service; they were collocated but in a building remote from their parent Department and from the SIS (which then also lost Jones back to full-time work in the Air Ministry); contact between the scientists and SIS was thereafter through a Joint Scientific and Technical Intelligence Committee, under the JIC. At Churchill's instigation, Jones returned to MoD in 1952 as Director of Scientific Intelligence, but the allegedly promised reintegration of nuclear intelligence under him did not happen, he returned to academe un-succeeded, his department being downgraded and placed under the non-scientist Director of the Joint Intelligence Bureau.[10]

Within the MoD and its still distinct Service Departments, there was initially no unified Intelligence Staff, each Department operating its own Intelligence organisation, but a Joint Intelligence Bureau was formed in 1946 to deal with economic, logistic, scientific and technical aspects. Responsibility for the JIC was transferred from MoD to Cabinet Office in 1957. When the 'unified' MoD was created in 1964, all Services' Intelligence Departments were amalgamated into the Defence Intelligence Staff, whose main effort was directed towards the Cold War. Another area of Defence reorganisation of particular relevance to the D-Notice Committee was Special Forces. After WWII the expertise of several such units (including Long Range Desert Group, Special Air Service, Special Boat Section, Small Scale Raiding Force, and the Royal Naval Experimental Submarine Flotilla) became a largely Reservist responsibility, but the SBS became a Royal Marines responsibility in 1946, and events in Korea and in Malaysia soon caused re-establishment of the Regular SAS, active thereafter in many other parts of the world.

Governmental Reviews of Security

The Attlee Government in March 1948 announced that, for security not political reasons, it intended to bar communists and fascists from employment in the Civil Service in connexion with work 'the nature of which was vital to the security of the State'; a Tribunal was established to hear appeals from civil servants threatened with transfer from secret duties or with dismissal. Positive Vetting of civil servants, and of others such as the military, started in 1952. From 1956 the scope of its consideration was extended from political affiliations to character defects. After the Vassall affair, the Admiralty set up a Security Department in 1961, and the other Service Departments did so in the following years; attempts to form, as recommended by Lord Radcliffe, one civilian-manned Joint-Service vetting organisation took rather longer.

In 1956, following publication of a Parliamentary Report into 'The Disappearance of two Former Foreign Office Officials',[11] the Government established a Conference of Privy

Counsellors to study security. They concluded that, whereas formerly the main threat had been espionage by foreign powers through professional agents, it was now from communists. In particular it identified the Communist Party of Great Britain as a major threat to security, and recommended that its members and their associates (including spouses), having been identified, should then not be allowed access to information which they might betray.[12] The 1956 Report found nothing notably wrong with the then security arrangements, but did recommend additional measures, including refusal to employ certain individuals in some circumstances even though nothing had been proved against them; it did however draw the line at giving the authorities extra powers to detain such suspects or prevent them leaving the country.[13] The Labour ex-Minister Herbert Morrison described the recommendations as 'repugnant to our traditions and destructive of morale', but they were introduced.[14]

In 1952 Churchill, alerted to the extent of Soviet bugging of British embassies and other official buildings, tasked MoD with investigating; a two-year review was led by its future Chief Scientist.[15] In June 1957, following adverse media comment about some British interception cases, Prime Minister Harold Macmillan[16] set up a further Committee of Privy Counsellors under Sir Norman Birkett[17] to 'inquire into the interception of communications' [this particular type generically referred to in the Press at the time and since as 'telephone tapping'], based on the practices of the authorities over the previous 20 years.

The Committee reported in October;[18] 'following the example of the Secret Committee of both Houses of Parliament appointed in 1944 to consider the same problem', they did not publish evidence given to them, but did reveal in Appendices which Departments during that period had arranged interception of communications, and how many cases.[19] The Report criticised the previous Home Secretary for having made available transcripts of intercepted telephone conversations to the Bar Council when it was considering a professional misconduct case, and it made several detailed recommendations about handling interception warrants. Bearing in mind the 'cable-vetting' affair of 1967 (see Section 7), it is noteworthy the Report did not mention the secret interception of cables by the authorities, although the Committee had been briefed on and accepted this activity. The Report gave 'C' little concern.

The Privy Councillors summarised: 'The origin of the power to intercept communications can only be surmised', but had been recognised as lawful in various statutes for at least 200 years; there was a difference of view about where the authority to tap telephones came from [but not about its legality]; the power to intercept was exercised for the detection and prevention of crime and for the preservation of the safety of the State; this power, then exercised almost exclusively by the Metropolitan Police, the Board of Customs and Excise, and the Security Service, was used 'with the greatest care and circumspection, under the strictest rules and safeguards, and never without the personal considered approval of the Secretary of State'; the use of the power had been effective in the case of both crime and of security; the exercise of the power 'in these limited spheres' should be allowed to continue under the current constraints; the interference with the privacy of the ordinary law-abiding citizen or with his individual liberty was 'infinitesimal', only arose as a by-product of the pursuit of wrong-doers, and was not 'harmful'. The future Minister Patrick Gordon Walker[20] alone dissented somewhat from the comments on continuance without change and the degree of interference with individual liberty and privacy.

Following the conviction of the 'Portland' spies and Blake, the Government set up an independent Committee in 1961, again under the Chairmanship of Lord Radcliffe, 'to review the security procedures and practices currently followed in the public service and to consider what, if, any changes are required'. In August, in response to a PQ from George Brown [21] about complaints in the Press concerning a D-Notice of 27 July 1961 ('Classified Weapons and Equipment: and Air Photography and Diagrams'), the Prime Minister [Macmillan] added to the Committee's remit the examination of the D-Notice System, 'both generally and with particular reference to' that particular Notice.

The Report attempted a definition of 'security': 'the safeguarding of such information in the possession of the Government as would by its unauthorised disclosure cause injury to the interests of the country' [correct in essence, but far too vague and all-embracing to be useable per se by the D-Notice Committee then or now]. The Report's recommendations, which were finally accepted by the Government in April 1962, covered the organisation of all aspects of departmental security, security classifications, personnel security and vetting procedures in the Foreign Office, Services Departments and Armed Forces, security in industry, physical (including documentary) security and security training, and, in its Chapter 9, 'the D Notice Procedure.'[22] Although its review of the D-Notice system was timely, the Report was mainly an overdue review of wider security systems, which in the post-WWII relaxation had become slack, amateur, and little related to Cold War realities.

Nevertheless, the further major security case later that year (Vassall) was followed in 1963 by another tribunal, again chaired by Lord Radcliffe, investigating the background, because of possible involvement peripherally in the case by a Government Minister. During this hearing, two journalists, Reginald Foster of the *Daily Sketch* and Brendan Mulholland of the *Daily Mail* were jailed for three and six months respectively for refusing to name their sources, and another *Sketch* writer Desmond Clough would have accompanied them to prison had an Admiralty Information Officer not come forward to reveal himself as the source.[23] In 1965 the Prime Minister [Wilson] had to order a further investigation, this time by the Standing Security Commission chaired by Lord Justice Winn,[24] following the convictions that year of FC Bossard and of Staff Sergeant PS Allen for selling secret documents to foreign governments (Soviet and Iraqi respectively). These cases revealed continuing serious deficiencies in personnel security procedures of Government Departments, in particular MoD, and led to further recommendations.[25] This succession of inquiries was part of the pressure which led to the Government setting up a Royal Commission on Tribunals of Inquiry, considering inter alia the degree to which evidence should be heard in camera.[26]

29

MEDIA CONTEXT[27]

Formal censorship of the Media was quickly terminated when the War ended, but Government was initially slow to abandon some habits of control, for example reluctant dissemination of official information, and strings attached to visits offered to the Media, including the requirement to submit copy on completion. Editors put their foot down; the NS told its editor members they should once more take full responsibility for what they published, subject to the OSAs and D-Notice guidance, and should decline to accept official invitations having 'censorship' conditions.[28]

Nevertheless, although the British Media have usually watched hawk-like for any attempt by government to restrict their freedom, they were ready in the early years of the Cold War to concede, when pressed, that they were fairly treated. In September 1954 the Director of the UN Division of Human Rights queried the adequacy of protection of sources of UK media information; the NPA not only gave a favourable interpretation of the assurances given by government in 1939 on OSAs 1911 and 1920, but also stated 'this Association is of the opinion that adequate protection for the sources of information of news personnel already exists in this country.'[29] The Press were preoccupied at the time with their own poor labour relations, which resulted in March 1955 in a national newspaper strike.

Those attempting to operate local (commercial) radio stations might have disagreed with this sanguine view of governmental attitudes to the Media. Of the pre-war continental stations broadcasting specifically to Britain, only Radio Luxembourg afterwards restarted, remembered now mainly as a popular music station, but of wider content (during the War used by the Germans). Establishing other independent radio initiatives was resisted by government (and the BBC); the Pilkington Committee of 1960 found 'no evidence of public demand' (none had been sought), the Government postponed any decision two years later, and from 1964 whenever off-shore stations such as Radio Caroline operated, government used many ruses, at home and abroad, and Acts (for example, the Wireless Telegraphy Act 1949, the Continental Shelf Act 1964 and the Marine Broadcast Offences Act 1967) in its efforts to prevent such 'pirate' stations from operating, despite their growing audiences.

The decade 1950–60 also saw widespread but ultimately vain resistance by the Press to the growth of broadcast news. The BBC had withdrawn in May 1945 from its wartime agreement with the Press on restrictions on BBC news broadcasts, now undertaking only to give the NPA and NS prior notice of any major changes in scheduling and coverage. In 1950 the NPA gave evidence to the Broadcasting Committee chaired by Lord Beveridge,[30] opposing 'Sponsored Radio' [i.e. commercial not BBC], initially a successful campaign. The Television Act 1954 nevertheless established commercial television and set up the Independent Television Authority. In 1955 the NPA complained formally to the BBC about the latter's decision to introduce an early sports bulletin on Saturday afternoons, including the football results. In 1957 the BBC wrote to the NPA and NS warning it intended to increase the number and content of news summaries interspersed in the Light Programme and Home Service. In 1958 BBC TV introduced a Sports and Results programme from 2 p.m. to 4.45 p.m. on Saturday afternoons (Independent TV had already done so). By 1959 UK television set ownership had risen to 24.5 million.

In 1960 the NPA gave evidence to the Broadcasting Committee chaired by Sir Harry Pilkington,[31] arguing against non-press commercial interests owning radio stations, on the grounds that only newspaper organisations could operate them satisfactorily; the NS, initially divided on this issue, eventually came in behind the NPA, but it was to no avail.[32] The first transatlantic television transmission took place (via the new Telstar satellite) in July 1962. The Television Act 1963 introduced the ITA Code on standards (portraying violence, etc), and gave the Authority increased powers over schedules and advertising (cigarette advertisements were banned from 1965), with a further Act the following year. Intelsat was formed in 1964, to further media and other commercial use of satellite communications. BBC2 was launched in 1964, and the first TV News at Ten was broadcast in 1967.

In the post-war years, the centralisation and amalgamation of the Press continued, both in London and the provinces. The Guild of Editors was founded in 1946, to address the interests of provincial editors separately from those of their increasingly metropolitan proprietors. The 1949 Royal Commission on the Press was set up by the Labour Government in part in reaction to widespread press support for the Conservatives in the post-war election, and in part at the behest of the NUJ, which was dissatisfied with proprietorial attitudes. This led to formation in 1953 of the General Council of the Press, responsible for overseeing its self-regulation and for dealing with complaints from members of the public. It was however regarded with distaste, by the Press as an imposition, and by government as ineffective.

In 1957 *Picture Post* ceased publication. In 1959 the *Manchester Guardian* dropped its local identity, and moved its main printing to London. In 1960 the *Evening News* absorbed the *Star*, and the *News Chronicle* despite its million plus circulation was absorbed by the *Daily Mail*, in 1961 the TUC sold its interest in the *Daily Herald*, and when IPC later took over Odhams, it took over the *Herald* completely. The many other amalgamations and closures, in London and the provinces, caused government in 1961 to set up the Second Royal Commission on the Press, chaired by Sir Hartley Shawcross,[33] mainly because of anxiety that the range of political and local democratic expression was being eroded. Its Report[34] made recommendations on competition (for readers, for advertising and between each other), production efficiency, distribution, newsprint, ownership and variety of opinion, economic remedies, what is now called 'transparency', amalgamations, and the reconstitution of the General Council of the Press. It also led to press anti-monopoly legislation being introduced in 1965.

Meanwhile, *Reynolds Weekly News* had become the *Sunday Citizen* in 1962 (but in 1967 ceased publication), the *Sunday Telegraph* and *Sunday Times* Colour Supplements had been launched in 1961/2, *The Observer* following in 1964. Because of continuing dissatisfaction with its performance, the General Council of the Press was reformed as the (also unsatisfactory) Press Council that year. In 1964 too the *Daily Herald* was renamed as the *Sun*, which in 1969 was sold to the then Australian Rupert Murdoch,[35] already the recent purchaser of the *News of the World*. In 1966, the *Daily Worker* became the *Morning Star*, and the Canadian Roy Thomson,[36] already owner of the *Scotsman* (from 1953) and the *Sunday Times* (from 1959), bought *The Times* from the Astors, soon putting news on the front page for the first time.

More generally, the total circulation of British national daily newspapers reached its peak (17 million) in 1950, with both the *Daily Mirror* and the *Daily Express* achieving 4 million. Technology used by the Media continued to change, and advances in photo-composition and web-offset printing continued progressively through the 1960s. The 1958 Report of the Advisory Committee on the Inland Telegraph Service reflected the rapid decline in the use of the telegram, by both Press and public, as alternative services (then principally telephone and telex) improved. The problems between proprietors, journalists and blue-collar staff which had been apparent in earlier decades and were to come to a head later, were manifest in particular in a month-long Press strike in 1955 and a six-week regional press strike in 1959.

Proprietors such as King and Thomson not only controlled many national and provincial journals, but also had major shareholdings in publishing and commercial television. Some of the more famous Press figures died during these decades (Southwood in 1946, Camrose in 1954, Beaverbrook in 1964, Kemsley in 1968), but their dynasties and those of the Harmsworths continued, albeit in less 'baronial' style. Others emerged (such as Robert Maxwell),[37] and a generation of notable journalists flourished as editors, or moved visibly towards such imminent prominence (amongst others David Astor, Arthur Christiansen, Hugh Cudlipp, David English, Harold Evans, William Haley, Denis Hamilton, Simon Jenkins, John Junor, Larry Lamb, and William Rees-Mogg).

One trend of this period was growing sensitivity of politicians to leaks about their confidential business to the Media. Eden was enraged by revelations of controversy about plans to end conscription in late 1955, and when President Eisenhower's personal message to him deploring the use of force at Suez was revealed in the Press in 1956; Macmillan was irritated in late 1958 by similar disclosures by Chapman Pincher about the future of the deterrent and in 1960 about the cancellation of the Bloodhound missile; Wilson obsessed about even more topics later that decade. Leak inquiries revealed little, indeed usually concluded that it had been a combination of open source material (often foreign), political gossip, and intelligent journalism.[38]

An Adjournment Debate on the Press took place in the House of Commons on 7 February 1967. This was sparked by widespread concerns about levelling off of readership numbers, continuing amalgamations and concentration of ownership in fewer hands, a perceived fall in journalistic standards, and the poor state of Press industrial relations. It was an unusually well-informed and measured debate, with only occasional Party partisan points being made. Other concerns expressed included those about chequebook journalism, and the strained relations between Press and politicians. The President of the Board of Trade Douglas Jay,[39] himself an ex-journalist, led those who said it was not for government but for management and unions to sort out the current problems. Gordon Walker summed up: 'All sections of the Press must realise that it is in effect on public trial at the moment', and emphasised that 'the Press works on public opinion, but public opinion must also work on the Press.'[40]

30

RETURN OF THE COMMITTEE

Although media censorship had ended on 2 September 1945 (and postal and telegraph censorship almost entirely by 30 September), the Ministry of Information lingered on.[41] Admiral Thomson was charged with implementing reactivation of the Admiralty, War Office, Air Ministry, and Press Committee. By mid-September he was 'beginning to despair of Mr Will' of the NPEC for moving too slowly, and he asked Burnham (still running War Office Public Relations) 'to take some firm and positive action regarding the question of establishing machinery for the preservation of military secrets in peace-time.'[42] It took some weeks formally to obtain agreement from diverse parts of the Media, not due to reluctance, merely to seeking volunteer members.[43] Meanwhile the Interdepartmental Committee on Security continued to debate the desirability (in the eyes of the Security Service and the War Office) of retaining Defence Regulation 3 (reporting of spy arrests and trials) 'for a little while longer, as its mere existence acted as a deterrent against persons who would otherwise divulge war secrets'. The Home Office asked DGSS to reconsider this position, feeling it would be difficult for government to justify retention now that censorship had ceased. Fortuitously at this moment the Media formally agreed to reactivate the AWOAMPC, and the Security Service therefore agreed to revocation of the Regulation from the beginning of October; the War Office following suit on courts martial.[44]

Before the Committee had re-formed, there was a small foretaste of matters to come. On 28 September Chapman Pincher[45] wrote in the *Daily Express* about atomic bomb weights. This caused governmental consternation, not only because of the article's impact on British relationships with those leading the American atomic programme, but also because, with no AWOAMPC in place and censorship having already lapsed, no action with the *Express* was considered possible. Action might have been taken under the OSAs had British leakage of information been behind the story, but eventually it was concluded the article had been based on facts already in the public domain, embellished by Pincher's 'imagination'.[46]

Re-establishing the D-Notice Structure for the Cold War

Even before war in the Far East was over, DMI had become concerned about the number of secret matters appearing in the Press. In late June, the Security Service and the Defence Departments, through their Joint Intelligence Committee, had begun to discuss this problem and books by temporary officers and civil servants of the 'now it can be revealed type'. The post-war AWOAMPC met for the first time on 3 October 1945. Sir Arthur Street, about to retire as Air Ministry PUS, was in the Chair and familiar with the pre-war work of the Committee, but his fellow Permanent Secretaries were new to it, as were all the Press representatives, now including William Will, ex-Chairman of the wartime NPEC (one of the two

NPA representatives, the other being yet another member of the Robbins family, Alan Pitt Robbins);[47] there were as before also two NS representatives, one from the SDNS, one from the PTPWNPA, and one from the News Agencies – a representative of the BBC was 'in attendance' for the first time, as was Thomson. Street opened by stating the Government hoped to see the Committee revived, and this was formally agreed.

On future Committee membership, it was suggested representation might include BBC (agreed),[48] Scottish Newspaper Proprietors' Association (Weekly Press) (not agreed because Will said present arrangements were adequate but PTPWNPA representation should be increased to two), Newsreels Association (not agreed), British Film Producers' Association (not agreed), photographic agencies (not agreed), Empire Press Union (agreed), Association of American Correspondents in London (not agreed), foreign Press correspondents (not agreed), and book publishers (not agreed). Rationales for all these decisions are not recorded; one can only speculate that there may have been press prejudice against audio-visual upstarts; and that non-Imperial foreigners were excluded because of security considerations, and anyway Committee advice would largely have been ignored by them.

The position of the *Daily Worker* (publishing again latterly during the War because the Soviet Union had become an Ally), was also discussed, as it was not a member of the NPA; Will undertook to speak to its editor, since 'he did not think there would be any difficulty in getting that newspaper to accept the principle of the D.Notice procedure and the D.Notices when issued'. Robbins asked whether other Government Departments, such as the Ministry of Supply and Aircraft production, were also to join the Committee, but the Chairman replied firmly 'it was intended to confine representation to the Service Departments'. Similarly dismissed was the memorandum Will had distributed to editors at the end of the War listing the many wider topics on which Departments had wished to be consulted; 'It was the general view that D.Notices should only be drawn up on matters concerned with defence security and must be specific in form', i.e. that, apart from a few general Notices, D.Notices would normally be issued as required at the time on specific stories. This was the practice which led to the System acquiring its media reputation, 'exaggerated by early television dramatists when characters they created declared "Slap a D-Notice on it" '.[49]

On distribution of Notices, Street proposed that 'if the Secretary enjoyed the confidence of the Committee he could take action on receipt of a D.Notice from a Department without the Committee being called unless some question of policy or principle was involved'. The Press side did not accept that, arguing the pre-War Committee had not met often enough. It was agreed the AWOAMPC should meet monthly for the time being, when 'non-urgent D.Notices should, if possible, be considered in batches', while on the more urgent ones the Secretary should consult with Will, who in turn would consult his Media colleagues and decide whether a special meeting should be held. It is remarkable that such a system, so unsuited to the realities of Media deadlines, should have been agreed; it was perhaps indicative of the mutual suspicion between Media and officials which immediately re-emerged in reactivating a system dormant for six years.

On the machinery of distribution, Henry Martin of the Press Association offered to handle urgent D-Notices as before through his office, sending them by direct printer to the London Media and by Creed (teleprinter) to the provincials. After Thomson reassured that during the War this had been done in case of urgency and that no breaches of security had occurred, the PA offer was accepted, with non-urgent messages to be sent out by the Secretary by post. Press members found the wartime categorised distribution lists unnecessarily complicated and asked that their members should receive all Notices; but it was agreed thenceforth to exclude all Irish Republic newspapers, even though some were still then members of the British NS; the Committee undertook, as the NS representatives were unwilling to do so, to inform these Irish editors that they were now beyond the British Press Pale.

Contrary to Thomson's previous advice about the need for a central point of contact to reflect the more joint nature of Services' matters, Street told the meeting that, when information and/or guidance was required, editors should approach the press section of the relevant department, 'and that these sections should undertake such inter-Service consultation as might be necessary'. The Media Members wisely merely 'took note' of this impractical and (as it turned out) short-lived arrangement.

Martin said the Press Association could no longer provide the Committee's Secretary. Although why is not recorded, he was well aware of the time and expense which in the Committee's earlier years the work of the Robbinses, father and son, had cost the Association. Street, clearly pre-alerted to this decision, stated that whoever took over would need an office, staff and machinery to carry out his work, 'and he would record it as the view of the Press Members that the salary and expenses of the Secretary should be met from public funds'. He, his successor as Chairman (Henry Markham[50] of the Admiralty, which now therefore assumed administrative responsibility from the Air Ministry), and one representative each from the NPA and NS would form a sub-committee to select a Secretary and agree the arrangements [the decision that the Secretary and his administrative support should be a charge to public funds has, in one form or another, remained in force ever since]. Finally, it was agreed that, should any member of the Committee be unable to attend a meeting, he should be able to appoint a stand-in.[51]

There were already press queries about publication of information on the wartime espionage trials. The Home Office was asked by the Services whether what had been agreed by the Lord Chief Justice was intended to apply only to cases of which the Press were already aware, or whether they should now inform the Press about other cases too. Its ruling was that, as an official statement had been made about all cases, it should be left to the Press to ask for further information, subject in each case to the Security Service being consulted to ensure that still sensitive information was not revealed. This policy quickly became known to the Press, before it had been formally announced and while Admiral Thomson at the MoI was still trying to obtain agreement from the revived AWOAMPC to a D-Notice about it. The *Sunday Dispatch* on 28 October carried an article gratefully but incorrectly implying that the complete proceedings of wartime spy trials could now be published, and this sparked immediate interest from other papers. The Home Office referred journalists to the War Office, who, while saying that there was no security objection, also reminded them there was still a DoRA Section 6 Court Order in force.

Editors therefore sought clarification from Thomson, whom the muddled official line precluded from giving any; he warned officials that, unless authority to publish was given, the Media were likely to defy the Order and risk the consequences. As the Home Office noted: 'This would be most unfortunate from our point of view since there would probably be nothing we could do about it, and the effectiveness of the proposed arrangements [ie to maintain the Defence Regulation in place but allow controlled publication] depends on a belief on the part of the Press that they cannot disregard Court Orders with impunity'. In hindsight, it seems unlikely the newly unshackled editors and their legal advisers would have meekly accepted that view.

The Media Members of the Committee indicated informally they now thought this was not a suitable subject for a D-Notice, as they did not wish to be associated with what appeared to be a de facto continuance of some aspects of censorship; any pronouncement should be issued by a Government Department. The Home Office felt it should not be the one to do so, because, although the impetus for the continuing restrictions came from its subordinate Security Service, Home Office officials did not wish to be held responsible for subsequent censorship of trial details as they were raised by the Press. Instead, it considered such an announcement should come from the War Office, as the Press were more likely to accept it from a Department already associated in editors' minds with security restrictions. When the Media Members' position was formally confirmed at the AWOAMPC's next meeting (see below), it was therefore the War Office which issued the instruction that articles about such trials should still be submitted for clearance.[52]

In the days following the AWOAMPC's October meeting, the sub-committee on the Secretaryship agreed the ideal candidate would be Admiral Thomson; he was not only experienced in matters of censorship and highly knowledgeable about the Media, but also widely known and well respected by both sides for the fairness and independence of judgement he had shown during the War. He was not however accommodated thereafter within a main Ministry building, but operated initially from the office of his post-war employers, Cable and Wireless, in Electra House on Victoria Embankment; the D-Notice Secretaryship was still considered to be a part-time post, something which could be fitted in with some other, full-time, job. The salary was £500 per annum plus some taxi fares; the ever-parsimonious Admiralty initially attempted to delay paying him, arguing he was still on demobilisation leave (merely interrupted by events since 1939), but it did concede he would be allowed occasional use of a room, Roneo machine and typist – given sufficient notice.

This appointment was announced formally by Markham when the Committee next met, on 8 November 1945. Also now there, as full members, were a second representative of the PTPWNPA, and the first ever representatives of the BBC[53] and the Empire Press Union.[54] The Committee discussed a draft D-Notice on a topic previously covered only in very general terms, now proposed by the War Office on behalf of the still non-avowed Secret Intelligence and Security Services: secret agents. The requirement was not in dispute, as all agreed their identities and activities merited protection; the debate was whether this should apply only to current and future agents. The War Office PUS Sir Eric Speed[55] succeeded in gaining agreement it should apply also to former agents, the rationale for avoiding disclosure [then and now] depending not on how long the agent had been 'retired', but on any personal security considerations, on there still being necessary secrecy surrounding the operations/techniques in which he/she had been involved, and on the need to reassure present and future agents that their personal security would not be threatened by publication; all this subject however to such activities and identities not already having been put widely in the public domain in other ways.

Because the secret Agencies were still not acknowledged to exist even in 'Private and Confidential' (and sometimes 'Secret') documents of the Committee, editors were asked in the Notice to seek advice from the War Office when considering articles/broadcasts about matters concerning agents. Sensitivity about the still then ambiguous position of the USSR was shown by further amendment of the draft Notice, where reference to 'unfriendly or hostile powers' was changed to 'other powers', lest it should 'offend certain countries who might possibly get to hear of the D.Notice' [assumedly via the *Daily Worker*].

A draft Notice was also tabled on publication of wartime stories, but Media Members confirmed their unanimous objection to a Notice being used to promulgate de facto continuance of censorship. A suggestion that the still extant MoI should issue the advice instead was also rejected, 'because it might possibly cause an unfavourable reaction'. As pre-planned, Speed therefore announced the War Office would handle it; he did not however mention the supplementary advice of officials about editors being relatively conditioned to accept restrictions from his Department.

Markham returned to the subject of the many American correspondents in the UK, who became just as aware of sensitive information as British colleagues, but whose cabled articles to the USA were beyond the Committee's advice. Thomson however suggested that 'from his experience during the War, American press correspondents (or at any rate the more important of them) could be thoroughly trusted'; it was agreed to uphold the decision of the previous meeting not to include them on the distribution of Notices. Finally, observing the last D-Notice issued had been D.942 of 3 September 1939, Markham suggested a new series should now be started; it was agreed the Notice about secret agents (and 'the British Special Air Service') should be No.1.[56]

While Thomson was absent on his first leave since before the War, the Admiralty asked in mid-November that an immediate Notice be issued asking the Media to refrain from publishing pro tem anything about the transfer of some surrendered German submarines from Lisahally to the Russian Navy in the Soviet zone of Germany. The reason was that the transfer was under the terms of the post-Potsdam Tripartite Naval Commission's agreement, which would itself remain secret until formally approved by governments. There was also fear of sabotage and a wish not to offend Soviet sensibilities. Will consulted those media colleagues he could reach, then told Markham that 'as a question of defence security was not involved', they did not consent to this request going out as a Notice; the Admiralty had to make its own approach to interested parts of the Media.[57]

Simultaneously, the War Office requested the issue of a Notice about Biological Warfare Research, seeking to prevent disclosure of the identities of British scientists and establishments involved. Knowing of Media Members' concerns about this, Will managed to bring a quorum of them together with the Deputy Director of the War Office Special Weapons Department, Brigadier Wansbrough-Jones,[58] and the Scientific Adviser to the Army Council, Professor Ellis.[59] They explained that, while the Government had 'virtually decided' to publish a hand-out on the 'beneficial results for public health in general' resulting from this research, it was nevertheless considered that, if ten or so scientists involved were known publicly to be experts in biological warfare, whenever they in future published some unconnected research, 'it would indicate to possible enemy agents the nature of work in which he was an expert, and so disclose the exact direction in which our Biological Warfare research had been proceeding'. Similar considerations applied to the establishments concerned and to linked university and private laboratories.

The Media side's objection to the Notice was that it was of 'a somewhat indefinite character', and that, coupled with the Government's intention to issue a hand-out, it would cause confusion in newspaper offices which would lead to inadvertent breaches. They would have preferred a complete ban of information about Biological Warfare, 'particularly having regard to the moral issues involved' [a curious non sequitur, particularly for newspapermen], but the Brigadier pointed out the Americans were involved in the research too, and might well publish information invidiously forbidden to the British Media. Other press suggestions were for the British and American Governments to postpone any publication 'until a decision had been reached about handing over the control of Atomic Bomb Warfare to an international body'; and to send out the desired advice not in a Notice but in a letter from the Lord President of the Council. Above all, the Media Members felt that D-Notices should not be issued unless they could 'impose a full embargo in definite terms, incapable either of loose interpretation or of oversight on the part of those they affected'.

A few days later the Brigadier wrote announcing the War Office had decided not to pursue the matter further with the Press at all, because of the 'high probability' the information about Biological Warfare research would anyway be published in the American Press. He added, however, that the meeting with the Media Members had been useful to the authorities in providing 'most useful guidance as to the advice we should give to the scientists, whose names we wished kept secret, as to their own conduct'. In addition, the War Office now knew 'fairly precisely how our standard security measures should be directed' through official means, rather than with the aid of the Press.[60]

Taking stock of his first few months as part-time D-Notice Secretary, Thomson wrote: 'This Services Press Committee job is no sinecure, for the Service Departments keep on requesting issues of D-Notices – six in all since November 1 – and the press members need a lot of persuasion to accept them'. When the Committee next met, on 15 January 1946, it had three new draft Notices (ostensibly from the Service Departments) to consider. The first was worded: 'No publication of information about official cyphers'. After some Media side questions on detail, it was amended to: 'No publication of information which gives any particulars about methods or systems of official ciphering, including those of Foreign Governments'.

The next draft started: 'No publication of information regarding methods of concealing equipment sent to assist prisoners of war in escaping, nor of the identities of nationals employed by us to assist in escapes'. Several on the Media side queried suppressing the latter identities, suggesting they deserved recognition which might lead to reward. Markham pointed out that concealment of identity was for their own safety, 'particularly in Eastern European countries where conditions were disturbed and where they might be subjected to personal injury from ill disposed persons. Cases had occurred where helpers had actually disappeared completely leaving no trace'. After discussion, the wording was amended to read: 'No information . . . to be disclosed regarding the identities of nationals in European countries who assisted our prisoners of war or "Evaders" to escape unless they have been officially announced'. It was agreed to review this after six months.

The third draft started: 'No disclosure of information regarding weapons before they have been issued to and are in general use by our armed forces . . .'. The Media side questioned where in practice the line might be drawn between secret items and those which could be publicised, giving as examples two types of the same weapon issued for experimental purposes only, on which legitimate wider opinions might well have varied considerably. Speed agreed to take this draft back for clarification, and the Committee also agreed with a Media suggestion that the term 'Secret List' should be incorporated in the draft 'as a distinguishing expression', even if for some equipment there was currently no such list in existence.

Turning next to broader policy, the Committee discussed again whether D-Notices should ever be issued on matters which were not national security matters but 'undesirable in the public interest'. Markham explained officials were not attempting to reverse the decision of the October 1945 meeting that only national security matters should be covered by Notices, but merely suggesting that a draft Notice should not automatically be turned away on these grounds, and that each Notice should be treated on its merits. This was agreed without discussion. In passing, the Media side suggested that, when the Government had confidential matters of a *political* nature to convey to editors concerning non-publication, it might well use the Lobby Correspondents.

The Media side then raised a D-Notice which had been rejected previously out of Committee. The President of the Board of Trade, Sir Stafford Cripps,[61] had made an announcement about German scientists and material transferred to Britain after the War ended (to work on secret defence projects, although he did not say so). When the Press had consequently approached Admiralty representatives in Barrow, press officers had attempted to suppress the story, alleging a D-Notice was in the process of issue, but this was before the Committee had even been informed of the case. Meanwhile the *Daily Mail*, based on PA local sources, had published the full story. Markham said he had received a somewhat different account of the details, but nevertheless 'accepted the conclusion that there was evidence of creaking in the mechanism, which might not unfairly be attributed to novelty', and he undertook to investigate. He also reassured the Media side that the German scientists had indeed come to this country of their own free will, adding that 'he thought he could say that their families were being well cared for'. The Media side also criticised the Government for having made the announcement through the President of the Board of Trade instead of through the Lord President of the Council, thus giving the impression the scientists were involved not on defence work but on commercial projects; Markham replied this was not the Committee's business, but he had 'taken note of the dissatisfaction of the Press Members in this connection'.

Finally the Committee gave further guidance to Thomson, firstly about the optimal day of the week for meetings (as often happens, the London and the provincial representatives had different ideas of convenience); and secondly about refining the distribution lists, telling him that even small local papers should continue to receive Notices, because often they were the first to hear information, and might otherwise inadvertently publish something sensitive, which would then be picked up by the national Media. However, they also told him that if he was in doubt about the distribution of particular Notices he should be guided by the Service Departments and by the Media Members; Thomson must have considered privately this was all teaching granny to suck eggs. The trivial side of the Secretary's role is recorded here periodically as a reminder that, time-consuming and tiresome though it may be, easy movement requires lubrication.[62]

At this stage, the Security Service began again to take more interest in the AWOAMPC. Its tenuous link with the Committee was through the War Office's department MI11, from which it heard afterwards of a recent meeting of the Armed Services' intelligence departments to discuss the distribution of the new D-Notices. MI5 had no copies of the Notices, and no contact with Thomson, and was again focusing on the amount of information perceived as secret being published in the Media. Concerned about the wide distribution of the content of the Notices, a Security Officer wrote in mid-January 1946: 'Unless the whole problem is handled extremely carefully, D-Notices will merely become a "Child's Guide to Espionage".'

Over the following weeks, the Security Service (which acted then on behalf of all the secret Agencies) helped draft the new D-Notice No.1, which applied to them all, vetted the distribution list (now about 500, including book publishers), and established direct contact with Thomson. Its representatives, many of whom had military experience, commented too on other Notices, for example that D-Notice No.4 (Equipment) pointed out to the Media (and therefore others) exactly where to look for new secret equipment, although conversely the wording was 'unhelpful in that journalists will not know what parts of a ship are J1361 or J1362 unless it is painted on them in large letters'. Prompted by Guy Liddell, Thomson later enquired of the Joint Intelligence Committee about sending copies of Notices to Commonwealth and Dominion Governments; it was decided that if such advice was considered desirable in those countries, the approach should be made (only to the Dominions) through their High Commissioners in London.

In their eagerness to control the content of the Notices, the Security Service desk officers even considered having a representative on the AWOAMPC, but Lieutenant Colonel EM Furnival Jones[63] quickly rejected this, feeling the Press would not take kindly to it, and anyway that to discuss sensitive matters would embarrass the Committee's Official Members, for whom instead their briefs would include the arguments. As a fall back, his subordinates wished at least to pre-clear any draft Notices which went to the Media side; but eventually they came to realise that, although Security Service concerns about the distribution list remained, there were also media considerations which it was not well placed to assess; a modus operandi of iterative discussion with the Secretary soon therefore came into play.[64]

The AWOAMPC returned to the draft D-Notice on weapons and equipment at their 18 March 1946 meeting. Will had had second thoughts about the phrase 'or are already in use by the Services', which he felt would confuse editors, because weapons in use would normally have been removed from the Secret List. Other Media Members supported him in the long and detailed drafting session which then (and frequently in the future) took place as the eminent civil servants and journalists attempted to find a form of words reflecting the views of both sides. Eventually a wording was crafted, of committee-like density:

> It is important in the interests of National Security that there should be no disclosure of information regarding weapons or equipment before it has been officially released, whether such weapons or equipment are being developed for service purposes in Government research establishments or are already in experimental use by the Services. This does not preclude the Service Departments from asking the Press to refrain from disclosing particulars of material or equipment which is in current use by the Services.

While in drafting mode, the Committee also remodelled a paragraph covering the difficulty which provincial editors allegedly had in knowing whether to seek information from the local or the London Services' authorities; the resulting prose did not remove this difficulty but it did promise that 'Every endeavour will be made to deal expeditiously with such queries'. Sir William Brown[65] reported the Air Ministry was replacing the periodic D-Notices on aircraft and engines by one 'comprehensive' Notice, and Speed announced the War Office had withdrawn its draft Notice about V2 Rockets.[66]

Contrary to the declared intention, no further meeting was held in 1946. The D-Notices which had been discussed, and others agreed out of Committee, were duly promulgated.[67] The Clerk of the House of Commons told Thomson (he already knew) that the Clerk no longer had the wartime power to refuse a PQ which touched on a subject banned by a D-Notice. Instead the two of them agreed that, whenever such a Question was tabled, the Clerk would immediately alert the D-Notice Secretary, who in turn would alert the sponsoring Department. The Clerk suggested the Department could then deal direct with the Member who had raised the question, either to attempt to persuade him to withdraw the Question, 'or take such other action as they considered necessary.'[68]

Although the principle that PQs about D-Notice-related matters are not stopped by the Parliamentary Clerks, or by any other official, has remained in force since then, the procedure which has evolved is somewhat different. Any PQ is forwarded to the Department of the Chairman of the Committee (now ex-officio PUS MoD), which decides by whom the response should be drafted. If the Question concerns purely factual aspects of Committee business, it is normally passed to the Secretary to provide the response, which, for administrative propriety, is returned to the Clerk of the House through MoD's parliamentary section. Although the D-Notice Committee is independent, it responds to parliamentary queries of any kind, as is proper in a Democracy. The Secretary informs the Committee, normally at a routine meeting, of such Questions, and of any other very occasional approach from an MP.

The first post-war book on espionage had been submitted to Thomson as early as Christmas 1945: 'They Came to Spy', by the *Daily Telegraph* Crime Correspondent S Firmin. It had already been cleared by the Home Office and Scotland Yard, and, having quickly skimmed through it, the Secretary sent extracts for expert advice to MI5, who sent parts of it on to MI6. By April nothing had been heard, and Thomson complained on behalf of the publisher. Furnival Jones explained the complications of having to consult so many authorities, even about such details as whether it was in the public domain that his own Service had had its wartime headquarters in Wormwood Scrubs Prison. As a token of goodwill, the author was offered through Thomson a discussion on some of the content with, amongst others, Lord Rothschild,[69] and in due course the book was not only published but serialised during 1945/6 in *Leader* (which also explained to readers how Thomson had helped).[70]

Thomson himself was also causing concern to the Security Service as an author. Not wealthy himself, and anyway believing the story of wartime censorship should now be made public, he decided to write a series of articles about it for the *Sunday Dispatch*, with active encouragement from Rothermere. In June 1946, he was asked by his MI5 contacts not to mention that German telegrams from the Irish Republic had been secretly routed by the Irish through England, with the agreement of de Valera (who had also, helpfully to Britain, banned weather reports for the duration, and authorised some other secret co-operation). Thomson reluctantly agreed to self-censor, but declined to show MI5 any more than a few selected passages from his articles, and also quietly told an American friend, who passed the story of the Censor being censored to the *Chicago Sun*, where it was duly published in mid-July. The Security Service easily discovered all this, but decided not to take any further action against Thomson 'in view of the particular relations which at present exist between him and the Security Service.'[71]

A few months later, Thomson did however submit the manuscript of his wartime memoirs 'Blue Pencil Admiral' to the Security Service Legal Adviser. As with the content of his serialised articles, although it was a frank and detailed account of the censorship system and of many of the matters it dealt with, it did not contain anything seriously damaging to national security; with a few deletions of minor detail, it was duly cleared in late 1946 and published. The War Office too at this time had a relatively relaxed attitude to wartime memoirs, and at an October meeting with the author Captain Sykes present, agreed to the publication of the then still unwritten history of the SAS in WWII.[72]

Although no AWOAMPC meeting was held in the second half of 1946 (because of Markham's death), discussion of related matters continued in the Departments. The Admiralty, for example, considered how much information should be released about ships under construction and in commission. As happens, there were good intentions at the outset, and the agreed principles were that as much as possible should be given to the public, consistent with security, and that it should be 'authentic'. However, early Cold war concerns quickly then surfaced about the Soviets gaining operational advantage from disclosed (or stolen) British research and development information. The draft Notice which was in due course produced for the AWOAMPC reflected more of the latter concern than of the former principle and of realism about how much was already in the public domain.[73]

Other matters included government guidance to WWII senior officers, discouraging them from giving so many interviews, and the increasing concerns about leaks, discussed by the Chiefs of Staff in December; these included an *Evening Standard* article about Sweden asking for the loan of British radars to locate launch points of Soviet rockets falling on Sweden (a request consequently rapidly withdrawn), an *Observer* article about Kenya being considered as an alternative British base to the Suez Canal Zone, and a Reuters report that Britain was considering agreeing to the granting of American bases in Canada.[74]

In late October 1946, Thomson consulted the Joint Intelligence Secretariat about the Media's unwillingness to accept D-Notices originating from the Ministry of Supply, seen by them as a Department dealing merely with industrial matters (including the use of atomic energy), even though some in the Media were already aware that it was also the Department responsible for secretly developing atomic weapons. Officials wrangled for several months, discussing whether instead of using D-Notices they could use OSA threats to prevent publication of atomic weapons-related articles and broadcasts (Thomson had privately already warned editors of this possibility). The Ministry of Supply also debated whether it would be possible to conceal from the public the location of the 'Pile' (stockpile) of nuclear weapons, but this was immediately and tersely dismissed by Dr JD Cockroft[75] as 'quite impossible' for practical reasons. The Head of the Atomic Weapons project therefore wrote to the Cabinet's Military Secretary in December 1946 suggesting the JIC might sponsor atomic weapons D-Notices, but finally the favoured option was for a Service Department to do so on behalf of the Ministry of Supply.[76]

31

BEGINNING OF COLD WAR
CONSIDERATIONS

The 22 January 1947 AWOAMPC meeting considered draft D-Notice No.10 (non-publication of movements of uranium and thorium), a ban not already covered by the Atomic Energy Act. The Services considered that knowledge of stocks available in Britain would enable a 'foreign power' to estimate the number of atomic weapons the UK would be able to produce and how long it would take. It was at that time impossible to differentiate between the development of atomic energy for commercial and for military purposes, and, the reasoning went, the foreign power might therefore assume the worst and be encouraged to build up its own supply of atomic weapons. Officials believed the American Press did not mention such movements.

The Press Association had already been approached direct by the Ministry of Supply, asking for no further reporting of uranium consignments to Britain; Martin considered this should have been requested through the AWOAMPC. The Chairman agreed, then revealing the draft D-Notice about deliveries had originated in that Ministry. Media Members had many objections to the wording as being much too wide (for example, pitchblende was included, which also had commercial use); 'everyone' knew we were developing atomic weapons, so a foreign power would know we must be importing fissile materials; chairmen of commercial companies might well refer to these materials at their Annual General Meetings, which the Press should be able to report fully; there was no way of preventing disclosure of such movements in their source country; and there had been no mention of a reporting ban in the Atomic Energy Act (although when pressed, Media members admitted non-disclosure would have been no more acceptable to them if it had have been so included). The new Chairman, Speed, expressed some sympathy and agreed to take expert advice.

He referred next to the existing D-Notice No.8, which advised against the publication of information on the new heavy tank and its trials.[77] The Media side, while agreeing to the need for a Notice, now felt it would be impossible to prevent leakages once the tank was deployed to the British Army in Germany for trials. Speed however claimed the security precautions would be adequate, for example sheeting the tank whilst in transport would ensure armour thickness could not be observed, and unauthorised persons would be excluded from adjacent areas. Media Members accepted these assurances, but suggested the Notice should be reissued as a reminder before trials began in April. The suggestion that agreed Notices would have to be reissued at intervals worried the new Admiralty PUS, JG Lang.[78] Thomson pointed out that this had been necessary during the War, because newspaper staff changed regularly, and current staffs were not fully conversant with D-Notice procedures. In apparent ignorance [unsurprising] of similar pre-war agreements, the Committee later decided a summary of extant Notices should be issued annually.

Will next raised his concern about D-Notice No.9 (lists of aircraft whose details were/were not publishable), agreed out of Committee since the previous meeting, and on which he had concurred because the technical Press members had led with the Air Ministry. On reflection he was unhappy with the passage relating to 'Private Venture Aircraft designed and built on the initiative of a manufacturer for military use', because of difficulty in differentiating between those for civilian and for military use. Air Ministry representatives explained it would be clear from the outset of preparation of drawings what its use would be, and that anyway no Private Venture aircraft could be designed for military use except to the order of a Service Department. The Chairman persuaded that, as the Notice had already been agreed, it should stand, subject to six-monthly review.[79]

One lingering dispute between the Admiralty and the Media (led by the BBC, whose representative frequently consulted its Air Correspondent) was resolved by Thomson in March 1947. The Department had in November drafted a Notice asking that mention of the use of helicopters in anti-submarine warfare should not be published. The Media had pointed out this was in the public domain, and that the Notice needed to be more specific about relevant new trials. The Notice now agreed covered only the types of aircraft being used, tactics and any special equipment embarked.[80]

Discussion of the draft D-Notice (now No.12) on atomic information had continued between Thomson, officials in the Ministry of Supply, and the Security Service.[81] At the 10 April 1947 AWOAMPC meeting, the Chairman said MoD and Chiefs of Staff attached particular importance to the Notice, and invited Wansbrough-Jones to deal in greater detail with points raised previously. The Scientific Adviser reiterated the 'reasonable estimate' a potential enemy could make from knowledge of uranium quantities (and of thorium, which enabled uranium supplies to be stretched) as to likely stocks of atomic bombs, adding 'Our own ideas of the future shape of our defence forces demonstrate how vital such information would be'. A further consignment was due shortly, so the Notice was urgently needed.

On the Media side's points, firstly that censorship in the country of origin was not possible, he explained that the Canadian Government owned the mine, controlled shipments, and published no information. Belgium did not include Congo uranium shipments in trade returns, and no Belgian press mention of shipments had occurred. On omission from the Atomic Energy Act of a ban on mentioning uranium movements, this had been 'to avoid equipping the Minister with permanent powers of censorship'; the whole Act had been drafted, at the request of scientists, 'to give the maximum freedom to public opinion, reliance being placed on the discretion and co-operation of the Press as and when required. The possibility of an effective control by the UN Atomic Energy Commission was also given due weight'.

On potential statements by commercial company chairmen, Wansbrough-Jones did not think they would refer to difficulty in getting supplies or their arrival. On information emerging from the American press, he referred to 'the well-known American sensitivity on this subject . . . by various means they would undoubtedly restrict reports of movements of stocks'. He also considered that, if some reports did appear in the American press, because 'the Press in that country was less responsible than our own . . . the accuracy of such reports would be far more discounted than corresponding statements in the British Press' [some might disagree]. Finally he maintained that, after the busy initial 6–12 month period, any leak of information was unlikely, because a potential enemy would by then be unaware of the quantity of basic stocks. The Service Departments would therefore be willing to review the Notice early the following year.

In discussion, the Official side gave assurances that Board of Trade and other government publications would not make reference to uranium movements within the United Kingdom, and conceded that, if information on the subject were released in other countries such as Belgium, the British Press would be free to publish it, and the Notice would be amended. On this basis, the Media side reluctantly agreed the Notice, and it was duly issued in mid-April. [An infraction did occur subsequently, when the *Yorkshire Post* of 9 October 1947 carried an article headed '£1,060,073 of Uranium Ore Bought by Britain' (from the Belgian Congo); however it transpired this information had been published in error by the Belgian Colonial Office.[82]]

Lang referred to the draft Notice on information on warships under construction, and to the recent Parliamentary Naval Estimates Debate, during which a Member had complained about the paucity of information being issued about the Navy. The Admiralty had attempted to counter by claiming 'very full information' had been issued pre-war [older Media members present might have remembered otherwise], and that this had prejudiced the Navy's position when it came to exchanging confidential advanced technical information with other countries, as was now being proposed by the United Nations as a confidence-building measure. Until the UN information exchange scheme 'reached a greater degree of reliability', the Admiralty therefore wished no announcement in the early stages of building, and only information on the 'general characteristics' of a new ship just prior to launching, until it was eventually commissioned [i.e. until the full crew joined and the ship came into service]. Even then the Admiralty would not publish details such as types of radar fitted.

The Media side unanimously rejected Lang's argument and draft. The technical Press representatives could not accept a blanket ban on articles about details of equipment and machinery. It would be impossible to keep secret the details of a ship until just before its launch, when hundreds of shipyard employees had been working on her, and many others in the locality would also be familiar with the general characteristics of even a 'novel type'. It would also prevent proper discussion of the Government's Naval policy, for example the balance between different classes of ship. The Press could not remain silent either on the implications for industrial questions of the shipbuilding programme. The D-Notice went much further even than was the case with the House of Commons, who were being denied information about the cost of individual ships, whereas the Media were being asked not to refer to any details at all of those under construction.

Some Media members indeed felt the request was not suitable for a D-Notice at all, and suggested instead merely a letter from the Admiralty to editors, each of whom would then decide for himself 'whether the Government was justified in departing from long-established practice'. Lang expressed some sympathy with these trenchant media views, adding 'the Admiralty well realised the news value, especially in the local press, of much of the information he was asking the Press to withhold.' He was merely seeking the co-operation of the Media 'in the new policy decided on by the Government'. The Chairman intervened, asking Lang to withdraw the draft for further work, as it was clearly unacceptable to the Media side.[83]

During the following months, discussion continued between Thomson and the secret Agencies on details of the D-Notice System. His point of contact was now almost invariably the Security Service's Legal Adviser, Bernard Hill,[84] who was concerned in particular about the presence on the distribution list of the communist *Daily Worker*, and who wished in vain to see all draft Notices before the Committee did (by April 1947 there were 12 Notices in force); Thomson suggested MI5 should disregard 'what is not essential to keep secret'. Others were more concerned about, for example, leaks to the Media on British deployments to and within Palestine during the last bloody months of the British mandate there. In December, Colonel Vivian listed for Thomson those matters which MI6 was particularly concerned to protect, including organisation, training and operational methods, personnel, 'clandestine functions', its responsibility to the Foreign Office, cryptography, 'strategical deception', and (as an afterthought) past members.[85]

In December a Media Member of the Committee was in trouble with his Official colleagues, Speed as Chairman telling the Periodicals representatives that the excuse for a breach (albeit inadvertent) of D-Notice No.9 (Aircraft/engines) given by *Aeroplane*'s editor was completely unacceptable, and placing it on the agenda of the next meeting. This was delayed until 18 March 1948 because Speed was ill. The Acting Chairman, the new Air Ministry PUS Sir James Barnes,[86] obtained agreement to the Services' request that the 'under 6-monthly review' D-Notices Nos.2 (Escape and Evasion), 9 (Aircraft details), and 12 (Uranium, etc) be retained. The Committee heard a report of infringements of Notices by the Press in the previous 12 months; as examples of those periodically reported, these were:

- (March 1947) – *Kentish Times, Daily Mail, Evening Standard, Glasgow Evening Citizen* – all connected the name of Sir Percy Sillitoe with MI5 (contrary to D-Notice No.1).
- (September 1947) – *Aeroplane* – published prohibited details of aircraft (contrary to D-Notice No.9).
- (October 1947) – *Daily Graphic* – 'Gave details of counter intelligence methods and activities' (contrary to D-Notice No.1).
- (January 1948) – *Daily Graphic* – published details of RAF jet fighters and bombers (contrary to D-Notice No.9).

The PTPWNPA representatives drew attention to information on the aircraft Secret List being published in American journals on sale in Britain, and asked that something be done. All agreed there was no point in giving copies of the Notices to American correspondents, and felt that 'the proprietors of US newspapers would have to be consulted if there were to be any suggestion of setting up a committee in the USA analogous to our own'. After considerable discussion of this 'distinct gap in the machinery', it was agreed 'the position should be explored at an early date' through the British Delegation in Washington, and then reconsidered by the Committee.

The Chairman raised disclosures about secret aircraft in the roneoed bulletin *Southern Flying*. It transpired this was privately edited and circulated by 'a youth of 18 in association with another youth also under 21'. A full Air Ministry investigation into the oeuvre of this enterprising pair had revealed that most information was obtained from other privately circulated bulletins, from visits to aircraft firms, and from a visit to the Radlett aircraft exhibition the previous year; furthermore, most of the information was correct. This stimulated Committee criticism of lax security in aircraft companies' house magazines. Barnes reported action taken: the Ministry of Supply had issued a 'special warning' to aircraft manufacturers not to divulge confidential information, and 'to exercise supervision over boys in search of information'; those responsible for the infringements in *Southern Flying* had been admonished; and the Air Ministry had undertaken to vet future issues of that bulletin before roneoing, and 'endeavours were being made to ascertain what other boys' flying clubs were in being.'[87]

Lang updated on the Admiralty's draft Notice about details of warships under construction. Despite much discussion with Media members during the previous nine months, it had still not been possible to 'produce complete understanding'. The Defence Departments were also keen to introduce a Notice banning publication of aerial photographs of certain key points, but, perhaps mindful of the Admiralty's experience on new warships, they wished first to discuss the idea in principle with the Media side. The Air Ministry explained that the authorities had become increasingly concerned since the War about the amount of information available from aerial photography, especially that which revealed, for example, the layout and production capacity of certain factories and centres of utilities.[88] Lengthy discussion of such sites ensued, with Media Members very dubious whether those they represented would accept what 'was almost going back to compulsory censorship. It might well lead to a photograph of a town hall being prohibited simply because the photograph also showed a power station or some other prohibited item'. They decided they needed a letter to newspapers/technical journals, seeking wider Media agreement to discuss this further.

Pitt Robbins complained about recent instances, particularly difficult for the provincial Press, where the Admiralty had enforced de facto censorship: an air attack exercise on the Home Fleet, and the return of the submarine *HMS AMBUSH*.[89] Lang explained that in the latter case the submarine had been returning from trials to provide information on which to base future submarine design, and therefore it was essential no secret details were divulged; and, although possible to brief the technical Press beforehand on areas to be avoided in articles, the Admiralty also had to allow for freelance reporters; submission of material was therefore the 'most satisfactory' way of dealing with this problem. The War Office (on behalf of all the Services and (although not stated) of MI5), asked that issue of D-Notices to the *Daily Worker* again be reviewed.[90]

On 17 March 1948, the Government sent a Top Secret Atomic telegram to the British Ambassador in Washington and the High Commissioner in Canada about work which had started in early 1947, known only to a few, on the development of UK atomic weapons. The project was not only secret on such matters as research location and weapon characteristics, but even on that this work was being done at all. Now secrecy was becoming 'ineffective', partly because so many people had to be involved in the project, and partly because sub-contractors not in the know could not be persuaded of the urgency of their input, thus causing programme delays.

Ministers therefore intended 'casually and incidentally' to announce the project, but wished to consult the AWOAMPC Media members beforehand about such an announcement; in the perceived unlikely event of adverse reaction, the Government would reconsider the whole question of publicity. First however the Government wished to know the views of the US authorities about this intention. Within a month, it was confirmed the US authorities had raised no objections, and the Security Service then supervised tightening up the wording of the draft announcement and of the lines to take in response to questions, consulting Thomson on this and on the timing.[91]

An unprogrammed meeting of the Committee was therefore held on 29 April 1948, at which Speed explained the Government had decided to state publicly 'that they were concerning themselves with the production of atomic weapons'. Before doing so, they wished to take the Media representatives on the Committee into their confidence, and he had had prepared a draft D-Notice accordingly for discussion. Wansbrough-Jones explained that, while UK atomic energy development continued to be generally 'for peaceful purposes', the Government had also been undertaking work on atomic weapons, hitherto 'under conditions of special secrecy', but now feeling 'the time had come to let it be known' this work was being done, 'to some extent dependent on the agreement of the Press to a "D" Notice on the lines of the draft now under consideration'.

He said the Notice's preamble was intended to indicate that nothing had been taken away from the Media's right to discuss the British atomic energy programme. All that the Media were now being asked to do was not to publish any information which might be of value to an enemy. Will asked how the Government intended to announce this information, and Speed replied that, while it had been the intention to do so in Parliament, the Government was now thinking of 'letting the information "slip out", in the form of a Parliamentary Question and Answer'. The Media side recommended however to the Government that the announcement should be a formal one, preferably made in Parliament, and that the D-Notice should be in the hands of the Media no earlier or later than the same morning of an afternoon announcement. The concern of the Media for parliamentary niceties appears to have been greater than that of politicians and officials.

The April meeting then discussed the content of draft D-Notice No.25. Of long-lasting significance, it read:

> It is important in the interests of national security that there should be no disclosure of information about, or reference to, the following matters relating to the development and production of atomic weapons (as distinct from information about the general atomic energy research programme and the production of fissile material, which are sufficiently covered by the provisions of the Official Secrets Acts and Section Eleven of the Atomic Energy Act, and are not affected by this Notice):
>
> (i)   The location or progress of work in the United Kingdom on the development or production of atomic weapons.
>
> (ii)   The design, methods of construction, weight and size of the atomic weapons which are being developed in the United Kingdom, and the materials which are being used.
>
> (iii)   The place or places where such weapons are stored.
>
> (iv)   The identity of those engaged on the work.
>
> (v)   The nature of the Government organisation which controls it.

The Media side queried why the location should be concealed, and the Scientific Adviser explained that work was in fact considerably dispersed, and that it would greatly assist a foreign power if it knew where to look. He was asked to detail which parts of the Notice were also covered by the Official Secrets Acts, and said 'pretty well the whole of sub-paragraphs (ii) and (iii), but probably not (i) and (v), and certainly not (iv)'. Further discussion led to the deletion of sub-paragraph (v). The Media side was also unhappy about the phrase 'the progress of work', since this would preclude the freedom of the Press to criticise the progress being made; the Chairman sympathised with this, which led to agreement to add a note saying that 'progress of work' in sub-paragraph (i) referred to factual information, and was not intended to prevent the publication of statements 'imputing lack of progress if in the view of the responsible editor there is such lack of progress in the general sense as demands comment'. The clause in brackets in the draft preamble was removed to a slightly amended second note, and a third note was added cross-referring to D-Notice No.12 (prohibiting information about the movements of uranium, thorium and their respective ores).

The Media side's recommendations were accepted by the Government, and the Notice was sent to editors the day before the parliamentary announcement on 12 May 1948; there was notably little Media comment.[92]

There was continuing AWOAMPC interest in the US Government's attempts to persuade the American media to accept some form of restriction of publication of security information. This was robustly resisted there, for example in a joint letter which 22 representatives of leading US publications sent to Secretary of Defense Forrestal in mid-1948. They declined any system of censorship, voluntary or otherwise, and suggested instead greater efficiency in the governmental security arrangements; the patriotism of editors would then suffice to prevent unwanted disclosure.[93]

Pitt Robbins and Thomson had meanwhile been discussing, as instructed by the Committee, the distribution of D-Notices to the *Daily Worker*. In order to avoid the newspaper realising it was being removed from the distribution of any Notice, and the possibility of this being raised by sympathisers in Parliament, they devised a complicated scheme under which there would effectively be two simultaneous series of Notices, only the less sensitive of which would be received by the paper. The Security Service opposed this however, and it was left to Thomson's discretion to decide when to omit to send a Notice to the *Daily Worker* in future.[94]

The 29 September 1948 AWOAMPC meeting nevertheless returned to distribution of Notices to the *Daily Worker*; the Services' representatives now felt this should continue, so it was agreed 'the disadvantages of omitting [that paper] outweighed the advantages'; only Martin of the Press Association disagreed, feeling strongly enough about it to ask that this be recorded in the Minutes. Next, the Chairman concurred with British Defence Staff Washington opinion on secret information revealed in American journals on sale in Britain: 'in view of the attitude of the US proprietors and editors, nothing could be done to improve matters'. The Committee decided, realistically, that no further action was worth attempting in that direction. This was a further example of the need for the governmental side to understand the limits of national censorship in an international media context, which has increased over the years as communications have become ever more global. The problem was and is of equal concern to the Media: no British editor wishes to be at a disadvantage vis-à-vis international journals and broadcasters, by dint of having to observe national constraints on publication not placed upon foreign competitors by their own governments.

The draft Notice about warships under construction was, after further detailed fine-tuning by the Committee, at last agreed. The revised version was much more specific and therefore more limited in scope than the original, concentrating on new equipment and weapons exclusive to the Royal Navy (where secret characteristics gave a performance advantage over the systems of potential enemies), on drawings and photographs linked to design, and on construction and trials. The Notice was issued the following month; in the Naval Estimates that year the Government, with the same security concerns in mind, gave only a global cost figure for ships under construction.[95]

On aerial photography of key points, the Media side had now obtained the agreement of editors generally to discuss this with officials. The list had been reduced by the Service Departments in the light of previous media comments, but discussion ensued on details such as whether photographs of aircraft factories could be published provided they did not show an adjacent airfield – would editors be able, for example, with the imprecise photographic definition of those days, to distinguish between a grass airfield and a football field? And did 'factories' include those making just engines and components? The Media side was also concerned about difficulties which would arise when journalists were officially invited to view air displays and exhibitions. The Air Ministry conceded the prohibition should include only 'important aircraft firms where new aircraft were assembled and tested', and that in some cases publication would be allowed 'by special arrangement with the authorities concerned'. Other key points affected included new and enlarged oil refineries, and nodal points of utility systems. The agreed Notice was issued immediately as D-Notice 33, 'subject to review if and when there is an improvement in the international situation.'[96] That review did eventually begin, when the Cold War had effectively ended, over 40 years later.

By now Thomson and Hill were working harmoniously; when DMI suggested to the Security Service in early 1949 that Thomson, because he had no official standing, should not be used for occasionally dissuading the Media from publishing matters which were not strictly D-Notice business, Hill gave the General a frosty response. During 1949, the Security Service continued however to be concerned about atomic security. When *The Times* published an article (21 March) headed 'Atomic Plant in Cumberland' [Sellafield], the Ministry of Supply was goaded into considering taking legal action against the paper, but instead in the end merely reminded the editor of the caution in the relevant Notice.[97]

Despite the decision to take no further action on American press publication of secret details of British aircraft, the concern remained, and was raised by the two PTPWNPA representatives at the 2 May 1949 meeting (after a briefing on 'The Arrangements for the Organisation and Conduct of Press Censorship in the Event of Emergencies', i.e. the updated WWII arrangements for use in future general war). The PTPWNPA reported there had been a great deal more information published in American magazines about British aircraft. *Aviation Week* had also published a 'very offensive' article blaming British editors for disclosing details of US aircraft during WWII. Once again, however, Committee discussion produced no new ideas as to how to cope with foreign publication of British information, beyond tightening up security in the Ministry of Supply and during media visits to British aircraft companies.

Other business included a review of two press infringements of D-Notices since the last meeting. The September 1948 issue of *Air Reserve Gazette* had referred to a rubber flight deck fitted in an aircraft carrier for experimental purposes, classified Confidential at the time, publication therefore contrary to D-Notice No.5; the Secretary had written to the editor 'who replied in a most courteous letter expressing his regrets'[98]. The December 1948 issue of *John Bull* had published an article referring to certain MI5 operations and to the connection of Sir Percy Sillitoe with the Service; again the editor had replied regretfully to Thomson, although the Secretary pointed out to the Committee that the infringement was 'understandable' as Sillitoe's connection with MI5 had already been published elsewhere, and it was not easy for the Press to distinguish between MI5's anti-communist activities (not covered by D-Notices) and its counter-espionage activities (which were, under D-Notice No.1).[99]

32

KOREAN WAR AND IMPERIAL DISENTANGLEMENT

As the Korean crisis developed, and a few weeks after initial British Commando landings at Inchon, the Committee was convened on 21 September 1950 to discuss media arrangements. The Chairman told them the War Office intended to give press facilities to cover the three-day embarkation of the main British Land Contingent, and tabled a draft D-Notice. Sir George Turner,[100] the War Office PUS, explained there was much more in the Brigade Group than the standard three infantry battalions, and why it was important therefore not to reveal the order of battle, composition, strength and equipment of the whole force. He thought it would be possible to prevent this by restricting journalists' access to the jetties when the three battalions themselves were to embark (American journalists had permanent passes to the jetties, but he thought they would 'co-operate'). The Media side pointed out however that foreign correspondents could hardly fail to observe British tanks, artillery, etc being concentrated in the vicinity of the docks, and the transport ships sailing. They said any Notice should specify precisely what should not be published, and enquired how foreign reports cabled home, and thence picked up in the UK, should be handled.

Turner acknowledged that expecting foreign reports not to be published in the UK would go beyond even what had been asked in WWII. After considerable discussion, it was agreed the D-Notice should be redrafted with specific prohibitions, making it clear that apart from the three battalions, nothing else about the Brigade's components should be published. The covering letter should remind editors of the wartime practice of stating the source of any reports from overseas [i.e. that they did not have the implied authenticity of British reports – a decreasingly convincing compromise]. Turner also revealed that the British contingent would be under command of the American Supreme Commander, General MacArthur, who would therefore decide the censorship rules in theatre, but that 'an excellent organisation' for briefing correspondents had been planned, and he did not therefore foresee much difficulty over censorship.[101]

Thomson made a complaint of his own against the *Daily Graphic*. When the Royal Marines Commandos had left the UK by air en route to Inchon the previous month, the Media had been invited by the Admiralty to witness their departure, but had been asked not to publish anything for a week, for reasons of operational security. The *Graphic* had nevertheless immediately published photographs of the Marines leaving, and had also falsely claimed they had done so with Thomson's authority. Several photographic agencies had complained about this breach of the embargo, having adhered to it themselves. Will felt this was a dispute between the paper and the Admiralty, which the AWOAMPC was not competent to deal with, as its duty was to consider D-Notice issues only. Pitt Robbins reported he had had a letter from Kemsley Newspapers (the *Graphic*'s parent group), saying the editor saw no reason for embargoes of this kind, and did not intend to abide by them 'unless the question of security was involved'.

Pitt Robbins had replied he disagreed with the editor's actions, because the *Graphic* had not only accepted the invitation knowing what the stipulations were, but had also failed to warn other journals and agencies it did not intend to observe the temporary prohibitions. Media members acknowledged the alternative to Departments imposing embargoes could be withholding facilities, but this would be as unacceptable as stipulating submission of copy for censorship by a Department, as had happened recently. The Committee agreed overall that such problems would be best dealt with by any embargoes being effected only through approved D-Notices; in exceptional circumstances when it was necessary to 'short-circuit' this procedure, the Department should still inform the Secretary.

This case also led to a more general discussion about whether it was within the competence of the Committee to discuss any matter not connected with the issue of D-Notices. The Chairman's summation was that 'he was anxious to obtain the maximum benefit both to the Press and Service members from the Committee's deliberations, particularly as the meetings were infrequent. It would be a pity, he thought, to restrict the scope of the discussions too rigidly, though formal discussions must be limited to matters relating to the preservation of defence security in the Press'. A similar pragmatic modus operandi has been adopted ever since. Will did report subsequently that, although his more purist view on this had been 'over-ruled' by the Committee, it was nevertheless shared 'very strongly' by the NPA. However, the NPA too has since then accepted the less purist modus operandi as beneficial. Furthermore, it is not just Defence security matters which are now within the Committee's purview.[102]

In his day-to-day work as Secretary, Thomson was when necessary ready to challenge officials as well as journalists. In October 1950, when MI5's Legal Adviser Hill wrote to him complaining about a Pincher article in the *Daily Express*, reporting the 'screening' of individuals under surveillance by the Security Service, Thomson responded robustly. 'If there is any real harm . . . I am largely responsible . . . I might add that my reply to his phone message was that he would find it difficult to make an article out of an explanation of this subject as there is not third degree in democratic countries and there seemed little he could say that was not obvious . . . "I presume it is OK to talk about the tapping of telephone calls?" he [Hill] asked. "That" I replied "has been talked about since the first World War."' Thomson reminded that he had discussed telephone tapping in his own book on wartime censorship, and that D-Notice No.1 referred to *secret* Intelligence and Counter Intelligence methods 'and I am quite sure that if the Press Members of the Committee had anticipated the inclusion of methods which were obvious to a child, they would never have agreed to the issue of the D Notice'. Thomson also recorded that, at the most recent Committee meeting, it had been agreed the Admiralty should inform him if there were indeed matters on which they required restrictions not already clearly covered by a D-Notice, and he challenged MI5 to do likewise. He cited as a possible example that 'the Daily Mirror rang me up at 1 a.m. the other night asking if it was safe to publish the news given in a Rome newspaper that Pontecorvo had gone to Russia and asking for confirmation that the story was true!'[103]

Thomson wrote the same day to Chapman Pincher 'for your private information', enclosing a copy of his letter to Hill, suggesting he showed it to his editor,[104] and adding as a quid pro quo: 'It is I think proof that you do well to ring me up before writing stories which you are doubtful about!' This close working relationship is also mentioned in the 1947–51 records of Pincher's old Department, the Ministry of Supply/Aviation, in which officials comment on the one hand that 'Pincher has once again succeeded in safely skating over very thin ice . . . reduces me almost to desperation at times', but on the other that he had usually checked with Thomson; and that much of his information came from the American Press (although the Americans themselves had been annoyed by leaks in the British Press about their microbiological research).[105]

When the Committee met on 7 February 1951, there were two contentious papers on the agenda. One detects, reading between the lines of Thomson's terse official record, that the atmosphere between the two sides was somewhat thunderous. The first issue was once again whether the communist *Daily Worker* should continue to receive D-Notices. Martin was dubious whether he, as PA editor-in-chief, had the authority to cut out a newspaper which was a PA subscriber from the distribution of an emergency D-Notice sent out through his Agency. He also felt withholding D-Notices from the *Daily Worker* affected the liberty of the Press, and that Members were not therefore competent to take such a decision; he pointed out the newspaper was still being published without restriction by the authorities. Will felt withholding information from it must be a Cabinet decision, and that the paper should receive either all Notices or none at all. Several media colleagues were concerned that, if the latter, the *Daily Worker* might then expose the whole [still secret] D-Notice System, and they too questioned the right of the AWOAMPC to withhold Notices from any British newspaper. The Admiralty's Lang, supported by the War Office, opined that this Committee was the 'right machine to handle difficult problems of this kind'; although Media members might have qualms about the principle of restricting distribution of D-Notices, the practical issue could not be ignored: 'What was communicated to the *Daily Worker* would warn the USSR of matters on which Britain is anxious to suppress information.'[106] The Chairman suggested that, before any decision was made by Ministers, it would be reasonable to let them have wider media views; it was agreed to take soundings.

The other contentious agenda item was 'Restrictions on Publication of Economic and Industrial Information of Value to Potential Enemies'. Will opened by saying he saw no connection between the paper circulated with the agenda and the title of the agenda item. The representative in attendance from the Joint Intelligence Bureau explained what they were hoping to do was 'to restrict the information an enemy *must* have before he could deliver an attack, either by air or by sabotage, and so reduce our war effort'. Barnes added that the current D-Notice about aerial photography applied in general to establishments of a military type, while the restrictions now proposed were similar but in the field of industry. 'They were intended to restrict a different type of military information'.

Unsurprisingly, the Media side was not persuaded. 'The extent of the powers to be taken was indeed alarming.' The next step would be to extend the ban to all new factories as they opened, and to articles on coal and steel. All factories were important in total war, not just particular ones. 'These proposals were a revolution as far as the Press was concerned.' After discussion about the degree to which the proposals went beyond anything introduced in 1938 and used during the War, the Chairman and Lang suggested forming a working party 'to iron out the difficulties' and 'to explore the extent to which it would be reasonable to ask the Press to withhold information'. The Media Members were dubious they could agree even to this without first consulting their members.

Pitt Robbins referred to a statement in the agenda paper that 'no difficulty is anticipated in obtaining the co-operation of the industrial firms concerned', and enquired whether instructions had indeed already been issued to firms to withhold information, as 'Correspondents had met with difficulties in obtaining from firms certain types of information normally given in peacetime.' The JIB representative assured him that 'while an approach had been made to certain firms regarding their reactions to proposals of this nature, no instructions of any kind had been issued to them'. The discussion ended with agreement to form a Working Party to consider 'without prejudice' what it might be reasonable to withhold from publication about factories and similar installations and their production, but only in order to 'enable this Committee to consider what recommendations the Press Members might reasonably put to their governing body'. A bruising meeting probably left both sides feeling they had held their ground, prior to battle shortly being rejoined.[107]

A month later, Thomson wrote to Media members about the *Daily Worker*. He asked them formally to ascertain the views of their respective organisations, as had been agreed, but meanwhile gave them additional information, and a somewhat refined official view. He told them first that since 1948 'two or three "D" Notices, regarded as highly confidential, have not been sent to the *Daily Worker*, though the Committee were not formally notified to that effect.'[108] At first its editor did not comment on the omission [which would have been apparent from the gap in the numerical sequence], but in September 1950 he had done so when he did not receive D-Notice No.65, dealing with the first brigade group sent to Korea, and later the editor noticed reference to No.71 in a Reuters tape and queried non-receipt. Thomson told him that, as the *Daily Worker* had a correspondent with North Korean forces, it was 'impracticable on the ground of military security' that he should receive D-Notices 'bearing on the Korean campaign'.

While the editor had accepted that explanation 'with good grace', he had now complained about the non-receipt of D-Notice No.75 (radar countermeasures, issued the previous December), and asked for a discussion about D-Notices generally. An early decision by the Committee was therefore now needed. Thomson also felt it would now be impossible to keep the paper in ignorance of a change in policy by, for example, numbering only the Notices 'which contain neither secret information nor statements from which secret information might be inferred (about 75% of those issued)'. The *Daily Worker* would have to be informed of the decision reached. Having reminded that the D-Notice system was essentially one of co-operation between press (in the interests of its freedom) and government (in the interests of the security of the country), he ended: 'The point at issue is whether any purpose is served, and whether in fact harm is not likely to be done, by following this procedure in the case of a newspaper whose views appear to be at variance with the basis of the system, that is, a belief in the paramount importance of national security.'[109]

Also in March, Thomson complained to the Committee's new BBC Member, Tahu Hole,[110] about a broadcast version of 'The Great Escape'. The Secretary had previously asked publishers to seek his advice about escape and evasion books, and although this one had already been published in the USA, he had (at the Air Ministry's request) advised replacing phrases like 'the Escape Chain' by 'underground'. When Hole retorted the BBC was publishing nothing new, Thomson privately conceded it was acceptable to publish extracts, but said he had written in order to remind producers 'to keep an eye on that kind of story.'[111]

In early March 1951, Thomson had been asked to use his influence, rather than a Notice, in keeping from being published that Dr WG Penney[112] was to be appointed Head of Aldermaston, as his previous connection with weapons programmes was known, but that research establishment's connection with atomic weapons had not yet been disclosed. Thomson was uneasy about this interpretation of D-Notice 25, and agreed to send out an addendum to it covering only any reference to nuclear weapon stockpiles. By June, however, the pressure from certain journalists to publish what they knew about Penney was building up; after discussion of tactics with Thomson, Chapman Pincher wrote to the Ministry of Supply's PUS, Sir Archibald Rowlands,[113] saying the *Express* did not wish to be scooped by a rival not so compliant, and that it knew the AWOAMPC Media side had declined a D-Notice on the matter, on the grounds Penney was a scientist and therefore not covered by the D-Notice System.

Thomson had tried unsuccessfully to persuade the Security Service that some compromise should be found. Pincher had therefore attached to his letter to Rowlands a suggested Press Release which, without mentioning atomic matters, announced Penney was moving to Aldermaston from the Fort Halstead research establishment near Chatham. This caused an even more frantic reaction from Rowlands to Barnes: neither the Royal Arsenal at Woolwich nor Fort Halstead were known as having any connection with the atomic programme, and he therefore proposed a new D-Notice (25B), requesting no mention of the transfer of any staff between Woolwich, Halstead and Aldermaston. The AWOAMPC Media members and the *Daily Express* agreed, and it was issued in July 1951.[114] The D-Notice Secretary had fulfilled his role as an intermediary between officials and journalists in finding a temporary and compromise solution to an immediate problem, which, if imperfect, was nevertheless acceptable to both sides.

Further involvement for Thomson in atomic matters occurred through the next 18 months. On 1 August 1951, the *Daily Telegraph* reported a British atomic bomb test would be carried out in the near future, something the British and Australian Governments were keeping secret pro tem. When approached about this disclosure, the newspaper's acting managing editor, Malcolm Muggeridge,[115] replied abjectly that it had been an unintentional error, and the attention of the staff had now been drawn to the Notice. In May 1952, the Security Service's Furnival Jones proposed tightening up D-Notice 25 in the light of experience and of developments in the nuclear programme. By late November of that year, however, Ministers were beginning to conclude it was no longer practicable to maintain secrecy about the roles of Aldermaston and Capenhurst, in part because Penney and other scientists had been recognised attending preparations for atomic bomb tests in the Monte Bello islands.[116]

Discussion of distribution of Notices to the *Daily Worker* continued behind the scenes. The Security Service view initially was that, 'because of the increasing gravity of the world situation', omitting the paper from the distribution would be a non-starter. Sir Dick White as DGSS disagreed, saying that, as an organ of the Communist Party of Great Britain, the paper would leak any Notice. His Deputy RH Hollis[117] then argued with colleagues that if the paper did not receive D-Notices, it could 'scoop' other parts of the Media and, if action was then taken against it, claim it was unaware of the prohibition. Hill argued having two types of Notice would weaken the strength of the 'In Confidence' marking on them, to which Hollis countered that the *Daily Worker* would get all except the few limited distribution Notices. Thomson reminded that when a two-type scheme had been looked at in 1948, the Security Service had been against it. Nevertheless, this scheme was now put to Ministers, as being for Political rather than AWOAMPC decision.[118]

The 7 April 1952 AWOAMPC meeting opened with some media special pleading. The post-war shortage of telephone lines was so acute that new subscribers since 1948 were obliged to share. The Media side claimed that 'for security reasons it was not in the national interest that editors and senior members of the staffs of leading newspapers should be required to share residential telephone lines even with only one other subscriber. Editors and their deputies had of necessity to do a good deal of work at home and this sometimes involved telephonic discussions of confidential matters with Government Departments', and they were 'concerned at the possibility of breaches of security occurring as the result of a shared telephone line'. They asked for an arrangement whereby applications for exemption from sharing, after vetting by the AWOAMPC Secretary, could be specially considered by the GPO. They would 'undertake that newspapers would exercise all due restraint in putting forward applications'. The hapless Post Office representative in attendance for that item regretted it would not at present be possible to grant exemption to editors 'as a class', but that applications from individual editors and senior executives from national and provincial journals, and equivalents in the PA and BBC, if endorsed by Thomson, would be sympathetically considered. The Committee agreed to this 'compromise'; one assumes Thomson was well lunched by media staffs in the following months.

A Cabinet Office representative next briefed the Committee on arrangements for non-publication of certain industrial information, thrashed out after the previous meeting, and promulgated in an Advisory Letter of 29 September 1951. For security authorities these had been very satisfactory, the Media had been co-operative, there had been no complaints, and Thomson had been helpful 'in interpreting the letter to editors'. The letter was now being sent to an even greater number of firms, and some companies were even discontinuing the use in advertising material of previously published aerial photographs of their premises. The Media side's occasional difficulties had been treated sympathetically through Thomson. The Defence Departments were grateful that what had started as a row had been resolved with the Media side's help.

The CoI representative in attendance thanked Media members for their individual assistance in the preparation of D-Notices which it would be necessary to bring into operation, with a new Press and Censorship Bureau, in the event of a future major war. Progress included over 90% of the required censors having been earmarked, 70% of whom had previous censorship experience (the remainder were proving difficult to identify, and he asked Members for the names and addresses of any others who might be suitable and willing); the censors' handbook was complete, and the necessary forms and censors' rubber stamps 'were all in readiness'; a building near Fleet Street had been found, suitable subject to further works for which 'high level' approval had been sought; three provincial centres were planned, in Manchester, Glasgow and Belfast; and the Press Censorship Committee was exploring with the USA and Canada the possible co-ordination of censorship between NATO countries in an emergency. The Cold War was getting colder.

Will reported that, when the previous year the Advisory Letter on industrial matters had been discussed with proprietors, Burnham had suggested it would be very good if a booklet could be made available to editors and other staff, giving examples of the kind of information which should not be published. Will said the Media generally would welcome such a booklet, that it should cover not just industrial matters but also 'more general aspects of Service information', that it should be classified 'Non-Confidential' albeit 'For Personal Use Only', and that about fifteen thousand copies would be required. The Committee agreed the idea, subject to the Services finding the money for it.

Finally, the Committee returned to the distribution of D-Notices to the *Daily Worker*, which at its February 1951 meeting had been passed back as being for Ministers' decision not the Committee's. The Services had advised that certain Notices should be withheld from the newspaper; Ministers had accepted their recommendation that a new series to be known as 'DX' Notices should be initiated, which would cover atomic and 'other specially secret matters', and which would not be sent to the *Daily Worker*. The vast majority of Notices would remain in the D-Notice series, which would continue to go to the paper. Before this was implemented, however, officials wanted to give the Media side the opportunity to comment. For them, Pitt Robbins welcomed the procedure, although he hoped they would be informed if it was ever proposed to withhold 'DX' Notices from any other journal.[119]

In mid-January 1953, the Joint Intelligence Committee discussed an amended D-Notice concerning scientists and establishments involved with atomic tests in Australia. An unnamed official who attended their ill-structured, under-informed meeting started his subsequent report to the Ministry of Supply's Under Secretary (Atomic Energy): 'After a good deal of quite heated discussion (which left me with the firm conviction that the inclusion of the word "intelligence" in the title of the Committee certainly has no reference to its members . . .)'. Nevertheless the JIC did eventually submit a draft to the Media side; this was agreed and issued in late May, in conjunction with the Australian authorities, who issued a similar request to the Media there to seek advice before publishing details.[120]

In early 1953, Thomson was involved in a libel action brought against the Temple Press (publisher of *Aeroplane*) by Aviation Studies Ltd, with whom the Secretary had previously had much correspondence concerning use of information in routine D-Notices about secret aircraft and aero-engines, and republication of information from foreign journals. The plaintiff alleged an article in *Aeroplane* had imputed 'improper and unpatriotic conduct' and a breach of security on his part, and Thomson was called by the defence. The possibility that a D-Notice might be quoted in open court caused the Ministry of Aviation and Treasury Solicitor successfully to claim Crown Privilege, on the grounds that publication of AWOAMPC discussions and communications with others would destroy confidentiality and the System. There was official suspicion perjury might have been committed by one of the principals, but this suspicion could not be transmitted to the Court because of the very Crown Privilege agreed. Thomson did however give factual evidence, and the plaintiff won. The judge in his summing up said voluntary co-operation with the D-Notice System appeared to have worked satisfactorily; Thomson and the Treasury Solicitor concluded it had after all gone well for them.[121]

At the 4 February 1953 AWOAMPC meeting, the Committee returned to distribution of D-Notices to the *Daily Worker*.[122] While the Committee had discussed this inconclusively at their meetings in October 1945, March and September 1948, May 1949, and February 1951, in practice the Services Departments had all in different ways continued to limit the newspaper's access to their facilities and information. However, Thomson's draft letter to editors on the proposed 'DX' Notices had caused some of the Media side to have second thoughts, so this new procedure had not yet been implemented. Pitt Robbins explained that on reflection he was seriously concerned the contents of the letter would almost certainly become known to the paper, and he had therefore been discussing an alternative scheme with the Secretary. This was to cease numbering D-Notices, distinguishing them in future merely by their date of issue. After further discussion, including of suitable machinery for ensuring the *Daily Worker* still would not 'obtain knowledge of a D.Notice which had been kept from it', Pitt Robbins' proposal was agreed. When Thomson implemented the numberless Notices afterwards, there were no enquiries or 'unfavourable comments'.

At the same meeting, Pitt Robbins and Martin raised a condition placed by the Admiralty on a Press visit to *HMS RELENTLESS*,[123] that all written and photographic material be submitted for scrutiny before publication. *The Times* had refused to accept the condition, and had not sent a correspondent, alleging this was not an isolated instance. Lang said it was standard practice when the Admiralty wished to let the public know about some new equipment, but did not want to disclose other, secret equipment the correspondents might become aware of during the visit. 'The scrutiny was not censorship', and was restricted solely to keeping secrets out of the reports, and pointing out errors of fact, not to preventing comment. He agreed it would be possible for a correspondent subsequently to publish something cut out on security grounds, 'but he reminded members that there was certain action which could be taken in such an event'. He also considered the Admiralty had more difficulty than other Service Departments in preventing correspondents from seeing anything secret.[124]

A Newspaper Society Member, James Palmer,[125] disagreed with his London colleagues, saying he would have accepted the invitation, ignored the condition and sorted out the problem as usual on the spot with local naval authorities. However, even he agreed the Admiralty conditions had been too mandatory, and that it would have been better to have asked the Press for co-operation in ensuring that classified material was not published; 'if this could be done the Press themselves would be very severe in dealing with offenders'. Others views included that the Press did not object to photographs being scrutinised; the Admiralty ought to follow the Air Ministry in having off-the-record talks beforehand at which journalists were briefed about what not to publish; and during a recent visit to the Admiralty Engineering Laboratory, where the Press were required to submit copy, no similar restrictions had been placed on visiting industrialists. Lang undertook to review Admiralty procedures.

Aviation security also remained a concern to Departments, and the interpretation of Notice No.9 had been constantly revisited. In mid-1952, for example, the Air and Naval Staffs had extended the period before which a new aircraft could be shown on the ground at the Farnborough Air Show (and thereafter reported on by the Media in some detail) from after ten hours' flying time to a year or more (although it could overfly the Show, and be reported on in general terms before then).[126] At the February 1953 meeting, the Committee returned to the linked subject discussed at previous meetings, 'Publication of Classified Information on RAF Matters in the Overseas Press'. Barnes admitted his paper was 'rather indeterminate'. It noted a marked increase in the latter half of 1952 in such publication, especially since the annual Society of British Aircraft Companies' Display. Much adverse comment in British technical journals led to Thomson being asked by the Air Ministry to approach the London representatives of the overseas journals principally concerned, to do what he could 'by friendly suasion with the Editors etc concerned' to prevent D-Notice No.9 matters appearing in their columns. As for the mainly freelance journalists who probably supplied the information to these publications, until they could be 'found out, and suitably dealt with', it was considered best to concentrate on the journals themselves.[127]

Barnes felt that, although there was not much leakage of British naval and military information in the overseas press, the time had come to approach the Association of US Correspondents in London, to suggest they should not transmit to the USA any British Service information (especially air matters) covered by D-Notices [which they neither received, nor were bound by]. This might be followed by a further suggestion they should also not send back similar information about US forces stationed in the UK (British editors would also have to agree not to report such information). Barnes acknowledged American correspondents would have to seek agreement from home to such self-censorship, which might not be forthcoming, but considered the approach ought anyway to be made.

The Air Ministry paper must even then have seemed out of touch with realities of global information and with American attitudes to interference from other countries. However, such overseas publication of information prohibited in the UK was something which the British technical press then felt increasingly strongly about, even more strongly perhaps than officials did about leakage. Supported by other Media Members, Alfred Chalkley[128] led in complaining bitterly the 'Government was adopting a negative attitude to the whole matter'. He suggested: prosecution of those in Britain responsible for the leakages; looking at the [legally enforced] US security methods (particularly on visits to aircraft factories) as his impression was there was very little leakage of secret aircraft and military information there; and paring down D-Notice No.9, as the System was so misused that it was in danger of 'breaking down'.

Sir George Turner stressed that, even where there had been foreign leakages, the British Press should avoid giving confirmation to such reports. He cautioned against saying the D-Notice System was breaking down; 'the voluntary system had worked well in the past and under present day conditions if it were discarded it would be necessary to introduce some alternative machinery which would probably be less acceptable to the Press'. Nevertheless, Barnes said he had some sympathy with the Media views. He promised OSA prosecutions would certainly be considered (but asked Members not to mention this), adding he would be 'surprised' if American security arrangements were more effective than the British. The Committee agreed Thomson should keep up his efforts to persuade foreign correspondents in London.

Other business included the machinery for notifying the Media of courts martial in USAF establishments in the UK involving British citizens (none are recorded in subsequent meetings). Will suggested [yet again] that meetings should take place more often, and the Secretary was asked to enquire of Members once a quarter whether they wished to have a meeting; if in any quarter there was none, there would automatically be one the following quarter.[129]

When Churchill had a stroke in June 1953, the authorities decided this information should be kept from the public, for reasons to do with national morale and the Prime Minister's role in the unstable Cold War international relations. Although this was only tangentially to do with national security as defined in the D-Notices, Thomson was asked to use his good relations with the Media to help dissuade them from publishing any news of Churchill's temporary incapacity, which he successfully did. More importantly perhaps, Beaverbrook and Rothermere (the only two proprietors aware of the stroke) agreed between themselves the information should not be published.[130]

At the 13 October 1953 AWOAMPC meeting, Lang, Pitt Robbins and Martin tabled their agreed paper on 'Conditions Governing the Grant of Facilities by the Admiralty'. It contained just two short sections, asking for 'consultation' before publication to avoid 'unwitting disclosure' of information inevitably seen during visits, or (in the case of exercises at sea) scrutiny of material either onboard or later through the Chief of Naval Information. Both were intended for use in conjunction with a handout to be provided beforehand. Martin and Will said they were still not happy with the form of words used, which 'savoured too much of censorship' and would therefore be unacceptable to editors. They wished to insert 'recognising that any form of peace time censorship would be unacceptable to the Press' in the Admiralty request, so that editors would understand their interests were being safeguarded.

Lang resisted this, pointing out the 'formula' as drafted had been used for the past few months without complaint from the Press. Questioned as to what would happen if an 'over-zealous' Naval Officer insisted on scrutiny or cancellation of a 'reporter's script', he retorted that 'the Admiralty would know how to deal with the officer'. Henry Turner (CPU), supporting the Admiralty wording, would even have preferred to see it strengthened; he urged it should be 'made perfectly clear to Commonwealth correspondents that they should submit their material for scrutiny' or some of them would be 'inclined to take their chance and not do so'. After further discussion, Media members agreed to the Admiralty paper, unusually by a vote, subject to its being found satisfactory in practice. Martin and Will asked that their dissent be recorded; and so it is.

The Committee returned to publication of secret UK aviation matters in the overseas Press. The Secretary had continued efforts to persuade, but the Association of US Correspondents in London had now said its members were not prepared to co-operate with the D-Notice system. *Aviation Report* was still unhelpful (although there was in fact no evidence they were publishing classified as opposed to speculative material). However, *Interavia* had recently appointed an Englishman as London editor, and its Swiss owner had agreed the London office at least would honour D-Notices and check RAF material received other than from London. On the intended amendment of D-Notice No.9 (Secret list of aircraft and aviation parts), it had so far proved impossible to draft a new Notice which both met perceived security requirements and would be acceptable to the Media. The Air Ministry therefore proposed the traditional British way out, an interdepartmental working party, to which it was hoped the Media would give evidence on detailed changes they thought should be made, prior to AWOAMPC reconsideration.

Pitt Robbins read the Committee a letter of complaint from the publishers of *Jane's Fighting Ships*, criticising the Admiralty's recent instruction to the Navy that this publication was not official, and that regulations regarding unauthorised disclosure of information to any unofficial publication therefore applied equally to *Jane's*.[131] The publishers had reminded that all the material used about the Royal Navy was submitted to the Admiralty for scrutiny before publication, and the Department's decisions invariably abided by; they could not therefore understand why they were being singled out in this way. Lang did not regard this as discrimination, but said this was the only publication in the Fleet which could easily be mistaken for an official document. It was clear furthermore that some naval individuals 'had spoken injudiciously' to *Jane's* compilers, and that was the reason for the Admiralty Fleet Order. The Secretary was asked to explain to *Jane's* accordingly.

Finally at this meeting, Palmer returned to the Advisory Letter of 29 September 1951 (now known as the 'War-Potential Letter') on aerial photographs of key utilities and factories; he claimed it was being interpreted too strictly by the Services, and a good deal of useful publicity was therefore being lost. The Services were tasked to review the wording of the letter and its implementation, prior to discussion at the next meeting. That this subject was being raised again by the Media, only two years after it had apparently been resolved, is indicative of a conflict which ran through to modern times: the balance between on the one hand preventing the gathering from the air (and now from space) of intelligence and targeting information on key points, and on the other hand publishing information which is or should be in the public domain.[132]

That month, the Air Ministry complained when BBC Scottish News reported a tank landing craft had put in to Campbeltown in bad weather, carrying radar equipment for the Isle of Tiree. The Ministry alleged that this disclosed the presence of a secret military radar station on the island. Thomson's investigation showed however there was also a civil (air traffic control) radar station there, which had previously been well publicised by the Ministry. It was agreed that journalists could not be expected to know which equipment was destined for what site on such dual-role islands, and that they should not refrain from reporting such incidents for fear of inadvertently disclosing military consignments.[133]

A case-study of that time concerned a Jersey man (Eddie Chapman) who had been recruited by German Intelligence during the War and parachuted into England, where however he had reported to the authorities and been used by MI5. His many post-war attempts to sell his story had been headed off by Thomson and the Security Service, but eventually he gained permission, and his book and serialisation in the *News of the World* were discreetly vetted by the Secretary (although the *Daily Mail* and *Daily Herald* then revealed the reason for the delay). However, the author also had an Australian publisher, who serialised the unexpurgated story in the *Sydney Sun Herald*, including the names of other agents. It also transpired the full story had been reported in the French and American press, but suppressed in the UK by the authorities' use of the OSA. Thomson now (December 1953) argued with Hill that once a story had been published elsewhere, he could no longer advise the British Media they could not publish the same information.

Hill disagreed, arguing this should not apply to information coming from former British agents. Officials decided to make it a test case with the Media side, and because there was no imminent meeting, a Notice including the Hill interpretation was cleared through four Members of the Media side in mid-January, 'earnestly' requesting non-republication. Arthur Christiansen did insist this Notice was accompanied by a confidential letter from the Secretary to a selected group of about 30 'reputable' editors, predominantly in London, giving the rationale: for reasons 'impracticable to explain to all editors', but predominantly because most British editors did not see the very few foreign journals in which such articles appeared, whereas if all the British Media published such disclosures, this would hamper discussions with secret Agency opposite numbers of other countries [not of potential enemies]. This rationale has not been accepted by subsequent generations of the Media side, nor was it even at that time by the equivalent Australian and New Zealand Committees.[134]

One advantage of the D-Notice Secretary having a good working relationship with the Media is that he often hears of potential disclosures while they are still being planned. Thus there are fewer surprises, and it is also easier to negotiate over a first idea than over something on which a good deal of work has already been done. In late 1953, the *Evening News* told Thomson that in the quiet season of January/February they intended to run a series on 'the Secrets of MI5'. Thomson reminded that strictly speaking they should not use that heading, MI5 not officially existing, but after the usual advice about nothing on methods, identities and current operations, they worked out an acceptable series of old war stories; Thomson asked for only minimal amendment (for example taking out reference to British operations in New York before the USA entered the War) and indeed suggested some improvements. On publication, the paper claimed official approval for their series, which irritated Thomson and Hill, until they discovered the *Evening News* had separately also sought and been given clearance for the finished articles from the Home Office.[135]

In February, at a delicate stage of secret negotiations with the Mau Mau leadership in Kenya, Thomson was asked to rush through a Notice advising against mentioning these and 'General China'; before that day's press printing deadline, he did not have time to consult Media representatives, and was immediately criticised by them. A few days later, he was asked to rush out a Notice about photographs of the secret hull design of the submarine *HMS EXPLORER*. Because again he could not contact Media representatives before the deadline, he did not issue a Notice this time, and he was criticised by the Official side. Afterwards Pitt Robbins gained the agreement of his colleagues that, rather than a Government Department decide what Notice should be issued in an emergency, it would be sufficient for the Secretary to gain the agreement of at least one Media representative.[136]

The 17 May 1954 AWOAMPC meeting revealed that the first draft of the non-confidential booklet for journalists on sensitive security subjects had not met with Burnham's approval; a second draft was now with him.[137] Martin returned to the attack on Admiralty visits, and to his previous questions about refusal to submit copy for scrutiny; the Admiralty had said a freelance journalist would not be invited again, but no answer had been given about a newspaper reporter. He wanted to know whether a newspaper too might be barred from future visits, which would imply censorship. The Admiralty replied no cases had yet arisen, and each would be treated according to circumstances. If a reporter visiting a ship transmitted his report therefrom as was usual by wireless, it could be picked up by potential enemies, a breach of security so important where NATO exercises were concerned that, if the Media were not prepared to co-operate, 'the Admiralty might be compelled to discontinue the practice of providing facilities' during naval exercises. Martin could accept its application to exercises but not to routine visits to ships and submarines; he was reassured the condition was very rarely applied to these.

The Media side raised again publication of aerial photographs of factory and utility key points (the 'War Potential Letter'), stating bluntly the current arrangements were 'not working well'. The original intention had been that only in cases of doubt would editors submit photographs for decision by Services Departments, but in practice the latter had placed such a wide interpretation on the Letter that some editors now submitted all aerial photographs, or, if short of time, declined to publish any. Other editors found that, having been asked not to publish certain photographs, these then appeared unchallenged in other journals. The possible value of an aerial photograph to an enemy needed to be balanced by other factors, including the values of giving technical information to experts, of 'giving potential customers at home and abroad an impression of British technical accomplishments', and 'of informing public opinion in a democratic country'. A 'less strict' interpretation of the War Potential Letter was needed.

Although the Chairman confirmed very few breaches of security had been due to aerial photographs, a Wing Commander gave the Committee a lecturette on use of such photographs by Intelligence Officers in establishing the productivity and economic value of a plant, in preparing scale models, and (to a much lesser degree) in target identification. His Ministry was not concerned so much about photographs revealing locations as about those revealing details. Sir George Turner spoke of his own experience of the use of aerial photography by the Germans during the War, but thought perhaps the Services were now playing too much for safety first. He suggested the Letter be redrafted to be more specific about what needed to be protected. In agreeing, other points made were that the Press was sometimes blamed for photographs taken by commercial firms from chartered aircraft; that there was no objection to aerial photographs of 'warships in movement' as long as shore establishments were not also shown; that there were however good grounds for allowing some aerial publicity photographs of shipyards because of the growing foreign competition; and that it would help if the Services when appropriate suggested photographs which *could* be published, subject to deletion of any secret details.

Pitt Robbins now proposed the title of the Committee should be changed to incorporate the word 'Broadcasting', adding that he rather than the BBC's representative was raising this 'since he could not be suspected of having a vested interest'. He also proposed other parts of the Committee's 'cumbersome' title should be changed at the same time. He suggested 'Defence, Press and Broadcasting Committee', but other members thought 'Defence' was connected solely with the Ministry of Defence[138] and might also be confused with Civil Defence. It was pointed out the Committee was already known colloquially as the 'Services Press Committee', and after a short discussion, it was agreed to change thenceforth to the title 'Services, Press and Broadcasting Committee' [SPBC].

Pitt Robbins again raised the issue of immediate D-Notices (when there was not time to consult the Media side), referring to a recent Admiralty request not to publish photographs of a submarine being launched that day. If Notices were issued without the Committee's authority and subsequently had to be withdrawn, the Press might thereafter ignore Notices and the whole system would break down. It would be possible to arrange for one or two Media Members always to be quickly available for the Secretary to consult in an emergency. Thomson explained that in the case referred to, the newspapers had been about to go to press, and even consultation by telephone might have taken 15 minutes; he hoped that, in such emergencies, the Committee would back him in any action that he took on their behalf. The Media side assured him he would have their backing in such circumstances. Martin even went so far as to say that, if Thomson was not immediately available and it was a real emergency, the Department concerned should telephone the duty Press Association editor and ask him to issue the message without delay.[139]

33

EQUIPMENT DISAGREEMENTS

The Sandys Crisis

In September 1954, a Political event severely disrupted the Media/Official relationship. The Minister of Supply, Duncan Sandys, addressed a Society of British Aircraft Constructors dinner on the eve of the Farnborough Air Show. Taking the opportunity to publicise achievements of the British aircraft industry to an international audience, he ran through many matters of little military significance, such as increases in output and workforce, exports of £60 million a year, improved gas turbine engine performance, developments in rocket motors and helicopters, and the new P1 fighter. Then, at the end of his speech, he without forewarning talked about current vertical take-off aircraft trials, something then covered by D-Notice No.9 (Secret Aircraft List).

The Press was not amused.[140] Next day Norman Robson[141] wrote on behalf of SPBC Media colleagues to Thomson, registering 'a very strong and formal protest', requesting that the Chairman take up the breach of required security with the Minister, and calling for an early Committee meeting. 'If we are to retain the confidence of the newspapers in observing "D" Notices, respect for all that is entailed must also be shown by politicians.' Next day, Pitt Robbins wrote from the General Council of the Press a similarly curt and even stronger letter to Lang (acting as Chairman in Barnes' absence on holiday):

> I think it is only right to tell you that all the Press members of the Defence Notices Committee take a very serious view . . .[referring to] the ludicrous position in which the newspapers were put when they did not know whether or not they could report a Minister's Speech without contravening the Official Secrets Act. They feel that unless Mr Sandys has some satisfactory explanation it is useless for the Committee to continue its work. I might add that personally I have no intention of continuing to serve on the Committee if its decisions are not accepted by Ministers as well as by newspapers.

The *Daily Mail* complained in a leading article that it had several times been refused permission to publish information about the aircraft, and the *Daily Sketch* protested in leading articles that the Ministry of Supply had stopped it publishing relevant photographs, even though when airborne the plane was in public view. Sandys discussed the furore with his acting Permanent Secretary, F Musgrave,[142] and it was agreed an early meeting of the Committee should be called, to pacify the Media or at least to listen to their complaints. Meanwhile, no new amending D-Notice had appeared about this aircraft.

At the special meeting on 22 September 1954, Musgrave said his Minister very much regretted 'that his reference to the vertical take-off project should have caused the Press Members to think that he was in any way circumventing the normal procedure for the release of Defence information. The Minister also wished to make the point there was no substance whatsoever in the suggestion made in one newspaper at least that he had used security as an excuse to save up a titbit for use in his speech . . . It was not an aircraft in the sense in which the term was used in "D" Notice No.9. It was a rig or structure for the purpose of holding together engines in order to try out the effect of diverting jets in a downward direction, although it might lead one day to vertical take-off aircraft in the full sense'. And so the loyal Musgrave went on, through the Minister thinking it right to give a 'boost' to British aviation, the Ministry often having made past announcements without criticism, being surprised at Press reaction this time, 'and rather at a loss to understand it'. The Ministry had now drafted a statement (with a photograph of the 'rig', doctored 'to ensure that it revealed nothing secret'), intended as a press release unless considered more convenient as a D-Notice No.9 amendment.

A long and tetchy exchange followed, between Officials who knew they (and Sandys) had handled badly something which was within a Minister's right to do, and Media representatives who had a point about the mishandling but exaggerated their own right to be consulted beforehand. Pitt Robbins reiterated the difficulty editors faced, suggesting that to the man in the street [and actually to officials too] the 'object' was an aircraft, but now they were being asked to accept that it was not an aircraft and therefore not subject to the D.Notice. By what authority therefore had the *Daily Mail* been refused permission to publish information about it in mid-August? Musgrave said it had been and was still a secret project, and there were many items of Defence equipment not specifically mentioned in D-Notices.

Barnes asked why the Press should have been in any doubt about publishing an official handout (a press release issued two hours before the speech, to the London Press only). The Media side retorted there were occasions when the Press was asked not to publish something a Minister had said publicly, and that the air correspondents already had a good deal of information about the project, but had been given no guidance on how much of it could be published. They considered it a breach of the 'gentlemen's agreement under which the Committee operated if the normal machinery was to be by-passed by Ministers'. Officials strongly upheld the right of Ministers to decide when and how to release information, even if the Committee might interpret and inspire announcements; Turner claimed that, if it were otherwise, it 'meant in effect putting the Committee above Government'. However, Musgrave said he would advise his Minister that in such future cases the Media should be given 24 hours' notice and advised as to the extent which they could report former secrets.

The first draft of the subsequent Minutes included Barnes suggesting the Ministry of Supply should be represented on the Committee, that the Media side had agreed, and that Musgrave should be that representative. However, even in circulating this, Thomson admitted there was a difference of view (initially between him and the Air Ministry's 'short-hand writer' and Assistant Under Secretary) as to what had actually been said; Pitt Robbins and Robson also had different understandings. When Barnes saw Thomson's letter informing them of these differences, he immediately wrote a stiff note to the Secretary; he took 'strong exception to it', since [quite clearly] he had himself 'very deliberately' drafted that paragraph, and he ordered that it stand; Thomson could only apologise for his 'discourtesy'. It was a fitting tail-note to a sorry affair. Yet the meeting had nevertheless served its purpose in allowing both sides to present their views (and to let off steam), and to come to a kind of agreement which might head off mistakes in future such circumstances.[143]

When the SPBC met again on 3 December 1954,[144] no direct allusion to the Sandys affair was apparently made; but a certain sharpness in tone between the two sides remained. First sweeping up minor matters arising, Barnes said the unclassified booklet on security matters had now been approved by Burnham, who had also written its foreword; it had not however been distributed because, from what was known of Media views on the War Potential Letter, which figured later in the agenda, the same criticisms could apply to the Booklet. Barnes then formally proposed the Ministry of Supply should have a representative on the Committee, Pitt Robbins seconded it, and it was agreed;[145] but the War Office's Turner placed on record that this did not imply departure from the principle that official representation should be confined to the Defence Departments, for whom the Ministry of Supply were the supply authority and therefore 'had an interest in most of the more important questions before the Committee'; they were 'simply making a convenient practical arrangement' [as will be seen, this continuing strong official aversion to the involvement of other Government Departments did not last many years longer, change being forced, as usual, by events].

The Committee debated at length the main agenda item, the draft D-Notice replacing No.9 (Secret Aircraft Lists). Media members immediately said the draft had been in their hands so short a time it had not been possible to consult the technical Press, and anything said must therefore be 'preliminary'. Officials explained the thinking behind the revised Notice, which they thought gave 'the maximum freedom' while maintaining 'minimum essential security safeguards'. They had tried to be more realistic about how long information which should be safeguarded could be expected to remain secret. The distinction between military and civil aircraft had been removed in recognition that aircraft engines, for example, might include features applicable to both. Technical Press representatives reminded that civil engines were built for export, and therefore needed publicity at an early stage.

Referring to disclosure of secret information in foreign publications, the Officials said the draft asked the British Media, if they repeated the information at all, to state the foreign source and not add further comment based on their own knowledge. To the Media side this was an unrealistic hope, as it would be 'invidious' for British correspondents to appear to have been ignorant of a matter (on which in reality they were well informed) until alerted to it by the foreign Press. Officials countered with somewhat two-sided arguments that there was a danger the British Press would discriminate in their selections from foreign journals, and that 'A good many of the foreign press disclosures were inaccurate and might mislead, but the fact that something was repeated in the British Press would tend to confirm it.'

On 'Advance Publication' of information about new aircraft and engines, officials acknowledged a time came in any project when so many people had knowledge of it that security had probably been compromised. New projects would therefore be kept under review and placed on the Advance Publication List as soon as it was felt this point had been reached. Media members welcomed the principle, but thought the transfer to the Advance Publication List would still come too late to forestall leakages; 'there was a lot of wishful thinking about security in the Service Departments', and they suggested aeronautical experts in the Media be consulted about when the transfer should take place.

Further detailed discussion followed on other parts of the draft Notice, including difficulties perceived by officials in having an 'Open List' including any aircraft, however old, which might go into action against an enemy. Technical press members pointed out there would usually come a time when full details of an aircraft would anyway be known to such an enemy. These members also raised a specific Air D-Notice then under consideration, concerning a Rolls-Royce Turbo-Propeller engine, asking that inclusion of information on the method of application of air cooled turbine blades be reviewed. This and other somewhat arcane detail is recorded here in outline as an indication of the level of minutiae into which the Committee sometimes went, of the role it had assumed as a negotiating body in such matters, and of the problems caused when D-Notices suggested by the Official side were either too specific or not specific enough to be used as practical guidance by editors.

Finally the Committee returned to the revision of the War Potential Letter. Media members said 'there was considerable disturbance' over part of the revised Letter. Being more explicit, it 'had made editors realise more clearly what they were up against in trying to carry it out'. Those responsible for security failed to appreciate there were thousands of factories involved, all of which depended on the technical Press to find methods of raising their efficiency, and discussion of factory layout was key to this. The Secretary was asked to read out two letters received from the Ministry of Fuel and Power and the British Electricity Authority indicating the difficulties they foresaw in complying with the Letter, 'in keeping the oil companies in line', and in the Minister complying with his obligation to make his full annual report without amending legislation. Barnes undertook to pass these comments to those currently reviewing security of economic and industrial information.[146]

There was then another long interval between meetings, while routine business continued, for example a Notice in February 1955, clarifying the advice on Cyphers, because the previous one did not cover GCHQ's role in breaking Soviet messages and employees involved in doing so. The Committee's interest in American attempts to control disclosure also continued, for example when in early 1955 the new Director of the Office of Strategic Information, Karl Honoman, published his philosophy and objectives (fact-finding, advice, discussion with editors on how to handle information within a free Press, dissemination, and operating on a voluntary basis without recourse to censorship); the American Society of Newspaper Editors responded that they regarded the new Office as 'the most serious threat to freedom of information that has developed in the Eisenhower administration.'[147]

In October 1955, Hill updated Thomson about the official position on vetting books and articles for publication: all insiders and ex-insiders were bound by the OSA and should submit their manuscripts to their old department for permission/vetting; for all others, it was a voluntary matter, for the D-Notice System if they so desired. As to prosecution of editors/publishers, under the then OSA this would only be considered if it was apparent they knew information originated from a Crown employee.[148]

There were occasions when Thomson's exceptionally cordial relationship with the Media was mildly misused by officials. In October 1953, he had persuaded the *Daily Sketch* not to publish a story about a Russian agent alleged to have been involved in the flight of Burgess and Maclean; this was not a matter of national security, as Thomson freely admitted to the Editor, but because the purveyor of 'this scandalous story' was considered by MI5 to be 'a thoroughly discredited person.'[149] In January 1956, an MI6 training exercise for some of its recruits required them to obtain the contents of a briefcase carried by another MI6 employee playing a role and following the (oblivious) Home Secretary out of a building. Unfortunately the role-player had missed his train, and the recruits unwittingly abducted instead a Stationery Office clerk who happened to follow the Minister out of the building. Subsequent interrogation of the terrified clerk elsewhere reached the ears circuitously of the *Daily Express*; at one stage an MI6 safe house was being watched by two reporters who were being watched by MI5. Again Thomson managed to persuade Pincher and his editor not to publish the embarrassing story, purely on grounds of personal friendship, rather than of damage to national security.[150]

Thomson was involved in another unusual incident in February 1956, as intermediary between MI5 and the Press. He invited Pincher to his Belgrave Square office, to pass on Hill's request that 'maximum prominence' be given to a story concerning the defectors Burgess and Maclean, who had by then appeared publicly in Moscow. Hollis was concerned that Burgess in particular might return to Britain, because (until Anthony Blunt provided it in 1964) there was no hard evidence against Burgess; it was feared he might then do further damage to the Security Service and to Anglo-US relations. Britain was still hoping to receive again from the USA 'the great prize' [Macmillan's phrase] of American atomic know-how. Burgess had recently provided information for a book about himself (KGB-aided but to be published in Britain), which included secret details of the brief period he had spent with the SOE during the War. The Pincher article ('Beware the Diplomats') duly pointed out that, should he return, he could face prosecution for breaches of the OSAs; Burgess did not return. Subsequent D-Notice Secretaries have not knowingly taken part in such manoeuvrings.

In late April 1956, in the wake of the unwelcome publicity caused by the Commander Crabb debacle, Hill met representatives of the Agencies to discuss press handling and how the D-Notice System might have been used; they clearly did not know Hill and Thomson had been told *not* to take the Press into their confidence. Hill thought adverse publicity could have been avoided if action had been taken early, not through proprietors (except Beaverbrook) but direct to editors. D-Notice No.1 as revised since 1945 had been accepted by the Media and in his opinion gave the necessary protection to the secret Agencies. Hill told Hollis, who agreed, that the Media had the right to criticise and 'the duty to campaign when they consider there has been a breach of liberty on the subject.'[151]

This coincided with the *Daily Express* revealing that White was to become 'C' and Hollis DGSS. Hill wanted to tighten up D-Notice No.1 on this point, but Thomson thought that, while the Media were content to accept the advice not to publish the identities of members of the secret Agencies, they did not consider this included their Heads. Nevertheless, when he put a draft to them, the SPBC Media side accepted it; Thomson consequently issued a D-Notice on 27 April 1956 reminding the Media of the previous guidance on these agencies, and adding some additional explanation. 'May I ask you to bear in mind that the task of the Intelligence Services in a democratic country is far from easy and earnestly request you, when in doubt, to act on the principle that as little publicity as possible should be given to their activities?'

Thomson's rationale for such requests included justifications on which editors, then and now, have quibbled in individual cases. 'Published reference . . . to what may seem to be obvious methods of counter espionage work, when related to particular cases or persons, create an awareness and vigilance in the minds of agents which may well enable them to circumvent the precautions taken to deal with them . . . Even the humblest member of the Intelligence Staff possesses information which would be of value to our potential enemies. Once identity is established, an agent at least knows whom to try and subvert . . . the enemy's comparative ignorance of similar information about British Intelligence [referring to Intelligence successes in the last War] also contributed in no small degree to those successes . . . Unless special attention is called to [practical training exercises by the agencies], they would not be noticeable to the ordinary observer.'[152]

Now as then, these are all the kind of grey area justifications which, in his discussion of individual stories with journalists, have to be weighed by the D-Notice Secretary against other considerations, such as how widely some detail is already in the public domain, whether or not something known to the average member of the public is therefore likely to be obvious to an agent/terrorist, and whether there is any clear and justified public interest in the publication of certain information in the possession of the Media. Usually it is not the story but one or two details therein which become the focus of discussion.

Another example of how attitudes change over the decades concerns broadcast plays. MI5's Hill told Thomson in July 1956 that he had negotiated with the BBC (who had undertaken to negotiate a similar agreement on his behalf with the ITA) that all future plays with an Intelligence content would be referred to the D-Notice Secretary, something which would not have been accepted as standard practice by those institutions even one decade later. But times change: it was then the same moment when MI5, like other Government Departments, moved to a five-day week.

Meanwhile MI6 informed Thomson (as usual through Hill) that the SIS was reviewing its relationship with the Media. Hill and Thomson thought the pressure on and from editors for 'scoops' made it unlikely that the Press would temporarily 'hold off' on stories about the Agencies, but they agreed to talk to the new 'C'. Hill wrote a philosophical piece soon afterwards, pointing out that since the insistence of Parliament in 1695 on discontinuing annual licensing of the Press, all offences involving the Press had been tried in the ordinary courts of the land by judge and jury, thus effectively freeing the Press from 'any amount of Government control'. He quoted Mr Justice Roche,[153] who had ruled much more recently that 'It is the duty of the Press to look into abuse, and find fault and criticise on behalf of the public.'[154]

34

SUEZ CRISIS, AND
'WAR POTENTIAL'

In early August 1956, shortly after Nasser had nationalised the Suez Canal, Thomson sent a Private and Confidential Letter to editors at MoD's request, covering early preparations for the Suez campaign. This asked that non-routine movements of units, equipment and stores to and within the Mediterranean should not be reported, nor strengths, destinations of men and materiel, and details of equipment; nor should Britain's 'Mediterranean strategy' be discussed. The direct cause was a *Times* article of 3 August, which appeared to be a major leak of plans for Operation MUSKETEER (codeword for re-occupation of the Canal Zone).

Subsequent investigation showed this was probably not a leak but the result of local correspondents near UK Defence bases making intelligent guesses about what was afoot, coupled with loose talk, which enabled the paper then 'to cook up an authoritative-looking statement which in fact is purely speculative'. The Prime Minister (Eden) had quickly met several editors-in-chief, and they had agreed the Media would accept 'reasonable guidance' from Thomson. A subsequent meeting of officials agreed censorship should not be attempted, but that Thomson should issue forthwith 'what can best be described as a pseudo-D-Notice'. It was also agreed there should be a press conference once or twice a week, and the Air Marshals later reluctantly agreed to let correspondents fly in 'practice flights' of Valiant and Canberra aircraft, and attend debriefs after operations.[155]

The immediate confusion caused by Thomson's request led however to a thinly-attended SPBC 'Emergency Meeting' on 14 August 1956. Lang as Chairman said it had been called because he understood the Press was having difficulty operating the guidance in the Letter, but Robson retorted it was not the Press who were having problems but the Defence Departments, who were 'getting worried by what they considered leakages of information. If they would let the Committee know their troubles, the Press Members would gladly see how far it would be possible to meet them'.

Concerns represented by these Departments, and Media side responses included: movements of ships in the Mediterranean area (particularly at Malta and Cyprus) should not be referred to, 'other than those which were self-evident' – Robson pointed out such matters were already covered in the existing D-Notice, but the British Press could not be expected to withhold information from Malta which was 'circulated to the world' by others; Lang hoped even so the Press would make it harder by, for example, reporting 'ships leaving Malta were sailing East' rather than '[specific] ships are going to Alexandria' – Robson pointed out that much news from Malta was based on 'fairly well-informed' waterside gossip, beyond the responsibility of the Committee; the Army was concerned about reports of Order of Battle, troops' destinations, dates of movements from Germany, Cyprus and Malta, and 'names of known senior officers engaged in the operations' – it was the Air Ministry representative who countered that these officers were using civil airline planes, for whom passenger lists were then published, and 'from which the Press could obviously draw their own conclusions'; Robson thereupon made the suggestion [a timelessly unpopular one with senior officers of the other Services, the Civil Service and Ministers] that senior officers should travel instead in RAF transport aircraft.

Also requested by the Services was that photographs of embarking troops should not include packages clearly marked 'Cyprus' or 'Malta', and that the strengths of units deploying should not be indicated by referring to them as, for example, 'the Parachute Brigade' or 'the Second Battalion' (excuses were made that this was an accidental contravention 'of the understanding arrived at by the editors at the Prime Minister's meeting'). The Media side seems to have been little impressed by the Services' concerns, and agreed only that Departments should initially take up any complaint with the journal concerned; only if circumstances justified further action should they return to the Committee. Nevertheless, Thomson published a clarifying further Notice after the meeting.[156]

Thomson was meanwhile aware that not only were the country and Media divided over the operation, but so were Ministers and officials, in particular those concerned with its legality. Although the legality of any operation is not directly a D-Notice Committee matter, any doubts about it inevitably affect media readiness to accept advice. In this case, it was known to officials that the Attorney-General and Solicitor-General (both of whom considered resignation), supported by their Departments and the Foreign Office, disagreed not only with the Lord Chancellor's view that the operation was lawful on the grounds of self-defence of British nationals, but also that the Lord Chancellor was constitutionally permitted to give such advice, not being himself a Law Officer. Eden then said the decision was taken on the basis of policy not law, and the Law Officers had to accept this, subject to it being made clear to Parliament that this was so.[157]

When the Suez landings began on 1 November that year, Thomson was therefore asked to issue an even more draconian Notice, which caused considerable media disquiet about the degree of self-censorship requested. Despite the country being fiercely divided by the politics behind the operation, the Media nevertheless generally supported the Armed Forces carrying it out, and published very little that contravened the letter or spirit of the Notices, not wishing further to endanger the Servicemen involved, a significant number of whom shared the public disquiet. Because of the relative weakness of Egyptian forces, the fighting was soon over, so the need for a high degree of security and for non-publication soon decreased. The British and French Governments yielded to US pressure for a ceasefire, and subsequently to withdraw their forces. By 12 November Thomson was able to cancel the Notice of 1 November.[158]

Post-Suez

Although temporarily disrupted by Suez, co-operation between the Intelligence agencies of Britain and the United States continued, such were their common interests. In January 1957, Thomson wrote a Secret and Personal Letter to editors referring to a mutual UK/US concern about covert listening devices used by Warsaw Pact Intelligence Services. He mentioned a past report in an American journal, picked up more recently in the British Press, about such a secret technical device; this also revealed that the Russians knew their devices were now known to Western Intelligence agencies, who were taking precautions. Thomson acknowledged the Press reports could not prejudice something the Russians already knew about, but confided in editors 'we have good reason to believe that the Soviets do not pass on discoveries of this kind to the satellite countries', against whom Britain also had to operate 'under present conditions', and who therefore would indeed benefit from such Western Press reports. Thomson therefore asked editors, without their sharing this information with their staffs, to consult him about any such articles.[159]

In the wake of the Suez withdrawal, media comment reflected not only the political controversy but also unhappiness with arrangements made for them by the Services. *The Times* suggested to the NPA a joint meeting with MoD Press Officers, 'to discuss immediate Press arrangements in the event of the outbreak of fighting on any scale, in any part of the world . . . sure that they [MoD] would agree that the experience which all newspapers suffered during the Suez episode bears out the need for the Defence Department to take a more realistic account of the needs of the Press – and that in their own interest'. Although MoD's John Newling[160] replied these matters were already under study by Defence and Foreign Office officials, representatives of both sides met in May 1957 to discuss 'Press Facilities in an Emergency'. This was not under SPBC auspices because matters for discussion concerned the mechanics of arrangements, not the content of reporting. This was a change from the pre-1918 concept of the breadth of the Committee's interests. Furthermore, the meeting having been an NPA suggestion, the Press delegation was led by Lord Burnham himself (as not only a proprietor, but also a Major-General and former MoI military adviser) and only the London newspapers were represented.

Accreditation arrangements prior to and during the Suez operation had been poor, but the solution now discussed (a pre-nominated pool of cleared, inoculated and uniform-owning correspondents) showed an ignorance of systems formerly tried unsuccessfully. Much subsequent correspondence was devoted to vain attempts to agree the distribution of places to the various media if the MoD allocation were 6, 12, 20 or 40. When actual crises did arise later, such as Aden, Cyprus and the Middle East from 1958, and British Guiana in 1962, accreditation arrangements were immediately found wanting, both in numbers and coverage; Reuters for example were particularly angry at being excluded from representation at the latter intervention.[161]

On communications, the Press had found the military and civil channels inadequate at Suez, and wished the Services to provide Press-dedicated equipment. Again this was an old problem, which the Services reasonably once again declined to solve; this time, 'Cable and Wireless mobile teams' were suggested as a possible compromise. On Press facilities, it was agreed that correspondents' transport to theatres of operations would be organised by MoD on repayment, but thereafter accommodation, rations and transport would be provided free by 'the major Service concerned'. Subsequently the 1942/52 handbook on 'Regulations for Press Representatives Accompanying a Force in the Field' was revised, the 1958 version being nevertheless very similar to those recorded in earlier chapters, reflecting operations and Press technology of previous decades.[162]

Back to Normal

Despite acres of drafts painstakingly prepared through the early post-war years, progress on wartime censorship plans was infinitesimal, any enthusiasm gradually waning. By late 1956, the retired Naval Captain in the MoI charged with producing revised regulations could only report he was 'not making much progress'. The booklet eventually produced has never been used in subsequent smaller-scale conflicts; notionally, in updated form, it might form the basis of any full new censorship system, if major war again appeared likely, as part of Government War Book preparations.[163]

In mid-January 1957, the *Daily Express* carried an 'Intelligence Report' by Sefton Delmer,[164] which revealed Soviet bugging devices and the extent of British knowledge of them, much to the consternation of the secret Agencies (even though Delmer's source was the Foreign Office). Thomson suggested the relevant D-Notice needed revision to cover this, but was unable to convince those he consulted on the SPBC Media side. Hill and Thomson therefore gained the approval of 'C', Lang (as SPBC Chairman) and Hollis for a briefing by the last named of two Media members (Robson and Pitt Robbins) in the Secretary's Canning House office; as a special concession they were given details of the Satyr device (a British reconstruction of the Soviet battery-less bugging system).

Even this did not convince them, however, and as a compromise a Private and Confidential letter to editors was drafted. Although the existence of the devices had already been disclosed in the USA and elsewhere, the rationale again was that the Soviets did not always pass on such Western disclosures to their satellites. This time the Media side did agree to issue the letter, but Haley of *The Times* immediately wrote privately to object that if something had been published abroad, it was impossible for the British Media to ignore or suppress it. The official and equally private reply was that it was other editors who were the problem, because *The Times* did not indulge in such stories. With even more finessed justification, it continued that articles about British security in the Press in the USA were not always passed by Soviet agents there to Moscow; furthermore, 'two or three Press members' of the Committee had been convinced after a secret briefing that 'the security people had a good case and authorised writing'. Haley accepted this exaggeration of the truth in gentlemanly silence.

'War Potential', Interception of Communications, and Nuclear Sites

In April 1957, examination having been completed of increased security required by the advent of the Hydrogen Bomb, Thomson wrote a further letter to editors on 'War Potential'. He announced that necessary precautions had been reduced even beyond the diminution in his June 1955 letter. In an era of developing nuclear deterrence theology, it was nevertheless still undesirable to allow a potential enemy 'too much information' which would allow calculation about *conventional* weapons, stocks and reserves, as this would enable assessment with some certainty of the degree of risk when planning any war. Sabotage was a further consideration, as was the usefulness of aerial photographs to an enemy's conventional and nuclear targeting.[165]

When the SPBC met on 18 September 1957 (no minutes have survived, but circumstantial clues do), its purpose was to discuss the draft Report of the Privy Counsellors under Sir Norman Birkett on telephone tapping. Thomson's view, with which Hill agreed, was that as the Report mentioned telephone interception, a reworded D-Notice would be required, which would allow the Media 'to comment freely on the correctness or otherwise of MI5 telephone-tapping', albeit not mentioning particular persons so listened to, nor the methods used. When the Birkett Report was published in late October, the Media side agreed with his/Hill's draft; updated guidance on reporting such intelligence-gathering was issued immediately afterwards in a Notice, followed in late November by a Secret Letter from Thomson to a wider distribution of editors than he had previously thought necessary.

The interpretation differentiated, at Hill's insistence, between 'intercepting' and 'listening'. The Secretary repeated the guidance he had given in his similar letter of January that year on Soviet devices, but added that it had become of even greater importance since the Privy Counsellors' Report, because of 'a tendency in the Press to suggest among other things that microphones and other devices can be inserted in telephones for over-hearing conversations. Devices of this nature bear no relation whatever to the practice of tapping telephone wires, which, as pointed out in the Report, has sometimes to be adopted by the Security Authorities'. In other words, although telephone tapping was now in the public domain, stories about 'other secret technical devices which are not part of a telephone circuit' should be checked out through the Secretary before publication.[166]

This follow-up action had been sparked by a Chapman Pincher article of 1 November 1957 ('*Every phone* can *easily* be a live mike'), which the angry MI5 Legal Adviser described as having done 'more harm than any other article he had written', a dressing down which was passed on to the journalist by Thomson. It transpired Pincher had not seen the January letter from the Secretary, whom he assured he might not subsequently have written precisely as he did. Nevertheless, the same edition had covered the Privy Counsellors' Report, and Pincher pointed out that, although it did not cover other technology linked to the domestic telephone system and already in the public domain, this potentially enabled much more intrusive bugging of the public.

Thomson himself was sharply criticised by Hill two months later, after he did not advise non-publication of GCHQ matters already revealed [by ex-National Service signallers] in the Oxford University *Isis* magazine, and republished in the *Daily Express* and *News Chronicle*. These Hill described as the 'most irresponsible acts committed by any newspaper since the War', and he set the police to investigating them as OSA breaches. He was 'astounded' by Thomson's advice; the Secretary robustly pointed out (and Hill had to agree) that what had been republished did not in fact contravene the Notices. He did concede he should have forewarned Hill, who was now concerned Thomson's advice might complicate any litigation, and he agreed to ask through the PA that the information in *Isis* should not be further republished pro tem. This request had to be withdrawn a few days later when Frank Allaun[167] asked a question in Parliament about the case. When the *Daily Mail*'s legal adviser then rang Hill direct for clarification, he was told he would 'publish at your peril'. When the Government decided the case would not be pursued, Thomson wrote a strong letter to Hill, pointing out media legal advisers had throughout had a contrary opinion to his, that the initial *Isis* article had caused little interest until the involvement of the Oxford Police and the Security Service had become known, and that, if litigation were necessary, it would have been better merely to have told the Press that certain matters were sub judice under the OSA. Hill did not want to prolong the disagreement, but told Thomson in essence not to get involved in legal matters beyond the Notices.[168]

At a more routine than usual SPBC meeting on 3 July 1958, an NPA representative SR Pawley[169] complained that, despite Thomson's clarifying letter of the previous February about the locations of ballistic rocket sites, the Press was still finding it difficult to interpret the Notice. 'It appeared that they could publish a protest received from a village but elsewhere they could only do so if there were more than one airfield or other Air Ministry property in the neighbourhood.' Officials replied it was difficult to go further in explanation; it was acceptable to publish a local protest, but 'there was surely no need to reveal the site was being erected in the field next to "Farmer Giles' farm"'; freedom to publish any site location would lead to disclosure of the layout of one or more missile-launch squadrons.

Subsequent discussion did nothing to convince the Media side, who pointed out that editors would find it difficult to judge what to omit from stories which might involve not just protest against the missiles, but also local planning restrictions or 'some speech by the local vicar'. No further action was agreed; a Notice over a year later was limited to asking for non-publication of the *complete* list of ballistic sites and their organisational and communications details.[170] This is an example of how difficult it is rationally to prohibit something readily apparent to the public, even more so now in these days of satellite photography.

Robson raised efforts by the Services to censor photographs taken during 'Minor Operations'. He suggested that unless such censorship could be carried out in-theatre, it seemed impracticable to have it, since, quite apart from non-accredited British correspondents, 'there was nothing to stop an Arab or other local taking a photo and either hawking it around to the highest bidder or mailing it by the next post'. There was also the then newish practice of newspapers using photographs cut from television films. The editor-in-chief of the Press Association Charles Jervis[171] added that the Committee should anyway resist any censorship of photographs other than for security (rather than 'propaganda') reasons, and that the Press would never agree to any such censorship 'unless all loopholes for avoiding censorship were fully covered'. The Secretary was tasked to report the Media side's views to the Cabinet Office.[172] Realism seems to have been accepted subsequently by officials, and no further Letter/Notice was issued on this. It was however a forerunner of Committee discussions in the following decades on the problems caused to officials by the globalisation of visual reporting in British and foreign Media.

At the same meeting, Robson referred to a list of Atomic Energy Establishments declared Prohibited Places under the OSAs, and asked how and why they had been selected, how this had been communicated to the Press, and what reference, if any, could be made to their existence? If there was an accident, for example at Windscale, what could the Media report, and could they take a photograph? Officials said the prohibition was not on the name of the place, but on photography. The Technical Press representatives challenged the number of AE Establishments on the list, since many (such as Dounreay, Calder Hall and Harwell) dealt now principally with commercial research and development, but Officials explained there was still some defence work done at such Establishments. The Media side continued however to be concerned that Prohibited Place censorship, so widely applied, could be used to impose censorship without consent on non-defence matters (or even on some low-level defence matters); the Chairman invited Defence Departments (and de facto the Security Service) and the AEA to review the number of AE Establishments on the list.[173]

The rumble of public opposition to nuclear missile bases in some places continued to pre-occupy the authorities, and to cause problems to the Secretary of how to give practical advice to the Media when a public demonstration was imminent. In August 1958, for example, Thomson wrote to editors (excluding the *Daily Worker*) referring to a protest march at Mepal (Cambridgeshire) two days later. He referred to the 'difficulties' which editors might have in view of requests made previously, and advised it would 'not be regarded as an infringement of those requests if the place of demonstration is described as "an RAF site near Mepal"'. He also warned however that leaflets issued by the march organisers described Mepal as 'an RAF rocket base under construction', and pointed out the base was a Prohibited Place and publication of any information about such places without permission was therefore a contravention of OSAs. The wording of Thomson's letter looks to a modern eye a little too much like passing on to editors an official threat, rather than a helpful reminder.[174]

On the other hand he did not intervene when there was an explosion at the Atomic Weapons Research Establishment Aldermaston in February 1959, in which two men were killed. It was a conventional explosives not nuclear accident, and the Government immediately made a factual statement and set up a Board of Inquiry. Its Report was critical of some handling procedures and complacency, but again the Government was quick to report to Parliament, and there was therefore no media suggestion of cover-up nor speculation about a nuclear risk.[175]

When the relationship between the Security Service and the Police changed in October 1959, giving the latter an additional supporting role, Thomson wrote to a 'Very Limited Distribution' of editors. 'May I worry you with another Secret Letter? I have been asked to inform you that new arrangements are being made to extend collaboration between the Metropolitan Police and the Security Service in secret counter-espionage work, outside the existing close liaison between the Special Branch and the Security Service. Whilst it is appreciated that normal Police activities are not covered by the "D" Notice procedure, I should be grateful if you would make no mention of these arrangements, as to do so would alert hostile intelligence services. An example of this collaboration might be assistance by the Police in Security Service observation on a known hostile intelligence agent. This of course is in no way intended to restrict an editor's duty to report on criminal matters.'[176] Similar arrangements continue to this day; in practice, the distinction between 'normal' Police activities and their support of the Security Service has caused each Secretary fewer problems than the occasionally leaky rivalry between the two organisations.

In 1960 the US authorities were looking at ways of tightening up their own security, and asked to see copies of the UK's D-Notices. Thomson was told by the Security Service this would only be agreed to if Notices handed over were given a formal security classification, because it was considered that the UK Media would withdraw from the System if it became known to the British public they were co-operating with the authorities. This point was duly made when the Notices were forwarded the following Spring, prior to the Bay of Pigs debacle. President Kennedy's appeal to the US Media to exercise discretion in publishing security matters was reported, for example, in the *New York Times* of 28 April 1961; a British official in Washington scribbled with accurate foresight 'We hope the President's appeal will be heeded by the Press, but have our doubts.'[177] It was not long however before the British Media were indeed revealing more about the D-Notice System to the public.

At the 30 March 1960 SPBC meeting, again discussed was the officially requested 'rule' that British Media articles repeating foreign press reports, on matters covered by D-Notices, should always make clear that the source was from abroad. Officials explained this was to minimise the credibility of damaging information, but the Media side now even more strongly felt this unacceptable. It was agreed examples of the practice would be gathered before the next meeting, for subsequent further discussion.[178] A year later, on 21 March 1961, there was in fact only brief discussion because no such cases had since occurred, and the matter was again deferred; Robson did however emphasise that times had changed since 1951 and that there was 'growing restiveness' in the Press about attempts (increasingly ignored) to stop the republication of information from foreign Media sources. He pointed out that British Defence correspondents also uncovered information additional to foreign reports, but the Defence Departments took the line that nothing could be published until officially announced. Lang retorted that just because it had been found out it did not mean it was publishable, but because the two sides of the Committee were 'a long way apart' on this, he would again see if the Notices could be better drafted.

The Media side mentioned the Blue Streak rocket, no longer a weapon but to be used for civil purposes; the Aviation Ministry explained that some militarily relevant technical details were still secret. The Admiralty announced some relaxations in the publication of details of new ships, for example submarines could now be reported at the laying of the keel like other vessels, and details of displacement, weapons systems, main machinery, complement, etc could now be given at the launch of any ship. New general guidance on aerial photography had now been agreed. Finally the Committee agreed with a Media suggestion that the time had come to review and discard the many obsolescent D-Notices;[179] not exactly an official thaw, but a mood change, in the hard-fought detail, as always.

35

FALLOUT FROM THE BLAKE CASE, AND THE KUWAIT CRISIS

In 1959, a Polish defector had informed the CIA and thence the British authorities that the SIS officer George Blake[180] was a spy for the Soviets whose information had led to the death of at least 40 agents in Warsaw Pact countries. The defector also provided information about a separate group of spies supplying the USSR with secret naval technological data from the Naval Base at Portland. As part of preparations for the 1961 trial in camera of Blake, Thomson issued a Private and Confidential Letter on 1 May 1961, telling selected editors for their personal information that Blake was an MI6 employee and therefore covered by the D-Notice of April 1956, but asking them, if they mentioned any of his published appointments, not to mention this connection, nor MI6's connection with the Foreign Office. He added that there was also a special reason for the request in this case, 'in that the lives of MI6 employees are still in danger'. The record shows that 'every editor played ball'.

In the following days, Thomson vetted 'an enormous number' of articles about the case submitted to him by the Press, and although David Astor[181] of *The Observer* came to see him querying the need for the Notice, he left apparently satisfied with the rationale. On 5 May however Reuters informed Thomson that a West German newspaper was carrying a report that Blake had given information to the Soviets which had enabled them to arrest six agents working for Britain behind the Iron Curtain, a story the Agency presumed they should not put on their tapes nor even pass to the PA. Thomson (and no doubt MI6) felt it likely this leak had originated from the Soviets in an attempt to gain information. After consulting a few in the Media (SPBC Members and others), he asked editors not to publish information from foreign sources that 'tended to confirm what they have been asked to conceal'.

All the Saturday papers complied with 'this somewhat unusual request', but next day *The Observer* not only published the German report, but also presented it as though it had originated in London. This article became known to some other newspapers the previous evening; the *Sunday Telegraph* rang Thomson saying it therefore really could not suppress the story any longer. Thomson readily agreed, and informed others accordingly. In complimenting the managing editor of the *Telegraph* group on 8 May on the previous restraint, he mentioned that happily the Notice had 'already almost achieved its object . . . [although] there are still one or two agents in jeopardy' [almost all the remainder of those who had survived Blake's treachery having by then been moved to places of safety by MI6].[182]

For once, Thomson under-estimated the furore. Although they had been compliant, editors were however far from convinced the Notice had been realistic. Others too, including MPs, were concerned that information openly available in other countries was being kept from the British Public. Two PQs to the Prime Minister about the D-Notice system were tabled for 11 May; this concern caused the Cabinet Secretary to contact the SPBC Chairman, Sir Richard Way,[183] about more fundamental matters. Referring to previous discussion in which Way had said he thought the time had come for some changes in the 'secretariat arrangements', Sir Norman Brook[184] passed on a request from Macmillan for a report on the D-Notice procedure. The Prime Minister wished to be advised whether existing arrangements were 'adequate for dealing with cases where a major security threat was involved', whether a decision to issue a Notice always had ministerial approval, and, if not, at what level the decision was taken.

'C' meanwhile passed Brook a telegram from the British Ambassador in Beirut, reporting that, until the BBC had broadcast articles in British newspapers on 8 May saying Blake had compromised British Intelligence activities, the case had hardly been mentioned in the Arab Press, but now it had been widely reported, implying the collapse of British intelligence-gathering in the region. White commented inter alia: 'So long as it is merely a question of a few foreign newspapers playing a British story, international repercussions are not likely to be great. Once the British Press is unleashed, with all the domestic repercussions and furore that this entails, the international repercussions immediately become very much greater. Hitherto, we had looked like getting by in the Lebanon. Since the British Press's hey day of May 7 and 9, this looks much less likely.'[185] Nevertheless, with advantage of hindsight both MI5 and MI6 thought the use of the D-Notice had been an error, and that taking editors into their confidence would have worked better.[186]

On 9 May, Brook chaired a meeting of senior officials to discuss damage to the D-Notice system caused by the restrictions imposed at their request in Thomson's Notice. They agreed there were some occasions when media interest was so great they would refuse to accept advice not to publish, and that this attempt to muzzle them over information in the foreign Media had been 'ill-judged'. They also reaffirmed that the D-Notice System was 'still very valuable' to defence secrets and to the business of the secret Agencies. Some officials wanted to use the Blake case to tighten up official secrecy; others felt that, on the D-Notice System at least, the Media would resist any attempt to tighten up, especially because of the disagreement over foreign sources.[187]

Separately, Thomson and Hill were now concerned about the survival of the System, and that nothing else should be done to inflame the situation. The former realised he had not handled the case well, and that he should have consulted Robson on 1 May. On 11 May he wrote to editors taking the blame for not having ab initio represented the likely media reaction sufficiently well to officials. Privately to Hill he said that, had he consulted the senior Media members of the Committee (Robson, Pitt Robbins, Jervis), he knew that they would have followed the official not the Media view of the matter; he had therefore recommended to Way that there was a 'need to reorganise and rejuvenate the Committee'. Hill sought directly from Robson an assurance the Media were still prepared to accept the D-Notice system, and received it, subject to allowing republication of foreign reports and to amending Notices affecting the Armed Services; but Hill also took the opportunity to point out that the substance of the PQs appeared to have originated in Press leaks of the Notices.[188]

Meanwhile the answers to the two PQs had been worked on for the Prime Minister, in an attempt inter alia to counter Press allegations that the D-Notice had been issued for the Government's 'own political comfort'. The first question, tabled by Marcus Lipton,[189] asked which Minister was responsible for D-Notices, and details about their circulation. He followed up by describing the D-Notice System as a 'relic of wartime censorship for the purpose of concealing information which a potential enemy already knows'. The Leader of the Opposition, Hugh Gaitskell,[190] criticised the additional publicity generated by attempting to stop publication of something already in the foreign Press. Macmillan replied that the System had been operating since 1912, and that 'an element of time' [i.e. the time needed to move agents to safety] was involved which he could not discuss.

The second question, tabled by Richard Marsh,[191] asked by what authority the Government had requested the British Press to refrain from publishing information already in the foreign Press. There was rather wider questioning on this by Gaitskell and others, and the gist of the Prime Minister's replies was that it had been necessary for security reasons to hold Blake's trial in camera, and that the Government was aware but could not disclose where leakage about Blake's MI6 connection had come from (although he did hint it had been planted, without revealing by whom). He repeated there had been some advantage of time gained in issuing the Notice. Nevertheless he accepted overall responsibility for the way the affair had been handled.[192]

Meanwhile, Way sent Brook his answers to the Prime Minister's internal questions about the D-Notice System, although he started by pointing out that he had been SPBC Chairman only since 1 April, that the Committee normally met no more than once a year, and that his predecessor Sir John Lang, who had been a member of the Committee since 1946 and Chairman since 1955, was better placed to give a view. He nevertheless went on immediately to say that, although the Committee was 'a good forum for discussion on the general subject of security', there was a good deal he was not happy about. The most obvious weakness in his view was that the System had 'no machinery, in the normal government sense, behind it'. It was not based on any one Government Department, the Chairmanship rotated, and the secretariat was not even housed in a Department. Against these defects there were however certain other factors, in particular that 'Thomson himself is quite extraordinarily persona grata with the Press [who] will co-operate with him in circumstances when they would co-operate with few other people'; and the System 'has gone along extraordinarily smoothly since the War, when one considers the very delicate ground which this whole subject covers and the fact that it is all based on a voluntary arrangement, except for the Official Secrets Acts themselves'.

On balance however he felt a sounder basis was needed, bearing in mind Thomson was now over seventy; Way's plan was to replace him in due course with 'a normal Government official', probably a part-time member of the PR staff. Recent events had made this medium-term planning more urgent. He also considered there was no urgent need to change the System whereby most Notices did not have any ministerial approval, since they were 'of a most routine type', about weapons and other such matters, but he acknowledged the System was not currently designed to deal with 'major security interests' involving Departments beyond the military ones; none of the senior officials on the Committee, nor their Departments, had had anything to do with the Blake case, which made it inappropriate (and 'absurd') for the Committee to have been considered the forum for resolving such a problem.

Referring to Brook's perception that Press Members of the Committee 'have recently been restive about the D Notice procedure generally', he said this was not about the System per se but about the restrictions in certain recent Notices. If the future use of the Committee were to include cases like that of Blake, he suggested three changes: all the Departments concerned should be represented on the Committee, it should be chaired by the Cabinet Secretary himself, and the secretariat should be situated in some central Department such as the Cabinet Office. Finally he alluded to the 'level of representation' of the current Media Members of the Committee, which he compared unfavourably to the official level ('all Permanent

Secretaries'). His summation was that 'we should not pretend . . . that the present machinery is what it is not, namely, a machinery and procedure competent to cover the whole range of Government security.'[193]

The Prime Minister responded by asking for a wider review of the D-Notice System. The Second Secretary in the Treasury, Burke Trend,[194] recommended to Brook that the Radcliffe Committee [already tasked to review security in the wake of the Blake and Portland cases] 'could take this topic in their stride with only marginal, if any, stretching of their terms of reference', and that Radcliffe, because of his WWII role, could make a major contribution. He added 'But I think it would be helpful if, before letting Radcliffe loose, we put a few of our heads together and tried to decide what sort of recommendation we should like Radcliffe to make'. A meeting of senior officials, including the Heads of the secret Agencies was accordingly convened in early June.

Beforehand, Hollis sent Brook a note about the D-Notice procedure as seen from his Service and MI6. As it affected their work, he said inter alia that 'from 1945 to date the 'D' Notice procedure has been of immense importance to the Security Service in its day to day workings. It has by and large over a period of sixteen years secured that no information has been published identifying officers of the two Services, nor has any information been published about the secret intelligence methods and activities of the Security Service'. It had operated well even during the trial of the Portland spies, where eleven of his staff gave evidence anonymously, and, although it had ultimately failed in the Blake case, MI6 had gained very valuable time before it failed. 'I think all agree that too much was asked of the "D" Notice in the end'. On counter-intelligence, Hollis wrote: 'There is no doubt that the operation of the existing "D" Notices covering the activities of GCHQ, the Atomic Energy Authority, and Air and Defence Weapon Development has greatly assisted the work of the Security Service . . . It has made the enemy work hard for his information and show his hand, instead of obtaining it by reading the national and technical press.'[195]

Discussion at the meeting was summarised in a memorandum, the gist of which was that the D-Notice System had worked well in the past and that something at least similar was needed for the future. It concluded the D-Notice procedure would not always be adequate to deal with cases where a major security interest was involved, especially where there was likely to be 'more than usual public interest'; that Ministers might need urgent advice whether the procedure was appropriate in a particular case; that the SPBC should be 'brought under the aegis' of the MoD [which had not actually been represented at the meeting]; that MoD should be responsible for advising Ministers whether the procedure was appropriate in any particular case; that the Minister responsible for the particular matter should remain responsible for any approach made to the Media; and that it would be necessary to consider what should be said to the Media if such changes were made.[196]

The Permanent Secretaries of the five Defence/Aviation Departments met on 13 June to discuss these thoughts, transmitted to them by Brook. The general feeling was that the Blake case alone did not justify major changes to the SPBC, that senior officials not on the Committee did not fully understand the nature of its normal work and its dependence on the co-operation of the Media as equals in the system, and that 'Brook's proposals slightly missed the point'. There was no need for the Chairmanship system to be changed, but there was a need for the organisation of the official side and its relationship with the Secretary to be improved. The MoD's PUS, Sir Edward Playfair,[197] responded accordingly to Brook, cautioning that it 'rests on the good will and the cohesion of the committee and the consequent willingness of the press members to accept an equal share of responsibility for the working of the system. The more we make the machinery look official, the less likely we are to retain this willingness'. The current 'critical mood' of the Media members would make them less likely to agree to substantial change.

The combination of an MoD Chairman and a new MoD Secretary [ie both from the central and more 'political' Services' Department] would cause suspicion. The Chairmanship rule should change only gradually, when the PUS MoD was next by normal turn in the Chair. As to the Secretary's position, they attributed some of the difficulties in the Blake case to Thomson frequently giving guidance to the Media of 'which neither the Committee nor sometimes the Departments concerned have any knowledge'. Their suggested remedy was to appoint an 'official link' with whom Thomson could liaise, and who would intervene when he thought higher authority or Ministers should be involved. This post might be considered as 'Joint Secretary' but 'for tactical reasons' should be called 'Liaison Officer'. This position would be even more essential when, within the next year or so, Thomson retired.[198]

The Liaison Officer would also act (under the Chairman) as the expert within the governmental machine on the D-Notice System, the lack of such expertise having been part of the problem in the Blake case. It would be difficult to find a suitable replacement for Thomson, as it could not be a serving civil servant, and the job entailed part-time but often, without notice, all-hours work. Another retired officer living in London would be best, with Joint Secretaries as a second best option.[199] Having ascertained that Way agreed with this line, Brook was concerned however about the reaction of other 'Civil' Departments and of Ministers, 'who are, I think, looking for some change and will need some persuading that none is necessary.'[200]

Kuwait Crisis

Another crisis involving the D-Notice Committee now however interrupted the debate. The Iraqi dictator General Kassim[201] was threatening to invade Kuwait. On 3 July 1961 the *Daily Express* contacted MoD and warned they had a story about the air routes being used by Britain to reinforce its troops in Kuwait. The paper was persuaded not to publish, but late that night rang back to say the story was in the first edition of *The Times*, and that they too were therefore going ahead with it. The articles mentioned troops and aircraft being deployed from Cyprus and elsewhere, and the possible diversion of an aircraft carrier in the Mediterranean to join the one permanently stationed East of Suez. The Government was most concerned, not about disclosure of these movements, but about the international political fallout from disclosure that air reinforcement was being effected by overflying the territory of CENTO Allies Turkey and Persia.

The Minister of Defence Harold Watkinson[202] minuted the Prime Minister explaining that the information had come to the Press from paratroopers talking to British reporters in Kuwait, and pleading that it was impossible to stop all troops from speaking to the Press, although he would try. The cover note to Macmillan from his own office was less calm: 'So it has turned out that the *Daily Express* have a better sense of responsibility than The Times . . . the [former's] office – with all its many and great faults and sins – is at least run by people with a modicum of intelligence and knowledge of the world. I venture to suggest that we should see that The Times gets it good and proper in the neck for this most disgraceful, cheap, thoughtless and unpatriotic story.' As Watkinson had pointed out, however, the proprietor would have an easy answer if confronted: a D-Notice had been suggested two days previously, but it had been 'turned down by the Press side and we had acquiesced in this.'[203]

Later Way recounted to Brook what had happened: after an emergency Cabinet meeting the previous Sunday, at which the Kuwait reinforcement was approved, Thomson was asked to seek agreement to a D-Notice about the air routes to be used. Despite his best efforts, he had been unable to persuade Robson as de facto leader of the Media side, to whom Way himself then gave the salient points: it was a military operation, with a 'dubious reception' in Kuwait; unnecessary information about routes might endanger the aircraft; there were political overtones about the overflying of foreign countries; and even if the UK Press based its articles on foreign reports of the previous day, this would still give the benefit of 24 hours' extra security.

'Robson reacted robustly to all these points', based on the impossibility of keeping troop deployments/routes of this scale secret. The information would be freely available in the foreign Press, the degree of confirmation by the British Press would be 'marginal', and the British Press was not prepared to be 24 hours behind the foreign Press in publication. The Media side were unanimous. Way concluded the Media would only agree to a D-Notice 'when they are convinced of the security purpose which it fulfils'; on this occasion Thomson and he had been unable to convince them, nor would any higher level intervention have made any difference.

Playfair commented there was no purpose in taking this particular matter further with the Media, the immediate urgency having disappeared 'under the accumulation of reports, plus our announcement that the build-up is practically finished' [nor had the Egyptians made difficulties about British ships transiting the Suez Canal]. However, such a case might blow up again, and the Embassy in Ankara had reported that Turkey had been deeply offended by the leakage and had reminded that the UK had promised 'to let nothing out'; the British Ambassador thought overflying rights might indeed be endangered. Playfair added however: 'I have rung Brooks and urged that, if the Turks do stop our overflying rights, and Ministers become indignant, he should do his best to prevent them tearing up the "D" Notice system and throwing it out of the window.'

Playfair told Way he thought there were nevertheless two matters on which to follow up: firstly to prevent any 'servant of the Crown' revealing such routes and to consider ways of stopping information about flight plans becoming known; and secondly, having thus achieved greater security at source, to come to some agreement with the Media, changing the role of a D-Notice from 'wicket-keeper against fast bowling to that of a longstop.'[204] He suggested a further meeting in due course with Robson 'in no spirit of reproach', to work out a refined understanding of the 'rule' that nothing should appear first in the British Press on matters of this kind without attribution to a foreign source [no further progress having been made on this by the SPBC since it had been previously discussed in Committee]. The whole affair had nevertheless enhanced rather than reduced Playfair's support for the system of voluntary co-operation with the Media.

Macmillan commented more briefly on Way's report that there was 'a certain confusion in the minds of editors' and indeed in the minds of the military about the 'security' of troop movements. There was only a remote risk that an enemy might shoot down an aircraft, but there was a far more serious political risk that publicity about routes might enable an enemy to build up pressure on friendly governments 'who are not in a strong internal position' not to allow overflying by the British. Furthermore the Turks had referred not to foreign Press reports but to those in *The Times* and *Daily Express*. Macmillan suggested these points be used in future discussions with the Media.

Way was unconvinced it would ever be possible to prevent troops talking to the Media. 'The average junior soldier is unlikely to be very skilful at evading being "drawn" by well directed questions from newspaper correspondents.' And to put an embargo on journalists talking to Servicemen would do more harm than good. He thought anyway that very little information came from troops (although quotes were useful for giving 'an air of authority' to a report), but that most of it came from local sources used by resourceful foreign correspondents. He agreed to try the only-after-the-foreign-Press line with Robson, but was not optimistic of success, 'because I know how extraordinarily sensitive the Press is over requests that they should not publish things which they know will be reported in overseas newspapers'.

Brook meanwhile returned to the future of the D-Notice Committee machinery, agreeing to try to convince Ministers the only changes should be the addition of MoD's PUS to the Committee and the provision of an official 'link' for Thomson to consult in the more political cases. This should be someone 'at the centre of the Whitehall machine', and he suggested the Secretary of the Joint Intelligence Committee, or in his absence the Cabinet Secretary's own Private Secretary. He would 'deprecate' this official becoming known to the Media as Thomson's Liaison Officer, but if they found out, 'there would be no question of his being consulted direct by journalists'. Agreeing, Way pointed out that most of the Secretary's business would continue to be of a level to be done directly with the Department concerned. He said he would welcome a talk with Brook about Thomson's successor.[205]

It is clear that by now doubts were beginning to grow amongst officials about Thomson's ability to sustain his previous performance, due to age and increasingly poor health. Following a conversation between Macmillan and Michael Berry, the latter sent the Prime Minister a copy of a memorandum about Thomson's Kuwait route negotiations with the Media, from one of the NPA representatives on the SPBC (presumably his Foreign Editor Pawley), which ended 'The question of overflying was not raised specifically. If it had been and a case made out, I think the non-Services side of the Committee would have agreed.' The tiny scribble by Brook on the note says: 'I wd *not* be surprised if this were true. The suggd D Notice was in good terms – "the routes by which B. troops in K. are reinforced". How quick off the mark *is* the Admiral? Maybe no-one told him the real reason (overflying) + he didn't tumble to it. It *might* be that, at 80, he is too old??' [This 10-year error in Thomson's age implies Brook did not know him well.]

The Media nevertheless still retained great affection for Thomson; after the Blake furore, the *Sunday Times*, while referring to his own admitted error of judgement in not foreseeing the unfavourable reactions to the Notice, reminded that at the end of WWII Beaverbrook had offered him the editorship of one of the *Express* columns, and the editor of the *Daily Worker* had invited him to dinner. The *Sunday Times* described him as 'this talkative, endlessly affable old sailor . . . unless the British Press is willing to endure the muddle that exists in the U.S. over publishing "classified" and "unclassified" information, it is hard to think of any significant improvement on the system of informal discretion that this most unusual Admiral has built up between himself and the newspapers of this country.'[206]

In mid-July, Brook summoned senior representatives of the Foreign Office, the MoD, the still separate three Services Departments and Ministry of Aviation, the Treasury, JIC, Cabinet Office and Downing Street (actually Admiralty House, where the occupants of No.10 were temporarily situated during refurbishment), to discuss the circumstances of the Press refusing to refrain from publishing information about overflying. Points made included: there were differing views of the actual attitude of the Press (referring to the apparently opposite reactions of Robson and of Berry); Thomson might have ab initio made clearer that the Media were unlikely to agree to the request; the Press regarded security vis-à-vis the D-Notice System in a more limited way than Government did (especially where there was great public interest); if less formal guidance than a Notice had been given, less damaging reports about overflying might have appeared; if this issue was to be followed up with the media, the points about publication in the foreign Press and British Press allusion thereto being regarded as less damaging should be used; and more effective use should be made of Army public relations officers [and by implication less use by the Media of comments from talkative troops]. The decisions made by officials were: the Services should complete their measures to prevent leakage from the Forces; Way as SPBC Chairman should prepare a paper for further discussion with the Media, based on views about publication in the foreign Press expressed at this meeting; depending on this paper it might be appropriate to reopen the Kuwait case with the Media; and meanwhile no final decision should be taken on the changes to D-Notice Committee administration under consideration separately.[207]

Thomson had not been present at this meeting, and another recurring theme is that officials have been unwise to hold meetings about the D-Notice System without the D-Notice Secretary being present, to help them avoid coming to erudite decisions which the Media, if present, would have regarded as unrealistic in practice. When Way a few weeks later produced the required paper, the three-page prose thicket was a proficient summary of the arguments, but added nothing which would have convinced the Media to agree that matters widely known abroad should not immediately be published in the UK. Nevertheless, the MoD did believe it could make it more difficult for the Press to obtain information directly from troops and charter companies' personnel, and that by sometimes not following normal air traffic control procedures and by maintaining radio silence, it could prevent tracking of the routes [the 'enemy' throughout this debate was perceived as being the Media rather than foreign intelligence].[208]

The Government was not however always bound by desire for complete secrecy. When the Portland spies had come to trial in 1961, it had been keen, unusually, that the public should be as widely informed as possible about it, in order that 'the extent of the Soviet spy system in this country' should be realised. This entailed inter alia allowing to be revealed in Court and published the activities of several unnamed members of the Security Service. This relaxation in policy was also, it was claimed, some recognition of the restraint the Press had shown until the trial started in not publishing anything which might have prejudiced the case against the spies.

Conversely, in a subsequent minor OSA Section 2 case in Bath, a newspaper published some details of how the Security Service had allegedly conducted an investigation, and leaked that an unnamed offender was about to be arrested. Thomson therefore issued a Private and Confidential Letter in mid-July 1961, telling the Media that, had the offender in this case been a spy and thus alerted, it would have been difficult or impossible for the Security Service to provide sufficient evidence for the Police to arrest him. He reminded that the advice of the Secretary should be sought, as was still requested by the Notice issued in April 1946, before publishing anything about the methods, activities or identities of secret agents.[209]

USA Concerns

One invariable concern when British spies were revealed, and when the UK Media disclosed matters which also affected Allied security, was the impact on the secret intelligence and security relationship with US authorities. At this time, however, the Kennedy Administration was itself concerned about disclosures in the American Media. In mid-1961 the British Ambassador in Washington, Sir Harold Caccia[210] sent a report to the Foreign Secretary on 'President Kennedy's Difficulties with the United States Press'. He commented on the remarkable 'lack of security precautions ... considering the tense struggle with world communism', and on the wealth of details published, military and other. 'This had perturbed the Administration for some time but action has been triggered off by the actions of the Press before and during the abortive Cuban invasion.' The attitude of the powerful American Press, the Ambassador said, was that their first obligation was to their readers rather than to security.

The President had attempted to deal with this by calling for a system of security censorship, but this had been 'received coldly or with active hostility' by the American Media. The possibility that the Americans might adopt something along the lines of the British D-Notice System was remote. In appealing to US Media to censor themselves, the President had made a mistake 'because [they felt] leakage of information is primarily the fault of the Administration', and the President could take strong measures to remedy that.[211] The USA has never subsequently adopted anything like the D-Notice System, for reasons of differences in culture, constitution and size. Much though many individual Americans, official and media (and public), have over the years been intrigued by the British system, the USA has retained its mix of considerable freedom of information and of draconian use or threat of litigation.

36

'WAR POTENTIAL' AGAIN, AND THE RADCLIFFE REPORT

The War Potential Letter, twice amended since its fractious inception in 1951, was again amended on 27 July 1961, the Committee emphasising the purpose of the revised restrictions was 'to safeguard the deterrent and to preserve secrecy on classified weapons and military equipment required for waging limited war.'[212] Thomson's letter reiterated that the prohibited list included, until officially announced and only with prior advice 'from the appropriate Department', all new weapons and equipment. A tougher prohibition still was placed on details of code name, design, performance and maker, and on rates of output, numbers ordered, trials and stocks of nuclear weapons, guided missiles, aircraft, weapons, vehicles, warships, and electronic equipment. The same restrictions on the publication of aerial photographs without prior consultation were repeated, but now applied only to Defence (including USAF) sites and to factories developing new weapons and equipment, of which the appendices listed 25 industrial airfields and 33 contractor companies.[213]

This mildly-intentioned Notice however caused immediate and widespread outrage in the Press, completely unforeseen even by the SPBC Media side. This stemmed from what the Press wrongly but understandably read into the phrase 'until officially announced'. This was taken to mean that nothing could be published about new weapons and equipment until there had been an official Departmental press release, and that journalists could no longer consult the D-Notice Secretary about such stories but had to go to the relevant Department. This interpretation was initiated by Chapman Pincher in the *Daily Express*,[214] who described the new Notice (without first consulting Thomson) as 'A determined attempt to muzzle the British Press, radio and TV by subjecting them to military censorship on a wartime scale'. He (and others) attributed this to the Conservative Government's desire to suppress censure about overspending on Defence equipment programmes (of which there were several recent examples) and about 'security blunders'. Having openly described the D-Notice System, Pincher claimed that the 'new restrictions abolish this system and put the power of censorship firmly in the hands of Government officials'.

Way immediately commented to Brook: 'It is somewhat ironical that within a few hours of my telling you yesterday that the old D Notice procedure worked perfectly well in the somewhat limited field of information about weapons, etc, the *Daily Express* should publish a vehement attack, and George Brown put down a question to the Prime Minister, on precisely this aspect of the present system.' Way pointed out it was not the substance of the Notice (in reality narrowing not widening its scope) which was significant in this case, but the fact that the Media side of the Committee had agreed it. This implied a need, as discussed previously, to look at the 'level of representation' of the Press side of the Committee. He was meanwhile raising with Robson the apparent loss of media confidence in their SPBC representatives over Notices (which strictly speaking were still 'Private and Confidential' and whose contents should in theory not have been detailed by the Press), and how to re-establish that a D-Notice 'is not evil in principle, even though there may be arguments about its interpretation.'[215]

As Labour Deputy Leader George Brown raised the matter twice in the House of Commons, once on a point of procedure, and once as a Question to Macmillan.[216] In the latter, he suggested in passing the Media should look to their level of Committee representation, and asked the Prime Minister to refer the revised Notice to the Radcliffe Committee already sitting. Macmillan, while pointing out the Notice's true intention, agreed immediately.[217] Being at the time deeply embroiled in, amongst many other problems, negotiations to join the European Economic Community in an era of Britain's comparative economic weakness, he must have been only too relieved to have the Radcliffe Committee to whom to pass yet another D-Notice hot potato. Brook was quick to tell Way he did not propose 'to trouble the Prime Minister again about this at this stage', agreeing to refer the matter back to the SPBC. Way soon afterwards received a letter from Robson deploring the campaign mounted by the Press against the Notice. Because of the holiday period, it was however mid-September before SPBC members could return to the subject, by which time tempers had cooled somewhat.

Despite the parliamentary interest which this affair caused and the strongly worded Press concerns, publicly voiced disquiet about its content was nevertheless not seen as calling the D-Notice System itself into question. A *Times* leader of 4 August 1961, for example, took Brown and Macmillan to task for referring to D-Notices as 'restrictions'. It said this incorrectly implied censorship, whereas D-Notices were 'an entirely reasonable and sensible practice', providing editors with advice they needed to avoid endangering aspects of national security, safeguarded by the presence on the Committee of Media representatives, and having 'no binding force'. It mentioned that abuses of the System had been very rare on both sides, and that it resolved occasional frictions. 'It is inevitable that Whitehall should occasionally cast longing eyes on the opportunities for suppression that a badly run control of "D" Notices would provide. It is also true that some sincere opponents of the ugly spectre of censorship are ready to shout before they are hurt'. *The Times* and others therefore welcomed the referral of the War Potential Notice to the Radcliffe Committee, remembering the way that during the War he had seen to it that 'untenable arguments in favour of alleged security were never made a pretext for trying to suppress any item of legitimate news'.

The 12 September 1961 SPBC meeting returned first to the Kuwait overflying dispute. Officials made points agreed with Brook, in particular about withdrawal or refusal of overflying rights potentially prejudicing the success of military operations and the safety of Servicemen. Way's impression was that the Media side (and especially Robson) was somewhat embarrassed by the speed with which they had rejected the draft Kuwait Notice; they now merely noted the Government's points and said they would bear them in mind in any future such case. His summation to Brook afterwards was: 'The Press side would never admit specifically that they were wrong in any particular case, nor will they ever generalise or commit themselves to any particular course of action on future hypothetical cases. Nevertheless, I believe that the discussion did some good.' Experience in other cases over the previous and subsequent years has been that officials are equally often reluctant to admit themselves wrong and to agree to hypothetical courses of action, for equally bad and good reasons.

The September SPBC meeting then discussed the offending 'War Potential' D-Notice of 27 July. Way commented afterwards that 'it is important to remember that there is a good deal of disagreement on the Press side itself. Those national newspapers who aim at exclusive stories in the Defence field want as much freedom as possible to publish information which they manage to obtain under the counter, whilst the rest of the national Press and the whole of the provincial Press, who do not or cannot expend any effort in trying to uncover exclusive Defence information, are rather in favour of clearly defined and strictly observed restrictions, "equal misery for all" so to speak'. At the meeting, it was agreed there had been misunderstanding of the Notice's intention because of a nicety in the way it had been worded, and that an explanatory letter should be issued (which Thomson duly did on 12 October). It was decided also not to issue a revised Notice because the matter was simultaneously under discussion by the Radcliffe Committee. Furthermore the SPBC's internal review of the Notices was also under way; by the end of the year, revisions had been agreed, for example reducing eight previous Notices on Defence to one.

On the calibre of Media representation on the SPBC, Way had already mentioned this (and his views above on London/provincial Press differences) in his evidence to the Radcliffe Committee. The Media themselves had also already reacted to the criticism by planning to strengthen their side of the Committee with more substantial personalities from the Newspaper Society and the Newspaper Proprietors' Association. On the official side, the Services Departments were now being brigaded by Mountbatten under a strengthened MoD, and its PUS joined the Committee at the beginning of 1962.

The Radcliffe Report

As evidence to the Radcliffe Committee, in September 1961 Thomson prepared a briefing memorandum about the SPBC, including a historical summary and the then modus operandi of the Committee, in particular of himself. He described how the Director of Public Relations of the Department concerned would pass a draft Notice to the Secretary, who scoured it for points he knew would be unacceptable to the Media and negotiated any changes with the Department. Thomson then took it personally to available London-based Media Members of the Committee, and, having achieved their concurrence, sent it to all the other Media Members for agreement. Non-urgent drafts often entailed going to and fro between Media and originating Department. If agreement could not be reached, and always if departing from established principles, the draft was discussed in Committee.

If the Notice was urgent, the Secretary had only to get the agreement of one Media Member (after the Blake case, two). Notices included only enough information to give an indication to editors of what not to publish, rarely confidential, so that if they fell into the wrong hands they would not tell a hostile agent [or presumably a hostile journalist] what he should try to find out. The SPBC Media members were however always 'put fully in the picture' beforehand, either by Thomson or in Committee, so that they could 'come to the correct decision'. The Central Office of Information distributed the non-urgent messages, while Thomson still roneoed and despatched urgent ones himself, keeping a supply of addressed envelopes in his Belgrave Square office for this purpose. Some very urgent Notices, and those of a temporary nature (such as one prohibiting reporting Field Marshal Montgomery's visit to Palestine until after it was over) were distributed via the Press Association tapes; Thomson did not like this method because they could then be seen 'by all and sundry within the newspaper office, from the Editor to the office boy', while on the other hand letters were opened by the editor himself, who then decided who on his staff should see it.

All Notices went to all morning, evening and Sunday newspapers throughout the country, to British News Agencies and to the London editors of Commonwealth News Agencies and newspapers; other journals and the broadcasters received Notices according to their content (none were now sent to Eire or to foreign News Agencies, nor, if 'basically confidential,' to the *Daily Worker*). The quarterly summary of D-Notices in force was useful to busy news and night editors as a quick check 'at a glance' as to whether a subject was covered by a Notice, and advice was then normally sought from the Secretary by telephone. Thomson ended his memorandum:

> *Infringements*. Editors occasionally, although never deliberately, infringe a 'D' Notice. As the whole 'D' Notice procedure is on a voluntary basis, the Fighting Service Departments consider it preferable to make use of my personal friendship with editors throughout the country. They accordingly ask me to write a personal letter to the offending editor. This invariably stops further infringements of the particular subject in question and produces an expression of regret on the part of the Editor, which I pass on to the authorities.[218]

The SPBC met on 2 March 1962 to discuss that part of the draft Radcliffe Report[219] which dealt with D.Notice procedures. Way confirmed that the MoD would henceforth be represented by its PUS,[220] and that the first SPBC representative of Independent Television News was Geoffrey Cox.[221] Way explained the Prime Minister had consulted the Opposition on the draft Report 'and was disposed to publish it' [he had already given George Brown an undertaking to do so], but before reaching a final decision wanted to obtain media views. This could be done either by Macmillan writing to certain 'leading figures' in the Media, if the Committee felt unable in this case to speak authoritatively for the bodies they represented, or by comment in Committee. As Way and Thomson had foreseen, the Media representatives, full of 'amour-propre', responded immediately they 'saw no need for the Prime Minister to seek other views' than their own.

Their views on the relevant 32 paragraphs were subsequently accepted on presentational accuracy, but not on Radcliffe's 'final further point' on the differing needs of the National and of the provincial Press (see below). Although some thought publishing details of the D-Notice System might jeopardise security, and Sir Maurice Dean[222] considered only the three very brief conclusions should be published, generally the Committee was in favour of full publication.

The published Report covered first many other aspects of security before addressing 'The Value of the D Notice System'. 'In our view the system makes a valuable and effective contribution to protecting the disclosure of "military" information which needs to be concealed and which it would be useful to other Powers to possess. By its operation Her Majesty's Government succeeds, year in and year out, in keeping out of newspapers, radio, and television a great deal of material which, so far as we can see, could not be kept out in any other way.' That clear endorsement aside, the latter sentence is grammatically interesting to the historian, as it implies that at that time, unlike now, there was an official perception the system was 'operated' by the Government, and that the Government's success was somehow not completely dependent on the agreement of the Media. Perhaps Radcliffe's implication was unintended.

The Report considered what alternative there might be 'to maintaining a system of this kind'. It acknowledged the Media did acquire 'a very considerable volume of information on secret matters which, prima facie, is of interest and importance to the public', and that their sources were 'not by any means necessarily illegitimate or reprehensible'. It discussed the limitations of using OSAs 1911–39, which were confined mainly to information about 'prohibited places' and that obtained through 'wrongful communication' by or through an official; furthermore they were not an invariably clear indicator to an editor of whether he was within or without the provisions of the Acts. While OSAs were 'a restraining influence at the back of editorial life', they did not provide a 'working code', nor was there 'a lively expectation' in the Media that minor breaches of security would be followed by criminal prosecution. 'It must be taken, therefore, that the Official Secrets Acts are not an effective instrument for controlling Press publication of that kind of "military" information of some though perhaps no great individual importance which it is nevertheless most desirable to keep from hostile intelligence.'

Where no censorship effectively existed, an effective instrument was therefore provided by the D-Notice System. It appeared to suit the needs of both sides; officials because it provided a centralised and quick means of communicating requests and warnings to the Media before damage was done, and with the authority of a Committee on which the Media representatives were known to be in the majority; and the Media because, without being mandatory, it enabled an editor to obtain guidance before publication whether some item of news was considered by the Government to be sensitive. 'According to the evidence we heard, neither side wishes to abolish or in any substantial way to amend the present system'. They also considered whether there was any inherent danger to security in the circulation of D-Notices themselves, and concluded that, 'in one form or another it is a commonplace of a newspaperman's life to be a confidential recipient of secret information', and that therefore both sides well understood the need for discretion.

Looking to the future, the Report considered first the standing of Committee Members, confirming that the Officials should be the Permanent Secretaries of Departments concerned. It did not consider that increasing the level of representation of the Media side [presumably by proprietors or more editors themselves joining the Committee] would make any difference, since the Media did not regard D-Notices as 'necessarily binding on them by the mere fact that their form had been agreed before issue by their representatives on the Committee'.

The Report was however concerned about 'the critical question for the future – the personality of the Secretary'. In view of what followed a few years later, this was a prescient observation, as was their description of the incumbent's working life, which still largely holds true today. 'It is upon the work of the Secretary and not upon what can only be very infrequent meetings of the Committee that the operation of the D.Notice system depends. His work involves much more than the various procedures that lead to the issuing of a D Notice. Since in most cases such Notices will not be acceptable to the Press as a whole if they are intended merely as blanket stops on a particular subject . . . he has to provide in himself something like a continuous advisory service of voluntary censorship so as to pass, amend, or reject copy that falls within the range of subject embraced by the Notice. This is an exacting task arising at unpredictable hours and often demanding an exercise of rapid and experienced judgement on the part of the Secretary or in other cases urgent consultation with the experts in the Department directly concerned.'[223]

Admiral Thomson was praised, noting his 'special qualifications and personality', and the knowledge and goodwill brought to the post from his time as wartime Chief Press Censor. Two important qualifications for his post were suggested: 'Negatively, the Secretary should not be himself drawn from journalism; positively, he must be familiar with the ways of the

Press and have a sympathetic personal approach in his relations with them.' They also suggested the Secretary's status should be raised by making the holder of the post a Committee Member, subject to Media side approval [this has never been pursued, nor desired by any Secretary, as far as is known], and that, because of the workload, two men should be 'allotted to the task'.

The Report's second recommendation, which bore in mind the voluntary nature of the System, 'trenches upon the very delicate subject of Press freedom', and for these reasons 'must not be subjected to overstrain', as it had been when difficulties had arisen over the issue of Notices to a 'quite exceptional' degree that summer. Three points had been brought home to them by their Inquiry:

- When queries on copy were made, the Government side must provide a prompt and authoritative answer, preferably through the Secretary.
- The agreement of the Media side to use the System was based on it normally being for defence matters, the publication of which would be prejudicial to the national interest, and it should only be departed from 'on special occasions when the subject is one of grave and obvious importance. . . There is always likely to be resentment if a Notice is thought to have been dictated by "political" considerations, or if it is thought that the official side is trying unreasonably to suppress here matter which is already public knowledge abroad'.
- No news in media possession should be held up by officials in the name of security 'when there is reason to suppose that the real motive of the request or pressure is the convenience of the Department or its political chief'. Such complaints 'are a standing grievance with the Press and they do more than any other single thing to prejudice the system of voluntary co-operation in the withholding of news which is represented by the D Notices'.

Finally, as instructed, the Radcliffe Report addressed the D-Notice of 27 July 1961 ('Classified Weapons and Equipment: and Air Photography and Diagrams'). It mentioned the similar preceding Notices of 10 December 1951 and 13 February 1956 and the 'War Potential Letter' of 11 April 1957, and that the Media side had never been altogether satisfied with the form of these documents, in that they had been too comprehensive in their restrictions. Despite the intentions of the new Notice to reduce the area of prohibition, the inclusion of 'Until officially announced' meant the Notice had not been 'happily drafted'; nevertheless, there had since been a further SPBC meeting, the Notice had now been rewritten to the satisfaction of those who had complained, and the matter was therefore closed.

The affair did however raise one further point in the minds of Radcliffe's committee (the two paragraphs of the draft characterised by SPBC Media members as 'offensive and substantially incorrect', but which Radcliffe insisted should stay in): how was it that a Notice which had been approved by the Media side had immediately provoked widespread media criticism, and why were these criticisms not voiced through the Committee but 'by immediate public representations'? 'There is, it seems, a conflict of interest which divides the Press on much that relates to information on defence subjects.'

This was described as between on the one hand those journals which did not have the resources and/or inclination 'to work up news on these subjects on their own initiative', and therefore found detailed instructions 'congenial'; and on the other hand those ('including some London dailies and some technical journals') which had specialist contributors, to whom it was 'essential to get what advantage they can out of their individual effort', who 'much resent, therefore, any system which tends to hold them to the same line as the others', and who therefore wished to publish all they could, subject to security considerations as discussed with the Secretary.[224] The Report considered the latter group entitled to their view, and that the public did not lose by such activity. It was something, the Report concluded, which those drafting D-Notices should bear in mind. Furthermore, referring to the Secretary's post, 'for this reason alone active assistance in scrutinising copy and helping to get it passed is one of the services that will be expected of its occupant in return for observance of D Notices'. This has certainly been one of the services to the Media expected of successive Secretaries since then.

Just before publication, Way had commented to Thomson on Cabinet discussion of the Report, which indicated a wish by some Ministers to 'enforce' protection of a narrower range of information, and make more OSA prosecutions: 'All this is pretty meaningless to me. One cannot enforce D-Notices; and the vision of a prosecution under the OSA is likely to remain a vision.' Thomson replied that if he was told what the really important defence secrets were, he could concentrate on getting the Media to seek advice on those, as MI5 and MI6 did 'with much success' over their agents.[225]

One side effect of the Radcliffe Committee's wider recommendations was that the Public Records Office (forerunner of today's National Archives at Kew) reviewed the security classification of official records which were or might come into its custody. The Keeper sent a note in early April 1962 to his Inspectors: 'Do we know anything of the Services, Press, and Broadcasting Committee + would you regard their papers as public records?' In due course he received the reply: 'I have not come across the SPBC before' [despite the publicity of recent years], and that there was doubt whether its papers were official records under the Public Records Act 1958; to this the Keeper minuted: 'If any of the IOs come across this Committee, I should be interested to know more about it.'[226]

There that matter rested, and it is not surprising, in view of the non-statutory, unique and anomalous quasi-official administration of the D-Notice System, and the then secrecy about its operation, that the PRO staff was not only somewhat ill-informed but also somewhat confused about its archival status. Fortunately, Pitt Robbins had arranged the transfer of the Committee's early minutes to the new Secretary in 1945, and in due course, as the ever-expanding MoD ran out of storage space, subsequent Secretaries transferred these and other Committee material to The National Archives. There those records which earlier survived war damage, and later excessive weeding, are well-catalogued and freely accessible.[227]

37

POST-RADCLIFFE

Early in 1962, George Thomson suffered a stroke, and in late March an Acting Secretary had to be appointed. This was the Deputy DPR for the Army and later for the MoD, Colonel 'Sammy' Lohan,[228] already therefore well known to the Media. Thomson did in due course return to part-time work in early 1963, reduced by his doctor to six cigarettes a day, but working from home on a reduced annual salary of £1,000, and in uneasy tandem with Lohan, who continued to be first port of call for media enquiries about Defence matters. On secret Agencies matters, however, Hill preferred to continue to deal with Thomson; he also took an unusually prominent role in looking for a suitable permanent successor for him, and, when the somewhat resentful and status-conscious Lohan refused to allow Thomson to share his secretarial support, Hill obtained the agreement of Way and Hollis to acquire a supply of SPBC-headed paper and have Thomson's official letters typed by his own MI5 Secretary. Any conspiracy theorists in the Media of the time do not seem to have been aware of this symbiotic friendship; any of the present day may rest assured such practices have not occurred since.

Admiral Thomson finally retired because of ill health at the end of 1963; he had received a knighthood in the New Year Honours for his highly-regarded work over 22 years as wartime Chief Press Censor and as D-Notice Secretary. He died aged 77 in January 1965, and the large and diverse attendance at his memorial service at St Bride's in Fleet Street included editors and many others from the Media, as well as officers from his old Service and the great and the humble from Defence and the several other walks of life with which he had been connected. It was a reflection of how important his perceived conciliatory, independent and popular personality had been to the relationship in this field between government, media and public, and to the evolution and continuing usefulness of the D-Notice System.

Hill had no feeling against Lohan, however, and had interviewed him in late May 1962 as the possible permanent successor. Lohan told him correctly that the Media would only accept a Secretary who did not hold any government appointment, and that he himself might be prepared to take on the job when he retired from the Army at the end of that year. Hill minuted 'I think if we cultivate him properly he will do all he can with the Press to see that the Intelligence D-Notice is honoured. I think we should get on well with him if he was appointed Secretary.'

Lohan became the 'permanent' Secretary on his delayed retirement from the Army at the end of 1963. One earlier side effect of his acting appointment was that officials' wish for a 'Liaison Officer' as a link between Departments and the D-Notice Secretary had been set aside. Being already an official, with an office in a Ministry building, linked in his other hat with the MoD PR system, and having, it was then thought, sufficient security clearances, it was now decided there was no need for an additional link to Departments. This was only partially an adequate arrangement and a wise appointment, as subsequent very public events were soon to show.

Under Lohan's acting stewardship, the D-Notice System had already again been in the news. On 14 September 1962, after it was announced the Admiralty clerk John Vassall had been arrested and charged with espionage offences, Lohan dealt with media enquiries about the application of D-Notices to this case. His advice was complicated by also dealing with similar enquiries as the MoD's Deputy DPR. In later evidence to the Vassall Inquiry Tribunal, he claimed this distinction had been 'clearly understood and recognised by the Press'; on potential conflict of interest and official misuse of the grey area between the two different roles, it had been confirmed with Hill and other officials that D-Notices could not be used 'to suppress newspaper speculation of a merely embarrassing nature'.

In practice however the danger of confusion did arise. In October 1962 Chapman Pincher went to see Lohan about the Vassall case, and the Colonel said he could not comment in his MoD capacity. However, when Pincher asked him questions in his D-Notice role, specifically whether there was any connection between the Vassall and the Houghton (Portland Naval Base) cases, Lohan 'inferred that there was no connection'. Pincher suggested in that case the lead must have come from a Russian defector, to which Lohan laughingly replied 'no comment', while also agreeing a number of American correspondents were 'touting' that story. Questioned further, he said there was no objection to publishing a story that the lead had come from a Russian defector, although this did not mean it was true. He later commented on other Vassall stories in the *Daily Herald* and *Sunday Pictorial*, and did ask for some deletions from drafts concerning references to MI5 and MI6 agents.[229]

When Pincher was later questioned by the Radcliffe Tribunal in January 1963, he gave the perhaps inadvertent impression that Lohan was largely the source of his story about Vassall being caught as a result of information from a defector, and that this was in Lohan's capacity as MoD's Deputy DPR. Sir Robert Scott explained the actuality to Way, adding 'it might be argued perhaps that Lohan need not have acquiesced in the publication of the statement about a defector'. This less than ideal mixing of roles had subsequently to be explained to others inside and outside Whitehall.[230]

In late April 1963, at the Campaign for Nuclear Disarmament Easter March on Aldermaston, an 'underground' group called 'Spies for Peace' distributed a pamphlet which revealed information about Regional Seats of Government (war emergency headquarters), details of which were covered by a D-Notice.[231] The breach of security was widely reported, and questions asked in both Houses of Parliament on 23 April. Macmillan responded that the information in the pamphlet seemed clearly to have come from a widely distributed [but classified] document used in a recent NATO biennial command and control exercise (FALLEX), that the precise locations of the Regional Seats had not previously been published for obvious security reasons, and that, although the information disclosed in the pamphlet was not seriously damaging to the national interest, the deliberate breach of security was serious and strongly to be condemned. He said the relevant D-Notices would remain in force and praised the Press for 'so loyally keeping to the regulations'.

The Opposition's questioning however followed the line also taken in a *Guardian* leader the day before: 'logic is carried beyond reasonable limits when, after hundreds of demonstrators have visited a site, its location remains unpublished'. George Brown and Harold Wilson both queried whether something widely known should remain covered by a Notice, but Macmillan retorted that the D-Notice covered wider aspects, and maintained it was not the Government's duty to publish every detail simply because some information had leaked out. The Opposition did not pursue this further, possibly because they anticipated a more profitable debate on the just published Vassall Tribunal Report. Not even all Macmillan's own side were convinced, however, and a few days later Captain Henry Kerby [see next Section] asked the Minister of Defence if he would set up an immediate inquiry into the value of the SPBC and D-Notices as a means of media censorship, as operations of the Committee had 'broken down'; the Minister assured they had not broken down, and that the 'Press had accepted advice in this matter most loyally.'[232]

Afterwards, Lohan sent editors a Private and Confidential letter, referring to likely Press follow-up on both 'Spies for Peace' and on Vassall, reiterating the previous advice on Secret Intelligence and Security Service matters which should not be published. In the chatty style which was a hallmark of his letters, he added: 'Believe me, every bit of this "D" Notice is important. A few days ago an article mentioned an address from which one branch of the Security Service worked (incidentally I have been assured that this breach was entirely unintentional and will not be repeated). But the upshot of this article was that some of those people who hold security in contempt made nuisances of themselves at the address mentioned. We all realise that in a country like Britain, the task of the Security Services is tremendously difficult; but they have their job to do today, tomorrow and at all times; I feel sure you will agree it is quite plainly wrong to give any help to those people who wish to impede their work – quite apart from the clear security aspects.'[233]

Lohan was by now in more relaxed communication with Hill. In early June the Colonel said to him 'There is really only one way to get at Editors, that is to take them out for a meal and work on them; but I have singularly failed to get an expense account [from his parent Ministry].' He claimed he was out of pocket as a result, but 'I do what I can'. This hint led to Lohan being granted an 'entertainment allowance' by the Security Service, as became more widely apparent a few years later.[234]

In late June 1963, the new Cabinet Secretary Sir Burke Trend held a meeting of senior officials to discuss the appointment of a permanent successor to Thomson, and other outstanding D-Notice Committee business. There was general agreement 'the only suitable candidate' was Lohan, who 'had effectively filled the post for the last year in Admiral Thomson's absence and in doing so had given wide satisfaction in Whitehall; he was known to and liked by the Press; and he was willing to continue to undertake the work on a part-time basis'. However, the meeting also agreed that Lohan's two posts had sometimes conflicted, that it was 'unwise' to continue this combination, and that the Secretary should be 'a distinct and separate appointment'.

Other administrative arrangements agreed at this meeting were that, although Way's move from the War Office to the Ministry of Aviation gave the opportunity to change the Chairmanship permanently to the PUS of the MoD, it was preferable for Way to retain the role pro tem; that the Secretary should be collocated in his building (then Shell-Mex House) and paid by his Department;[235] that Lohan could not be paid less than Thomson's half-rate of an Information Officer (then £1,300 to £1,400 per annum) but that he would be permitted also to have a secondary job [other than in a Departmental PR role].

In view of what happened a few years later, it is fair to Lohan to record that the then satisfaction of Whitehall with his performance included his willingness to be an occasional channel through which Ministers (via officials) leaked to the Press matters which they wished to become public unofficially. When for example an arms deal with Saudi Arabia particularly lucrative to British Industry was concluded by MoD, the Foreign Office wished there to be no publicity for this; the Minister of Defence Harold Watkinson wished however that his Department should gain credit for the deal, and Lohan passed this on discreetly to Chapman Pincher.[236]

The 'Dolnytsin' Case

In early 1962, a Soviet Intelligence Officer Anatoly Golitsin had defected to the West, and after remaining in the USA during his initial questioning by intelligence services, came to England for continued debriefing. The UK Aliens Office received an enquiry from the *Daily Telegraph* on 11 July 1963, which revealed to the Security Service the paper was aware of this. Every effort was being made at that time to ensure the defector's identity and whereabouts did not become public, because it was considered his life would be in danger from Soviet agents. Hollis called on Way with Hill, discussed the options (do nothing and accept widespread publicity, approach the *Telegraph* only (but other journals might also know of the defector), or issue a D-Notice).

Lohan, when summoned, advised the latter course, and that the only way of ensuring a Notice reached all national newspapers before that evening was to issue the Notice by PA tape; this was duly authorised. The Private and Confidential Notice not only asked the Media not to mention the presence in the country of a defector who was 'providing important intelligence information', and mentioned the 'positive danger' to his life, but also stated his name; however the surname given was Dolnytsin (the name of another Soviet intelligence officer already working in London), which at least one newspaper was thought already to have acquired.[237]

Before sending the Notice out, Lohan managed to consult seven of the eleven SPBC Media Members, who agreed with its issue and, unusually, advised not mentioning the US link because it would give credence to a recent *Newsweek* article about weaknesses in British security. Lohan also rang the managing editor of the *Daily Telegraph* to tell him what was happening, who initially accepted the advice in the Notice; but he later rang back to say he could not guarantee the story would not come out anyway, because it had come from an American source. The paper therefore intended to publish the story, but he agreed still to omit the name. Late that evening, Lohan was rung at home by Chapman Pincher to say the *Daily Express* intended to carry the story, because they knew the *Telegraph* was (even though this was before the first edition of the latter had been printed).

Lohan then spent the night hours on the telephone trying to dissuade other papers and the two television news companies not to publish. Both the latter and some papers (including *The Times*) did agree to hold off until the story had been carried in the foreign Press. Lohan was not in possession of all the facts, so he did not counter a media assumption the defection was recent. On 13 July the *Evening News* also published a photograph purporting to be of Dolnytsin, and, after consulting Hollis, Lohan therefore issued a Private and Confidential Letter reminding that the Notice was still in force, and asking that photographs and other details which might lead to identification should not be published. In discussion subsequently with picture editors, he accepted photographs with a blocked out face and fudged background.

Trend called together Way, Hollis, the JIC Chairman, other officials and Lohan to discuss what more to do. The *Daily Telegraph*'s editor had already confirmed to the Foreign Secretary that the information published came from a source in the USA, and the British

Embassy there had been asked to find out more, including 'any hint' as to the *Telegraph*'s Washington sources. On whether the issue of the D-Notice was justified, it had been believed that other papers also had the story (the *Daily Express* did); giving the defector's name had been intended as evidence of taking the Press into the Government's confidence. Ministers had not been consulted about this, because, having originated from the Security Service, it was 'self-evident' the matter should not be disclosed in the Media.[238]

This meeting of senior officials agreed that, because of the growing number of Notices concerning MI5 and MI6, it should not be a requirement on every occasion to seek approval, but that it would be desirable for officials to warn Ministers of any case 'likely to have political repercussions'. It would not be desirable, officials thought, 'to inspire' Parliamentary Questions about this case, but the best way to answer any media queries was that the disclosure of the defection was not due to any breach of British security, and that it was not customary to disclose what advice was given to Ministers by officials [such advice is still not disclosed, on any subject, even under the current Freedom of Information Act].

Hollis was asked to check with his Legal Department whether in theory the *Daily Telegraph*'s article could lay the paper open to prosecution under the OSAs, and whether publication of information contained in a D-Notice could lay any journal open to similar prosecution. He reported back afterwards Hill's advice that for a journalist to be prosecuted successfully about an article, it would be necessary to show he had 'received his information or some material part of it from a person in Crown employment and that this person had not received the authority of the head of his department to give this information'. There was no evidence that the *Telegraph* had received its information from such a source in this case. On the second question, Hill had told Hollis: 'a D Notice has never been regarded as information entrusted in confidence within the meaning of the Act, and he [Hill] considers that no newspaper would receive a D Notice on those terms.'

Meanwhile the British Ambassador in Washington Sir David Ormsby-Gore[239] had talked to the President and the US Attorney General about the case, and telegraphed to London they were both 'entirely relaxed' about it, although they did wonder why the defector had been named. He added: 'The President himself was extremely critical of recent [American] news-paper articles suggesting that there was bad feeling between our Security Services. He said that it was always possible to find someone in a vast organisation like the CIA who would be led by a journalist into making some critical comment about the British', but that nobody who counted would lend themselves 'to such foolish backbiting.'[240] By other means, the *Telegraph* itself later confirmed the source was an (unnamed) American in the USA.

The case was raised twice in Parliament. In the House of Commons on 18 July, the Prime Minister replied to Labour MPs that the defector's name had been given to editors as a confidence-building matter, and that the newspaper story came from a foreign source; he denied it had been leaked in Britain for political advantage to counter criticism of the Government's record on security.[241] In the Lords, the Foreign Office Minister of State replied on 22 July that it had been thought right to take editors into confidence because one of them had asserted he had acquired the name from a foreign source, and that it might therefore be published abroad anyway, and then republished by other British editors, had they not been cautioned not to do so by the Notice.[242]

However, the *Daily Telegraph* pointed out again on 23 July that the relevant D-Notice had not as normal been circulated to editors personally in a 'Private and Confidential' sealed envelope, but had been sent out on an open PA teleprinter circuit, subscribed to amongst many others by the Soviet News Agency Tass. This was in fact incorrect, although the credit for what actually happened was due to the Press Association; Lohan established post hoc that his request for a very limited distribution had been interpreted by the PA in such a way that the message went only to the national papers and to a reduced number of provincials, and certainly not to Tass. Nevertheless, the tape message would have been widely seen within all those newspaper offices; despite a degree of urgency, this had not therefore been a good way of disseminating theoretically very sensitive information.

Way told Hollis on 22 July that Lohan was having 'a difficult time' with the Media side of the Committee, which felt that they should have been told the defector had been in the UK for 18 months. Hollis explained that Golitsin was still being debriefed, and that the publicity had inevitably damaged the confidence which he (and other potential defectors) had in the British authorities. Hollis also thought the 18 months had been mentioned in the draft he had seen, but had been removed by someone [Way does not appear to have been able to verify this subsequently].[243]

At the 'full and frank' 24 July 1963 SPBC meeting, the Media side reflected the widely and strongly held adverse view of the official line on the Notice. They criticised especially that it had conveyed a sense of urgency by giving the impression 'Dolnytsin' had recently arrived in the UK, whereas, because he had been here for some time, the danger to his life had thereby been exaggerated; if the Media members consulted by Lohan had known this, they would not have agreed to the Notice [in fact neither Lohan nor even Way had been aware of the date of defection]; and that, even if the Media side had been persuaded of the need for a Notice, it should merely have asked editors not to publish anything about a Russian defector without first consulting the Secretary. The Official side countered by stressing that at least one newspaper had intended to publish that evening, the rationale was justified, there had been no intention to mislead editors, and the length of time since defection was considered irrelevant. The two sides therefore agreed to differ.[244]

This case caused further fallout from the Press. William Haley, editor of *The Times*, wrote to the MoD, as being responsible for the Government side of the SPBC. He claimed *The Times* had always taken D-Notices seriously, even when, as in the Blake case, it had put them at some disadvantage vis-à-vis their competitors. The 'Dolnytsin' affair had however caused the paper 'to lose confidence in the whole "D" Notice system'. The Notice had been disregarded by the *Telegraph*, *Guardian* and *Daily Express* and then others, and a defection described in the Notice as 'recent' was in fact 18 months ago; it was difficult therefore to see how it could have serious consequences for national security. *The Times'* continued reticence in reporting the story had moreover harmed its own reputation. Either D-Notices must mean what they say and be observed, or they had no validity at all. The whole system depended on trust. He reiterated that transmission by PA tape meant the Notice could have been acquired by 'Communists'.

Haley was invited to come and talk to the Prime Minister, who after much inter-Departmental correspondence and a high-level meeting of officials, was provided with copious 'briefs' by Way and Trend. When Macmillan and Haley met on 29 July it was not in fact much of this which the editor really wanted to discuss. At the end of the Prime Minister's long repetition of governmental justification, Haley thanked him politely and said he had only one comment to make, namely that, instead of using PA tapes, the message could have been sent around to London editors and the main provincials by car.

What he wanted mainly to put across (not recorded subsequently in the minutes of their meeting but in a separate letter to Trend from the Prime Minister's office), was that, once Admiral Thomson had retired, the D-Notice System 'did not work . . . The whole thing revolved around the Secretary . . . The point was that he had to be trusted and he had to be a man who would himself probe any story so as to satisfy himself of all the facts. Unless there was a good Secretary there was always likely to be some breakdown in the system'. This strong criticism of Lohan's performance came ironically only a few days after the Civil Service had approved the Colonel's confirmation in the post and its remuneration. Trend had however already asked Way to defer action on that approval, and now wrote to him apropos of Haley's opinion: 'I suppose . . . we had better reconsider Lohan's position?'[245]

Meanwhile, on 1 August, Commander Kerans[246] asked the Prime Minister in Parliament whether he would institute an enquiry into the 'D' Notice System. Macmillan replied that, with the agreement of the Media side of the SPBC, the Government had decided to change the way in which the Media were consulted about Notices concerning sensitive subjects, which it was hoped would also produce a more secure and simpler system; Marcus Lipton also voiced concern that the wide distribution of the Notices drew attention to otherwise unnoticed security matters.[247]

Afterwards, the Prime Minister wrote to Trend about 'an acceptable replacement for Thomson', adding that it was clear somebody must be found who enjoyed the same confidence and regard of the Press. He also instructed that 'any D-Notice on a subject affecting politics, espionage, and security in the broad sense' should be issued only with the Prime Minister's agreement, or in his absence that of the Foreign or Home Secretary as appropriate. Trend sent a letter accordingly to all the relevant Permanent Under-Secretaries in late August, setting down all the new arrangements agreed.[248]

On finding a permanent 'replacement for Thomson', Way sounded out as many Media members as he could quickly reach, but of the eight only Harman Grisewood[249] of the BBC considered Lohan should not continue as Secretary. Others thought Lohan should be excused for his inexperience in the post, and should not be judged by one case. There were 'some reservations about his complete acceptability', but also a feeling he should not be made scapegoat for something where others had also been in error, and that his removal would reflect badly on the SPBC as a whole. In late August the Prime Minister endorsed that Lohan should stay on.[250] As will be seen, there were many who within a few years came to regret this triumph of inertia over judgement, but by then there was a different Prime Minister.

Meanwhile Lohan had attended a meeting of senior officials called by Trend on 26 July to consider suggestions by Sir Bernard Burrows[251] of the Foreign Office about improving the machinery for using D-Notices on matters of 'high political content', and other related documents. It was agreed that there was no point in adding representatives of the Foreign Office or No.10 to the SPBC, because the Committee hardly ever met except when there was a contentious Notice (or 'other objections') to be discussed, and business was normally done by phone. However, it was thought there would be advantage in politically sensitive cases in the Secretary seeing at least one Media Member in person, and taking with him an expert from the Department concerned to explain the rationale; if an SPBC meeting had to be called consequently, that expert should also attend it. On requests for such Notices, it was agreed the Department concerned should consult other Government Departments and Ministers first if necessary, and it was also suggested that Trend consider whether the Secretary should himself inform No.10 'of any politically sensitive case in which the D-Notice procedure was being used.'[252]

A few weeks later, the satirical magazine *Private Eye*[253] identified Menzies and White as being 'C' and DGSS, causing Lohan to send a further letter to editors about naming the Heads of the secret Agencies, in breach of the longstanding Notice of 27 April 1956. No other journal had followed the magazine's example, but Lohan felt it necessary to spell out the rationale for keeping the identities of the postholders secret. 'From the point of view of national security it stands to sense that if the movements [appointments] of the Heads of the British Intelligence Services become common knowledge, then one thing must lead to another; it would not be long before their associates also became known and that, in turn, must lead to the whole structure and methods of the Intelligence Services becoming known to the wrong people.' When the *New Statesman* mentioned MI5 and MI6 in an article the same month, albeit favourably in an otherwise critical piece by an ex-Foreign Office man about his old Service, Trend and Caccia at first considered litigation rather than D-Notice action, but concluded this would be unlikely to succeed.[254]

Lohan's rationale was not that used in later years: that revealing the identities of these senior officials would lead to disclosure of secret operations and contacts with which they had been involved in recent years (also hard always to sustain convincingly). There is a stronger, but still not always decisive, argument about maintaining a certain mystique which gives enemies pause for thought, and about building a reputation for tight security which encourages informers and allies to assist British Intelligence without fear of exposure. Currently (2007) the names and photographs of the Heads of the Secret Intelligence and Security Services are in the public domain, and no deleterious effect has so far been observed. On the other hand, the advice is still applied as vigorously as possible to protecting the identities of all others who still are or have relatively recently been involved in undercover operations, other than those who have, usually with permission, chosen subsequently to pursue a more public role and not to conceal their antecedents. This advice is almost always observed by the British Media, despite leaks from abroad and from a few dissident insiders.

The Heads of the secret Agencies came up in another context in late 1963, when the editor of the *Sunday Times*, Denis Hamilton,[255] in conversation with the Prime Minister's PS Sir Philip de Zulueta,[256] suggested that because Lohan's knowledge of security and intelligence matters was 'not very helpful', a few 'responsible' editors should have direct access to 'C' and the DGSS. Way was immediately dubious, but agreed to attend a meeting called by Trend, bringing with him Lohan. All agreed that, even were the Heads willing to do this (and they were then reluctant), the understanding thus gained would reach only a small part of the Media, the D-Notice System would be weakened, and the editors not included would be enormously resentful. Hamilton had not asked for a reply, so it was decided just to say nothing, and to treat any further approach by an editor 'on a case by case basis.'[257]

In January 1964, Lohan having moved into his Chairman's building (Shell-Mex House in the Strand), in a small office shared with his Secretary, he subsequently complained to Way that those in a neighbouring office were listening to him through the walls, and asked for a better room with an outer office. In his routine business, he was attempting unsuccessfully to persuade the Film Producers' Association to be represented on the SPBC, and with equal lack of success to have the classification of the Notices downgraded (Hill agreed until it was pointed out that the only Secret Notice was the one covering his area). He was also in correspondence with the Home Office Civil Defence and Fire Service Department, because the BBC was embarrassed by councils passing to their local press details of the Corporation's plans for emergency communications in the event of war.[258]

In April 1964, Colonel Lohan's reliability was again called into question, this time by officials. When secret discussions were being held with the Russians about exchanging Greville Wynne[259] for 'Lonsdale', Trend held a meeting to discuss how to keep this from being disclosed until the exchange had been successfully completed. In the event, Chapman

Pincher published the story in the *Daily Express* ahead of other papers, albeit after it had been confirmed that Wynne was safely back in British custody at the border crossing. Officials suspected this scoop had come from Lohan, because of his known friendship with the journalist. When confronted by Way with this accusation, Lohan 'was explosive in his reaction', claiming that far from giving information to Pincher, he had spent a whole evening restraining him from publishing a story he had already acquired from other sources. A few days later the Security Service confirmed to Trend that an investigation had cleared Lohan of suspicion on this occasion, and Lohan was informed accordingly.[260] In June 1964, having again consulted representatives of the Media side, Way told Trend lukewarmly there was now 'no reason for not confirming' Lohan as the permanent replacement for Thomson, and it was agreed.[261]

In June 1964, Lohan began again to number 'D' Notices'.[262] The first such reiterated concerns about electronic transmissions intercepted by the Soviets, especially those involving secret defence research and development projects, and military trials and exercises, as evidenced by the activities of the Russian intelligence-gathering 'trawlers' which accompanied NATO exercises in which the Royal Navy and/or US Navy participated. Particular areas in which media discretion was requested were the technical characteristics of defence radar and radio equipment, and the operating details such as frequencies and transmitting times. Publication was however acceptable if details had already been published in other countries or where the location could not be concealed (eg the giant 'golf-balls' at Fylingdales).[263]

At the short 13 August 1964 SPBC meeting, the Media side attacked the MoD for lack of progress on overflying; this had been under discussion for three years, yet an urgent Private and Confidential letter had been needed in May. The Media were still sceptical about the rationale, because of the visibility of British troop movements to the foreign Media. Another indeterminate discussion ended with Way inviting the MoD to define some categories of overflying information to be protected. In his routine report, Lohan reported very few breaches of security in the past year, but an increase in aerial photography and films.[264]

In October 1964, the *Sunday Telegraph* broke the story, originating in Moscow, of the background to the trial and sentences of Greville Wynne and his Russian contact Oleg Penkovsky.[265] In an effort to forestall whatever the Soviets might say to discredit the SIS, Lohan wrote a limited distribution letter to editors in early October, hoping they would observe 'the spirit of the 'D' Notice' of April 1946 about the Service. 'I do beg of you, then, if the Russians seize this easy opportunity to create embarrassment, that anything they have to say about MI5 or MI6 is not pursued in depth; that is to say, please do not seek interviews or publish photographs of the people concerned or their home surroundings.'[266] In any similar circumstances today, it would not be acceptable for such a blanket request to be issued; advice from the Secretary not to publish would concentrate on specific details, genuinely damaging to security.

Early Years of the Wilson Government

When Harold Wilson's[267] Labour Government came to power in October 1964, one of the early changes introduced by the new SofS for Defence, Denis Healey,[268] was to collocate the Services' Public Relations Directorates, and to invite Edward Pickering,[269] the *Mirror* Group's editorial director, to advise him on how to improve reporting on Defence matters.

The *Sunday Telegraph* of 11 April 1965 reflected widespread Media hopes that Pickering's Report might 'break the rigid pattern in which Whitehall conservatism and the customary Ministerial instincts towards self-preservation have cloaked themselves in the Official Secrets Act . . . For 13 years in Opposition Labour critics, led by Mr George Wigg,[270] now Paymaster-General, clamoured for this change'. The paper also however criticised the way in which Healey's centralisation had been effected, because amongst other things it had finally removed 'the peppery, temperamental deputy, Colonel LG "Sammy" Lohan, who handled the newspapermen', who had been 'retired to D-Notice pastures'.

In December 1964, the SPBC reconsidered advice given the previous May about overflying, and Lohan issued a further Letter. He further emphasised the danger to the lives of British troops in theatre if they could not be reinforced from the Strategic Reserve in the UK, and if tactical surprise were lost through premature disclosure. He acknowledged the disadvantage to the British Press of not publishing deployment stories originating from foreign sources, but warned of the danger of the latter 'maliciously speculating' in the hope of receiving confirmation in the British Press. 'In the circumstances you will no doubt agree', he said, not to draw attention to such flights, and to delay the mention of initial troop movements during crucial phases until they were announced officially.[271]

Despite Harold Wilson's initially carefully cultivated relationship with the Media, already by early 1965 his Government was expressing serious concern about the number of leaks of Cabinet discussions, a preoccupation fanned by the *Sunday Times* appointing a 'Whitehall Correspondent' specifically to poke into areas not covered by the traditional and more controllable Lobby Correspondents. In late February, the Head of the Civil Service warned his colleagues about 'special risks of embarrassment from a concerted attempt to reveal the advice which civil servants are thought to be giving Ministers'; and the Prime Minister issued instructions that Ministers were not to give interviews to journalists without a PR adviser present 'at a time when sections of the Press appear to be making somewhat feverish efforts to penetrate the normal confidentiality of Government business'. This message was in itself not to be revealed, but inevitably it was, and on 15 June Wilson was harried by the Opposition about it in the House of Commons.[272]

Defence business was equally leak-prone, and after the *Daily Telegraph* revealed the cancellation of the TSR-2 aircraft in early January 1965, and Chapman Pincher followed up in the *Daily Express* on the American replacement for it, and Healey's other Top Secret plans for major cuts in Defence spending, a leak inquiry was instituted across Government Departments and the British Aircraft Corporation. It revealed a very large number of those in the know, all of whom denied being the source. It was however a political embarrassment not a national security breach, and no D-Notice action was considered.[273]

In June 1965, 'Justice' (the British section of the International Commission of Jurists) published the report of a Working Party chaired by Lord Shawcross on the Law and the Press. This was a sequel to the jailing of two journalists during the Vassall Tribunal, and inquired into the extent to which existing laws of contempt of court, libel and official secrets hampered the Press in publishing matters of public interest, 'within the limits of what is necessary for the protection of the liberty of the subject and the security of the State'. It made recommendations for changes in law and legal procedure, and on the right of the Press to criticise judicial decisions, but concluded it would not be right to give journalists a special privilege to withhold sources of information. On the OSAs, it recommended it 'should be a valid defence to show that the national interest was not likely to be harmed and that information had been passed and received in good faith and in the public interest.'[274]

On the D-Notice System, the Justice Report recorded the claims of some witnesses that OSAs were invoked to prevent, through Notices, the publication of information sometimes already in the public domain abroad, which could not possibly affect security, the real purpose being to protect government servants. 'We feel that this does not make for good government since it can lead to protection of inefficiency and malpractice, stifle the needful exposure of public scandals and prevent the remedying of individual injustices.' Such comments clearly apply also to governmental practices and official secrecy at any period in history, and not just to or even principally to the cautionary advice in D-Notices but to much wider and more profuse information given out, both openly and unattributably, by governmental sources. In the case of the D-Notice System, any tendency to abuse is at least constrained by the Media Members of the Committee. In practice too, although litigation using the OSAs lurks in the governmental armoury, the Acts were not and are not invoked by nor linked to D-Notices, nor may the Government use any information acquired solely through the D-Notice Secretary in order to initiate litigation; this remains an unwritten but agreed and unbreached principle of the system.

The Justice Report may nevertheless have been one of the many nudges, the others coming more insistently from the Media side, which caused the Committee to start yet again reviewing the D-Notices still in force, to bring them up to date and to improve their texts in the light of experience gained in applying them. On the official side, this work was conducted interdepartmentally under the auspices of the snappily titled 'Working Party on Security Restrictions on the Collection and Publication of Information in the UK', apart from those Notices concerning MI5 and MI6, on which the SPBC Secretary was tasked to liaise direct with the secret Agencies.[275]

Government confidential business continued to be widely leaked in 1966. In Downing Street, Wigg reported in March to Wilson the early results from two 'Books' he had caused the Labour Whips to produce, analysing the many unauthorised disclosures and known Ministerial/journalistic contacts; the insinuation Wigg made was that the leaks originated from Ministers wishing to puff their Departmental achievements.[276] Nevertheless three months later a further major but again inconclusive leak inquiry had to be conducted into media articles about the multinational rocket ELDO, the Prices and Incomes Policy, and the Seamen's Strike; Pincher revealed the diminution of the Ministry of Aviation, causing an official to comment that 'once a project comes to be discussed in the MoD and the Ministry of Aviation, he is often able to get wind of it'. MI5 were also asked to look at whether there was any pattern or trend in current leaks, and reported there was not. Again all these were matters of political embarrassment, but they contributed to the culture in which the D-Notice affair of 1967 was nurtured.[277]

By early 1967, by when there were 16 extant D-Notices, Departments had agreed with the Secretary that three of these should be cancelled altogether, and all but one of the remainder revised. Even with the unamended Notices, it was considered that 'Defence, intelligence, and security information which needs to be concealed in the national interest, has been effectively kept out of the Press both through editors themselves following the guidance of the "D" Notices and through advice given by the Secretary in cases of doubt. Only very rarely has a request not to publish from the Secretary been disregarded . . . the occasions on which his intervention has been successful have been numerous.'[278] One of the rare occasions when a Notice was largely disregarded was when in 1967 the *Sunday Times* decided, despite Lohan's despatch to it of the Secret Agencies Notice, to feature an exposé of the career and treachery of Philby, by then long in Russia. Parliamentary and public reaction was however predominantly then against the newspaper, not against prohibition of publication.[279]

There was nevertheless still one cloud concerning the D-Notice System, not on the horizon but again hovering over the Secretary himself. While the Media side of the Committee regarded his performance as at least satisfactory, his social habits were causing concern to officials, and his friendships with certain journalists (in particular Pincher) were beginning to cause concern to George Wigg, who as Paymaster-General had been given by Wilson special responsibility for security, both national and Party Political. In mid-1965 Hollis consulted Way about the official concerns, brought to a head by belated realisation that Lohan had custody of a Top Secret document about Government War Headquarters (codenamed TURNSTILE, one of only eight copies in existence, such was its perceived sensitivity). The Cabinet Office considered he needed this in case he had to handle media interest in these Headquarters.[280]

The problem was that, although he had been 'indoctrinated' for TURNSTILE in 1962, Lohan had not been fully Positively Vetted (PV'd) under the latest system, nor given the necessary additional clearances required for this codeword by 1964; at the same time, if he were now to be PV'd, his known heavy drinking and alleged womanising meant his Positive Vetting would be unlikely to be approved. Hollis and Way agreed that in practice the Secretary's post [at that time] did not require Positive Vetting because the criterion used was 'regular access to Top Secret material', which Lohan neither had nor needed. Nevertheless they decided to use the PV investigation machinery discreetly to look into the allegations made about the Colonel's behaviour and friendships.

When the investigation report was made in due course, it was 'not particularly helpful', since it adduced no evidence either that Lohan had ever leaked information to Pincher nor 'of his alleged loose relations with women'. That he lived beyond the means of his MI5-supplemented salary (lunching frequently at the Savoy Grill, it was noted), was explained by his wife's wealth. Way even checked on Lohan's reputation with a trusted member of the SPBC, David White of the *Glasgow Herald*, who despite Pincher's low popularity with other less prolific journalists, reported back no Press accusation that Lohan leaked to him.

Way recalled to Trend in February that even Thomson had been criticised by officials for being too close to the Press, 'even though we now regard him as having been a magnificent Secretary'. There was an element in Lohan's case too of 'give a dog a bad name', and it was 'a little ironical that the Ministry of Defence should have brought up the question of his security, when he had in fact been their own number two Public Relations Officer for many years'. Discussion about Lohan between very senior officials continued through to the following Spring, when the new DGSS Furnival Jones briefed Trend again, concluding that, while Lohan might not have been given a PV clearance had it been sought, 'I doubted whether he represented an unacceptable risk to security in his current position. In the afternoons however he was sometimes fuzzy with drink', and if there were dissatisfaction with his performance 'there might be an advantage in looking for a replacement'.

Trend wrote to Way in late March 1966 that, although Lohan's PV 'was not technically completed in the sense of being carried to the end of the fourth stage [the 'field' investigation of behaviour, interviewing of referees, etc], there are no grounds on which we could question his reliability . . . the balance of advantage probably inclines in favour of leaving him where he is. Nevertheless, I am not entirely happy about the position; and I think that you yourself share this feeling of residual dissatisfaction'. When Way wrote to Lohan about Trend's decision, Way's office (knowingly or inadvertently) enclosed a copy of Trend's less than fulsome expression of confidence. Lohan replied to the now retired Way, commenting: 'I must say that Burke Trend's letter was not the most joyful thing to start a Monday morning with . . . It really is disheartening to think he still dislikes me enough to wish to get rid of me. I wonder where the acid comes from.'[281]

The political pressure to remove Lohan as a presumed source of leaks continued however. The Chairmanship of the SPBC (and responsibility for the Secretary) had passed permanently ex officio to the MoD's PUS, now Sir Henry Hardman.[282] Trend told him at the end of April 1966 that, although he had 'no specific grounds for uneasiness', he was not wholly happy about the Secretary not being completely PV'd, which Hardman undertook to look into, and also reported to his Secretary of State (Healey). By the time Sir James Dunnett[283] took over from Hardman in June 1966, MoD had concluded (and so informed Trend, who agreed) that 'in all the circumstances' Lohan should be allowed to continue in post, without full clearances, until he was 60 in 1970.

Nevertheless, spurred on by Downing Street, Healey had his officials reconsider the case in June/July 1966 'because of the risk of Press leaks and a general feeling that he might have outlived his usefulness as Secretary'; once again he was advised there were insufficient grounds for sacking him and no alternative posts to move him to. Even when George Wigg voiced his 'personal misgivings' to the Head of the MoD Security Division in mid-July 1966, in the margins of a meeting about wider matters, he was assured it was a personality not a security problem, and that Trend was keeping it under review.[284]

On 6 February 1967, Healey however summoned Dunnett for a further talk about Lohan, and two days later minuted him with seven detailed questions about the Colonel's supervision, employment, performance and clearances. He emphasised that 'it is possible that the Prime Minister may press me on this in the near future'. Healey ended by saying that Trend 'seemed to have the impression that we were already taking steps to keep a special eye on Lohan'. On 17 February (a significant date, as will be seen), Dunnett sent Healey two replies. The first outlined the way in which the Committee and its Secretary operated ('normal for a year or more to elapse' between meetings, and he had seen Lohan only three times since taking over as Chairman about a year previously), explained again the employment and dismissal rules, confirmed that Lohan received very little classified material and that the demands on him were 'spasmodic', reported that MI5 were 'naturally reluctant' to say much about their use of Lohan (but that it did not involve any high degree of secrecy) and that they paid him not more than £500 a year for this,[285] and concluded that 'it was a great pity that he was ever put into his present job'.

The second minute dealt with courses of action now open, which he had discussed exhaustively not only with his own senior security and personnel officials but also with Furnival Jones. Having Lohan watched was ruled out because neither the DGSS nor the Home Secretary considered there were proper security grounds for doing so. Dismissing Lohan at a month's notice was ruled out because it would be hard to give any convincing explanation, not only to Lohan but also to 'his friends in the Press'. Upping his post to PV status was ruled out because it would be open to the 'comeback' of why this had not been done long ago, and that it was being done now to get rid of Lohan. The only safe course was therefore to warn Lohan formally about his indiscreet and inappropriate behaviour, and that if it continued his services would be dispensed with. Dunnett appreciated however that this course 'may not be acceptable to Ministers generally', and ended by reminding that Lohan was the servant not just of the Official side but of the Media side, and that any action taken would have to be explained to their SPBC representatives.[286] The reason for recording here so much detail of administrative discussion about one not very senior temporary civil servant becomes apparent in the next section, where events became even less 'joyful' for Colonel Lohan, or indeed for almost anyone else involved.

Summation

During the early years of the Cold War, the D-Notice System had been re-established, taking onboard many of the principles and practices developed before and during WWII, and developing new Notices to match new circumstances and the technological advances of the period. Most Notices and Letters had apparently been agreed without rancour or much difficulty, but some consistently (such as the War Potential Notices/Letters), and others suddenly (such as the 'Dolnytsin' Notice), had caused considerable and strongly felt disagreement, never fully resolved.

The apparently irregular meetings, the part-time nature of the Secretary's post, Lohan's controversial persona, the lower than ideal calibre of the Media side, and the rotation of the chairmanship between the Permanent Under-Secretaries, all leave a feeling of lack of continuity and focus, perhaps also a reflection of the less centralised organisation of Whitehall at the time, particularly of Defence and of the secret Agencies. Occasional Political focusing on the System had shown both that it had jarring defects, but also that it was accepted by both sides as preferable to the alternative of litigation. Its continuance and stability had yet to be seriously challenged, as it was about to be.

Section 7

THE 'LOHAN' AFFAIR, 1967

38

A SQUALL BECOMES A STORM

This tragicomic tale only merits a section of its own because it achieved very high publicity at the time, polarised the relationship between Government and Media, threatened the continuance of the D-Notice System, and seriously damaged the political reputation of the Prime Minister, Harold Wilson. He described it later as 'self-inflicted', and 'in personal terms one of my costliest mistakes in our near six years in office.'[1]

Narrative

Early afternoon on 16 February 1967, a Mr Robert Lawson[2] came by appointment to see the *Daily Express* defence correspondent, Chapman Pincher. Lawson had worked recently as a telegraphist in two cable offices (Commercial Cables and Western Union), and claimed he had discovered that all cables and telegrams handled by both companies (and all other similar UK companies and the Post Office) were collected daily by a Ministry of Public Building and Works van and taken to the Admiralty building for vetting, being returned 48 hours later. He thought this had been routine practice for at least two years. He told Pincher he had recently offered the same information to the *Daily Mail* and to the University of London Students' Union magazine *Sennet*.

Pincher knew covert examination of communications of suspected spies was normal practice in many countries, but this allegation was of much wider interception. He made further enquiries with the MoD, whose PR Branch had already been approached by the *Mail*'s defence correspondent the day before. The Chief Press Officer had been too busy on 15 February with press conferences (about the 1967 Defence White Paper) to investigate the enquiries that day; only when Pincher rang did he consult the security authorities. Based on their initial advice, the CPO told the *Mail* there was absolutely nothing in the 'ludicrous' story and the whole thing was 'nonsense'; this MoD 'line to take' was based on the unstated facts that it was indeed not the MoD which examined cables to and from overseas but the secret Agencies, and that no telegrams (internal UK messages) were vetted.

Pincher later on the 16th was given a similar response, but he had already been in touch with another contact (and angling friend), the Director of Public Relations of the GPO, Turlough O'Brien,[3] who told him it was not true *all* cables were intercepted as alleged, but some were, which he (O'Brien) regarded as publicly known. However, Pincher felt there was indeed something in the story, and phoned Lohan (another close friend as well as an official contact), who also saw no particular security problem in the story, advised there was no prohibitory D-Notice, and suggested Pincher consult the MoD (being unaware he had already consulted its PR Department and the GPO).

Coincidentally, that same day the Government Assistant Chief Whip Charles Morris[4] sent the Paymaster-General George Wigg a Strictly Private and Confidential memorandum, headed 'Press Disclosures – Chapman Pincher, "Daily Express"', referring to 'our conversation' and enclosing 'our file relating to the above', covering the period 15 November 1965 to date. 'It would seem that there are 26 reports covering a multiplicity of issues where the source is open to question', which he had asterisked for Wigg to peruse.[5]

This file was part of the analysis being undertaken by the Government because of Ministers' concerns about the high number of leaks of politically sensitive information from many Departments, referred to in the previous chapter. Wigg and Morris were matching known journalistic contacts, hoping to establish who the civil service and parliamentary leakers were. This had achieved one 'success'; Wigg confronted the MP concerned, closing down that channel. Such collation/analysis was however time-consuming for the Whips, and in the long term achieved little else; nor were official leak enquiries any more productive. Pincher was just one of several journalists under scrutiny. At this stage there was little in his dossier other than his prolific output, and Lohan had not ever been mentioned by Wigg to Morris.[6] Pincher was well known to Wigg socially, their relationship being notably cordial until the *Daily Express* had begun regularly to attack the Prime Minister. Because Wigg had been given special responsibility by Wilson for security matters, both national and political, he was therefore perhaps on the look out for a leak cause célèbre. He was also 'a natural conspirator.'[7]

The next day (17 February), the secret Agencies and Foreign Office Security Department became aware a cable-vetting story might be published, and an emergency meeting was convened there. Lohan was not invited, allegedly because he did not have the necessary high security clearances, but a Security Service officer did contact Lohan beforehand, explained the concerns to him 'in a very guarded way', and asked him to act as decisively as possible to get the story suppressed. After talking to the two defence correspondents concerned, Lohan reported back that the *Mail* had agreed to drop the story, on condition they were not 'scooped' by anyone else, and that the *Express* had agreed to hold the story until the following Monday (20th), when further discussion with Lohan would take place. Pincher said later the arguments used by Lohan had been based not on the Notices but on general security and on political embarrassment: 'It would cause a diplomatic furore – all the foreign embassies would immediately think their cables were being examined, and there would be a hell of a row.'[8]

The meeting of officials later that day was chaired by Christopher Ewart-Biggs,[9] and it was agreed inter alia that the Security Service should brief Lohan to continue his efforts to dissuade the *Express* from publishing. He should base his approach more on the OSA than on the Notices, albeit without giving Pincher any 'gratuitous information' about the actual interception of telegrams and the extent and purpose of it. The officials decided that the D-Notices of 27 April 1956 (Intelligence and Security Services) and of 30 October 1961 (interception of foreign communications) were relevant.

Relevant parts of the two D-Notices stated:

- Notice of 27 April 1956. '. . . In requesting secrecy on the items listed below, I would emphasise that they refer to two branches of the British Intelligence Services – MI5 . . . and MI6 . . . The reasons for the requests made, in so far as I am permitted to give them to you, will be found in the appendix to this letter . . . Will you please in the national interest make no reference to the following: (i) Secret intelligence or counter intelligence methods and activities in or outside the United Kingdom. . . .'

- The appendix included a note: 'Certain methods employed in Intelligence work are to some extent a matter of common knowledge and it is thus understandable that editors would not normally regard them as secret methods. Published reference, however, to what may seem obvious methods of counter espionage work, when related to particular cases or persons, create an awareness and vigilance in the minds of agents which may well enable them to circumvent the precautions taken to deal with them. Such references do serious harm in assisting a foreign Intelligence organisation to build up a picture on the basis of which it conducts its operations, both offensive and defensive.'

- Notice of 30 October 1961: '. . . (2) The various methods used in interception of foreign communications for secret intelligence purposes. In this connection the Committee request that you will not refer to the fact that on occasions it is necessary in the interest of defence for the Services to intercept such communications.'

After this meeting, the Foreign Office PUS, Cabinet Secretary, Foreign Secretary, Home Secretary and later the Prime Minister were informed by early evening of the situation, which was apparently 'under control'. Still however concerned about the implications, Ewart-Biggs rang Lohan (they did not previously know each other) at home during the weekend, and he and a Security Officer also rang Lohan on Monday 20 February before he met Pincher for lunch, to reiterate the official line. The perceived dilemma, and therefore the central matter in these telephone discussions, was how far the D-Notice Secretary could go in what he revealed to Pincher, and what arguments he could use.

Although Lohan should have been the authority on the use of D-Notices, in this case he was being told by officials what to do, on some aspects against his better judgement. He foresaw, but did not ultimately resist proceeding with, two difficulties. Firstly, the 1961 Notice referred to interception for 'secret intelligence' purposes, yet Lohan would have to convince Pincher without revealing what was actually involved. On this Ewart-Biggs agreed Lohan 'should not lean too heavily upon these words' in the Notices, but should attempt to argue it involved 'an area of activity generally falling under "D" Notices and to give the impression, without going into details, that what was in question was a matter of defence of the Realm.'[10]

Secondly, Lohan would have to try to counter Pincher's contention that the story involved a large-scale invasion of privacy, and therefore had a public interest justification; this should be done by pointing out the legal authorisation of the interception, and, again without going into details, the extreme selectivity of the interception, done only for national security reasons. The 'diplomatic furore' argument had now been dropped, which was just as well, because Pincher had by chance dined during the weekend with the Israeli Foreign Minister Abba Eban, whom he had asked (without saying why) about diplomats' expectations of having their cables read by host governments; Eban confirmed diplomats expected cables not in code might be read.

Lohan and Pincher met on 20 February for lunch at L'Ecu de France in Jermyn Street, the latter's favoured restaurant for such meetings with contacts.[11] There were slight but significant variations in their subsequent recollections of what was understood between them when they parted, some two hours later; these were central to what transpired during the next ten hours, to the very high-level and public aftermath, and in due course to the Radcliffe

Report. Lohan's aide-memoire to the Radcliffe Committee[12] described how he had followed the official line, adding his own comments about the 'stupidity' there would be in trying to read the content of every telegram, but that useful intelligence was gained from studying patterns of activity.

He said Pincher had argued against him that the interception of cables was 'absolutely parallel' with telephone tapping [now in the public domain] and opening mail, and could not therefore be described as a 'secret intelligence method'. Pincher also reminded Lohan of the part he [Pincher] had played in having telephone tapping specifically excluded from the D-Notice of 31 October 1957. Lohan argued back that a different medium was now in question, but Pincher 'was particularly angry about what he claimed was interference with individual privacy', and because Lohan would not deny that Press messages were 'not excluded'; Pincher persisted in his contention this degree of interception was not of long standing. Nevertheless Lohan later claimed: 'At the end of our discussion I was reasonably sure I had convinced Pincher. We parted with good feeling and Pincher said he would represent my case in all fairness to his Editor.'

Chapman Pincher's recollection, summarised by solicitors retained by the *Daily Express* for the Inquiry,[13] was somewhat different. Lohan had produced the two allegedly relevant D-Notices, already well-known to Pincher, they had agreed neither could reasonably be applied to this case, Lohan had put them back in his breast pocket and they were not referred to again. Lohan had endeavoured to persuade Pincher 'to prevail upon the Editor not to print the story', and Pincher had agreed to pass on Lohan's request, but said it was wholly a matter for his editor. As they stood on the pavement outside the restaurant waiting for a shared taxi, and 'in an extremely good mood' according to Lohan in his later oral evidence, Pincher joked that were Lohan the editor he would publish the story, would he not. In his own later oral evidence, Pincher however said that he had prefaced this remark by saying that if he [Pincher] were the editor, he would not agree to suppress the story.

Lohan went next to the *Daily Mail*, where he talked to the defence correspondent and the managing editor, about their still stopped story. Afterwards, neither considered he had been asking them to observe the two Notices, indeed they formed the clear impression he was *not* relying on them in making his case. The reason they agreed not to publish was because Lohan 'inadvertently' referred to a particular current security operation. In later oral evidence to the Radcliffe Committee, the new *Daily Mail* editor Arthur Brittenden[14] confirmed the paper's decision not to publish was because of their understanding that a specific operation might be prejudiced, and because he considered Lohan's approach was in itself 'equivalent to a D-Notice'; on which Radcliffe commented [correctly]: 'Not all members of the Press . . . would accept such a principle as sound doctrine'.

Whatever the intra- and post-prandial conversation with Pincher had actually been, when Lohan returned to his office at about 3.30pm, he rang Ewart-Biggs and other officials and told them the *Daily Mail*'s editor had definitely agreed not to publish the story; and that, although the *Daily Express*'s editor had told Pincher to write the story up so that he and the paper's lawyers could consider what decision to make, Pincher had told Lohan he did not think the *Express* would publish it, at least that evening; if, on the other hand it was decided to publish, he would tell Lohan in advance.[15]

Lohan mentioned to the Security Service Legal Adviser that the *Express* considered they were not precluded by Section 4(1) of OSA 1920 from publishing; he was told that in this particular case the Government 'were pinning their colours to the 'D' Notice mast', and if there was still a risk of publication, he should now tell Dunnett as SPBC Chairman. Lohan did this, but again with an optimistic assessment of the *Express*'s probable course of action. At about 7pm, the Foreign Office DUS Denis Greenhill[16] briefed the Foreign Secretary George Brown on the events of the day. Brown suggested he [Brown] might ring the proprietor of the *Express*, Sir Max Aitken,[17] to ask that the story be suppressed. Greenhill however advised him, in the light of Lohan's assessment, 'to handle the matter through the normal channels', and Brown departed to dine at a friend's Hyde Park house.

Meanwhile, Pincher had briefed his editor Derek Marks[18] and submitted his article; at 6 p.m. an editorial conference was held, and at some time between then and 7 p.m., Pincher rang Lohan, still at his office, to say he would not know the decision definitely until about 8.15 p.m. During this call (or possibly an earlier one), Pincher also mentioned to Lohan that the informant Lawson had told him that if the story did not appear in the British Press, he would take it to a foreign agency; Lohan asked Pincher to ask Lawson to phone him about this (Lawson did not, but meanwhile Lohan rang the Press Association and asked them to watch out for any such foreign-based news). Pincher agreed to ring again when Lohan arrived off the train at his home in Charing (Kent) at about 9.30pm. Pincher then left to catch the train to his home in Ewhurst (Surrey), and soon afterwards the editor and deputy editor departed for an *Express* dinner at the Garrick Club.

They left the night editor with the instruction the cable-vetting article would be the lead story unless meanwhile a more contemporary story of higher priority came in. No bigger story did arise, and at about 7.40 p.m. the Night Editor therefore ordered Pincher's story to be telephoned to Glasgow and Manchester, where printing of the next day's edition started earlier than in London (9.30 in Glasgow, 9.45 in Manchester, 10.05 in London). Pincher rang the Night Editor at 9 to learn what decision had been made, and as pre-arranged, then rang Lohan at 9.30, giving him the unwelcome news. This sparked a hot-wire crisis in that pre-mobile phone era of comparatively cumbersome communication; the Radcliffe Report dryly observes: 'Between the hours of 9.30 on the 20th and 1 a.m. on the 21st, a great many telephone conversations took place between the various authorities concerned.'

The now alarmed Colonel immediately rang the *Express* to check what he had been told by Pincher, and made a vain last-ditch plea to stop the story; the Night Editor told him not only did he not have authority to do so, but the first editions were already being printed. Lohan rang his Security Service contact, who rang Ewart-Biggs, who rang Greenhill, who rang the Foreign Secretary, who instantly wished to talk to Aitken. Having learned from the Night Editor that all senior *Express* staff were carousing at the Garrick Club, the call was transferred to its hall porter, and Aitken was summoned to the lobby phone to talk to Brown. Brown did not know Aitken was speaking from the Club, and because he himself was on an open line, could only talk 'in very guarded terms'; he was therefore not specific about what the story was.

Aitken anyway knew nothing whatsoever at that stage about the cable-vetting story, but said the Editor was with him, which Brown believed meant in the office. Aitken agreed that if something infringed D-Notice advice, it should be stopped, and Brown returned to his dinner, thinking he had achieved suppression of the story. Aitken meanwhile returned to the table, and he and Marks had a discussion at cross-purposes, since the latter at first thought Brown must have been referring to some other security story which definitely *was* covered by a Notice; indeed he telephoned his Glasgow office from the Club to verify whether this was so. Meanwhile the presses in all three cities rolled inexorably on. Only at 10.30 pm did the Editor ring the Night Editor in London, hear the full reality, and immediately rush back to his office.

The speed of the action in this Whitehall/Fleet Street farce now speeded up even further. Lohan had meanwhile rung the *Daily Mail*, as he had undertaken he would do should another paper decide to run the story, to tell its Editor (who was also out dining with friends that evening) he was now free to publish. When Lohan then almost immediately afterwards heard from the Foreign Office that Brown had persuaded Aitken not to publish, he rang the *Mail* again to tell them to kill it after all, because the *Express* was not now going to run it; only to be told that this could not be so, since the *Mail*'s night editor had a copy of the *Express* first edition in front of him, including the story. Lohan agreed without reservation the *Mail* was indeed therefore entitled to publish. Marks shortly afterwards rang Lohan and, in response to his reproaches, said Pincher had assured him the D-Notice Secretary had agreed the story was not covered by any Notice.

Nevertheless, because of further messages from Brown now conveyed to him by the Foreign Office Press Adviser, and because of Lohan's protest, Marks became sufficiently concerned that he tried to contact Aitken and Pincher, but could reach neither; he therefore decided at about 11.45pm to kill the story in all further editions, and gave instructions to his staff accordingly. He informed the FO of this, and then, at about 00.30am, rang Lohan, to whom he said he assumed all other papers were also being stopped; the Colonel replied that this was impossible, since he knew that not only the *Mail* but also now *The Times* were running the story. Marks therefore countermanded his own recent instructions.

The *Daily Express* article, although prominent, was relatively short. Headlined 'Cable Vetting Sensation, Security check on private messages out of Britain', with a strapline of 'With telephone tapping in the news – a new controversy which will be a parliamentary flashpoint is revealed today by Chapman Pincher', it read:

Thousands of private cables and telegrams sent out of Britain from the Post Office or from commercial cable companies are regularly being made available to the security authorities for scrutiny.

This 'Big Brother' intrusion into privacy, which ranks with telephone-tapping and the opening of letters, was disclosed last night.

It is certain to lead to a flood of questions in Parliament where a Bill to prevent unauthorised telephone-tapping was given its first reading yesterday.

The check can be applied to all cables and telegrams received from abroad whether by individuals, companies or embassies. The embassies are allowed to send messages out in code but companies may use only accepted commercial codes.

Passed on
There is no hold-up or censorship of the cables. But on the morning after they have been sent or received they are collected and sifted by a Post Office department concerned with security.

Then any cables believed to be of special interest are passed to the Security Services. They are studied there, copied if necessary, and returned to the Post Office and cable offices after being held for 48 hours.

Most of the original cables and telegrams go out through the Post Office, which owns the former Cable and Wireless Company. Cables passed through private companies – mainly branches of foreign companies operating in Britain – are collected in vans or cars each morning and taken to the Post Office security department.

The probe is conducted under a special warrant, signed by a Secretary of State under Section 4 of the Official Secrets Acts and regularly renewed to keep it valid.

In advance?
Its purpose is to provide intelligence for the security, military, and criminal investigation departments. A regular check on cables may reveal the activities of persons or organisations suspected of operating against the national interest.

But while the cables are being vetted, there is nothing to prevent information being passed to the Exchequer, the Board of Trade, or any other interested department.

This could provide the Government with advance information of confidential trade negotiations and other private deals.

It has not been possible to establish when this routine cable probe was first introduced, but I understand that it has been in operation for several years.

Footnote: An 'anti-tapping' Bill introduced into the Commons yesterday was sponsored by the Liberal MP Peter Bessell.'[19]

Parliamentary Escalation

There the action for the night ended, but during 21 February the strength of the political storm increased. 'Now began the time when No.10 was dominated by the D Notice affair.'[20] The affair might still have been resolved in the calmer light of day in a low key way, but, coincidentally, there was in the pre-planned House of Commons business for 21 February an innocuous Question to the Prime Minister about the D-Notice System. The questioner was Sir John Langford-Holt, and he wanted merely to know the number of D-Notices issued by the SPBC since 1964,[21] a not uncommon type of question asked periodically by MPs. Before the debate Wilson asked the Leader of the Opposition Edward Heath[22] to meet him, explaining that, even if Sir John's only indirectly connected question was not reached, he intended to take the opportunity to 'deal with the points made in that [Pincher's] article'. When he summarised the background, Heath interjected that the Government had no sanctions when the advice in Notices had not been followed; Wilson agreed the system depended on good will and confidence, and thought the SPBC 'would want to get back to the status quo'. Heath said he found the article 'somewhat extraordinary', and Wilson commented briefly on the 'series of leakages of information' to Pincher.

In the House of Commons, Wilson gave the specific answer to the Question as originally provided by his office, but then went beyond this to launch his own attack on the *Daily Express* (although he did not name it) about that morning's cable-vetting article. 'I would like to add one comment', he said. 'As the House knows, the system under which these Notices are issued has worked well on a voluntary basis for many years, and that means on the basis of confidence and trust between the authorities concerned and the Press. The procedure is described in chapter nine of the Radcliffe Report [1962], which stresses that "its success depends upon good will and, in effect, on very little else". Unfortunately, the confidence and trust which are the basis of the whole system have been called into question by the action of one newspaper in initiating this morning a sensationalized and inaccurate story purporting to describe a situation in which, in fact, the powers and practice have not changed for well over 40 years.'

Langford-Holt sought an assurance it was the Government's policy to keep D-Notices to an absolute minimum, and issue them only in cases where national security was involved. Once more, Wilson went beyond a simple reply. 'Yes, I can certainly confirm that it is the policy of the present Government, as it was of the previous Governments ever since this system was initiated. What I am concerned with today is a clear breach of two D-Notices, in spite of the fact that the newspaper concerned was repeatedly warned that they would be contravening the Notices. This creates a difficult situation for the other newspapers who have honoured this arrangement with us.' Marcus Lipton asked for confirmation there was 'no substance whatever in the alleged censorship of cables, private and business, emanating from this country'. Wilson now prudently stuck more closely to his 'line to take' brief, replying merely that he would neither add nor subtract from what he had already said.[23]

The Storm Increases

This brief but significant parliamentary exchange was the catalyst for what now became a much wider politico-media affaire d'honneur. In the next day's *Daily Express* (22 February), under the headline 'A Charge Refuted', Pincher referred to Wilson's allegation the paper had knowingly and after warning breached two D-Notices. 'This is completely untrue. Yesterday, after Mr Wilson's statement, Colonel Leslie Lohan, Secretary of the Defence Notice Committee, confirmed what he had told me previously – that though he had requested non-publication of the information, the D-notices referred to by the Premier did not apply.'

Pincher gave his version of events, detailing his role with the 1962 Radcliffe Committee, and consequent amendment to a D-Notice. In support of Lohan, he not only said the Secretary had 'used all his powers of persuasion to induce the *Daily Express* not to publish' the previous day's story, but also that 'Colonel Lohan, who took over as secretary after the Radcliffe Report, has been scrupulously fair in ensuring that D-notices are not misused to suppress information just because it happens to be embarrassing to the Government'. He ended: 'If the cable probe has been going on unchanged for 40 years as the Prime Minister told MPs, why was the Government at such pains to prevent disclosure of facts? My inquiries show that though sporadic checks of cables have always been permissible under the Official Secrets Acts, the ROUTINE vetting of all cables is more recent.'

The Times made a similar point in its leader of 22 February: 'If the story is wildly inaccurate, why invoke D notices? It would not be disclosing anything to foreign intelligence agencies since it would not be disclosing anything at all.' It considered there were 'reasons for being dissatisfied with the lecture the Prime Minister read yesterday about D notices', and that, if the story 'is anywhere near correct, it discloses a practice about which the public has cause to be concerned'. The *Daily Telegraph* in its leader the same day also criticised Wilson: 'Although the Prime Minister's statement on "D Notices" yesterday may have sounded weighty, it was little more than a red herring. The important matter was not whether a "D Notice" was technically infringed [the newspaper thought not], but whether the *Daily Express* was right or not in alleging that official scrutiny of cables, designed solely for rare occasions of suspected danger to the security of national defence, has been used for other purposes.' Referring to a recent Parliamentary Question to Wilson about sanctions against Rhodesia, the paper alleged the Prime Minister had 'used in an extreme degree the technique, permissible within limits, of evading questions of public importance by the red-herring method . . . these diversions had a disturbing undertone. They took the form of demanding – and smearing – sources of information and threats of the Official Secrets Act'. Other newspapers, including those otherwise supportive of the Labour Government, reflected similar disquiet about Wilson's reaction to the cable-vetting story.

Official Reaction

The avid media interest and high-level political involvement caused Dunnett, in both his hats (PUS MoD and SPBC Chairman), to request emergency meetings the same day of officials from the Foreign Office (Messrs Greenhill and Ewart-Biggs), MoD, Home Office, and Post Office. The first meeting (chaired by Greenhill and attended also by Security Service, SIS and GCHQ officers) discussed information which would be needed for any inquiry. What embarrassed officials most was the realisation that the only legal authority for the interceptions was a Home Office warrant or warrants signed in 1921, but never (as then intended) renewed since. Indeed, nobody could even find a copy of the warrant(s) to check what was specifically authorised; it was suggested that Cable and Wireless might possibly have a copy in its archives. It transpired subsequently that the current Home Secretary was entirely unaware of this authorisation until Pincher re-disclosed the interceptions. Officials were additionally doubtful about the legality, beyond the probable original warrant authorisation, of handing cables not just to the Cable Companies but now to the Post Office and to GCHQ; they suggested a six-monthly review and re-signing, preferably by the Foreign Secretary, as he was responsible for the 'beneficiaries' of intelligence thus garnered, SIS and GCHQ.[24]

Lohan attended part of the second meeting, chaired by Dunnett. Discussion focused on events at and since the 17 February meeting chaired by Ewart-Biggs. They confirmed Lohan had been asked 'not to lean too heavily on paragraph (2) of the "D" notice of 30/10/61 in order to avoid the risk that the newspapers might scent a separate story'. It was the Security Service Legal Adviser, Bernard Sheldon[25] who, after consulting GCHQ, had passed these 'instructions' to Lohan, with Ewart-Biggs and someone from GCHQ ringing him subsequently (it was also GCHQ which had originally suggested the 'nonsense' response by the MoD Press Office).

Officials concluded there were 'two possible constructions to be put on these events': either the *Express* had deliberately deceived Lohan, relying on his failure to insist on the applicability of the two Notices; or, because Lohan had not insisted on the Notices, the *Express* might have genuinely thought they were free to publish. Against the latter interpretation were the facts known to officials that the paper had consulted its legal branch, that the *Daily Mail* had only published when it knew the *Express* had, and that Lohan had only been informed publication was going ahead when it was too late to stop it. Dunnett told the meeting he had now been requested by the Cabinet Secretary to obtain statements from Lohan on whether, after the Prime Minister's statement in Parliament, he had indeed reaffirmed to Pincher the two D-Notices did not apply, and also on Pincher's claims in the *Express* that morning.[26]

Lohan's three-page minute to Dunnett later that day, while not consistent in every detail with what emerged later, showed the differing recollections between him and Pincher of what happened at and after the long L'Ecu lunch [it is difficult now to say to what degree both accounts were coloured by intervening events and reactions]. Lohan's minute concluded: 'You ought to know that I have kept the Foreign Office, the Security Service and GCHQ appraised of every step I have taken. I acted to the best of my ability on all advice given (this was plentiful and somewhat contradictory). I think it would be improper in this particular minute to speak of matters relating to the briefings I received from the Foreign Office, the Security Service and GCHQ, since I realise the tremendous stress and difficulties my advisers were under. The kindest thing I can say is that the briefings were not consistent and could not in any circumstances support the contention that I was asked specifically to tackle the *Daily Express* and *Daily Mail* on the basis of the two D notices of 27th April 1956 and 30th October 1961. In the case of the first one, the argument had already been rendered untenable by the past history of telephone tapping and, in the second, any emphasis would have disclosed to Chapman Pincher the true nature of the operation. For what it is worth, I think Pincher and his Editor genuinely believed, in spite of what I had said to the contrary, that this interception of telegrams and cables was the responsibility of the present Administration. The motive behind publication was political and the fear of being scooped by another paper (the informant had said that he had given the story to foreign as well as British news agencies).'

This minute was immediately forwarded by Dunnett to Trend, referring to 'anxieties' he had already expressed orally to him about the briefings given to the Colonel by the Foreign Office, Security Service and GCHQ. Nevertheless, as Trend observed in forwarding the minute to Wilson's office, Lohan had apparently told Pincher that 'matters of national security were at stake', and if this were so, 'Chapman Pincher loses a potential alibi', since he and his employers had been made aware of 'the one thing which is at the root of the whole "D" Notice procedure, ie national security, *was* involved.'

Lohan wrote separately to Dunnett about his telephone conversation with Pincher immediately following the PA report of Wilson's Parliamentary comments on 21 February. He alleged Pincher opened by saying 'Let us get this straight, since we do not want to go on calling one another names. Am I not right when I say you agreed with me that the D notices did not apply to our story?' Lohan had reiterated his version, and Pincher had allegedly agreed that Lohan, having put the Notices back into his pocket, nevertheless went on to argue at great length 'why it was not in the public interest to publish your story'. Nevertheless the journalist had persisted in his belief that the Notices had no relevance, as evidenced by Lohan's putting them away, and said the *Express* was going to refute the Prime Minister's allegation. Lohan felt it useless to continue the conversation. 'I did, however, once again tell him that all my arguments, and he well knew it, were conducted in the spirit of the D notices and could have no other basis.'

Parliamentary Action

Heath rang Wilson's Private Secretary early on 22 February to say that, in view of the *Express* refutation, he considered it most important the matter was cleared up publicly, and offered to put down a Question to the Prime Minister. Officials headed this off, and Wilson postponed a visit to Liverpool that afternoon in order instead to discuss the matter face to face with Heath. Wilson said his statement the previous day had not been based on the Lohan and Pincher discussions, but on 'telephone calls to high executive levels in the *Daily Express*' the previous evening [presumably Aitken and Marks]. Having run over the sequence of events in detail, Wilson 'added parenthetically that, as Mr Heath would know, there had been a close relationship between Colonel Lohan and Mr Chapman Pincher over the years and this incident would probably upset that relationship. Indeed there had been a continuing problem about leakages of information and it was possible that Colonel Lohan might have been concerned in some of this'.

Wilson said he intended to make a further statement in the House next day. He thought there should be an early SPBC meeting, and he might refer to such a meeting in his statement, as it was very much a matter for media authorities to consider. Heath agreed, wishing to be kept in close touch, and asked whether Wilson was still of the view Pincher's article was an infringement of the D-Notices. The elliptical reply is revealing: '. . . a meeting at the Foreign Office on Friday under Mr Ewart Biggs had been advised that to publish the information about the interception of cables would be an infringement of the "D" Notices and that the meeting had decided the subsequent course to be followed with the *Daily Express*'.

Heath asked if he could see copies of the two Notices [it may strike non-Politicians strange that the Leader of the Opposition had not already done so], and when Wilson agreed and outlined their purpose, Heath commented [correctly] that he thought the earlier one had been issued after the Commander Crabb affair, when he (Heath) had been Chief Whip; also that it was strange telephone tapping was not covered by a Notice. Wilson later dropped in on Heath to discuss whether the postponement of his visit to Liverpool should publicly be attributed to 'pressure of work' or to his meeting with Heath on this matter; the latter was agreed, and Heath handed back to Wilson's Private Secretary the loaned documents, commenting that he presumed that the relevant word in both Notices was 'methods'.

The cable-vetting affair was indeed again raised by Wilson in the House of Commons on 23 February. He explained that, since his previous statement, the *Daily Express* had excused its action by challenging what he had said, but, having had from the SPBC Chairman a full account of what had occurred between Lohan and Pincher, he need only repeat his previous comments. He suggested both the Government and the Press would now need to consider what lessons could be learnt from the 'incident', and in what respects it might be possible to improve the System 'without endangering the basis of mutual trust, confidence and good will which has enabled it to work for so many years with so little friction, in their joint interests'. Heath however replied that, because of the conflicting evidence between the Prime Minister and the newspaper, the matter could not be left there, and suggested the matter might best be resolved by three backbench Privy Counsellors investigating and reporting to the House.

Wilson countered it should be left to the SPBC in the first instance to consider what lessons might be learned, but Heath persisted, referring to the 'great anxiety' in the Press, and claiming it was not just a matter of 'future arrangements', but also of clearing up what had happened. Other MPs asked questions about the role of the D-Notice Secretary when a matter was not specifically covered by a Notice, about why it was so important to prevent disclosure of something which had been standard practice for over 40 years, and whether an independent inquiry under Lord Devlin (then Chairman of the Press Council)[27]could be set up. Wilson remained adamant the SPBC should investigate first, and only 'if there was anything left open, or in dispute', would he then discuss it further with the Leader of the Opposition.[28]

There was more adverse media comment on this debate next day. For example, *The Times* defence correspondent Charles Douglas-Home[29] asked why, 'on this tenuous case, have the Government bent all their efforts towards Mr Pincher for the publication of this story – particularly when newspapers in the past have broken D Notice agreements without such attendant upheavals. Cases that come to mind in particular are the first mention of MI6 during the Blake case of 1961, and the confusion over the Russian defector in 1963. There seems no doubt that the Government as a whole intend if possible to stop up Mr Pincher's sources and are taking extraordinary measures to deal with him. This irritation has been particularly pronounced since the ending of the Defence Review last year, when Mr Pincher wrote about the aircraft carrier controversy.'[30]

'But Mr Pincher maintains that Ministers admitted openly to American journalists, as early as November 1964, that leaks to him were going to be stopped. The Government has widely questioned civil servants and politicians in their search for the source of leaks to Mr Pincher and they now believe they have identified the prime source.' Douglas-Home also reported that Pincher ('one of the most assiduous inquirers with Colonel Lohan as to the propriety' of his reports) was dismissive of these efforts, pointing out his receipt of the award the previous autumn of 'Reporter of the Decade' (ironically, presented by Wilson himself) as evidence of his continuing successes.

The day after the debate, Heath minuted Wilson he had 'given further thought' to the whole affair. He saw 'four major questions': the conflict of evidence (now also involving *Daily Express* executives); whether the Notices did in fact apply to the article; whether scrutiny of cables should be covered by Notices; and any necessary changes to the System. In view of Press and public disquiet, and in fairness to those concerned on both sides, Heath considered some form of inquiry was needed, and that the SPBC was not the right body to carry it out. He therefore reiterated 'most strongly' his suggestion that an all-party Committee of three Privy Counsellors should be appointed, citing the precedent of the Macmillan Committee of 1957.

39

ANOTHER RADCLIFFE INQUIRY

Largely because of Heath's letter, the Cabinet Secretary convened a meeting of officials that afternoon (24 February), attended by Dunnett, Sir George Coldstream,[31] Greenhill and the Prime Minister's Principal Private Secretary 'Michael' Halls,[32] to discuss what to recommend to Wilson. Trend acknowledged 'it might be necessary to conduct an enquiry', to consider what in fact had happened between Lohan and Pincher, the adequacy of the 'D' Notice procedure as such, and the powers to intercept cables and telegrams and the use made of those powers. In discussion it became clear Heath intended to up the political ante by making his letter public. Officials agreed any enquiry into the facts would inevitably lead to further enquiry into the powers to intercept cables. For this reason, although an SPBC meeting should go ahead, it was undesirable the SPBC should conduct the Enquiry, both because its Secretary would be a subject of it, and because details of the intercept procedure should not be revealed to Media Members.

Officials also decided to recommend that, if a Committee of three Privy Counsellors were to be convened, it should be chaired by 'a judicial figure'; Lord Radcliffe immediately came to mind because of his relevant previous experience. Powers possibly needed, in particular to compel the Press witnesses to reveal the sources of their information, were discussed, but it was felt those could be given at a later stage if required. The Enquiry might take up to six weeks, and, because no official secret had been revealed improperly [sic], there was no need to involve the Security Commission. Finally the officials agreed draft terms of reference for the Enquiry; they bore only passing similarity to those shortly to be given to Radcliffe by politicians.

Meanwhile, Halls rang Heath's Private Secretary, and told him Heath must decide for himself whether to publish his letter to Wilson. 'But he must also decide whether he wishes to continue the arrangement whereby matters affecting security are discussed between the Prime Minister and himself on Personal and Privy Councillor terms, including the disclosure of matters which cannot be fully communicated to the colleagues of either, or whether he wants to use each occasion for making these matters the subject of public controversy. The Leader of the Opposition will no doubt recall Mr Wilson's role on the Philby case. Published or not, Mr Wilson will reply to the letter.' Just over half an hour later, Heath's reply came to Halls: he regretted such a message had been sent, because there was nothing unusual in his [Heath's] letter; it set out in detail what Heath had asked in the House, in no way infringed the private talks, contained nothing not already public, and he had warned Wilson that he would have to do this. It was 'always understood that these private talks did not inhibit action of this particular kind'.

That night Wilson wrote to Heath, replying to 'your letter which I received this evening [a conciliatory use of the not uncommon ministerial subterfuge that one's civil servants have been acting without one's complete knowledge]. Like you, I have been giving further thought to this question'. He said not only did he now agree to the Privy Counsellors' Enquiry, but that he had spoken on the telephone to Radcliffe, who had confirmed he would chair it, and agreed terms of reference. These were: 'To examine the circumstances surrounding the publication of the article in the *Daily Express* of February 21 entitled "Cable Vetting Sensation"; and to consider what improvements, if any, are required in that system in order to maintain it as a voluntary system based on mutual trust and confidence between the Government and the Press in the interests alike of the freedom of the Press and of the security of the State'.

Reaction in the SPBC

Unaware of this decision, SPBC Media members were meanwhile highly displeased about Wilson's previous public indication that the Committee should be the body initially to investigate the dispute, about which they had not been consulted. One of the NPA Members even tendered his resignation; Lee Howard,[33] the *Daily Mirror*'s editor, explained he did 'not feel able to attend any SPBC meeting that may be called in the immediate future to discuss the dispute between the Government and the "Daily Express". Any such meeting would be a gross abuse of the functions of the "D" Notice Committee, which in my view exists solely to provide a link between the Government on the one hand, and the voluntary acceptance by the Press on the other of the need to restrain publication of certain information in the national interest. I know of no "D" Notice which would have any direct bearing on the story published by Mr Chapman Pincher in the "Daily Express". If no such notice exists, as I believe, I cannot see what possible function the Committee can fulfil in considering this dispute between a most reputable journalist and a disapproving Government. The "D" Notice Committee is not an instrument of censorship but a voluntary body. It has been a privilege to have represented the National Press on it; but I cannot participate in any attempt to use the Committee in a way which was never intended – and particularly to rule upon the conduct of a journalist of high integrity and his newspaper'. He ended by paying tribute to Lohan's performance as the Secretary.

His fellow NPA Member, LJ Dicker,[34] while sympathising, decided to stay on, stating in his own paper when an SPBC meeting was called to discuss the affair, that there was no question of sitting in judgement on conduct, but that 'It is more a matter of whether the D-Notice procedure was properly used and whether any such Notice was ever transgressed.' In the event, the meeting did not take place, having been overtaken by subsequent develop-ments elsewhere in the immediately intervening days. Meanwhile, as their representatives on Radcliffe's Committee, Heath nominated John Selwyn Lloyd,[35] and Wilson selected Emmanuel Shinwell,[36] both ex-Ministers of Defence. Jeremy Thorpe,[37] pressed unsuccess-fully for a Liberal Party Privy Counsellor to be added to the Committee of Enquiry. Wilson left it to Radcliffe to ask for what powers he needed, and for more if required as the Enquiry proceeded. Radcliffe decided he needed no powers of compulsion, at least to start with, and announced his intention of opening the Enquiry in the second week of March.

Wilson formally announced the Enquiry in Parliament on 28 February, engendering a further (and repetitive) debate, short but prickly. An interdepartmental working party under Ewart-Biggs was set up to produce an official narrative of events and 'a paper dealing with the substance of the matter'. The Treasury Solicitor was tasked to provide legal advice to the Enquiry, but it was agreed by officials its terms of reference should not include whether an offence had been committed; an examination of that would be carried out separately. For unexplained reasons, the MoD chose this moment to arrange a security check on all Media Members of the Committee. Lohan himself wrote an aide-memoire, recording (possibly with a little immediate hindsight/self-justification): 'for the last three months the newspaper world has become over-excited and over-sensitive about the topics of telephone tapping and interference with mail. Rightly or wrongly Fleet Street felt persecuted and suspicious. The atmosphere was ripe for an explosive protest about these issues'. He listed long-standing weaknesses he perceived in the D-Notice System, in records, filing and the Notices themselves. Nevertheless he saw only two 'major upsets' since May 1962: 'Dolnytsin' and this. He had been in direct contact throughout with Sheldon of MI5 and GCHQ.

Press Action

The Press, in all its forms, was not meanwhile silent. On 26 February, *The Observer* supported the D-Notice System, but suggested there was a widespread feeling amongst defence correspondents that Notices were 'too vague'; the *Sunday Times*, however, published alleged quotes from Lohan criticising the handling of the dispute, which caused Wilson to instruct Wigg to visit Dunnett at home that very Sunday and ask for comment; Dunnett did not reply in writing until 8 March, when he relayed Lohan's denial of the direct quotes attributed to him, although he did admit he had drawn the reporter's attention to certain remarks about the status of the Secretary contained in the 1962 Radcliffe Report.

On 28 February, London University's Student Union magazine *Sennet* published an article by Pincher's informant Robert Lawson. This included that when the *Daily Mail* had rejected his story, he had gone first to the London School of Economics magazine *Beaver*, which had also turned down his story because 'there was no political significance' [one assumes its editor did not subsequently become one of the great names in British investigative journalism]. The report included four grainy photographs of alleged bags of cables being transferred to and from the boot of a private car outside the Great Northern Telegraph Company offices, and ended by pointing out that for a security check to be effective, it would also have to cover all outgoing telex and telephone calls; 'Is the Government prepared to deny categorically that these means of communication also are not subject to similarly thorough investigation?'

The Spectator Publishes the Two Notices

This amateur effort nevertheless caused the Prime Minister to write further to Radcliffe three days later, by which time the *Daily Sketch* (1 March) and the *Evening Standard* (2 March) had picked up the *Sennet* article; the *Economist* of 4 March wondered why Wilson was making so much of something which was not really news. Even more worryingly for the Government, on 3 March *The Spectator* included two articles on the whole affair. The less damaging acknowledged Wilson had some points in his favour, but chided him and his advisers for their lack of understanding of how the Press worked; it also recorded that what the Media as a whole now suspected was 'nothing new has been told the enemy but that ministers have been caused embarrassment. Many readers probably think that this whole affair is a storm in a teacup, the newspapers striking attitudes, editors seeking martyrdom. They should think back a little to Profumo, Vassall, Crabb and the other cases in which press and opposition took the cat-o'-nine-tails to the government and flayed and flayed. To put it crudely, the newspapers smell blood; and Mr Heath, just like Mr Crossman in the Profumo case, is playing it with quiet subtlety. When I heard that Lord Radcliffe had been asked to head the probe, I could hardly believe my ears: "the word is like a knell"'.

Much more serious to the Government, and at that time to the SPBC, was the article in the same issue by the political commentator Alan Watkins.[38] He described Wilson as 'highly conscious of the press', and noted recently 'a certain edge' came into his voice when discussing newspapers, a situation very different from 'the cosy one that existed in 1964–66'. Watkins described adversely the Official Secrets Acts and their draconian use, and, in marginally less unfavourable terms, the D-Notice System and its application in this case, including the possibility a current secret cable-monitoring operation would be prejudiced. What caused the most upset, however, was that *The Spectator* published, for the first time ever, the complete text of a D-Notice, indeed both of those in question. It did so to question the wording and the rationale in detail in the remainder of Watkins' piece.

Wilson wrote to Radcliffe that he might well be asked in the House whether the terms of reference of the Enquiry should be extended to enable it also to consider 'these additional matters and any others of the same kind'. He hinted at what he hoped Radcliffe's response would be: 'If you agree, I would propose to reply that in my view the second part of the terms of reference would presumably involve consideration of all recent breaches or alleged breaches of the system, but that the construction of the terms of reference is a matter for your colleagues and yourself and that, if you felt they should be extended, I should of course respond appropriately.'

Radcliffe deflected this suggestion: 'My own feelings about the current newspaper demonstrations are that they are only a part of the current controversy about the rights and wrongs of the original *Daily Express* publication, and that nothing of value for the future would be likely to be gained by extending the Privy Councillors' enquiry into such matters'. However, the Privy Councillors did in the event decide to investigate *The Spectator*'s publication of the notices, and Watkins and his editor Nigel Lawson[39] were in due course summoned to give evidence.

The *Spectator* articles gave the affair further legs across the Media. Although the *Daily Express* had deliberately refrained from comment since the announcement of the Enquiry, Pincher now (3 March) took the opportunity to correct some details in the Watkins commentary. He denied his newspaper had ever been told a specific current operation might be prejudiced, and that Lohan had told him initially there were two applicable Notices (both points confirmed by Lohan). He also quoted Lohan on how Watkins had acquired the contents of the two now published D-Notices: having called on the Colonel in his office, saying *The Spectator*'s copies of the Notices were missing, he was shown the Notices, having been reminded by Lohan the contents should not be published in full or in part. The *Economist* of 4 March, having described Lohan as someone 'whom journalists like and respect', now complimented Lee Howard on having had the 'guts' to resign, summarising the Government's behaviour towards the Press as leaving 'a very bad taste in the mouth'.

At a thinly attended SPBC emergency meeting on 15 March 1967, Dunnett said he would welcome views before he gave evidence to the Radcliffe Committee. Changes to official representation were mooted by him (without objection from the Media side), including membership for the JIC Chairman and Home Office PUS, so that the secret Agencies' interests might be better reflected, plus an AUS from the MoD, whose role would include being the Secretary's official point of contact.[40] Because hurried consultation was sometimes needed, he proposed that a DPBAC Vice-Chairman should be formally selected by the Media side, better to co-ordinate their views and interaction; Media Members were however against some retired journalist being selected as Vice-Chairman, because the incumbent needed to be completely up to date with current media matters.

Dicker and Cox thought the system already normally worked well, and that perhaps security clearance of the Media side would enable better explanation of rationales to them. Media members considered there was little problem with 'technical' Notices, but that the 'broader areas of political security' were becoming more important and more problematical. Lohan complained the method of circulation of advisory letters which he had inherited was chaotic, but that once the review of D-Notices was complete and they had been issued in loose-leaf books, the situation would improve. Dicker suggested *The Spectator* should be reported to the Press Council, but others thought that this and other matters should await the Radcliffe Report.[41]

Officials' View of the Future of the D-Notice System

The MoD-led Inter-Departmental Working Party which had been considering revision of the D-Notices since 1965 rapidly brought its work to a head, making recommendations for incorporation in a Cabinet Office paper on the D-Notice System 'and possible improvements to it in the light of recent events.'[42] The Cabinet Office paper was submitted to the Privy Counsellors on 16 March, and appears in the eventual Report.[43] Uncompromising in its view that the *Daily Express* had deliberately 'infringed and thus inflicted damage upon the "D" Notice system', and that *The Spectator* had been similarly underhand, it was well balanced on how effective the System usually was, on the key role of the Secretary, and on the short-comings in official procedures and organisation which had contributed to the debacle.

'With each infringement of the system, and given the present popular cult in intelligence and security matters, the area of secrecy protected by the "D" notice procedure is progressively eroded; but a great deal remains that still requires protection . . . Press criticism in the recent episode has been directed more to the question whether the system should have been invoked in this case rather than against the system itself. Nor does any alternative to the present system seem feasible'. The recommendations were generally pragmatic: the Media side should confirm Notices were not for publication; official guidance to the Secretary should be given by one lead Department as appropriate on each occasion (preferably in writing); there should be some system of appeal when the Secretary was unable to persuade an editor; in any such cases the Chairman should be informed early enough to be able to intervene personally; the Foreign Office DUS [responsible for security and intelligence matters, including those concerning MI6 and GCHQ] and the Home Office PUS [responsible for matters concerning MI5] should be added to the SPBC in lieu of two Services' PUSs; and one of the SPBC Media members should be chosen as Vice-Chairman (and point of consultation for the Chairman in an emergency or on points of procedure). Wilson scribbled on the draft 'This is good. On para 12 [appeal procedure] wd it be possible to bring in *Devlin*, who is I think a Privy Councillor (or who if not could become one) + who carries the confidence of the Press'.

Behind the Scenes

Officials had also been drafting and redrafting with Wigg and Wilson a further letter from the latter to Radcliffe. A revealing minute from Trend to Halls of 23 March says: 'I ought perhaps to record that Trevelyan [the Secretary to the Enquiry Committee][44] suggested that Lord Radcliffe ought not to be given too much time between receiving the letter and meeting the Prime Minister . . . on the grounds that, if he is given too much time to think about the implications of the letter, he may write, even before meeting the Prime Minister, and say he can't take on anything more! . . . There is nothing particularly secret about the contents of the letter; but it might do no harm to send it in double envelopes if it is to go through the post'. Mandarin-craft of an advanced degree!

In the multi-enveloped letter sent to Radcliffe on 28 March, Wilson said he had been thinking over some of the broader implications of the Enquiry 'to which I shall have to give rather careful consideration when we receive your report . . . You will know what I have in mind – those aspects of your Enquiry which bear upon some very important, but also very sensitive, areas of public policy, which may even involve, in the extreme case, the lives of men and women. Although these issues are not formally within your terms of reference, I am concerned that we should not be thought, merely because the questions are so delicate, to have been in any way reserved or inhibited in taking you and your colleagues fully into our confidence in this respect but that you should all feel that you have been enabled to consider them as fully and frankly as you wish'.

'At the same time, the way in which you treat them in your report is clearly a very important consideration from the Government's point of view, if we are to achieve the dual purpose of reassuring public opinion about the sensitive practices in question without prejudicing national security and the public interest'. He asked Radcliffe therefore to come and talk about the problem, and said he would 'greatly welcome your help and advice before you reach the stage of concerting firm views'. Radcliffe willingly agreed, and responded to this warning shot that 'There are certain implications which will arise out of our Report, however we express it, that need a great deal of consideration!'[45] Trend a few days later minuted Wilson to dissuade Radcliffe, when he met him on 6 April, from recommending a separate inquiry into 'current practice', which was 'perhaps the most sensitive of all areas of covert interception of communications', but which had now 'unfortunately excited a degree of public interest'.[46]

There was also an international dimension to the concerns, emphasised by a note for the record in the Prime Ministerial archives. On 30 March the British Ambassador in Washington, Sir Patrick Dean,[47] referring to the Radcliffe Enquiry, informed Wilson that Norman Birkett[48] had told him that in his view the interception arrangements were necessary, and that he (Birkett) was personally satisfied the arrangements were carried out for entirely the right motives with security and the public interest in mind.[49] The Prime Minister did not need reminding about American sensitivities concerning the sharing of intelligence thus gleaned by the British system, in particular where it concerned American citizens and organisations, which the United States NSA was precluded for constitutional reasons from directly acquiring itself by covert means.[50]

One of those whom Radcliffe interviewed informally and alone was the DGSS, Furnival Jones, who recorded afterwards that the two questions they focused on were 'could D-Notices about the Security Service be made more specific?' and 'did he [DGSS] have any ideas for a different system of controlling disclosures in the Press?' He said the system normally worked well, but depended on both sides having confidence in the Secretary; in Lohan's case this was not full in Whitehall, but in the Media he had no evidence otherwise. 'The task of the Secretary was an unenviable one and I doubted whether any man would be regarded as ideal at all times by all sides. He had to run with the hare and hunt with the hounds.' Despite its imperfections, no alternative system appealed to Furnival Jones. Radcliffe commented nobody else had any ideas for an alternative. The DGSS also briefed Radcliffe more fully about the system for requesting GCHQ interceptions, and emphasised its value in counter subversion.[51]

At a lower level of input to the evidence collection, Lohan in mid-April told Trevelyan there was no trace of any SPBC Terms of Reference. After his death, Thomson's daughter had handed over all records from his flat, but these included only a potted history. Lohan added a 'cri de coeur' about his own situation: he had to be available at all hours, he had made 112 trunk calls from his home in the past year, and received up to 30 incoming calls per day there. He had to work at high speed to meet media deadlines, and in Shell-Mex House he felt like an 'orphan'. It was supposed to be a half job but was full-time, and he was paid initially only 50 per cent (later 75 per cent) of the salary of a Chief Information Officer (Class A). It was a lonely job too – 'I fall slap in the middle between the Civil Service and the Press' in working conditions.[52]

On 12 May, the Media side met in the *Daily Telegraph* Fleet Street offices to select a Vice-Chairman, who they agreed had to be London-based. They asked Lohan to chair the meeting. After discussion there were only two possible candidates, Dicker and Pendred, but the latter declined to stand, because he felt the Vice-Chairman should be from a newspaper not periodical background. Dicker was keen to do the job, so was selected.[53]

Submission of the Radcliffe Report

The Committee of Privy Counsellors worked from mid-March to mid-April. As well as Lohan and Pincher, they interviewed representatives of the *Daily Express*, *Daily Mail*, *Daily Mirror*, *Spectator*, *Daily Telegraph*, MoD, Foreign Office, Post Office, and the secret Agencies.[54] Senior officials agonised with Trend over whether the probably unfavourable conclusions should be included, and on what line to take on the preferred form of future D-Notices, with the secret Agencies preferring them to be as imprecise as possible; Trend summed up the dilemma: too much detail, too much disclosure; too little, too little weight. There was also official sensitivity to criticism that Lohan had not been included in the initial Foreign Office meeting.[55] When the Privy Counsellors had finished their evidence-taking, and had deliberated on their conclusions but not yet completed drafting their Report, Radcliffe went in late April to lunch privately with Wilson at Chequers. The Judge advised considering the whole affair as 'a storm in a teacup', and explained the Report's conclusions to the Prime Minister, who, at what was an entirely affable meeting, raised no particular concerns.[56]

When finalised, the Report was dated 17 May 1967, and was from then formally in the hands of the Government, but it had still not been released to the public by the start of the second week in June. Meanwhile, as early as 15 May, Trend (after discussion with Wigg) had minuted Wilson about the Privy Counsellors' 'Summary of Conclusions', recommending that, when he saw Radcliffe next day, he should try to persuade the Judge to modify the conclusions. When the complete draft was seen by Wilson's political advisers they became even more concerned, stirring him to share their fears; from then on direction of the considerable interdepartmental discussion was in the Prime Minister's own hands.

Wilson and Radcliffe Disagree

When they duly met, Wilson told Radcliffe his primary concern was that responsibility ultimately lay with him for the security of the State. He then complained that the Conclusions (he had not yet read the whole Report) 'taken by themselves, appeared on the one hand to be highly critical of the Government and on the other to exonerate the *Daily Express* from all blame for publishing the article in question'. He understood the whole Report gave a more balanced view, but it was the Conclusions which the Press would seize on. Wilson therefore wanted to make clear that the Government would feel free to decide the extent to which it would accept the Report.

He thought the 'problem which therefore remained was that the Report might be taken as giving support to the view that the Press was now virtually free to publish stories bearing on national security'. The Government's dilemma was that it could not be too precise in D-Notices 'without an unjustifiable breach of security, but that if too ambiguous, the Notices were not effective . . . The Government might even be forced to consider legislation although this would be highly contentious'. He might therefore consult the editors on what steps should be taken to protect secret information.

Radcliffe thought the Prime Minister was 'exaggerating the effect of the Report on the Security and Secret Services and, indeed, exaggerating the political significance of the Report'; after initial reaction, a more balanced appraisal would take place. His advice was that it would be 'tactically unwise' to attack the *Daily Express* as the facts did not support the case. He doubted whether the Media would ever publish information 'if it was clear that it might prejudice a current security operation'. He believed the Press would accept his recommendation on the redrafting of the Notice of April 1956, 'which had virtually been interpreted out of existence'. He also opined that any calling together of editors, in particular to consider legislation, 'would only be counterproductive and stimulate continued interest in the matter'.

Wilson disagreed about the political impact, saying he would have to stand by the statement he had made in the House that the two D-Notices did apply to the story, which had been on the best advice available to him from his civil service, diplomatic and security advisers. He discussed with Radcliffe introducing some form of appeal or arbitration machinery in such cases, but the Judge doubted whether this would be acceptable to the Media, although he was not against Wilson's other proposal that Lord Devlin might become the Chairman of the SPBC. Radcliffe also suggested the Secretary should be 'a person of considerably greater ability than Colonel Lohan, more hard-headed, and his relations with the Press should be more formal and austere'.

Wilson agreed on the latter point, conceding the Government had been at fault in not requiring the post to be Positively Vetted; in future 'the indefensible situation must not be allowed to recur in which the Secretary was deliberately excluded from a meeting to deal with an incident or deliberately kept in ignorance of certain relevant, if secret, information'. He also revealed to Radcliffe that Lohan's conduct had been under close scrutiny before this incident because of the suspicion he had disclosed secret information to the Press and was a security risk. He showed Radcliffe 'certain papers relating to Colonel Lohan', and asked whether these would influence the Report.[57] 'Lord Radcliffe was obviously deeply shocked by what he had read', Halls recorded. He said they indicated 'grave misdemeanour' on Lohan's part and possibly provided the basis for charges under the OSAs. He agreed they threw further light on the Lohan/Pincher relationship, but 'he felt bound to point out that he had anyway formed a low opinion of Colonel Lohan's credibility as a witness'. He did not however consider his Committee could now 'take cognisance' of the papers he had just been shown (or would have done previously).

Wilson finally returned to the unwelcome Conclusions of the Report. He asked Radcliffe to consider publishing the report without the Conclusions. The Judge, after due reflection, said an amendment to the first draft of the Conclusions had already caused his Privy Counsellor colleagues 'some difficulties', and 'in consequence they had only now been persuaded to sign the Report'. He did not think therefore he could now go back to them and suggest the Conclusions should after all be omitted. He raised no objection however to the Prime Minister's wish also to publish the non-secret part of the evidence taken, which Wilson saw 'might go some way towards establishing the relationship between Colonel Lohan and Mr Chapman Pincher and provide ammunition for the use of the House when the Report was debated.'[58]

40

THE STORM BECOMES A
HURRICANE

Wilson Decides Future Handling

A week later, 23 May, Wilson summoned Healey and Wigg, the Lord Chancellor, Attorney-General, and senior officials from Departments directly concerned, to discuss how to respond to the Report and its supporting evidence when published. It was decided publication should be on 8 June, with a House of Commons debate the following week. The principal political decisions of the meeting were that, for reasons of counter-balance to the starkness of the Conclusions, the non-secret parts of the evidence taken by the Radcliffe Committee should be published; and that a White Paper should be published simultaneously with the Report, giving the Government's response.

This should draw attention to the 'central dilemma', namely the balance between precision and generalisation in D-Notices on highly sensitive matters. It should also show that action was already in hand to rectify shortcomings, and to take any disciplinary action (Wilson wanted first to consult Trend about that concerning Lohan). The idea of a 'trusted figure' such as Lord Devlin as a 'court of appeal' should be floated, as someone whose decisions would ideally be accepted by both sides.

There was some discussion of how far the White Paper should go in drawing attention specifically to Lohan's 'lapses'. 'It was clear that without his errors the errors of others would almost certainly not have sufficed by themselves to have led to the gross breach of security which had occurred . . . On the other hand, to the world at large he would appear as a relatively minor figure and too great an emphasis on his shortcomings, particularly when he had not been specifically criticised by the Committee, would be represented publicly as an attempt to find a scapegoat for the Government's errors. It would also call into question the Government's wisdom of having employed him as Secretary of the Committee. Much would depend on the drafting of the narrative part of the White Paper. If this could expose the part played by Colonel Lohan without directly accusing him of major responsibility for the debacle, this would suffice.' The Wheels of Power sometimes grind exceeding small.

Burke Trend, who had already been investigating with the Permanent Secretaries 'the faults of machinery and personnel which had been exposed by the present case', undertook to circulate a separate internal paper shortly. Finally, it was recorded that the Foreign Secretary, George Brown, whose Department was clearly in the firing line and who was away in Moscow, had gained Wilson's agreement that his position on the matter should be 'reserved' until after his return and taken into account before any final decisions were taken.[59]

It is interesting to read Wigg's assessment of events at this stage (24 May), before politicking climaxed: the Radcliffe Committee, by allowing witnesses to be represented by

Counsel, became like a court 'concerned to protect individuals from injustice', whereas such investigations should be like Boards of Inquiry in the Services, concerned only with establishing the facts;[60] Lohan might have falsified evidence of when *Daily Express* messengers came to collect copies of Notices from him around the day of publication of the cable-vetting article; Marks had been fully aware of the arguments against publication; and the Foreign Office and GCHQ were blameworthy in that cable-vetting was not covered by the OSAs, so the employees of the cable companies for 47 years could not have been prevented from talking. Trend too picked up the latter point, and asked other questions about whether the Foreign Office had kept the MoD sufficiently informed after the first crucial meeting, and about why records had not been kept by officials of critical calls. The Departmental responses duly came in, largely denying they had done anything 'improper or insufficient.'[61]

On 24 May, in the margins of discussion of Middle East crises, Wilson mentioned receipt of the Radcliffe Report to Heath, and, following constitutional propriety, asked him to read it and to discuss the excisions needed and the programme for handling it (complicated by Wilson's imminent visits to Canada/United States). Trend too was working on this programme, on possible disciplinary action against Lohan and O'Brien, and on the publishable version of the official evidence, about which Ewart-Biggs was leading a feverishly-paced working party. 'In so far as we may wish, for our own reasons, to modify any of the evidence which was given when Counsel was present', Trend asked significantly, 'how far are we inhibited by the fact that the transcripts of such proceedings were made available to Counsel, who still have them?'[62] Next day, when it seemed [inconclusively as it turned out] that the veracity of Lohan's account of his advice to Pincher might depend on receipts given to humble *Daily Express* messengers, Wilson authorised exceptionally the 'forensic examination' of these mundane scraps.[63]

Trend's major motivation was to advise the Government against getting drawn into the deeper and deeper problems he foresaw if matters continued to be played up rather than down. Greenhill's major concerns were that the full evidence revealed that Foreign Office control of cable-vetting had over the years become somewhat loose, and that the publicity might induce journalists to probe the sensitive relationship in this field with the United States, not as regards a specific operation but generally.[64] Although all telegrams were initially collected, only those categories authorised by Ministers were retained and analysed by GCHQ staff (about 2–3 per cent of the total). About 100,000 telegrams a day were thus processed, about one third of which were addressed to or originated in the UK. The information given to the Radcliffe Committee did not cover the content or disposal of the intelligence thus gathered, nor do the arrangements have relevance to more modern international communications. The cover story to the cable companies (clearly not entirely effective) was that the collection was for government 'accountancy purposes'; strangely, not all the companies had been required to sign a 'no disclosure' agreement.

Wilson Accuses Trend and Officials

The minute in which Trend asked the question above about doctoring transcripts also asked his fellow Permanent Secretaries (and by implication their Ministers, including now the Home Secretary): 'does anybody wish to raise any objections, of principle or of practice, to publishing the expurgated evidence?' When Wilson saw this, he was furious. His consequent telephone call on Sunday 28 May to Trend (who was on weekend in Deal, Kent), and his comments when the Cabinet Secretary answered his summons the same day to No.10 for a

20-minute dressing-down, were recorded by Halls in as angry a Top Secret Note for the Record as one is likely to find in Prime Ministerial archives:

(i)   The Prime Minister made it quite clear that he had got the impression that Officials were back-tracking on the decisions that he had reached; they were attempting to prevent publication of the evidence, or to water it down to such an extent that it would be meaningless.

(ii)   He certainly would not accept Trend's proposal that there should be a meeting of Ministers on Tuesday.

(iii)   He considered it particularly naïve to have made the reference to the Home Secretary [Roy Jenkins] and could not understand why Trend thought it might be necessary now to bring him into this matter.

(iv)   The various decisions which had to be reached on the Radcliffe report would be taken by himself and he was not prepared to put this into commission with his colleagues.

(v)   He accepted that the Foreign Secretary's position had been reserved about publication and he could deal with that himself a deux with the Foreign Secretary. But he did not accept that any other Minister's position had been so reserved and he was concerned to see that Trend was inviting further reservations.

Trend justified his minute as seeking to present all the facts needed by the Prime Minister in reaching a decision about publication of the evidence, and as reflecting the problems which the Ewart-Biggs working party had found in deleting some of the evidence (which would make it look 'a bit odd'); and the Home Office had been added because it was responsible for MI5, which was marginally involved. 'The Prime Minister made it clear to Trend that the post mortem on the publication of the *Daily Express* article, and the various analyses which had been made since the Radcliffe Report had been presented to him, clearly showed that the Official machine had badly mishandled the matter and had, moreover, given him advice which had now been found in some respects to be incorrect. Sir Burke Trend must take this fully into account in recognising that the Prime Minister would be free to make whatever statement he decided was appropriate when the Report was published.'[65] The threat of parliamentary exposure of perceived official shortcomings could hardly have been more bluntly put.

Next day, without referring directly to Wilson's angry comments, Trend punctiliously forwarded the recommended expurgation of the evidence, stressing in his covering minute that the Ewart-Biggs working party was aware the evidence was to be published, but rightly felt the Prime Minister should be aware of the implications of that decision. Trend added there were only two points he thought now needed to be considered further: whether publication of the evidence would expose 'us' to any legal risk or would inhibit any disciplinary action, and whether such publication 'by exciting further speculation about the interception of cables, will focus attention on activities which we would much rather continue to conceal'.

This polite, reasoned and reasonable further questioning of Wilson's judgement drew a response from the Prime Minister which, if less angry, was just as robust. In an eight-page Top Secret and Personal minute to Trend the same day, he repeatedly alternated between acknowledgement of the force of the arguments of officials against publication, and assertion of his own intentions as to the political handling, including if not publication then parliamentary exposure; between a resigned acceptance of official advice and a somewhat bitter and intimidatory defiance of it.

> I think the Committee make quite a powerful case against publication. Clearly they have not, of course, considered the arguments for publication. I had not realised that this Working Party was in fact being given any remit to consider whether the evidence should be published . . . Their job, as I understood it, was to prepare a list of the deletions from the evidence as given so that nothing affecting security would appear . . . Their arguments against publication are compelling and I studied their political assessment of the position with considerable interest. They are, I am sure, right in saying that with so extensive a volume of material, hostile critics in the Press, with their well-known selectivity, would be able to find additional sticks with which to beat the Departments concerned. Inevitably the Committee was less well fitted to consider the other side of the picture, namely, what will be the end-product of the publication, the Debate in the House . . . But clearly on a political matter such as this I must accept the evidence of Mr Ewart Biggs and his colleagues. I can only wish Mr Ewart Biggs' political perception had been as acute when he briefed me for my Statement in the House.
>
> My inclination now is to wash my hands of the whole affair and let the machine decide how this should be handled. Indeed, I feel I have no alternative. Once an inter-Departmental Committee has produced a unanimous Report of this kind . . . I could only secure the publication of the evidence by making clear to all my well-briefed colleagues that I must insist on publication . . . but I have to reckon with the comments which will appear under the signature of a number of political journalists about the disagreement which I overrode. So probably the right thing for me is to accept that now this Committee has reported, the issue is closed. I think the Official machine should now take all the other decisions required, up to and including publication.

Wilson then turned to other aspects of the case. 'The rear guard action will no doubt now turn to the question of the White Paper – first as to whether it should be published at all, on which I gather there are doubts, and second, if published, whether the present draft should be emasculated.' Again, having established that he himself would like the draft further toughened, he said 'would not feel disposed to stand out' against the collective judgement of officials. Similarly it would be wrong for him to interfere in the enquiry into the behaviour of Lohan and into his relationship with Pincher, which he regarded as 'the fundamental issue here . . . I think the machine has done a very good job on it and, since the cobbler should stick to his last, I feel probably that I should not intervene any further'.

'But of course after publication the issue moves into the political sphere, where as a not inexperienced cobbler I have both rights and duties. I should not propose to take any further Official advice on how I should address the House of Commons . . . the advice I received on February 21 has proved somewhat counter-productive so far as I am concerned . . . I feel I should give the House a full and frank account of what has taken place . . . qualified only by my overriding duty to see nothing affecting security is made available to them . . . the central question is one raised by Radcliffe, though not answered by him, though he knew the facts, why the Secretary of that Committee [SPBC] was not present at the meeting on

Friday, February 17' [in the Foreign Office]. And he went on to say that he would feel bound to reveal why Lohan had not been trusted, and how the Director of GCHQ had ruled that Lohan could not be made privy to the sensitive cable-vetting information because he had not 'undergone appropriate security procedures. The House, of course, may well ask why, as I did'.

Wilson said he would infer other official shortcomings about Lohan and his lack of clearances. 'I think the House is entitled to know how this situation arose, and on this at least my own position is beyond reproach. I am not sure I can say the same about the Departments concerned over a period of many years . . . In view of the way things are moving, I think my posture in the House and in the subsequent Debate should be one in which I thank the Committee for their Report, that I express certain mild queries about some of the conclusions in the light of evidence they received, and that I explain to the House the real answer to the questions the Committee failed to answer and, indeed, failed to pursue . . . I am losing the urge to fight this matter any further, but . . . thereafter I speak to the House of Commons on the basis of full disclosure – subject only to security considerations'.

> Clearly the whole issue is capable of being represented as a two-way vendetta between Beaverbrook newspapers and myself . . . It is true of course that a much milder predecessor of mine, Stanley Baldwin, decided that such an issue had to be fought to the finish, and history has, I think, recorded that he was right and that he won. I rather tend to feel that after a major storm of the kind we have had, a storm which is still to reach its climax, an honourable peace might well be negotiated, and I have some very clear ideas about how this could be brought about. But I do not like peace negotiations from a position of weakness, even humiliation. A good healthy, bloody deadlock provides the best climate. And since such a deadlock is clearly not now going to emerge in advance of publication, perhaps I might be left to consider how it might be contrived in the Parliamentary situation after publication.
>
> So, if I reach the conclusion – and my mind is not finally made up – to wash my hands of the pre-publication phase, and leave it to those more expert than myself, concerned as they must be with their preoccupations . . . I shall be somewhat intolerant of intervention by the Official machine once we move into the political phase. I can assure you I shall consult the Paymaster General, whose concern for security matters is beyond all doubt. Indeed, I feel that after nearly three years of Parliamentary silence he might well wind up the Debate, since I trust his ['political' deleted in manuscript by Wilson] judgement implicitly in this matter.

Having uttered this ultimate threat, Wilson did however offer a final and personal twig of peace to Trend, in a handwritten postscript: 'In other words, Burke, I know when I'm beat, provided that the last battle is fought under my direction. But I wanted you to be absolutely clear that whatever disagreements we have had – and I respect your motives and concern for my interests as you do mine – this whole sad episode will make no difference whatsoever to our relationship on other and more important matters.'[66] One is left with a strong image of a Prime Minister at bay, alone in his study except for his faithful bloodhound George Wigg occasionally licking his writing hand.

After the Cabinet Meeting the next day, Sir Burke Trend went to see the Prime Minister, with the Paymaster General present. Wigg said he did not consider the expurgated version of the evidence offended security at all; he also reminded Wilson that the personal letters in his possession could not be used. Trend reiterated the official arguments,[67] but Wilson disagreed that the evidence itself would damage security, and pointed out it was the Report which admitted the existence of MI6. Wigg went even further, saying it was the actions of the Foreign Office which had already damaged security; 'all sophisticated intelligence services had been alerted and there was already evidence that [foreign cable] traffic was diminished'.

When invited by Wigg to say what he would do in the Prime Minister's position, Trend said that Denis Healey, advised by Dunnett, would be in favour of publication, while George Brown, advised by his officials, would be against. The Attorney-General's advice should now be sought about both legal and 'natural justice' risks. He admitted he was on balance still against publication, and urged a meeting of Ministers concerned. He wanted to be sure that, if the Prime Minister decided 'to go it alone', he (Wilson) realised the implications and 'did not get out of the present situation only to find himself in a worse mess'. Trend also mentioned his own position vis-à-vis Lohan and the lack of clearances, and ran through the 1965 discussion of Lohan's possession of Turnstile documents.[68]

Wilson returned to the attack on the Ewart-Biggs working party, and its conclusion that there were 'serious difficulties and disadvantages in publishing the edited versions of the evidence'. He said 'it seemed to him that the official machine was going to great lengths to protect itself. He had been given unsound and misleading advice. He had, for example, been told on the morning when he drafted his reply to Sir John Langford-Holt's Question that Colonel Lohan had informed the newspaper concerned that to publish the article would be contrary to the "D" Notices, while it was clear that he had not said this [an interesting interpretation by Wilson]. So much which had been happening recently seemed to him to be the official machine finding means of obstructing him. He wondered what would not happen to the draft White Paper' [of which meanwhile draft after redraft had for several days been bouncing around Whitehall like pinballs].

He ended the meeting by saying that, if the 'official machine' was genuinely seeking to carry out his instructions, he would do his best to 'protect those concerned'. If not, he would decide his own course of action. Meanwhile his 'conclusion' was that officials should proceed on the basis that in principle he was in favour of publishing the expurgated evidence, and that he wanted to take the latest draft of the White Paper with him to North America. On his return he would decide how he would act in Parliament. After Trend and Wigg had gone, Wilson saw Healey then Brown alone; the former agreed with publication and the latter 'withdrew his objections.'[69] Trend rapidly put action in hand to carry out the Prime Minister's wishes, to inform Lohan and O'Brien of what was happening and that they would then 'have to face certain disciplinary proceedings', to inform the Privy Councillors and outside witnesses concerned, to complete the White Paper, to complete the legal checks, and to plan a timetable for publication.

Before Wilson left for North America, the draft White Paper had been considerably revised to take into account his own points (including 'emphasise the *Daily Mail*'s role'), and, as a sop to its concerns, some of the Foreign Office's own version of events. The Attorney-General had advised against any disciplinary action being commented on by Ministers until after the Debate. He had also been concerned that the earlier draft had been in its tone too hostile to the Radcliffe Report. Heath had meanwhile been to No.10 to read the Report (and had alarmed the Prime Minister's Office by asking for some notepaper; Wigg and the Cabinet Office were rapidly consulted, and, rather than being frisked as he left, the Leader of Her Majesty's Opposition was merely rather unnecessarily reminded of the sensitive nature of the Report's contents).

Wilson again met the Ministers and senior officials concerned on 7 June, when the arrangements for the publication of the Radcliffe Report and the Government's repudiatory White Paper were finalised (Trevelyan was in the unusual position of having a major hand in writing both). Having been presented with the voluminous papers only the night before, the rest of the Cabinet was then effectively presented with a fait accompli on 13 June, immediately before publication later that day. They could only caution against making Lohan a scapegoat for what they perceived as the faults principally of senior civil servants. Richard Crossman in his diary characterised Wilson as having for the first time taken 'the strictly presidential line' by refusing to allow prior discussion by Ministers of his handling of the case; and Barbara Castle thought he had 'gone off his rocker', although she also recorded Wilson's lingering doubts about the course chosen, and his anger at 'intolerable slackness among top civil servants', and his blaming the Conservatives for not having put Lohan through the positive vetting process.[70]

The Lohan 'Disciplinary' Committee

Even before the Radcliffe Report and the White Paper had been finalised, however, the long planned internal Civil Service investigation had begun into whether any offence had been committed. Although Wilson had personally authorised forensic examination of Lohan's receipts for Notices signed by *Daily Express* messengers [one of whom was briefly the most humble witness to appear before the Radcliffe Committee], there was even so no conclusive proof that the Colonel had altered a receipt to support his rather than Pincher's version of events. Lohan was summoned on 31 May and 1 June to appear before a small committee of senior officials to be, in his word, 'interrogated'. Because told he was entitled to have a 'friend' present should he wish, he understood it to be a disciplinary committee. A la Kafka, no allegation was made against him, and neither was it explained to him in what way his conduct had been called into question. Afterwards, Dunnett reported on 5 June to Wigg that he had been 'very conscious throughout my interview with him of the points made by the Prime Minister[71] . . . but he was very much in control . . . whatever Lohan's view of the events . . . he is certainly not going to welch on his contacts.'[72]

Lohan himself however felt this summons compromised his position as the 'middle-man' between the Government and the Press, as it destroyed the necessary independence from official pressure which the D-Notice Secretary must be seen to have. Because he considered his position was now 'untenable', he therefore tendered his resignation on 9 June. The news that Lohan had appeared before 'a disciplinary committee' had appeared the same morning in the London Day by Day column of the *Daily Telegraph*, edited by William Deedes (as it happened, Lohan's MP).[73]

The MoD immediately launched an investigation into this 'leakage of official information'. This revealed Lohan had told Pincher on 31 May he was involved in an internal enquiry, but allegedly nothing else 'of importance'. Pincher had then telephoned an MoD AUS, his friend John Drew,[74] who had merely tried to find out Pincher's source, also hearing of the *Express'* suspicion the Government was delaying the publication of the Report until some suitable day on which there was even worse news. On 6 June Lohan had reported to the MoD Press Office that, the previous evening at a *Newsweek* party attended by several politicians, an unnamed official had told a journalist (who had contacted Lohan next day) the Radcliffe Report would come out 'in Pincher's favour', but 'the skids were under Sammy'.

This official turned out to be a Wing Commander in the MoD Press Office, who denied he had used those words, allegedly being unaware of the Lohan enquiry. Deedes had told Lohan on 8 June 'a senior official' had rung him and given him the whole story;[75] the same day Deedes accosted two No.10 Press Officers in the House, and 'with what one can only describe as a gleam in his eye, and rubbing his hands' remarked 'I think we are going to have some fun next week over "D" Notices. I hope you chaps are ready to cope'. These vignettes are not atypical of the timeless ways in which official information travels quickly from the inner recesses of Whitehall over the back fence to neighbours in Parliament and the Press; such gossip is the dopamine of public life.

The MoD, in response to widespread media questioning sparked by the *Telegraph*, denied any disciplinary action against Lohan, but made it clear that he was subject to Civil Service regulations. 'In accordance with normal practice . . . inquiries have been made of various persons who were concerned in an official capacity with the events and circumstances leading up to the Radcliffe Enquiry, and naturally Colonel Lohan was one of the people of whom such enquiries were made'. Reporting the resignation subsequently, *The Times* of 10 June added: 'Members of the Services, Press and Broadcasting Committee from both sides of the fence are believed to be very concerned at the course of events leading up to Colonel Lohan's impending resignation. His Whitehall colleagues are reported to be indignant at the way he has been treated'. From its Press Office staff, MoD quickly lined up an acting replacement as SPBC Secretary, Thomas Cochrane (see below), who wisely advised this should not be mentioned by the Prime Minister until the Media side of the Committee had been consulted.

Wilson meanwhile had been in search of a sympathetic ear in the Press, and on 9 June rang Hugh Cudlipp at the *Mirror*. He explained he could not say anything about the Radcliffe Report before it was published, but it would 'reveal a lot of material . . . which would not be very nice'. Colonel Lohan had 'some very odd contacts'. He hoped people would not think Lohan had been victimised. He (Wilson) would welcome the opportunity to discuss the background with Cudlipp, not the disciplinary aspects but simply fact-finding to see how the D-Notice System could be improved. Cudlipp agreed to meet with Wilson in the Commons the day before the Report and White Paper were published; on that occasion, unlike their telephone call, no Civil Service ears were listening, so no record remains.[76] If however the Prime Minister thought Cudlipp would be willing or able to dampen media criticism, he was anyway wrong.

The Radcliffe Report

On 13 June, the Radcliffe Report and accompanying White Paper were at last issued, the latter an apparent surprise to those outside the inner circle. Part I of the former summarised the characteristics of the D-Notice System as previously covered in more detail in Radcliffe's previous Report of 1962, and reiterated 'The Secretary's office is therefore the central point of the system'. This part also alluded to the 'special occasions' when 'the Secretary finds himself urging with respect to a particular piece of news that has suddenly broken that, whether or not it is covered by a "D" Notice or even if it is not so covered, it is undesirable, unwise or unsafe that it should be published. It may be a very sensible thing to offer such advice in a particular context. But action of this kind falls outside the "D" Notice system'. In such cases it was wholly within an editor's discretion how he responded. The point was made as particularly relevant to this case.

Part II of the Report reprinted Pincher's article of 21 February, and then asked and answered three questions:

–   Is this article an accurate account of the facts with which it purports to deal?
    The Radcliffe Committee concluded the practice described was authorised, long
    established and used, and properly carried out to the limited degree justified.
    The Pincher article itself 'was not inaccurate in any sense that could expose it
    to hostile criticism on that score'.
–   Is it a breach of any one or more of the 'D' Notices?
–   Is it contrary to anything that can be called the procedure or conventions of the
    'D' Notice system? The Committee answered these two questions together.
    Having detailed the relevant parts of the two Notices, it unravelled the
    conflicting strands of the narrative to produce the most likely sequence, as
    described earlier in this History, and reviewed all the evidence. Their conclusion
    was that 'it would not be right to say that the article amounted to a breach of
    the "D" Notices; and that there was not any procedure that required an editor
    to observe a "stop" on publication on those . . . exceptional cases . . .where the
    Secretary, on behalf of the Committee, maintains that a "D" Notice request is
    involved and the editor is unable to agree that it is'.

Part III of the Report turned to 'Possible Improvements to "D" Notice System'. 'We have come to the conclusion that there is not much in the way of alteration that can usefully be recommended for the "D" Notice system. It is not that anyone familiar with its working thinks of it as perfect or as so constructed as to offer a guarantee that mistakes or breaches will never occur. It is, after all, a voluntary arrangement, embracing a very large number of independent publications, directed to securing the suppression of certain categories of news which arise, often under great pressure of handling, in unpredictable forms and combinations. But what was emphasised to us by a number of witnesses was that, despite its imperfections, it has worked effectively for a number of years, and, so far as we could learn, its working has not been the cause of any substantial dissatisfaction to those who are party to it. This is a striking fact when it is recalled that we are speaking of a free Press which is alive to the importance of asserting its independence of Government control. It indicates a sense of responsibility and editorial care that are very much to the credit of all concerned.'

The Committee continued that it considered that any significant attempt to make the arrangements more watertight might make it break down under the strain, and that it could think of no alternative which could be put in its place. It set itself against suggestions of 'breathing space' pauses or appeals, for practical reasons of time pressure and of finding an acceptable independent arbitrator 'ready to carry out at very short notice the delicate work of adjudication'. The current case had been an exceptional one, and improvements in procedures and liaison could be made, as well as 'a closer delimitation of the functions of the Secretary'. The Report ended by making 16 conclusions and recommendations. These were that:

(1)   No new practices had been introduced in recent years in the interception of
      telegrams.
(2)   The *Daily Express* article of 21 February had not been generally inaccurate.

(3) There was no simple answer to the question of whether the article had breached the October 1961 D-Notice, based on the words of the Notice.

(4) A narrower reading of the April 1956 Notice had prevailed in practice than the literal wording implied, and it would not therefore be right to say that the *Daily Express* had breached this Notice.

(5) The SPBC was invited to rewrite the Notice of April 1956, and some wider restriction was suggested.

(6) The October 1961 Notice, although cryptic, had not been breached.

(7) There was no evidence that the editorial decision to publish had been taken 'with a deliberate intention of evading or defying "D" notice procedure or conventions'.

(8) 'There is not much in the way of alteration that could usefully be recommended for the "D" notice system'.

(9) It was unsatisfactory that the SPBC Secretary should be the Government spokesman on questions that lay outside 'D' Notices and turned on national interest.

(10) The Secretary should report at once to the SPBC Chairman if in an unresolved dispute with a newspaper on application of a Notice, or on a matter to which current Notices had no apparent application.

(11) The SPBC Chairman might on occasion wish to ask the 2nd PUS of the MoD to act as his Deputy on Committee business.

(12) The Secretary ought to have a Deputy.

(13) 'Effort must be made to see that the Secretary is properly informed as to the facts that lie behind any "D" Notice request'.

(14) Two of the three 2nd PUSs in the MoD [there was then still one for each Armed Service] should be replaced on the Committee by the Home Office PUS and the Deputy Under-Secretary of the Foreign Office.

(15) It was accepted that the Editor of *The Spectator* had published the text of the two relevant Notices under the misapprehension that his journal was not a participant in the system; but all Notices should be treated as confidential documents and withheld from publication.

(16) The Committee of Privy Counsellors did not agree with the editor of the *Spectator*'s suggestion that there were certain circumstances of public interest in which, after warning the SPBC, an editor should at his discretion publish a confidential Notice.

The Government's White Paper Response

It is little wonder these conclusions were disappointing to a Prime Minister and coterie who had chosen to put so much political energy into the follow-up to Pincher's article. Nevertheless, the Government's simultaneous White Paper,[77] far from burying the unwelcome outcome, exacerbated it. The Paper started by re-justifying the official position: 'It is the duty of the Government, in the light of all the advice they have received and the information they possess, to record that the effect on national security of that publication has been to cause damage, potentially grave, the consequences of which cannot even now be fully assessed. It is to examine the circumstances which led to this state of affairs that the Government feel it necessary to present this White Paper.'

Having welcomed the Radcliffe Report, and accepted its recommendations on the operation of the D-Notice System, the Government then went on, through 14 pages of closely-argued prose, to disagree or quibble with almost all the rest of it. It said none of the officials, nor Lohan, had fully appreciated the significance of the 'limited information' on which Pincher had initially asked for advice. Lohan had failed to tell officials he had told Pincher on 16 February the Notices did not apply, and had failed to make clear to officials he had doubts about the instructions given to him after the 17 February meeting chaired by Ewart-Biggs. Lohan had missed the implications of Pincher's jocular remarks as they left their 20 February lunch, and had therefore failed to inform his Chairman or officials of the true position, with the result that there was no opportunity to make a high-level intervention until the article was already being printed. Radcliffe's Committee considered Lohan should have been invited to attend the initial Foreign Office meeting, but this was not possible because 'matters to be discussed were of the most secret nature and only those officials who had gone through the appropriate security procedures could properly attend'.

The *Daily Express*, the White Paper went on, 'must bear the direct responsibility for what happened and the development of events leaves little doubt that there was a determination to print'. Picking out relevant sentences from the Radcliffe Report, it criticised Pincher in particular for having ignored Lohan's 'urgent appeal on behalf of the Government for the suppression of the story', about which there was no disagreement, and for having failed to keep Lohan informed about the editorial decision-making, especially at about 6.30 p.m. on 20th. 'It was the nation's security that suffered as a consequence.'

The White Paper then dealt with 'The Three Main Issues'. On the accuracy of the *Daily Express* article, it disagreed with the Privy Counsellors: 'It would be contrary to the public interest to say in what detailed respects the article was misleading. The Government do not, in any event, take the view that these are decisive in assessing the nature of the article or the impression which it was intended to, and did, convey. The Government adhere to the view that the article was, in the words of the Prime Minister in the House on 21st February, 1967 "sensationalised and inaccurate" . . . [it was] intended to convey, and succeeded in conveying, the impression that the Government were responsible for introducing new invasions of privacy or for distorting existing procedures to this end. These imputations are in no way borne out by the facts'.

On a breach of the D-Notices, while accepting the Radcliffe Committee's views about interpretations of ambiguous phrases, the White Paper pointed out it was not just the Press who were involved in such interpretation, but also the Government, and only it had all the necessary background; 'The difficulty is that to establish the applicability of these "D" notices beyond doubt, it is necessary to have a full knowledge of the activities involved'; but for reasons of security it was not always possible to disclose to others any background on these activities. When the Prime Minister had been speaking in the House about the relevance of the two Notices, he had been 'expressing the clear and unanimous conviction of all those who carry responsibility in these matters that the *Daily Express* article in question was in breach of "D" notices'. Based on the same evidence as had been available to the Privy Counsellors, the Government therefore disagreed that the Notices had not been breached. On any failure to observe D-Notice procedures, the Government did however accept the *Express* had not been at fault, 'since the editor, according to his evidence, was not made aware, in time to be of value, of the official view that the publication would involve a breach of "D" notices. It is regrettable that this was so'.

Finally the White Paper addressed 'Improvements to the "D" Notice System'. About the relevant Notices it commented: 'Any Government is, however, faced with a basic dilemma. On the one hand it is impossible to draft all "D" notices in precise and specific terms without revealing far too many of the secrets which the system was designed to protect; "D" notices in precise terms could not, in any case, hope to give comprehensive coverage; and they might well require statutory reinforcement in the long run . . . But on the other hand, "D" notices of a general nature can only give protection if there is complete trust on both sides. Under the present system, the Press must be prepared to accept official interpretations of the applicability of certain "D" notices to particular cases, subject, of course, to the ultimate responsibility of an editor to take the final decision'. It concluded that in these circumstances the current system was viable, that the present incident had arisen out of a series of avoidable misunderstandings and the failures by the *Daily Express*, and it asked the SPBC urgently to review the wording of the D-Notice of April 1956.

On the D-Notice System in general, the White Paper welcomed the Radcliffe Committee's conclusion that not much in the way of alteration was needed. 'The successful operation of this system over a period of years is a remarkable fact', protecting the rights and privileges of a free Press 'which, with the potent weapon at its command, must guard the public interest', while also paying 'proper regard to national security'. In supporting the recommendations about the role of the D-Notice Secretary, it observed that in this episode the fact that 'he based his main case on wider arguments meant that he ceased to speak with the authority of his Committee', whereas in such cases it should be for Ministers to decide how the Government's case should be made. On Lohan not having had the appropriate security clearances to have been given the complete picture, the White Paper claimed that before this case officials had already been reviewing the clearance requirements; in future the Secretary would have the full security vetting and necessary clearances. The Radcliffe Committee's other recommendations concerning the system were accepted, subject to agreement by the SPBC.

41

ROCKS ALL AROUND

Parliamentary and Press Reaction

Radcliffe Report and White Paper were immediately and widely headlined throughout the Media, and there was a brief initial debate in Parliament. Led by Heath, the Opposition concentrated on the Privy Counsellors' rejection of Wilson's previous accusations against the *Daily Express*, on his rejection of their major conclusions, on the position of Colonel Lohan and his summons to the Civil Service investigation, and on what personal responsibility Wilson took for the faults revealed.[78] That evening both Chapman Pincher and Lohan were interviewed several times, on BBC and ITN television news, on the widely watched late night programme '24 Hours', and on radio.

The Press that evening (13 June) and on the following days treated the story with varying degrees of colour, from very comprehensive extracts of both documents in *The Times*, *Telegraph* and *Guardian*, to more selective extracts in most other papers, with much prominence to theatrical details such as the Garrick Club and L'Ecu. The *Daily Mail* included a photograph of Colonel Lohan sitting on an Embankment bench in the June sun, watch-chain across waistcoat, bowler hat on lap, luxuriant moustache over jutting lower lip, above a caption 'My position is now impossible'. The *Daily Express* gave major coverage to its exoneration by Radcliffe. The widespread ridicule of the Prime Minister for his reaction to the Privy Counsellors' Report gave cartoonists much delight.

On his vetting, Lohan immediately spread the word to the Press that he had indeed been positively vetted within the previous two years and 'many times before.'[79] The angry and embittered Colonel spoke freely to the Press in the following days about other aspects too. He told the *Daily Telegraph* the criticism of him in the White Paper (of which he was clearly aware a few days before it was published) was 'so great in fact that my effectiveness as secretary has been completely destroyed', and that 'It is all very well for people to talk in hindsight, but if this situation arose again I would act in exactly the same way.' He was the subject of the main interview in the *Sunday Times* of 18 June, where he was described as 'loud and jolly, fond of good lunches, frantically extroverted, full of jokes and funny voices, loved by all defence journalists'. He complained his many successes were never mentioned, and 'could only imagine that someone has been out to get me and ruin the voluntary system. Not Mr Wilson, just someone important in Whitehall. I suppose that what will happen now is that a committee of civil servants will take weeks deciding whether some story is good, bad or indifferent. That won't work. I think the D Notice was the best system'. He clearly thought it would not survive.

Meanwhile political correspondents were being intensively briefed by both Labour and the Conservatives, the latter more gainfully; 'Tories Find Radcliffe "Trap" for Wilson –

"Incriminating" Phrase' was the *Daily Telegraph* headline on 15 June. The Opposition believed Wilson was vulnerable 'out of his own mouth' on his decision to reject the main Radcliffe findings, referring back to what he said when he first established the Committee of Privy Counsellors the previous February – 'to rely on their judgement on all of these very difficult problems'. The newspaper reflected what many others were saying: 'What puzzles many MPs is why Mr Wilson should have got himself into such a needlessly awkward situation. He is not the first Prime Minister to find great difficulty in ever admitting that he was wrong.'

Follow-Up to the Publications

Wilson summoned Wigg, Trend and Dunnett on 15 June to discuss follow-up actions. These included Dunnett interviewing Lohan imminently about whether he did intend to resign; if not, sending him immediately on unpaid leave because of his 'recent actions in relation to the Press and Television'; recovering any classified papers in his possession, including letters to and from Sir Richard Way; arranging that the SPBC meeting requested by the Media side should not take place until after the Commons Debate on 22 June; and sending a holding letter to editors about the relevant D-Notices now being revised in the light of Radcliffe's recommendations. Wilson also asked the head of the Civil Service Sir Laurence Helsby to investigate and report on the history of Lohan's PV process, by close of business the next day.[80] It is unusual for such minutiae to receive so much top-level attention.

When Dunnett saw Lohan next day, the Colonel accepted immediately he was subject to Civil Service regulations, saying his resignation letter was being typed, but that he was being pressed by the SPBC Media side not formally to resign until the Committee had met. Dunnett ran through the PV position, and Lohan agreed he had never been taken through the final stage, but repeated what had been said in the Way correspondence ('he clearly knows it pretty well by heart', Dunnett reported). When formally warned about handing over official documents, Lohan laughed at the idea he might contravene the rules. His final point was that one of his four sons was still being educated and 'costing him about £700 a year'; he was anxious therefore to find another job, perhaps as a Queen's Messenger, and he very much hoped 'the present trouble would not prejudice his chances.'[81]

Healey duly reported the outcome of this interview to Wilson, and that the Paymaster General was content. Lohan's resignation letter included: 'One thing is important; on no occasion did anyone tell me that the lives of Servicemen or Secret Agents were in danger. Had I been able to use this ploy I should have been only too delighted.' He ended by pointing out that the public statements about his lack of access to highly secret information meant the Press now believed 'I have hoodwinked them for years by pretending to know matters about which I knew nothing because I was a security risk. This should be put right. I pray that this rotten affair can now be killed once and for all and I can resign with some dignity. I need another job and as things go now, I am being slandered out of the business.'[82]

Wigg and Wilson Fight Back

Meanwhile the paranoid atmosphere in Whitehall persisted. Even British ambassadors abroad were sent instructions not to comment but to report local reactions; only Madrid responded: there had been considerable interest (one paper headlining 'Farce of the D-Notices') because Spain also had an OSA and 'a Government given to prying, phone-tapping.'[83]

In London, Wigg was homing in on details in Helsby's report on Lohan's PV, including his suspicion that Way had deliberately sent Trend's adverse 1965 comment on Lohan to the Colonel (despite an immediate investigation then which had concluded it was an office mistake). Officials were already writing papers on the future of the D-Notice System, as envisaged by themselves and some Ministers.[84] At the beginning of the week in which Wilson was to meet editors at 10 Downing Street, he was in Paris for talks,[85] but the post-Radcliffe conflict was large in his mind. On 19 June, a Flash Secret telegram was sent to 10 Downing Street by Halls in the British Embassy in Paris, 'to be deciphered personally by Le Cheminant',[86] the Prime Minister's junior Private Secretary, with instructions to Wigg to obtain transcripts of all the television interviews given by Pincher the previous Tuesday (13 June), and to examine them 'to see whether what Chapman Pincher said in these interviews went further than what he said in evidence to Radcliffe'. The Prime Minister also wanted the Paymaster General to know that 'after further reflection he thinks that the line which he and the Paymaster discussed on Saturday night for his speech in the debate is not (repeat not) sufficiently aggressive.'[87]

Wigg immediately set to with the Whips Office to comb for discrepancies the transcripts of the dozen programmes in which Pincher had taken part or been quoted. That evening Wigg sent the Prime Minister three points: firstly on the timing of the first (17 February) reference to 'diplomatic furore' ('It is clear that Pincher is lying' [but it seems Wigg misunderstood what had already passed between Pincher and Lohan]); secondly on the conversation with Abba Eban during the following weekend ('Apart from the despicable behaviour of Pincher in going into this aspect of security with a Foreign Minister of a Foreign Power, Pincher also shows that he is continuing his lies about the pressure put on him to discontinue his story' [the slight variations in Pincher's words were not in fact incompatible, and he did not tell Eban why he was asking the question]); and thirdly on whether Lohan had replied to a question from Pincher during their lunch that there was no specific operation involving spies in progress [the two wordings on 'in progress' were similar, unless the qualification 'at that time' was given a particular and precise significance]. In the intensive political discourse of the following weeks, these weak 'discrepancies' found by Wigg did not feature noticeably.[88]

Wigg Briefs Wilson

The same day, George Wigg sent Wilson two other briefs. The first was about the forthcoming meeting with editors: 'There is little doubt that the editors will be a hostile audience (although you will have friends),[89] but they are undoubtedly aware that their own position is far from strong since if they fail to meet any reasonable proposals or are deliberately obstructive, this can redound to their known discredit'. Wigg's suggestions included that Wilson should stress the Government wished to maintain and strengthen the D-Notice System, not to follow (as had been suggested by a few in the Press recently) the American and continental example of legislation; that the Government considered the discussion confidential, the meeting being billed merely as the first of several to secure continuance of the System; that the Government wished to liberalise the System rather than make it more restrictive; that the 'most profitable line of approach' might be to investigate reconstituting the SPBC so that it enjoyed full Government and Press confidence and support; and that the Committee should play a more active role in ensuring the full observation of D-Notices and in managing 'difficult cases'.

Wilson should suggest the appointment of a new and eminent Chairman, independent of both government and official circles, possibly a Privy Counsellor, security cleared and fully briefed, and 'readily available to deal with matters of importance immediately as they arise'; there should be two Deputy Chairmen, one a similarly independent person, the other a senior official; and the Secretariat should be augmented to include a Secretary and a Deputy Secretary (together with supporting staff), one of whom would be an ex-official now employed in Fleet Street, the other a civil service information officer, both appropriately security cleared and briefed. If Lohan's position were raised, Wilson should say this would be dealt with in the House on 22 June. Wigg's brief ended: 'Please at all costs remember your audience will be hostile and *ignorant*. So give them a tute [tutorial] – *teach them* what it is all about.'[90]

The other Wigg brief, classified 'Secret', was a 'fuller account' of the Media meeting which had taken place on June 16 at the offices of the Newspaper Proprietors' Association, with 15 editors present. It had been called 'to consider the attitude of the NPA to the meeting you have called for Wednesday next, June 21'. Wigg had not of course been at that meeting, but had clearly been debriefed by someone who had, referred to in this brief as 'my friend.'[91] Lee Howard, having resigned from the SPBC, had been put in the chair, and, the 'friend' reported, the hatred of Wilson personally of the IPC and *Express* Group editors 'had to be experienced to be believed'. The informant recommended that Wilson nevertheless did not dodge any differences with them.

The NPA meeting had decided editors should act individually rather than collectively, and a collective boycott of the Prime Minister's meeting had been rejected; because the IPC editors had backed the boycott proposal, the informant wondered whether Cecil King was behind the idea, but neither King nor Cudlipp had lobbied the informant, who also thought Berry of the *Telegraphs* had told his otherwise hostile editors not to support a boycott; Marks had decided that because his position at the meeting with Wilson would be 'impossible', he would not attend. Discussion of the extent to which the Prime Minister would exploit the meeting included Harold Evans[92] of the *Sunday Times* mimicking how he thought Wilson would use it in the House of Commons; the general view of the editors had been that the Prime Minister's meeting was a 'diversionary tactic' [i.e. to dampen the attacks on his handling of the affair in the Press]. 'The responsible elements at the meeting made up, for the most part, by those who had taken the trouble to read the Radcliffe Report, were in favour of meeting the Prime Minister because he would otherwise be able to claim that they had not responded'[93].

A marked difference of opinion over the treatment of Lohan had emerged amongst the editors; Maurice Green[94] of the *Daily Telegraph* suggested some written, financial or job offer support for him, but this was opposed by Arthur Brittenden of the *Daily Mail*, who contrasted the different advice Lohan had given to his paper and to the *Express*. Brittenden also 'inferred that Lohan had been looked after quite well [financially] in the past. My [Wigg's] friend, who thoroughly understands the workings of the *Express* newspapers, confirms that the suggestion was not explicit and, indeed, it would be quite impossible for anyone to be explicit about the subject of past help. If it had been given neither Brittenden nor anyone else would know' [Did Wigg protest too much?].

Wigg also reported his 'friend' was convinced that, if at any time from 16 February, a direct approach had been made to Marks himself at the *Express*, the story would not have been printed; and suggested that by mid-evening on 20 February 'the atmosphere on both sides had become mildly alcoholic and by that time the fear of being scooped would become so great the problem would be very difficult indeed to handle'. Wintour of the *Evening Standard* and 'Gould of the *Daily Sketch*' [actually John Gold of the *Evening News*] had attacked the whole D-Notice System, but had not been supported; however, Wigg and/or his informant said that if Wilson persisted with his Court of Appeal idea, the opposition might grow very considerably. The 'friend' believed Pincher had convinced himself the Government was using the security procedure improperly for political advantage.

Wigg summed up this conspiratorial brief: 'The opposition which the Government and yourself must face is basically emotional and ignorant. There has been little study of what the row is all about and the job you have to do is to formulate the differences – you have got to explain that you are concerned with security, the liberty of the subject and putting right the damage caused by the irresponsibility and inefficiency of individuals. My friend believes you can do it, but don't under-estimate the task ahead of you, particularly the long term task of mending fences over a very wide area.'[95]

Wigg also harried the Secretary of the Radcliffe Committee, asking why the Privy Counsellors had not paid more regard to officials on whether the two relevant D-Notices applied to Pincher's article. Radcliffe replied firmly this had turned on Colonel Lohan's position. The Committee had felt that, since 'there could be no definitive ruling on the interpretation of a D-Notice', it was necessary to approach this question from the point of view of those concerned with the actual working of the system, namely the Media and the successive Secretaries (as 'also the Government spokesman on "D" Notice matters'). In practice over the years, these had come to understand the 'limited' interpretation of the wording of the Notices in question. Officials on the other hand were not in direct contact with the Media in these matters, and therefore 'it is irrelevant what views officials might privately have held on this matter'. Radcliffe acknowledged this view was not however spelt out anywhere in the evidence.

This argument was difficult for Wigg and officials to stomach, but in logic it is impeccable. It also highlights why the D-Notice Secretary and officials must have a close understanding of each other's positions, the lack of which, as Radcliffe perceived, was at the heart of the whole debacle. Wigg wrote to Wilson that, having discussed this with Trevelyan, he (Wigg) now realised the Committee had accepted it when 'Lohan got himself across as the "D" Notice king . . . assisted in this by Greenhill's evidence as the Deputy Secretary in the Foreign Office responsible, who did not know what the two "D" Notices were'. Wigg still found it 'astonishing' the Radcliffe Committee had accepted Lohan as the one expert official giving evidence on behalf of the Government who, because he was not PV'd or indoctrinated, 'knew little of what the operation was about.'[96]

Wilson's First Meeting with Editors

On the morning of the 21 June meeting with editors, Heath tabled an amendment to the Government's motion (which approved its own White Paper on the D-Notice System), for debate in Parliament next day; in effect the amendment censured Wilson for rejecting the main findings of the Radcliffe Report. Late that afternoon, 32 editors and managers[97] (and Dunnett, and Wilson's private office and press staff) gathered at 10 Downing Street. Wilson opened as briefed on the confidentiality of the meeting, but immediately departed from Wigg's more confrontational line. He said the Government 'had come to the conclusion before February that the D-Notice system needed to be examined'. He acknowledged there had been 'serious shortcomings' in the Government's handling of this case, but it was of unusual character, as it was not one of the Defence Departments which was involved as the lead, but the Foreign Office; liaison with the D-Notice Secretary had therefore had to be improvised, and the SPBC Chairman had not been informed until 7 p.m.

Before throwing it open to discussion, he detailed what 'the Government' had already considered as possible solutions: an 'independent' appeal procedure, and the involvement of a Privy Counsellor (either as the recipient of appeals, or as Committee Chairman), despite the time factor difficulties; the interpretation to editors of the 'precise meaning of D-Notices' by the independent person, but without informing them of precisely why a Notice was being issued; the recruitment of the Secretary and possibly also the Chairman from Fleet Street (he mentioned Donald McLachlan[98] as a possible such Chairman, with a senior civil servant as his Deputy). Having restated that it was of course for each editor to make the final decision on publication, he then almost threw it open for discussion, but first asked the editors to suggest how they would like to take matters forward, himself suggesting that before further meetings of the present sort, the Media might like to delegate discussion to their members on the D-Notice Committee.

Two present with SPBC experience, Windsor Clarke[99] and Lee Howard, immediately asked 'what particular points had prompted the Government before February to think the "D" Noticed system needed to be reviewed. They pointed out that it had, in fact, worked well over the whole period since the War'. Wilson had to admit he had no particular case in mind, but that the Chairman was a busy civil servant, often abroad, and for this reason 'the Government had felt before February that there ought to be a Chairman who was free to devote himself more fully, when the need arose, to the "D" Notice arrangements.'[100] Moreover, Wilson continued, there was the question of whether the Secretary 'ought not to be cleared from a security point of view so that he could be fully briefed on the background'.

Clarke, supported by Christiansen[101] of the *Sunday Mirror*, commented that all had worked entirely satisfactorily when Admiral Thomson had been Secretary; perhaps the post did indeed need to be upgraded, and an independent person with the right clearances appointed, and with a Deputy. Wilson said that, because of his wartime experience, Thomson had been 'in rather a special position', that, if the system were to be based on trust when Notices did not apply 'it would create difficulties in a case where, for example, two Editors were involved, one of whom was considered trustworthy and one who was not'.

Wilson returned to his point that the Secretary could only properly operate 'within the scope of the meaning of existing "D" Notices'. Where, as in this case, the Secretary had to extend his operations outside this field to wider matters in the national interest, a chairman independent of government would be more likely than a civil servant to have the confidence of an editor. Clarke, Sir Gordon Newton[102] and John Junor[103] expressed concern that such an SPBC Chairman would be responsible for making direct requests to editors to refrain from publication on matters which were not covered by existing 'D' Notices. Others agreed that in such cases of non-D-Notice 'national interest', any direct approach should only come to editors from Ministers. Wilson said he was referring only to the limited field of security and intelligence matters; the Government's suggestion was that, in such cases, the Chairman would be acting more as an 'honest broker' than as Chairman of the Committee.

Several editors suggested that, in cases where the Notices did not apply, they would expect to be given sufficient evidence to convince them about the request for non-publication, something which nobody had been able to do in the cable-vetting case. Wilson countered that, while high trust was needed to enable the system to work, there were some highly sensitive matters which the Government could not reveal at all, and he doubted whether editors would want to be placed in the position of knowing such material.[104]

Richard Dinsdale[105] said he did not see how editors could be expected to accept an independent Chairman 'as a sort of referee'; Wilson used the 'honest broker' description again, and said the Government too would 'probably' have to accept the independent Chairman's view even if he did not agree with its 'ideas on the scope of national interest'. Lee Howard asked what view the Government would take if the Media were to decide the current system had worked well and did not need change, to which Wilson replied 'the Government would of course have to consider carefully any such advice. But nothing was perfect and, in any case, the Government would itself want to make changes to its representatives on the 'D' Notice Committee, including the Chairmanship', which would not be a full-time appointment; but it should be paid, and he thought the Press would wish to discuss the terms and how the salary should be financed. Lee Howard said he was puzzled by the 'loose talk' about the 'spirit' of the D-Notices; Wilson explained Radcliffe had referred to the way in which Notices had come to be interpreted in a certain way over time; this, Wilson considered, weakened the system, and tighter drafting could overcome the difficulty.

Summing up, the Prime Minister invited further discussion, and, perhaps realising his ideas about an independent Chairman had not found favour, suggested his functions might be limited to 'the field of "D" Notices'. Harold Evans said it might not be easy to surmise the view of the Press as a whole from the limited group of editors present, but Wilson said it was up to the Media as to how they consulted and for how long. Meanwhile the SPBC would continue as it was pro tem, specifically to redraft the two relevant D-Notices, and to make intermediate arrangements for the Secretaryship of the Committee.[106]

House of Commons Debate on the White Paper

Next day (22 June) in the House of Commons there was a late debate on the affair. Even before discussion started, the Conservative Opposition attacked the Prime Minister for delegating the opening of the debate to the Attorney-General, Sir Elwyn Jones.[107] The Government's line was that what was at issue was not the 'mere interpretation' of the Notices nor the Press conduct in this case, nor even the Prime Minister; 'It is the fundamental question of a nation's security and how, in a free and democratic society, it can be preserved'. A full explanation of the background would not be possible for security reasons, but Jones ran through the public story, including that all officials involved ('save, perhaps, Colonel Lohan himself, who at all material times, unfortunately, kept his reservations to himself'), had been convinced the relevant Notices applied, and that had been the basis of the Prime Minister's 21 February statement to the House. 'Accordingly, there can be no substance in the charge that the Prime Minister deliberately misled the House' [cries of dissent from the Opposition] when he said the *Daily Express* had been repeatedly warned it was contravening the D-Notices.

Anthony Barber[108] tabled the alternative Opposition motion, accepting not the White Paper but the Report of the Privy Counsellors. He described the White Paper's 'over-riding purpose' as being 'to establish the infallibility of the Prime Minister against all the evidence and contrary to the findings of the Radcliffe Committee'. He attacked administrative incompetence and the idea of a Court of Appeal, referred to the 'universal condemnation' of Wilson's 'arrogant' behaviour in the face of the opinions of others, including editors, and gave a detailed critique of events, some of which he characterised as 'pure comic opera'. Finally, referring to the new allegation by the Government that the *Express* disclosure was a potential 'danger to men's lives', Barber asked why the Foreign Secretary had not therefore intervened earlier. He challenged Wilson to admit he had made a mistake.

Shinwell announced his intention of pouring a little oil on troubled waters, as the Opposition seemed more interested in castigating the Prime Minister than in the need for safeguarding national security. It was important to consider 'motivation' before discussing what had happened, and, although Wilson could perhaps be criticised for not having ascertained all the facts before intervening, he was justified in taking his stance because of his concern for security. Shinwell confirmed he himself thought the article should not have been published, but then, referring to the rejection of the Privy Counsellors' report, caused laughter by asking the Prime Minister 'It is all very well to dissemble one's love, but why kick us downstairs?' He went on to give his assessment of the personalities and relationships involved. 'In a James Bond story one meets professionals. Here we met amateurs'. Pincher was just doing his job, but Lohan ('a very interesting [and later in the speech 'strange'] character') was the only one 'who really might be incorporated in the next James Bond film'. But the Foreign Office did not trust him, would not give him all the facts, and 'would not have him on the premises' when they decided to instruct him. In this respect Lohan had been badly treated.[109]

Selwyn Lloyd reminded the House the D-Notice System was voluntary, that orders could not therefore be given by officials, as some of them had appeared to think, and that the Secretary was the servant of the whole Committee. He urged that the System should not be over-formalised, and did not think asking a Privy Counsellor to be available day and night would work. Wilson intervened to say this was something being discussed with editors, but that because of the time factor, he agreed this idea was 'probably the wrong answer in the circumstances'. Other Conservative MPs attacked Wilson for implying without foundation that the Pincher article had put 'men's lives at stake', and Lohan's MP William Deedes criticised that, despite his effective acquittal, the Government had allowed 'the good name of an official to be sacrificed in this way'.

One name-blackening intervention organised beforehand by Wigg was by *Tribune* journalist Raymond Fletcher.[110] Having criticised the *Daily Express* and lampooned the excessive reaction of the Opposition, he said he had 'a serious accusation to make'. This was that Fleet Street was 'buzzing with rumours to the effect that Colonel Lohan had been the source of many of Chapman Pincher's stories . . . in the past'. Fletcher also advocated giving potential enemies 'every scrap of information that we have'. The Soviets must have found this parliamentary contribution almost as amusing as that this MP was Wigg's choice of spokesman; in 1999, publication of the defector Mitrokhin's book revealed Fletcher had been a KGB agent.

After a long and stormy debate, Heath wound up for the Opposition, saying there were two issues: national security, and the honour and integrity of the Prime Minister. Heath had seen the whole Report, including the unpublished sections, and, while agreeing these should not be published, the protection of national security and making this compatible with a free society should not be used 'as a cover for muddle and incompetence in an Administration'. Nor was it acceptable for the Prime Minister not to apologise when the Privy Counsellors had found him wrong. The Attorney-General had pitched 'the matter too high' in claiming the issue was one of the nation's security; they were dealing with just one important aspect of intelligence-gathering, and 'I have seen no evidence that men's lives were at stake.' He criticised Wilson for not having wanted an Enquiry at all, and for having made his attacks under cover of privilege. He urged the Prime Minister to take the honourable course and withdraw them; otherwise the House could 'only conclude that it is in keeping with the character of the right hon. Gentleman, as he has displayed it on so many former occasions'.

Wilson accused Heath of being obsessed with him, rather than talking about policy. He denied bias against the Press. Security had from the outset been his concern, and this had been endangered by the *Daily Express* article. The Government would have failed in its duty if it had accepted every conclusion of the Radcliffe Report. The aspect of security concerned in this case was not its purely negative sense – that of protection; as Radcliffe had explained, it referred to 'certain wider intelligence purposes which concern this country's international relations'. He also referred to the point about men's lives being endangered: 'I have not said that men's lives have been endangered by this particular article, or the events which followed it, but, equally, I cannot say that they are not being endangered. [*Laughter*]. . . . The tragedy is that they may have been endangered, or may in the future be endangered. We shall never know'.

Wilson ended, responding to earlier questions from Messrs Barber and Deedes about Lohan's Positive Vetting, by saying the Colonel's relationship with journalists (especially Pincher) had also been of concern to the previous (Conservative) Government. He revealed that consideration had been given in early 1964 to Lohan's suitability for the post, and that he had not been given 'full positive vetting clearance'. This additional information was to lead to the next stage in the Lohan affair. Meanwhile, when the House divided at the end of the debate, the Opposition motion was comfortably defeated, and the Government motion carried, both by margins which reflected its majority of seats in the House.[111] Not all Wilson's Ministers were happy however, in particular blaming the continuing influence of Wigg ('evil genius', 'Harold's Rasputin'); afterwards, however, Wilson claimed that, until Deedes had raised Lohan's name, he had not intended to mention him, and that Trend not Wigg had been the adviser who had originally set the ball rolling; Trend later retorted, however, that he had tried to get Wilson to accept the Radcliffe Report.[112]

Afterwards, Wilson wrote to Healey: 'The Debate being over, I feel it is right now that the dead should bury their dead, and with the greatest relief I now propose to disengage myself from this extremely wearying subject'. All disciplinary procedures should now be dealt with through normal Departmental channels; on other matters, including Lohan's future as Secretary, there was now no need to consult Wilson or other Ministers. The Prime Minister would henceforth concern himself only with broad policy, interdepartmental co-ordination, and talking to editors about the future.[113] But it was not to be.

42

LOHAN IN THE SPOTLIGHT, AND RADCLIFFE BITES

Lohan next day challenged, through the Media, Wilson's end-of-debate statements about him. Radcliffe and Selwyn Lloyd (Shinwell declined to comment) said publicly they could not remember anything being said in evidence to them about an inappropriate relationship between Pincher and Lohan. There was no let-up in wider Press criticism of Wilson's handling of the affair. The *Press Gazette* of 24 June commented adversely on the ideas put to editors: 'Mr Wilson's transparently unhappy idea of shoving an ex-editorial man into Col. "Sammy" Lohan's job was a washout from the beginning. It suffered from the wishful-thinking syndrome that may have given Mr. Shinwell his place on the Radcliffe Committee – with similarly unpleasing results for No. 10'. Almost all national and provincial editors were wholeheartedly against major change to the structure of the D-Notice Committee, and the Chairman and Secretary coming from the 'newspaper world'.

Pincher himself wrote a mocking piece in the *Daily Express* on 24 June, headlined 'The Love of Two Colonels', in which he responded to the Prime Minister's insinuations he had been 'unduly friendly' with Lohan by pointing out he had been just as close socially to Wigg until they fell out in 1966 over Pincher's 'criticisms of his idol, Mr Wilson'. Pincher also clarified that the '1964 inquiries into Colonel Lohan, which the Prime Minister mentioned so mysteriously', had followed his scoop on the exchange of Lonsdale for Greville Wynne, reminding that Lohan had been suspected then of tipping Pincher off, whereas he had in fact persuaded the *Express* to hold the story until it was certain that the Soviets could not withdraw from the deal.

In more jocular paragraphs, Pincher compared Lohan's fondness for a drink with Wigg's enthusiasm for gambling on horses, and confessed that he (Pincher) had given gifts both to Lohan's wife and to Wigg; the former was as a thank you for the visitors' book from her old home,[114] the latter was a salmon caught by Pincher during one of his Scottish angling trips, for which Wigg had thanked him 'on behalf of himself, his secretary, and her cat'. Even this anecdote later became part of further memoranda between Wigg and Wilson, after a Labour MP put down a Parliamentary Question to the Prime Minister about the article.

Meanwhile at its 26 June 1967 meeting, the SPBC had accepted Lohan's resignation.[115] The Committee's statement issued afterwards thanked him for his services to them, and added 'The Press Members of the Committee wished to record the fact that they had full confidence in the Secretary'. The MoD issued its own statement, explaining that under his contract Lohan's resignation could not take effect until 1 August, but that he had asked to be relieved of his duties immediately 'because of circumstances that are now public knowledge', and, as he had had no annual leave since taking up the appointment in January 1964, he was being sent on paid leave. Lohan told the Press he had had several job offers, was anxious to clear up the slur on his character made in the House by Wilson and Shinwell, and would sue anyone who made similar remarks outside Parliament.

In his place, the SPBC now formally appointed as Acting Secretary Mr 'Tommy' Cochrane,[116] who, apart from his trade mark bow-ties, was a low-key operator very unlike his now notorious predecessor. He was immediately granted direct access by GCHQ, but not TURNSTILE clearance by the Cabinet Office, nor an 'entertainment allowance' by the Security Service. The MoD's DUS (Admin) hastily concocted Terms of Reference for him, which covered the official side of his duties beautifully, but which were almost wholly silent about the D-Notice Secretary's arcane relationship with the Media.

The 'Smearing' of Lohan

The Conservatives decided to bring the 'smear' about the improper Lohan/Pincher relationship back to Parliament for discussion. Sir Richard Glyn[117] tabled a Question on 27 June about what specific inquiries were made in 1964 into Lohan's conduct, which Ministers were involved, and who was responsible for allowing Lohan then to continue in post. Wilson at first gave a guarded answer, and offered to show relevant papers to the Leader of the Opposition; but when Heath and others followed up, his replies were seen as further blackening Lohan's name.

Wilson said the 1964 enquiry into Lohan's suitability to remain as Secretary had reviewed his 'over-close association with journalists', and that this particular anxiety was not wholly allayed. However, 'it was decided, taking everything into account, to allow the Secretary to continue in his office, which was not then a positive vetting post, for the time being'. This had not been revealed to the Radcliffe Committee because 'it was not known to any Minister or me until some days after the Radcliffe Report was published'. He said that, having been challenged by Barber and Deedes in the previous debate, 'I gave the reply and kept it to the very minimum'. He acknowledged 'my full share of responsibility and share it with my predecessors that these decisions were taken'.

Heath, who by now had seen some of the correspondence concerning the 1964 enquiry and its follow-up, asked whether it was correct that in March 1966 'very senior officials had recorded their conclusion that they were all satisfied that there were no grounds on which they could question Colonel Lohan's reliability?' An angry exchange followed between Wilson and Heath about the misuse of quotations from in-confidence papers, but this led to further criticism of the Prime Minister for having mentioned the doubts about Lohan at all. In the end, the Prime Minister said that the right answer was for Heath to see all the relevant papers and to suggest what, if any, action should be taken.[118] As The Times remarked, 'half an hour later no one had got anywhere and Colonel Lohan . . . was no better off than he was at the start of the rumpus'.

Seeking allies in the Commons, but ostensibly for 'procedural reasons', Wilson gave Thorpe as Liberal Leader a long briefing next day, 'on Privy Counsellor terms.'[119] He reminded Thorpe of the convention accepted by Wilson as Leader of the Opposition at the time of the Philby case, that he could not question officials (in that case 'C') except in the presence of the Prime Minister, and said he would not allow Heath to publish selective parts of the Helsby Report.[120]

Lohan continued to put his case to the Media, writing in The Spectator of 29 June that he had been 'slandered out of business by half-truth, untruth and innuendo'. He criticised some of those involved in the cable-vetting affair; many officials had no idea how the D-Notice

System worked, and believed the Press was there to be manipulated. 'Chapman Pincher is poison to Whitehall . . . Some idiot somewhere must have formulated the theory that I actually conspired with him, so that the story could be written and the Government embarrassed. To support this stupid and untruthful theory my reputation had to be ruined'. Lohan also now took his case to the General Secretary of the Institution of Professional Civil Servants, William McCall.[121] Because Lohan had already resigned, McCall's options were limited, but they decided to concentrate at least on retrieving the Colonel's reputation. McCall therefore immediately (30 June) wrote to the Prime Minister making two requests: that the Colonel's 'personal position should be taken out of the public and political arena' until IPCS representations were made on his behalf, and that there should be 'an investigation along the lines of the procedures well established in the Civil Service.'[122]

Sir Richard Way wrote lengthily to the Prime Minister from retirement, giving his recollection of events, 'in view of the prominence which has been given recently to Colonel Lohan's service as Secretary'. He was subsequently warned off from having any discussion himself with Heath or Thorpe, and tartly told that some errors in the dates in his accounts showed the dangers of retired officials speaking from memory.

Helsby meanwhile reported to Wilson his further findings on Lohan's PV. In addition to reminding of the detailed Positive Vetting regulations, and in particular of the position of Ministers in relation to any individual (fundamentally a PV is a departmental not a Political responsibility, for constitutional reasons), Helsby told Wilson that the senior officials concerned advised against showing the private letters to Heath, although they hoped Wilson would allude to them orally so that other supporting documentation could be so shown.[123]

Wilson Grapples with Heath and Home

When Wilson saw Heath later that day (29 June), he did not in fact mention the private letters to him, but had a tetchy discussion about access to officials and the use of other papers which could be seen. Later that day, Heath returned accompanied by Sir Alec Douglas-Home,[124] who had been the Conservative Prime Minister when the 1964 enquiry had begun. Wilson and Helsby showed them the latter's full Report on Lohan's PV history (the oblique reference to private letters went unnoticed). Douglas-Home asked why the PV information had not been shown to the Radcliffe Committee; Wilson replied they had known it was not a PV post. Douglas-Home also expressed concern about the apparent injustice to Lohan, the impression having now been given publicly he had committed some serious security offence, when his defects were primarily his drinking and alleged womanising. Heath concentrated on Ministers' knowledge of the case, and on why Lohan had had access to documents for which he had not been cleared. Wilson returned again to the 'over-close relationship' with Pincher, and other alleged leaks, including over Vassall. Wilson closed the meeting by offering further meetings, with senior officials present, and further access to documents.[125]

Afterwards, Wigg commented to Wilson inter alia on the use of the PV procedure which had been made by Way in 1964 'as an instrument of personnel management . . . a fairly common practice'; Helsby was now about to write to all Permanent Under-Secretaries forbidding such use in future. The DGSS (Furnival Jones) wrote, having investigated the Vassall allegation (also alluded to by Pincher in his Radcliffe evidence), confirming Lohan had consulted MI5 at the time; MI5 (after consulting the US authorities because of the defector link) had authorised Lohan to confirm the story, and Lohan could not have been the source because he was not one of the very few officials who knew about Vassall. Furnival

Jones had little doubt however that 'Pincher drew the right conclusion from the eventual reply and the twenty-four hours' delay that preceded it.'[126]

On 4 July Heath and Douglas-Home again went to see Wilson (with Trend and Helsby also present at Heath's request). At the end of another long discussion of now familiar points, Heath referred to the use made by MI5 of Lohan, which indicated surely he could not have been considered a security risk; Helsby said the retainer paid had been for 'titbits of information that he brought to them from Fleet Street', they had not given him any sensitive information, and 'he was in no sense taken into their confidence'. Heath also referred to a *Sunday Mirror* article of 2 July which had mentioned the involvement of a Tory MP, which he presumed was Captain Kerby (see below). Heath wished to place on record that 'it was quite unusual for the Paymaster General to speak to his (Heath's) Chief Whip on a security matter', and he had now forbidden it.[127]

Heath subsequently discussed the matter with the Shadow Cabinet, and then saw Wilson again twice on 5 July. He stated that nothing now seen invalidated the Radcliffe Report, and in fairness to Lohan therefore, an impartial enquiry should be held, as McCall had requested. After further tetchy exchanges about parliamentary handling, Heath published his letter accordingly that evening. Wilson had little option but to agree, and announced the same day that 'an appropriate impartial procedure' would be available to Lohan, to 'deal with Government statements which he considers unfair'. To ensure freedom from political influence of any kind, this would be an internal Civil Service enquiry, headed by Helsby as Head of the Home Civil Service, accompanied by Dunnett and the Treasury Solicitor, Sir Harvey Druitt.[128] McCall was satisfied this group was 'an appropriate impartial body', and Lohan was reported in the Media to be 'delighted'. To those less directly involved, the notion that an enquiry by three senior mandarins could be free from the influence of political considerations of any kind must have given delight of a different sort.[129]

Radcliffe in the House of Lords

The House of Lords debate on the cable-vetting affair took place next day, 6 July. As the *Guardian* reported: 'With a passing word of sympathy for the Prime Minister, Lord Radcliffe yesterday quietly cut into a thousand tiny pieces the White Paper that had rejected his committee's report on the D Notice affair. Like the result of last year's Cup Final, the committee's findings still stand, he told the Lords. "You might say that you do not agree with the result and that the referee had given the wrong decision. But it would not be very much good saying that you rejected it – even if you had a loyal vote to support you". Conservative peers chuckled and Mr George Wigg, seated on the steps of the throne, looked distinctly glum'.

Most other newspapers prominently ran similar stories. Under the headline 'D notices White Paper savaged. Scathing attack by Lord Radcliffe', *The Times* described his point-by-point criticism: the 'weighty' opening paragraphs about national interest were nothing more than a lot of good general phrases, the passage on the alleged inaccuracies in the *Daily Express* article was 'not worth the dignity of a White Paper', and he saw no reason for altering the conclusions of his Committee. 'On security, Lord Radcliffe was even more ruthless. Government always tended to want not a free press but a managed and well conducted press, he said. It was the job of a newspaper to be wary of these sometimes subtle, sometimes obvious inducements . . . He would be sorry to see a system of complete trust. 'A beautiful sentiment, but you certainly cannot order it by White Paper'. Lohan had been put before the

Committee by the Government as a witness as to fact, without any hint as to his 'suitability or capacity'. Radcliffe ended: 'Although I feel no resentment at the attitude taken by the Government, I feel grave doubts about their wisdom and their observations on the nature of "D" Notices.'

When the Lord Chancellor, Lord Gardiner,[130] defended the Government's position by re-iterating points of detail, he was sharply rebuked by another judge, Lord Shawcross (like Radcliffe a crossbencher), who said he could see nothing in the *Express* article which could have endangered lives. Lord Goodman regretted the White Paper, but attacked Radcliffe too, while the ex-editor, Lord Francis-Williams,[131] criticised the *Express*, but also attacked Government Departments concerned for having misled their own public relations officers into telling 'lies'.

Lord Carrington[132] summed up for the Opposition: it said a lot for the Press that, despite intense competition, there had been so little trouble previously over national security or the D-Notices. Finally Lord Chalfont[133] repeated the Government's line that 'With the full knowledge of many facts that cannot be made public, publication of the story in the *Daily Express* of February 21 did positive harm to our national security, the extent of which we may never be able to assess'. He ended with a swipe at his old trade, commenting that, but for the 'myth' of the scoop, about which only other journalists cared, much of what had been under debate might never have arisen.[134]

Wilson and Helsby

Even before the Helsby 'procedure' had started, Wilson summoned him to remind that, although this was a matter for officials, there would be political follow-up when he (Wilson) 'would be free to decide his course of action'. Helsby pointed out his examination was bound by Civil Service procedures 'to be limited to the complaints that a Civil Servant had against the Government as an employer', and that it would be quite inappropriate for him to sit in judgement on what others outside Government might have said. Wilson continued to press Helsby on the extent of the enquiry, on its timetable, and on the use of private letters from a Tory MP to Wigg, which Wilson had now authorised to be passed to Helsby.

In the following days, Helsby received from McCall a draft undertaking that Lohan and the IPCS would not comment on the Helsby Committee's findings, on the understanding the Government would be similarly bound. That Wilson would be thus precluded from comment was clearly however a step too far, and Helsby negotiated an amendment that both sides would 'accept the Committee's findings without argument'; this was a more realistic appreciation of the later reactions of both Wilson and Lohan, as it turned out.[135]

A Press View

Meanwhile, Wigg was pursuing correspondence with those who he thought were not giving the Government fair reporting (he complained to the BBC about its 'flagrant anti-Government performance'), and with those whom he thought he could influence in the Press. For example, he wrote to Michael Berry of the *Telegraph* Group on 7 July: 'As one who relies almost exclusively on the DAILY TELEGRAPH and SUNDAY TELEGRAPH for my newspaper reading, I was most interested to read the debate in the House of Lords yesterday on the "D" Notice system'; he went on to recommend the views expressed by Arnold Goodman[136] ('one of the most trenchant and devastating speeches I have ever listened to') on the relationship between the Government and Press. Berry courteously apologised that neither his newspaper nor even the Press Association had carried Goodman's speech, but 'since you have invited me to agree with his opinions I should add that I do not think they are well-founded'. Berry pointed out the Radcliffe Committee had not, as Goodman, censured Max Aitken, nor had it found that the D-Notice system had collapsed because of lack of goodwill by the Press. He ended: 'My own conclusion would be that there is no difficulty in dealing with the Press provided you are frank with them. There are as many patriots in Fleet Street as anywhere else.'

Wigg replied he had not meant to impugn the patriotism of the Press, but the Government's good faith should also be accepted by the Press, as the *Express* had failed to do. Berry responded that good will was not enough, and that 100 per cent trust would never be possible. 'So far as "D" Notices are concerned there is only one man who can allay the suspicions of both sides and that is the official on the "D" Notice Committee who actually speaks to the Press'; it was essential the Secretary should understand the Media and be properly briefed by the Departments. The consensus amongst editors was that 'the present system works perfectly well and that it was only an attempt to use a "D" Notice which did not really apply that led to all the trouble'. Wigg came back on that last point, but Berry, closing the correspondence, quoted from the Goodman speech which Wigg had so admired: 'there must be an infinite number of views about how you can construe a "D" Notice'. For once, Colonel Wigg seems to have been lost for a contradiction.[137]

The Helsby Report

On 7 August, the Helsby Enquiry Report was published by the Treasury. In sum, it concluded the D-Notice System had worked well until the cable-vetting incident, that Lohan deserved credit for 'his considerable contribution' to it during his tenure of office as the Secretary (who is 'the central figure in the working of the system'), that his post had not hitherto required Positive Vetting and that he had been cleared under a previous vetting system (pre-Radcliffe Report on Security Procedures, 1962), that there was never any doubt about his loyalty to his country nor any addiction to rumoured 'abnormal practices', that he had not been the source of the substance of a newspaper story, that he had been neither careless nor incompetent in his handling of the cable-vetting story; and that he had been handicapped therein by certain inadequacies in the operation of the D-Notice System on that occasion, for which he was not responsible. But it also concluded that he had made 'several errors of judgement', that his association with Chapman Pincher had been allowed to develop in a way which had adversely affected his ability to discharge his responsibility in the cable-vetting incident, and that the 'Government statements at issue were in accordance with the facts, and, having regard to all the circumstances, were not unfair.'[138]

The Media the following day were disappointed by this even-handed judgement. 'Greyer Than Grey' was a typical caption in the leader in *The Times*; 'In some 500 words of opaque prose, the trio of eminent civil servants . . . seem to have succeeded only in further obscuring those issues'. The Government's statements were 'not unfair, perhaps, in the sense that the soccer player who fouls an opponent while the referee's back is turned is "not unfair". Colonel Lohan must regard this report as a mixed blessing; and neither does it particularly become its authors'. The *Sunday Telegraph* of 13 August, under a headline of 'Clear as Mud', said two fallacies underlay all government thinking on the matter: that the D-Notice Committee was an organ of Government, and that Lohan should have acted as a conventional civil servant; it forecast strong press resistance to any government attempts to transform the Committee.

The private assessment of McCall, who had represented Lohan throughout the Enquiry and had amended the first draft of the Helsby Report, was that Lohan had never been in any way disloyal, that his distaste for the Government and its reductions in Defence spending had been driven by his personal concept of patriotism, that his sensitivity about his own status had led him to resent Dunnett's apparent distance, and that he had been in ways an over-trusting innocent when the poor relationship between the Government and Pincher/*Express* came to a head.[139] McCall nevertheless felt Lohan's reputation had been recovered by the Helsby Enquiry insofar as was possible, and he therefore put out a public statement that he accepted its conclusions.

The Government was nevertheless displeased by the reaction in the Media. On comment about the Helsby Report, for example as made on BBCTV ('So it is honours even'), Wigg minuted the Prime Minister on 9 August complaining 'In other words, the statement that was put out by Turnhill [the commentator] on the BBC news is a classic example of what is wrong in the BBC. The statement is inaccurate, it contains expressions of opinion unsupported by facts and, in my judgement for what it is worth, it is not even second-rate journalism.' Wilson scribbled on this that they might consider a formal approach to the Director General of the BBC about this and an earlier programme considered as biased.[140]

The Helsby Report did not however mean closure on the cable-vetting affair. On 1 September, the Prime Minister held a meeting with Chalfont, Wigg, Trend, Dunnett, Greenhill and other officials, to consider 'the next steps in the revision and strengthening of the "D" Notice machinery, particularly the appointment of the chairman and secretary of the "D" Notice Committee'. He reaffirmed that in future these two would deal only with 'D' Notice questions, and that if there were any other grounds for objecting to publication, 'such as national security', it would be the responsibility of Ministers or senior officials to take action. No one present appears to have asked what more precisely the Prime Minister meant by 'national security'. The discussion focused exclusively on the potential post-holders, mainly on that of the Secretary, because 'The Press seemed to be interested only in the future secretary', and because Cochrane 'would need to be replaced by someone of higher standing who carried more weight with the Press'.

Possibles were Brigadier Thompson,[141] Admiral Denning[142] or some Major-General. Possible Chairmen were Donald McLachlan, late of the *Telegraph*, a retired ambassador, or Lord Head,[143] of whom the latter was favoured. Wilson wished to test reaction to these choices at his next meeting with editors on 7 September, and asked to have Thompson's reaction (via Chalfont) before then, but he did not wish Head to be approached beforehand.

Chalfont also reported his recent meeting with Denis Hamilton of the *Sunday Times*, to discuss the damage done by the paper's series on the workings of MI5 and MI6. The editor-in-chief had said D-Notices were not 'a force at present', but that he would now ensure the reporting of his paper would be constructive and not attack the present secret Agencies, only expose their 'ineptitude' of 1945–60; he would also discuss the full substance of the articles beforehand with Ministers or officials (not with the D-Notice Committee) in exchange for information on their accuracy. This was assented to, but without any official approval or guarantee of immunity from prosecution, indeed the Government said it would formally repudiate articles when published.[144]

Wilson's Second Meeting with Editors

The meeting with much the same group of editors (except this time Marks of the *Express* did attend) was duly held on 7 September. Wilson again made a long introduction, saying he had not received any concerted Press view since the previous meeting,[145] but wished to try the further thoughts of the Government on the editors. He reaffirmed the system would be concerned only with D-Notice matters, and that if other appeals for non-publication 'in the national interest' were to be made, this would be done by a Minister or senior civil servant. The Government wanted some 'greater identification of the Press with the Committee, especially in connection with the Chairman and Secretary'. The latter would be given the necessary clearances if not already a civil servant. There seemed to be some advantage in the Secretary being drawn from the Press, perhaps from amongst the existing defence correspondents, such as Brigadier Thompson, and in this case the Press might wish to pay half his salary.

At the end of this 20-minute speech, according to the leaked report of the meeting in the following week's *Press Gazette*, 'there was an embarrassingly lengthy complete silence'. Harold Evans in due course said there were two questions: was it in principle right that the Secretary should be drawn from the Press, and was the present rather numerous gathering the right forum for discussing such a problem. Windsor Clarke said he thought editors preferred 'a firm distinction' to be drawn between the Press and the officers of the Committee, as the latter merely sought the co-operation of editors. Consequently he felt the Committee's staff should be nominated by the Government, although being acceptable to the Press. Nobody currently or previously from the Media should therefore be Chairman or Secretary, and the Secretary might best come from outside the Civil Service if of the right calibre, such as a former member of the Armed Services.

Wilson said he was anxious for firm views from those present. Having a senior civil servant as Chairman had worked well, 'but difficulties were apt to arise on intelligence questions'. Selecting someone from outside governmental circles would obviate the suspicion the D-Notice System was being used for political purposes. He would even accept an Opposition politician as Chairman.[146] Media opinions varied about the merits of an independent Chairman vis-à-vis a senior official, but independence from politics was agreed. A consensus in favour of retaining the status quo eventually emerged. The Prime Minister clearly now realised his initial intentions on the SPBC officers were never going to achieve editors' support, and he closed the meeting by saying a suitable candidate for Chairman and a Secretary would be selected, who would both be or become civil servants; he would consult the SPBC about their acceptability.[147]

Boer War Correspondents 1900 (*Getty Images*).

Light Cavalry Reconnaissance in Boer Territory (*Getty Images*).

Leading Members of the Early Committee: Sir Graham Greene (top left), Sir Edmund Robbins (right), Lord Riddell (bottom left) (*National Portrait Gallery*).

Zeppelin Bomb Damage London in World War I (*Getty Images*).

THE AUTHOR

Admiral Thomson, WWII Chief Press Censor and D-Notice
Secretary 1945–63 (*MoD*).

Traitors Philby (left) and Blake (right) in Exile with their Soviet Wives (*Associated Press*).

D-Notice Secretary Under Fire: Colonel 'Sammy' Lohan 1967 (*Associated Press*).

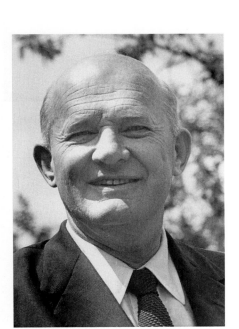

1967 Cable-Vetting Affair: Harry Chapman Pincher (top left), Colonel George Wigg (right), Captain Henry Kerby (bottom left) (*Associated Press*).

The 1967 Radcliffe Committee: (left to right) Mr Shinwell, Lord Radcliffe and Mr Selwyn Lloyd (*Press Association*).

Cartoons: Harold Wilson after the Radcliffe Report (*Daily Express*) (top); Sir Colin McColl is outed as Head of the SIS (*Tom Johnston*) (bottom).

D-Notice Secretaries: Major General Kay (top) (*General Kay*), Rear Admiral Higgins (bottom) (*News International*).

D-Notice Secretaries: Rear Admiral Pulvertaft (top) (*MoD*), Rear Admiral Wilkinson (bottom) (*Edward Hill*).

MoD Officials and Military 1964–1989 (*MoD*).
At a dinner party in April 1989 to celebrate the 25th anniversary of the establishment of

1. Sir John Nott.   2. Denis Healey.   3. George Younger.   4. Lord Zuckerman.
9. Sir Robin Butler.   10. Sir Clive Whitmore.   11. Sir Frank Cooper.

the unified Ministry of Defence, some of those mentioned in this book:

5. Sir Michael Quinlan.   6. Lord Lewin.   7. Sir James Dunnett.   8. Sir Henry Hardman.
12. Kenneth Macdonald.

Anti-terrorist Operations in Northern Ireland: Royal Marines Man an Early Observation Post over Belfast (*Press Association*).

43

CLEARING UP THE DAMAGE

In the still swirling Whitehall waters, some took advantage of the confusion. Lieutenant Colonel Maurice Oldfield[148] of MI6 reported to Trend that MoD's John Drew had recently lunched with Pincher, and heard of an imminent *Daily Express* book on the cable-vetting affair. Drew told Oldfield he was discreetly running Denning for the Secretaryship, and that meanwhile the D-Notice machinery was in complete disarray, and not being 'resuscitated in any recognisable form'. When Oldfield asked whether he had told his PUS all this, Drew replied he was not going talk to Dunnett about anything, but Oldfield could use the information as he wished.[149]

The SPBC met at short notice on 19 September 1967. Dunnett informed them Lee Howard felt he could now continue to serve on the Committee once re-nominated by the NPA, and that the Radcliffe recommendations on official representation would be implemented by the addition to the Committee of the Home Office PUS, Sir Philip Allen,[150] and the Foreign Office DUS, Sir Denis Greenhill. After brief discussion, inspired by *The Spectator*'s role in the Radcliffe Inquiry, it was agreed that 'journals of opinion' should be invited to be represented on the Committee, and the Secretary was instructed to write to the PPA accordingly. It was also agreed that drafts of revised D-Notices (other than the two involved in the cable-vetting incident) should now be circulated to all SPBC Members, and a sub-committee formed to discuss them. The existing drafting sub-committee had already completed its work on D-Notices Nos. 10 and 11 (Intelligence Services, and Cyphers and Communications respectively), to meet the recommendations of the Radcliffe Committee, and these were approved.

On the 'Future Composition of the Committee', the Media side having previously discussed the option of either a senior civil servant or a distinguished independent as Chairman, Dicker as new Vice-Chairman confirmed they were unanimous it should be the former, and that it should be the MoD's PUS. On the Secretaryship, Dicker said he could not support the appointment of Brigadier Thompson, not because of 'any selfish reluctance on the part of the *Daily Telegraph* to contemplate the loss of their Military Correspondent', but on a point of principle. This (supported by his Media colleagues) was that it would be wrong to appoint as Secretary anyone who had been 'closely connected with a particular newspaper', which would inevitably give rise to doubts about his impartiality.[151]

For similar reasons, it was agreed it would be inappropriate to appoint any *serving* government servant, who might be perceived as being biased in favour of the official view. 'The Secretary must be seen to be independent and not to be seeking further advancement in his career', so a retired Service officer or civil servant would meet the requirements. Previous Press experience was not essential, since, provided he had the 'right personal qualities, the necessary understanding to work with the Press could readily be acquired'. It was further agreed the Secretary should be fully positively vetted and codeword cleared, and that he should have a Deputy. The Committee also felt it desirable the Secretary should be formally required to notify the Chairman as early as possible of any disagreement with an editor. Dunnett reminded it had been suggested the Press might pay half the salary of the Secretary, 'in order to establish his position as a servant of the Committee as a whole'; the Media side responded that there would be 'considerable practicable difficulties' in such an arrangement, and that because of 'the comparatively small amount of money involved', they doubted it was worthwhile. The Media attitude to the Secretary would not be influenced, they asserted, by whether or not they had some responsibility for his salary.[152]

Probably prompted by Downing Street, Dunnett raised the *Press Gazette* leak about the Prime Minister's meeting with editors, and asked whether the Media side had 'any idea how it came to be published'. Lee Howard said editors who had attended had been 'equally astonished' to read it; others felt that, while the journal 'should have realised that the article ought not to be published', it was not a matter for the Committee but for the No.10 Press Office. Dunnett can have expected no different reaction. Finally Mike Ramsden[153] raised yet again the 'greater restraints' the British Press were under than their foreign counterparts when publishing information about new aircraft; it was agreed to remit this problem to the new sub-committee drafting revision of the relevant Notice.[154] Later that day, Wilson accepted the SPBC views, and Dunnett undertook to produce a list of retired officers for the Prime Minister's consideration 'as possible candidates for Secretary.'[155]

Dunnett wrote to Halls next day listing 16 candidates, including two ambassadors, a member of the Security Service, (extraordinarily) 'C' himself (then Sir Dick White, proposed by the Foreign Office), four Major-Generals, four Colonels, a Naval Captain, a Commander (proposed, almost as extraordinarily, by Lohan), Brigadier Thompson (despite the SPBC blackball), and Admiral Denning. Of these, Dunnett marked as non-starters the more junior officers, and, after discussion with Chalfont, gave as 'front runners' Denning and one of the 'extremely likeable' Generals who was highly thought of by Greenhill. Halls scribbled a note to Wilson that Wigg was 'v critical of this, since as you know he feels that this is a put up job to get Denning, who still seems to be the best' [the latter phrase seems to be Halls' own comment, but reflected the preference of senior civil servants, hence the 'put up job']. Wilson scribbled back 'I'd go for Denning despite our suspicions, I think he's probably the right man.'[156]

Denning was sounded out positively, the SPBC Media side concurred happily, delicate negotiation over pay and allowances took place,[157] and agreement was given Denning could retain two non-executive directorships acquired since retirement, and his local church commitments (but not connections with his local Conservative Association). His appointment was announced on 4 October and was well-received in the Media, as was his own description of his role: 'To safeguard not only the security of the British people but also their legitimate right to know'. He was allocated an office in the MoD Main Building, and started work on 16 October 1967.[158]

Meanwhile, Cochrane as Acting Secretary had been responsible for the successful revision of the D-Notice (No.11) about Cyphers and Communications. The key paragraph eventually agreed by the whole SPBC, and promulgated on 22 September, now read:

You are requested not to publish anything about:

a. HM Government's codes and cyphers;
b. Details of duties and numbers of employees in defence and diplomatic communications establishments (in personal identification the place of work and grade may be given; but this information should not be enlarged upon without first consulting the Secretary);
c. The nature and extent of interception by HMG of any form of communications, or of transmissions such as radar, for the purpose of national security; this includes the establishments and the personnel, methods and arrangements involved.'

The Notice ended that otherwise 'discussion of the subject in general terms is not precluded', but requested 'extreme discretion' in the use of disclosures made abroad about British codes, cyphers and interception. The same day a less radically revised Notice (No 10) about the British Intelligence Services was also issued by Cochrane.[159]

These Notices did not please all. Derek Marks of the *Daily Express* wrote to Dicker on 29 September, saying they were totally unacceptable. The retention of advice about no republication of foreign articles on British ex-agents meant, for example, that if Maclean, Blake or Philby made comments, only the foreign Media could report them. The new Notices were too wide and sloppily drafted, and, whereas before editors had been encouraged to consult the D-Notice Secretary if in doubt, now it was implied they had no such discretion. He also gave as a hypothetical example the retired agent who opened a pub, but whose identity could not be reported [this was a misreading; what possibly should not be reported would be that he was an ex-agent].

Furnival Jones and Oldfield met on 9 October to discuss the new arrangements. The DGSS said some editors wanted direct contact with MI5 and MI6; 'C' was not against this. Dunnett had suggested there might be two D-Notice Committees, one for Defence matters and one for the secret Agencies whose Secretary would be a Security Service officer, able to speak with authority for them. Fortunately this suggestion, which would have been increasingly difficult and inefficient to operate when terrorism became of greater concern, was not attractive to anybody and was quietly dropped. The idea of direct editorial access to the Agencies was also put on ice, DGSS and Oldfield agreeing it should not be 'institutionalised' and would need political approval.[160]

A further SPBC meeting was called on 10 October 1967, to consider the objections to the new Notices voiced by Marks. These were rejected, with no support for his views, and some irritation amongst the Media side that he had gone public with them. Formal approval was given to Denning's appointment.[161] This was again welcomed in the Media in the following days, even the *New Statesman* of 20 October merely and mildly asking 'D-Notices: All Ship-Shape Again?'

Final Twists

There were three final twists to the Lohan 'rumpus'. The first was in late September when the now retired Lohan was banned by Dunnett from reviewing, for *The Spectator*, Greville Wynne's autobiography 'The Man from Odessa', the manuscript of which the Colonel had discussed with the publisher when still in post.[162] The second and more curious twist was the correct deduction that the 'someone quite senior' who had leaked information to Deedes out of sympathy for Lohan was none other than the MoD's also now retired AUS, John Drew. At a meeting between Wilson, Wigg and senior officials on 18 September, Helsby had reported that 'an Under Secretary in MoD, now retired' [clearly Drew], had told Pincher and McCall the MoD had been pressed by No.10 to dismiss Lohan *before* the cable-vetting article. Drew was also under suspicion as being a source of the leak in the third 'twist' recorded below.

The meeting debated what might be done to prevent Pincher publishing this additional information, either by use of the OSA or by [almost incredibly] D-Notice action; the justification would be that, if Drew were 'mentally disturbed' or 'bitter', he might talk to the Press about intelligence matters too, thus threatening national security. Dunnett was instructed to produce a brief for Ministers on Drew, who thus became the focus of high-level and hostile (but discreet) scrutiny not just of this misdemeanour, not only of his recent performance and of previously undetected sinister undertones in what he had said to the Radcliffe Committee [in reality merely ambiguous], but also of his whole past career.

This career had contained more sensitive matters than most: from 1940–5 he had been employed on Deception Plans and Psychological Operations, and afterwards had frequently held similar intelligence appointments; his AUS (Personnel and Publicity) post had been cover for more exotic responsibilities, such as 'community relations' in Malaysia and Hong Kong, the discreet encouragement of some Saudi tribes to make trouble against the Yemenis, and deception plans for the V-bomber force which carried the airborne nuclear deterrent. In the MoD he dealt inter alia with officers from MI5, MI6 and GCHQ, contacts he was alleged to have enjoyed and kept up 'to an extent that his continuing official duties may not have fully justified'. He had also been responsible for public relations, and had enjoyed too his relationships with some journalists, particularly Chapman Pincher.[163] He had also, on his recent retirement, made two small manuscript amendments to his final OSA declaration form [he must have been almost the only retiree ever to have read that small print], although when informed such changes were impermissible, he had signed a non-defaced form.

Colleagues interviewed by the MoD sleuths suggested Drew resented he had not advanced further in the Civil Service, and, worse still, 'that he had a streak of loyalty to some of his colleagues which could, on occasion, lead him to extremes'. Chalfont minuted that, on brief acquaintance, he remembered him 'as a man of rather inflexible habits, classic reactionary political instincts of the Panglossian type, and generally regarded by his contemporaries as sound but not brilliant'. Posterity should remember him more kindly; Dunnett and Helsby, to Wigg's dismay, recommended to Wilson, who did not demur, that this was a case of misplaced loyalty, and that to take any further action might be counterproductive ('he is the kind of man who might well make a fuss [to Media friends] about what he would claim to be unfounded allegations'); as matters stood 'we are not at risk of his leaking secret information over the whole span of the knowledge that he has acquired.'[164]

Captain Kerby

The third and even more colourful twist was again initiated by Chapman Pincher.[165] He did indeed reveal that Lohan's dismissal had been under consideration over a month before the cable-vetting incident, mainly as the result of a report to the Paymaster General by an unnamed Conservative MP. The name was soon revealed elsewhere as being Captain Henry Kerby.[166] This had not been disclosed to Lohan until during the Helsby Committee's investigation, and ironically the Colonel was suspected of being the source of the leak to Pincher. McCall denied this, and, because Drew was also a possible leaker, it was decided by the authorities that nothing could be done about it. Lohan commented in Pincher's article that this information explained 'many peculiarities of the case'.

There were indeed even more bizarre peculiarities in what had been happening earlier in this affair. Kerby, disenchanted with his own Party leaders (who he felt did not sufficiently recognise his talents), had taken to feeding information to Wigg and sometimes directly to Wilson, not only about his multifarious contacts at home and abroad, but also about the inner workings of the Conservative Party, including its 1922 Committee. On 20 December 1966, Kerby had attended a small private party in an Ennismore Gardens bedsit, given by two *Telegraph* journalists. Amongst the score of guests were Lohan, whom Kerby knew ('slightly' he alleged, but in fact well, as they had met over the years at the houses of both Admiral Thomson and Pincher). During the evening, Lohan took Kerby aside and, 'in his *foghorn* voice and the worse for drink', asked a favour: he wanted Kerby to put down a series of Parliamentary Questions about Wilson/Wigg appointees, drafted with supplementaries by Lohan, which would 'put that bloody bastard Wigg on the spot once and for all' and 'blow him out of the water.'[167]

Lohan's aim, he said, was to show that Wigg had no power over MI5, MI6 or the D-Notice System, and he alleged that this was part of a campaign being masterminded by two Tory Privy Counsellors, Deedes and Sandys, particularly the latter (although he wanted to keep a low profile). Lohan also claimed even Wilson did not trust Wigg, as shown by the Prime Minister's close questioning of Lohan when they had previously met, about who Wigg's Press contacts were. Kerby agreed to meet the Colonel in the New Year, and meanwhile reported the conversation to Wigg, commenting that Lohan 'must be mental', and asking for instructions. Wigg welcomed this opportunity to deal with the garrulous D-Notice Secretary, and gave the green light to Kerby, who duly arranged to meet Lohan for lunch on 26 January.

Immediately afterwards, Wigg received a further vividly written Kerby note. Lohan had claimed Wilson was unwell, and in order to undermine him, it was necessary to undermine Wigg. To do this, a 'moral' case à la Profumo must be found, and Lohan thought he had it. A *Times* journalist had seen the Foreign Office Minister Lord Chalfont, whom Wilson had made a Life Peer and appointed at Wigg's suggestion, at the White Tower restaurant, very drunk and 'with his finger up' a most attractive woman not his wife [no wonder Radcliffe appeared shocked when Wilson showed him this Kerby note; there has never been evidence to support such allegations about Chalfont]. Lohan suggested Kerby should write a 'more in sorrow' letter secretly to Wilson about this, followed up by Parliamentary Questions targeted at Chalfont's recent assumption of additional responsibilities for Defence aspects of foreign policy. Before this, they should tip off their mutual friend Pincher, whom Wigg had recently threatened that Lord Goodman would 'do' him. Kerby accordingly arranged a Parliamentary Question about Chalfont on 23 January,[168] which Pincher duly picked up in the *Daily Express* on 3 February under the headline 'Farcical! The only word to describe Lord Chalfont's job', causing Kerby to write gleefully to Wigg that the plan was working.

The conversations with Lohan continued, with Kerby's convivial encouragement, covering Sir Solly Zuckerman's[169] close relationship with royal circles and desire for a hereditary peerage, and his close relationship with 'McLoughlin' of the *Telegraph* and the Tories generally; that the Security Service were pro-Wigg except for an unnamed 'Admiral'; that Trend and the top civil servants were fed up with the Government, as was the National Press;

that if Wilson resigned, George Brown would only last 'a weekend' and then the Government would slide to the Left, with Mrs Castle as the probable focal point; that Lohan's best source was his MP Deedes and his worst enemy Sir William Haley of *The Times*; that Wigg operated in a triangle with Goodman and Robert Maxwell (who ensured Wigg was 'never really short of lolly'), and much more in the same libellous vein, all excitedly reported by Kerby to Wigg.

Risible though this now appears, it demonstrated that Lohan was not an appropriate person to be the D-Notice Secretary. It was these scrawled Kerby notes which had caused Ministers to reopen attempts to rid Whitehall of him, and which were the hidden background to the reaction to the cable-vetting article.[170] As early as 21 February, Wigg had authorised Trend to show the Kerby notes to Dunnett, 'for information only' and not to be used as the basis for any action; although this must also have been to protect Kerby, 'The Paymaster took this line because this was a matter affecting an individual civil servant and . . . the information was unconfirmed.'[171] His cover not having been blown, Kerby had gone on meeting and writing to Lohan ('My dear Bob' Lohan called him) all through the succeeding months, and reporting back to Wigg. Kerby also wrote a diatribe against Pincher, with whom he had had an outwardly jovial telephone conversation: 'the source of Harry's . . . disgraceful article [is] the KCB who is Harry's fellow-Jew and Zoologist and long-standing and most intimate buddy.'[172] Kerby also told Wigg that Pincher was a close friend of the Soviet Embassy 1st Secretary and senior GRU officer Anatolij Strelnikov, although he did concede Pincher was on the Soviet Embassy blacklist.

Kerby's role was almost blown by a *Sunday Mirror* article in early June, which caused Lohan to write asking Kerby's opinion as to who the informer could be. Kerby's letters to Ministers frequently included an underlying message, then and in later years, that he wanted to leave Parliament (he had Berger's disease, and underwent a serious operation on his legs in mid-1967), and that he hoped for a title and for other government-connected work: 'Once RESIGNED from the rat-race, might it not *then* be possible for at least a *slice* of bread to come my way?'[173]

With the Advantage of Hindsight and Experience

Looking back 30 years later, and reminiscing on the impact of the affair on the first Wilson Government, Michael Foot[174] recalled that 'Harold had absolutely relaxed from his big election victory . . . Then, suddenly, the deluge . . . He had lived by the press and television. He then got an artless question from Sir John Langford Holt, MP for Shrewsbury, who had never hurt a fly. Harold started on this question with a long tirade against Colonel Sammy Lohan and D-Notices and, in 20 minutes at the despatch box, absolutely infuriated the press, whom he had previously enchanted. Those who live by the press have their problems.'[175] Others considered Wilson to have been badly advised at key moments, not just by Wigg, but also by the Cabinet and Foreign Offices.[176]

Reviewing the Lohan Affair here 40 years later, the initial feeling is of astonishment that the mixture of, on the one hand, a communication failure in routine business between two men of middling importance, and on the other hand, the prior obsession of some rather unusual politicians with these two, were together allowed to become a major event at the highest Political and Departmental level. Even those who were involved have differing opinions as to how this happened. Some see conspiratorial reasons alone. But it has predominantly the hallmarks of the traditional Great British Cock-up: a confluence of minor matters in a sequence and intensity which, had they been foreseen as a hypothesis, would have been dismissed as highly unlikely; important principles subverted by the venal traits of those concerned with upholding them; judgements made by otherwise intelligent men whilst under pressure and experiencing surges in the bloodstream of alcohol and/or of testosterone; complex and sophisticated higher organisations being rendered inadequate by failure to ensure basic human interaction; and lack of understanding of how the situation looks to those in a different 'tribe', or even to the general public.[177]

The Radcliffe Committee fulfilled its role in establishing *what* had happened and in making sensible proposals for small changes to the D-Notice System. But it was not asked to establish *why* those involved behaved as they did. It did allude in passing, especially in its lines of questioning, to some of the contributory factors. One was the friendship between Chapman Pincher and Colonel Lohan, of which the latter said in his evidence: 'I go so far as to say that I consider him one of my very great personal friends, apart from work'. Such a degree of social intimacy blurred the professional sharp edges of their discussion in this case. In principle, the D-Notice Secretary should, if possible, have a thoroughly friendly working relationship with the editors and journalists (and officials) with whom he interacts; but he needs also to maintain a certain distance and dispassion, if he is to remain independent in his judgement, as Radcliffe wisely observed.

Alcohol too played its part in reaction to events, not only at the lunch at L'Ecu, where drinks before and a bottle of wine with the meal were shared – not excessive for two men of the world, but enough to allow the odd nuance to be misinterpreted. That evening by chance others too were imbibing, not excessively perhaps by the time that the presses were about to roll, but enough for there to be misunderstandings and, at a time when every minute and detail counted, haziness in grasping the import of what was afoot. The Media, even in today's less lunch-rich London working world, are one of the remaining bastions which correctly perceives that regular selective lunching opens minds, doors and, most importantly, mouths. The sensible D-Notice Secretary lunches with the Media and others almost as often as he is invited, but does not mix such opportunities for general gossip and mutual understanding with pressing a case for non-publication of some sensitive matter.

The D-Notice Secretary must also keep in systematic contact with all those, journalists and officials, with whom he might at some stage in future have dealings; and vice versa. That there was a lofty disdain for Lohan, merited or otherwise, amongst some officials is apparent in the evidence to the Radcliffe Committee. It was one reason why he did not have all the clearances that he needed, why there was so little face-to-face discussion by officials with him at crucial points, why telephone communication was inadequate, and why aspects of the D-Notice System were so little understood by some officials. When the System is under pressure and events are moving fast, there is not time to build relationships, understanding, good will and trust; all that must have been done previously when business is at its normal pace.

But whatever the mistakes of those in the engine room, none of them would have led inexorably to what happened politically, had they not coincided with other trends in the Government, and in the Media. These included firstly ministerial over-sensitivity to the hostility of the Beaverbrook press, and specifically to the unusually well-informed articles of Pincher in the national security area[178]; and secondly the desire in some parts of the Press to attack ministers and officials by sensationalising their hidden activities, come what may. Such attitudes are ever-present and inevitable to some degree in government and media. When the trends are adverse, it behoves both sides to seek at key moments to return to a sense of proportion and to public frankness. It also behoves other institutions involved to act as a conciliatory bridge, and to function effectively themselves. It must be acknowledged that in this case the Services, Press and Broadcasting Committee was not then in sufficiently good shape to do so; and that Colonel Lohan, a worthy man in many respects, was nevertheless not the right man to be the lynchpin of the D-Notice System. That said, he was unfairly made the scapegoat for the collective shortcomings of a great many others.

Section 8

LATTER YEARS OF THE COLD WAR, AND NORTHERN IRELAND, 1967–90

44

SECURITY, POLITICAL AND MEDIA CONTEXTS

This is a summary for the period of the security concerns of British governments, and therefore of the Media and D-Notice Committee. The Vietnam War still dominated US attention (causing public opposition in the UK too, viz the 1968 Grosvenor Square riot), until major military support for South Vietnam ended in 1973 and the war in 1975. In Greece the Colonels' Regime (1967–74) affected British interests in Cyprus and NATO. In 1968 the 'Prague Spring' was ended by Soviet suppression; two Czech intelligence officer defectors, Frolik and August, and the KGB officer Lyalin, brought information to the West which led to unmasking some Soviet agents and sympathisers. Nevertheless a degree of détente with the USSR started in the late 1960s, including Strategic Arms Limitation talks (SALT 1 signed 1972), continuing until the early 1980s; peaceful or proxy rivalry and political and military confrontation nevertheless continued.

Divergence between the major communist powers climaxed in 1969 in the Sino-Soviet Border dispute. The Cambodian Civil War lasted from 1970 until communist Khmer Rouge victory in 1975, followed by imposition of its murderous regime until Vietnamese intervention in 1979. Having been vetoed by President de Gaulle in late 1967, Britain reapplied to join the EEC in 1971, and (with Ireland) joined in 1973. In 1971, Britain expelled 105 KGB and GRU intelligence officers in protest at the level of espionage in the UK. US-China dialogue led to the visit of President Nixon to the People's Republic in 1972. The 1972 Franks report recommended repeal of Section 2 of OSA 1911, and the introduction of an Official Information Bill. The nominally Marxist Allende regime in Chile was overthrown in 1973. Lieutenant and Mrs Bingham were convicted of passing secret Naval information to the USSR in 1973. A five-month oil embargo was imposed by OPEC countries on the West in late 1973, causing a three-day working week in Britain.

In 1974 the incoming Labour Government secretly agreed to continue the planned Chevaline enhancements to nuclear missiles. Secrets of the wartime communications decoding system were revealed in Britain from 1974, when without authorisation the WWII head of the SIS Air Department, Group Captain Winterbotham, published 'The Ultra Secret'. As Portugal withdrew from her African colonies, long-running civil wars involving Marxist forces started in Angola (1974–2002) and Mozambique (1977–92). The Royal Navy was embroiled in 'Cod Wars' against Iceland in 1972–3 and 1975–6. The Bulgarian dissident Markov was assassinated by poison-tipped umbrella in London in 1978. The British Embassy in Tehran was attacked by a mob later that year. The Government made proposals on OSA Section 2 reform in 1978 (Cmnd 7285); a Private Member's Bill on Freedom of Information was introduced in 1978, but fell when the 1979 election was called. Vietnam saw off Chinese border incursions in 1979, the same year the SALT 2 Treaty was signed, the Conservative

Government opted for Trident as the replacement UK nuclear deterrent, and Anthony Blunt was named as the 'Fourth Man' (with Burgess, Maclean and Philby, and, revealed later, Cairncross).

More lastingly significant events in Iran were the overthrow of the Shah and establishment of an anti-West Islamic Republic there in late 1979, and the taking of American hostages, a crisis not resolved until early 1981, after an abortive April 1980 rescue attempt, which contributed to the election defeat of President Carter. Even more significant for the future was the Soviet invasion of Afghanistan on Christmas Day 1979, the start of an almost ten-year sapping and ultimately unsuccessful war, in which local resistance groups (including Taleban) were supported by the West and Pakistan. The 12-year Salvadoran civil war started in 1980, involving Marxist and Cuba-supported elements, and similar Cold War concerns were behind the US invasion of the Commonwealth island of Grenada in 1983 (about which Britain was not fully consulted).

At home, the 1980 Iranian London Embassy Siege brought the SAS to a media prominence it has not since lost. The announcement that year of US nuclear cruise missiles being stationed at Greenham Common and Molesworth sparked protests over the next few years, there and elsewhere in Britain, including a CND march of a claimed one million in London in 1983. A White Paper on the 'Interception of Communications in Great Britain' was published in 1980 (Cmnd 7873). In 1981 there was a strike by some unionised GCHQ employees, which led to controversial de-unionisation in 1984. A further Freedom of Information Private Member's Bill was introduced in 1981, but was opposed by the Conservative Government and defeated. In 1981 too, Chapman Pincher published a book ('Their Trade is Treachery') based on information provided by the disaffected MI5 officer Peter Wright, including allegations the ex-DGSS Roger Hollis had been a Soviet agent (subsequently investigated by Lord Trend, and not supported by him or by defectors); a consequent 1982 Security Commission Report (not published in full) led to changes in procedures and organisation.

This Report attracted little media interest because the Falklands Islands conflict, and subsequent reinforcement of defences there, were the dominant British security (and political) events of 1982; South Georgia was invaded by Argentina in March 1982, and the Falklands War lasted from April to June. In the early 1980s a number of spies were exposed in the US/British Secret Communications Interception agencies, including Geoffrey Prime at GCHQ in 1982; this led to the Government's avowal of what was now widely in the public domain, namely GCHQ's principal function. In October 1983, Islamist suicide bombers attacked peacekeeping force barracks in Beirut, killing 292 Americans and 63 French. In 1984, Britain and China agreed the date (1997) for the transfer of Hong Kong to the latter. The Foreign Office clerk Sarah Tisdall was convicted for leaking information about the arrival of American cruise missiles in Britain. In 1984, a Data Protection Act was passed, and the MoD underwent further centralisation of common functions of the Services.

In 1985 the MoD senior civil servant Clive Ponting, who had leaked information about the sinking of the Argentinean cruiser *General Belgrano*, was acquitted after successfully pleading a public interest defence. The same year, the disaffected MI5 employee Michael Bettany was jailed, and the ex-MI5 officer Cathy Massiter revealed the extent of surveillance of CND and other British anti-government organisations; the Bridges Inquiry found no interceptions had been improperly authorised, and Massiter was not prosecuted. In 1985, Abu Nidal terrorists attacked Rome and Vienna airports, and in 1986 USAF aircraft (controversially) from Britain bombed Libya because of President Ghadaffi's support for terrorist groups. In retaliation, the British journalist John McCarthy and others were kidnapped in Beirut, later to be joined by the Archbishop of Canterbury's emissary Terry Waite (neither of whom was released until 1991). In October 1986 the UK broke off diplomatic relations with Syria over the Hindawi plot to blow up an El Al aircraft.

In 1987, the Attorney-General started legal proceedings against the *Daily Telegraph* to prevent the publication of extracts from the book 'Spycatcher' by Peter Wright; this added, to information in Pincher's 1981 book, the allegation that there had been an MI5 plot against Harold Wilson (something Wilson had himself implied to two BBC journalists soon after resigning as Prime Minister, but which Wright admitted to BBC Panorama in 1988 had been untrue). When publication of the book moved to Australia, the British Government lost its case there (and its later appeal). Similarly the UK High Court rejected a permanent press ban and the Government's contention that an insider was bound to permanent silence 'in all circumstances', but upheld the Government's right to prior restraint, and the duty of confidentiality of its employees. Meanwhile in the USA, the Reagan Administration was also attempting to tighten up on government secrecy.

In 1988 a Private Member's Bill to reform Section 2 of the OSA by narrowing its scope, raising the damage criteria, and allowing a public interest defence, was defeated by the Government using a three-line whip on Conservative Members. In December 1988 Libyan terrorists blew up a Pan Am flight over Lockerbie, killing 270. Parliamentary pressure, the Spycatcher case, the Ponting acquittal, terrorism, and other security concerns of the Government induced it in 1989 to pass the Security Service Act (which put it on a statutory basis, coincidental with a number of internal reforms), and a new Official Secrets Act. OSA 1989 tightened up in several areas, removing the public interest defence for Secret Intelligence and Security agency matters, and potentially making it more difficult for journalists to use an 'already in the public domain' defence.

Internal economic problems in the Soviet Union, the drain of the Afghan War, and the realisation that competition with the US Star Wars programme would probably be unachievable, led to President Gorbachov introducing Glasnost and Perestroika reforms in 1986. These in turn encouraged the Solidarity movement in Poland and other pressures within Warsaw Pact countries. Solidarity supporters were successful in the 1989 Polish elections; the Soviet Government abrogated the Brezhnev Doctrine vis-à-vis its satellite countries, which in turn achieved regime changes. The symbolic Berlin Wall started to come down in November 1989, and in Malta the following month the USA and USSR signed an agreement formally ending the Cold War.

Early in 1990, the British journalist Farzad Bazoft was hanged as a spy in Iraq, and a month later Britain seized 'Super Gun' parts destined for there. At the end of July 1990, Iraq invaded Kuwait, amongst other things capturing a British aircraft at the airport and using the passengers as hostages (released in December). The Gulf War to drive Iraqi forces out of Kuwait lasted three weeks in January/February 1991. The Pound Sterling joined the European Exchange Rate Mechanism that October (it was extracted after the costly Black Wednesday the following September); Mrs Thatcher resigned in November.

The Warsaw Pact was dissolved in mid-1991, the USSR that December. NATO confrontation with the USSR, and concomitant nuclear theology, had dominated British security policy for over four decades. Disengagement from the colonies continued throughout the period (48 countries left the Sterling Area), and although operations were still undertaken around the world (for example military intervention in Anguilla in 1969, and maritime blockade off Beira 1966–75 to prevent oil reaching Rhodesia), they were very much secondary to standing Cold War deployments. The British Army and RAF were focused principally within British Corps boundaries in West Germany, while the Royal Navy focused principally on operating and protecting the submarine-launched deterrent, and on locating and shadowing the large Soviet submarine fleet. Similarly the major focus of the Secret Intelligence and Security Services and GCHQ was on the Soviet threat, and countering Soviet activities worldwide. These were the predominant national security preoccupations.

Domestic Terrorism and Other Problems

Nevertheless, a domestic security problem was of almost equal concern: countering Irish Nationalist terrorism in all parts of the United Kingdom and against British official and military representatives in Western Europe, and dealing with Unionist terrorism and intercommunal violence in Northern Ireland. Irish Nationalist activity in the border area had effectively ceased in 1962, but Protestant and Royal Ulster Constabulary reaction to the Northern Ireland Civil Rights Association campaign which started in 1967, and increasingly violent confrontations, led to additional troops being deployed to the Province in August 1969. The split in the Irish Republican Army at the end of that year, into Provisional, Official and other factions, was followed by paramilitary actions against the security forces, and the first death of a soldier in early 1971. Internment of activists, mainly Nationalists, started in August 1971 (and lasted until 1975), 3,000 Catholics fled temporarily that month from Protestant harassment to the Republic of Ireland, and the number of troops in the Province increased to 12,500. In October that year the IRA bombing campaign spread from Northern Ireland to London (notably the Post Office Tower).

In January 1972 the 'Bloody Sunday' shootings by the Army in Belfast led to a further upsurge in Catholic support for the IRA, and to Protestant counter-action, and the Government imposed Direct Rule from Westminster. After the Sunningdale Agreement, power-sharing was introduced, but the IRA campaign continued. In addition to the continuing high level of violence in Northern Ireland, the 'Balcombe Street' bombers were active in Great Britain in 1973–4, including Whitehall, the Old Bailey, the Houses of Parliament, the Tower of London, Guildford, Woolwich, Birmingham, the London Hilton, and Green Park Underground Station. In the same period a number of stories of a 'dirty tricks' campaign by Security Forces in Northern Ireland reached the Media, which in due course led to the removal of the Information Officer Colin Wallace and a tightening of civil control. At the end of 1974, the Prevention of Terrorism Act was passed.

The escalation of killings in Northern Ireland in January 1976 caused Harold Wilson to order the deployment of the SAS there. There were further bombs in London's West End in 1976, and the British Ambassador to Ireland, Ewart-Biggs, and a junior official were killed by a roadside bomb in Dublin. Britain continued to have severe economic problems, culminating in needing to borrow from the International Monetary Fund in 1976, and the 'Winter of Discontent' 1978/79. In the year that Mrs Thatcher[1] became Prime Minister (1979), the level of terrorist violence continued, for example with the assassinations of her supporter Airey Neave in the grounds of the Houses of Parliament, of the British Ambassador in The Hague, and of Lord Mountbatten in County Sligo and the murder of 18 soldiers at Warrenpoint the same day.

In 1981, hunger strikes amongst Nationalist prisoners ended after 5 years and 10 deaths, and bombings in London included Ebury Bridge Road (1981), Hyde Park and Regents Park (1982), and Harrods (1983). In 1982, Sinn Fein won seats in the Northern Ireland Assembly for the first time; and the Animal Liberation Front sent letter bombs to Downing Street. In 1984 the violent 12-month Miners' Strike started. In October that year the IRA bombed the Brighton hotel where the Conservative Cabinet was staying during the Party's annual conference. There were race riots in autumn 1985 in Brixton, Toxteth, Peckham, and Tottenham. The Anglo-Irish Agreement was signed in 1985, but the Northern Ireland Assembly was closed in mid-1986; counter-terrorist operations and terrorism continued at a high level, including such atrocities as the bombing of the Enniskillen Remembrance Day ceremony in 1987. This came soon after 'Black Monday' on the London Stock Exchange. In March 1988, the SAS shot three IRA members planning a bombing in Gibraltar (a jury later decided they had been killed lawfully). Later that month at the terrorists' funeral in Belfast, a UFF member opened fire in the cemetery, killing six, and, at the funeral procession of these, two British Corporals who drove into the area in error were taken away and shot by the IRA. That October, mirroring even more severe restrictions in the Irish Republic, the British Government introduced a ban on the voices of terrorists being broadcast in the UK (although their words could be spoken by actors), not lifted until 1994.

However, also in 1988 the SDLP leader John Hume initiated talks with the Sinn Fein leader Gerry Adams, which, with the secret contacts between the British Government and Sinn Fein already under way, began to lead gradually towards a reduction in violence. In early 1989 the Nationalist solicitor Pat Finucane was murdered in Belfast by 'Loyalist' paramilitaries, and in September that year there were heavy casualties when the Royal Marines School of Music at Deal was bombed by the IRA. In 1990 there were poll tax riots in Britain; and in the same year, the IRA bombed the Baltic Exchange and assassinated the Unionist MP and ex-Minister Ian Gow. In February 1991, the IRA launched mortar bombs into the garden of No.10 Downing Street, and a few days later bombed Victoria and Paddington stations. Secret talks nevertheless continued between the British Government's representatives and those of the IRA in Sinn Fein.

Although the Cold War was the predominant security concern of the period, the campaign against Northern Irish terrorism had more direct impact both on the UK population and on much of the British Army (particularly the infantry, bomb disposal and intelligence units and Special Forces) and on the Royal Marines. It made them increasingly experienced in such operations, which stood them in good stead thereafter in other parts of the world where communities were at war with each other. It also had a significant impact on police forces, not just the RUC and Metropolitan Police, but also other forces in mainland target areas. The secret Agencies were increasingly involved in these operations and the negotiations.

Inevitably some secret counter-terrorist operations by the Security Forces, not all of whom always co-operated easily, became increasingly controversial as they later became more widely known.[2] The bombings and killings in Northern Ireland during this period, and the extent of the security apparatus built up to counter them, although they together achieved much less national and international publicity than those in the rest of the United Kingdom, were nevertheless far more devastating pro-rata, in damage, disruption, casualties and impact on daily life. The IRA campaign in Great Britain and certain parts of Western Europe did however have a more insidious effect on public security generally, and barriers, armed guards and surveillance devices gradually became the norm, from Downing Street to Defence establishments to airports. Even the houses of some 'ordinary' citizens were affected; the search under the car for a bomb became the norm before each journey for even the most junior member of the Services and for his/her family.

Media Context

During this period there was much change in the organisation, regulation and technology of the UK Media. Old favourites such as the *Boy's Own Paper* (established 1879) closed (1967), newspaper groups continued to change business hands, and broadcasters made changes too: regular colour television programmes on BBC2 from late 1967, and on BBC1 and ITV from 1969; BBC's Radio One launched in 1967, its Light, Third and Home Service programmes being renamed, and its local radio stations starting the following year. In 1968 the *Daily Herald* was transformed by IPC into the *Sun*. In 1969 Rupert Murdoch bought the *News of the World* and then the *Sun*. The London Broadcasting Company started the first legal local commercial radio station in 1973, followed by many others. In 1974 the BBC introduced CEEFAX, and in 1978 started broadcasts of parliamentary proceedings. *The Observer* was sold by Astor in 1976 to the Californian company ARCO. In 1977 Trafalgar House bought Beaverbrook Newspapers. Rothermere merged the *Evening Standard* and the *Evening News* in 1980. At the end of 1980, the Independent Broadcasting Authority awarded the first breakfast television contract to TV-am. Murdoch bought the loss-making *Times* and the *Sunday Times* from Lord Thomson in 1981, and in 1982 he gained control of Satellite TV (renamed Sky, and merged with BSB in 1990 as BSkyB). Channel 4 started broadcasting in 1982. Robert Maxwell bought *Mirror* Group Newspapers in 1984. The *Independent* started publication in 1986. Conrad Black[3] gained control of the *Telegraph* Group from Lord Hartwell (Michael Berry) in 1987.

In communications technology, satellites began to be used from the mid-1970s. Satellite consumer television was launched in the USA from 1976, Britain following a few years later, and satellite dishes were available from the early 1980s; the first licensed cable broadcast system started (in Swindon) in 1984, the same year British Telecom was privatised. The first mobile phone call in Britain was made in 1985, but expansion of use was initially slow and handsets large. A rudimentary internet came into being in early 1983, and the World Wide Web was under construction by 1991, although widespread use of personal computers by the public was still a few years away. The extent of the implications of these developments for the Media and for security did not become fully apparent until later.

Industrial relations in the Media worsened; *The Times*, for example, suffered a year-long shutdown 1978–9. Following changes in trades unions legislation, 1986 was a key year in British Press history; there had been lengthy negotiations the previous year between several unions and Murdoch's News International, who wished to remove 'Spanish practices' of over-manning, demarcation and ghost workers, accumulated over many years across Fleet Street, and to replace them by terms unacceptable to the unions, including use of new technology, flexible working, and no-strike clauses. News International had meanwhile been building a new plant at Wapping and secretly negotiating with the electronics workers union to man it. When 6,000 News International workers went on strike in January 1986, they were issued with dismissal notices, and production of *The Times*, *Sunday Times*, *Sun* and *News of the World* was switched to the new plant. In the acrimonious picketing and other action which followed, a large police presence ensured the plant could continue to operate, and the strike collapsed in early February.

Other parts of the Press soon followed suit, and also moved to new premises; the old ways of Fleet Street had been permanently changed. In another aspect of the new wave of Press production, the *Today* newspaper had finally been launched in March 1986 by Eddie Shah,[4] with computer photosetting and full colour offset printing (the first national colour national, sold to Lonrho four months later, the following year bought by Murdoch's News International, closed 1996). Another indicator of feelings in the industry at about this time was the founding of the Association of British Editors in 1985, as an organisation independent of proprietors, seeking to attract members from the National Press (the provincial editors already being served by the Guild of Editors) and from other media.

On regulation of the Press, because of Labour Party concerns about the perceived pro-Conservative bias of the majority of newspapers, the returning Prime Minister Harold Wilson set up a Royal Commission on the Press in May 1974. When it reported over three years later, it had not found strong anti-Labour bias, and it played down the impact of technology on competition; a minority report argued however that this and other market pressures now worked against the desirable diversity. In July 1989, against a background of public and media dissatisfaction with the Press Council, the Conservative Government set up a special committee of enquiry under DC Calcutt[5] to study privacy matters. It recommended that self-regulation by the Press should be given a further chance, but that the Press Council should be replaced by a Press Complaints Commission, which duly took its place in early 1991.

Meanwhile, the electronic media had been subjected to three enquiries: the Annan Committee (1974–7) on the future of broadcasting, the Hunt Committee (1982) on the expansion of the cable networks and on broadcasting policy, and the Peacock Committee on the financing of the BBC. The second ITV franchising round took place in 1968, followed by others in 1974 and 1982. Broadcasting Acts were passed in 1972 and 1973, and the ITA became the Independent Broadcasting Authority, responsible also for the regulation of independent local radio stations. The Broadcasting Act of 1981 removed certain political prohibitions and set up the Broadcasting Complaints Commission. Mrs Thatcher commented later on the 1985 Peacock Committee: 'Broadcasting was one of a number of areas . . . in which special pleading by powerful interest groups was disguised as high-minded commitment to some greater good'; she had particular misgivings about television licences and the position and efficiency of the BBC.[6] The subsequent Broadcasting Act 1990 began the deregulation of ownership of commercial broadcasting, replaced the IBA and Cable Authority by the Independent Television Commission, the Radio Authority and the Broadcasting Standards Council, and attempted to place obligations on TV companies (including the BBC) to procure up to 25 per cent of their output from independent producers.

All these changes, and other media trends of the period, in due course impacted directly or indirectly on the day-to-day work of the D-Notice Secretary. One media trend particularly perceived by the Secretaries and by officials from the early 1970s was an increase in investigative journalism in intelligence and security matters. Probable reasons included changes in public attitudes to authority, which started in the late 1950s, developed in the 'Swinging Sixties', and were well established by the mid-1970s. These manifested themselves too in a growth of the 'fringe' press, and coincided with the increase in the pervasiveness of and competition within television, the release of wartime records, 'spy scandals', dramatic events such as the Iranian Embassy siege, and above all the impact of domestic (i.e. Northern Ireland-related) terrorism. Increased investigative journalism was matched, in the perception of the Media at least, by increased governmental counter-action, including litigation. There were elements of truth in the perceptions of both sides; but in reality neither side is as scheming as the other fears, as is usually evident to the D-Notice Secretary operating in the no-man's land between them.

45

REVISION OF THE NOTICES 1971, AND EARLY CASEWORK

After the Lohan Affair

As the Lohan storm receded into the past, the swell from it continued to toss the vessels of State and Media around, albeit more gently. In mid-October 1967 the Press reported that a forthcoming American book[7] about to be serialised in the *Saturday Evening Post*, disclosed the names of the Heads of MI5 and MI6. The *Daily Express* of 19 October therefore published the names as a challenge, arguing the convention of non-publication could not be applied to something already published abroad, and claiming the D-Notice System was wrongly being used. The new D-Notice Secretary Admiral Denning responded to consequent enquirers that the System had never been used to prevent British republication of such facts appearing in foreign journals [a correct description of the Committee's policy, if a slightly elastic version of historic reality].[8]

Selwyn Lloyd later said on the BBC's '24-Hours' programme he doubted that any great harm had been done by the disclosures, and that the D-Notice system had worked well, but suggested the right response of the British Media in such situations should be reviewed. Two days later *The Observer*, under the headline 'Cleaning Up the D-Notices', pointed out the voluntary system was very vulnerable, because if a newspaper chose to 'wreck' it, there was very little that the Government could do; old-fashioned appeals to editors' patriotism and good sense could only work if there was a 'clean-up of anachronistic provisions' such as not naming the Heads of MI5 and MI6. The newspaper also commented on the lack of anyone other than the D-Notice Secretary to whom the Media could go to ask questions about the way in which the secret Agencies operated, as was possible in the USA. In Parliament, the Prime Minister said the American book was detrimental to the secret Agencies' efficiency, and therefore contrary to the national interest, but that the Media were not stopped from re-publishing matters released abroad by outsiders, as long as they quoted the source; and that they should consult the D-Notice Secretary in such cases.[9]

Denning meanwhile quietly and methodically got on with re-stabilising the D-Notice System and re-establishing confidence in it. The revision of the 12 Notices required much to-ing and fro-ing, initially between Government Departments, and later, when drafts were released to the Media side, even more consultation and redrafting. When, for example, Ramsden of *Flight* saw the revised D-Notice No.4 (Aircraft and Aero-engines), he wrote to Denning in mid-June 1968 saying it was still too verbose and complicated to be useful to journalists, security classifications were out of date, and there were too many gradings of equipment; he suggested new principles, based on the more 'enlightened' attitude of government compared to post-war, and on collaboration with the more open USA being now greater than that with France. So it was back to the drawing board for the working party.[10]

Sometimes the disagreements were between officials. Lohan had tried to get the Civil Defence Department to update the February 1962 Notice on sensitive sites as long ago as early 1966. After several years of discussion between Home and Cabinet Offices, the eventual draft covered underground works, coastal depots and pipelines for the storage and movement of emergency petroleum reserves; regional seats of government (33 from Dover Castle to scattered old barracks, in addition to the main complex at Corsham); emergency communications facilities; secret control centres for the national grid and railways; and hidden floodgates in the London underground railway system. Officials decided to conceal that some establishments had NATO functions (not covered by D-Notices), but an honest Commander in the Cabinet Office persuaded them this would be discovered by the Media, and would cause distrust; the published Notice added mention of the NATO link.[11]

Surviving records for this period are notably thin, but what few there are confirm a similar pattern of activity to that before and since. When for example in late December 1967 an explosion occurred at the Royal Ordnance Factory Bridgwater, causing casualties and severe damage, the local ITV station hired a light aircraft, and its cameraman was seen by an Army patrol leaning out and filming from low-level overhead. MoD asked Denning to take it up with the ITA, who apologised for the contravention of a 1961 D-Notice (the new No.6 concerning aerial photography had not yet been agreed), sent a copy of the complete film to the Army for checking, undertook to remind staff of the existence of the Notices (which were previously locked away in managers' safes), and suggested the new Notices be sent direct to news editors of each ITV company.

Although records of Denning's dealings with publishers have apparently not survived, he wrote to their Association in September 1967, mentioning the current work on D-Notice revision, copies of which would be distributed only to those 'publishers who are more liable to publish books which may be affected by the Notices', but reminding that from time to time other publishers did also publish such books or those 'which might be affected by the Official Secrets Act'. He said that in the past these had often been brought to his attention so late in the production process that 'any alterations or deletions which may be advisable, would be an expensive matter.' He suggested publishers and authors consider sending him a copy of the manuscript as soon as it had been decided to go ahead with publication.[12]

In late October 1967 Greenhill circulated a Foreign Office/SIS think-piece that linked it with the 'almost pornographic interest in intelligence matters that has been aroused' by articles in the *Sunday Times* on 'Philby: the Aftermath'. At the time the editor Harold Evans was also threatening to accept an invitation from Philby to send a journalist to Moscow to interview him, for a substantial fee for the benefit of his abandoned family; the Foreign Office deployed moral arguments and threats of legal action against Evans, George Brown intervened with the proprietor Lord Thomson, the newspaper decided to leave it to a literary agent ('the *Sunday Times* are sinning by proxy' said Greenhill), and the immediate initiative fell through.

These matters had refocused attention on the Foreign Service, which thought it had begun to live down the Burgess, Maclean and Philby treachery and to reform; and on MI6, which was portrayed as 'an upper class racket' coming off worse against the Soviet professionals. Greenhill suggested what was now needed was publicity about the improved political control and recruitment by merit, and allowing the naming of 'C' and selected editors to meet him;

the Philby and Lohan affairs had seriously damaged the Government/Media relationship in this field, and it was no longer possible to deny the existence of the secret Agencies.

The reaction to this piece amongst senior officials was generally favourable, with hesitations only over naming Heads of Agencies. Furnival Jones (DGSS) thought this should be done only through the D-Notice System and with appropriate caveats on what information should still not be published (photographs, addresses, movements, etc). White ('C') agreed with this but advised they should wait and see whether the D-Notice System would again function. Trend was both sceptical about trusting the Press and also concerned about the 'constitutional implications', writing to the PUS of the Foreign Office: 'People like you and I are not public figures in the normal sense and can speak and act only through our Ministers', and that the limelight would be unwelcome; 'perhaps I have got all this wrong and am simply being stuffy and old-fashioned'.

Trend would indeed have preferred to stick with the former 'neither confirm nor deny' policy on secret intelligence matters generally, and sent the think-piece on to Wigg in the hope of a sympathetic view. This he duly received by return: 'Are we prepared to run the risk of death by a thousand cuts? I am not, so I would not be prepared to give away information until it has been clearly established, if not by agreement with the representatives of the Press then at least by Ministerial decision, just how far we are prepared to go. Having taken such a decision, we should not go one millimetre beyond that point.' Wigg's greater concern, however, was whether it would be possible to 'bring about the restoration of some kind of a "D" Notice system'; it would be 'in the long term interests of Press and Government alike'. He foresaw that the absence of such a system would in practice lead not to legislation but to a free-for-all, and 'the policy of scoop with the consequent unscrupulous overtones that we have come to know so well'. The Press should be persuaded of this point, and meanwhile there should be 'no tooth-paste approach of a gentle squeeze always producing a little more.'[13]

Lecturing to the Royal Commonwealth Society in late November 1967, Chapman Pincher used his enhanced fame to criticise Government censorship, giving examples: use of the OSAs in 1950 to conceal that construction of atomic reactors at Windscale allegedly used the wrong concrete (porous to radioactivity); Wigg's threat of OSA prosecution of Pincher in 1965 if he revealed a senior Minister had left 'sensitive' papers in a restaurant (sensitive only in that they revealed a disagreement between the Minister and the Home Secretary over housing coloured immigrants); and the secret attempts to be rid of Lohan. Whereas in the first two examples the D-Notice System had rightly not been involved, Pincher went on to describe other examples where Lohan had been used by the Government, in his view wrongly, for political purposes (the Kuwait overflying case, and a request not to publish a speech by Egypt's President Nasser about the 'wrapping up' of the MI6 network in the Middle East at the time of the Blake trial). He also criticised the new D-Notice Secretary, with whom he never had a close relationship and rarely consulted, for saying D-Notices could in some cases have wider application than purely defence matters.

His recent adversary George Wigg, about to become Horserace Levy Board Chairman (charged principally with modernisation of racecourses, of which he was a long-standing aficionado), was also giving interviews and writing articles. In The Times he argued that the Press should be more ready to 'accept its obligations' and, surprisingly in the light of recent events, that government should be less concerned with its own image. Amongst other attacks on the Press, he criticised the 'disregard of the public interest . . . revealed in what has been called the savage contempt with which a minority of newspapers treats the D Notice system'. He saw this however in terms of Party politics, not of a wider malaise between the governmental machine and the Media: 'Was it fortuitous that the first public challenge to the D Notice system came during the life of a Labour Government?'[14]

Indeed, the Beaverbrook group in particular continued to embarrass the Wilson Government. Pincher attacked its over-reliance on the Americans in satellite reconnaissance, and included two words ('keyhole' and 'talents') in the text which were relevant secret codewords; although he did not mention them as codewords, the authorities concluded they had been leaked to him.[15] The Prime Minister's Office enquired whether Pincher had checked the article out with Denning (he had not), but then Halls commented to the Cabinet Secretary: 'The last thing I would want to do is to get the Prime Minister involved with the *Daily Express* or with Chapman Pincher. We have had enough of that.' A check with the Americans anyway elicited that everything had already been published elsewhere.[16]

The official assessment was now that, apart from the *Daily Express*, Media doubts about the D-Notice System had largely disappeared. This was not entirely so; when Dicker became too ill to continue work, the editor of the *Evening News* told fellow-editors 'This whole question of D Notices has become such a major issue between Fleet Street and Downing Street that I think we would be wise to have a discussion before agreeing to replace Mr Dicker', and two NPA meetings were needed before the London editors voted by 11 to 4 to continue to be represented.[17] Nevertheless, the general attitude on both sides was to give Admiral Denning time to re-establish the working of the System, thus achieving 'fundamental change' in the relationship.

During these years, the SPBC seldom met formally unless there was a major matter to be discussed; business was carried on by correspondence and informal meetings between Dunnett and/or Denning and individual Media members, particularly the Vice-Chairman. The Media side also met periodically in the Vice-Chairman's office. In December 1967, Dunnett sounded out his official colleagues about a change in title for the Committee, since the Services Departments were now all brigaded under the MoD, and wider interests were indicated by the representatives of the Home Office and FCO on the Committee. Trend suggested being more radical still and replacing 'Services' by 'Security', although he recognised this might 'raise unnecessary qualms in certain quarters'. Denning and others thought this might indeed imply to the Media side a 'thin end of the wedge' extension of coverage to political and economic affairs; 'it would certainly be on these grounds that the "Express" group would criticise it'. Trend gave way, and Dunnett suggested 'Defence, Press and Broadcasting Committee', to Dicker. The latter was however terminally ill, and shortly afterwards Windsor Clarke was chosen by the Media side as his replacement; it was he who agreed the change of title in early 1968.[18]

A contrary perception to those of Pincher and Wigg above was voiced in the 1968 Annual Report of the Press Council, where its Chairman Lord Devlin discussed situations in which something alleged by a reader to be a lie was claimed by the editor to be from a secret and undisclosable source. As an example of how deadlock could then arise, he cited the cable-vetting affair of the previous year, which had been resolved only because the Radcliffe Inquiry had been set up. 'Had it not been for this very exceptional procedure, the case might have passed into currency as another example of press irresponsibility . . . There are too many people ready to prefer an official accusation to a newspaper denial.'[19]

Routine business included disagreements in early 1968 between the BBC and MoD, when the latter's Police illegally confiscated film of Claud Cockburn outside Aldermaston, and Tam

Dalyell[20] in a PQ asked why the Corporation had been given and then refused permission to enter the Microbiological Research Establishment at Porton. There was a spat with the *People*, which published an article in mid-June 1968 about the collapse of a TA paratrooper during escape and evasion exercises, including that his mother had been prevented, by use of a D-Notice, from publicly criticising the resistance-to-interrogation training involved. A Colonel from the Joint Service Interrogation Wing was summoned to brief the concerned Media side. This led to their proposing further changes to the draft Notice, which allowed mention of safeguards used in the training, and encouraged media discussion with the Secretary if these appeared to have been breached.[21]

In July 1968, Denning was summoned by the House of Commons Committee of Privileges investigating the passing by Dalyell to *The Observer* of a Select Committee document about the Porton Down Defence Chemical Research Establishment. Denning told the Committee there was nothing in the subsequently published article he could have asked to be excluded, although when he had given prior advice to the paper, he had not realised the Select Committee Report in question had not yet been published. Dalyell was nevertheless reprimanded for breach of privilege.[22]

The few remaining records of this period show that Denning had re-established the working relationship with Security Service Legal Advisers (who still represented also the interests of SIS and GCHQ until these Agencies acquired their own Legal Departments in much more recent times). Thus, for example, the Secretary consulted before giving the *Sunday Times* advice on a Soviet spy case in November 1968, when the *Daily Express* the following spring sought advice about the security threat it perceived in the 'explosion' in the number of Chinese restaurants in the UK (MI5 declined to comment), and when the *Sunday Mirror* in August 1969 ran a story about the arrest in London of a Soviet spy; in the latter case the Security Service had been prevented by the Foreign Office from publicising their success, but after it had been leaked by the police, Denning did persuade the editor not to mention an American connection.[23]

The revised D-Notices involved in the cable-vetting fracas had been agreed by September 1967, but it was not until March 1969, after much word-by-word tussle, that the others had generally been agreed by both sides of the Committee, as had that they should continue to be called D-Notices. Even then there was one still in dispute, the new No.4, concerning once again Aircraft and Aero-Engines, on which the Ministry of Technology and the Media side (led by Ramsden of *Flight*) were unable to agree. By mid-November 1969 this had been negotiated down to one sticking point, the Media side being unanimous in their view they should be free to conduct informed discussion of new projects up to the point where the specification was officially approved; so many projects had run into trouble in the past that the public should be aware of the issues involved as early as possible. Dunnett told his opposite number at the Ministry of Technology, Sir Ronald Melville,[24] that, if agreement could not be reached, there might be no D-Notice at all on this subject.

Fruitless negotiation went on through to the following summer. The MoD became inclined on balance to accept the Media side's wording, which allowed an editor in the possession of secret information, especially about a new aircraft, to publish something which he regarded 'as essential to free discussion of the validity of such projects', having taken advice through the DPBC Secretary. Melville still disagreed, on the grounds that officials should not appear to condone even technical offences under the OSA. He foresaw problems too in collaborative projects with other countries (e.g. the Jaguar and Multi Role Combat Aircraft projects), where there was normally an agreement on 'no release without mutual consent'; and in that, if editors were given the right to decide what was essential to publish, it could not be denied to members of Parliamentary Select Committees. The Media meanwhile were not silent on the official attitude.[25]

Windsor Clarke as Vice-Chairman also pointed out to Dunnett one fallacy in official thinking, that D-Notices were 'in effect, guidance to the Press as to the kind of things they may publish without running the risk that they might be infringing the Official Secrets Acts'. On the contrary, the Media side 'would feel that D Notices are, in purpose and in effect, guidance to editors as to what in the national interest ought not to be published. There may be a consequential and valuable effect in preventing unwitting involvement with the Official Secrets Acts, but we do not set out to relieve an editor of his proper editorial responsibility in this direction.' Dunnett took this point, but stressed one of equal importance as a principle of the D-Notices' relationship to the OSAs: 'We cannot escape the fact that the Official Secrets Acts exist and that if the "D" Notice system does not work as intended then the question of the infringement of the Acts is bound to arise, and it is in this connection . . . that the "D" Notices are important. I cannot imagine a situation ever arising in which the Government would contemplate proceedings under the Official Secrets Acts if the action of the editor concerned was covered by a "D" Notice.'[26]

There are signs that Dunnett, already dealing with the continuous political and administrative problems of his large and fractious Department, was finding that the DPBC was taking up an irritating amount of his time. He told his Deputy Under-Secretaries that Denning handled day-to-day problems efficiently, but was not so good on 'political' issues such as revision of the D-Notices. Dunnett also had to handle the linked intelligence matters personally, such as MI6's concerns about an imminent book on Blake's escape by one of his accomplices. Dunnett therefore now made his AUS (Defence Staff) Denning's official minder in such matters.[27]

In May 1970, charges under the OSA were brought against a Colonel who was the British senior observer in the Nigerian civil war, the editor of the *Sunday Telegraph* Brian Roberts,[28] and the journalist Jonathan Aitken,[29] all accused of offences concerning a UK Government confidential report on that war's progress. The prosecution opened by quoting Admiral Denning, who had previously told the *Telegraph* that publishing the document would not 'fall foul' of D-Notices because it dealt with the forces of another country and did not affect British national security; he had however added that if it was an official document, it might be subject to the OSA. When the case resumed the following January, he was called as a prosecution witness, and closely questioned by judge and defence about the System. He explained he could only advise, not direct, and that the whole Committee would have had to agree to a Notice being raised specifically to stop this publication, had it been justified; he added he did not give advice on what might merely embarrass the Government, which could impose a Confidential classification 'unreservedly': it had 'often happened before, I am afraid.'[30] The defendants were later all acquitted.

While an early October 1970 DPBC meeting was still being arranged, Chapman Pincher interpreted a leak about the impasse on the draft Aviation D-Notice into 'Bid for tighter gag on defence news', and a 'determined move to impose tighter censorship on the reporting of defence information by newspapers is being made by senior officials in Whitehall . . . strongly contested by newspaper representatives on the D-Notice Committee.'[31] In reality, Dunnett was losing patience with the Ministry of Technology, and he warned his Secretary of State Lord Carrington that the technical Press was 'incensed' about the way the UK Editor of *Interavia* could pass to his European editor information which could not be published in

Flight and other UK publications; 'we may be heading for a bit of a bust-up, logical though our position is'.

With Carrington's support, Dunnett summoned officials from the Ministry of Technology and told them that, rather than risk the whole D-Notice System foundering, he intended to accept the latest Media side wording He thought the risk of editors behaving irresponsibly was slight. Without Melville there, the Ministry of Technology officials readily agreed, accepting that ultimately this was for the MoD to lead on, and that it would have to go to Ministers for decision. The key paragraph now read: 'Editors may discuss in general terms the validity of unlisted and projected new aircraft or engines which have been publicly referred to by the Government, or feasibility studies relating to them based on information officially released or which has appeared in the foreign press, but are requested to withhold publication of detailed technical data received from other sources except where it is considered by the editor to be essential to informed discussion of Government policy. Should any editor be in doubt he is requested to consult the Secretary of the Committee.' The inelegance of this caveated prose is a reflection of the many sub-committee pens which had scratched their mark on the multiple drafts.

Carrington wrote accordingly at the end of August to his opposite number at the Ministry of Technology, with copies to other Ministers involved and to No.10 Downing Street. The Foreign Office were concerned at the impact a row with the Media side might have on the implementation of Notices concerning the intelligence services, although Sir Alec Douglas-Home himself commented he thought that the Press 'play brinkmanship and too often go over the edge'. The Attorney-General Peter Rawlinson[32] had more substantive concerns about the relationship with OSAs. He considered that an editor who knew or should have done that he was contravening the Acts 'would strictly be committing an offence whether or not his subsequent publication of the information was in breach of a D Notice'. Although he acknowledged that in practice such a prosecution would damage the System and the Government's relations with the Media, he advised that the wording should avoid a potential defence that, even though information had been *communicated* to an editor in breach of the Acts, its *publication* was permitted under the terms of the D-Notice. He urged therefore that either the Notice or some other accompanying communication to editors should make clear the Notice did not condone a breach of the OSAs.

The Minister of Technology John Davies[33] was convinced the technical Press was making a major issue of principle out of what had started as a minor practical problem. He pointed out to Carrington that neither *Flight* nor *Interavia* had had any problems with his Department over the years, and that there were now only four types of aircraft affected by the draft Notice No.4 (Harrier, Jaguar, MRCA and Nimrod). He agreed damage to the D-Notice System needed to be avoided, but cautioned against leaving it to an editor to decide whether he needed to seek advice in this field. He agreed some Notice was better than none, and hoped that at the forthcoming DPBC meeting it would be possible to persuade the Media side to alter its position slightly.

When the DPBC[34] met on 7 October 1970, the restatement of the 'as far as we can go' Media side position included that the 'D Notice system was entirely separate from the Official Secrets Acts'. They therefore did not want a Notice worded in such a way that an editor could cite it as a defence if he was prosecuted under the OSAs. Dunnett privately saw this position as in reality unlikely to be that of the defence in any prosecution, but let it pass since it met the Attorney-General's concerns. The Media side then withdrew for a lengthy reconsideration of its position, saying on return they were now prepared to consider amending the final sentence of the disputed paragraph to: 'In such a case [the editor] is requested to consult the Secretary of the Committee'; this removed the official concern about it being left to the editor to decide whether to seek advice. Dunnett therefore recommended acceptance to Ministers.

The Media side also suggested that the new Notices should be accompanied by a full Introduction, covering how the D-Notice System worked, the underlying principles, and the relationship between the Notices and the OSAs. All happily agreed, but parts of the wording of this new Introduction now became fresh bones of contention. Trend as Cabinet Secretary tempered his approbation by querying whether it was wise to quote from the Radcliffe Report of 1962 that, by means of the D-Notice system, the Government 'succeeds year in and year out in keeping out of the newspapers, radio and television a great deal of material . . .'; some damage might be done by the implication that this was still a governmental objective, since 'Keeping things out of newspapers, radio etc, is not nowadays a very "with-it" concept'. The Prime Minister Edward Heath himself took an interest in the wording of the officials' draft, suggesting an addition to make clear it in no way changed the existing system.[35] The Media side had meanwhile redrafted the official version of the Introduction, but, in ignorance of Mr Heath's words, omitted them. This caused much subsequent angst among officials, and to-ing and fro-ing in unsuccessful attempts to find a way of re-inserting them. In the end, Heath was persuaded to accept this unintended slight, but he instructed that if any of the Press tried to suggest that there had been a change in the existing procedures, the correspondence about the omission should be disclosed.

The Law Officers' Department had also proposed an amendment, clarifying the relationship between the D-Notices and the OSAs, by adding a new phrase: '. . . *and D Notices should not be regarded as providing full guidance on what may or may not be a breach of the Acts. Moreover*, the Acts cannot therefore be regarded as providing full guidance on what should or should not be published on a particular subject in the interests of national security. The D notices provide such guidance and offer the editor who is in doubt . . . a point of contact in the Secretary. . . .' The Media side (who had already attempted themselves to insert a late amendment elsewhere, much to Dunnett's irritation at having to restart the clearance process with Departments) attacked this apparently innocuous succession of sentences, and in particular the 'full' in the new phrase.

By now it was late May 1971, and Dunnett asked whether, if he could not persuade the Media side about the word 'full', the Law Officers might withdraw their amendment. His un-PUS-like words reflected his anger: 'The Press side . . . are being extraordinarily stupid and difficult . . . we are, I am afraid, dealing with an extraordinarily childish set of people who still do not understand what D Notices are about'. He may be forgiven for his exasperation at this tedious, minor but high-visibility addition to his concurrent burdens, which now included escalation in Northern Ireland, a new Government and severe pressures on the Defence budget. A solution was eventually found in late June at a meeting between officials led by Dunnett, and Windsor Clarke and Alastair Stuart [36] for the Media side: the contentious sentences including 'full' were deleted and the request to consult the Secretary moved to a position which covered all situations. It had taken about four years of protracted negotiation since the Lohan affair to achieve a new set of Notices.[37]

Denning (who was simultaneously manoeuvring the Franks Committee interaction through the DPBC) accordingly issued the twelve revised D-Notices and their General Introduction on 16 August 1971 (see Appendix 4). These received a mixed but generally passive reception in the Press; 'Bid for tighter gag on defence news' said Pincher in the *Daily Express*, while the *Daily Telegraph* the same day (19 August) described the changes as making the Notices 'up to date and more permissive'. Minor changes to Committee personnel details and to the Equipment Lists Annex to the Aircraft and Aero Engines D-Notice were then issued periodically up to the next major review in 1981.

Denning had also approached the Publishers' Association during the staffing of the Notices. It continued not to wish to be represented on the DPBC, but did republicise amongst its members the Notices and the Secretary's availability to give advice, advising Denning who should receive a copy of the new Notices (only those 'who are more liable to publish books which may be affected by "D" Notices'). The following year he reminded officials of his role vis-à-vis books (the same conventions apply to this day): books by 'insiders' are dealt with by the Department for whom the author worked (although the advice of the D-Notice Secretary is often sought, for example as to the degree to which details are in the public domain, consistency, etc), while books by others are dealt with directly between the Secretary and the publisher/author (should they wish to discuss the manuscript).

An indication that the D-Notice System had settled back into general acceptability appeared in the American *Time* magazine of 5 July 1971, in an article about the debate in the USA provoked by publication of secret Pentagon papers, on 'how – and where – to draw the line between a government's right to secrecy and the duty of the press to inform. In Britain, for nearly 60 years, the problem has been partly solved in fuzzy fashion' by the use of the D-Notice System. Denning was quoted as claiming there had been no serious violation during his tenure; 'I've received the utmost co-operation from the press . . . Whenever they've applied to me, they've always played the game. I never try to kill an article'. He and others in Britain did not however think such a system would work in the USA, because of its size and diversity, because they perceived the US Press as lacking perhaps 'some of the inhibitions of our press here', and because of the absence in the USA of the necessary trust between government and press, 'a virtue that is, to say the least, an American rarity' [in *Time*'s opinion].

Giving evidence to the Franks Committee in December 1971, Pincher expressed a less favourable view of the current D-Notice regime. Having criticised Section 2 of OSA 1911 for being at the root of officials' belief that everything was secret, he reminded that there were non-sensitive aspects of even the most secret matters, although journalists were uncertain where the line would be drawn; as an example, he had once obtained ministerial approval to publish a photograph of a nuclear bomb's exterior. He claimed that until the 'D-Notice row' journalists had had no problem at all in knowing where the line was, because of their close relationship with Thomson and then Lohan; 'But now that situation has gone, and we manage on our own'. He conceded however that this was partly because, in the Cold War stalemate, there was less defence news; 'it is not like it was; the nuclear situation is static.'[38]

Relationships within Whitehall were also not always full of mutual respect. When the Vice-Chairman Windsor Clarke was about to set off in 1971 for a lecture tour in the Far East, including to a multinational Press audience, he asked Dunnett whether there was anything useful to Britain which he could cover in his speeches. The Chairman minuted his MoD colleagues 'I have some reservations about putting him in touch with the FCO since, even now, their appreciation of what D-Notices are all about leaves a good deal to be desired'; and instead he asked his own AUS (Defence Staff) to brief Clarke. In the same period, Clarke's own views about some of his colleagues showed as little admiration; one was 'an hysteric' and another 'too precise and pedantic.'[39]

D-Notices as the reason for non-publication of information were occasionally cited by those not entitled to do so: in late 1970 a Foreign Office official tried to stop the BBC interviewing a Briton recently released from captivity by the Chinese authorities, and Chief Constables and regional MoD Commands attempted news blackouts on Service aircraft crash sites. In early 1971 Denning issued a Notice reminding that D-Notices should not be invoked except through the Secretary.[40] Conversely, conspiracy theorists in the Media occasionally quoted D-Notices as the reason why something had not been disclosed, when in reality it was purely at the behest of the police or officials; for example, in September 1971 when robbers of Lloyds Bank in Baker Street allegedly also acquired photographs compromising VIPs, some newspapers claimed that a specific D-Notice had been used to suppress this information. There is nothing in the archives to support this claim; furthermore, by autumn 1971, not only were there Standing D-Notices (which did not cover this kind of story), but also any such involvement by Denning over political/royal embarrassment could not have been concealed from the sensitised Media side of the Committee.

Not everything which came the D-Notice Secretary's way was without humour. In February 1972 the Chief Press Officer at No.10 complained to the Prime Minister's PPS Robert Armstrong[41] that a nameless Minister had told *The Times* editor (Rees Mogg) over lunch the Cabinet was to discuss Northern Ireland and make a statement imminently. 'It really is intolerable . . . that a leak of this kind should occur'; he asked whether the Prime Minister wanted it investigated. Heath replied he supposed it ought to be, 'but it's a bore'. Trend did not dissent from all Ministers being questioned, but cautioned he had reservations about the possible outcome, because of embarrassment if the Minister concerned was detected. A few days later Armstrong scribbled a note to the Prime Minister: 'I now learn that the Minister concerned was the Prime Minister . . . William must have read more than was intended into what you said. The question of a leak inquiry falls.'[42]

One detects in veiled media references that Denning's relationships with Government Departments were not without occasional tensions. A diary item in the *Daily Telegraph* of 30 March 1972 alleges he had been forbidden to attend the launch of a new book about WWII espionage ('The Game of Foxes'), on the grounds he might be asked questions which 'could only be answered in an indiscreet manner'. He did however attend an informal lunch in the publisher Hodder's offices afterwards, and there he explained he had asked for some changes in the book, 'largely because, even after 25 or 30 years, certain people still needed to be protected by anonymity'. That some officials and possibly Ministers were no longer entirely happy with him is reflected in private correspondence at the time between No.10 and Dunnett, who was being chased to appoint a new Secretary; Dunnett commented it was 'not an easy post to fill.'[43]

However, a successor was found. In December 1972, Admiral Kenneth Farnhill[44] succeeded Admiral Denning. Whatever the opinion of others, Trend wrote warmly to the latter, who responded that his appointment had not been 'without its exciting and traumatic moments' but that 'nearly everyone' had been co-operative; however, being 'constantly available 24 hours a day tends in time to become rather irksome'; a sentiment which at the age of 68 was understandable. *The Times* (9 November 1972) described him as 'a popular and distinguished secretary' of the DPBC.

One of Farnhill's early initiatives was again to contact the Publishers' Association, who were as ever co-operative, but declined DPBC membership. The Security Service asked him whether D-Notices were issued to editors in Northern Ireland; they were, but in living memory no editor had ever sought advice. Behind this question was concern that interception of telephone calls there would become known; Farnhill advised case by case intervention rather than a proactive letter, as this would merely alert papers to the practice (he was unaware that discreet political pressure had been brought to bear on *The Times* while he was advising it against publishing such a disclosure). He took a similarly pragmatic view when in February 1973 *Time Out* (now run by a 'leftwing collective', albeit one of no concern to MI5) published the text of D-Notice No.10 (British Intelligence Services); 'least said, soonest mended', he wrote. MI5 characterised the difference between him and his predecessor as that Farnhill considered himself 'more a judge [between officials and the Media] than an advocate [for the official line]'; the same brief commented there was now more 'embarrassing' material published abroad and in the fringe press.[45]

In July 1973 Farnhill intervened with the Independent Broadcasting Authority on a 'World in Action' programme about GCHQ, pointing out that technically the location of the establishment was covered by the D-Notices; the IBA decided not to include it, even though, as Thames TV and the Press pointed out, it was widely known and indeed included in *Whitaker's Almanack* and in recruiting advertisements for radio officers. In the programme, the Home Secretary Robert Carr[46] assured the participating journalists the Government intended to abolish Section 2 of the OSA, as had been recommend by the Franks Committee the previous year, and that there was no intention of further impeding investigative journalists.[47]

In August 1973, the American *Newsweek* magazine named Maurice Oldfield as new Head of the SIS. Marcus Lipton MP immediately announced he would ask the Prime Minister to 'withdraw the D-Notice' preventing such publication. 'Not Much of a Muzzle', commented the *Guardian* (11 August) in a not unfriendly leader, which nevertheless drew an immediate riposte from Clarke as DPBC Vice-Chairman. This was discussed at Farnhill's first DPBC meeting, which did not take place until 16 months after he became Secretary, on 24 April 1974. He reported that two events had focussed particular media attention on the D-Notice System in the past year: firstly, the son of the former Chief of the SIS[48] had appeared in court on a drugs charge, which had initially entailed attempts to limit disclosures about 'C', but Farnhill had eventually advised that, because his identity had already been published abroad, restrictions no longer applied. The second had been a 'World in Action' programme about GCHQ, on which the Vice-Chairman[49] complimented Farnhill that 'the collective responsibility of the Committee had been safeguarded.'

The main item on the agenda, raised by the Chairman, now Sir Michael Cary,[50] was whether the domestic conflict in Northern Ireland should be covered by D-Notices, which currently applied only to external threats. This 'delicate situation' meant that, while coverage could not 'properly' be given, 'to those taking part, the situation had most of the characteristics of a war'. He did not think it would be right to draft a new Notice, but he sought opinions. In discussion there was agreement only that 'the case for doing something in this area did need to be kept in mind'. An example was given of someone whose murder had followed a disclosure made in court that he 'had been helpful to the police', published without restriction in the Media; however, much such information was published in the Republic of Ireland, where the DPBC had no locus standi.

The Media side were united that it would be wrong to interpret D-Notices as being applicable to the security situation in Northern Ireland 'but circumstances could alter cases'. It was accepted nevertheless that some parts of the Notices (for example, those concerning weapons and intelligence) 'could in certain circumstances apply to events in or concerned with Northern Ireland, and the Secretary had to use his own initiative and discretion in dealing with these'. If he ever needed to extend the coverage of the Notices [on security grounds], he should first use the emergency procedure for convening the DPBC. He should never allow the System to be used to 'prevent political embarrassment or . . . to cloak matters outside its scope even though there were good reasons why these should not be publicly discussed'; any such restrictions should be requested of the Media by ministers or officials themselves.

Finally at this meeting, Clarke once more raised the non-naming of the Heads of the secret Agencies. The Media side (he claimed) were 'not greatly concerned either way about this', but the fact that the information always quickly got published anyway 'weakened the authority of the "D" Notice system'. Cary said he had 'a certain amount of sympathy with this point', but at least it still prevented 'C' from becoming 'a public figure'. The Foreign Office representative, Sir Geoffrey Arthur,[51] reiterated the line that, once the identities were published there would be difficulty in drawing the line on information about those Services as a whole. Cary said he would consider it further.[52]

In early May, Farnhill was asked by the BBC if he would participate in a 'Nationwide' programme about the D-Notice System. Because there were political considerations, he consulted Cary, who supported his desire to do so, as did Arthur on behalf of the Agencies; both felt the relatively new Secretary had already shown that he would be well able to handle a full broadcast discussion and to decline to be drawn into any aspects of concern to politicians. The idea was rapidly scotched however by the Prime Minister, who felt 'very strongly that Admiral Farnhill should be asked to decline any such invitation, and also that no alternative speaker with inside knowledge should be offered'. Wilson did not feel it would be possible, even if the BBC so desired, to discuss the D-Notice System 'in the abstract', and that sooner or later the discussion would turn to specific cases and examples, including Wilson's personal involvement in the 1967 events. The Cabinet Secretary added: 'The BBC are in general marginally more critical of the D Notice system than the Press', and that it was unfair to expect Farnhill to cope with 'some pretty difficult off-the-cuff questioning' without either appearing to stonewall or embarrassing the Government. His final point was that, since the Lohan affair, the Secretary had managed 'to operate discreetly and successfully in the background to the satisfaction of all parties. The Prime Minister does not think it would be helpful to him or his work to give him this kind of publicity.'[53]

The Secretary's interventions with publishers did not always receive a good press. In May 1974, *The Observer* published a critical article sparked by Farnhill's suggestion ('It might be useful if I had a look at the draft') on a book called, ironically, 'The Invasion of Privacy'. The paper described these interventions as 'those semi-friendly warnings [which] ever so gently squeeze the wrist of a major publisher'. In fact Farnhill advised no deletions from the manuscript, which included paragraphs about D-Notices and OSAs being used to keep public and Parliament 'in a great fog of ignorance about the security services'. The book argued principally for a right to individual privacy in the face of intrusion by media, electronic surveillance, credit agencies and 'computer banks', and in particular by the police and governmental agencies.[54]

At the 11 November 1974 DPBC meeting, the main discussion concerned the threat to offshore fuel installations. When Farnhill had tabled this, an FCO official had commented acidly that at least he was taking an interest, whereas the MoD was reluctant to allocate resources to defence of platforms and pipelines; and that it was 'absurd' that currently the major responsibility for their protection lay with the Chief Constable of Aberdeen. Farnhill's argument was that, although the installations and their pipelines and shoreside facilities were not government-owned, and were not therefore covered by D-Notices, they were perceived as potential targets for terrorists and for enemies in war. The authorities had agreed that, because of the increasing strategic and economic importance, there were national security implications, but also hoped media coverage would not be unnecessarily curtailed.

Farnhill suggested the only such matters deserving protection by D-Notices were current or planned military defensive measures. He also considered that linked Special Forces, tactics, techniques, special weapons and devices, and classified design details of naval protection vessels, were already adequately covered by D-Notices Nos. 1, 2, and 3, and that the only novel aspect now requiring discussion was application to these non-government installations. He proposed merely an additional note to D-Notice No.8 (Civil Defence etc), reminding editors of application to offshore fuel installations. However, although the DPBC agreed the justification, it concluded there was no justification for amending the Notices, nor that they should apply to security measures taken by the operating companies themselves. The Media side was divided as to the best way of communicating this grey advice to editors, and did not want it to be seen as in response to the Secretary's initiative; it was eventually decided therefore the Vice-Chairman would inspire an editorial enquiry, and the Secretary would then publicise his reply.[55] Journalists can be just as Machiavellian as bureaucrats. When however in 1979 the BBC sought to make a 'Nationwide' programme about the Royal Marines' role in defending the rigs, its approach to the MoD was rebuffed to the Director-General by the Cabinet Secretary personally.[56]

Closing the 1974 meeting, the Chairman gained general agreement that they should meet 'at regular though not too frequent intervals even if there was no special matter to be discussed so that they could keep in touch and be informed by the Secretary of events occurring in between meetings.'[57] Once again Committee activity had fallen to a sluggish level, but the new Secretary intended to be more pro-active than his distinguished but weary predecessor. It is noteworthy that there was no discussion at the meeting of the implications for the D-Notice system of new legislation then being introduced by the Home Secretary, Roy Jenkins,[58] to combat rising IRA terrorism. Within the JIC however, there was a flurry of interest in the DPBC: the MoD's failure to brief Farnhill before an Israeli visit reported in the *Sunday Times*, and the Secretary's consequent complaint, led to his briefing that Committee about the System in January 1975; they agreed he should be informed about future possible breaking stories.

The next meeting was not until 1 September 1975 (no record apparently survives), when the DPBC agreed the Australian authorities' request to continue to protect the whereabouts of the Petrovs. Because the Australian Media did not fully support their D-Notice System, the Australian authorities regarded it as decreasingly effective; by February 1978 the British High Commissioner in Canberra was reporting the strong opposition of the local Media to the continuance of their System.[59]

46

IMPACT OF IRA CAMPAIGN, AND PROTECTION OF OFFICIAL INFORMATION

In January 1976, uneasy about the continuing policy of not naming Heads of the Secret Agencies, Farnhill reminded the Committee of recent Press articles about 'C' (Oldfield), adding that some had now gone further and disclosed his address and other details, causing concern as to his personal security.[60] While Farnhill had no strong reason then to anticipate a marked increase in media interest in the Intelligence Services, he clearly did so, and asked for confirmation the current interpretation was still correct. He also again highlighted the anomalous interpretation of Notices, applicable only to external enemies, even though the same methods, techniques and individuals were increasingly being used against an indigenous terrorist group not covered by the Notices. He sought advice as to how to deal with this anomaly.

After the 18 February 1976 DPBC meeting, which included the annual review of D-Notices, Windsor Clarke wrote to editors telling them that, while no changes had been considered necessary, both sides of the Committee had been concerned that domestic terrorism was creating problems which 'might well have a bearing upon the purpose and effectiveness of D Notice No.10 covering intelligence activities'. This applied for example to information published abroad which would normally therefore be accepted as republishable in the UK, but which now would be useful to 'domestic' terrorists who might not otherwise have been aware of it. He referred to dangers of assassination, bombing and kidnapping. The Committee did not at that time wish to broaden the Notice to cover this area, but did feel 'they would be justified in bringing this difficult situation to the attention of editors.'[61] It is not recorded how editors reacted to this opaque guidance.

Terrorist and counter-terrorist activity meanwhile increased and the Media themselves had differing views as to how best to report such events. In late 1976 the Home Office approached the new DPBC Chairman, Sir Frank Cooper,[62] asking him to review advice to the Media on reporting the activities of the security authorities. Following an inconclusive DPBC meeting on 28 September 1976, Cooper reiterated the reluctance of the Committee to be drawn into internal security matters, but Robert Armstrong (now DUS at the Home Office) wrote with a plea at least to continue the debate. Nevertheless, his Department (and the Security Service) would 'not want to do anything that might damage the effectiveness or acceptability of the D Notice system for its proper purposes; and we doubt in any case whether the DPBC would itself be the right forum for a substantive discussion of the problems with which terrorism confronts the media'. However, it had been the Media side which had themselves originally raised the anomalies, and Cooper and his Home Office counterpart Sir Arthur Peterson[63] considered that further discussion should preferably again be initiated by the Media rather than by government. 'We think that the press and the broadcasters have become more keenly aware of the problems for them and have also learned to live with the risks – or at any rate with the fears of the risks – of encroachment upon press freedom.' They hoped for at least some informal DPBC discussion, initially in private between Clarke, Cooper, Armstrong, Peterson and Farnhill.[64]

Routine business meanwhile continued. One case in which the Secretary declined to intervene concerned a leak to Chapman Pincher in July 1976 about the supply of arms, including cluster bombs, to Kenya. Commercial overflying of the 'CENTO route' for this purpose had been refused by Turkey, so RAF aircraft were discreetly used. Disclosure of this was considered by Farnhill to be a matter of political embarrassment rather than of national security. A governmental leak enquiry was set up, but it transpired so many people knew about the deliveries that no source could be identified; the report reminded there had been similar unsuccessful leak enquiries following Pincher articles in 1968, 1971, and 1974.[65]

Agee and Hosenball

The magazine *Time Out* of 20 May 1976 included an article by Duncan Campbell and Mark Hosenball (respectively British and American journalists) entitled 'The Eavesdroppers', which described US-UK Signals Intelligence (Sigint) activities worldwide. It was based mainly on information already disclosed in the USA by an ex-NSA employee, and Farnhill did not intervene because of this public domain consideration. However, GCHQ subsequently pointed out it also included a paragraph about monitoring IRA communications, and electronic techniques used by UK security authorities to jam IRA radio-controlled bombs, details not previously published. The consequent leak procedure was eventually halted, however, because experts decided this story could possibly have been written as a result of intelligent technological journalism, and because the Security Service was already investigating other matters concerning Campbell and Hosenball.

On 17 February 1977, the Home Secretary announced that Hosenball and an ex-CIA 'whistleblower', Philip Agee, were to be deported at the request of the American Government. Farnhill had little to do with this cause célébre. That evening he was rung at home by *The Times* and *Sunday Times*, wanting to know his reaction to the *Time Out* article, which they presumed was the reason for the deportation. On 'a friendly and non-attributable basis', Farnhill pointed out the article had been published several months previously and that he had not been consulted beforehand, but his memory was that most of it had been material already in the public domain and much of the rest was speculation (the dangers of which he nevertheless reminded).

The next morning, the editor of the *Evening Standard* Simon Jenkins[66] similarly consulted him, referring to a recent *Economist* article on Hosenball and the D-Notice System. When Farnhill explained he had not seen the *Time Out* article before it appeared in public, Jenkins asked what his reaction would have been if he had been consulted. Wary about a hypothetical question, Farnhill replied he would probably not have advised against publishing information already in the public domain, but might have argued that some of the speculation was covered by D-Notices; he mentioned that D-Notice No.11 (Cyphers and Communications) specifically drew the attention of editors to the dangers of enlarging on information published elsewhere. When Jenkins told him he was assembling a 'dossier' to present to the Home Secretary, and had found nothing to justify Hosenball's deportation, Farnhill helpfully (but possibly somewhat beyond his remit) suggested that, while everyone was assuming the *Time Out* article was the reason, it was 'at least possible that there were other undisclosed reasons'.

The following week, the *Guardian* sought advice from Farnhill on an article on links between American and British intelligence services, sparked by the Hosenball/Agee affair. He advised against publication of several details, and the *Guardian* decided not to publish. A version of the article immediately appeared in the *Red Weekly* (24 February) and the *Socialist Worker* (26 February). Although the information was certainly covered by D-Notices, all was even so fairly innocuous and the allegations would have broadly been known to or assumed by the Soviets: that GCHQ existed and what it did, that the Intelligence Corps and MoD provided considerable extra manpower to it, that it was linked to the NSA, that MoD costs did not appear on GCHQ's balance sheet, that its employees were subject to the OSA, and that it was not only hostile countries/organisations which were monitored by GCHQ and by implication NSA. Farnhill was correct in the advice he gave, but the blanket secrecy then imposed by government was so extensive that it was a temptation to the disaffected to breach the 'softer' aspects of it.

The Public Domain

Returning to the applicability of D-Notices to domestic terrorism, Farnhill was despatched to sound out Clarke, who was strongly against formal DPBC discussion, but tolerated informal discussion with just those representing the news media (i.e. NPA, NS, SDNS, BBC and ITN). This duly took place, and did lead to a brief discussion in a full Committee meeting on 23 March 1977. There was also then 'exploratory' discussion of the linked matter of republication of secret information not officially released but already in the public domain. Farnhill sought guidance because, despite the now accepted convention that information published abroad could be re-published in the UK, there was no guidance on similar information already published in the UK, whether (inadvertently or deliberately) without reference to the D-Notice Secretary, or against his advice. There was also no agreed definition of 'publish'; information might be available somewhere but not accessible to the public without the kind of investigative resources which the Media then had; but, when intelligently put together by the Media with other information in its possession and published, it could potentially be genuinely damaging to national security. This debate was the forerunner of many more over the years about how to decide when information has become 'widely in the public domain'.

After the meeting and the Media side's own private discussions, Clarke wrote to Cooper and Farnhill summarising their views. They had 'considerable sympathy' both with official concerns about inadvertent publication of some apparently innocuous detail which was in fact key to intelligence of wider importance [what became known as the 'jigsaw' effect], and also with the Secretary's difficulties in giving advice on such matters 'for which there is little or no precedent for guidance'. They did not however think it would be possible to produce an 'acceptable' amendment to existing D-Notices to meet these difficulties, nor did they favour 'a proliferation of Private and Confidential letters', as these tended to devalue the Notices. They were also very conscious the Home Secretary was currently preparing an amendment to OSA Section 2, and felt the whole question should be left until his proposals were known.

Clarke sent an accompanying handwritten note to Farnhill, which, in the much later internet age, still has resonance. 'We [the Media side] found it impossible clearly to define a "fringe" publication when it came to overseas (or, indeed, domestic) publication of sensitive material. Nevertheless, we would be unanimous in discouraging editors from regarding something in such a publication as *automatically* meeting the requirements covering re-publication in UK. Our feeling was that cases would have to be judged within the individual circumstances so far as possible. If, therefore, you receive an inquiry about such a published item, and if after considering the nature of the publication itself and the details published (perhaps being malicious, speculative, or simply designed to draw an official comment) you felt the need to counsel the utmost caution upon your inquirer, the P&B Section would feel that this was an entirely appropriate and proper course. I offer these comments with the full approval of my colleagues, as a matter of guidance for you in view of the fact that it has not been possible to frame a formal Section statement on the fringe publications question.'[67]

To this day, a similar modus operandi applies in such cases. The guidance above to the Secretary may sound remarkably indefinite to anyone who has not been involved at the Media/official interface, but it was practical. Similar guidance today in such areas of modern uncertainty has likewise to be practical rather than over-prescriptive. In each case, the onus is on the Secretary to make an initial judgement as to which side of the public domain line he considers the detail of the information to be, and then to attempt to persuade either an editor or an official or both of his view. So long as the Secretary is no less intelligent and well-informed than the one to be persuaded, an agreement can almost always be reached in negotiation, which meets both the information and the security aspects of the public interest.

In response to Clarke's formal letter, Cooper said he thought that, although no conclusions were reached, the discussion had at least alerted all to 'a very difficult area in terms of both sensitivities and definition'. His 'own personal inclination' was to take a far more relaxed view 'about events of 30 or more years ago than of current affairs'. He wished only to emphasise two points 'in case the subject comes up in conversations in and around Fleet Street': there was no question of trying to prevent publication of matters from investigation and foreign journals, merely to avoid the damage that the sum of this could do; and 'I have to admit that there are still those in official quarters who would like to be able to use D Notices to block loopholes and compensate for security failures and some on occasion seek to do so. They are rapidly disillusioned and this will continue to be the case. In those departments which are covered by D Notices, the system is generally understood, as is the need to preserve its integrity; elsewhere this is not always so and one could be forgiven for thinking that such knowledge as some people have is on a par with that of (and perhaps derived from) those authors and script writers who cause their characters to announce that they will 'slap a D Notice' on whatever is momentarily causing them embarrassment!'

Government Attempts to Amend the OSAs

Cooper's letter to Peterson the same day highlighted other media concerns, especially the Government's wish to amend Section 2 of OSA 1911, legislation which both sides for different reasons found unsatisfactory, and on which the Franks Report of 1972 had recommended its 'catch-all' provision should be abandoned. Franks had also recommended the establishment of a joint government-media 'classification committee', to advise editors on what should not be published on matters not of national security but national interest, for example foreign affairs and treasury matters generally. The Callaghan Government decided to progress this idea, but in 1978–9 the Media were generally hostile to self-censorship where security was not concerned; 'Our task is to seek out information and to uphold the public's right to know.'[68] The DPBC Media side wanted nothing to do with 'classification', and indeed had growing concerns about Government intentions even on national security.

Cooper reported to his colleagues that Windsor Clarke had been surprised by a hardening of attitude amongst the Media side since the March meeting, a 'vague sense of unease' that officials regarded the D-Notice System as a convenient means of suppressing embarrassing publication, typified by recent attempts to suppress factual information in a 'fringe journal'. More specifically, Clarke wrote: 'It is, to put it bluntly, a belief among some of my colleagues that the Home Secretary is planning a new Official Information Act or a measure of that kind, that will be unacceptably restrictive and repressive from a Press and Broadcasting point of view. Individuals who believe they are well informed harbour this fear and have adopted the attitude "Concede nothing until we know what the Home Secretary proposes". I think there is a fear, too, that it will be implied that because we co-operate over the D Notice system there is no reason why the media should not co-operate over other restrictive measures. As I think I have mentioned before, we do occasionally encounter the "Uncle Tom" jibe from people senior enough to know better, and perhaps this makes one or two of our people unduly sensitive.'

Cooper put down a marker that, when more was known about the intended new Act, its impact if any on the D-Notice System would need to be considered by the DPBC. Peterson acknowledged this as 'another example of the [media's] fear that the replacement of section 2 of the Official Secrets Act will turn out to be, not an improvement in press freedom, but the substitution of an armalite for a blunderbuss'. Meanwhile they would 'have to rely upon the natural reluctance of the mass circulation papers to crib material from and thus acknowledge a debt to the fringe publications. And the outcome of the Aubrey-Berry-Campbell affair may have a bearing on this: I expect you will have seen that the Attorney-General has approved charges under section 1 of the Official Secrets Act 1911, and that may give some people cause for thought'.

The subsequent 'ABC' trial, another contemporary cause célèbre, was so called because not only the three defendants, but more piquantly three anonymous witnesses Colonels A & B and Mr C, shared these initials. The case was sparked by that of Agee and Hosenball, deported because they were alleged to have published disclosures about the CIA without US authority, but for whom the then 'fringe' magazine *Time Out* campaigned. The journalist Campbell was charged with receiving secret information from the ex-Sigint soldier Berry, who was charged with providing it, and another journalist Aubrey with abetting them.[69] D-Notice System involvement in the ABC affair was tangential in theory, but Farnhill's position was tested in practice. Whilst the case was still in process, Cooper wrote in mid-December to Sir Antony Duff at the Foreign Office[70] and the other DPBC Official Members, referring to the discussion at the March 1977 meeting; he explained that reporting of the Committal proceedings (8 November) had highlighted the problem for the technical Press in particular of determining what was publishable. Farnhill was being asked for guidance in such a way that officials thought it was aimed at 'provoking him into writing something which may be useful to Campbell's defence' at the subsequent trial. For the time being he could anyway only reply that he could not comment on sub judice matters, but Cooper warned his colleagues that, whatever the outcome of the ABC case, the DPBC would need to return at its January meeting to republication of sensitive material.

Before the 24 January 1978 meeting, Cooper and Clarke arranged that the latter would propose a small sub-committee to consider specific points, rather than have further inconclusive general discussion. Although Armstrong (now promoted to PUS Home Office and therefore a DPBC Member) wished the Security Service Legal Adviser Bernard Sheldon to be on the sub-committee, Cooper thought this would be a step too far for Media members. Farnhill had met the latter separately to brief them on six of the cases he had had to deal with in the previous three years, 'involving writers, publishers and film and TV producers', in which he had been asked for advice on matters not strictly covered by the then D-Notices, for example domestic terrorism and historical security stories.[71] There was no criticism but some unease amongst Media members about this de facto extension of his remit, although it was accepted there was then no alternative source of advice for the Media. Farnhill stressed that in such cases he always made clear he was speaking personally from experience and not as the DPBC's representative. No conclusion was reached, but the Media side was concerned they might thus be drawn into matters beyond the latitude they were given by those they represented. Similarly there was no Media side agreement on whether the development and expansion of material already in the public domain should be restrained if it resulted in a damaging article.

Farnhill later minuted his Chairman on the unease about his growing role in advising on 'historical' stories. He attributed the increase in his work on intelligence and security manuscripts as being due to the dam broken by 'Ultra' disclosures since 1974, release of wartime intelligence records, CIA disclosures and the US Freedom of Information Act. Books by their nature required much more time and negotiation than advice on Press articles or broadcasts. It was helpful to publishers to have one person (the D-Notice Secretary) involved rather than some book-clearing department, and discussion in an atmosphere of goodwill often strayed slightly beyond pure D-Notice advice. He reminded that in 1974 the Minister for Defence had announced in Parliament that anyone wishing to publish his wartime intelligence memoirs should consult his former Department or the D-Notice Secretary. He recommended that he should continue the practice at least until OSA Section 2 was reformed; he foresaw however that even if intelligence disclosure was then criminalised, the Media would still need the D-Notice Secretary's advice. DPBC inability to agree on all this meant in the end that the proposed sub-committee was never formed; D-Notice Secretaries since then have continued to deal with 'historic' matters, with the Committee's de facto consent.

Meanwhile more routine D-Notice business continued. In early December 1977, at Farnhill's prompting, Cooper had written to Palliser at the FCO about the imminent appointment of the new 'C'. 'I think we can take it as axiomatic that, even if the appointment is not announced, it will leak very quickly. It did on the last occasion. We will then get enquiries to the Secretary of the "D" Notice Committee about what the papers should do. For example, on the last occasion, the *Daily Mirror* was persuaded not to publish a photograph and details, and these were promptly published in the same time scale by the *Daily Telegraph*.' Clarke's advice was that D-Notice No.10 alone would be insufficient to prevent leakage, possibly after publication of the name abroad, and he recommended therefore a letter to editors from Downing Street.

Cooper agreed, discussing with Palliser such variations as giving editors the name in confidence and asking them not to reveal it, or allowing them 'to reveal the name once only, if we could be confident – and there might be great difficulties in this – that the papers would not use it again whatever the circumstances'. About the difficulty at least he was right; as Clarke himself made clear to the Chief Press Officer of No.10 when he met him a few days later at the annual Newspaper Conference: there were strong media feelings about the subject, and a mooted private meeting of a senior official or Minister with editors would probably be counterproductive, in the light of 'the not entirely happy or satisfactory' history of such meetings.

The Cabinet Secretary now took the lead, as coincidentally the DGSS was also due to be relieved. He obtained Mrs Thatcher's agreement for her Chief Press Officer to act as suggested by Clarke, also referring to the personal security concerns in the latter's letter to editors the previous April. Armstrong also himself briefed 'appropriate people from the 'heavies', in relation to the MI5 appointment'. Initially it made some difference to general media reticence about identifying the two new Heads of Service; but, even though not named in the Downing Street letter, it was quickly and widely known who they were, and in the following months this information percolated into the public domain. In the eyes of the Media, there were many others with similar personal security concerns but without the protection of anonymity, and the risk was considered to be outweighed by the public interest accountability of their senior positions.

In mid-June 1978 *Peace News* (which had named Colonel B, and been convicted for contempt of court) published a three-page article ('A Gentlemen's Agreement') about the D-Notice System. It gave full details of the DPBC membership and of the Notices, and described the application of each Notice. It was critical of authorities' actions in the various areas covered, but gratifyingly accurate and fair about the D-Notice System itself. A former Conservative Minister suggested the Director of Public Prosecutions should investigate this 'breach of security', but Farnhill said he would 'not be losing any sleep about it . . . It is merely a system for helping the Press make up its own mind. I express an opinion but the final decision on what to publish rests with the editor.'[72]

The White Paper discussion document on Reform of the Official Secrets Act appeared in July 1978. As a central part of the repeal of OSA 1911 Section 2, the Home Secretary referred to 'an informal committee on classification', but it was not immediately clear whether this was to be a temporary and advisory one to set up a new system (and therefore of no direct concern to the Media side) or a permanent one effectively ruling (to editors as well) as to what could be made public (and therefore of direct concern and, in Clarke's view, likely to receive a hostile reaction from across the Media). The Media side discussed this on return from their summer holidays, by which time it was clear there was little likelihood of precise legislative proposals being made in the foreseeable future (the Callaghan Labour Government had many more immediate problems).

After the 28 November 1978 DPBC meeting, Cooper nevertheless reported to Ministers and colleagues that the 'Press and Broadcasting Members expressed some fairly trenchant views, of which I believe you will wish to be aware'. These centred on the classification committee, about which they spoke 'with surprising unanimity and something approaching vehemence'. The formal part of the meeting again made it clear that the Media side believed that the D-Notice System could not survive 'in parallel with a statutory system backed by criminal sanctions'. The DPBC should continue to concern itself only with security against external threats and not with matters classified for other reasons, nor with advice about classification or legal matters. In the subsequent informal discussion, a strong media interest emerged in a Freedom of Information Act proposed in a Private Member's Bill by CR Freud,[73] containing appropriate national security exemptions. If the 'classification' idea were to go ahead, the Media would require some organisation to consult which could give 'authoritative answers immediately or with very little notice'. The DPBC 'Uncle Toms' calculated no government would ever be able to sustain a Press facility which could reliably match the speed required by media deadlines and still meet the requirements of political clearance, let alone one where potential criminalisation was involved.

The Cabinet Secretary, now Sir John Hunt[74], mulled over these media objections with senior colleagues. Cooper said media views would ultimately depend on the extent of criminal sanctions which could be applied against them. All agreed on the need to keep the DPBC yet not extend its role; Armstrong thought editors and their legal advisors would learn to use the proposed system in making enquiries, although 'Departments would need to be very careful how they answered such inquiries, for fear of prejudicing subsequent proceedings. But editors would be very chary of making inquiries of this kind, since the mere fact that they had done so might subsequently be used as evidence that they had reason to believe that the document came within the categories protected by the Act.'

This did not sound a very slick system, and Farnhill had no difficulty in picking it to pieces and showing how in practice it would not work in detail, because of how the Media actually needed to operate. He also pointed out the Media would still need to seek advice on linked matters which were not specifically covered by the classification committee, and would continue therefore to turn to a system they knew and consult the D-Notice Secretary, who would however now be forbidden to get involved in classification matters. The MoD on this occasion sided with the Media against the Home Office, Cooper's deputy describing the proposed Act as (in media eyes) 'a Frankenstein's monster.'[75]

By mid-1979, however, with Mrs Thatcher's Government two months into power, it was clear that, despite the Media side's continuing concerns, and although the classification committee proposal was likely to be dropped, Ministers had decided nevertheless to proceed with plans to reform OSA Section 2 as part of the new Official Information Bill then passing through Parliament. At the 18 July 1979 DPBC meeting, the Media side reiterated their remaining major concerns. They were relieved the classification idea had been dropped, but considered that the creation of an offence of unauthorised disclosure by a private citizen, in circumstances when he had reason to believe that the information in question was protected by the Act, would make impossible the publication of matters of legitimate public interest without high risk of media conflict with the criminal law. They were also worried about the likelihood of creeping over-classification of information, and the potential for improper use of ministerial certification.

Ministers were taking a close interest in the Media side views. Against their arguments, Armstrong took a firm Home Office line (with support from the Foreign Office): it was too late to attempt to allay their fears of the Bill itself; there could anyway be no complete answer to their worries, since there were bound to be occasions when the Press would risk conflict with the law; it would be intolerable to create a situation in which a citizen could knowingly disclose protected information with impunity; the Media would be at risk only over a relatively narrow range of information. He conceded that they regarded the narrower focus of the Bill as in practice increasing the risk, but said they had only themselves to blame by having done so much over the years to discredit OSA 1911 Section 2. 'One effect of the new legislation may well be that editors will err on the side of caution in publishing secret material in the defence and foreign relations field. However unwelcome that may be to the journalists, is it an unmitigated disservice to the public service?' Nevertheless, in the light of 'the recent history of official secrets prosecutions', it was not at all likely editors and journalists would be brought to court unless the Attorney-General was satisfied there was a strong case. They would also, Armstrong claimed, 'enjoy' the protection of some possible defences in the draft Bill. It would not be Ministers but a court which might require a journalist to reveal his source, but more probably he would be asked what steps he had taken to ascertain whether the Act applied to the information in question. The DPBC discussion had been very useful in learning of media anxieties, and he agreed the Committee should not only remain in being but should also 'keep right out of this area'; but that was his final view.

Cooper was more sympathetic to media anxieties. He told official colleagues there was not only apprehension about the draft Act, but also 'the (almost paradoxical) fear that Ministers are moving away from a system of voluntary co-operation towards a much more rigid alternative which will exert pressure on editors to consult Government Departments before they report or discuss certain matters'. Assurances of prosecution only in 'blatant' cases did not allay this fear. The D-Notice Secretary was in fact consulted in practice on matters more diverse than the Notices 'where no help can be obtained from Government Departments', both sides tacitly accepted this, it increased the goodwill of the Media, and would be likely to continue whatever the OSA said; it had 'become, in a curious way, part of the system.'[76]

In the light of media concerns, Hunt conceded in early August that some additional machinery might possibly be needed, separate from the DPBC, to advise editors and others on whether 'serious injury' would be caused by publication. Farnhill, continuing to put media views strongly to officials, pointed out they would be unlikely to be content to wait and see how the new legislation worked in practice, since they suspected its provisions were aimed not just against Crown Servants but against them too. He queried whether advice on 'serious injury' would in fact be advice or 'on the basis of "disregard it at your peril"'.

The debate between senior officials continued into the autumn of 1979, and the draft Protection of Official Information Bill continued to be amended. In early November, Farnhill was sufficiently concerned about the way things were moving to write privately to Clarke. He referred to Press comment on the proposal that a Minister's certificate (that something caused or would cause serious damage) should not be contestable in the Courts; this would cast doubt on continuation of the D-Notice System, because, even in the unlikely event that the Media side agreed to extend coverage of the Notices to the whole proposed OSA coverage, the opinion of the Secretary would not be worth seeking; only the Minister concerned could decide. This was in contrast with the current System, where the agreed convention was that an editor who had followed the Secretary's advice could, in the unlikely event of being prosecuted at all, plead the advice in his defence.

The Media side agreed. In late November, Clarke wrote to Cooper that during the past few days

> the P&B section of the DPBC has hung together by a thread which is still under considerable strain. Like several others, I have received private assurances that the Government is having a major re-think of the Protection of Information Bill and that amendments will be introduced which will, in effect, re-write the main aspects of the Bill. However, some of my colleagues feel that the fact that the original Bill could be introduced at all is evidence enough that the Government
>
> (a) has failed to appreciate the admittedly unofficial advice which has been offered (as a matter of goodwill rather than anything else) on the philosophy of the Bill, and
>
> (b) so takes the D-Notice system for granted that Ministers seriously believe that it can continue to function while, under clause 1(1a) of the Bill criminal

sanctions are held in reserve at the discretion of Ministers over the whole defence and foreign affairs fields.

Clarke urged Cooper urgently therefore to call a special DPBC meeting, to explain the current situation to the Media side ('we should avoid an adversary climate if possible'), because he feared that otherwise there might be several 'formal resignations'. He felt he was exceeding his 'P&B writ' in writing thus privately to Cooper; 'My reason for so writing is that if the D-Notice system is to come to an end I believe it should be done by an understanding which, if short of agreement, at least avoids acrimony, while if it is still useful (and I think we all take your word on this point) the very shaken confidence in its validity should be restored without undue delay'.

Having received this plea, Cooper told the new Home Office PUS, Sir Brian Cubbon,[77] that he was keen to have a meeting before Christmas 'if only to give an opportunity for the Press side to calm down and let off some steam and to feel they are being consulted and that their opinions are valued. I need hardly say that the help they give over the D Notice system is worth repaying by giving particular attention to their susceptibilities'. He hoped Cubbon would be able to tell them something 'about the future course of events', and allow them, without commitment, their say 'at the beginning of our rethink of the legislation'.

Cubbon however was not keen to have a meeting at which the Media could let off steam while he could say no more than three sentences: 'the Government is not at present proceeding with the Bill [the Prime Minister had announced this on 20 November]; this does not mean that the Bill will not reappear or that it will reappear in its present form; I cannot say more at this stage'. He felt Ministers were 'in a tricky position'. Until they had some idea where they were going on the matter, any discussion with the Media could be difficult, since it might appear that these were 'with an empty sheet of green paper in front of us'. On the other hand it would be foolish prematurely to revive controversies about the present Bill, and he did 'not intend to engage in discussion of a Bill which the Government has decided not to proceed with at present'. Cooper however insisted (although the meeting was delayed for other reasons by six months).

In August 1979 came two reminders that many of the security versus publication issues faced in the UK were common to other democratic countries. The JIC Secretary sent Farnhill the transcript of a lecture given the previous month to the Washington Chapter of the National Classification Management Society by the senior NSA classification specialist. He highlighted the quantity of sensitive information made available to the Soviets by the US Media, balanced the need for security against vital freedoms of speech, press and justice, and suggested improved legislation, dialogue with the press, and 'policing up our own act'. Of more direct concern to UK secret Agencies were moves in the USA to improve political control, particularly of the CIA.

This coincided with a more general discussion in Whitehall about the collective impact of measures which would give greater publicity to the secret Agencies. The SIS view was that these must eventually impair the quality and quantity of the intelligence obtained by the Agencies, who would no longer be able to elicit the co-operation and trust of agents and allies to the same degree as in the past. It disagreed with a previous observation by the MoD's Cooper that the UK should consider abandoning the blanket refusal to speak about any aspect of intelligence matters. It considered that once this convention was abandoned, there would be a very 'slippery slope', with no way of drawing a line on further disclosures; the more that was given out, the more journalists would probe and expose. It cited examples of such slides in other countries, and commented on the conflict for the CIA between the oath of secrecy to the US Government and the duty to Congress.

Farnhill prompted Cooper to respond, pointing out that the SIS had read more into his remarks than intended [Farnhill may have drafted the original letter, but Cooper would not have signed unless it completely reflected his own view]. The greater openness suggested was only where to give unattributable help to the Media would be advantageous to the SIS and to public understanding of its role. Cooper wrote to the Cabinet Secretary, saying he did not wholly accept the 'slippery slope' argument; the MoD had on occasion found being helpful to the Media 'had paid off hand over fist' [the Media might have had a somewhat different view]. Armstrong replied he agreed with Cooper, but 'we are clear that the Prime Minister would not', so there would be no change of policy for the present.[78] The SIS argument has been used by it and by other secret organisations before and since, and is still a policy adhered to in principle, but with modulations in practice.

At the 15 January 1980 DPBC meeting,[79] Cubbon confined himself on the OSA Bill to reassurances that, although there was no way in which a criminal law could be constructed to give immunity to a responsible journalist (because 'responsible journalism' was not a concept known to the law), nevertheless the Home Secretary would take account of media views in drafting any legislation (and indeed was due to meet representatives at the International Press Institute in February). The DPBC position would depend upon what eventually emerged in the legislation, and the Media side's views would be taken into account before the legislative process began.[80] Afterwards, Cooper commented to Armstrong (now Cabinet Secretary) on the 'widely differing perspectives between HMG and the media on the effects of a Protection of Information Bill. We regard legislation as rectifying the defects in Section 2 of the Official Secrets Act which . . . had been the subject of much adverse comment by the media itself, particularly the catch-all nature of the official information protected. The Press side of the DPBC at least see the Bill as a medium for inhibiting comment and discussion in many areas on which they have a legitimate duty to inform the public'.

Armstrong retorted there was 'now no amendment of Section 2 of the OSA 1911 which the Press will accept.' The Bill had brought the Media 'hard up against the prospect of living with legislation which defined precise categories of information which would be protected by sanctions; and they did not like it. The Blunt affair came as a heaven-sent excuse to turn on the Bill; but, if they had not had that excuse, they would have found another'. Armstrong thought the Media would now prefer to 'stick to Section 2', and he saw not much future 'for any kind of deal which trades up-to-date legislation on the protection of official information for some kind of commitment to "open government"'. He nevertheless reiterated that the DPBC remained valuable, and that it and the trust built up over the years should be retained.[81]

Cooper sought to be proactive, and set his own Ministry to work while the Bill was 'in suspense', asking it whether it would be preferable either to retain OSA Section 2, or for the Protection of Information Bill to be enacted, or for some different legislation to be enacted – and, of course, if so, what? In late February 1980, after much civil and military security directorates staffwork, the 'clear consensus' in MoD was reported to him: retain Section 2 – at least until 'a suitable opportunity comes to introduce legislation acceptable both to Ministers/Whitehall and to the media/country' [philosophically and constitutionally an interesting pairing]. Meanwhile 'Section 2 protects the MoD's interests that matter'[82].

Cooper reported this, which accorded with the view of the DPBC Media side, to Cubbon, adding three points. Firstly, 'we should not underestimate the difficulties in attempting to legislate in the face of Press opposition, since, regardless of logic, it would be regarded as "repressive" unless it was coupled with measures relating to open Government going a good deal beyond anything Ministers have been prepared to contemplate so far'. Secondly, if not ideal, Section 2 was adequate as long as the case was good, whereas past difficulties had arisen because 'the offences prosecuted could be regarded – rightly or wrongly – as marginal to the national security interests of the United Kingdom'. Thirdly, at a time of manpower reductions [the Government's then intention for Whitehall], replacement of Section 2 by a new system of classification would cause 'considerable upheaval in the conduct of normal business' and 'considerable doubt and uncertainty'. Cubbon agreed; the real question, it seemed to him, was not the obviously serious offender, whom Courts were likely to punish, but 'lower down the spectrum (whether actions by disclosers or receivers) that should not be tolerated but against which the law is in practice powerless. Only time can answer that'. Which within a decade it did.

47

WIDER CONCERNS ABOUT THE
D-NOTICE SYSTEM

In the late 1970s and early 1980, Duncan Campbell wrote a series of *New Statesman* articles revealing then sometimes classified national security information. That about the still publicly unavowed Secret Intelligence and Security Services caused other editors to seek guidance from the new D-Notice Secretary Admiral Bill Ash[83] as to the standing of D-Notices 10 (British Intelligence Services) and 11 (Cyphers and Communications). In February 1980 he therefore sent an apparently routine and innocuous short letter to all editors confirming that the two Notices were still 'in force', and that the 'need to protect the information on the intelligence services covered by these two Notices is unchanged and remains of the first importance in the interests of national security'. He asked that editors continued to be guided by them, adding they were 'kept under review' by the DPBC.

A month later, the *New Statesman*'s editor Bruce Page[84] wrote lengthily to Ash, reminding that the System was voluntary, whereas the implication of the Notices' wording was otherwise, that matters previously raised by the journal (phone tapping, mail opening, and the intelligence services' real costs) were all of public interest, that the goodwill on which the System depended could be extended to the DPBC but not necessarily to the organisations covered by the Notices, that it was 'an open question' whether a system set up 'in exceptional times' could be 'extended and institutionalised', that 'during the 1970s the intelligence services in many western societies' had, by their actions and attitudes, lost the confidence of large sections of the public, that if the Notices were indeed kept under review it was remarkable that they had not been amended since 1971, and that (in the *New Statesman*'s view) there were civil and political liberties threatened by the intelligence and security agencies. The Committee should therefore be aware of their lack of 'credence' with 'many serious media organisations', and 'as a contribution to public understanding', the editor intended to publish this correspondence.

Ash replied tersely (and perhaps impetuously) that this representation of the D-Notice System was so tendentious and wide of the mark that he did not think anything would be gained by joining issue on it. Page duly published the correspondence as part of an article by Duncan Campbell entitled 'The D Notice Quangette': 'The D Notice system is one of the great mysteries of British journalism. Many members of the public believe it to be a means for the Government to suppress news of their favourite grievance. Even quite experienced journalists working on a "sensitive" story fear – absurdly – that their efforts may be frustrated by the arrival of the D Notice carrier, despatched urgently from the Ministry of Defence.' He pointed out that one of the reasons why the System had 'broken down' was ironically its 'deep secrecy'.

Campbell gave an accurate description of the System and how it operated, the names of those on the Committee, the list of 1971 Notices and the gist of their content. He criticised the very existence of the System as unnecessary, since editors would not 'wittingly publish information which endangers life or serious national interests' [but did not suggest how either of these dangers might be assessed]. He reminded readers of past problems over advice provided, such as the 1961 equipment Notice and the 1967 attempt to suppress discussion of the traitors who had fled to Moscow; and that compliance with the advice in the Notices did not prevent journalists being prosecuted, as in the 1970 *Sunday Telegraph* case or the 1977 ABC trial. He ended by suggesting some new system, 'a more genuinely representative interface between Fleet Street and Whitehall which sought to open up the government and not to close down press investigation'. This article attracted immediate attention in other journals, and on BBC radio's 'World at One' on 2 April, where Robin Day interviewed both Page and Ramsden, who gave their equally strongly held but contrary views about the D-Notice System.[85]

While the Media were thus focusing on the D-Notice System itself, the Government was focusing on protecting official secrets, albeit with some despondency. The Bill had been tabled a few months earlier in the House of Lords, seeking to toughen the OSAs and in particular to replace the 'discredited' Section 2 with something applicable more effectively to Secret Intelligence and Security. It had not only been criticised by the Media, but had also met considerable resistance in Parliament. At the beginning of May, Cubbon wrote to Cooper, putting work on hold until a more favourable political moment arrived, and acknowledging the difficulty which meanwhile the Law Officers would have in exercising 'their responsibilities under Section 2' in the face of what one of his subordinates referred to as the Media continuing 'to flex their muscles by exploiting leaks of one kind or another.'[86]

The DPBC Media side met on 1 May to discuss the *New Statesman* onslaught. There was a wide variation in views, from David Chipp of the Press Association[87]whose growing doubts about the System's modus operandi had been brought to a head by the affair, through a few who considered no change was necessary, to the majority opinion that some changes were indeed overdue, and that a more fundamental review than the annual one was necessary. Windsor Clarke wrote accordingly to Cooper, asking that this be put in hand. Ramsden followed up to Clarke at the end of May, suggesting that D-Notices should be published, so that they were seen to be sensible, as the only way to correct Press suspicion and misunderstanding.[88]

House of Commons Defence Committee Inquiry 1980

The public correspondence with the *New Statesman*, and earlier agitation from such as Peter Hennessy[89] in *The Times*, stirred parliamentary interest once more in the functioning of the D-Notice System. Dr John Gilbert[90] gained agreement of colleagues on the House of Commons Select Committee on Defence (HCDC) that they should study the subject. The MoD, as sponsoring Ministry for the System where Parliament is concerned, started inter-departmental work in April on the necessary background paper for the HCDC, although Gilbert (acting as Chairman during this study) did not formalise and announce the work until mid-May. He told Cooper then that, although their interest had been stimulated by the *New Statesman* controversy, they were in no sense beginning the enquiry with preconceived notions or setting up a 'lynching party'. The initiative was because the System had never previously been formally addressed by the House, and because time had elapsed since the

Radcliffe Committee had looked into it.[91] Hennessy in *The Times* pointed up the additional background that a new consideration was the security implications of Northern Ireland.[92]

Cooper commented to his staff he 'would guess we shall be pressed most on grounds that there have been so many breaches it is a waste of time.'[93] He was also wary about commenting on comparable practices in the USA and Europe, since this 'could rapidly get us into deep water over the OSA, Freedom of Information Acts etc'. His officials considered what historical aspects the Enquiry might consider: 'As Colonel Lohan's real crime was to get too closely involved with certain Conservative back-benchers, it seems all the more likely that the Defence Committee may interest themselves in the matter'; however, they also acknowledged that since 1967 the Secretary's post had been filled by 'a series of Flag Officers [Admirals] selected for their breadth of experience, personal qualities and maturity of judgement.'[94]

Meanwhile the DPBC Vice-Chairman had different concerns, in that Chipp had decided not only that he would be standing down from the DPBC, but also that he intended (Clarke thought) to put in 'a very adverse view' of the D-Notice System to the HCDC; he expected Chipp's evidence to be 'emotional and ill-argued', but was even more concerned that the resignation would be coming at a time 'when it can be based on no reason of substance'; privately Chipp also thought that some of the Committee's Media representatives had become too close to officials in their perspective.[95] When Chipp shortly afterwards wrote to Cooper courteously enclosing his HCDC submission and explaining his rationale, it was not however the System itself but its image which concerned him most: 'D Notices look like a conspiracy and this impression is fed by ill-disposed or ignorant people, including some civil servants, who believe the system has powers and functions which we know it doesn't have. Now we may all know that we are lily-white but others don't and the D Notice system quite frankly has a bad general press. It is thus counter-productive.' He intended to try to disband it from within, but if the majority of his Media colleagues disagreed, he would 'quietly' leave the DPBC.

The HCDC took evidence, written and oral, from officials and from those in the Media who wished to give it. Ministerial permission had to be sought to provide even parliamentarians with copies of the still classified extant 12 Notices, and the MoD was also asked to provide information on comparable practices in other countries.[96] Media written evidence was received from the Guild of Editors, NS, PPA, SDNS, BBC, IBA, the *Daily* and *Sunday Telegraph*, *Daily Mail*, *Daily* and *Sunday Mirror*, *Daily Express*, *Guardian* (where the editor and his staff disagreed but the former gave way), *Flight*, Thames TV (all the foregoing, in sum, for continuation); individual members of the NUJ (critical of the 'non-accountable' and 'captured' Media members of the DPBC as much as of the system); *Defence*, the *New Statesman*, PA (its editor-in-chief, at least), and London Weekend Television (all for discontinuation). Individual critical comments included Harold Evans' view that the Committee was 'dying of senility', while Bruce Page characterised those in the Media who supported continuance by 'You will always find people ready to kiss their chains.'[97]

Amongst even those who were for continuation, views varied, several wishing its Notices and organisation to be made public in order to remove the wrong perceptions of its role. Others were motivated in part by fear of it being replaced by something worse, in particular draconian use of the OSAs. Hennessy, speaking personally as a Whitehall correspondent rather than for *The Times*, listed the pros and cons of the System, referring to it touching 'a strain of deep ambivalence in many journalists, including those who are convinced that Whitehall remains the citadel, the Monte Cassino, of excessive secrecy in the western world'.

The deputy editor of *The Times*, Louis Heren,[98] writing personally, felt his newspaper applied adequate self-censorship without the need for the DPBC, and that the system was 'a hangover of the days when . . . the men in Whitehall knew what was best for the country'. Chipp, while not agreeing the System was sinister, or a threat to open government or the free flow of information, nevertheless felt that 'the whole ethos of the last quarter of the twentieth century must be against such cosy press-official consultations.'[99] The longest media submission came from the *New Statesman*, co-signed by Page and Campbell, enlarging on the original article.[100]

Some official consternation was caused by Page's stated intention to discuss the detail of the 12 extant Notices in public session of the HCDC, and by Gilbert's refusal to consider a closed session, having already asked the MoD to consider with the DPBC and others public discussion of the Notices. The Security Service (unlike SIS and GCHQ) considered that, although there were 'disadvantages in publication, we would be unlikely to find them insupportable'. When the transcript of Page's evidence was circulated for comment on the thus publicised contents of the Notices, the MoD decided the time had come to accept publication, but it felt this should nevertheless properly be a decision for the DPBC to take. Ash felt a rapid decision was impracticable, and that the Committee would not want to have to 'salami-slice' D-Notice revision under this pressure, but, prior to the planned DPBC meeting two weeks later, he rapidly asked Departments concerned to confirm his view there was little if anything in the Notices which could not be published. This Departmental trawl confirmed that, apart from one small detail in D-Notice No.8 (Government War HQs etc), there was no classified material in the D-Notices, although there was still official concern about potential longer-term and political implications of declassification.[101]

When Sir Frank Cooper gave evidence he did so partly in public and partly in camera. The HCDC pressed him to agree that the contents of D-Notices could be debated in public, and he undertook to discuss this with the DPBC.[102] The gist of his evidence was that officials wished the System to continue, but that some updating was needed, that the calibre and independence of the Secretary were vital to its successful working, that whatever emerged in revision of the OSAs there was no direct connection between such Acts and the D-Notice System, that a two-tier system of Notices was theoretically possible, that there would be difficulties in covering domestic terrorism in the Notices, that information published abroad should continue to be publishable in the UK, and that there was a difference between leaks of inside information and leaks of classified information. In camera, he talked about the need for the secrecy surrounding Chevaline,[103] how the more secret aspects of operations in Northern Ireland were covered in practice by existing D-Notices, about the lack of reach to those few journals outside the system ('a small loophole'), and whether the Media members were truly representative of the Media as a whole ('debatable', but he thought there was no widespread dissatisfaction).[104]

Admiral Ash also gave evidence, despite being relatively new in post. He had already observed the Notices were in need of a more radical overhaul than was possible at an annual DPBC meeting (only one change, to Notice No.4, Aircraft and Aero Engines had been made since 1971), and that the system suffered from widespread misconceptions about it which could only be removed by increased public knowledge. When asked how often he was consulted by journalists, he said written requests from the Press for advice were very rare because of the short timetable to which the newspapers worked, but slightly more frequent from the broadcast media, and that oral requests in his six months in office had numbered about 30, of which he gave some examples: queries from the provincial Press about local manufacture of certain weapons, and from the national Press about the transportation of nuclear material and Government preparations for war on the civil side; in all of this, the most he had advised was omission of a few words. He confirmed that, where something contrary to a Notice was published inadvertently (unlike the *New Statesman* case), he merely wrote to or rang the editor for future reference, and that there had been no instance in recent years where a request from either side for an amendment to a Notice had been turned down by the Committee.

He was quizzed on the lack of a Notice dealing with IRA matters, and later returned to give evidence in camera on this. He explained that the topic had 'caused considerable difficulty for the Committee', because although there was no published definition of national security, the DPBC had always excluded matters of internal security, and any broadbrush change to this would intrude on the 'freedom of the press to discuss large areas of subjects'. However, he considered that 'with the growth of various forms of terrorism in recent years', it was something Committee would have to look at in the review of the Notices which it had recently decided to undertake. When questioned about Cooper's in camera concerns that it would be difficult to define exactly what aspects should be covered, and about links with journalists in the Republic of Ireland, Ash said he had in mind terrorism in general, not just the Irish dimension, but that subjects like the NITAT facilities[105] would need to be covered.

His in camera session ended with two hypothetical questions. The first was on weapons information, and on where the line should be drawn between keeping a deficient capability secret, or 'having to expose it to have it remedied'; Ash replied this would have to be dealt with case by case in discussion between the Secretary and the Media. The second was in which circumstances he would think it necessary to consult Ministers; his opinion was that, in the very rare event that this might happen, he would raise it through his Chairman and it would probably concern something likely to become a political issue, or the operation of the D-Notice System as a whole rather than an individual Notice.[106]

From the Media side of the Committee, open evidence was given principally by Windsor Clarke, who explained that, although he was called Vice-Chairman of the DPBC, his actual role was to act as Chairman of and Spokesman for the Press and Broadcasting Members.[107] He criticised fellow-journalists for their lack of knowledge of the System and their utterly incorrect insinuation the Media representatives were paid 'Uncle Toms' of the Government. He distributed to the HCDC the letter he had written to *The Times* in 1973 after the Granada TV 'World in Action' programme had alleged that the DPBC had ordered cuts in broadcast programmes; he had been so 'incensed' that he had pointed out that it was not a censorship organisation. He suggested to the HCDC that some similar public statement about the D-Notice System was now required.

When it was suggested the Secretary's detailed reports to the DPBC on his contacts with the Media might regularly be published, Clarke was however against the idea, on the grounds that editors and journalists would not welcome their private discussions being made public, revealing contacts and other, as yet unpublished, information; but he could accept unattributable and more general reports which gave the public an indication of the kinds of enquiries recently made and advice given. He supported the intended review of the Notices. On their publication, his only concern was that a two-tier system might develop, of what could and could not be put in the Notices themselves, as opposed to in a classified annex.

Clarke was teased by Bruce George[108] about the apparent disparity between the Press complaints over D-Notice constraints on investigative journalism, and the apparently low number of actual approaches to the Secretary. Clarke countered it would be a poor investigative journalist who was deterred by the existence of the D-Notice System, and that, although he would have no objection to having such a journalist on the Committee, as was sometimes suggested, the fact was that ultimately it was editors who decided what was published.

On the Media side's modus operandi, he revealed they then met separately about four times a year to discuss general media/government matters, such as the implications of the Government's recent draft Bill on the Protection of Official Information, and how it might compromise their freedom and independence in relation to the D-Notice System. He had similar views to those of Ash about the distinction between national interest and national security vis-à-vis weapon system deficiencies. He also agreed with Ash's view of the *New Statesman*'s article as 'tendentious', and defended the System robustly, refusing only to be drawn in public on the views of the one dissenting (and unnamed) and ex-Media member of the DPBC (clearly Chipp, about whom Clarke stayed behind afterwards to talk briefly in private).

Finally, questioned about the views of the foreign Press about the D-Notice System, he replied that in his experience European and Japanese journalists tended to admire it but think it could not be applied in their country, while Americans found it harder to understand, since the size and complexity of their country would make it impossible to implement. He agreed too that in the unlikely event of a large part of the British Media deciding no longer voluntarily to use the system, it would cease to function[109] Cooper at about this time was in correspondence with his opposite number in Australia, where the official (but not media) view of its own D-Notice System was then similar to that of UK officials.[110]

The Government's position on OSA reform was meanwhile summed up in a letter of 26 June 1980 from the Home Secretary William Whitelaw[111] to the Attorney-General and other Cabinet colleagues. He apologised to the Law Officers for the difficulty caused by the decision not to proceed with the Protection of Official Information Bill ('torpedoed by the Blunt affair'), and conceded that neither of the remaining alternatives (reforming Section 2 or 'soldiering on for as long as we can with the 1911 Act') was attractive. The Media opposition to the former (as expressed in the DPBC and more widely) caused him to think nothing further should be done by the Government 'unless and until events force us to consider the matter again'. Meanwhile he suggested that the Attorney-General's position might include the reassurance that prosecutions could only be brought with his consent, as the safeguard against prosecutions not in the public interest. Mrs Thatcher's conclusion was that 'there may be political advantage to be gained from talking about reform in this field, but there is precious little political advantage to be gained from actively trying to do something about it.'[112]

Amongst all this HCDC and OSA work, the normal pattern of consultation between media and D-Notice Secretary went on, the trivial aspects sometimes causing him the most time-consuming work. In April 1980, for example, a producer with the BBC in Norwich wrote for advice on a never until then told 'very good wartime story', concerning the repatriation in 1945 of American servicemen buried in the UK. Allegedly special trains had been built and tracks altered to achieve this 'massive operation'. It was kept secret, the story went, in case the relatives of the scattered British dead became aggrieved that the same was not being done for them. Would the producer be contravening the OSA if he now revealed it? Admiral Ash spent many days trying to help, but despite contacting at least nine Government Departments, he found only that all wished to avoid having any responsibility for a decision on this deadly secret. Archives do not reveal whether the tale was ever told by BBC East Anglia.[113]

On a more important administrative matter, Ash became aware of the increasing number of informal contacts between the Security Service's Legal Adviser Bernard Sheldon and some journalists. These occasionally crossed with contacts Ash had with the same editors and journalists. It was therefore agreed he and the Legal Adviser needed to maintain closer contact and better co-ordinate their dealings on any particular story.[114] This closer practical liaison has continued through to modern times, when both the Security Service and the SIS have nominated points of informal contact with the Media; these are not one of their separately organised and now myriad Legal Advisers, but in each Service an officer with the credibility of an operational background and direct access to DGSS/'C'.

On 1 July 1980 the DPBC met to discuss the initial questions that were being asked of it by the HCDC, especially whether understanding and acceptance would be improved by wider publicity, whether the Notices themselves should be published, whether a more thorough review than normal was now needed, and whether terrorism should be covered by D-Notices (Cubbon afterwards interpreted Clarke as prepared to consider this); the only agreement was to start the review. Meanwhile the *full* contents of the Notices should not be made public (the Media side were as divided as officials on this), as they had been drafted on the basis that they would be Private and Confidential.

The HCDC circulated its Report on 'The D Notice System' in August.[115] The Report balanced the case for and against continuation of the System. 'For' included advice provided to editors in addition to the general admonitions in the OSAs; that it was designed to prevent publication of information damaging to national security in a way not done by the OSAs; and that the alternative (litigation) could be something worse. 'Against' was that it was a form of censorship (albeit voluntary); that freedom of the Press was compromised by media participation in the System; that the position vis-à-vis the law was confusing; and that because the System was little used it was obviously unnecessary, since editors would not deliberately publish matters damaging to national security. The conclusions (by a majority vote) were that the System as currently constituted was 'failing to fulfil the role for which it was created'; but that it was important to prevent damaging publication, and the layman/editor could not always know what was damaging to national security. The HCDC, and most of those who gave evidence to it, therefore considered that an advisory system such as the D-notice one was necessary.

The somewhat vague recommendations for improvement included making Notices more accessible, usable and public, improving their drafting process, and increasing media confidence in the processes. Having considered a continuation of the existing official/media system or alternatively a system operated entirely by officials, it plumped for the former, since the Media seemed content with it. Finally the HCDC recommended that a genuine attempt by an editor to comply with D-Notice advice, in particular publication after assurance from the D-Notice Secretary that some information was not covered by a Notice, should normally preclude prosecution by the Government.

When the Attorney-General's Department saw the latter recommendation, however, it pointed out that: 'This proposition depends upon there being an exact equivalence between subjects covered by D Notices and information protected under the Official Secrets Acts. But this is not the case. The Officials Secrets Acts cover a wider area than the D Notices and there is therefore information which would not come within the terms of any of the D Notices, but the publication of which would prima facie be an offence under the Official Secrets Acts.' In any case, its comment concluded, the decision whether or not to prosecute was not for the Government, and so no Government could agree to non-prosecution; and it would be 'constitutionally improper' for an Attorney-General, whose responsibility in a quasi-judicial capacity it was, 'to fetter his own discretion by giving any general undertaking or assurances that he would not prosecute in a particular category of case'. Although the OSAs have since been amended, the non-relationship between them and the D-Notices remains the same, as does the gentlemen's agreement rather than guarantee on non-prosecution.

Reaction to Parliamentary Criticism 1980

Ash immediately set about drafting Terms of Reference for the full DPBC Review, reflecting the tone of the parliamentary criticisms, but when the Cabinet Secretary saw the first draft he swiftly expressed 'substantial and extensive reservations' and rewrote them. He thought the Terms of Reference had gone a great deal further than was necessary both in 'knocking' the existing system and in pre-judging the result of the review. MI5's Sheldon also expressed concern at attempts to define national security in relation to domestic security; he stressed that the Media would often be in no position to judge whether or not a threat originated outside the UK, and that much of the value of the D-Notice System to his Service was that it allowed it to obtain intelligence by secret means 'in the same area as the British press', whereas 'publicity can have considerable bearing upon our ability to do so effectively'. When however the MoD omitted any definition of national security from a subsequent draft, Armstrong asked the redrafting project leader, Cooper's deputy Sir Arthur Hockaday[116] to have at least a general definition re-instated, so that the Media could not choose their own. Armstrong's version got around the continuing reluctance to include domestic terrorism per se in the coverage of the Notices by adding 'externally organised or assisted subversion or terrorism'; but he thought this definition would still have to be classified.[117]

Detailed discussion of the modalities of the review continued between officials, and then with the DPBC Media side, through the autumn of 1980. One linked issue which emerged was confusion over the direct if informal relationship between the Security Service and some parts of the Media. Cooper told Armstrong that, while he expected no difficulty in the D-Notice Review over the protection of Defence information, he foresaw problems over the extent of protection demanded by the secret Agencies, because of the existence of the parallel channel of communication. Armstrong saw less danger in this channel, commenting that, 'in the case of the BBC, the Box [Box 500 was MI5's address] gives as well as gets value'.

Armstrong nevertheless convened a meeting of senior officials on 1 October to discuss what Ash himself saw as a minor problem. He highlighted to Cooper two prime factors: firstly that, while the Government's policy was formally not to discuss most matters concerning the secret Agencies, the D-Notice Secretary needed to do so, for reasons of confidence and credibility; secondly, the Security Service (which still acted then for all three Agencies) was not allowed overt contact with the Media, but for practical reasons had 'fairly extensive informal contacts' with them. The difficulty caused by these two factors together was that the Agencies were normally trying to suppress stories entirely, and that when such sub rosa negotiations failed, the advantages of the D-Notice System to both sides were not available. Ash cited three recent cases in which the outcome had been unsatisfactory to the Agencies, where the D-Notice Secretary had not been asked to become involved: a *Sunday Times* story on Menwith Hill, a 'World in Action' programme about Little Sai Wan, and a BBC Panorama documentary about secret intelligence.

Ash's view was that the lesson of such cases was that 'the D-notice system should habitually be regarded as an instrument of first, rather than last, or no, recourse'. He also considered the most difficult areas were those concerning not external threats, but internal security and the interface between this and an external threat. He did not however feel the problem required any major change in existing arrangements, nor that intelligence and security matters should therefore be excluded from coverage altogether, to the detriment of the Agencies.[118] This view was subsequently accepted by senior officials. Since that time, the D-Notice System has coexisted harmoniously with the limited direct contacts between now all three Agencies and the Media. This three-way relationship is not cosy, but it is normally practical. The same meeting of officials also discussed potential problems of publication of the Notices. The SIS was against publication, the Security Service broadly for it. GCHQ, while content for HMG's interception of communications to be acknowledged, did not want its role in this to be avowed. All agreed it was difficult to define the latter in a way acceptable to both sides.[119]

The DPBC met on 14 October 1980 to discuss its response to the draft HCDC Report. Clarke handed over as the P&B Spokesman to Ramsden, who was thus in post for the Review, and it was the latter who suggested the revised form of words incorporated in the final Terms of Reference:

> To review the operation of the D Notice system, including the nature and extent of official information to be protected by the system, the form of the guidance and advice by which protection is sought, and the organisation and arrangements for formulating, distributing and making known the guidance, and for keeping both the guidance and the system under review.

The Media side also said that it would be difficult to reach a view on some elements until the Government had defined more precisely what it wanted to protect. In discussion it was agreed to make a joint public announcement about the Review and its Terms of Reference, that some definition of national security would be required, that the Media side would need to carry with them the organisations they represented, and that the term 'D-Notices' would continue to be used.[120]

When the HCDC Report was published in late October, the DPBC (through the SofS for Defence as its de facto parliamentary voice) agreed with all the conclusions except that on non-fulfilment of its role; he pointed out this was not supported by the evidence, which was that 'the great bulk of information on national security which the Government believes it is its duty to protect has been effectively preserved from publication as a result of a sense of responsibility of the greater part of the media and through the influence of the existing D-Notices and the action taken by the DPBC to administer the system in the light of current circumstances.'[121]

The D-Notice System and the Non-Avowed MI5 and MI6

In late November 1980, Ash took stock of 'Media Activity in the Intelligence Area', summarising the points recorded above. The year did indeed end with that recurring bone of contention, non-naming the secret Agencies. In mid-December Cubbon wrote the customary letter to his two dozen or so fellow Permanent Under-Secretaries, the Queen's Private Secretary, the Parliamentary Commissioner and senior officials in the Legal Departments, informing them that the new DGSS from March 1981 was to be John Jones.[122] 'As on previous occasions, there will be no public announcement either of the fact that these changes are occurring or of the identity of the new head or deputy head of the Service'; the accompanying Home Office Press Officers' brief justified non-publication on grounds of 'national security'.

Ash immediately minuted Cooper with his concerns about this continuing practice, pointing out that, since 1977 'the publication of the names of the Intelligence Services had become rather more commonplace and the guidance given in D-Notices ... has been questioned both in the press and in Parliament'. He regarded leakage as likely, and was concerned about the impact on the D-Notice System's credibility; but, because official views were unchanged, he suggested at least altering the justification in the defensive Press brief, to reflect what had in fact been the major 1977 concern, the personal security of the Heads of the Agencies.

Cooper the same day fired off a letter of mild protest to the Cabinet Secretary, reminding that in 1977 it had been felt D-Notices were unlikely to be sufficient to avoid disclosure, and that the Prime Minister's Office should write to editors; he suggested this should now happen again. Cooper also agreed with Ash that the Media might be more sympathetic to the personal security justification. Armstrong replied a few days later that, while in 1977 the Press Secretary at No.10 had indeed sent such a letter to editors (including by mistake the editor of the communist *Morning Star*), it had been decided not now to repeat this process, because 'editors will no doubt have what was said at that time in their minds if and when they hear about the new appointment'. Despite this remarkably optimistic and detached view, Armstrong did however agree the Press brief be amended more or less as suggested.[123]

48

THE DPBC REVIEW 1981 TO 1982

The brief preliminary response to the HCDC Report was published in January 1981,[124] welcoming its conclusion that the D-Notice System should be retained, as 'a necessary and beneficial service for both' government and media, and reporting the agreed Terms of the Reference. Chipp elsewhere continued his personal campaign, telling the Commonwealth Press Union: 'I don't think I am suffering from the general paranoia of a reporter in thinking that restraint on our freedom to report is the great danger we as journalists face worldwide, and certainly in Britain. The attack is insidious and slow and is often justified by what are superficially very worthy motives.'[125] The remainder of the Media side readily progressed the Review, reflecting the much greater interest now being taken by broadsheets and the BBC in challenging official secrecy. In late February 1981, Ash told the Official side that the BBC's Alan Protheroe[126] had asked for guidance on whether it would contravene the D-Notices to show an organisation chart of one of the Secret Agencies in a projected Panorama programme about US/UK intelligence and security. The BBC did not intend to submit the programme for scrutiny because it was of a 'philosophical nature', contained opinions not operational details, and had been carefully scrutinised by Protheroe in the light of D-Notice guidance. Ash had however felt unable to give advice without knowing more detail.

Simultaneously the FCO expressed concern about the latest draft of the revised D-Notice No.10, which would effectively 'have taken a significant step towards public avowal of the hitherto unavowed agencies and their activities. Ministers have not yet considered whether they wish to move in this sense'. Before such a draft could be put to the Media side therefore, political approval would be needed, as Ministers would have to deal with consequent Parliamentary Questions. Middle-ranking MoD officials also had concerns about the relationship between the revised D-Notices and the classification of official documents, and inserted in the draft a clause directly linking the coverage of the Notices with the classifications Top Secret and Secret (and even occasionally down to Restricted). This was later rejected as a criterion by the Media side.[127]

Grappling with such detail, the Official side made slow progress in producing the first draft of the revised Notices. At the thinly-attended 5 March 1981 DPBC meeting, the only paper ready for even 'preliminary consideration' was Ash's General Introduction. The Media side view was that the Introduction's definition of information to be protected was too wide, that repeat publication of information already in the public domain should always be accepted (officials still argued some repetition could be 'prejudicial'), that the roles of Vice-Chairman and Secretary should be better defined along the lines of the 1967 Radcliffe Report, and that the Government's security classification system was 'at best of purely academic interest to Editors' and should be omitted (officials accepted both the latter points).

No deadline for the draft Notices was set, and it was the new Vice-Chairman Ramsden who afterwards kept up pressure on officials, also making it clear he expected to see terrorism somehow included in the coverage, particularly in the Notice concerning the Intelligence Services. He also hoped for publicity for the Review, including a press conference when completed. Ash wrote to his Australian opposite number announcing the intention of scrapping the aged Notice about the Petrovs; not only were they not in Britain, but other defectors were not similarly protected by a special Notice (the Australians agreed to this). The Notices on the Intelligence Services and on Secret Communications were held up by the knock-on effect of the concurrent passage through Parliament of the British Telecommunications Bill. Ramsden's intervention did however cause Cooper to tell officials to speed things up.

With the expansion of the use and sophistication of radio and radar since 1971, Departments wished to expand the coverage of the relevant Notice, to include for example radars used to detect Soviet aircraft approaching British air space; even so they doubted whether their proposals would have much 'effect on Duncan Campbell and the editors who support him'. GCHQ opposed 'for presentational reasons' the amalgamation of that Notice with that covering their own activities. The draft Photography Notice was causing even more anguish to officials; arguments about 'War Potential' sites of previous years were now complicated further both by the known interest of Irish terrorists in economic as well as governmental targets, and by the already detailed products of satellite photography. Officials would have preferred the Media always to consult about publication of photographs of Defence establishments, and only to use those issued by the MoD; however, this being probably unacceptable to the Media, a fall-back negotiating position of voluntary consultation was prepared.

GCHQ also continued to press for non-republication of damaging information published abroad or in 'fringe' journals, because it brought it to the attention of a wider audience, and because republication in mainline media gave 'a semblance of authority'. As to 'transition to war', officials considered attempting to extend D-Notice cover to all 'civil establishments vital to the life of the community', and excluding such places from maps. However, the practical difficulties of defining which locations were involved, and likely objections of commercial owners to prohibition of photographs wanted for publicity purposes, caused this official desire reluctantly to be suppressed; similar realism dictated that only those nuclear establishments belonging to the Government could be covered.[128]

Casework continued as normal, for example when the BBC *Panorama* programme broadcast critical comments about MI5 activities by a former officer; on D-Notice advice, the BBC Director-General Sir Ian Trethowan[129] ordered the producer to omit ten to fifteen minutes of details, including the identities of the Heads of the secret Agencies, even though by then their names had been published elsewhere.[130] In book publishing, the manuscript of 'MI5: British Security Service Operations 1909–45' by Nigel West[131] was offered to Ash, and was at first considered by that Service to contain too many disclosures to be acceptable (198 MI5 names plus 30 WWII double agents); through the Secretary the author persisted, showing how much was already in the public domain; ultimately the only major deletion negotiated by Ash was the chapter on MI5's long co-operation with the Irish G-2 branch.

In mid-May 1981 the DPBC's four officials[132] and the Secretary met to discuss what Notice revisions could be put to the Media side. They agreed first, reflecting the policy of not according domestic terrorists the same standing as foreign enemies, that no reference be made to terrorism. The exception was one sentence in the Introduction referring to the dissemination of sensitive information which put national security at risk: 'It can also be of value to terrorist groups who lack the resources to obtain it through their own efforts.' They discussed how to define national security, agreeing it would have to be addressed during the Review, but that meanwhile they would not differentiate in the document (as the Media side had wished in previous discussions) between national security and national defence, 'thereby avoiding exposure of intelligence and security as separate subjects'. The Security Service had concerns about any mention of 'subversion' in connection with the police, and was against avowal of any specific secret Agency (but content with 'the security and intelligence services'). Officials were constrained by maintaining the primacy of the police (not D-Notice covered) in combating domestic terrorism, and by the non-avowal policy.

Cooper suggested it would be necessary to form a government view of whether or not to publish the Notices openly; on balance officials favoured such publication, since this would make future dealings with the Media easier, but it would be necessary to retain the ability to promulgate a confidential Notice if necessary. Particularly if this were done, it would be necessary to obtain Ministerial approval of the new Notices, since their policy of non-avowal of those Services would be affected; this produced the chicken and egg situation that Ministers could not be approached before the Media view on open publication was known, but the official position could not be revealed to the Media until Ministers had approved it. All agreed however that, although there was concern that the Media increasingly did not regard articles about the secret Agencies as damaging, the D-Notice Secretary was best placed to deal with this.[133]

Ash meanwhile discussed with Ramsden other possible administrative changes, such as replacing the ex-officio Press Association membership by a corporate Agency one,[134] and whether all the Media members should be drawn from journals which actually took 'an active interest' in defence and security matters. Ash was also in correspondence with the Home Office about the HCDC recommendation that compliance by an editor with a D-Notice should guarantee immunity from OSA prosecution. The Government's lawyers again pointed out OSAs covered a wider area than D-Notices, and that the Government could not give any assurance of non-prosecution, since initiation of prosecution was exclusively the responsibility of the Attorney-General acting in an independent quasi-judicial capacity.[135]

The full DPBC met on 1 July 1981, and gave muted response to the Cooper proposal to issue the Notices in shorter, less detailed and more consolidated form, as a body of general guidance, perhaps even as a 'Code of Conduct'. The Media side was divided about open publication of the revised Notices, Ramsden and some being in favour but James Bishop[136] and others were against, on the grounds it would undermine a rationale for the Committee, namely Official/Media discussion of matters which could not be conducted in open forum; if the system were open, the Government could just as well give guidance unilaterally. Similarly Bishop was against a 'Code of Conduct' approach, since every editor must be free to make his own decision and few if any would be bound by a Code. Clarke (still a DPBC member) countered that, whether the system was open or closed, the reasons for non-disclosure could be more freely discussed than if the Government alone issued guidance.

After further discussion, the Committee agreed certain principles/practices by which the remainder of the Review subsequently took place. The current practice of separate (preferably one page) Notices should be retained. Guidance should be so framed as not to inhibit debate on matters on which the public should be informed, differentiating between broad policy/strategy (in which the Notices should not be concerned), and detailed matters which it was proper to protect. Balance was needed between avoiding too much detail and enabling editors quickly to make judgements without further consultation, with more emphasis on national security in 'near war or peacetime' not just in total war. The importance of trust in the unbiased judgement of the Secretary was emphasised.

Open publication of the Notices, and repetition of information already published elsewhere, were both discussed inconclusively and left for further discussion, as was the detail of the draft Notices, and organisational aspects. Finally Ash told the Committee that a national newspaper had asked for a photograph of the DPBC in session; some members felt there would be benefit in this when the Review was complete, others felt this novel idea 'needed further consideration and that the application should be refused for the present'. It was 2002 before this happened; the seeds of openness require gentle nurturing.

Work once again proceeded slowly through the in-trays of both Official and Media Members, for example on whether articles about the 'financing' of the secret Agencies would be damaging, and about whether terrorism should be covered (the Media side's interest in this had been re-kindled by an MoD amendment pointing out the usefulness of satellite photographs to terrorists). It was 4 November 1981 before the DPBC re-convened. After noting the formal withdrawal from the Committee of the Commonwealth Press Union (a reflection of the changed relationship between Britain and the Commonwealth countries, rather than disagreement with the rationale of the D-Notice System), the Committee immersed itself in the detail of the draft Notices ('with some vigour' on the Media side, for example resisting the secret Agencies' wish that their past members should invariably be covered). The BBC representative, Dick Francis,[137] with his Northern Ireland experience in mind, also raised the lack of reference in the Notices to terrorism, and asked the extent to which the phrase 'potential enemies' included terrorists. Cubbon explained the Notices were [then] intended to protect information 'from enemies in the classical sense, ie those who constituted the external threat'. The reference in the Introduction to terrorism was sufficient reference to 'the incidental (albeit important) benefit in D Notices' that some information which was also of value to terrorists would be protected too. On republication, the Committee accepted an Ash compromise, saying that although no automatic ban was sought, there should be no elaboration, nor confirmation of accuracy.

On dissemination of D-Notices, it was now clear that nothing remained in the redrafted Notices which required retention of the 'Private and Confidential' marking, and that therefore continuing to keep them from public knowledge would only cause adverse comment. The Media side was still divided however on whether the Notices should be distributed below editorial level within their organisations, or whether this would degrade the importance of the Notices in the eyes of editors, and also 'might inhibit reporters in the execution of their task'. Against the latter view was the feeling that it would be only a short time after issue that the revised Notices would be published 'by one means or another', and so perhaps the solution was a 'liberal interpretation of the principle of the Need-to-Know'. Summing up, Frank Cooper took this impracticable compromise as a consensus against 'wide and open publication'; he suggested as sufficient a combination of reporting the result of the review to Parliament, and of leaving it to editors to promulgate as they wished within their own organisation. The Official Members of the Committee must have been quietly amused at the institutional nervousness of some Media Members about openness, an apprehension that was to recur amongst their successors almost 20 years later. Nevertheless, at least the new package of Notices had now effectively been agreed, also reducing the previous 12 Notices to eight.[138]

Ash continued to tidy up the Review's organisational aspects. His report commented yet again on the irregularity of DPBC meetings, and the adverse parliamentary and Media comment on this.[139] He suggested spring and autumn meetings, at both of which the Secretary would account for his stewardship in the previous half-year, and at the latter meeting the System and Notices would be formally reviewed. The D-Notice distribution, which had again developed in ad hoc way, should again be reviewed, in particular to decide whether some of the 'fringe' press should be included. He was still awaiting Media side views on their own representation, but no change was recommended in the Official side, the Secretariat,[140] nor the location of its office; despite the advantage to the perception of independence which a non-Ministry location would bring, it was still considered that the advantages of ready (and secure) communication with officials outweighed this.

By the end of November 1981, Cooper felt confident enough to report to the Cabinet Secretary that the Review was effectively completed, and to seek ministerial blessing before the final Review meeting with the Media side in mid-December. The only HCDC recommendation not eventually addressed by the DPBC was that concerning an editor who followed D-Notice guidance being given immunity from OSA prosecution; finally considered to be legally inappropriate for the DPBC to address, it was passed to the Home Office for comment direct to the HCDC; in the absence of formal agreement, the convention has since been maintained nevertheless that information acquired by the D-Notice Secretary from the Media has not been used to initiate or support litigation.

The Official side was content with the draft, but Cooper acknowledged 'In one or two places we have had to bow to pressure from the press and broadcasting side on the score that information has come so widely into the public domain that it would be unrealistic to seek to deny the use of it, or where they have made a strong case that, in present-day conditions, the press should not be denied the right to discuss subjects in broad terms.' On dissemination, he thought the next DPBC meeting would agree that the new Notices should be sent to editors personally, but making clear there was no DPBC restriction on the extent to which they could be 'made generally available within newspaper and other offices'. An appropriate cover note would be formulated after the meeting to inform Parliament, and thus the public.[141]

This was indeed what was agreed at the next DPBC Meeting on 12 January 1982;[142] also that there should be an extra NPA member (representing the Sunday national newspapers), that the 'fringe press' should be given the Notices if they asked for them, that there should be two meetings a year and an annual review of the Notices, and that there should continue to be a full-time Secretary, and an Associate Secretary as required from the MoD Press Office. After this meeting, a further approach was made to the Publishers' Association, again firmly resisted by it. On the other hand, it was the Media side themselves who even more firmly rejected an approach by the Guild of Editors seeking separate representation on the DPBC; this was partly because editors were already sufficiently represented on the Committee, but mainly on the grounds that if the Guild was thus allowed to join, any similar request from the National Union of Journalists would also have to be agreed.[143] On 31 March 1982, Cooper and Ramsden jointly signed their brief formal report to the HCDC, summarising action taken since its 1980 Report; this was widely reported in the next day's media.[144] The Australian authorities (and Media) immediately complained about the dropping of the Petrov Notice, until it was quietly pointed out to them that prior agreement to this had been obtained by Ash's opposite number there.

Security Disclosures

In 1982, to the dismay of the secret Agencies, the ex-Bletchley Park WWII code-breaker Gordon Welchman[145] published the UK edition of his book disclosing much more detail about

'Ultra'. Ash had represented beforehand to his publishers the potential damage this could do to the security of current secret communications interception work, and also, on behalf of GCHQ, had pointed out that Welchman had not sought permission from his previous employer (GCHQ) to do so. However, because the American publication was already widely available, as Ash conceded, Penguin persisted and published. GCHQ expressed its disquiet to the NSA, who consequently withdrew Welchman's American security clearance, much to his upset.[146]

49

FALKLANDS CONFLICT 1982

MoD/Media Interaction

Although war with Argentina had been a possibility since before 1976 (when the Callaghan Government first started again secretly talking to the Argentine Government about some form of shared Falklands responsibility),[147] there had been no detailed planning for conflict, and there was therefore no agreed Media strategy when the crisis started. At first the MoD was reluctant to allow correspondents to accompany the Task Force as it sailed south, but editors who had the ear of the Prime Minister persuaded her to allow this. There were some who felt that the generally reluctant attitude to the Media of the military derived from American experience in Vietnam, but, as this History has recorded, the corporate dislike of correspondents near the front line went back to Victorian times, for reasons of both security and administration.

One other point of friction between media and authorities before and during the Falklands conflict was the wish by many of the former to report as dispassionately as possible. Those who referred to 'British troops' rather than to 'our troops' came in for much criticism, Prime Ministerial, military, public, and from other parts of the Media which were more overtly patriotic. The Press Association, although a British agency, also had other problems with the authorities over the Falklands War; its editor-in-chief, ex-D-Notice Committee member David Chipp, battled successfully with the MoD firstly to increase the number of journalists allowed to embark with the Task Force, including one from his Association, and then over imposed restrictions on reporting.[148]

Reuters, as an international News Agency, had to explain to both British and Argentine authorities that it was not a British company, but whereas the latter refused to let Reuters correspondents accompany their forces, Britain did eventually allow one to do so; he was de facto subject to local naval and military censorship, but Reuters as a whole 'did not feel bound to take any account of the 'D' Notice system in London'. When, for example, Ash phoned to complain that the Agency had reported the British Fleet was near Ascension Island (en route to the Falklands Islands), and asked whether the Reuters editor was not concerned for the security of 'our forces', the German editor replied he was not British and that security was Britain's concern not Reuters'. The Agency did however attempt to hold back stories which might endanger lives, although post hoc even Reuters wondered how it could have judged this adequately without some expert advice.[149]

There was some confusion both in the MoD Press Office and in the Media about channels of communication, with a number of newcomers drafted in on both sides who were not conversant even with the normal peacetime channels. For example, the *Daily Mail* editor David English[150] complained vehemently to Ash in early April that, having heard the large luxury liner *SS Canberra* was to be requisitioned to carry troops to the Falklands, his defence correspondent was contacted by 'a representative of the D Notices Committee' with a request not to publish the information, because it would alert the Argentinians to the scale of the operation; the information was then announced in Parliament. English wished to register 'the strongest possible protest at this scandalous mis-use of the D Notices procedure', and threatened to disregard D-Notice advice in the future. Ash said he was the only 'representative of the D-Notice Committee', and had not spoken to the *Mail*'s Correspondent, but, given the name of the person who had made the erroneous request (probably in the MoD), he would take it up.[151] Such abuse by junior officials of the name of the D-Notice Committee has been an occasional irritation throughout its post-WWII life.

As the naval Task Force was rapidly embarking personnel and equipment and preparing to move south, and while diplomatic manoeuvring continued, the MoD's 2nd PUS and DPBC member, Arthur Hockaday, gathered officials on 6 April to discuss whether and if so how to institute censorship of the output of those journalists accompanying the Task Force, and possibly the Media in the UK too. The sensitive matters identified were mostly those covered in D-Notices; it was agreed 'anything resembling censorship would be very badly received by the media', but that journalists would nevertheless respect the need for discretion in certain areas, and that there would be 'a measure of' de facto control over embarked journalists.

It was therefore agreed that no system of censorship of despatches would be set up, but that Sir Frank Cooper would brief editors next day, hopefully thereby reducing appearances by 'armchair strategists' (mostly garrulous retired admirals and generals) about whom the Prime Minister had already expressed anxiety. Guidance would also be given on the principles of self-censorship to be observed, and instructions issued to officials and military about contacts with the Media, and communications from Task Force personnel to their families. Although Ash was involved in these discussions, and many D-Notice principles were incorporated, there was no suggestion that the D-Notice System in itself would suffice to handle the expected volume of reporting.[152]

Cooper duly briefed editors, and a week later his Office recorded: 'Since then the reporting of military information has been reasonably restrained. The Secretary of the D Notice Committee and PR staffs have been consulted about the publication of several specific items and their advice generally has been observed. There has been rather more speculation about our intentions than we might wish – though this has been so varied and conflicting that the Argentinians have probably gained little from it.' However, there were 'signs of restiveness amongst Editors, with Defence Correspondents being pressed to obtain more information', so Cooper had a further talk with the editors on 20 May. Ash had also been having problems with poor co-ordination concerning D-Notice advice, between the MoD (as his sponsor Department) and the Sub-Committee of Heads of Information chaired by the Prime Minister's Press Secretary.

Based on daily contacts with the Media, Ash contributed to points covered by Cooper: media unhappiness over the radio blackout imposed on the Task Force as it moved south, and shortcomings in satellite communications from *HMS HERMES*; the shortage of additional places for journalists; official/military unhappiness over breaches of security, including TV film of a Major giving the size of the amphibious force; reports of departures of ships from Ascension Island; and speculation about secret military assistance from other countries. Officials were also concerned about stories (especially on BBC TV) based on Argentinian disinformation.

The wider history of official/media interaction through the course of the War was investigated and commented on subsequently in the Beach Report (see below). As expected, when the 'hot war' started at the beginning of May, media interest largely switched from equipment and covert matters to current overt operations; the D-Notice Secretary's role reduced accordingly. Nevertheless Ash was still much involved, suggesting that at Cooper's third meeting with editors he should raise the 'increasing tendency for editors to disregard D Notice No.6, particularly as it relates to Sigint and the part that Sigint plays in current operations'. He gave as an example an article in early editions of the *Daily Mail* of 5 May (displaced in later editions by the missile damage to *HMS SHEFFIELD*), which discussed ways in which the Task Force Commander would make use of Sigint.

At his third meeting with editors on 6 May, Cooper raised this continuing speculation about operational plans, continued reporting of assistance from third countries (putting such help in jeopardy), and media harassment of Service families. Editors countered with complaints of the paucity of information being provided by the MoD (compared with the deluge of Argentinian information, however inaccurate), delays in announcing operations which were over (eg sinking the *General Belgrano),* the MoD's inability to confirm or deny stories from other sources (for example, a fabricated US report of a major naval battle, about which MoD could only say it 'had no information'), and non-return by the MoD of media film and photographs from the South Atlantic. Editors asked what lay behind recent ministerial criticism of UK Press coverage, and suggested any media harassment of families would be avoided by the MoD providing photographs of Servicemen in the news.

In the days that followed, Ash clearly felt he was not being kept adequately informed about some topics on which he was being consulted by the Media. For example, on 11 May he complained he lacked an up-to-date assessment of the need to protect information on Chilean assistance to the UK; he was quickly told the need was still there, even though the Chileans were also helping the Argentinians with humanitarian tasks such as picking up *Belgrano* survivors. When Cooper met editors again next day, although there was still 'simmering discontent and suspicion' of the Government amongst editors, he thanked them for their helpful reaction to his previous complaints, and briefed on revised reporting, transmission and photographic arrangements. Regular pooling of Task Force journalists' reports had not proved welcome to them, and, for security reasons, the MoD would not allow them access to the staging post and communications centre of Ascension Island. The Chief of Defence Staff, Admiral Lewin,[153] explained why some reports of casualties had to await next of kin being informed, and he thanked BBC and ITN for providing the MoD with film footage they had acquired (but not used) of Argentine Forces in the Falklands Islands; this had proved valuable to the MoD by showing, for example, that there were no Mirage aircraft based at Port Stanley airfield.

Ash meanwhile continued to give advice to officials and media about specific stories or trends. For the Commodore commanding Clyde Submarine Base he helped draft a 'not for publication' letter to all Scottish editors about the threat to the operational security of submarines, caused by identifying when and where particular boats deployed (information useful not just to the Argentinians but also potentially to the Soviet Navy's technical intelligence). To the BBC, Ash remonstrated about continued reporting of covert Chilean assistance to the UK. For Peter Hennessy of *The Times* and *Economist* he took up with officials the MoD's heavy-handed re-vetting (by PR staff of all people) of already vetted copy from the Task Force (the re-vetting was soon widely ignored by the Press); Ash pointed out too that officials were wrong in sometimes expecting him to fulfil this vetting role.[154]

When Cooper met editors again on 21 May, he asked that the now frequent Special Forces raids on the Islands should not be reported in detail, but added that reporting of their widespread nature would on the other hand be helpful. There was still general media disappointment that the Task Force was technologically unable to transmit live television pictures from the South Atlantic; and it was explained that, unlike the Army, the Navy did not have photographs of Servicemen other than Commanding Officers readily available for the Media (strangely they were then kept onboard the ships in theatre). The MoD's Chief of Public Relations[155] explained the complications in deciding which Task Force correspondents should be allowed to accompany the landing forces, but at least the Media had now agreed to some pooling of their despatches.

Ash became particularly agitated two days later when the *Sunday Times* published an article which contained 'clear and blatant breaches of D Notice No.6', by referring to intelligence on Argentinean forces derived from Sigint in such detail that both GCHQ and JIC expressed concern; he went to see the editor. Even more widespread governmental concern followed over the quantity of radio information transmitted to the UK by correspondents ashore in the San Carlos landing area, 'giving details of incidents before official confirmation was available and before any consideration had been given to the security implications for our own forces'. The SofS for Defence[156] wanted not only to know how 'local control' of correspondents could be improved, but also suggested additional supervising officers should be provided from amongst officers whose ships had been put out of action.

The MoD asked Ash to point out to the *Daily Star* it was using disinformation 'possibly being supplied by an Argentine agent'; this concerned British helicopters in Chile, but the editor revealed it had in fact come from a long-standing CIA contact. Similarly Ash investigated a *Mail on Sunday* article about the French allowing British Harrier pilots to train against French Air Force Mirages, which originated in the French newspaper *L'Express*; he felt he could have asked British newspapers not to re-publish this immediately (although the Argentine Defence Attaché in Paris must surely have seen it), but Whitehall decided that in this case 'other considerations' dictated the story should be widely known.[157]

At Cooper's sixth meeting with editors on 9 June, editors' concerns included that they did not know where their correspondents were (all 28 were now ashore with 3 Commando Brigade or 5 Infantry Brigade, but the MoD too did not know exactly who was where), and that a few correspondents (especially Max Hastings)[158] were filing much more material than others (investigation showed he was filing more 'background' reports, thereby having easier access to scarce communications). Several editors had complaints about apparent censorship (for example that photographs of the recaptured Goose Green and Darwin showed no devastation or casualties; in fact no censorship had been applied to these Press photographs); and about continued MoD re-vetting of material filed, some on grounds of 'bad taste' rather than security (the MoD's CPR conceded he had occasionally asked for deletion of 'gory details of casualties' to spare distress to families).

Further complaints concerned the with-holding of the Servicemen's names (done initially to make more difficult Argentinian interrogation of any prisoners), and mis-reporting of casualties, in particular those the previous day in *HMS PLYMOUTH* (initially reported as many but in fact few) and in Royal Fleet Auxiliaries *Sir Tristram* and *Sir Galahad* (initially reported as few but in fact heavy). Cooper could only explain the difficulties of accuracy in a confused state of action, with initially limited communications. Finally editors were briefed on media arrangements after repossession of the Islands was completed. 'There could be no question of completely free access for the world's press, since the numbers involved

– of the order of thousands on previous experience – would swamp local resources.' However, the charter of a special ship to take a limited number (about 100) of foreign and additional British correspondents to the Islands was under consideration, if the Media would collectively pay the £1million involved, and this problem was left to a smaller meeting to discuss. The editors were described by the MoD recorder as 'in a niggling mood (although few of them seemed to share the same niggle).'

Disputes with the BBC

Repossession of the Islands was completed by the Argentinian surrender on 14 June. At the last meeting between Cooper and editors on 16 June, the latter were reported as being 'in a more relaxed mood . . . though still pressing MoD for improved facilities'. Vetting of copy was over (other than some local restrictions, for example concerning air defences of Stanley Airfield), arrangements for additional correspondents were still under consideration (the charter ship idea had been replaced, on grounds of cost, by planned one to two day visits in light aircraft, if Chile and Uruguay agreed). The only sour note was a furious row between Cooper and the BBC representative that day, who accused the MoD of deliberately diverting BBC film of bomb attacks, to return by the slow sea route; 'Sharp points were made about the "public's right to know" and the MoD's responsibilities for not jeopardising the lives of Servicemen'. It was indeed the end of a very intensive and emotive period for all concerned.

Attention, official and media, now turned to lessons learnt. As early as 18 June Ash wrote to the DPBC's BBC representative, Alan Protheroe, about a Panorama 'Falklands Special' programme on 15 June, and 'about the extent to which the D Notices were disregarded'. Sir Robert Armstrong similarly wrote to the BBC's Director-General, referring in particular to reporting British (and friendly) intelligence-gathering aspects as 'shockingly irresponsible'. He pointed out it was not yet clear Argentina had agreed to a complete cessation of hostilities, adding that 'if she continues hostilities from the mainland, the success of our operations and the lives of our servicemen may well be significantly prejudiced by what was contained in that programme.'[159]

Fortunately Argentina did indeed confirm cessation of hostilities shortly afterwards, but hostilities with the BBC rumbled on. Trethowan replied he was 'surprised' by Armstrong's letter; 'We were not at all happy about several aspects of it ourselves, including the intelligence section, but for programme and journalistic reasons'. He went on to say how careful the BBC had been throughout the conflict to avoid endangering operations, and that, before the 15 June Panorama programme, Protheroe had consulted Ash on the more sensitive points. 'I am sure you appreciate that "Panorama" is not, to put it mildly, the only source of information out of London available to the Junta.'[160] Cooper explained to Armstrong that Protheroe's enquiry to Ash had been 'confined solely to the extent to which it would be proper to make reference to Chile now that operations had ceased', and the reply was that, although Chile's involvement had now been disclosed, it was still very sensitive, and any reference should be 'only in the lightest terms'.

Cooper suggested to Armstrong that, 'irresponsible' though the BBC had been, senior officials should now be concerned 'with the increasing tendency of BBC programmes (and of certain other elements of the "responsible" media) to regard the specifics of intelligence collection, and in particular communications interception, as an "open house" for comment and speculation, rather than with pursuing too far the iniquities of this particular programme. The extent to which this is tolerable is a matter on which there is, I believe, a need for some further clearing of minds internally'. In this perception of a media trend, he was supported by 'C'; events of subsequent years have proved them right about the closer interest the Media have since then taken in intelligence matters, and in commenting on them.[161]

Trethowan, about to hand over to Alasdair Milne,[162] made placatory farewell calls on Cooper and Armstrong in late July. In preparation, Ash briefed his Chairman on GCHQ's experience that programmes about secret communications interception heightened the communications security awareness of Argentina and other countries, to the disadvantage of the UK. Ash also doubted whether the then D-Notices could really be applied to the UK intelligence relationship with the USA [present Notices do, albeit only to the degree it impacts on UK National Security]. He highlighted three areas in which 'Panorama' had ignored D-Notices advice: reference to daily sharing of Chilean intelligence, including radar observations; speculation that a British Sea King helicopter with an intelligence-gathering role had crash-landed in Chile; and references to covert small ship operations in Chilean waters.

Ash also listed other BBC programmes of recent years on intelligence, including one in mid-June which had greatly concerned the SIS because it detailed US/UK intelligence-sharing,[163] Radio 4 and 'Panorama' programmes in 1980–1 on 'the Profession of Intelligence', and extensive coverage of the *New Statesman* articles on telephone tapping. Ash pointed out these were previously areas in which the fringe 'radical' press had been active, but were now of regular interest to the BBC and mainstream press. Ash also briefed Protheroe about these concerns before Trethowan met senior officials, so the Director-General too was well-prepared for the discussion.[164]

With advantage of hindsight, Protheroe had approached Ash before the BBC had worked out a sufficiently detailed script; Ash should have asked more questions about detail in view of the sensitivity of the topic and of the unfinished South Atlantic business; the DPBC should have taken more interest in the follow-up and in the trend perceived by Cooper and 'C'; and senior officials should have given more thought to defining the boundaries between what was properly in the public interest to know and what was properly in the public interest to conceal. However, all this happened at the end of a wearing period in public life, and perhaps no lasting harm was done. But neither was there lasting improvement to the understanding between Government and Media on reporting intelligence matters.

Special Forces

On completion of the Falklands War, one other peg in the ground of future relevance to DPBC business was planted by the Director of Public Relations (Army), Brigadier Ramsbotham[165] in a mid-June note to all editors. Acknowledging that 'some extra reports' about Special Forces (SAS and SBS) had been released, because they had not been related to their non-Falklands roles (although when there were heavy SF casualties in a helicopter crash, the Media had accepted Ramsbotham's plea to delay publication until families had been informed), he reminded it was now necessary to 'revert to the old understood convention that we do not release names or photographs of individual members of the Regiment, or details of the specialist techniques that they employ for their various roles'. He particularly cautioned journalists who had met SF members during the Falklands campaign, and heard from them tales of previous exploits, that they should not repeat them. If in doubt, they were to consult the D-Notice Secretary.

Post-Falklands Conflict Inquiries

As soon as the conflict ended, the Media attacked the MoD over its handling of both journalists and information during the preceding weeks. This criticism was reflected by DPBC Media members in their own meetings, although a feeling that government was becoming increasingly hostile to media was not unique to Britain (the International Press Institute commented that worldwide the Media were 'losing out to legislation and to violence').[166] Various formal reviews into the conflict were set up,[167] and five concerned the D-Notice Committee directly: the MoD's own internal Inquiry, the HCDC Inquiry into 'The Handling of Press and Public Information during the Falklands Conflict', an MoD-commissioned Study by University College Cardiff into the relationship between the Media and the Government in a time of armed conflict, the Report on 'The Protection of Military Information' by the Study Group on Censorship chaired by General Beach,[168] and the DPBC's own review. Armstrong noted with concern to Cooper that the HCDC had appointed as Inquiry media advisers Chapman Pincher[169] and Simon Jenkins, the latter having already arranged to co-author a book on the conflict with Max Hastings; the Cabinet Secretary asked colleagues to formulate co-ordinated guidance to their Departments as to what might be said to non-'official' Inquiries.

In his brief written evidence to the HCDC, Ash reminded that the revised D-Notices had been issued to the Media only a few days before the Argentinian invasion of the Falklands, and that it had been decided to see whether they proved adequate before issuing any additional guidance for the conflict. He reported that, although from the first weeks the number of media enquiries had increased appreciably, it had not been necessary to issue additional Notices; he acknowledged a longer war might have made this desirable 'on the sensitivity of particular subjects'. Overall, his assessment was that, judged by the number and nature of requests for guidance, and the very small number of breaches of Notices which had occurred, 'the system played its intended part in influencing them [the media] to exercise care (as they did) over the publication of information'.

In July 1982, the HCDC began taking oral evidence, principally on shortcomings in the MoD PR system and on the inadequacy of facilities for deployed journalists; there was little criticism of the D-Notice System's subordinate part. Ash being on leave in New Zealand, Cooper wrote to the HCDC Chairman in mid-November summarising two DPBC meetings since the conflict (26 July and 18 October 1982):

At the outset of hostilities the number of queries and requests for advice addressed to the Secretary increased appreciably from all elements of the media, though these fell away once the arrangements for briefing and consultation had begun to take shape. Requests for advice came particularly from the regionals. Initially the queries were straightforward and fell clearly within the ambit of the D Notice system but, later, increasing difficulty was found in preserving a distinction between requests put to the Secretary in relation to D Notices and which could be dealt with in the name of the DPBC as a whole, and those for action which related to other means of controlling the publication of information – for example, the vetting of copy – which lay outside the Committee's province.

Hence at the first meeting the Committee took a broad view on the need, in any future warlike operations, to divorce the D Notice system from whatever censorship processes the Government might find it necessary to institute. Further thought needed to be given to the arrangements for the D Notice system in such circumstances and the point at which any changeover might take place. At the meeting last month I informed the Committee that the MoD accepted that it had a major task on its hands to look at the question of whether any more measures were necessary to protect military information in wartime. This would cover the practical and policy aspects and the Ministry would require help and counsel from outside.[170]

The comments at the two DPBC meetings themselves (although no detailed record seems to have survived) were somewhat pithier, both about the MoD's media handling performance and about the D-Notice System's role (the descriptions of the latter varying from 'totally irrelevant' to 'a useful contact'); Protheroe also said that D-Notice No.6 (Secret Agencies) was too wide and 'an obstacle to carefully judged, contextual reporting.'[171] At the second meeting there was also discussion on and agreement to the D-Notice files being eventually deposited through the MoD in the Public Records Office; it was left to the Secretary's discretion as to when each file might be thus deposited, there being no perceived need to observe the then official 30-year rule except in the case of official documents. In the light of the random nature of media archives and commercial pressures, this was a wise concession by the Media side, without which this History would contain many more gaps.

The eventual HCDC comment[172] was: 'The role of D-Notices during the conflict was small, but not insignificant . . . Individual editors stated that D-Notices had not been invoked against them during the conflict, although there were different views about the role which they might have played in other circumstances'. The editor of *The Times* (Charles Douglas-Home), for example, thought D-Notices might have more importance in future conflict, since journalists with the Task Force had had to submit to censorship as a precondition of accompanying the troops, but would not have done so if they had free access to the battle zone. Conversely, the Press Association editor-in-chief (still Chipp), criticised the D-Notice System as unworkable. The HCDC concluded that, in the face of such divergent views, there was probably only limited scope for D-Notices in wartime conditions, noting D-Notices had been superseded by censorship during WWII, but accepting the D-Notice Committee itself was reviewing the operation of the System during conflict. The campaign had been perhaps a useful reminder that every war is different, as indeed is the environment in which each takes place; subsequent larger-scale operations, albeit well short of global war, showed the D-Notice System can have a part to play, as active as those involved wish it to be.

Non-Falklands Activity

During this Falklands-related activity, Ash was still dealing with the day-to-day enquiries from the Media, for example over the Prime case and consequent publicity about GCHQ, books on intelligence or similar security matters (GCHQ was particularly concerned about a new 'insider' American book 'The Intelligence War'), and articles such as 'Russian Spy Trapped by Girl Agents' (*Sunday Mirror*, 12 December). He also proposed in March 1983 that the DPBC archives should be deposited in the Public Records Office; although the Media side suggested that these could be released to the public after as little as five years, at the Secretary's discretion, official security concerns postponed this initiative. On books, at the request of the DPBC he had a further meeting with the chief executive of the Publishers' Association, to discuss once again 'the D Notice system in relation to book publishing generally, and the possible membership of the PA in the DPBC in particular'. He reported afterwards the general attitude of goodwill towards and understanding of the D-Notice System amongst the Publishers' Association Council; but as before there was also concern that they should not give their members any cause 'to believe that the Association would act as the agent of the D Notice system in seeking to protect information'. The Association however reminded its members of the D Notice system by a notice in *Bookseller*, and encouraged contact between publishers and the D-Notice Secretary.[173]

The won't-join-the-Committee-but-will-accept-the-guidance policy remained the position of the Publishers' Association until 2008; it was one which D-Notice Committee representatives of other parts of the Media always found hard to accept. But in practice in his relationships with individual publishers, the D-Notice Secretary very rarely found the absence of a Committee representative a significant drawback. Indeed publishers, although no more fond of self-censorship than any other part of the Media, have usually been just as likely to seek guidance. The prospect of having to withdraw a book after publication, as a result of government litigation about some information or photograph adjudged post hoc damaging to security, is a good deal more daunting financially than an injunction against a newspaper or television editor, who has merely to amend an edition or canned programme. It must be conceded however that books' authors, who have 'pride of parenthood' about their manuscripts, are a good deal less philosophical than publishers about altering their work, even in some small detail. This author is no different.

The DPBC discussed non-participation of the Publishers' Association at its 23 May 1983 meeting, because of its concern (reported afterwards in the Press) about the number of books being published which purported to give details of the 'personalities, activities and methods currently or recently employed' by the Intelligence agencies. The new DPBC Chairman Sir Clive Whitmore[174] commented to Armstrong afterwards that he was impressed by the Media side's concern that the Notices should be effective, as exemplified by their attitude to the Publishers' Association. He added, however: 'But in the final analysis the press and broadcasting members are as aware as all of us that D Notices will continue to have little influence with those who are disposed to disregard them until some way can be found of making the prospect of successful prosecution credible once again as an ultimate sanction'. Had the Media side been aware of this comment, they would have wished it expressed otherwise, since it implies a more direct connection between Acts of Parliament and the D-Notice System than exists; it implies editors choose to seek advice mainly because of fear of litigation, which is incorrect. They would however have shared Whitmore's wish that all parts of the Media equally would consider D-Notice advice, since otherwise the responsible are journalistically (and indirectly financially) disadvantaged vis-à-vis the irresponsible.

MoD and Beach Reports on Censorship

The MoD's own internal review of the media aspects of the War had started in late July 1982. Although it was accepted that interaction with the DPBC should be included, participation by Ash was appropriately tangential. When a concurrent independent study was first mooted, Ash did however caution against it being headed, as MoD first intended, by someone from the Media, arguing the Media tended to be 'suspicious of their kind who take part in Government projects to protect information'; he thought it unlikely therefore any Media figure of substance would wish to take it on. This view was accepted and led to the selection in November 1982 of the retired General Beach, known and respected also outside the Services.

Ash noted the potential implications for the D-Notice System of a reminder from Ramsbotham as DPR (Army) to those establishing the Beach Study: there was a link with separate discussions already under way amongst the security authorities, including the Metropolitan Police, on control of Media access to information about Northern Ireland-related operations.

Ash had an amicable exchange with Ramsbotham on the relationship between PR, censorship and the D-Notice System. The Brigadier correctly cautioned against taking the Falklands conflict as other than a 'unique experience', and against there being 'two levels of censorship in tri-Service operations controlled by MoD'. Censorship should, he considered, be imposed from above, to a common standard passed down the operational chain, rather than added later at a higher level over what those on the ground/at sea deemed appropriate. Similar principles applied to use of the D-Notice System, in which the trust of editors depended on consistent application throughout the chain of command. Its role and its Notices needed therefore to be properly understood not only by the journalists and editors involved, Ramsbotham said, but also by PR Officers and censors (he believed censorship should be an operational not a PR responsibility).

Ramsbotham hoped that, because this had clearly not invariably been so during the Falklands conflict, the DPBC role in future war would be 'considered against a more normal situation. This applies particularly to the visual media, whose ability to transmit sensitive operational information was so fortunately restricted by technical reasons, and not therefore subject to what could have been considerable censorship problems'. In a further minute, he commented that if censorship was clearly dictated by the operational chain, not by PR Officers, 'the D-Notice Committee could exercise its correct function', and the separate censorship would be accepted by the Media for the operational measure which it actually should be.[175] Although this view is theoretically correct, subsequent campaigns have shown however that the D-Notice System and the MoD have to work also with the reality of Political PR.

When it finally emerged, the MoD's internal Review did not mention the D-Notice System at all in its brief Report, 'The Falklands Campaign: The Lessons.'[176] On the HCDC Report, the MoD commented[177] on the role of D Notices merely: 'The Defence, Press and Broad-casting Committee has reviewed the usefulness of D Notices during the Falklands campaign. Its experience and views will be made available to the working party on censorship.' When in autumn 1983 a joint Media/MoD exercise ('Eternal Triangle') was held, Ash did not take part, although it was chaired by the ex-DPBC Member David Chipp, and assisted by current DPBC Member Alan Protheroe; both declared it an undoubted success, but castigated the hostile attitude of *The Times*, *Sunday Times*, *Guardian* and *Daily Telegraph*, who had alleged an attempt to corral the Press, putting its freedom at stake, rather than accepting it as a trial of operational MoD/Media practices.

The Beach Censorship Study Group had meanwhile taken evidence inter alia from Cooper and Ash. Others who gave evidence and the Group itself, whether media or official, generally considered the D-Notice System existed, worked quite well, and should therefore continue to have a role, albeit with some fine tuning. Future scenarios and technologies were still then difficult to predict, but those with a Defence background were on the whole less stringent than those from the Media about how much censorship might realistically be demanded, and Beach himself emphasised the international dimension.[178] The Beach Report[179] recommended that in transition to war, the 'voluntary arrangement with the media' should normally suffice, and that in limited conflicts:

- There should be no formal censorship System, but a voluntary system based on that in existence.
- The D-Notice-based system should be used more widely than in the Falklands campaign, with, if necessary, an augmented Secretariat.
- The Notices would, however, probably require augmenting by more specific guidance appropriate to the circumstances of the conflict.

As to any future major conventional war (i.e. against the Soviets, but nuclear war was not covered):

- Guidance on information to be protected should be prepared in advance, and discussed with the Media through the DPBC, which, despite differing views as to its continuing relevance, was nevertheless a representative and useful consultative body.
- The D-Notice Secretary should be used in a senior role in any wartime censorship system, because of his experience of the needs and ways of the media.
- The DPBC should be used in a consultative role on policy during war; but complaints/appeals about wartime censorship should be handled by a separate body.
- Matters already published in other countries should be publishable in the UK, as was already the D-Notice convention.

A postscript to Media/Official aspects of the Falklands Conflict was provided by Frank Cooper, recalling later a visit to the Pentagon in March 1983. Apart from admiration about the conduct of the operation, the most frequent question put to him by those who had served through the Vietnam War was: 'How do you fight a war in the face of the media?'[180]

Back to Normal

In September 1982 Ash had been offered for advice the manuscript of Nigel West's new book 'A Matter of Trust', about post-war MI5 Operations, which the Service had separately learned of and discovered was based in part on the recollections of a disillusioned ex-Security Service Officer, Arthur Martin. The same October day that the Secretary decided he would like to see the draft, the Government unknown to him was granted an injunction against 'Nigel West'. The Thatcher Government was not prepared to rely on the D-Notice System in circumstances in which it was becoming increasingly concerned about Britain's secret intelligence and security reputation. Ash therefore had to stand aside while litigation and official clearance were pursued.[181] The book was nevertheless published later in 1982, and the publicity caused by litigation greatly increased sales, the New York publisher even using the Attorney-General's affidavit on the dust jacket. The television rights were bought by another writer who, having consequently insisted on meeting Peter Wright, later co-wrote 'Spycatcher' with him (see below). Use of the D-Notice System on 'A Matter of Trust', rather than litigation, might perhaps have meant that this precise chain of events would not have occurred.

In May 1983, Ash heard from Australian sources that a new book ('British Intelligence and Covert Action') was shortly to be published there and in Britain, including coverage of manipulation of Third World states and interception of commercial information. The publisher declined to offer a manuscript for checking but said it would follow the advice which Ash then gave. The Australian Government had meanwhile taken out an injunction against the *National Times*, which only managed to continue its serialisation of the book after it had removed passages as required by the Hawke Government. The book did indeed contain details which Ash would have recommended omitting, including some names; the Secretary could only write after publication pointing this out.[182]

The 1 November 1983 DPBC meeting carried out the annual review of D-Notices. No significant changes were considered (MI5 and the Home Office had previously disagreed with a GCHQ proposal to mention specifically the interception of communications), but discussion did ensue about the applicability of Notices to US Defence activities carried out in and from the UK. Whereas NATO activities were covered indirectly, because Britain's national security depended on the Alliance, the Committee's guidance to the Secretary was to act with care where the Americans were pursuing their purely national objectives.

The recommendations in the Beach Report were discussed by the DPBC on 16 January 1984, with John Grant,[183] a member of the Beach Study Group and former DPBC Member, also present. The Chairman explained that an interdepartmental Working Party was currently being set up to consider further action, and that it would find it helpful to have the DPBC's preliminary views. These included that:

- 'The range and complexity of news-gathering channels used by the media now and in the future, and particularly of the automated communications available to them, would make any system of mandatory censorship inoperable'; censorship would therefore have to be voluntary.
- The UK Media would co-operate with a system of voluntary censorship, and this would be improved 'if deliberate action were taken in peacetime to develop the relationship between the media and Whitehall'; Exercise Eternal Triangle was a good example of the kind of measure required.
- Most foreign correspondents in the UK would wish to conform to guidance issued, rather than risk expulsion; thought should be give to the problems which journalists from potentially hostile countries might cause in transition to war.
- In a major war involving allies, it would be essential to have a combined system of protection agreed beforehand; this needed pursuing with NATO.

The Committee very much favoured Beach recommendations directly concerning the D-Notice System, adding that if the D-Notice Secretary were to be directly involved in any censorship system, as opposed merely to giving the benefit of his experience, the DPBC would need a replacement Secretary. The only doubt was the practicability of putting together a specific set of guidelines for a non-specific limited war.[184]

Ash, alongside more routine matters such as advising in September 1983 what might be omitted from a BBC 'Newsnight' programme on cruise missiles, continued to be involved with Beach follow-up work, including giving evidence to the University College Cardiff study team.[185] At the 1 May 1984 DPBC meeting,[186] he reported the Government had taken legal action on a book ('GCHQ – The Negative Asset') while he was still in negotiation with the publisher; the Media side warned such litigation made it difficult to continue to support the System, a message subsequently passed to the Cabinet Secretary. On follow-up to the Beach Report, the Interdepartmental Working Party had concluded by July 1984 that most recommendations could be accepted, but not censorship in the UK ('impracticable and undesirable') nor the full general war organisation (principally because of the major manpower and resource implications, but also because NATO (and the UK Media) would not welcome a system that was 'markedly more restrictive than those of our major Allies'). In its place, MoD now proposed a system of 'intensified guidance' to replace D-Notices in wartime, with the DPBC retained in an advisory capacity. The initial reaction of Ramsden was that any involvement in a censorship system was likely to be unacceptable to the DPBC Media side, as it amounted to 'a function of Government' in general war.

Following up the 'Negative Asset' discussion, Whitmore wrote to Armstrong on 29 May, recording his 'unease that the D-Notice system could be put at risk' because some in the Media believed officials were trying to extend application of the Notices beyond the agreed point. There had been 'gentlemanly, if occasionally difficult, discussion' about the 'tendency for the Government to regard the D-Notice system as just another part of its own panoply of instruments for protecting information and accordingly to see the Secretary of the Committee as an arm of the Executive.'[187] It was something Whitmore felt the DPBC Chairman needed to watch.

Armstrong replied: 'The D-Notice system is in essence a gentleman's agreement. We cannot be expected to deny ourselves other recourse, when we are dealing with authors or publishers who are not gentlemen. Nonetheless, it may still be right to start the process by seeing if they are prepared to behave like gentlemen.'[188] Were there a media equivalent of the Cabinet Secretary, he might well make a mirror observation about officials and the politicians whom they assiduously serve. The D-Notice Secretary must invariably perform his duties as though he is a gentleman; in this he is helped by having acquired, during long previous worldwide military deployment, expertise in rascal-recognition.

Despite Ramsden's reservations, a paper was put to the 3 October 1984 DPBC meeting, describing the 'intensified guidance' organisation as 50 to 100 high calibre, trained and exercised staff (available at one week's notice), controlled by a Ministry, operating a 'stop-list' system which would be compiled beforehand with the help of the DPBC, but which would replace D-Notices. In general war, the DPBC would then remain as merely a channel of communication with the Media. The Media side (not previously consulted about this cost-cutting solution) doubted whether there could be an effective censorship system in circumstances of contemporary media technology, and whether, if D-Notices were suspended, there was any role for the DPBC in general war. They agreed the DPBC should have nothing to do with implementing censorship, but that it had a potentially useful role in advising on the setting up of any system the Government decided to introduce. Ash pointed out that one of the reasons for the decreasing use of the D-Notice System through the Falklands conflict had been the difficulty of divorcing advice (based on the equivalent of 'intensified guidance') from censorship. The term 'intensified guidance' was unanimously disliked, presumably because of its Orwellian undertone. Whitmore undertook to represent these views in further work, and consult the DPBC further before anything was submitted to Ministers.[189]

A further DPBC meeting was therefore held on 20 November 1984. The MoD draft White Paper and accompanying submission to Ministers were now deliberately vague about the advisory organisation for use in general war; it said merely the DPBC would be consulted about its role, and mentioned the embryo organisation might be implanted in the DPBC womb. Ramsden said there were concerns about some wording in the draft White Paper, especially use of 'guidance' when 'censorship' was meant. There was also too much emphasis on the difference between 'limited' and 'major' [or general] war, when in practice there was little difference where censorship was involved. In lengthy discussion, points included that:

- 'Censorship' implied submission of copy, excision/amendment and sanctions; but 'the full panoply of censorship as existed in World War II would be impractical in any future war'.
- 'Guidance', in the sense of the peacetime use of the D-Notice System, might be inadequate for the Government in wartime, but it should be possible to maintain an organisation based on similar principles; it was this intention which underlay the idea of 'improved guidance' [as, with bureaucratic nicety, it was now termed].
- It was accepted the Government would wish to back up any wartime censorship system with the possibility of sanctions, and their extent and nature would influence the attitude of the Media to any proposals; but the DPBC should play no part in setting up sanctions.
- All the Media side were content to advise on wartime arrangements; some felt the DPBC should be suspended in wartime, replaced by a broader media advisory body, as in WWII [because of the short-term nature of the institutional memory (official and media), they were seemingly unaware of the limited influence which that ad hoc body had had compared with the AWOPC in WWI].

The Committee completed the annual review of the Notices (no amendments), before hearing Ash's last customary report of previous months' business before his imminent retirement.[190] The Beach Report was shortly afterwards accepted by the Government.[191] Although some Beach principles have survived, those recommendations which required creation of a permanent infrastructure of dormant organisation, and of investment and training, lingered semi-forgotten in the Whitehall haze, while other more pressing current problems emerged to centre stage. When future conflicts did subsequently occur, as will be recorded, the then peacetime organisation was adapted ad hoc as required, with the D-Notice System (including once again the Press Association) fully involved. Thankfully, such ad hoc-ery has not so far needed to be tested in a major and lengthy war.

Postscript

Before he retired, Admiral Ash was involved in late 1984 in one further Falklands-related intervention, namely the publication of extracts from the diary of the ex-Supply Officer of the submarine *HMS CONQUEROR*, Lieutenant Sethia. The major sensitivities concerned the sinking of the *General Belgrano*, still then surrounded in political and legal controversy; but from a security point of view Ash's concern was not about these aspects, but that the diary also contained operational and technological details which would be of great interest to the Soviet Navy. As both PUS MoD and DPBC Chairman, Sir Clive Whitmore therefore personally saw those in the Media thought by Ash to be considering publication of extracts, namely the editor of *The Observer*, Donald Trelford[192] and the Chairman of Granada Television, Sir Denis Forman.[193] Neither still had the diary or extracts in his possession, the former decided not to use the information he had, and the latter, although the programme had already gone out (without the operational and technological detail), agreed he too would consult Ash or his successor before any further use of the diary.[194]

50

BACK TO ROUTINE BUSINESS

In its new-found enthusiasm for regular six-monthly meetings, the DPBC met on 23 May 1985, firstly to hear the Acting Secretary's[195] report of his recent work. This included the *New Statesman*'s wish to publish unspecified operational and technical details of *HMS CONQUEROR*'s attack on the *General Belgrano*, and in particular of the submarine's towed array sonar, allegedly given to *Guardian* reporters by the retired Chief of Defence Staff, Lord Lewin; the magazine accepted the information was covered by D-Notices Nos.1 and 2, but asked in its columns of 18 January whether Admiral Lewin had thereby been in breach of the OSAs; Kay had replied there was no direct connection between D-Notices and the OSAs.[196]

Kay also reported that the *Sunday Times* had in March wished to publish photographs of the retiring and (not yet announced) incoming DGSS, John Jones and Antony Duff; but the newspaper had accepted Kay's advice that photographs would make things easier for terrorists, blacked out Jones' face and omitted Duff's, informing its readers this was 'at the expressed wish of the Security and Intelligence Services'. The next issue of the *New Statesman* had however ridiculed the *Sunday Times*, and published a photograph of Duff en clair. Kay had decided to take no further action, mainly because it would 'have given a measure of official recognition to an appointment which at the time was no more than media speculation'. Duff himself, already a public figure, was 'not unduly bothered.'[197]

Further discussion of the Beach Report was postponed for a year because officials were far from ready, but it was agreed to invite Chipp to send a Press Association representative to DPBC meetings, because its views were needed when discussing rules for the Media in wartime; Ramsden was deputed to approach him, and duly reported back at the 25 November 1985 meeting that Chipp had said the invitation should await his successor as editor-in-chief the following year. The Acting Secretary's six-monthly report included an article on Ultra by the WWII Codebreaker Welchman, which the journal *Intelligence and National Security* wished to publish. Because of his anguish at his NSA security clearance having been withdrawn, Welchman insisted the D-Notice Secretary was consulted. When Kay sought expert advice about any damaging information in the draft, GCHQ said no deletions could now be usefully suggested, but asked Kay not only to tell the journal this did not indicate official approval or acquiescence, but to emphasise Welchman's legal and personal obligations to seek permission before publishing anything on his wartime work. Kay had declined to do this, as it went beyond the DPBC role and would damage its credibility. Whitmore and the Director GCHQ subsequently agreed that 'the wholly proper management action' should be kept separate from the operation of the D-Notice System, and that the latter would write himself to Welchman.[198]

In mid-December 1985, the Head of a secret Agency, this time SIS, was again in the news. The D-Notice Secretary 'received information'[199] that the *Sunday Times* was planning to publish an article two days later which would include the name and photograph of 'C'. Kay rang the defence correspondent, who subsequently confirmed the story would concern changes at the top of the intelligence world, including the Cabinet Office (whither the previous 'C', Sir Colin Figures, whose identity had already been divulged, had gone as Intelligence Co-ordinator). The intention was to say that the name of his successor, although known to the paper, was being withheld at the request of the authorities, accompanied by a doctored photograph. Even so, Kay gave the usual personal security warnings.

An hour later another *Sunday Times* journalist rang him, and it soon became clear he was unaware of the previous conversation with the defence correspondent.[200] He reported that, in the Editor's absence, the deputy editor had decided that, although other (domestic) details would not be revealed, the new 'C' Christopher Curwen[201] should be identified. His rationale was that all previous 'Cs' had been identified during their term of office, either through foreign sources or because an Honours List had provided a clue, and that anyway the new appointment was the result of a 'shake-up' in the SIS ordered by Mrs Thatcher. Kay spoke to the deputy editor, reminding him of the Notice's advice, and of the terrorist threat to 'C' and his family, and assuring him there was nothing non-routine about the appointment. The deputy editor argued that too much weight was being given to the terrorist threat, pointing out the senior military involved in Northern Ireland apparently needed no such anonymity; Kay countered that, unlike the military, the SIS were involved only in covert work.[202]

The internal editorial conference at the *Sunday Times* lasted that evening until well after 9pm, and Kay then heard the name would be published, partly because, if that paper did not publish it, some other organ would, holding the *Sunday Times* up to ridicule, and partly because, it was assumed, other precautions would make it difficult for a terrorist organisation to attack the Head of the SIS (a rationale which, to those with direct experience of anti-terrorist operations, smacks of touching faith in the security forces, naivety, or cognitive dissonance). On 15 December the *Sunday Times* duly published the story ('New Spymaster at MI6'), which was picked up to varying degrees thereafter by *The Observer* and *Sunday Express*. The *Daily Telegraph* the next day however accepted Kay's advice not to publish the name, and the *Sunday Express* apologised for not having consulted.

On 15 December Curwen's home was broken into, the Bomb Squad was called, and, although nothing was found, the Media got to know of this too; who broke in, why, and who told the Media, were not discovered. On 16 December Curwen himself phoned Kay to say *Sun* reporters were outside his house, but after the Secretary rang the night editor, they were withdrawn. Next morning, Curwen rang Kay again to report that, as he left home, he was approached by an *Evening Standard* reporter and photographer; after Kay's intervention with that paper, no photograph or other domestic detail was published, and even the name (but not the fact of the break-in) was omitted.[203] This whole vignette is not entirely atypical of the D-Notice Secretary's picaresque role. As Kay said to the *Guardian* afterwards ('People at Large', 21 December 1985): 'I don't measure success in percentages. It's a voluntary system and sometimes advice is taken and sometimes it's not'; the newspaper commented: 'Won three, lost two, drawn one'.

Whitmore nevertheless decided with Ramsden's agreement that the incident merited a special DPBC meeting on 24 February 1986, to discuss the *Sunday Times*' action and reasoning. Kay told the tale, adding he had had similar discussions with *The Observer*, who, although they shared the *Sunday Times'* opinion about exaggeration of the terrorist threat to senior Intelligence Officers vis-à-vis other senior people, had nevertheless initially accepted his advice. Kay felt there was a further argument he should have used, and which he had incorporated in a draft amendment to D-Notice No.6 tabled at this meeting, namely that public identification of one Intelligence Officer could lead to the identification of others, for example successors and predecessors working overseas in designated SIS posts whose cover was a normal diplomatic appointment.

The Media side readily accepted the well-known operational and personal security rationale concerning all secret Agencies personnel, except about their Heads. Officials argued that these were not like the Heads of the US agencies, who were normally already publicly known political appointees; the senior UK military and police were likewise already necessarily public figures. They felt that once the Heads were avowed, the Media would turn their attention to the Deputies and Heads of Departments; disclosures would provide an "idiot" terrorist with information he would not otherwise be able to access; and that the security of the families of the Heads was also at risk. The Committee were reminded of their earlier (1976) guidance to editors on this subject. After further discussion, the Media side, led by Keith Whetstone,[204] agreed the amendment now proposed could be approved, and that the reason to be given to editors for this 'routine' change was that, in view of the heightened interest in the identities of the Heads of MI5 and MI6, the DPBC had decided it would be 'helpful' if the guidance were 'set out more positively'.

Finally Kay[205] referred to a *New Statesman* article of 14 February ('New D Notice Gag'), which he said 'purported to discuss' the small D-Notice amendments issued after the 1985 review and reflect comments made to Duncan Campbell by Kay, but in which there were 'wide differences' to what had actually been said. Campbell's opinion was that the amendments extended the coverage of the Notices on details of plans to take over hospitals, transport, food and fuel supplies, and to conscript civilian labour (even if 'to be handed over to US Forces'), on photography or diagrams of nuclear or cruise missile convoys, and any photographs of intelligence agents 'whether or not involved in domestic political surveillance'; Kay had explained the more prosaic reasons for the amendments.[206] Campbell nevertheless alleged the defence spokesmen of both Opposition parties had pledged to end the D-Notice System, Paddy Ashdown[207] referring to the new amendments as 'another component of the Government's prison of secrecy'.

The then hostility of the *New Statesman* to the System was not traditional; a former editor Paul Johnson[208] now wrote: 'When a self-confident government and a powerful newspaper come into conflict over national security, the result is almost certain to damage all three . . . I continue to believe that something on the lines of Britain's old "D-notice" system is by far the best way of regulating this sensitive area in a democracy. When I was an editor I never once felt that receiving a D-notice was an infringement of my rights . . . A system of voluntary co-operation, which imposes restraints both on governments demanding secrecy and editors wishing to publish, is particularly desirable in the war against terrorism, where the armed forces, police, reporters and television crews are all in the front line.'[209]

The Committee returned to this at its 28 May 1986 meeting, concluding that, although the hostile article had not impaired the D-Notice System's credibility, it showed the importance of removing misunderstandings among journalists about the Committee's workings; the Secretary should enlist the help of the Media Society and the Institute of Professional Journalists. A step in 'demystifying' the DPBC had already been taken by publication of recent Media appointments to the Committee, including those of Colin Webb,[210] the new editor-in-chief of the Press Association (who thereby restarted its otherwise unbroken connection with the Committee), and of the editor of *The Observer* Donald Trelford.

The General's final report included two requests for a copy of the D-Notice system from members of the public. He had been mindful of the cautious guidance given to editors in early 1982 about promulgation of the Notices, and had therefore decided to interview the two applicants to establish their bona fides. One he had concluded wished only to criticise the Police and Security Service, and he declined to give him a copy of the Notices; to the other, a researcher from the Oxford University Press, he had given a copy of the Introduction and the titles of the Notices, and offered to brief her further as necessary. The Committee however felt that, as the contents were not confidential, it was now acceptable to supply the Notices on request to members of the public who showed 'a genuine interest'. Certainly today there is a steady flow of requests and queries from members of the British and foreign publics, all of whom (even the small minority who appear not entirely rational) are given the desired information, in addition to that on the website, subject to the provisions of the Data Protection and other limiting Acts.

Kay told the Committee that, on a manuscript submitted for expert advice ('GCHQ and the Secret Wireless War 1900–1986', by Nigel West), GCHQ had said that, while there was nothing which endangered security as covered by D-Notices, they would prefer that books on such subjects were not published. Once again, they hoped therefore he would tell the publisher that clearance did not imply official approval, and again he had declined to do this. The Committee endorsed his view that the Secretary should confine himself strictly to three questions in vetting manuscripts: 'Is the information covered by a Notice? If so, will publication endanger National Security? And if so, can the piece be amended so as to be acceptable from a security point of view without ruining the story?' These are three of the criteria still applied not just to books, but to all matter referred to the D-Notice Secretary. There are of course others too, including 'Is the information already widely in the public domain?' and 'Is there some over-riding aspect of public interest at stake?'

Desultory follow-up work by officials on the Beach Report meanwhile continued. Immediately before the 12 November 1986 DPBC meeting, Admiral Higgins[211] circulated two papers for discussion, on the annual review of the D-Notices, and on 'Intensified Guidance to the Media in Time of War'. The only significant addition to the first was a sentence in the rationale for D-Notice No.6 (British Security and Intelligence Services'), pointing out that disclosing the methods used in past successes against certain countries and organisations 'may well prompt them, or others, to adopt effective countermeasures in the future'. The second paper was now a rather thin (after 18 months, just three pages) distillation of the 1942 Ministry of Information D-Notices. The Media side was told merely that areas which would be covered in 'Intensified Guidance' included (in addition to Defence information) Foreign Affairs, the Home Base, Trade and Industry, Intelligence, Finance, and Government; the only Appendix, on the Military aspects, was itself just a list of sub-headings.

Before turning to these, Higgins clarified that publication of Peter Wright's memoirs ('Spycatcher') in Australia was not a D-Notice matter, but a legal and political one. Not mentioned in the minutes was a 'Spycatcher' connection with a book which was causing much unjustified official concern: 'Official Secrets' by David Hooper. On the broadcasting side, Higgins reported full co-operation from the BBC, ITN and TV-am News over the Campaign for Nuclear Disarmament mass trespass at the Royal Naval Armament Depot at Coulport, in not showing footage of sensitive areas. Similarly he had had a 'useful' meeting with the editor of the new newspaper, *The Independent*, Andreas Whittam-Smith[212] over its recent article on GCHQ's involvement in detecting a bomb plot against an El Al aircraft; the DPBC agreed that, although this did not strictly concern British national security, the role of GCHQ in helping to counter international terrorism was properly covered by D-Notice No.6, and something on which editors should therefore seek advice.

In discussion of proposed D-Notice amendments, although GCHQ was keen to stress that any disclosure invariably led to a tightening up of target communications, the Media side felt the proposed wording gave 'too much reinforcement to the prohibition of any history of code breaking and there had to be some time limit'. It also suggested the Committee was being used to enforce discipline upon ex-employees of GCHQ, whereas the existing wording already adequately covered the point intended. The amendment was therefore dropped. There was no further attempt to define national security; as a Security Service Legal Adviser pointed out, trying to distinguish between the internal and the external threats was unlikely to make it easier for editors to decide whether D-Notices applied to a particular case.[213]

On 'Intensified Guidance', the MoD's John Blelloch[214] said officials had quickly realised there was no point in trying to reinvent the wheel, hence the reliance on the WWII procedures (nothing further was said about setting up an embryonic organisation to interpret and administer the 'guidance' system for general war). Officials also now accepted that censorship in the field would not be practicable, and that instead there must be reliance on escort officers keeping correspondents from sensitive areas and information. More widely, technological changes since WWII 'made control of communications almost impossible and whatever information was fed into it the media would still retain access to many sources outside Government control. For this reason the Government felt unable to support Beach's recommendation on the need for censorship'. Blelloch felt this made explicit guidance to editors even more necessary; advising the Government on a system of voluntary censorship in time of war would be a new role for the Committee [not true, but WWI was a long time ago].

The DPBC agreed the official approach so far was logical in its aim of highlighting areas where editors would need 'to exercise care and if necessary seek advice'. It reiterated however it would not be involved in administering the system if ever brought into force, nor quoted so as to give it authority, nor did it wish the term D-Notices to be used [the nomenclature view was rescinded during further work], but it did wish to be consulted again when more detailed work had been done by officials.[215] Afterwards, prompted by Ramsden, Higgins did attempt quickly to dispose of one small irritation by suggesting substitution of 'Government' for 'Intensified' Guidance, but this was considered by officials to have draconian undertones. Eventually it became known as 'Written Guidance', a term so neutral and undeniable that nobody could object.

A few days after the meeting, Ramsden rang Higgins with second thoughts on the coverage of terrorism, specifically on counter-terrorism which involved only the Police, such as extreme anti-hunt and anti-animal vivisection violence; these were not within the interests of the DPBC. It was agreed to return to this at a future meeting. Higgins' own view was quite clear: 'terrorism [of the IRA sort] is a threat to the realm and therefore a matter of national security, and thus properly subject to D Notice procedures'.

In the later months of the year there were two more Parliamentary Questions, both from Dale Campbell-Savours,[216] the first on 21 November asking how many books had been discussed between the D-Notice Secretary and their publishers; he was told 36 since 1967, but they could not be named because of the short-term confidentiality expected by publishers and authors. The second question[217] asked specifically whether Chapman Pincher's book 'Their Trade is Treachery' had been submitted 'for consideration by all' the DPBC members;

it had not in fact been submitted for advice,[218] but there was philosophical discussion as to whether to reply 'No', and thereby breach the principle of not revealing anything about consultation, logically therefore having to say 'Yes' about future books which were so submitted. A longer answer was agreed, which restated the principle and answered neither yes nor no. If the Neither Confirm Nor Deny practice was good enough for nuclear matters, it was good enough for the confidentiality of publishers.

51

THE 'ZIRCON' AND
'MY COUNTRY RIGHT OR WRONG'
CONTROVERSIES

Duncan Campbell had been commissioned by the BBC in 1985 to research and present a series to be called 'Secret Society'. In view of his known propensity for upsetting the Government by his exposés in the *New Statesman*, particularly of security and intelligence matters, the BBC may be said to have underestimated the problems he would in due course cause the Corporation; he certainly added excitement to the work of the D-Notice Secretary. When the BBC's autumn 1986 publicity launch highlighted the series, Higgins started to remind DPBC Member Alan Protheroe (as also Assistant Director General responsible for BBC News) that advice might be needed (described in the then BBC DG Alastair Milne's memoirs as 'remonstration noises').

The BBC Governors too became interested in the series when it became known that one episode would concern Zircon, a spy satellite being secretly developed by the Thatcher Government with American assistance (one of the then BBC Governors was Daphne Park,[219] an ex-SIS officer). Concern on the government side had started some months earlier, when GCHQ became aware that BBC TV Scotland was filming Menwith and other secret communications sites, that there was a Campbell connection, and in August that the journalist had, during an interview with the ex-MoD Chief Scientific Adviser, Ronald Mason,[220] revealed he was aware of the exceptionally secret Zircon Project. GCHQ did not, however, immediately inform the sponsoring Department (MoD) of this, so when that month the 'Secret Society' series was announced by the BBC, it was not realised that this included anything about Zircon. Similarly uninformed, Higgins routinely wrote to the BBC in September offering advice, and Protheroe, who knew little about the series at the time, undertook to get back to him in due course.

In early October Campbell interviewed the Chairman of the House of Commons Public Accounts Committee, Robert Sheldon,[221] probing him about the high cost of Zircon. Such was the secrecy surrounding the project that Sheldon knew nothing about it, despite its size, and he angrily terminated the interview and contacted the Comptroller and Auditor General, Sir Gordon Downey,[222] who also knew no detail of the project. Surprised, he contacted Sir Robert Armstrong, and it was agreed that, as a first step, Sheldon should contact his predecessor Joel Barnett,[223] now Vice-Chairman of the BBC Governors, to restrict Campbell's use of the interview. Due to a previous departure from normal practice in the BBC Contracts Department, however, it was Campbell/*New Statesman* not the BBC/*Listener* who owned the material of the programme.

Because the D-Notice Secretary is kept informed about specific operations/projects only on a need-to-know basis, Higgins too had been unaware of the Zircon project, and its relationship with the deterrent force. Realising now what else was in the Secret Society series, and its significance, he chased up the BBC. Protheroe, seeing this was building into something which would become very Political (and political inside the BBC too), was concerned to limit the D-Notice System's involvement strictly to the national security aspects. He delayed broadcasting the series, something which was immediately leaked to the Press, who linked it with Conservative claims of BBC left-wing bias, and with the Government's recent injunction of a *New Statesman* article considered to be highly damaging to Britain's relations with Saudi Arabia; but these articles did not mention Zircon.[224]

Meanwhile officials were rapidly soothing bruised internal relationships; Downey, Armstrong and the Treasury PUS, Sir Peter Middleton[225] agreed a form of reassurance for the future: 'Where, in the interests of national security, large projects are excluded from the Annual Confidential Defence Projects Statement, the C&AG would consult the Chairman of PAC in any circumstances which would normally justify a report to Parliament.' Armstrong, with the far-sighted refinement of Cabinet Secretaries, added that he would prefer the insertion of the words 'expect to' between the first 'would' and 'consult', because 'I suppose that it is possible that there might at some stage be a Chairman of the PAC of whose discretion it was not possible to be as sure as we can be of Mr Sheldon's.'[226]

Higgins had other occasion to go back to Protheroe, because on 1 November a BBC TV Scotland producer hired a helicopter and overflew parts of the Clyde Submarine Base, photographing a classified submarine propeller and depots where Polaris missiles were maintained/stored, something on which Higgins hoped Protheroe would seek advice before broadcasting. Instead, Protheroe talked privately to Whitmore after the November DPBC meeting, saying he had now seen the rough cuts of the first four of the series, and that they were 'very broadcastable', the underlying theme being there was too much secrecy in the UK. The first three parts he thought were acceptable from a national security point of view, but the fourth, about Zircon, he feared might contravene the OSA.[227] It seemed to him Campbell might have deduced the existence of Zircon from a British Aerospace press release about communications satellites, but had worked out that the apparent orbit was more appropriate to spying on the USSR. Whitmore concluded from this conversation that Protheroe probably knew even more about Zircon, so decided to take him into his confidence, and confirmed it was indeed a GCHQ project. He explained why the Soviets must not know in advance about the project, and that it was classified Top Secret 'Codeword' because of the American link. It was certainly something covered by D-Notices. Protheroe accepted this, and agreed to reconsider broadcasting that part of the series. He cautioned however that, if it was pulled, Campbell would certainly take it elsewhere.

When Whitmore reported this conversation to selected colleagues, the Director of GCHQ, Peter Marychurch[228] pointed out the British Aerospace press release had actually concerned Skynet not Zircon, and that what Campbell had said to Mason and Sheldon indicated he must indeed have some other source, a matter of great concern. Nevertheless he considered that, even if Campbell did publish elsewhere, it would have much less credibility than if the BBC broadcast it. Protheroe came to see Whitmore and Marychurch in early December, explaining that the BBC might anyway, for editorial reasons, wish to shorten the series from six half-hour slots to one 2 1/2 hour programme, which might resolve the problem; and that if Campbell then took the Zircon material elsewhere, that was the Government's problem not the BBC's.

Protheroe therefore told his Director General in mid-December that, for security reasons, he thought the Zircon episode should not be broadcast; Milne over Christmas decided to pull it. The angry Campbell made sure this cancellation was leaked, and on 18 January *The Observer* published 'BBC Gag on £500M Defence Secret'. Campbell also wrote an article for the *New Statesman* of 22 January 1987, which the Government attempted to stop by an injunction against him and the journal. The article linked its information to four unnamed senior defence officials and a former GCHQ employee. The Attorney-General asked the Special Branch to investigate what officials saw as a prima facie breach of OSAs, and to find the sources of the leak to Campbell. The police raided his home and the *New Statesman*'s offices. Campbell retaliated by organising a viewing of the cancelled programme for MPs,[229] even though the BBC had ordered its employees to return all copies; this took place not in but close to the Houses of Parliament, the Speaker having ruled against it being shown on the premises.

Meanwhile at the BBC, the Governors turned on Milne, and on 29 January he was sacked. Two days later the Glasgow offices of BBC Scotland (which had made the Zircon programme) were raided by the Strathclyde police, who arrested and interrogated the visiting Protheroe under the OSA (which ironically he had signed four times in his military and BBC roles), and (against his will) removed papers and footage. Although he received little support from the BBC Governors, this caused widespread media outrage, and the same public shock waves as (at that time even more so than now) in the case of any venerable maiden aunt allegedly caught in flagrante delicto.[230]

Higgins had played no part in the latter and more dramatic events. Having offered his advice to the BBC about the programme, once it became a highly politico-legal matter, he withdrew from further involvement. Nevertheless, the affair had become a major politico-media event; the Media side of the DPBC had additional concerns that the Government and police action, widely perceived as being over heavy-handed, would indirectly tar the DPBC's reputation. A considerable head of steam built up amongst them, led by Ramsden, who rang Higgins at the beginning of February, firstly to complain that he and the rest of the Media Members had not been informed about what had been going on; Higgins explained his role had been limited to the earlier stages, and that Protheroe had been concerned *not* to involve the D-Notice System but to deal with Whitmore 'on a personal basis'. Secondly Ramsden said that he was 'horrified' at the Government's raid on the BBC Scotland offices, and 'uneasy' about his own continuing position as Vice-Chairman. Other Media members shared his concern; 'It did seem as if there was an intent not to pursue a specific offence but to carry out a trawl of the Campbell files to see what might be found there. Throw in "Spycatcher" and you have a period of heavy passage and not a little sophistry.'[231]

Higgins replied, pointing out that the Attorney-General had been acting in his independent role as a Law Officer, and that the police raids had not been ordered by him per se, but had been in response to his request 'in the ordinary process of law' to investigate a prima facie offence [it subsequently emerged the Metropolitan Police Special Branch also considered methods used by Strathclyde Police were unnecessarily heavy-handed, but a degree of rivalry has perhaps to be allowed for]. Higgins stressed that the police action had nothing even indirectly to do with the D-Notice System. Ramsden nevertheless continued to agitate through to the spring among his colleagues for a meeting to discuss media concerns.[232] In this he was widely supported, for example by *The Observer* Editor, Donald Trelford: 'It is the government's job to keep secrets, part of a reporter's job is finding them out. An editor's job is deciding whether to publish them or not. In doing this he may take advice and hold a story in the name of national security (by using the D-notice system, for example, which seems to have been curiously inoperative over the Zircon affair).'[233]

The OD(DIS) v The D-Notice System

At the end of 1986, in response to the Prime Minister's dissatisfaction with co-ordination of the Government's response to the increasing publication of intelligence and security matters, the Cabinet Office machinery for security matters was overhauled.[234] Interdepartmental monitoring and reaction was now the responsibility of a Cabinet sub-committee known as OD(DIS) and its subordinate sub-committee of senior officials OD(DIS)(O), then chaired by the Cabinet Office Deputy Secretary Christopher Mallaby.[235] Its terms of reference included 'Arrangements for action in respect of unauthorised publication on security and intelligence and cognate matters'. Mrs Thatcher took a close personal interest in their work, and required ministerial approval of many individual actions which previously had been the responsibility of officials.

In her strategic aim, she was justified in seeking improvements in co-ordination and ministerial oversight; at the 'tactical' level her interventions in practice hindered and delayed solutions being negotiated. This was particularly so where the D-Notice System was concerned. Her attitude to litigation had changed since the earlier years of her Premiership, for several reasons: the relationship between media and politicians had continued to deteriorate into mutual negativity, television in particular exaggerating the tendency to simplify, sensationalise and personalise politics; and greater commercial competition within the Media had led to more 'White Knight' campaigns and commentators. Politicians, thrust more visibly into the spotlight, reacted increasingly by attempting to manipulate news. Thatcher had been particularly angered by the Falklands reporting, by 'Spycatcher', by hostile reaction to her support for the Tripoli bombing in April 1986, and by criticism of anti-terrorist legislation introduced to combat the IRA.[236]

In February 1987, Higgins was involved in the vetting of 'Molehunt' by Nigel West. Embarrassment about delays caused by OD(DIS) interference on political aspects was masked by the fortuitous involvement of the Treasury Solicitor (because a previous legal undertaking applied to the book's content). Higgins voiced concerns to Whitmore as his Chairman that in future he would be invited by the Cabinet Office to report to them matters (not just about books) which should properly be between the D-Notice Secretary and the publisher/journal, but which instead would then be 'under the influence of the higher levels of Government where political considerations are always likely to creep in'. The integrity of the D-Notice System would thereby be affected, which the Media would soon realise. Furthermore, delays caused by political involvement would mean that the quick response needed by the Media could not be provided.

Within days he was minuting Whitmore again, complaining that on 'An Affair of State' by Kennedy and Knightley (about the Profumo case), he was being prevented from consulting the publisher while awaiting a ministerial decision. He listed a dozen intelligence-related books which he knew were then in the publishing pipeline, on which he foresaw similar delays and interference in his normal negotiation between the Media and intelligence/security officials. The only way of anticipating the hindrances now involved would be to give the list to Mallaby for advance discussion with Ministers as to what they wished to become involved with, but this would make Higgins de facto part of the Government machinery. He had made the Security Service Legal Adviser Bernard Sheldon and the Treasury Solicitor JB Bailey[237] aware of his concern, 'but others may not find it so easy to accept in view of (Prime) Ministerial interest'.

Whitmore was equally alarmed, and undertook to discuss the problem with the Cabinet Secretary. By late March, Higgins was reporting further to him: 'In two months, we have moved from the situation where I sought advice at my own level from Government Departments and based my actions and reactions to the media on that advice, to a situation where my actions and reactions are now subject to Ministerial decision and detailed control, down to the wording of letters and phone calls, by the Cabinet Office'. He did not see how the D-Notice System could survive such direct political control. Whitmore wrote immediately to Mallaby, reminding him the D-Notice System was voluntary and depended on the Media accepting the independent 'honest broker' role of the Secretary; but that the OD(DIS) was drawing Higgins increasingly into its workings as though he were just another official. This appeared now to be a 'lasting' situation, and he invited Mallaby to come and discuss the problem with him and Higgins.

In his briefing note for this meeting, headed 'OD(DIS) v DPBC', Higgins stated his 'Magna Carta', including that the DPBC and its Secretary must be free from political influence, that ideally the Secretary should not consult officials at all except to seek expert advice on detail, that he must then be free of political constraint in deciding the advice he gives, that it was for the Government Department concerned not the D-Notice Secretary to inform the Cabinet Office of events, and that it would not be acceptable for the Secretary to have to await even indirect direction from the Cabinet Office via the Department concerned before deciding what to do.

The Home Secretary, Douglas Hurd,[238] was meanwhile expressing concern, apropos of 'An Affair of State', that publishers without 'the full facts' were increasingly stating, when approached by officials, that they were satisfied their manuscripts contained nothing damaging to national security or in breach of the duty of confidentiality. He suggested Ministers needed to take stock of the emerging situation and, with the Prime Minister's endorsement, tasked officials to establish 'what could be done to put Ministers in a better position for handling cases like this in the future.'[239] As part of this fresh initiative, Mallaby asked of Whitmore at the end of March 1987 (a few days before they were due to meet) that Higgins produce a note 'on the extent of any change in the co-operation of the media with the D-Notice system, with a view to it being considered at a future meeting of the OD(DIS)(O)'.

Concurrently, there was a brief spat directly between Mallaby and Higgins over the Government's draft line to take on the broadcast of the BBC/Campbell Emergency Powers programme.[240] Higgins again pointed out it was essential for the Media to regard him as an 'honest broker' between them and the Government, whereas the line to take implied not only that he was a government official, but also revealed the BBC had submitted the film to him and accepted his advice on a few changes. With Whitmore's support, the line to take was duly amended, but was then queried by Mrs Thatcher. It was left to her PPS Nigel Wicks[241] to explain to her that 'we do not take the initiative in revealing such discussions, but are ready to confirm that they have taken place if the other party had first disclosed them'.

Mrs Thatcher was understood by Higgins then to find the D-Notice System irritatingly 'wishy-washy'; she was certainly not pleased with Mallaby's covering note to the Secretary's information on trends in media co-operation.[242] This recorded the experience of Higgins and Kay that, while the revised Notices of 1982 had resulted in a diminution in the number of enquiries, no change had been detected in the level of co-operation. Nevertheless there were some such as the *New Statesman* who never used the System, Pincher had never submitted a book manuscript, and Nigel West had not accepted all the advice on his two previous books on MI5 and MI6. Higgins recorded he had made a particular point of contacting publishers about forthcoming books, which in a survey of five-year periods from 1967 to 1986 showed variations in numbers of manuscripts submitted between 17 and 23; of these, books where amendments were requested varied from six to 13, of which between one and four were not wholly accepted by the author/publisher. No particular adverse trend was perceived in dealings with other parts of the Media either, although there were greater pressures currently from advocates of freedom of information, and increased interest in 'exposures' following the 'Spycatcher' case.[243]

When Whitmore, Mallaby and Higgins met a few days later, harmony was restored. All the points in the last named's 'Magna Carta' were agreed. His independence would be respected. He would deal with Departmental and secret Agency officials at his level as before. Departments would deal with the Cabinet Office, keeping the D-Notice Secretary advised as appropriate. He would not be involved in any ministerial decision-making, nor vice versa. When Defence/military matters were discussed in the OD(DIS)(O), MoD would be represented by a two-star civil servant. Mallaby would explain in the Home Secretary's 'stocktaking' that the D-Notice System could not be 'tightened up', and point out to Ministers that it covered national security not breaches of confidence. Whitmore would keep the situation under review.[244]

Back to Zircon

In the 12 February 1987 *Listener*, Protheroe had given his account of recent events, stating no direct approach had been made to the BBC by the Government demanding cancellation of the Zircon programme, but he criticised the 'Use and Abuse of the Official Secrets Act' over the years. In late February Campbell's solicitors agreed with the authorities he would not publish any genuinely sensitive information known to him, and the injunction on the programme was lifted (although police investigation continued). In March Protheroe gave Higgins a copy of the 'Secret Society' programme on wartime emergency powers, which he viewed and, having taken expert official advice, concluded that although 'one sided and generally unpleasant' about the powers, it was so full of conjecture as to cause no damage to national security. In April Higgins similarly received, viewed and found non-damaging the programme on 'Radars', which included cancellation of the costly Nimrod Airborne Early Warning project.

Based on his assessments, officials recommended to the Prime Minister that no legal action should be taken against the BBC to stop the first two programmes, and no comment should be made. Mrs Thatcher was not convinced, however, that the films would not prejudice national security, indeed considered they were intended to do so. In particular she considered that material on priority in hospital services being given to, amongst others, American personnel serving in wartime in the UK, as 'calculated to prejudice the Government's capacity to take difficult decisions'. Nor did she agree the Government should refuse to comment on the programmes, which were designed to portray it in a bad light, and should attract a response putting the case for emergency powers in wartime; it would do so if similarly published in a newspaper 'and it is not clear why the BBC should be treated differently'. She tasked Departments to consider how this should be done, and the effect of the programme on national security.[245]

Whitmore immediately saw difficulty in the Prime Minister's line; not only had Higgins already obtained Departments' agreement the programme could be cleared from a purely national security point of view, but also a Cabinet Office team had discreetly viewed the film after the police search of BBC Scotland offices, and given it a similar clean bill of health, something of which the BBC was almost certainly well aware. He hoped therefore that

Mrs Thatcher could be dissuaded; Armstrong subsequently achieved this, subject to deletion of the precise location (in East Anglia) of the NATO wartime civil agency for controlling shipping. This advice Protheroe was prepared to accept (but only from Higgins). The location was later leaked anyway in the *Guardian* of 29 April, allegedly inadvertently, after the Prime Minister had approved legal action to stop it appearing in Campbell's 'Secret Society' articles in the *New Statesman*.

Despite a long exchange of correspondence between Ramsden and Whitmore/Higgins, the Media side's concerns had not subsided appreciably by the 1 June 1987 DPBC meeting. Routine business was first dealt with: there were now two brothers at the table, Keith Whetstone, and the new Deputy Secretary Admiral Tony Whetstone.[246] Higgins reported that, although the 'Spycatcher' affair had continued to preoccupy the Media but not the D-Notice System,[247] it had nevertheless stimulated a significant upsurge in the number of other books on security and intelligence matters, some of which had been submitted for advice and small changes made, others had not required change nor even vetting, and in a few cases the publisher had declined to seek advice [but seemingly no damaging information was included]. He had also given advice to broadcasters, amongst whom there was a similar increase in intelligence and security interest. Dealings with the Press had included *The Independent* (which had allegedly revealed the name of an SIS employee in Afghanistan); and the *Guardian* Media File ('Welcome to the club, chaps',16 February) had reported his reminder to the growing number of free newspapers about using the D-Notice System, even when recycling news from other papers. He had also been active in discussing the D-Notice system with journalists and media lawyers, and at media seminars, in order to dispel some of the mythology surrounding it.

On Zircon, Whitmore reminded that the Secretary's involvement 'had been strictly limited to the early stages of the affair' and that the Attorney-General had been acting as a Law Officer, not subject to Ministerial direction. Cubbon confirmed there was 'a discontinuity' between the Attorney-General and the police, who had 'complete freedom of action within the law once the process had been set in motion by the Director of Public Prosecutions'. It was incorrect therefore to claim that the Attorney-General had ordered the search of the BBC Glasgow offices. Ramsden said he found it hard to accept that 'nobody in Government had been aware of the intention of the police to raid' the BBC's offices, and other courses had been open to the Government to bring to justice those who had leaked secrets.[248] 'He was particularly incensed that the BBC's offices should have been searched in this peremptory way when the BBC had fully honoured the spirit of the D-Notice system by deciding to withdraw the ZIRCON episode'. He wished to register with all Government Departments the Media members' strongest possible protest about the raid, which was 'an outrage against the freedom of the press of this country'. They saw it as 'a failure of the D-Notice system which was designed to prevent this sort of conflict between a Government which respected the freedom of the press and a responsible press which respected the needs of national security'.

In the lively discussion which followed, the Official side's case included: although the BBC had acted responsibly, it was the *New Statesman*'s contrary actions which had precipitated subsequent events; whereas the Government was a party to the D-Notice System, the police were not, and would have seen little difference in seeking possible sources of evidence between Campbell's home, the *New Statesman*'s offices, and those of the BBC; and that, although officials had sympathy with the Media side's dislike of police searching media offices, the action had been properly carried out in the name of the law. All agreed a clear separation must be maintained between the D-Notice system and the operation of the OSAs; Whitmore could do no more than agree to pass on the Media side's strong views to the Cabinet Secretary.

Passing quickly over the 'Working Arrangements between MoD and the Media in Time of War',[249] the Committee agreed a Higgins Note on the applicability of D-Notices to terrorism: 'the activities of the Security and Intelligence Services were adequately covered by D-Notice No.6 in whatever field they were operating and that no more specific reference to terrorism was required in either D-Notice No.6 or the general Introduction'. Although not specifically mentioned, this included covert activities of the military working in conjunction with those Services and the police, in particular the Special Forces and Intelligence units. Thus, in this low-key way, did the DPBC finally acknowledge its de facto involvement in the wider national security realities of the era.[250]

The Committee met again on 11 November 1987, unaware that further major controversies were about to come its way. Whitmore reported a visit he and Higgins had made to *The Independent* to discuss its recent three 'breaches' of D-Notice No.6; the FCO representative, now JDI Boyd[251] said two of the cases had involved secret interception of foreign communications, which were particularly susceptible to countermeasures and damage. Higgins reported a relatively quiet period [usually a warning sign] for book vetting, enquiries and advice. Most discussion was of two Beach Report follow-up drafts provided by Blelloch. On 'Proposed Working Arrangements with the Media in Time of Tension and War' [these applied only to those 'in the field', and to a major war], Media side comments included that reference to public relations implied just portraying information in a favourable light, whereas the Media was concerned with obtaining *accurate* information; it lacked an international (especially NATO) dimension; it did not seem to do anything to avoid the conflict between censorship in theatre and that in London which had so bedevilled the Falklands conflict; it (probably sensibly) did not address nuclear warfare; it would not be acceptable to ask war correspondents to undertake not to report morale-damaging aspects such as mismanagement of a campaign; but that the mere writing of the draft must have been beneficial in increasing MoD awareness of media needs in time of tension and war.

On 'Written Guidance to the Media', Blelloch thought that publication would in itself add to deterrence, by showing the Government's commitment. The Guidance had been drafted in general terms, so that editors and the intended Advisory Service could exercise common-sense about what was already in the public domain. The Media side, while generally favourable to the Guidance, thought the Advisory Service might have difficulty dealing with speculation; that again the international dimension was lacking; and that it was important to avoid the Guidance becoming just a 'Stop List', to which the media reaction would merely be 'What is there left that we can publish?' Blelloch undertook to incorporate all these comments in further work.

A fortnight later, Blelloch received another media view from Bishop, this time in his other hat as new Chairman of the Association of British Editors: there was no guarantee that any of the guidelines would be acceptable in reality to all the Media in a time of tension or war. While the MoD paper still referred to 'public relations in forward and rear areas of operations', he repeated that the Media's principal concern was 'acquisition and publication of accurate information'; while they would welcome guidance on matters not covered by current D-Notices which needed to be protected in time of war and possibly tension, this needed to be far more specific than the 'too generalised, and thus too potentially restrictive' guidance in the paper. Blelloch replied that the guidance had to be seen against the

Government's acceptance of the Beach recommendation that as much news as possible should be disclosed. Internally, his other lingering concern was how to give guidance on secret intelligence and security matters in an unclassified document; the Cabinet Secretary, now FER Butler[252] agreed it would need in war to be much more extensive than that in D-Notices, if it were to be of practical media use; it would therefore need to go into sensitive areas and explain why 'revelations are undesirable. Given the media's current obsession with security and intelligence, we shall need to be very sure that this particular section of the guidance will not be used to our disadvantage.'[253]

The FCO, on behalf of GCHQ, was meanwhile making one last effort to dissuade the BBC from showing the Zircon programme, the master copy of which was still in the possession of the senior Scottish Law Officer, the Lord Advocate. When the FCO approached Higgins, he pointed out that, if the film was returned to the BBC, he could hardly ask them not to show it, as all agreed it did not damage national security, the project was now public knowledge, and anyway much of the footage was about the Public Accounts Committee. The most he could do, if GCHQ had identified any damaging details in the film, would be to advise the removal of those. The FCO reluctantly agreed to the film being returned to the BBC, but hoped Whitmore (or Higgins, although he would not have agreed it was appropriate for the D-Notice Secretary to do this) would tell the BBC that to show it would 'still be damaging to national security'. There was also one official document which the search of the *New Statesman*'s office had revealed, and which included Top Secret 'Codeword' information, which the FCO hoped, being in English not Scottish jurisdiction, the police would find a way of returning to the Government rather than to Campbell.

As subsequently decided by the OD(DIS)(O), in late November (the day the film was returned to the BBC) Whitmore made arguments of general damage to the BBC's Deputy Director General, who retorted that, as no prosecutions had been brought, the request put him in a difficult position, on which he would 'reflect'. A few days later, Armstrong met the Chairman of BBC Governors, Marmaduke Hussey[254] and attempted to persuade him. Hussey thought however it would now be difficult to justify the BBC not showing it, but considered ways of minimising the damage, for example by showing the film late at night or by 'encapsulating' it in a more general programme about the Zircon affair.[255] A combination of government and BBC measures did indeed delay the programme further, but when the film was at last broadcast, it created little impact; and, whatever damage it had already done to relations between the Government, officials and the Media, it did no serious damage to national security.

Observer Article on GCHQ

Late on 11 December, *The Observer* rang the Deputy Secretary Admiral Whetstone, who had the pre-Christmas watch, and sought advice on a wide-ranging article on GCHQ, the declared outline being based in part on Duncan Campbell's investigations. After consulting GCHQ, Whetstone rang back the next day, and gave his advice as to what details would be damaging, and the paper revised its draft and rang through the sanitised version. It covered the Agency's internal organisation, its current tasking beyond national security, the use of the BBC monitoring service (of overt international sources) as collateral, the interception (with the alleged aid of the USA and South Africa) and breaking of codes to do with Portuguese anti-Marxist/Cuban operations in Mozambique, the listening post locations, and that GCHQ dealt in cryptology, all of which Whetstone was able to establish had already been separately put in the public domain, apart from some specific crypto operations/ techniques, which the paper also agreed to delete.

However, *The Observer*'s intention to publish had meanwhile reached the ears of No.10 Downing Street, and an injunction was immediately ordered. Whitmore managed to get this stopped, on the grounds that the correct D-Notice action had been taken and the advice accepted, that legal action based on what had become known through the D-Notice Secretary would seriously endanger the system's continuation, and that it appeared that no serious damage to national security would now be done by the article. In this he was supported by his Secretary of State, who nevertheless did 'not dissent' from No.10's wish to litigate. Whetstone felt the editor Donald Trelford should be warned privately that the Government might still, independently of the D-Notice System, consider litigation (based on its two-week-old and still in force injunction on all Campbell material), and phoned him mid-Friday. Trelford, having consulted his legal advisers, decided to hold the article, and published instead one critical of the Thatcher Government's actions, which it linked to the 'Spycatcher' case, on which judgement was imminent.[256]

'My Country Right or Wrong'

Shortly afterwards, Ramsden found it necessary rapidly to canvas the views of Media side colleagues, and ask for a special meeting on 21 December 1987. This was in reaction to further suppression by the Government of a BBC programme, this time an episode of Radio 4's series 'My Country Right or Wrong' concerning the Intelligence Agencies. The BBC had consulted Higgins about the content of the programme from late November, and a detailed discussion had been arranged for 3 December; but that day, after the *Daily Telegraph* revealed the extent to which past and present members of the secret Agencies had participated in the programme-making (the producer boasted of 'spies queuing up' to be interviewed) , the Government (as Whitmore described it to the meeting) 'felt obliged to seek to maintain the principle of the duty of confidentiality, and, without reference to the Chairman or the Secretary, a temporary injunction had been sought and obtained' [by the Home Office; this severe injunction was eased slightly by the Court on 9 December to allow the rest of the by then Higgins-cleared programme to be broadcast].

In the days before the DPBC meeting, the Media had quickly picked up that there was to be confrontation, the injunction having been made public by a BBC letter asking the Government to reconsider and reminding them of Higgins' no-damage assessment. Follow-up was typified by *The Independent* which carried interviews with Higgins, Ramsden and others as part of its summary of the dispute.[257] Higgins stuck to his guns ('we like him', said the BBC), also pointing out the Committee was not involved with the duty of confidentiality aspects being pursued by government. Bishop, in his Association of British Editors hat, called on the Media to withdraw from participation in the D-Notice System. Trelford commented: 'What we have is a situation where the Government is going behind the back of the D-Notice Committee and using the courts. And the courts are giving them much more than even the security people want. If they won't acknowledge that the D-Notice Committee is the right way of dealing with the Press then there is trouble ahead' (although he also went on to say that the System should be preserved 'because the alternative would be even less desirable)'. Newspapers from the nationals to the *Scotsman* to the *Birmingham Post* picked up the story, and Ramsden was interviewed on the BBC Breakfast programme and other channels on the morning of the meeting. All this coincided with the Government imposing a three-line whip on Conservative MPs to vote down a Private Members' Bill to reform OSA Section 2, something which Mrs Thatcher wished to do in due course by a (tougher) Government Bill.

At the DPBC meeting, Whitmore acknowledged that the separate legal action ('this twin track approach') had 'caused resentment and a feeling in the media that the D Notice system was not worth bothering with'. Cubbon explained that 'the Government in this case was not trying to prevent any particular disclosure, but to maintain the general principle that members of the Security Services should not speak publicly about their work without authority'. Ramsden accepted these explanations, but argued the Media nevertheless had a duty of discovery and disclosure in the public interest, and could not therefore accept that the duty of confidentiality at all times overrode the duty of conscience. 'That way lay censorship'. The Media side considered the Government had been wrong to seek an injunction, because in doing so they had disregarded both the D-Notice System and the duty of the BBC to publish information which the public had a right to know. It had put the System at risk by attacking the wrong target, the Media, rather than its own employees and ex-employees.

Officials counter-argued that, when it was impossible to know in advance which of its employees was about to breach confidentiality, the only practical way of stopping publication was to restrain the 'publisher'. It was then for the courts to decide where the balance lay between the freedom to publish and the duty of confidentiality. The Media side countered that, if Government was to proceed thus by injunction, the Media would resort to 'stealth', and despite the ring-fence around negotiation with the D-Notice Secretary, would become reluctant to seek his advice. The Government appeared to be making the duty of confidentiality 'the cornerstone' of its policy on the publication of information, thereby indirectly controlling what the Media could report, and this was a fundamental change in governmental attitudes to press freedom. It sowed the seeds of the demise of the D-Notice system, which some sections of the Media were already again becoming more reluctant to use.

'In the view of the media the Government's attitude towards it had hardened, and while the press still honoured the D-Notice System, the Government did not . . . Any assurance by the Government of the importance it attached to the D-Notice System would be more convincing if it contained a recognition that recent events had undermined the credibility of the System in the eyes of the media'. Whitmore accepted these concerns and the need to rebuild confidence. Finally it was agreed that Ramsden would make a short public statement reflecting the Media concern, the continuing importance which both sides still attached to the continuance of the D-Notice System, and that there would be a public official response to the Media concerns; all this to be read to the many reporters then waiting outside the MoD Main Building.

In the press next day, the Media side called on the Government to support the D-Notice System, and in the *Guardian* the normally mild-mannered Ramsden enlarged on his statement: 'I don't think Mrs Thatcher realises what she has put into jeopardy. She had always advocated the virtues of individual responsibility and self-discipline. Here is the Press co-operating with the Government in the national interest and she's in danger of losing members' support by her very rigid interpretation of the duty of confidentiality'. His alarm was shared even by the MoD. Before the DPBC meeting, its Secretary of State, George Younger,[258] had written to the Prime Minister explaining in detail how the System worked, and extolling its virtues. 'Inevitably, a voluntary system, and particularly one which operates in a grey area, is not watertight. It depends for its success on confidence and trust, and the relationship between the Secretary of the DPBC and the media is a delicate one . . . this voluntary system does work . . . and without the early warning the system provides . . . we should be faced more frequently than now with decisions on whether to take legal action after the event and after the damage had been done'.

Younger enclosed a list of 20 examples of the Secretary's advice having been accepted in the past year. These included a book about the IRA on which no official action had then been needed, the non-publication of photographs of sensitive areas of the nuclear deterrent base at Faslane, removal of the names/photographs/details of intelligence officers from books and articles, deletion of current cryptography techniques from an article intended for an academic journal, omission of Security Service addresses and telephone numbers from an article about a British Telecom billing muddle, non-broadcasting of certain details of vulnerable points in emergency oil installations, and omission of some technical details from broadcasts on Zircon.[259] Because of the Prime Minister's personal interest, Whitmore sent his draft official response on the DPBC Media side's protest to Younger, who sent it smartly to No.10. The letter made clear the seriousness of the situation: 'There were a number of indications before Christmas that the media were proposing to withdraw from participation in the D Notice system.' Younger and Whitmore reiterated their opinion of the importance of the System, and that 'there is no simple and obvious replacement for it.'[260]

Contrary to the belief of some on the governmental side, the Media have no effective mechanisms or aptitude for co-ordinating attacks on the Government. But occasionally it appears to the Media, individually and collectively, that they themselves are coming under attack from government, and spontaneous media indignation erupts. Every opportunity is then taken to needle the Administration, through columns and broadcasts, and through the Parliamentary Opposition. Not all are silent on their own faults however; at this time, the Director of the Press Council, in an article entitled 'Irresponsibility jeopardises press freedom', quoted the 1948 criticism by Sir William Haley (then of *The Times*) of 'newspapers who have moved into the entertainment industry – and not very high grade entertainment at that'; the Director feared (as others have done since) that the Press's own faults would lead to governmental regulation being imposed upon it. He still went on to lambaste the then Administration: 'Since the middle of last year the Government has scuttled from court to court, from country to country, from continent to continent and now, like a long-running play, back to London again in its attempt to keep from the British reader information and allegations about the history and conduct of its own security services' which were available to most of the rest of the world.[261]

A media-and-friends frenzy was indeed now under way, exemplified by the intervention of Tam Dalyell on behalf of Magnus Linklater,[262] editor of the *Scotsman*, over the book 'Inside Intelligence' by Anthony Cavendish (35 years retired from the intelligence world), incorrectly alleged to have been vetted by Higgins (it had not been submitted to him), but briefly injuncted by the Government on grounds of breach of confidentiality. The *Daily Telegraph* of 12 January featured a long and sympathetic interview with Ramsden ('D-Day on the D-Notice deal'), in which he explained the line that the Media side would be taking at the next DPBC meeting. On 13 January the new DGSS, Patrick Walker,[263] was deliberately named by the *Guardian*, *Independent* and *Times*. The BBC Chairman Marmaduke Hussey weighed in with the warning that the Government's tendency to seek injunctions consti-tuted 'a very serious threat to the liberty of the Press'. The Prime Minister's Press Secretary Bernard Ingham[264] countered this spontaneous media barrage by referring to the D-Notice Committee being 'a further impending casualty of the increasing anarchy in journalism', to be rescued, if still possible, 'only by facing up to the facts' [about the security (especially terrorist) situation].

In January, the OD(DIS)(O) met to discuss work ordered by Ministers to take place in the wake of the still awaited 'Spycatcher' judgement. The MoD representative stressed the importance of the present D-Notice System remaining in force, and that the Government should not use information given in confidence to the Secretary by the Media as a basis for legal proceedings; in this he was strongly supported by Mallaby. Officials therefore agreed to recommend that the Government's relationship with the D-Notice System should not be a separate subject in the ongoing work on tightening up controls, merely that its role should be borne in mind by those studying other proposals.[265]

In mid-January Mrs Thatcher summoned the SofS for Defence, the Home Secretary, the Foreign Secretary, the Attorney-General and their top officials to discuss the response to the DPBC Media side. Most present argued strongly for the retention of the D-Notice System. The discussion focused first on 'the undoubted overlap between national security and the duty of confidentiality owed by members of the security and intelligence services and others'. The Government insisted on the latter, and because of the difficulty of getting the Media to include it in the relevant D-Notice, the line agreed was that the Government reserved the right to take action if national security was damaged by a breach of confidence, even if the D-Notice Secretary raised no objection; and that advice on the duty of confidentiality could be given to the Media only by the Treasury Solicitor.

The Prime Minister's meeting then turned to a reassurance given in the draft that any information imparted by the Media to the D-Notice Secretary would be 'used by the Government solely to decide what advice to give the Secretary about the risk, if any, to national security'. This policy had been confirmed to No.10 before the meeting in a letter dated 8 January 1988 from Mallaby as Cabinet Office Deputy Secretary: 'we would not go to law on the basis of information obtained only through the D Notice system that a particular publication was on the way; and . . . any information provided through the D Notice system would not be used by the Government as evidence in any case we initiated on the basis of separate information'. Some argued that this would put the Government 'in an untenable position', by estopping it from preventing, if necessary by legal means, the publication of information which damaged security or breached confidences. It was pointed out by others, however, that the first time a Government so used such information given by the Media to the D-Notice Secretary, the System would collapse. If that happened 'there would be less prospect of the Government knowing about such damaging information before it appeared in the media', whereas some knowledge of an impending problem at least gave the Government the opportunity to try to discover through other channels informa- tion that 'could be used as a basis for legal action without infringing the confidences of the D Notice system. . . . The Government could maintain the required degree of freedom to use DPBC material as it wished by making the assurance referred to . . . above, "subject to the Government's overriding duty to preserve national security"'.

Changes to Whitmore's proposal centred on a view that only if the Secretary saw a full draft article or script (as opposed to having it read over the telephone), could he make a proper judgement, and indeed that he should avoid giving any opinion until he had done so [the Secretary, needless to say, was not at the meeting, and so could not point out that, even if the editor concerned agreed to provide the full wording (if it then existed), deadlines were often such as to make telephone calls the only possible basis for judgements and advice]. Finally 'it was agreed that it was very important to ensure that Government servants were the subject of proper contractual arrangements which included a term imposing a duty of confidentiality.'[266] The longer-term results of this meeting were reflected subsequently in amendments to the OSA and contracts, including eventually those affecting the Services' Special Forces.

Whitmore duly despatched the approved letter to Ramsden on 21 January 1988. He confirmed first that the Government continued to place great reliance on the D-Notice System, and hoped that the Media would continue both to share its view that certain information should not be made public in the national interest, and to consult the D-Notice Secretary. The critical paragraph now read:

> The D Notice System deals with information in specific categories, as set out in the Notices themselves. It is advisory and voluntary. It does not deal with the question of breaches of the duty of confidentiality owed by members and former members of the security and intelligence services to the Crown, a matter therefore which falls outside the remit of the DPBC Secretary. The Government's position, expounded at length in the Peter Wright case, is that members and former members of the security and intelligence services owe a lifelong duty of confidentiality to the Crown, and that the upholding of that duty is essential to the effectiveness of these services and thus to the overall security of the country. If advice on a question in this field is desired, the Treasury Solicitor would always be glad to provide it.

When Ramsden saw this, his immediate reaction was that the breach of confidentiality argument was 'an unrestrained Government licence to suppress publication of almost anything about the intelligence services, even if the editorial material complies with D Notices and even if it is already in the public domain (as specifically allowed by D Notices)'. He called a meeting of the Media side at the beginning of February, at which, with Higgins' assistance, a reply to the Official side was produced. Some present felt the Whitmore letter was so unsatisfactory that the Media should withdraw from the D-Notice System, but a majority felt that more influence was obtained by remaining in it and putting the Government 'on notice'.

Ramsden's consequent reply of 2 February to the Government[267] expressed continuing media concern that the Government was maintaining 'its present course of proceeding against the Media in the Courts rather than against those it believes to be in breach of their duty of confidentiality'. It saw inconsistencies in the Government's position which had threatened the D-Notice System. 'We cannot accept that the duty of confidentiality should become a Government licence to prevent the publication of material which complies with D Notices . . . We have to warn you again that [this] trust will not be forthcoming from the Press side of the Committee if the principle of absolute confidentiality becomes enshrined in any new law with no corresponding recognition of the value of Press freedom'. Whitmore acknowledged receipt, but there was no further government response.[268]

The Media side would have been even more agitated had they been aware of concurrent government action over another book on the SIS ('The Friends') intended by Nigel West, on which Higgins had been in contact with the publisher and author [see case history at end of next chapter]. In late January 1988, in the context of considering whether some Conservative Party steps could be taken to dissuade Allason/West from going ahead with the book,[269] Mrs Thatcher had directed that in Higgins' negotiations 'all communications should be in writing, the Attorney General should be kept in close touch and all written communications cleared by him before despatch'. Higgins and the MoD's OD(DIS)(O) representative Nicolas Bevan[270] pointed out this would be a significant departure from the agreement reached with Mallaby the previous April. 'The Cabinet Office', Higgins reported, 'suggest that it is only to apply to the present case but I doubt if that is how the Prime Minister sees it or intends it to be. A precedent is always a precedent, and there are a number of cases in the offing that could be difficult for the Government'. Higgins regarded the Cabinet Office instructions as 'unworkable', and in his negotiations with West he ignored them.

Mallaby wrote an apologetic letter to Whitmore, explaining that, such was the strength of the Prime Minister's feelings, she had 'not ruled out the possibility of using information obtained on the DPBC net for the purposes of seeking an injunction, even though this could break the DPBC system'. Mallaby said that, in this case, and if Whitmore agreed, he would prefer not to ignore the Prime Minister's instruction. In the event, the Law Officers shortly afterwards concluded that litigation was unlikely to succeed, and, as Higgins scribbled with satisfaction on his copy of Mallaby's letter: 'Since it is now agreed that the D-Notice machinery is the only possible way of limiting the damage of West's book, and without it Government would not have known of it, we are in a stronger position than usual to resist.'[271] And resist they did.

In February the HCDC Clerk warned the MoD that his Committee, having continued its predecessors' interest in the D-Notice Committee, was thinking of conducting a new investigation into it, 'particularly in the light of recent events'; however, they would await the White Paper which the Government had promised in the summer on official information and security. The MoD had had enough of political 'interest', however, and politely pointed out that the Government's views on the value of the D-Notice System had been set out in a letter from Whitmore to Ramsden as recently as 21 January. It predicted correctly that 'as a purely voluntary arrangement' the System would not be part of the Government's review, and it was therefore unlikely that the White Paper would deal with it 'in any degree of substance'.

Government Litigation in Early 1988

As an indication of the degree of Government/Media litigation at this point, and although the D-Notice Secretary was not directly involved in any case once litigation started unless asked by both sides so to become, the Legal Secretary in the Attorney-General's Department listed in May 1988:[272]

- The Wright case: in England and Wales, the Government's appeal in the House of Lords against its case lost in the Court of Appeal (against the *Guardian*, *Observer* and *Sunday Times*) expected to start in mid-June, interlocutory injunctions remaining in place meanwhile; in Australia, High Court had reserved judgement on British Government's appeal, but no longer any restraint on publication of 'Spycatcher'; in New Zealand, British Government was seeking from Court of Appeal leave to appeal against its decision; in Hong Kong, interlocutory injunction pending trial in place against *South China Morning Post*.
- 'One Girl's War' by Joan Miller (WWII memoirs of a deceased member of Security Service): injunction against publisher, awaiting outcome of UK 'Spycatcher' case.
- Zircon, and Lawrie [see chapter 52]: injunctions still in force, but Campbell in process of settling with the Government.

427

- 'My Country Right or Wrong': no date fixed for hearing, but increasingly unlikely to come to trial.
- 'Inside Intelligence': Injunctions granted in England against *The Observer* and *Sunday Times*, but no trial date fixed; in Scotland, however, interim interdict against the *Scotsman* refused by Court; the Government seeking leave to appeal to the House of Lords.

Mediation

The cases above were not eventually settled in accordance with the Government's wishes by litigation, although the use of it sometimes helped bring matters to a head. Insofar as they were resolved to anybody's satisfaction, it was by negotiation. There are some principles which are irreconcilable, in theory at least, but in day-to-day practice a clash between governmental and media interests, within the D-Notice System itself and more widely and publicly, can far more often than not be avoided by the Secretary's mediation. In this respect, concerning potential use by government of information given by the Media to the D-Notice Secretary, it is worth pausing to restate how politicians' inclinations have in practice been interpreted, since the Prime Minister's meeting above, by successive Secretaries, with the tacit understanding of both sides of the Committee and of those whom they represent.

The Secretary must operate 'Chinese walls' with the information which he acquires both from the Media and from officials. If these 'walls' need occasionally to be breached by the Secretary in order in a particular case to obtain expert advice, or to progress negotiation by him between the two sides, it must be with the specific permission of the 'owner' of the information. Even then, if the Secretary judges that something could become a matter on which the Government might be tempted to litigate, he must both remind the editor of that possibility, and also provide officials with only enough information for him to obtain the necessary advice. Even then, officials know that, although his enquiries of them may make them aware of a possible publication, they are unable to use this knowledge alone to initiate legal action; there must be some other source than the Secretary. This 'gentlemen's agreement' has not been breached, because, as was pointed out at Mrs Thatcher's meeting, to do so would not be in the interest of the Government beyond, possibly, the case concerned.

52

REFORM OF THE OFFICIAL
SECRETS ACTS

Zircon Again

The Zircon affair had rumbled on in 1988. A new interim interdict had been granted against Campbell in Scotland in late November 1987, specifically concerning his alleged informant and former GCHQ member Alexander Lawrie (linked with the Top Secret document found earlier that year by police in the *New Statesman*'s offices). By May 1988, it had been conceded that this interdict did not in fact stop the BBC showing the film. Higgins was asked by officials therefore to seek a viewing of the film (which had not been changed since the Cabinet Office team had seen it when in police hands), to which the BBC agreed. Having viewed it, Higgins explained to the BBC's new DPBC representative John Wilson,[273] for the record, that his function was strictly limited to offering advice on national security aspects, and, while he explained the general damage arguments, he 'offered no advice', i.e. he agreed that no further damage to national security would be done by showing it.

When the DPBC met on 24 May 1988, there was a new Chairman, Sir Michael Quinlan,[274] and Whitmore had replaced Cubbon at the Home Office, while Blelloch had passed his Beach Report work to Kenneth Macdonald.[275] Quinlan was warned by his predecessor that Ramsden now wanted to raise the proposed reform of OSA Section 2. The Government had begun to look at Section 2 again the previous April, and in mid-December announced in Parliament an intended White Paper. The draft claimed that the defect of the existing Section 2 was that it went 'too wide' (which is what the Media had long felt), although an unstated official reason was that in practice it had been found hard to bring successful prosecutions. Officials deliberately excluded any definition of secrecy/security, so that it would be for the courts not the Attorney-General to decide whether an offence had been committed.[276]

The Paper included arguments against a 'catch-all' defence of public interest because there was no longer a 'catch-all' offence as in the existing Section 2, and because it would 'destroy all hope of clarity in the law'. It also argued against an absolute defence of 'prior publication'. While Higgins thought the Media would 'squeal' about that, he did not think it would make much difference to the application of D-Notices; each story had to be discussed with the Media on its merits, and he occasionally did argue that repeating previously published information could still cause additional damage. He did immediately put down three markers: there should continue to be no direct link between the new Act and the D-Notice System; the revised categories of information to be protected might nevertheless require some rewording of the detail of D-Notices; and one new proposal in the draft Act might dissuade the Media from using the D-Notice System. This was that for an offence to be committed, it would be necessary for the 'discloser' [i.e. the Media] to know that harm could result. Clearly a prior warning from the Secretary that something might do damage would remove this defence. However, he felt this might not be a consideration with the largely responsible Media.[277]

Before addressing concerns about the draft OSA, the May DPBC meeting dealt first with continuing follow-up work on the Beach Report. A joint MoD/Media exercise in the Falklands Islands had shown that technological advances had already made the plans for television reporting unrealistic and in need of much further discussion between the MoD and BBC/ITV. The Media side still felt the draft guidance was so broad that it could 'inhibit the free publication of information which was the life blood of the media'. Further planning action now passed to the COI.[278] The BBC's Wilson raised once more the 'My Country Right or Wrong' case, saying he had not been convinced by Whitmore's reply to the Corporation in February, voicing strong concern that, once an interim injunction had been granted in future cases, the Government would obtain relevant transcripts and be in a position to vet what was broadcast; Quinlan reassured 'the future of these issues would fall to be seen in the perspective of the revision of the Official Secrets Act'.

When the OSA White Paper[279] was issued by the Home Secretary (Hurd) at the end of June, Ramsden asked Higgins to provide his assessment of the effects on the operation of the D-Notice System. Taking into account points made in recent debates in the Houses of Commons and Lords, Higgins confined his comments to the impact on D-Notice business, avoiding the wider concerns of the Media and various freedom of expression groups, and on this occasion discouraging the Media side from believing 'that the Committee offers them an easy avenue for influencing the Government's decisions'. He assessed that the categories of information covered by the White Paper, specifically Defence, Security and Intelligence, and International Relations, were likely also to cover the areas of the D-Notices (although the converse was not true), so that there was no incompatibility. He flagged up his previous point about the liability of the discloser, and its possible discouragement to editors to consult. On the lack of a Prior Publication Defence, he pointed out that this was not an absolute exclusion, and that it would be open to the defence in any trial to argue that all harm had already been done by the initial disclosure and none by the second. He conceded however that, until the final form of legislation was known, it was impossible to give a full assessment.

Ramsden consulted his colleagues by letter, and in due course sent Higgins two hypothetical cases to demonstrate their immediate concerns. The first, from Wilson, postulated a civil servant giving unauthorised information to a newspaper, which, when it consulted the D-Notice Secretary, was told he had no advice to offer against publication; but the civil servant was then charged and found guilty because the Government did not have to prove harm. The editor was found not guilty however, because his defence was that he did not know it might cause harm, and in fact it did not cause harm; 'the above suggests to me either that the proposed new law will make an ass of the D-Notice system or the D-Notice system will make an ass of the law'.

The second hypothetical example, Ramsden's own, concerned a multinational weapon guidance system which did not work; a secret British accident enquiry established that the problem was caused by emissions from public broadcasting stations and would need many years and millions of pounds to correct it; an Italian newspaper published this conclusion, but, although the D-Notice advice permitted publication on grounds of no damage to national security, British newspapers were precluded from doing so because there were several grounds for prosecution but no public interest defence.

Higgins passed these two cases to Home Office drafters for comment, and, admirably quickly, was able to pass their response back to Ramsden. Assuming that the leaker in the

Wilson example was a former member of one of the secret Agencies, it was indeed the intention there should be a difference in treatment, and that, unless the editor was charged with 'aiding and abetting', it would be necessary to prove harm, whereas no such test should be needed for members of the Agencies, who had quite different 'obligations'. On the Ramsden example, the prosecution would have to show that the disclosed information was official, that its further disclosure met one of the tests of harm, and that the editor knew this; but even so, as Higgins had already pointed out, it was still open to the defence to show that no additional harm had been done by the second disclosure [there was no consideration in the proposed Act of the British public's right to know what the Italian public knew].

Unsurprisingly, these answers, entirely logical to governmental minds, did not reassure media minds they would be able to pass on to the public information which they had acquired, and which did not endanger national security, was of public interest, and possibly known to the publics in other countries. In late September Higgins told Quinlan (and thus the Home Office) 'The media side is building up quite a head of steam on the White Paper proposals and Mike Ramsden has told me that they definitely wished to submit their views to the Government.'[280] It was no coincidence that at this time the Press generally, and some parliamentarians, began to campaign actively against aspects of the proposed Act, and against what was perceived as the drive by the Government to ever greater secrecy. The Guild of British Newspaper Editors produced a pamphlet ('Officially Secret'): 'This book tells how the role of the nation's newspapers as public watchdogs is being severely blunted by a pervasive, almost institutionalised secrecy in our society'. The *Press Gazette* of 19 September ('Journalists must all resist this relentless secrecy') took the then Conservative-supporting *Sun* to task for being almost alone in scoffing at the Guild's pamphlet, and wrote its own lengthy attack not just on the White Paper, but on increasing secrecy in local and utilities authorities, courts, and educational bodies. The Association of British Editors, still chaired by Bishop, warned that, unless a significant number of changes were made in the proposed legislation, it would prove unworkable and leave the Media 'exposed to harsh consequences that are not part of our current experience', citing four areas of particular concern: international relations, interception of communications, and the lack of defences of prior publication and of public interest.[281]

The DPBC Media side met in mid-October to formulate their collective response.[282] The short letter to Quinlan afterwards said the impact of the proposed legislation on the D-Notice System would make it 'unworkable'. It focused on clauses which would make any intelligence disclosure an offence, subject only to a test of harm which did not have to be proved to the Court, with no public interest defence and usually no prior publication defence. The D-Notice Secretary 'may consider that a proposed publication would not harm the national security; but how could he advise an editor accordingly ("offer no advice") knowing that the publication would be contrary to the Official Secrets Act? He could "offer no advice" knowing it to be in conflict with the law, and an editor might plead in court that he had cleared publication with the D-Notices Secretary. If this plea were not accepted by the court, the Official Secrets Act would have invalidated the D-Notice system.' One idea on which Higgins disagreed with Ramsden was that a government Law Officer should be appointed to the DPBC, to help prevent such conflicts between the law and the D-Notice System as had occurred over the Zircon affair. The Secretary saw this as 'a quite unworkable suggestion', and in this was supported by the Treasury Solicitor, who pointed out the reasons of legal propriety, independent responsibility, and practicality in the workings of the Committee (he thought the Media side would soon want their own lawyer present, something Bailey foresaw as going 'all the way to the Court door!')

The BBC was meanwhile in separate correspondence with the Home Office. In mid-September, Wilson wrote to Whitmore: 'You will understand that these are clearly matters of the greatest importance to any broadcasting organisation, particularly one with audiences at home and abroad.' The Corporation welcomed much of the White Paper, but had some disquiet about the apparent answers to two questions: 'Are there publicly important issues which should be discussed openly, which can now be discussed openly but which could not be so examined under the proposals in the White Paper?'; and 'Does the White Paper clarify matters in such a way that editors can more readily weigh the consequences of reporting such information as comes their way?'

His long and well-crafted letter ended by addressing the whole field of governmental secretiveness. 'Although the White Paper steers itself away from the question of public access to the general body of officially held information, the protection of necessary secrets cannot satisfactorily be considered in isolation. It is best seen as part of a general system which allows access to most information while guarding fiercely those facts which must not become public. The great danger is that a system which protects too much will be so weakened by dispute that it fails to protect the small body of information which needs to be kept secret. The quality of media reporting on current affairs would be improved in Britain if unrestricted official information were made available to journalists unequivocally. Such a change would make the protection of the nation's secrets easier.'

Wilson's whole letter encapsulated many of the timeless media arguments on official secrecy; the BBC, being itself a large and impenetrable bureaucracy, is often ahead of the rest of the Media in picking the holes in the output of similarly opaque governmental organisations. In this case, it took the Home Office over seven weeks to concoct Whitmore's response of 3 November. On general aspects of the White Paper, he pointed out that it was not written in legislative language, and that government's intention was in fact to narrow the criminal law so that it applied only to unauthorised disclosure which caused unacceptable harm to the public interest. Further, the criminal law, unlike civil law, was not concerned with balancing competing interests but with penalising conduct contrary to the public interest.

He reassured on the limited application of the new Act, but made clear that the 'Government does not consider that any person is justified in knowingly causing such a serious degree of harm to the public interest, even in the hope of doing good'; such a person should use other means. The Government did not intend that there should be no disclosure in the Media of any information relating to the secret Agencies, just that it should not be disclosed by insiders; disclosure by others would be an offence only if it was likely to damage operations and if the discloser knew this [a BBC point about *informed* discussion was not picked up]. The official line on a prior publication defence was similarly uncompromising: certain information was always harmful, whether or not it had been published before, but the prosecution would have to prove specified harm was likely. Finally, on the BBC's wider point on public access to official information, the White Paper was concerned solely with reform of the criminal law; 'freedom of information is a separate issue which does not arise from that reform' and 'a worthwhile objective in its own right.'[283] In many respects, media and the governmental perspectives remained as far apart as in Sydney Brooks' rhetorical question of 1907.

When the DPBC reconvened on 15 November 1988, Higgins referred first to an allegation by Rupert Allason in the House of Commons during the OSA debate on 22 July 1988,[284] that in 1982 the D-Notice Secretary (Ash) had passed officials information from a manuscript

('A Matter of Trust, MI5 1945–72') provided by Allason, and that this had led to the author being injuncted. Higgins' investigation confirmed Ash had never received a copy of the manuscript, and that the Security Service, alerted by Press references to the forthcoming book, had themselves obtained an advance copy 'by unauthorised means', and initiated the injunction. Most of the DPBC meeting was occupied by long discussion of the draft OSA. Whitmore foresaw little impact in practice on the D-Notice System. The Media argued that the 'class or description' clause would enable the Government to use it 'as a device to prosecute for reasons of political embarrassment rather than damage to national security', and that the Secretary's view that a prosecution was unlikely to follow 'no advice' from him was perhaps 'too sanguine'. After this discussion, the Committee swiftly rejected the idea there should be a government Law Officer on the Committee.

Macdonald (following the convention accepted by then that MoD's 2nd PUS rather than the Chairman spoke on MoD matters), said he would welcome an informal exchange on two matters concerning Special Forces. The MoD had become 'extremely concerned at press speculation' recently that the SAS had been deployed to Cyprus to rescue hostages held by terrorists in a Kuwaiti Airbus, and even more so at the discussion of the rescue techniques which might be used. He asked the Media side's opinion as to whether, now the crisis had passed, it would be worth briefing editors on the dangers of such reporting to the safe release of hostages. The Media side felt the use of Special Forces in countering such terrorist activity was so newsworthy that any agreement reached with editors in advance might not be honoured by all when a crisis arose, but that nevertheless such a briefing should be arranged. This should be modelled on that to editors a few years previously at the SAS HQ at Hereford. While agreements on reporting hostage incidents had been worked out three years earlier between the Media, police, Home and Scottish Offices, the DPBC considered such agreements would usually be inadequate for terrorist incidents, as most had an international dimension and would therefore attract international media; furthermore the quid pro quo on which they were based (unreported briefings during, in return for full publication on completion) could not be offered in ongoing security situations.[285]

Macdonald said the recent inquest into the deaths of IRA terrorists killed by Special Forces in Gibraltar showed the importance of protecting the identities of the members of SAS, SBS and their supporting specialists. This led to wider discussion of whether there should be a separate D-Notice on Special Forces. There was no firm view, but it was agreed that restraint in reporting of and speculation on SF operations should be urged on editors during the proposed briefing.[286] The subsequent visit by some 30 editors (including three on the DPBC) took place in January 1989; it was agreed by those present that some additional MoD guidance would be useful, and that, although not strictly DPBC business, the guidance should be discussed on behalf of editors in the DPBC before issue.

After the Official Secrets Bill had been published in mid-December, Douglas Hurd, as part of his drive to explain to and reassure the Media, had his Private Secretary write to Ramsden, picking up his points made since October. He emphasised there would indeed be a test of harm in the prosecution of any journalist writing about the secret Agencies, and that the defence could argue that the information did not fall within any 'class or description' in the Bill. There would 'inevitably be a period of adjustment to the new legislation, and the Committee may well wish to consider whether any changes are necessary in its manner of working'. This letter however drew from Ramsden an anguished letter to Quinlan: 'may I ask you for your reassurance that you understand our concern? . . . The Press perceives the proposed Official Secrets Act as law which will greatly extend the day-to-day powers of

Government officials to censor rather than to extend the freedom of information on which the working of democracy depends. We on the Press side of the D Notice Committee will be seen as accomplices in this'. The Media side felt the end of the D-Notice System was 'genuinely on the agenda.'[287]

A month later Quinlan replied, giving his and Whitmore's reassurances as to how the new OSA would be applied in practice, and that the Secretary would continue to be able to give advice based on national security criteria alone. 'As you know, Bill Higgins does not see any real danger that those to whom he talks in the various Government Departments will try to push him towards accepting any looser criterion. It will be a clear direction to him from the Committee collectively that he must reject any such pressure; and both Clive and I are confident that he will be able to do so. And if he is unduly "leant on" I would expect him to report that to us all at our next meeting, or earlier if necessary.'[288]

The full history of the introduction of OSA 1989 is something for a separate book, but as the internal Whitehall and the parliamentary debates continued, so they did in the Media. A typical contribution was that of DPBC Member and *Observer*'s editor Donald Trelford, who was described in the *Press Gazette* of 20 February as advocating that editors must test the new OSA by if necessary risking going to jail; he criticised the guillotine imposed by the Government on parliamentary debate, and warned that the proposed legislation was not a charter for liberty, as the Government was claiming, but a 'charter for State media'. A lengthy article in *The Times* of 22 February was based on an interview with Higgins 'in his sparse eyrie' in the MoD. His line was that the new law would make it more important for an editor to know whether what he wanted to publish would damage national security; 'If I tell him it isn't damaging, he's got a good defence. If I tell him it is damaging, and he goes ahead and publishes, then that will be a good platform in the prosecution's evidence.' This may not have been precisely what lawyers and officials were saying, but it was a message which journalists and courts might comprehend.

The Official Secrets Act 1989 was passed on 11 May 1989.[289] Looking back, one might say that both sides of the DPBC were right, and they were wrong. The new Act did not usher in an age of greater official openness, nor did it lead to an age of greater use of the OSA by the Government. In an area of conflicting but equally valid principles, no Act can be perfectly conceived and construed, nor even always be imperfectly acceptable. The important factor in the end is how such an Act is used in practice, and the saving grace in Britain is that using such an Act is an unpredictable and often uncomfortable option for a government. There are still many strong counterweights to the power of central government, including the courts, the Media, and, when roused, the public. In the field of national security, the imperfect D-Notice system has therefore generally remained, both for the Media and for government/officials, less imperfect than litigation.

A Publishing Case History

In December 1987, Nigel West (Rupert Allason) had submitted to Higgins for advice the manuscript of his new book 'The Friends', about post-WWII SIS operations. The Secretary immediately realised some of the 50 or so 'new' names in the manuscript were also covered by a previous injunction (on his book 'Molehunt') and possibly also by a 'Spycatcher' injunction, about which West needed therefore first to consult not him but the Treasury Solicitor. He told Allason accordingly, adding that he considered the book anyway did general damage. It was at this stage, before Allason had even responded, that the Prime Minister had intervened, ordering litigation [see chapter 51]. The Government eventually decided not to litigate because Allason was not a 'Crown servant', and it considered success under the then OSA therefore unlikely.

In early February 1988 Allason discussed the manuscript with Higgins, and, apart from two short passages and two codewords, their debate centred on names (after consultation with SIS experts, the Secretary now wished to discuss about 100), and their links with particular locations and periods. Higgins also pointed out that Allason's position as an MP of the ruling Party would give the information in the book added credence with hostile intelligence. The author quickly agreed some omissions and undertook to review other names, and also to consult the Treasury Solicitor.

Further negotiations, with reasoned concessions on both sides, reduced the number of disputed names to 15 by early March. Separately, Allason was in discussion (and not entire agreement) with the Treasury Solicitor about other injunction-related names; by mid-May, the Treasury Solicitor was alarmed when the *Daily Mail* published extracts from the forthcoming book, including 'Spycatcher' material. Higgins was not involved in the legal aspects, but he too wrote to Allason about the newspaper articles, enquiring what his intentions were about the names unresolved between them. Receiving no immediate answer, in late May he advised the publisher (Weidenfeld and Nicolson) against publication pro tem while discussions continued. The Secretary was also aware the *Sunday Times* was investigating a story linked to an individual in the book, but he decided the grounds for intervention would be weak.

A few days later, West made his final deletion of more names, and Higgins concluded he had achieved as much as he could. The book was published in June. It included seven names from 'Spycatcher', but the Treasury Solicitor decided he had insufficient grounds to obtain an injunction, as that book was by then already on sale in many other countries. In subsequent media interviews,[290] West briefly described his dealings with Higgins, and he responded to Higgins' final letter of mild disappointment about residual detail that he had used the System and made many deletions accordingly.

The publication was not the end of it for the D-Notice Secretary, as media interest was maintained by a PQ from Tam Dalyell[291] as to why Allason had not been injuncted, by the unhappiness of BBC Governor Dame Daphne Park at having been 'outed' (again) as an ex-SIS officer, and, in July, by the book being temporarily withdrawn from bookshops following legal action by Greville Wynne, who received an apology and damages. To media enquiries, the customary line taken by Higgins was that discussion had taken place with the author, there had not been complete agreement, but details of that interaction must come from the author; the Secretary's involvement did not imply official 'clearance', nor that everything in the book was accurate. On the Wynne case, Higgins was required to provide an affidavit to that effect.

Much later (1992), Higgins had to dust off his files when a constituent of the SofS for Defence claimed D-Notice censorship of those sections of that book and another, 'Blow Up Jewish Ships' by David Leigh (in which a few agents' names had been deleted, but Higgins' intervention had helped sales publicity); both alluded to alleged interception and destruction by Britain of ships carrying Jewish refugees in the mid-1940s, and other nefarious Palestine-related operations. Higgins was able to prove he had not asked for any amendments to West's manuscript to be made in the passages concerned. Nor, had he been asked to do so, could he have done so under the interpretation of national security in the D-Notices and the constant practice that matters of political embarrassment are not covered.[292]

53

BUSINESS AS USUAL AGAIN

Before the OSA process had been completed, 1989 had started with the *Guardian* revealing the identity and former postings of the new Chief of the SIS, Colin McColl.[293] This time, although there was ritual tooth-sucking on the governmental side, there was no great debate, nor D-Notice activity. In February a draft article on 'Nuclear Scotland' was submitted to Higgins by the *Daily Record* for advice, and, there being nothing damaging or indeed new, he offered none, but with the formulaic statement that this did imply all the facts were correct (they were not). Thames Television consulted on a programme about Blake, asking whether there had ever been a D-Notice on him; Higgins tracked down a copy of the Thomson Private and Confidential letter to editors of 1 May 1961 in the SIS archives, where curiously it had been upgraded to 'Top Secret'.

The DPBC met on 2 May 1989, and turned once more to OSA 1989, the Media side repeating their concerns and the Official side their reassurances; it was agreed a 'clear directive' should be issued by the whole Committee to the Secretary, 'to enable him to resist pressure from officials to depart from the national security criterion which must be the sole basis on which his advice should be offered'. Quinlan thanked the Media side for this indication that they undertook to continue their support of the D-Notice System, as the Government did. Higgins subsequently drafted the directive to himself, although he felt it was superfluous; indeed he and his successors have never felt under undue official or political pressure to depart from the proper practice, and have easily resisted what little there occasionally has been.[294]

In late May the BBC's Deputy Director-General John Birt[295] made a personal approach to the Cabinet Office with suggestions as to how Government/Media relations might be improved, including two about the DPBC: there should be a member of the Security Service on the Committee, and magazine and book publishers should be represented. The Quinlan response, although welcoming any approach 'to mend fences', was that the Media's current attitude had been coloured not by D-Notice activity, but firstly by the Government's actions over breaches of confidentiality, which had been behind the 'Spycatcher' and 'My Country Right or Wrong' controversies, and secondly by OSA reform. He pointed out that day-to-day advice to the Media was decided not by the Committee but by its Secretary, based on the eight standing D-Notices which had been agreed by amongst others the Security Service's Home Office representative; therefore having a Security Service representative would do no more than allow the Committee to quiz him directly. As to magazine publishers, they already had two representatives on the Committee, including the Vice-Chairman; and the Book Publishers Association, while encouraging their members to use the D-Notice System, still declined to be represented on the Committee. No more came of this Birt initiative, but it was an indication perhaps that media/official relationships were beginning to return to at least an uneasy modus vivendi.

This more relaxed attitude, encouraged by events in the disintegrating Soviet Union, was reflected too in reaction to articles which previously would have caused major Whitehall convulsions. In late May, Campbell published a further detailed article in the *New Statesman* on the Government's underground bunkers in Wiltshire, Middlesex and Buckinghamshire. The Cabinet and Home Offices now seemed not unduly concerned, and Higgins noted that, even had he been consulted, there was little or nothing he would have advised should be omitted.[296] One area which did still engender reaction, however, was secret communications, including those of Britain's Allies. On 20 September 1989 *The Times* published information about the interception of communications in the Middle East by American (and Israeli) intelligence. Although this was not strictly a breach of D-Notice No.6, which referred specifically to UK interception, and although a similar story had been published in the USA, GCHQ was concerned that publication would have reminded potential adversaries [and friends and neutrals] to tighten up their communications security. Higgins made no formal approach to *The Times*, merely informally reminding its DPBC representative of the point.

Between March 1987 and September 1989, the IRA carried out a dozen attacks on British targets in mainland Europe, from bombing barracks to shooting off-duty personnel and an Army wife. Campbell, in the *New Statesman* of 20 October 1989, claimed classified documents on counter-terrorism intelligence had fallen into IRA hands, showing the poor state and incompetence of Britain's intelligence/security operatives, some of whom he identified. The journal, as usual then, had not consulted Higgins, but his assessment was that, even had they done so, he would not have advised any deletions; there was no damage to national security, the documents being five years old, and the information was either already in the public domain, or self-evidently now known to hostile intelligence.

At the 1 November 1989 DPBC meeting, Ramsden (a Member since the mid-1960s) handed over as Vice-Chairman to Alastair Stuart. In his periodic report, Higgins warned that a member of the public might approach the Committee with the erroneous claim D-Notices had been involved in a conspiracy between the BBC and the Government to suppress news of an accident in August to the cross-Channel ferry *EARL GRANVILLE*. To this day, similarly fanciful claims are made several times a year by members of the public; they are a mildly diverting insight into the energetic eccentricities of British (and sometimes international) life.

Other subsequent examples of routine activity included Higgins declining to become involved over a *Sunday Times* article of 17 December 1989 on the Lockerbie aircraft bombing the previous year. In this the newspaper reported the activities of the MoD's Royal Armament Research and Development Establishment, and of one of its forensic investigators in particular, drawing a strong protest from the Establishment about the thus heightened terrorist threat to its employees. The name was however already in the public domain as a forensic witness in other cases, no other damage to national security was done by the article, and the authorities agreed it had not heightened the threat to RARDE. The same month, the *Sunday Times* and *Mail on Sunday* contacted the Secretary about a new non-lethal defensive system fitted in HM Ships, Laser Dazzle equipment. Higgins persuaded them that, especially in view of mounting tension in the Gulf, where such ships were deployed, they should not publish this information; they agreed. In early January, however, the Royal Navy informed him the Spanish magazine *Tiempo* had just published this information, and Higgins was immediately approached by several British national dailies. Although he argued against wider publication, he acknowledged his arguments were 'pretty thin', conceded the information must now be regarded as widely in the public domain and could be republished ('offered no advice'), and informed the two papers who had until then withheld the story. Before the 1990 Farnborough Air Show, *Jane's Defence Weekly* sought his advice about a special issue which would include the history of the UK's airborne nuclear weapons, and discuss the replacement of the free-fall nuclear bomb. The main concern was a 1988 Panavia photograph of a Tornado aircraft fitted with long-range tanks and a nuclear bomb. Having consulted aviation and security experts, Higgins concluded there would be no damage done to national security by publication of both the photograph and the article.[297]

Again, Naming Heads of Intelligence and Security Services

The BBC's Wilson had written to Quinlan in late 1988, restating the case for making public the names of the Heads of the Secret Intelligence and Security Services on appointment. He pointed out it was an 'unofficial tradition' for the Media to publish these names 'in defiance of your best efforts', and suggested publication could be accompanied by requests, which journalists would observe, not to publish home addresses and family details. He was not asking for the British Heads of Service to 'appear on a phone-in' as had recently happened with the KGB. Quinlan consulted the Cabinet Secretary, citing non-avowal of the SIS as now the principal reason for the practice; it was agreed a paper on the official position would be produced for the next DPBC meeting.

The DGSS, Patrick Walker, acknowledged his position was different from that of 'C', because the Security Service was by then avowed by Act of Parliament and had a higher profile. His name had been published several times, and his only concern was that his homes and family details should not be. Nevertheless, although the operational argument was not strong, he argued that attachment of a DGSS name to a previous post (for example in Northern Ireland) would cause his successors there to be identified, and also that there were family advantages in living 'comfortably under the fig leaf of MoD cover'. He cited how as a Catholic he had been for many years, without problems, an active member of a congregation in England which included many Irish members, but that when his appointment as DGSS was leaked to the Media, details of his (fortunately by then former) home area appeared also in the Irish magazine *Phoenix*, provided (he suspected) by an Irish parishioner. He countered Wilson's comparisons with other VIPs under terrorist threat with arguments of 'additional targets' and of inability to answer articles as other public figures could. He still therefore had reservations about appointments to his post being made public, and, while the SIS remained non-avowed, wished to retain the same policy on non-identification for both Services.

When the interdepartmental committee of intelligence officials met in mid-December to discuss the response, they concluded it was not practicable to have different policies for the three Agencies, and all should be protected at all times. Higgins, who as a non-official was not at the meeting, told them afterwards this was unconvincing and they would have to produce some better arguments; how could operational efficiency be affected if hostile intelligence agencies and terrorists already knew the names? His opinion was that justification, if at all, could rest only on personal security. He wondered whether any of the officials on the interdepartmental committee had ever met a journalist. Nevertheless, when the Cabinet Secretary handed the decision down to Quinlan for use at the forthcoming DPBC meeting, it was that there should be no change. There might be very occasional exceptions, such as the recent announcement of John Adye's[298] appointment as Director GCHQ, but this was because of the public interest in the unionisation dispute.

Quinlan duly reported this at the 9 May 1990 DPBC meeting. Alastair Stuart replied that the Media side were unconvinced by the arguments, and doubted whether the Government would be able to hold this line much longer, particularly in view of developments in the Soviet Union [where President Gorbachev had by now introduced the policy of Glasnost/openness, and the Head of the KGB had spoken in public]. However, they would support the policy for the time being, on grounds of operational and personal security.

Following up the Special Forces briefing to editors, Quinlan sought advice about the MoD letter to editors. The Media side could not accept that every terrorist incident was a threat to national security, and therefore did not agree to D-Notice No.1 (Operations and Plans) being quoted in the letter.[299] Officials countered that 'more often than not international terrorism had a political objective which involved the overthrow of established political order and the rule of law, and put at risk the interests and lives of the subjects of particular countries'. On comparison with other kinds of violent action, the Media side reiterated that their agreement with police forces on criminal hostage-taking was different; all the police required was a delay in full reporting until the incident was over, whereas in terrorism cases, for ongoing intelligence reasons, continued non-disclosure was normally needed. Although not totally convinced, the Media side was nevertheless aware of public sentiment about terrorist killings, and an amended letter to editors was agreed accordingly.

Application of the confirmed policy on not naming Heads of the secret Agencies followed swiftly. In the Queen's Birthday Honours List of June 1990, the DGSS (Walker) was due to receive a knighthood; as usual the announcement would list him as belonging to the MoD. Higgins and the Security Service Legal Adviser discussed how to handle this, agreeing it would be counter-productive to seek to prevent the Media from identifying him as DGSS. Quinlan's office checked with the Cabinet Office, who 'clarified' the action to be that, although nothing should be done pre-emptively by the Secretary, he should give advice as in D-Notice No.6 if asked. The only newspaper which did in fact comment on the knighthood was the *Guardian*, which not only did not consult Higgins, but also republished the name of 'C' (McColl); Higgins was thankful not to be asked to do anything about this by the two secret Agencies.[300]

Section 9

POST COLD WAR, 1990–97

Civilised bureaucracy rubbing up against decent journalism . . . an honourable way
of tackling a problem that has no truly satisfactory solution.

John Wilson, BBC Controller of Editorial Policy,
describing his experience as a D-Notice
Committee member, February 1993

54

IRAQ, TERRORISM, MODERNISATION

One hesitates to write any history of an era of which it is too early to have a true perspective, and which indeed has not yet ended. But in the spirit of openness and of freedom of information, it is appropriate nevertheless to record some of what has happened since the end of the Cold War, as it has involved the D-Notice System. With the importance in mind of confidentiality between the D-Notice Secretary and those who consult him, many names and details have been omitted in this more proximate section, but the gist is here. Similarly, the convention has had to be observed that official histories do not include matters concerning the administration in power at the time of publication, even where they are already in the public domain.

In the period from 1990 to the present, landmark operations directly affecting British national security include: the first Gulf War, disintegration of the former Yugoslavia and Allied interventions there, the (hopefully) final throes of Irish terrorism, post-colonial intervention in Sierra Leone, the general aftermath of '9/11', first and second campaigns in Afghanistan, the second Gulf War, and its aftermath. Some analysts characterise the difference in the national security situation between pre-1990 and now as: during the Cold War we knew the capabilities of the Soviet Union but not its intentions, whereas in the Anti-Terrorism War we know the intentions of terrorists but not their capabilities. This academic jeu de mots contains some truth, but is an over-simplification not especially useful to those 'on the ground' with whom the D-Notice Secretary works, nor therefore to him.

In the technology of warfare and communications, there have been very rapid developments in electronic equipment, and in its availability not only to public and non-public organisations but, in even the poorest countries, also to individuals, including those in the Armed Forces involved in security operations. These factors, and the exponential and uncontrollable spread of the internet since 1985 and of the World Wide Web from 1990, have all impacted significantly on the capabilities and organisation of those who use force internationally, of those who counter it, and of those who report these conflicts, also internationally. The speed of circulation and accessibility of information through international search engines since 1998, the growth of social networking such as blogs since 2002, and the easy availability of relatively cheap mobile phones incorporating cameras and internet access, have all changed the environment in which international media operate. Often trailing in the technological wake, similarly affected, is the machinery of governments.

The combination of new technologies and new threats has caused many governments, including that of the UK, to introduce countermeasures claimed to be needed to protect against terrorism, which have implications for media freedom. All these trends have therefore created new challenges for the working of the D-Notice System. Despite this, the principles and many manifestations of the underlying tension between the Media and the governmental sides have remained the same.

First Iraq War – UK's Operation GRANBY

On 2 August 1990, the forces of the Iraqi President Saddam Hussein invaded Kuwait. The USA and the UK immediately despatched units to Saudi Arabia to deter any incursion beyond the Kuwaiti border, while lengthy and ultimately unsuccessful diplomatic efforts were made to secure Iraqi withdrawal. On 12 October a Cabinet Office meeting discussed how to handle media aspects of the crisis. Higgins' prior advice to MoD representatives included that the embryo Military Advisory Service (MAS) should not be activated, as it was designed for transition to and use in major war involving the UK base, and was anyway not yet established. He suggested that reinforced MoD guidance should be adequate in the circumstances, backed by the D-Notice System (already being used by editors in queries about the crisis).

He also pointed out that, whereas the MAS had been intended to subsume the DPBC role, in this case 'normal' peacetime security matters would continue to require his advice. Furthermore, to suspend the DPBC and activate the MAS would send the message to media and public that, despite the diplomatic activity, war was in fact about to start. The COI agreed with this view, although it alarmed him by suggesting that, if the MAS were activated, he should be appointed as stopgap Chairman; for this he 'would not be a willing volunteer', especially as 'it could be a very sticky end of an unprepared wicket.'[1] All Government Departments subsequently agreed about non-activation of the MAS.

Indeed the arrangements in theatre had already been decided by the Americans (with the agreement of the Saudis, who also controlled access by journalists to their country by the issue of visas); the British system there was based on the growing Coalition's Joint Information Bureaux. Apart from 'registered' freelances already in theatre when the operation actually began, 'accredited' journalists were organised by Coalition authorities into escorted six-member Media Response Teams, who as part of their written undertaking also agreed to pool their work, and to submit to censorship ('vetting'). Other journalists depended on briefings in Riyadh, Dhahran, Washington, London and Paris. It remained only for the MoD in January 1991 to issue advisory guidance to editors in the UK, which reflected the US ground rules, as well as matters covered in less detail by D-Notices; the headings were Military Operations, Military Equipment and Capabilities, Military Losses and Casualties, Command, Control and Communications, and Intelligence and Information about the Enemy.[2]

These arrangements had been discussed in principle (symbolically under Any Other Business) at the 13 November 1990 DPBC meeting. The MoD claimed that four UK Media Response Teams (three land/air and one naval) were the maximum which could be handled in theatre. The Media side pressed the MoD for 'a clearly identified focal point to whom Gulf related enquiries could be directed', fearing otherwise confusion with the D-Notice System's continuing role; they did not wish Higgins to become involved in any official vetting system. They also stressed the importance of consistency between in-theatre and London/ Washington briefings, and hoped information sent by correspondents to London could be assumed already to have been vetted. They suggested too that MoD guidance should be classified; this 'would make it more attractive to journalists' and would not be resented by the public once the fighting started, although it was felt parliamentary interest would lead before long to its publication. During the campaign, the Committee should 'concentrate on categories of *information* rather than *activities*', leaving the MoD free to deal with individual incidents under its own authority.[3]

Higgins reported increased media consultation since the deployments to Saudi Arabia had begun. In September, for example, the RAF was passing photographs of its activity in theatre to the Press, as part of psychological pressure on Iraq and to sustain support at home. One such handout however inadvertently included a Tornado aircraft firing a still highly classified defensive flare (not yet used in any action against the Iraqis, as offensive operations had not begun). The MoD attempted to withdraw the photograph before publication; an acrimonious exchange with newspapers developed, only resolved by the intervention of the D-Notice Secretary, who obtained media agreement not to publish pro tem.[4]

More routinely at the November meeting, Higgins reported he had not needed to advise any changes to a book on the KGB by the Soviet defector Gordievsky (and Christopher Andrew), nor on a book about Burgess. He had however advised *Jane's* against publishing a book on 'Hostage Taking Terrorism – Incident response Strategy',[5] because of helpful information it might provide to terrorists; *Jane's* decided not to publish. He advised the BBC, on a programme about Blake, not to publish MI5 and MI6 names involved. Amongst bizarre public enquiries were whether a D-Notice had been issued to prevent discussion of Cornish tin miners' rights not to pay poll tax, why he had not prevented the *Mid Devon Advertiser* from revealing a Kuwait tanker was anchored in Torbay, and what D-Notice action he had taken about a gay brothel in Barnes.

On 17 December, classified papers and a laptop containing details of Coalition operational plans were stolen in the UK from the temporarily unattended car of the British Joint Force Commander. This news was not immediately made public, in the hope that whoever now had the computer might not realise its provenance and sensitivity, and would not therefore be tempted to sell it to the Iraqis. Inevitably the story was leaked (by the police, allegedly) and on 29/30 December Whetstone and then Higgins himself (returning prematurely from leave) successfully persuaded all editors by telephone not to mention the laptop, using the rationale in D-Notice No.1 (Military Operations).

However, early on 3 January, the PA editor-in-chief (and DPBC Member) Colin Webb told Higgins that the Dublin edition of the *Irish Times* that day mentioned the laptop. Hurried consultation within the MoD optimistically decided that the thief (or whomever he had sold the computer to) was unlikely to have read that newspaper, and, despite his doubts, Higgins was asked to continue to advise against mention. Lack of understanding by officials of how the international media churn hot stories around was highlighted a few hours later when the *Chicago Tribune* rang; by next day pressure across the UK Media to publish the full story had become impossible to contain, and the *Sun* informed Higgins it intended to go ahead; several other journals indicated similar intent. In late afternoon, the MoD conceded to Higgins, who told editors he was withdrawing advice against publication. The *Mail on Sunday*, which had been first to reveal on 29 December that it knew of the laptop, later complained that either the Deputy Secretary or the MoD had revealed its exclusive story to other papers, but Higgins was able to prove others had already been making similar enquiries.

One unusual feature of this incident was that, due to a lacuna in the official press system, it fell to Higgins at one stage to advise the Opposition Spokesman on Defence not to mention the missing computer during a broadcast interview. Quinlan undertook afterwards to ensure the D-Notice Secretary was never in future placed in such an inappropriate position.

The new Prime Minister, John Major,[6] had also been attacked for misleading the House on 20 December, when he replied to an unconnected question that no D-Notices had been issued since August, it being inferred he had known by then of the laptop theft; but by then no D-Notice action had indeed yet been taken. The *New Statesman* (11 January) had another tilt at the D-Notice System, uncharacteristically suggesting 'proper wartime censorship might well be preferable.'[7]

In mid-January 1991, Coalition forces launched air attacks on the Iraqi occupiers in Kuwait, followed by land operations just over a month later. By early March the operation had been completed, other than the establishment of no-fly zones in Iraq. Contrary to the early advice of the DPBC Media side, the MoD Guidance document was fortunately unclassified when issued, which simplified matters. However, the MoD had not provided the requested one 'focal point' to handle GRANBY queries, but left it to various members of its PR department to respond to the Media. Higgins had therefore remained the channel of queries about secret Agencies' activities.

He had also continued to receive other Gulf-related queries, particularly from provincial papers, about how to report local industries' roles in supplying British forces. Around RAF Chilmark local people became angry with their newspapers about articles on the Station's key role in logistic support; Higgins was able to reassure no damage had been done. He also refuted a report that he had prevented the Media from reporting the number of Soviet supply flights into Iraq. Usually he referred GRANBY queries to the MoD; and once the campaign began, the pace and brevity of the operation, the self-evident nature of the Coalition forces' dispositions and strength, and the military control of the journalists in theatre, all anyway meant little advice was needed for the duration. Afterwards Higgins assisted the Cabinet Office in rewriting the Guidance to the Media in Time of Tension and War, based on his experience and on advice in past and current D-Notices.[8]

When the DPBC met on 15 May 1991, the Media side voiced the considerable dissatisfaction felt during the campaign by those they represented. Points ranged from difficulties in obtaining visas for British journalists, limits imposed thereby on the number of UK Media Response Teams (problems allegedly not faced by American and French Media), 'instances where junior Servicemen had placed unrealistic restrictions on reporting', communications difficulties, being in an MRT (as opposed to freelancing) having hindered journalists rather than helping them, that only one MRT place had been allocated to a Scottish paper, and the arrangements for operational reporting and for briefing having been variable (with Washington and Paris being more informative than Riyadh and London).[9] Higgins was well pleased to have been on the sidelines.

In his periodic report, Higgins said he had 'offered no advice' on a book dealing with UK/US relations (including intelligence) at the time of the Suez crisis, but had advised removal of some names from a new Nigel West book on the WWII Special Operations Executive (of 17 names, only one eventually remained in dispute; West had shown six were already in the public domain, three had been agents only during the War and not since, and the author and publisher agreed to omit seven of more recent currency).[10] He had also had to correct a local Health Authority's attempt to misuse the D-Notice Committee's name in trying to dampen down press interest in a London pub kneecapping. While standing in, his Deputy had refused a request for D-Notice action from British Telecom, which had been publicly criticised by the West Mercia Chief Constable over delays in a new police communications system, linked to the then highly classified national security System X.[11]

Post-GRANBY

In the Gulf War follow-up, and with the Cold War being perceived as over, a certain euphoria about security in parts of the British Press caused occasional concern to Higgins. The *Sunday Telegraph* of 18 August, for example, included an article headlined 'Saddam Fell for Trojan Horse Trap'; this alleged that (circumstantially identifiable) British-made radio equipment sold to Iraq had been 'fixed' so that any messages sent could be picked up by the GCHQ listening post in Cyprus, relayed to Cheltenham, and passed on to the US NSA. It also alleged the Americans had similarly in the past sold 'fixed' encoding machines to the Argentinians. The paper had not sought advice in accordance with D-Notice No.6 before publishing the story. Such was the sensitivity on this occasion that not only did Higgins remonstrate, but the FCO's PUS (at the request of the Prime Minister) spoke to the editor Trevor Grove,[12] neither denying nor confirming the story, but confirming it was 'extremely damaging to the national interest', and hoping the story had not come from an irresponsible official source.

Through 1990 and 1991, the Royal Navy was having problems with some corrosion in pipework in nuclear-powered submarines,[13] including the deterrent force; as this caused limitations in their deployment, the information initially remained classified. Although once detected and technical limitations imposed, there was minimal danger to submariners and public, there was undoubtedly embarrassment and sensitivity to the views of international nuclear safety bodies. The Security Correspondent of the *Guardian* broke the story in June 1991, and, as the trailer to a Thames Television follow-up, in mid-September wrote a more detailed article on operational limitations. Until then the MoD had not asked the D-Notice Secretary to become involved, nor even informed him there might be media interest. Although this now attracted high-level attention, it was quickly concluded that national security was not significantly damaged by the information; the TV programme anyway dealt mainly with environmental rather than operational issues.

In late October 1991, after he had decided he did not need to offer advice on the new book 'Instructions from the Centre' by Andrew and Gordievsky (translations of KGB orders to its 'Residents' abroad), Higgins was asked by the Cabinet Office to delay passing his decision to the publishers until the Foreign Secretary had considered the possible implications for Anglo-Soviet relations. He agreed to do so only overnight, and then went ahead, on the basis that even if the Foreign Office was unhappy, there was nothing in the book which endangered national security; the D-Notice System would not therefore be used to hold it up further.[14]

D-Notices and Terrorism

At the 5 November 1991 DPBC meeting, Higgins reported his advice had been accepted on not publishing names of certain Security Service officers in connection with the collapse of the Bank of Credit and Commerce International; and on protecting the home address of Gordievsky at the time of arrival from Moscow of his family (although the Committee agreed this was a one-off stretching the coverage of D-Notice No.6). The major topic was again the extent to which terrorism should be covered by D-Notices. This internal debate had started in 1976, and been resurrected by events in 1981, 1986 and 1990. Terrorism had been defined in the Prevention of Terrorism Act 1989 as 'the use of violence for political ends, including any use of violence for the purpose of putting the public or any section of the public in fear'.

The Media side of the DPBAC had never accepted that this definition applied to all those who used violence for 'political' ends, for example the Animal Liberation Front; but the scale of IRA violence had caused most of the Media side by now largely to consider that brand of 'domestic' terrorism as de facto covered by the Notices.

For the Media side, Stuart therefore said they felt it would be useful now to take stock and see whether any change was needed in the DPBC approach. The after-effects of the demise of the Soviet Union, and 'the growing impact of regional powers, some of whom used the sponsorship of terrorism as a means towards their political ends', seemed 'likely to be of growing importance to the Committee'. A paper suggested by Robert Hutchinson[15] was tabled, in the hope that if there were to be change, it should be by deliberate decision rather than 'a process of drift'. It concentrated on categories of information rather than on activities, which met the official desire to cover counter-terrorist tactics and equipment (including that at airports).

One of three courses was suggested: a new D-Notice on terrorism; modifying an existing Notice; or maintaining the status quo. The Media side felt the first two courses would involve trying to define national security and terrorism, and that it would be impossible to find a definition mutually acceptable to officials; 'Definitions acceptable to the media would be so vague as to be unacceptable to officials, whereas those required by officials would be so all-embracing as to be unacceptable to the media.' They therefore favoured maintaining the status quo on the Notices, but [contrary to their previous views] encouraging Government Departments to seek informal agreements with the Media, similar to those with the Association of Chief Police Officers on criminal kidnappings and hostage taking.

The Official side welcomed the initiative, and the MoD's 2nd PUS JM Stewart[16] emphasised the subject was of growing importance to the MoD; many aspects of its 'response to terrorism, training, equipment and Special Forces operations were particularly sensitive, and unguarded reporting could undoubtedly put lives at risk as well as prejudicing the success of counter terrorist operations'. However, while he agreed a new Notice might be difficult, the existing Notices neither excluded terrorism nor did they automatically include it. He therefore considered it would be helpful to modify the wording 'to clear up the present ambiguity and make the circumstances where D Notices did apply more readily apparent to the media'. He offered to produce a draft for the next meeting; while this step was agreed, the Media side observed they were unaware of any such reporting to date which had put lives or operations at risk.

There was further discussion about protection of personal details of Heads of the secret Agencies, for reasons of personal rather than national security (despite officials arguing that there was an indirect effect on the latter, because agents/informers would be unlikely to help a Service which could not even protect its own people). The Committee accepted there were valid humanitarian reasons for inclusion, but said Government Departments 'should not become accustomed to asking the Secretary to depart from established D Notice criteria'. They concluded by agreeing the current eight D-Notices should remain in force unchanged.[17] When Higgins again discussed personal security with MI5 afterwards, it agreed the Media were more inclined to take advice from the D-Notice Secretary than from 'anonymous officials from a number of different Government Departments', and they did not want him to be restricted in so doing.[18] This favourable Security Service view of the System's pragmatism was also reflected in its Legal Adviser's response to a US Pentagon query: although a few in the Media wrongly accused it of censorship, 'In our experience, when the D Notice system is used it works extremely well.'[19]

The announcement in December 1991 of Stella Rimington's[20] appointment as the next DGSS caused a tidal wave of media interest, and Higgins and Whetstone were active in advising against publication of her home address and family details. Because of the Media side's unease over the applicability of D-Notices to these appointments, Higgins asked the secret Agencies yet again to justify his involvement, which they all again did, primarily on grounds of the personal security of those concerned and their families in the light of the increased terrorist threat. The Security Service also suggested DGSS should come and explain the threat personally to the DPBC [this never took place; Rimington wanted first a wider strategy on openness for her Service].[21]

In January 1992, having seen advertised a forthcoming book on covert anti-terrorist operations in Northern Ireland, Higgins approached the publisher and was shown a proof copy. He advised omission of details whose publication would endanger lives and be helpful to terrorists, especially the technique known as 'jarking' (secretly tampering with terrorists' weapons). The book brought into prominence again the roles and identities of Special Forces. Changes were negotiated, despite the reluctance of the author, Mark Urban, to accept some arguments. He pointed out that the authorities were not always best placed to rule on what should not be published, as the Media often knew better what was already in the public domain. It also transpired he had already written an article for *GQ* magazine (30 March), which included some of the material Higgins was recommending excluding, and that some unamended copies of the manuscript were already held by other journalists.

When the DPBC reconvened on 29 April 1992, under a new Chairman, Sir Christopher France,[22] the Secretary included in his routine report that Urban's publisher had now accepted advice to remove certain details of operational techniques, undercover identities and intelligence-gathering methods. Higgins also reported that although *Jane's* had declined in 1990 to publish a book on counter-measures to terrorist hostage taking, another publisher had now done so without seeking prior advice; he had subsequently pointed out damaging information it included, and received an undertaking in future to consult. He also refuted a complaint (to the SofS for Defence) that he had entered a public library and removed pages from a book about alleged British attacks on Jewish refugee ships in the 1940s [linked to the case recorded in chapter 52]. He said time spent dealing with requests for advice from commercial aerial photography companies continued significantly to increase.

Amongst the few 'breaches' of security by the Media was a *Sunday Times* article of 5 January which, in an otherwise non-damaging story ('Saddam helps Algeria make Islamic nuclear bomb'), alleged GCHQ was listening to telephone calls in Baghdad. The editor, Andrew Neil,[23] responded to Higgins' remonstration by pointing out foreign governments were well aware from previous publications that GCHQ was tasked with such interceptions, and that the countries involved in this article would not therefore have been told anything new. The reality is that laxity of some countries in communications security is tightened up after such reports, to the detriment of secret intelligence-gathering.

The main discussion concerned the MoD paper on D-Notices and terrorism. Officials reiterated their feeling that, well though the System worked on external defence matters, it had not been so effective in preventing publication of information 'likely to be of use to terrorists', particularly in the technical field. Examples given were remote electronic triggering of explosive devices (revealed in *Daily Telegraph* 20 May 1991), and how detonators could be detected (*Intersec, the Journal of International Security* in 1992). Terrorism being a threat growing in prominence now the Cold War was effectively over, Stewart said it was 'so often service men and women and their families who were the targets for terrorist attack both in

UK and abroad'. A new D-Notice was not considered necessary, but officials proposed that 'a potential enemy' in existing D-Notice No.1 should be agreed to include 'terrorist organisations and States sponsoring them'. In addition, there should be reference to the need to protect 'anti-interrogation training and tactics and equipment used in counter terrorism'; and in D-Notice No.6 a reference to countering terrorism in the list of responsibilities of the Secret Intelligence and Security Services and those working with them.

For the Media side, based on pre-meeting discussion, Stuart replied that, while they were very conscious of the anguish caused to the victims of terrorism, they had never accepted what appeared to be the rationale behind the official paper, namely that terrorism endangered national security. Even if the Grand Hotel Brighton bomb had killed all members of the Administration, 'the Government of the UK by democratically elected politicians would have continued'. The destruction of the Pan Am jet over Lockerbie, although outrageous, 'had had no bearing on national security whatsoever'. Nor could the Media side accept that Special Forces matters were merely, as the paper described them, 'intrinsically interesting'; legitimate public interest and public safety concerns justified media discussion of them. That said, the Media side was sympathetic to the concerns; although it did not accept the MoD paper's rationale and 'potential enemy' interpretation, it nevertheless had 'little difficulty' in agreeing the specific amendments proposed to the two D-Notices.

In discussion of this nuanced Media position, points made included that the D-Notice No.6 amendment was in line with the Security Service Act 1989 on its responsibility for countering terrorism; while it would be possible 'endlessly to debate a definition of national security', past governments had 'gone to considerable lengths to avoid doing so'. The MoD's paper could unacceptably 'open the way to D notice advice being offered on Police activities'; and the amendments should be presented to editors 'without any supporting rationale, which would be likely only to open the door to discussion and disagreement'.

The ultra-courteous France, summing up, thanked the Media side for their 'very thoughtful consideration', adding 'it was probably inevitable that neither side would accept the totality of each other's views, and while officials did not necessarily accept all the points put forward, it seemed wise to build on areas of agreement rather than disagreement. In that spirit, there was no need to debate the philosophy behind the paper'. In that true British spirit of pragmatism, the Committee agreed; and when the two amended D-Notices were subsequently issued to editors, they were simply 'asked to note the changes which are underlined.'[24]

Significantly perhaps, there is no record that at this meeting Higgins mentioned his recent tangential involvement in the Matrix-Churchill/Iraqi 'Supergun' case, then under initial investigation by the Trade and Industry Select Committee. This concerned a DIS technical expert who in January had given evidence to that Committee; he had used a pseudonym for personal security reasons, but his true name had inadvertently been mentioned in a BBC broadcast in March 1992. Higgins obtained BBC agreement to their discreetly changing it back to the pseudonym in the subsequently available transcript. Further problems arose later that year when both the BBC and ITN used an old United Nations film which showed the same expert in a slightly different context, even speaking to camera. Quinlan, both as his employer and as DPBC Chairman, spoke to the DPBC representatives of the two broadcasting organisations, who agreed not to reuse the same archive material until further notice.[25]

Avowal, and Northern Ireland

On 6 May 1992, during the Queen's Speech debate, in furtherance of more open government, the Prime Minister (Major) caused surprise by avowing the Secret Intelligence Service and referring to its Chief (McColl) by name. By the following afternoon the Media had discovered his home address; the SIS contacted Higgins, telling him the Press were 'camped on the doorstep' of 'C', and asked for intervention with the tabloids (they had already contacted the 'responsible broadsheets' themselves). Details of McColl's address and family were not subsequently disclosed by any part of the UK Media, although some gave hints, and the *Daily Mail* complained that the banning even of pictures of him as a young man was out of line with the open government policy. In the following days there was much jocular media comment, and on 9 May the *Mail* did publish a photograph of the young McColl, without the editor later being found hanging from Blackfriars Bridge.[26]

The editor of the *Mail on Sunday* did challenge Higgins over the policy, pointing out again that the Head of the CIA could be photographed. Higgins replied at greater than normal length (he later scribbled on his file copy 'Apparently much appreciated by Sir Colin McColl!'), denying the direct correlation, on the grounds there was no sustained terrorist campaign in the USA, but even so Mr Gates [Head of CIA] was surrounded by armed bodyguards at all times, and in the American political system was a public figure. Assassination was 'a potent and favoured weapon in the IRA's armoury' (although he did not say so, the PIRA was known to have targeted senior MI5 figures), as evidenced by the Brighton, Deal and London bombings and the murders of Lord Mountbatten, Airey Neave, individual servicemen, and the ambassadors Ewart –Biggs in Dublin and Sykes in The Hague, the latter two perceived as having SIS connections in previous posts. McColl would be a similar high-risk target, whose murder would be a boost for terrorists and a blow to national security. Nevertheless, Higgins also quietly wrote to the secret Agencies, suggesting that in future the Media's 'curiosity' might be 'dampened down if a more positive policy of releasing as much as possible were to be adopted', with a press release at the time of appointment giving 'quite a lot of biographical and domestic details', accompanied by a request not to publish photographs and addresses.[27]

Despite the DPBC's ambivalent attitude to domestic terrorism, Northern Ireland was de facto beginning to feature more often in the Secretary's work. One such case concerned the UDA/UFF activist Brian Nelson;[28] the Government did not comment publicly, the policy being not to do so on intelligence matters. Higgins was not involved until four months later; when BBC Panorama decided to make a programme on the issues raised, he was asked by the MoD's General Staff secretariat to intervene. He confined this to speaking to the BBC's DPBC Member (Wilson), reminding of the need for care not over the story as such, but over the revelation of details of 'tradecraft', in this case the specific techniques used by the Security authorities to recruit and manage informers, and the behaviour patterns of those who became agents. Wilson was able to reassure on these points, and to undertake that the script would contain generalities rather than specific techniques or clues as to the identities of other agents and their handlers. Higgins told the MoD therefore that, although the programme would undoubtedly be 'troublesome and embarrassing' for the Department, it would not in his judgement cause serious damage to national security.[29]

Pressure for Change

Pressure for a full review of the D-Notice System meanwhile continued from the Media, particularly from the Guild of British Newspaper Editors. Sir Christopher France initially resisted this, and was supported by the Cabinet Office, whose seconded diplomat

LP Neville-Jones[30] felt 'the D-Notice system serves us well' and that a full review should not be undertaken 'unless absolutely necessary.'[31] However, resistance was weakening: on 23 September 1992, France took part in a public seminar organised by the British Executive of the International Press Institute, chaired by Peter Preston.[32] The topic was 'the future utility and working of D Notices', and the other principal speaker was the ITN's editor-in-chief and DPBC representative, Stewart Purvis.[33]

He spoke critically of the System, suggesting its agreed advice was largely ignored by Government, that there were more modern and sensible ways of resolving matters to do with publication on national security and these provided better protection for editors, that the Committee was not representative of all the Media, that it was too secretive, that the coverage of the Notices was being extended to internal security matters, and that the Committee should be abolished and replaced by the relevant Government Departments giving their own guidance to the Media and answering queries on it. France defended its role, but announced the Committee had already decided nevertheless that a review of its role, organisation and Notices should be held imminently. The IPI seminar, and Purvis's comments, sparked lively press debate in the following days, some in the Media supporting him and rather more not; some of the latter feared it might be replaced by something worse.[34]

At the 20 October 1992 DPBC meeting, Higgins first obtained the Committee's agreement that henceforth minutes of their meetings would drop the 'Confidential' classification, and be marked just 'Personal', allowing recipients discretion as to how they were then handled. Most discussion was about the annual review of the D-Notices, and this time there was substantive discussion. France said changes in the international situation and the Government's moves for more openness meant that more was now required than relatively minor amendments. His indication at the recent IPI meeting that there was about to be a DPBC review had also raised external expectations. If the Committee agreed a thorough examination of the System was now due, they needed to agree the mechanics for carrying it out.

Stuart replied that, although wanting to know more about the Government's intentions on openness, the Media side entirely agreed; secrecy added to the belief there was something 'sinister' about the Notices.[35] They felt the Notices' wording now 'had an archaic ring', but should not be specific – that was the role of the Secretary in his advice – and should make it readily apparent to editors and others when to seek advice. The Introduction was important, and needed complete reshaping, not only to explain the working of the System, but 'to persuade the media that the system was user-friendly and to remove many of the misconceptions' about it; all agreed it should make clear that 'one aim of the system was to facilitate publication rather than to prevent it'.

A sub-committee (chaired by Moray Stewart, and later to include two DPBC Media Members) was agreed, as was that the first step should be for officials to carry out their own review, because the D-Notice System stemmed primarily from 'the Government's perceived need to protect certain categories of information'. The draft Introduction with 'philosophy and rationale' should be ready for Media side consideration early in 1993, but broader aims of removing popular misconceptions should be left for the review itself. A press release should be issued quickly (subsequently effected on 26 October by an 'inspired' Question in Parliament from Dr David Clarke, promulgated by the Press Association, and widely reported and welcomed in the Media the next day).[36]

This was Admiral Higgins' last meeting as the D-Notice Secretary. It is probable that, of all the post-WWII Secretaries, he had the most testing period of office, because of changes in international and national circumstances, and in the mood of the country and media vis-à-vis national security. He also faced greater than normal political pressures. He did much to maintain the reputation of the post for independence and integrity, and to publicise and explain the role of the DPBC. His replacement was, coincidentally rather than customarily, another recently retired Naval Officer, Admiral David Pulvertaft.[37]

55

THE D-NOTICE REVIEW, AND
SPOOK MANIA

Pulvertaft was within days asked for advice on a BBC TV 'Inside Story' programme entitled 'The Informer', claimed to include the first ever interview with an anonymous member of the IRA who had doubled as a Royal Ulster Constabulary agent. This caused alarm in Whitehall, because although the BBC's Controller of Editorial Policy (and DPBC Member) said the programme had been cleared with the appropriate authorities, none of the many authorities concerned could discover which had done so. This Northern Ireland 'first' was indicative of a trend in disclosures which faced Pulvertaft throughout his time in office.[38]

He was also almost immediately faced with media interest in the personal life of the DGSS Stella Rimington, and attempts to discover her home address; and the SIS sought assistance over one of their officers whose name had been mentioned in a minor Norwegian journal, sparking questions from the *Mail on Sunday*, where the Secretary's intervention prevented further disclosure in the UK. In January 1993 there was further media interest in Rimington and her family; her address had now become known to her local paper, the *Islington Gazette*, and thence to others, and the *Evening Standard* photographed her leaving home. Pulvertaft engaged in extensive damage limitation with those papers he knew were interested, on grounds of the threat to her personal security. She nevertheless had to move house, and take other precautionary measures. In early March, however, the *Sunday Times* published a photograph of her (with only her eyes 'masked'), and others followed suit. At about this time, her daughter's name and address were found on an IRA list. Pulvertaft's continuing efforts to discourage publication of details about the DGSS were, however, complicated by his awareness that behind the scenes the Security Service was planning a public booklet about its role, including Rimington's photograph.

In another personal security case at this time, his advice was different. The *Glasgow Evening Times* (8 February) published an article about the swimming pool at the home of the then Secretary of State for Scotland, Ian Lang,[39] including detailed aerial photographs of the house and grounds. The editor had sought prior advice from Pulvertaft, and (because Lang was not on the High Threat List)[40] been told there was no national security concern as defined by D-Notices. The Secretary was unaware that the Scottish Office Information Directorate and the Strathclyde Police Special Branch had separately asked the paper not to publish such details; nevertheless, when later informed of this, he did not change his advice. The Scottish Office was disgruntled, and although the editor pointed out that Lang's address was far from a secret in Scotland, the Office issued its own risk reminder to the Scottish Media.[41]

In March 1993, the publisher Bloomsbury announced its intention of producing 'a series of novels about SAS adventures'; this was indicative of a new sub-trend. Later that year, in addition to five other SAS books in the pipeline, the *Sun* reviewed the hitherto undetected 'The SAS at Close Quarters', which Pulvertaft found to be no more than a historical compilation of open source material by an ex-SAS soldier. When a further insider book was advertised (about the rescue by foreign SF (advised by the SAS) of passengers from a hijacked airliner in 1977), Pulvertaft decided that, although the MoD would have preferred some of the techniques used not to be publicised, it had been a foreign operation and therefore was not covered by D-Notices. By mid-1995 [leaping momentarily ahead] this early stream of SAS books had turned into a steady torrent, and the Head of the Security and Counter Terrorism Directorate in the MoD felt it necessary to issue 'ground rules' for their handling to HQ DSF. When he saw these ground rules, Pulvertaft took issue with some of them as being unsuitable for invariable application to books by non-insiders and to press articles, and potentially an impediment to his negotiations with publishers.[42]

In April 1993, it was reported that Paul Henderson of Matrix Churchill, who had become known publicly because of the 'Supergun' affair, was to publish his memoirs, 'including the story of his 20 years working under cover with MI6.'[43] Pulvertaft considered asking the publisher for sight of the manuscript, but the SIS advised that, apart from the names of a few of their officers, Henderson would not have had access to other still secret information. The Secretary therefore merely advised Bloomsbury to clear such names with him; in fact, Henderson used only pseudonyms.[44]

In Spring 1993, Pulvertaft suggested to the MoD that it would have a better relationship with the Media on secret equipment coming into service, if it briefed him better before the Media became interested. He cited a recent article about unpublished capability deficiencies in the new Type 23 frigates, which would certainly be of interest to potential adversaries.[45] Subsequent discussion with various directorates led, however, to no such systematic briefing of the D-Notice Secretary; it remained more common for D-Notice involvement on secret equipment stories to start reactively.[46]

The Review of the System

The most vocal Media side exponent of the line that the D-Notice System should be ended continued to be Stewart Purvis.[47] In mid-December he wrote via Pulvertaft to the Steering Group, explaining his view and rationale more fully. 'One of the penalties paid by a state as officially secretive as ours is that anything to do with 'secrets' or 'state security' inherits its own twilight world of manufactured myth and rumour. The D Notice Committee suffers accordingly, with many people believing that its role is to censor the media on matters of national security – a censorship with which the media are believed to comply. We know that the reality is somewhat different.' The gist of why he believed therefore that 'this quintessentially English arrangement' should be discarded was that a different and more open system was needed, both to remove the misperception, and also mainly to address the existing 'fundamental flaw': that the Media Members of the DPBAC 'mostly represent nobody other than themselves.'[48]

Stewart's Steering group of officials (to which Pulvertaft was attached) started therefore by asking whether it was still necessary in contemporary circumstances to have some system of advising the Media about security matters; if so, whether the present System met the need; and, if not, whether they should seek to change the System or substitute some other. Many individuals/organisations responded to the public invitation to contribute views, a few supporting the Purvis line in some way (including Channel 4, Liberty, and the NUJ), but the majority (including the Quakers) supporting continuation, albeit with improvements not just to the System but in governmental openness. The British Guild of Newspaper Editors, for example, was critical in particular of increased restrictions implied by extending D-Notice coverage to domestic terrorism.

Officials too concluded some system was indeed required, and that, despite acknowledged imperfections, they could not think of anything significantly better than the DPBC. Of Purvis' suggested unilateral system (with or without a consultative element), although they saw some advantage in the Government being able to issue and revise Notices without needing to seek media agreement, they thought the downside was greater: an even more adversarial atmosphere and a perception that government ignored media concerns. A suggestion that responsibility for the System should be transferred from the MoD to the Cabinet Office was also quickly and 'strongly' scotched by the latter, ostensibly on the grounds it 'might inadvertently' send the wrong signals to the Media about the 'suppression of politically inconvenient information'.

The MoD's Press Secretary/Chief of Information Gill Samuel[49] reported a journalists' view (based on a recent talk with a group from Channel 4): they had a 'natural aversion' to participation in a Committee which existed 'to suppress news'; DPBC Media members were 'establishment' figures not representative of the 'working journalist'; they preferred to deal with those in power rather than through 'intermediaries'; they would prefer a system which could be tested in the courts as in the USA; and they were sceptical that the review would be a real one. Samuel concluded therefore that the Purvis view was more genuinely representative of the Media at the 'operational level', and that 'a new breed moving in at the top from the ranks' of the working journalists might not in future be so co-operative.

Pulvertaft disagreed; he acknowledged the Press Secretary dealt with working journalists, as he did, but ultimately the decision whether or not to publish was made by 'editors, directors and publishers', who took other factors such as potential litigation into consideration.[50] He emphasised the DPBC did not suppress news, only any endangering detail, so that the story otherwise could be published; that the DPBC Media side all considered themselves journalists, but it was at the editorial level that responsibility had to be taken; that Government Departments all worked through their press officers, who were 'professional intermediaries' (he was too polite to remind Samuel that they were all therefore geared to the political wishes of their Ministers); that, separate from the D-Notice System, there were Acts such as the OSA which could indeed be tested in courts, but that litigation was retrospective and not preventive, and generally unwelcome to both sides; and that the demands of protecting national security meant great care would be taken over the review.

He added that the Purvis/Channel 4 view had received little support at the IPI seminar [media seminars do admittedly tend to be populated by 'non-working' and 'establishment' figures], and that the 'new breed' of journalists would in due course become editors themselves, when they would realise their responsibilities and might welcome advice [as has indeed happened]. At the same time, Pulvertaft was reminding the official Steering Group that only the Secretary saw the totality of D-Notice business; the System was quite different from any area of Ministry/media business in that it dealt solely with a defined area of national security [i.e. without the political dimension]. He expressed surprise at how comparatively little use the MoD itself made of the System, and suggested the Department could achieve more positive results if when appropriate it did so. He supported greater openness, acknowledging that if D-Notices were published, officials should expect that the Media might use the contents to probe areas of secrecy. He also cautioned that the widely recognised

'D-Notice' title gave him easy access wherever needed, and should not therefore be lightly replaced.[51]

When the Review Steering Group had progressed work sufficiently, they sent it to two designated Media side representatives, Colin Webb (PA) and James Bishop (PPA). They broadly supported the conclusions, suggesting only editorial changes, such as in the General Introduction stressing first the voluntary nature of the system, and removing the 'Nanny-ish tone' on the relationship between the D-Notice System and OSAs. In order to update the Media side, the Chief of Defence Intelligence briefed on post-Soviet threats, noting that British Forces (and ipso facto the secret Agencies) had since 1990 been involved inter alia in operations in the Gulf and Bosnia, 'neither event having been predicted much in advance'. It emerged that the Defence Intelligence Staff had not been consulted about the D-Notice Review until quite late in the work, and had then suggested its officials be included in the coverage of the Notices; the secret Agencies argued however that not all the DIS merited this protection, and that those who did could be included in the 'others under threat' category of the new Notice No.6. In the secret intelligence world, there exists a certain pecking order of 'threatenedness'.

At the 6 May 1993 DPBC meeting, the Secretary's report included that the twelve editors to whom he had so far given advice had all accepted it; that he had mediated between officials and London Weekend Television after it had filmed the interior of the Atomic Weapons Establishment Aldermaston from an external hydraulic platform (the programme went out minus some sensitive details of security arrangements); that the *Jerusalem Post* had run an article on the D-Notice System after the *Guardian* correspondent in Israel had had his credentials withdrawn by the Israeli Government for breaching local censorship; that the Defence Security Coordinating Committee intended with his support to review the excessively large number of high security establishments to which the aerial photography rules applied; and that he had continued the programme of publicity and of briefings about the D-notice System to a variety of audiences.

The announcement of the D-Notice Review had stimulated three Parliamentary Questions, and there had also been one about the System's involvement in the earlier announcement of Rimington's appointment as DGSS. Unusually, the Secretary had also led in the successful negotiation over a book by a former MI6 insider ('A Game of Moles' by Desmond Bristow), in liaison with the SIS [partly because the author lived beyond the reach of the Treasury Solicitor in Spain, where a Spanish version was also planned]; this later led to revised procedures for the secret Agencies (which officials described as 'a gloss' on the policy set out by the then Government in December 1988): the Agencies would clear all insider material, the D-Notice Secretary continuing to deal with the rest.[52] Nigel West's 'Faber Book of Espionage' had been cleared once the authoress Charlotte Bingham had agreed to her 'outing' as a former member of MI5, and (unknown to Pulvertaft) the former Deputy Secretary Admiral Whetstone had been given permission to spread the word about the D-Notice System by addressing a visiting party of senior members of the Russian Supreme Soviet.[53]

Updating on the Review, Moray Stewart said clear themes were emerging: a continuing need for some such system, Notices and Introduction needing to be simplified and less formal, and the role of the DPBC being better explained, possibly in an Open Government document. The Media side asked that work be speeded up, and time be allowed in the subsequent consultation phase for media organisations they represented to be consulted. The Committee discussed the alternative scheme suggested by Purvis. Stewart explained that the Working Group had decided this scheme would be less effective than a joint official/media system such as the current one. The Media side felt it might suit the 'big beasts' (national press and broadcasters, with their own lawyers) but not the Media as a whole,[54] and that 'it was better to improve the present joint system than abandon it'. The DPBC therefore concluded that, even though the Government had to initiate the content of D-Notices, 'the media exercised more influence by contributing to their content than declining to do so'. Stewart subsequently reported the likely outcome to the Cabinet Secretary, who informed the Prime Minister (Major had become closely interested after being shown earlier correspondence between Purvis and Pulvertaft).

Because of progress being made, Purvis himself was somewhat more comfortable, and wrote to Bishop welcoming publication of the Notices and a possible change of Committee name. He still preferred the Secretary to be more overtly a government official than a 'broker', and sought a more regular and fuller report on the Secretary's dealings with the Media, so that they would be 'party to the fine details of conversations which had taken place', which they currently were not (on which the Secretary commented 'nor are the officials'). The final hurdle in the work of the Steering Group was disagreement over how counter-terrorism was to be covered in the new Notices. As late as mid-May the Security Service was suggesting that, rather than occasional passing references to counter-terrorism, something more substantial was required, even if necessary a parallel system for the work of the secret Agencies. Seeing that this would torpedo the D-Notice System altogether, Stewart wrote to Whitmore [Home Office] hoping that 'you and Stella will be able to go along with a solution which is slightly less than ideal from your point of view but would preserve the system in the interests of all'.

The Security Service still pushed for a separate Notice, on the justification that foreign intelligence services continued to operate against UK interests and that successful counter-terrorist work depended crucially on exploitation of secret intelligence. Pulvertaft regarded this as unsaleable to the Media. His view eventually prevailed, the result being references to protecting counter-terrorism operations and operatives in the new General Introduction and Notices Nos.1, 2, and 6. Even so, when Stewart held a further meeting in mid-June to discuss this aspect, the two Media members thought that what little there was about terrorism in the drafts was 'bad enough'; but after some detailed redrafting they accepted it.[55]

An extra DPBC meeting was held on 19 July 1993 to consider the final paper from the Review Working Group. The underlying theme was that the future System should remain voluntary, advisory and on a shared basis; and the new D-Notices should be published, initially in an Open Government Document,[56] thereby demystifying the process and eliminating the notion of 'slapping on a D-Notice'. The Media side (who had met on 7 July and agreed their support) concurred that, subject to a few further small amendments, the Introduction, Notices and explanatory note could all now be published.

To emphasise the advisory nature of the Committee, it was also formally approved that titles should be changed from that moment to the 'Defence, Press and Broadcasting Advisory Committee' (DPBAC), Defence Advisory Notices, and the 'Defence Advisory Notice Secretary' (DA Notice Secretary) [although these titles remain to the present day, colloquially they continue to be the D-Notice Committee, D-Notices and the D-Notice Secretary]. The Open Government Document was agreed, for deposit in the House of Commons Library and elsewhere; but it was decided that the Committee rather than Ministers should take the lead in responding to expected media interest. Subject to wider consultation with media organisations being completed, announcement before Parliament's summer recess was planned, and indeed achieved on 23 July.[57]

In essence, the revised standing Notices[58] had been reduced in number from eight to six, with a 'Rationale' paragraph being added to each, and the text shortened and cleansed of Cold War allusions. The reduced General Introduction referred to the break-up of the Soviet Union and 'the UK's involvement in smaller-scale conflicts, the undiminished and currently high threat from terrorist attacks and the risk of weapons of mass destruction', as well as the continuing targeting of the UK by foreign intelligence services. The formerly long-debated wording of the D-Notice/OSA relationship was abbreviated merely to: 'Compliance with the DA Notice system does not relieve the editor of responsibilities under the Official Secrets Act.'

The result of the Review was widely reported on television the same evening, and next day in most national newspapers: 'Whitehall Gag Lifted' (*Daily Star*), 'Daylight on the D-Notices' (*Daily Telegraph*), 'Secrecy lifted from D-notice system' (*Financial Times*), etc. The *Guardian*, whose security correspondent had previously described the system as 'a peculiarly British practice', was the most muted ('Government revives press 'D notices'), referring to the Government [sic] having 'dusted down' the System 'in an attempt to make it more acceptable to the media'; but otherwise it reported the changes factually. The *Press Gazette* of 2 August summed up the generally warm media response (contrary to the expectation of the MoD Press Secretary) in its headline: 'Demise of the D-notice (Yes, we are allowed to tell you about it).'[59]

Silly and Serious

A more light-hearted (in retrospect) incident in May had shown another side of the Secretary's role. *The Times*[60] reported a drunk vagrant had managed to break into a (now former) SIS building in Pimlico looking for somewhere to sleep. A BSkyB team following up this story filmed the outside of the building, including SIS personnel entering and leaving, one of them a woman whose cover in then particularly sensitive work would have been blown had that part of the film been shown. Pulvertaft therefore negotiated with BSkyB that those clips were not used and were deleted from the archive. The only face shown was that of the convicted drunk, who said he had been surprised when told who the building belonged to, 'but it explains why they wouldn't give me bail at first – they must have thought I was James Bond or somebody'.

During 1993, the BBC's Peter Taylor was making a series of programmes, called 'States of Terror', about how democratic states respond to terrorist threats.[61] He was also writing an accompanying book, and the MoD was nervous about its Northern Ireland component, especially as Taylor had already told them of some sensitive matters he was covering on film; books, the MoD felt, always contained more detail. Knowing this, Pulvertaft asked the BBC's new DPBAC representative, Richard Ayre, to have a look again at the relevant chapter in the book, especially about covert 'fieldcraft'; he later received Ayre's assurance that nothing in it could damage current or future operations.

However, unknown to the Secretary, there had meanwhile been tetchy discussions between Taylor and the MoD, which had allegedly threatened a D-Notice would be 'slapped on' or that the Corporation might be taken to court. Subsequent calmer discussion included agreement that sections of most concern might indeed be vetted by Pulvertaft. He suggested to Ayre that 'a neutral' might come to the BBC to look at the relevant sections, thus avoiding release of the text; this gained a reluctant response, in view of how unhelpful the MoD had been compared with the RUC and the military in theatre. Ayre did however discuss with the

Secretary in some detail several of the matters of concern to the MoD. This enabled Pulvertaft to persuade MoD not to pursue the matter further, and instead give Taylor an unattributable briefing on agent handling which would enable him to recheck the content before publication/transmission. No serious damage was done.[62]

There were very few journalists to whom such a concession would be made by the security authorities, because very few were by now highly experienced in the security field. Very few could claim therefore that when they assured they were not damaging security, they were sufficiently knowledgeable probably to be right (even though disclosing embarrassing matters which the authorities would otherwise prefer to remain hidden). The few journalists in this category rarely need to consult the D-Notice Secretary, nor does he need very often to contact them, since they and their editors understand the Notices; few therefore feature by name in this section of this History. This represents self-regulation as intended, which is altogether different from subservience.

During the August 'silly season' of 1993, the Secretary was again involved in a Rimington domestic story. The *Sun*[63] alleged the secrecy about her move to a new house had been compromised by a Security Service press release announcing she had sold her former home. Stung by this criticism of something done under its new policy of greater openness, the Service complained to Pulvertaft; he then explained to the Media that the information had been deliberately issued so that the new owner of the former house did not become the innocent target of a terrorist using out-of-date intelligence. More importantly, he discovered a number of reporters from various papers were trying to find out Mrs Rimington's new address; he was therefore able to gain the agreement of interested national editors (and also of the editor of the local paper) that, even if discovered, it would not be published.

Even more 'silly season' was the case of the Cheltenham overground reservoir. This was adjacent to one GCHQ site, was due for infilling and development, and posed no great threat to its official or residential neighbours. However, BBC Radio Gloucester reported that the reservoir's relocation was urgent, because of flood danger to GCHQ's computer rooms. This sparked a flurry of Press interest, causing the Agency to ask Pulvertaft to intervene, on the grounds it might put ideas into the minds of terrorists. He quickly decided that not even the most stretched interpretation of any Notice could apply, and the least said the better. When asked by GCHQ therefore for a line to take instead (not his job) in response to any media questions, he tongue-in-cheek suggested 'we would all get our feet wet'; and, more seriously, not even to whisper anything about terrorism. The silly season was fortunately at an end, and the story died locally.[64]

56

BOOKS, AVOWAL, AND THE CHINOOK CRASH

The D-Notice Review having been settled, the DPBAC returned to routine business at its 27 October 1993 meeting. Pulvertaft mentioned another relevant Open Government document recently issued, outlining the central Intelligence machinery.[65] On the application of the new Notices, and particularly those which had caused most debate during the Review, the Secretary said he had had no difficulty in interpreting the phrase 'other individuals [who] are likely targets for attacks by terrorists' in D-Notice No.6. He was in reality still in discussion with officials about how he did so, since they would have liked this category to include a somewhat wider spectrum of people than the Committee had agreed. As an extreme example, there was an MoD policy of not disclosing the names of frontline pilots, because of the experiences of captured aircrew during the first Gulf War; Pulvertaft (and the court concerned) drew the line, however, at protecting the name of an RN pilot's wife charged with a drink-driving offence.

A less extreme example, and one which scraped into the 'covered' category, concerned an admiral alleged to have acquired a surplus MoD flagpole for his local church, who was 'door-stepped' by a *Mail on Sunday* team. The alerted Deputy Secretary asked the paper not to publish the admiral's home address, for security reasons, which was agreed, but that evening the editor rang Ponsonby at home threatening to sue him and to cease co-operation with the DPBAC. It transpired this was for 'breach of commercial confidence', the accusation being he had 'blown' the story to the *Sunday Express*; the good working relationship was restored when Ponsonby proved the latter had had the story before the *MoS*. More clear-cut was his reminder to the Editor of *Today*, who had published the photograph and general location of the weekend cottage of the Home Secretary, Michael Howard, who was most definitely on the High Threat List.[66]

At the October DPBAC meeting, Pulvertaft reported that on D-Notice No.3, although there was much information now in the public domain about the transportation of nuclear missiles within the UK, all accepted that the timing and security arrangements of convoys still required the protection of this Notice (in July however he had declined a Naval Security request to intervene on public discussion of other matters connected with the convoys). On aerial photography, the Government Departments other than the MoD had not yet finished their review of sensitive sites, and so he was still having to use old criteria under D-Notice No.5. The Vice-Chairman asked that the new D-Notice No.6 be amended to include the phrase 'highly classified' before 'operations', 'methods', 'tasks', etc, since not all matters in these categories needed protection; officials agreed. Stuart also once more raised the lack of representation of the Publishers' Association, about which he was taking soundings with its

Chief Executive. On membership, it was agreed the Secretary should approach BSkyB and Channel 4, in view of the independent TV sector's growth.

Although the D-Notice Secretary's involvement in matters relating to Northern Ireland had been increasing because of the personal security aspects, the previous reluctance of the Committee to become embroiled with domestic terrorism had so far made this still a tangential area. He did not receive press cuttings from Northern Irish papers (nor strangely did the MoD Library at the time), and only four Ulster papers were on the DA-Notice distribution list, all of them supporters of Unionism.

There was however increasing interest by television companies in the past and present situation in the Province, and the November 1993 BBC 'Spotlight' programme about an informer caused Pulvertaft (having offered his usual advice) to review his own monitoring of the Northern Ireland Media. He was also asked by the MoD to consider whether non-security forces individuals working in Northern Ireland who were known to be under threat could be covered under the new clause in the revised DA-Notice No.6, as 'other individuals who are likely targets for attacks by terrorists'; he advised however that the DPBAC would consider lawyers, judges and magistrates were outside its remit. He did give advice to the BBC that, in a programme about deployment to Northern Ireland for the first time of RN Sea King helicopters for anti-terrorist operations, it should not report some of the secret technical capabilities of the aircraft nor the duration of the deployment.[67]

Amongst his activities between meetings, Pulvertaft hesitantly approached the publisher of Chapman Pincher's forthcoming autobiography, 'Pastoral Symphony'; even though the author had never submitted his books for advice, the pre-publication publicity had mentioned his 'secret contacts'. As it turned out, this book was about Pincher's hobbies of fishing and shooting; he made maximum publicity out of the approach, referring to the 'prodnose' Secretary's 'monstrous' request.[68] Pulvertaft's request to see the manuscript of 'The Life of Graham Greene' by Norman Sherry (one name was omitted as a result of this intervention) had also drawn comment (in *The Observer* of 30 January 1994 and elsewhere), wrongly seeing a current Cuba link and an implication that Greene had been in MI6 when he wrote 'Our Man In Havana' (picked up in *Der Standard* of Vienna because of the tenuous 'Third Man' connection).

In a more genuine Soviet connection, Pulvertaft noticed in the November 1993 *Bookseller* that the publishing rights of the defector Oleg Gordievsky's autobiographical third book had been bought. In the event, a year passed before publisher and author were ready to discuss the manuscript with the Secretary; by December 1994 he was also receiving media queries about his involvement, to which he gave the usual answer: he would not discuss his dealings with one 'media outlet' with another. The pace hotted up when serialisation rights were sold by the author to the *Sunday Times*, and when *The Times* of 10 December carried Gordievsky's claim he was going to name 24 'establishment' figures who had been recruited as paid 'agents of influence' by the KGB; one, the *Guardian*'s literary editor Richard Gott, had already been leaked to *The Spectator*. Pulvertaft decided that, unless any of these names were also covered by D-Notice No.6 (which seemed unlikely, but he checked with the secret Agencies), he would not get involved in this media controversy.

Meanwhile the *Sunday Times* was being sued by Michael Foot over its allegation, based on Gordievsky, that he was one of the agents of influence. The final twist was then a suggestion put to the Secretary by conspiracy-minded journalists that D-Notice involvement had been part of a secret Agencies' cover-up which included the fingering of Foot by anti-Labour elements in MI5 (Pulvertaft knew this to be untrue, but he kept this to himself in order to avoid being drawn into a Political matter). The Secretary reiterated the more mundanely procedural DPBAC role in vetting books, including this one (a role which Gordievsky had publicly acknowledged). In the end, the Secretary's private assessment was that, given the 'dog bites dog' situation, the D-Notice System had come through fairly unscathed. The 'dog' allusion was of course purely idiomatic.[69]

Protection of Identities

Returning to pre-Gordievsky events, on 15 January 1994, the *Sunday Times* contacted the MoD Press Office about a story they were running next day on an SAS disciplinary inquiry into weapons lost during training in Oman. The MoD asked for Pulvertaft's help in protecting the name of one Staff Sergeant involved; he had previously taken part in operations in Iraq and Northern Ireland, one in particular giving direct cause for concern for his personal security if he were now identified. The newspaper accepted the D-Notice advice, did not name him in the article, and agreed to delete the geographic connection from their database, so that it would not inadvertently be used in future. At about this time Pulvertaft was also giving advice to the BBC on another programme on agent handling in the Province, and negotiating the omission of an SIS name from an *Independent* article on the illegal supply of arms to Azerbaijan.[70]

In spring to autumn 1994, Pulvertaft was asked to intervene in several cases involving personal security of others thought by officials to be of interest to terrorists, and he sometimes did so. These included the Attorney-General being photographed leaving home; addresses of the official residences of numerous senior officers of all three Services which were not within MoD establishments (the Media was then taking a prolonged interest in these houses and their staffs, following revelation that the Air Member for Personnel's wife had spent much public money on the décor of his residence near Cheltenham); the private addresses of other Ministers revealed en passant in unconnected stories (e.g. the former Defence Secretary Tom King's flat being in the same building as that of fellow Minister David Mellor's inamorata); a salacious *Daily Mirror* story about the wife of a former CO in Northern Ireland; and the SAS background of the new Chief Inspector of Scottish Prisons. He did not intervene over stories that MI5 had intercepted letters between the recent Chief of the Defence Staff and his mistress, since they were (like the media's 'Squidgygate revelations') 'total garbage' and nothing to do with national security.[71]

Late on 30 March 1994, the *Daily Express* rang Pulvertaft at home to ask his advice about a 'spy story' exclusive. The Russian Intelligence Service's Head of PR had tipped their man in Moscow off that the Head of MI6's Station there, John Scarlett,[72] was to be expelled. The Secretary's initial advice was that the paper should not repeat the Russian claim he was an MI6 officer, but describe him as a diplomat; and later that there should be no photographs nor home address details. This was a tit for tat expulsion which the SIS had hoped would be low-key, but the Russian/*Express* exposé and the subsequent activity by other parts of the UK Media soon made the actual position abundantly clear (even after following Pulvertaft's advice), without it ever being officially confirmed. On 2 April, an Agency photographer took a picture of Scarlett and his family arriving at Heathrow. Pulvertaft, having learnt of this from a press contact but not being able to reach all the papers quickly enough that evening, could only complain post hoc to Max Hastings of the *Daily Telegraph* when he published it; the editor replied with impeccable logic and ingenuousness that, since Scarlett was described by the authorities simply as a bona fide diplomat, the onus had been on Pulvertaft to alert him that this was not so and about the sensitivity of the picture.[73] They were not to know that Scarlett would a decade later become the most publicly photographed ever Head of the SIS.

The 20 April 1994 DPBAC meeting was joined for the first time by representatives of Sky Television and the ITV Network, bringing the Media side to 13 (giving better balance between written and audio-visual organisations), while the Official side continued to have four. The Secretary reported that the ever co-operative Publishers' Association had again decided not to be represented. Detailed debate took place over rewording DA-Notice No.6; following quibbles between the two sides out of Committee, and now across the table, over single phrases or words (even a 'the') considered by one or other to be too restrictive or too loose, agreement was eventually reached [space fortunately precludes here recording fully the output of these distinguished minds]. It was also agreed that in future changes to Notices need not, as in the past, await the annual review.

In his six-monthly report, Pulvertaft mentioned the introduction of the Intelligence Services Bill in Parliament in November 1993, the associated press briefing by the Foreign Secretary Douglas Hurd with Colin McColl of the SIS and John Adye of GCHQ, and the announcement that David Spedding[74] would succeed McColl (Pulvertaft had tried to dissuade editors from publishing their photographs but some youthful snaps did appear). He also described the new official Protective Marking System, which redefined existing security classifications; the MoD believed the only impact on the Committee might be a reduction in requests for advice, as the intention was to make officials more critical of unnecessarily high classification.[75]

Pulvertaft asked the Committee's guidance on whether there were ways of 'intercepting' photographs taken by unidentified photographers, for example on the doorstep of someone on the High Threat List, *before* they were offered for publication, but Members agreed there was no reasonable solution. On aerial photography, he reported progress in conjunction with the Cabinet Office in reducing the number of protected sites in Great Britain, from about 600 to about 30.[76] On one reported intervention he was challenged by Purvis: this concerned articles/broadcasts about an arms seizure at Teesport, where ITN knew from two public departmental briefings that the Security Service had been involved, something the Secretary had advised against publishing [there had been a left-hand right-hand situation with briefings from different Departments on different occasions]; this challenge was not recorded in the minutes, about which Purvis subsequently complained, and the omission was rectified.[77]

The FCO representative Sir Timothy Daunt[78] informed the Committee there was to be a change in the criteria under which former employees of the secret Agencies might publish or give interviews. In Parliament that day the Foreign Secretary (Hurd) announced that, bearing in mind their lifelong duty of confidence, they must apply for permission from their former employing Department to do so; such requests would now be looked at on their merits, more so for matters over 30 years' old than for recent activities, although even here permission might be granted in 'especially rare and exceptional' cases.[79]

How the Secretary Keeps in Touch

At the end of his routine report, Pulvertaft explained how he kept abreast of what was being published; this is an opportune point in this History to summarise how successive Secretaries have done so since the mid-1980s. The D-Notice Secretary is a one-man band, so there is a limit as to how much he alone can monitor. He (or, in his absence on leave, his part-time Deputy) does every day of the year scrutinise all the principal national newspapers and magazines, and a selection of others, and their websites. He also checks every issue of publications and electronic equivalents such as '*Bookseller*'. He is an avid if sometimes reluctant reader of and subscriber to media news and the multifarious publications and websites to do with, for example, media law, freedom of information, media regulation, and all areas covered by the D-Notices, academic, professional and populist. Otherwise he has to rely heavily on information from others. He receives press cuttings and other pertinent digests. Officials inform him as necessary of relevant matters which, openly or otherwise, come to their attention. Journalists, in seeking advice, are a steady source of information about their own intentions and (especially) those of rival transmitters of information/speculation (rivals not infrequently being inside their own organisation).

Above all, however, the effectiveness of the Secretary depends on his personal contacts. As a recently retired senior officer, he already has many contacts within the MoD and the Services. He has regular contact with the designated posts in the secret Agencies who have informal contacts with the Media. Because of his unique role, he has easy access when needed within other governmental and non-governmental organisations. He makes it his business to be known personally to as many editors/producers/publishers as will see him, and offers to brief those new in post who have not previously dealt much with national security. Above all he tries immediately to establish a good working relationship with those journalists, programme makers and authors who frequently deal with national security, by regular telephone contact, and, occasionally, over lunch. Contacts which are tangential to current casework are just as important as those involving specific persuasion or debate.

These personal relationships are important in ensuring both a flow of information and that the Secretary is rarely completely taken by surprise; they are essential in establishing confidence between the Secretary and his contacts, whether media or official, so that when advice is being given to either side or both (remembering the Chinese walls which he must maintain), it is more likely to be accepted, especially when there is time pressure. There are many grey areas in national security, where there is a possible genuine danger to lives or operations, but where it is hard to provide conclusive evidence; sometimes the public interest justifies taking the risk of publication, sometimes the risk justifies overriding the public interest pro tem. It is in such marginal cases that an official or an editor may eventually say to the Secretary: 'You haven't conclusively persuaded me, but because I trust your judgement, I will accept your advice in this case.'

Chinook Helicopter Crash

During the early evening of 2 June 1994, a Chinook helicopter flying in low cloud from Northern Ireland to Fort George in Inverness crashed on the Mull of Kintyre, killing all onboard. The passengers, en route to an Intelligence conference, included many leading members of the security authorities involved in the campaign against terrorism. They came from the Royal Ulster Constabulary, the Security Service, GCHQ, the Northern Ireland Office (NIO) and the Army. About two hours later, the Security Service contacted the Deputy Secretary, requesting D-Notice action to protect the identities of its members involved in the crash (it was not yet known then whether there were any survivors).

Pulvertaft (returning from leave to assist Ponsonby that evening) was faced with three different cultures in advising on how the casualties might or might not be reported. The RUC almost immediately indicated the wish to honour their dead openly, as the police officers were known members of their local community. The Security Service, for reasons connected with current operations, wished to prevent the identities of their dead being made public. The MoD wished to be open about the identities of the dead aircrew, but, for similar reasons to the Security Service, to protect the identities of the nine Army passengers with Intelligence backgrounds. Furthermore, in the confusion immediately following the crash, the publicity situation was changing hourly; the Secretary decided therefore not to issue a separate letter to editors through the PA, but to ask that a reference to DA-Notice No.6 be added to civilian and military casualty lists about to be issued by the NIO and MoD respectively.

As they came to terms with the magnitude of the crisis and loss, the authorities did indeed engender some confusion about news handling, reflecting the different chains of command and interests involved. In the middle of the next day, at a press conference given by the Northern Ireland Secretary and his senior military and police officers, it was announced that names would not be released 'for security reasons', and a few hours later the MoD confirmed its request that the Army personnel be covered by D-Notice action. However, at about the same time, the Northern Ireland Office, having concluded its stance was 'unrealistic' in the light of the understandable media interest, issued a new statement that 'after further reflection' the six 'NIO' civil servants (actually five were from the Security Service, and one (female) from GCHQ) would be named. The NIO added however that photographs, family details and addresses should not be published, being covered by DA-Notice No.6; shortly afterwards HQ Northern Ireland issued a similar statement about the Army dead. Because one of the 'NIO' names was well-known to the Media to be the Deputy DGSS, they immediately assumed all six were from that Agency (which at least protected GCHQ's wish that their involvement in Northern Ireland should not be acknowledged).

These rapid changes of message caused confusion in the Media, and Ponsonby (who had not been kept entirely in the picture) received many calls for clarification. That evening he discovered that the PA fax from Northern Ireland announcing the names had not included the DA-Notice rider, something which PA (London) then made rapid efforts to correct. At the behest of his family and his regiment, the photograph of one Colonel had, however, already appeared on ITV (where Purvis was particularly critical of the confusion) and on BBC News in the West Country, where he was well known. Despite much further discussion between the Deputy Secretary and the Media, the same photograph appeared in the *Sun* and *Independent*; the former did however remove from later editions the photographs of three Intelligence Corps officers, and its editor offered helpful advice about future handling, later agreed by the full DPBAC.

In the following days, intense media interest continued, and gradually further details emerged. On 7 and 8 June, Ponsonby felt it wise to issue further reminders to editors about photographs, addresses and family details, but on 10 June he was in disagreement with *The Times* over the use of the Colonel's already published photograph in its obituary. The following week, realising the impracticality of holding the DA-Notice No.6 line for all the Army personnel, Pulvertaft asked MoD to carry out a security assessment, and days later he was able to announce the reduction of D-Notice protection to just four Intelligence Corps dead; all the NIO dead remained on the 'no disclosure of details' list. There were also many other matters connected not with crash but with the former activities of those killed, which were covered by D-Notice advice followed fully by the Media.

Further complications arose over funeral arrangements around the country, with on the one hand the families and some parent departments wishing to give each deceased a 'good funeral', but on the other the police concerned about the risk to the personal security of the many figures from the Intelligence world wishing to attend. The Secretary's reaction was not to issue further D-Notice messages, but to advise the latter group 'if you don't want to be seen, either don't attend, or take precautions which make photography and other identification unlikely'. Over the next few years, as anniversaries and inquiries came and went, there were occasional requests for updated advice about identification and activities of those killed. More often there have been allegations of D-Notices being used to suppress information about the crash itself; these have all been untrue.[80]

The Chinook crash and its aftermath was the main topic when the DPBAC next met, on 26 October 1994. Pulvertaft concluded that, despite the confusion, the System had minimised disclosures which would have been damaging. The Committee agreed some confusion might have been reduced if reference in the casualty lists to D-Notice relevance had been explained as being at the request of the Secretary rather than of the Department concerned; that he would have been less unsighted if always on the distribution of PA messages concerning the D-Notice System (Webb agreed to arrange this); and that the growth of local commercial radio stations made his task of keeping all the Media informed of the System increasingly difficult.[81]

On more routine matters, Pulvertaft reported an unusually high number (14) of books in the pipeline about SIS-related subjects, in eight of which Pulvertaft had been involved in some way, but with minimal need for 'negative' advice. The Vice-Chairman referred to Pulvertaft's speaking note for the previous meeting, and to the difficulty of maintaining confidentiality and media trust, yet still allowing appropriate debate within Committee. The Secretary had attempted to cover this point in a draft amendment to the 'General Introduction', but this had not been acceptable to the Media side. After the meeting it became apparent that some Media Members, notably Robert Hutchinson of *Jane's*, had reservations about knowing too much detail of the Secretary's in-confidence dealings with individuals, since this could put the Media side de facto in the position of a tribunal or peer pressure group. Subsequent Media side guidance to the Secretary was that only two circumstances demanded reticence with the Committee: when sensitive security concerns were at issue, and when an editor, having accepted advice not to publish, retained 'dormant' information which he would expect the Secretary not to divulge to others [not only to officials, but particularly to rival editors]. Since that time, successive Secretaries have struck a balance found acceptable in the detail given to the Committee.

There had been continuing media interest in the 77 official residences (particularly after the HCDC published the running costs of each), and Pulvertaft had sent a reminder to editors in July that, while many were well known locally, the exact location of over half was not in the public domain and if disclosed would increase vulnerability to terrorist attack. It was however a Ministerial residence which caused the Secretary to issue the next reminder. One November weekend evening, about 150 protestors against the Criminal Justice Act invaded the grounds of the Home Secretary's Kent home. Because Howard was on the High Threat list, Pulvertaft immediately issued a reminder that the precise location or clues thereto should not be published; apart from the *Daily Telegraph*'s inadvertent mention of the house name, about which its DPBAC representative apologised, the remainder of the Media followed his advice.[82]

A more significant contact with an editor was over a *Time Out* article giving addresses and telephone numbers of many buildings used by the SIS, Security Service and GCHQ. The then somewhat more 'fringe' magazine had never been sent D-Notices,[83] so the editor was perhaps justified in pleading ignorance of the implications; having been provided with a set, he undertook in future to seek advice. Any damage and inconvenience to the secret Agencies was fortunately reduced by the SIS and Security Service having recently concentrated respectively in the very prominent Vauxhall Cross and Thames House buildings (although a London taxi-driver once assured this author (who refrained from contradiction) that it was common knowledge this was not really so, but was a deception plan).

57

SPECIAL FORCES, FORMER YUGOSLAVIA, INADEQUATE DA-NOTICES

By late 1994, Admiral Pulvertaft had been in post long enough to have experienced deficiencies in the D-Notices when applied to Special Forces. These included that past operations (unlike current and planned ones) were covered only if carried out in conjunction with the secret Agencies. Protecting SF identities had similar limitations; and equipment developed specifically for countering domestic terrorism was strictly speaking not covered. The Media side had themselves begun to consider this unsatisfactory in the light of modern security realities and media focus. The Secretary therefore engaged the MoD secretariats concerned (Home and Special Forces Directorate, and Legal Advisers) in dialogue which might lead accordingly to revision of the Notices.[84]

Protecting Special Forces identities became headline news in March 1995, when their Director and three officers were robbed at gunpoint by Serbs in Bosnia. The MoD failed to forewarn Pulvertaft; the first he heard was a BBC Radio 4 report, and articles followed in the *Daily Mail* and *Daily Mirror* of 18 March, the latter also naming the Brigadier (other journals followed). The Secretary did manage to persuade newspapers not to publish additional personal details of the officers, and even not to publish a photograph of the Director Special Forces (although, strictly speaking and illogically, photographs of SF personnel were not then covered by a Notice). However, unhelpful speculation about what the UKSF were planning in Bosnia was published as part of the mugging story, which the Secretary would have been able to discourage had he been involved from before the story broke. Failure by the MoD Press Office to alert the D-Notice Secretary about a breaking story has on other occasions too precluded him offering proactive advice to the Media, to the subsequent detriment of the Department and of Services personnel. This defect has sometimes been exacerbated by the MoD policy of never willingly volunteering any information about the UKSF.[85]

The 1995 New Year Honours List announced the award of the CB to SJ Lander[86] of the 'MoD', but when *The Observer* rang the Press Office for more details, the complete lack of any information caused the paper to deduce correctly he was a senior person in MI5. When Pulvertaft was later approached by a grumpy Security Service, he suggested either it followed the UKSF practice of listing awards without names, or it needed to forewarn him, so that MoD could refer any enquiries to him and he could give any advice necessary. The latter system was agreed, and has been used ever since; junior grades who receive awards are rarely of media interest, while the more senior are usually either similarly of no immediate media interest or already in the public domain.[87]

In routine perusal of the spring 1995 *Bookseller*, Pulvertaft spotted 'The Double-Cross System 1939–45' by JC Masterman.[88] Although such historical books are unlikely to cause security problems, some of those involved still living are unwilling despite the passage of time that their past secret activities should be known even to family. Their old Services retain a duty of care; unwanted identification also hinders recruiting of present-day agents, and derivations of some secret techniques/channels of contact are still in use. Pulvertaft's files showed Masterman had asked officials in 1968 for permission to publish a manuscript (written 23 years earlier), in order to champion international co-operation and to show the secret Agencies in a good light. For whatever (non-D-Notice) reason, however, permission was refused in the UK, and in 1972 he published instead in the USA.

Publication of the British edition was belatedly imminent; Pulvertaft discovered this was to include material not in the US edition, tracked down by 'Nigel West', who was also contributing a long introduction containing the names of about 50 WWII double agents of many nationalities. Rupert Allason agreed to submit the draft introduction, which, when checked, was considered to include identities of nine agents/handlers not previously disclosed. In the rapid exchange of correspondence with the Secretary which followed, the author was able either to provide chapter and verse of disclosure elsewhere, or to assure he had obtained the individual's consent. Where there was some greyness in interpretation of previous disclosure/consent, Pulvertaft tended to adjudicate in Allason's favour.[89]

Special Forces Again

The DPBAC met on 4 May 1995, under its new Chairman RC Mottram,[90] and quickly moved to the contentious amendment of DA-Notice No.6, now desired by officials to give the same coverage as the secret Agencies to the UKSF (and the Intelligence Corps). Special Forces had been again brought into greater media prominence by their then high profile role in Bosnia, described nevertheless in the draft as operating 'behind enemy lines'. The Media side did not altogether oppose extending the coverage, but felt the wording was too loose. They questioned whether editors would understand what was meant for example in the current fluid Balkan operational environment by 'defence intelligence organisations', 'enemy' and 'lines'. They queried undefined coverage of participation in previous operations, and 'agents'. Officials undertook to reconsider the draft. Pulvertaft sought guidance how meanwhile he should advise the Media if the UKSF were used to assist the safe withdrawal of UN Peace-keeping forces; after some discussion, it was agreed there would be sufficient justification to use DA-Notice No.1 (Military Operations).[91]

After this meeting, there was another incident in Bosnia, when the Serbs imprisoned about 30 British soldiers, of whom according to the Press eight were SAS [this was untrue]. MoD statements did not convince some newspapers otherwise, and Pulvertaft was left once again making the most of inadequate Notices to protect current SF covert operations and personnel elsewhere in Bosnia. Because of the Chief of the Defence Staff's concern about the potential damage of such speculation,[92] the Secretary considered issuing a general reminder to all editors; the MoD however was against this because it would be inconsistent with its policy of never commenting on SF operations.[93]

A different SF story broke in mid-June 1995, when the Government announced its support for Shell's plan to sink an obsolescent floating oil storage and tanker loading facility, Brent Spar, in deep water west of Scotland. Greenpeace (who later admitted miscalculation of possible pollution damage) organised world-wide protests and some activists occupied the facility. The SofS for Defence outlined options for military intervention, including use of the SBS, if so requested by the Department of Trade and Industry. What was already a high visibility case achieved extra media 'legs' when it was leaked that a relevant MoD letter had been signed by his Assistant Private Secretary, Princess Anne's husband Commander Laurence.[94] There was so little truth in the story, other than SBS responsibilities for oil installation security generally and the name of DSF (both already in the public domain), that Pulvertaft declined to take any action.

MoD alarm bells were meanwhile ringing about 'Andy McNab's' second book, 'Immediate Action'.[95] This was considered by the MoD Secretariat to 'cross a new line in the damage it threatens to the national interest', in that it confirmed SAS involvement in specific past actions and revealed details of training, techniques, equipment and tactics still in use against terrorists. A wide-ranging injunction was immediately proposed, but the FCO and Cabinet Office were lukewarm, and instead Pulvertaft was asked if he would contact the publisher. Within days, however, an injunction of less impact was approved by Ministers, and Pulvertaft withdrew immediately from involvement.

Difficulties quickly became apparent in enforcing a world-wide ban and protecting the MoD's copyright (claimed for the first time by officials, but dropped during negotiations). There was media hostility: 'If generals can write books, why not the heroes?' asked for example the *Sun*'s military commentator (himself a General) on 5 August. As litigation proceeded, Pulvertaft's brief involvement in this and past cases was included in the publisher's affidavits. This highlighted the unsatisfactory aspects for the D-Notice System of divided vetting responsibility, especially when it passed to and fro. Sufficient excisions were eventually negotiated between the MoD and publisher for publication in November, but with much further criticism of the MoD's handling and of the ex parte nature of its injunction.[96]

On the broadcasting front, Pulvertaft had opened negotiations with London Weekend Television about the intended dramatisation of 'The One That Got Away' by ex-SAS soldier Chris Ryan (previously vetted by the MoD and deletions ordered). The book's content had been compressed into a two-hour TV package. Having been assured no information would be added, Pulvertaft confined himself to warning about visually giving away current operational techniques which were not in the script, and to suggesting he might at some stage view the intended programme, bringing with him an 'expert'. This happened in January 1996, following a *Sunday Times* article, which alleged a falling out between Ryan and McNab over the detail of the story.[97] One of the two 'experts' chosen by HQ DSF to accompany Pulvertaft was, to his surprise, another member of the Bravo Two Zero patrol. Although there were no security concerns in the footage (but many errors noted by the patrol-member), LWT guessed the identity of the junior expert ('by his youth and size', the Secretary thought), and complained to Pulvertaft afterwards this had misused the D-Notice System, and possibly damaged the commerciality of the programme. The Secretary reassured that the expert's identity would not be revealed by him; but inevitably it was leaked elsewhere, in the many subsequent articles about degrees of heroism and blame. It also transpired that the MoD had separately seen a somehow pirated copy. All in all, one might say that, although Pulvertaft had played his part correctly, there had been Greater (Special) Forces at Work.

The BBC had meanwhile been considering how to dramatise 'Bravo Two Zero', but initially all were awaiting resolution of the MoD injunction against 'Immediate Action'. Peter Taylor had also long been manoeuvring to make an 'official history' series about the SAS, but despite personal appeals through senior officers who knew him, official agreement was not forthcoming. The MoD was then alarmed to hear rumours in December 1995 that the BBC had allegedly been approached by another retired general with an offer to make an unauthorised series about the UKSF, but when approached by Pulvertaft, Ayre denied this. The next BBC/MoD run-in was as it happened another Taylor series on the history of the IRA, but this was not announced until late 1996.[98]

A human interest story in which the Secretary became involved concerned an ex-GCHQ employee who had fallen in love with a Russian woman. The immigration authorities were convinced her ardour for him was not as great as her desire to live in Britain; the GCHQ man became increasingly desperate, coming to the attention of the *Daily Express* and the *Guardian*. Their angle was that security and other considerations preventing her from coming to the UK might result in him flouting the security rules forbidding him going to ex-Soviet countries. Pulvertaft intervened only to remind newspapers they should not mention details of the man's GCHQ employment and contacts.[99] In the run-up to the next DPBAC meeting, MoD's Equipment Security Branch proposed amending DA-Notice No.3 to cover not just nuclear weapons but *all* Weapons of Mass Destruction. They pointed out that, since the Gulf War, proliferation of these had become of increasing concern. This proposal was scotched immediately by the Director of Naval Security, who argued government could hardly on the one hand say that it was not developing Chemical and Biological weapons, and on the other then forbid all discussion of them.[100]

Towards a Further Review

The Media side meanwhile exchanged letters about how to amend the General Introduction to the Notices to cover the possibility, raised by Robert Hutchinson, of the Secretary being confronted with a situation where a failure of government resulted in a risk to national security, and where disclosure of the failure would also increase the threat to life or operations. The BBC's Ayre suggested one of the arguments against the D-Notice System was that it would always be vulnerable to abuse by government, and that therefore it was necessary to 'set a higher than usual level which the threat would need to attain before the Secretary could issue 'negative' advice'. He proposed some such criterion as '*highly likely* to lead to *imminent* threat to life or to *serious long-term* damage to national security', with each underlined element needing to be established to the Secretary's satisfaction. He also suggested acknowledgement in the Introduction that 'the greater the degree of error or negligence by government, details of which it is proposed to publish, the greater must be the editor's presumption in favour of publication'. Pulvertaft did not comment on this degree of media mistrust of government; but he did make the practical point in passing that a person whose life was threatened by disclosure would be unlikely to differentiate greatly between death being *imminent* or at some time slightly further into the future.[101]

At the 26 October 1995 DPBAC meeting, the Media side could still not agree MoD amendments extending coverage of DA-Notice No.6 to Special Forces and the Intelligence Corps. Having discussed at length beforehand, they 'felt that now was not the appropriate time . . . as this would give the wrong signal to editors'. No compelling reason to amend had yet been demonstrated. If meanwhile UKSF personnel were likely to be at risk, editors would 'act responsibly as part of their normal dealings with the Ministry'. The Vice-Chairman Stuart also referred to Press speculation that the Security Service was about to be given a new role in combating serious crime, and said that he had written to the Home Office PUS Richard Wilson[102] pointing out this would be a significant departure from the role which was the basis of current Notices. The Media side thought it better to await such developments before agreeing to amend Notice No.6. Pulvertaft reminded the Committee they had anyway asked him at the last meeting to set up a further review of the Notices, and a number of ideas had emerged from Departments, but none was yet ready for discussion by the DPBAC.

He also raised 'Public Access to SPBC and DPBC Papers'. The gist was that, although the Committee had agreed in 1983 to deposit its records as appropriate in the Public Record Office, none appeared so far to have been transferred. Because of confidentiality considerations (between Secretary and media), he had reorganised the filing system into 'Registered' and 'Unregistered' files; he intended to send the former (Committee and Departmental work) over 30 years old to the PRO, and to retain the latter (in-confidence negotiations with the Media over specific cases) for access only by researchers under 'Sponsored Access' arrangements. The Committee generally agreed with this, but the Media side added 'there was no need to be over-sensitive about the 'Unregistered' part of the records, as nothing which passed between an editor and the Secretary could be deemed to be 'in confidence' after 30 years.'[103]

In October 1995, 'Nigel West' sent the Secretary the manuscript of what later became his 'Secret War for the Falklands'. Lengthy discussion led to some disagreement between Pulvertaft and officials/Director Special Forces over names not in the public domain, disclosure of the precise role of *HMS ENDURANCE*, some SF activities, and some secret Agencies' details. Pulvertaft eventually sent Allason his list of what he considered to be covered by the Notices. The normal process of negotiation then occurred, including over newspaper serialisation, with the author citing public domain sources, including Argentine ones, before a solution acceptable to the many parties involved was reached in late March 1996.[104]

After the DPBAC's inconclusive discussion on coverage for the UKSF, the MoD informed Pulvertaft it was separately preparing 'ideas to put to Ministers to improve our present practices in the field of publications about the UKSF', and asked for his comments. Its draft paper reflected the greatly increased interest in the SAS/SBS by the Media and by authors (several of them ex-SAS), and was an attempt to induce the Media to consult before publishing such material. Pulvertaft did not agree with officials that the Media were concerned about the one successful legal case recently brought by the MoD. However, he agreed some clarification of the MoD's position might be useful. In commenting on the part of the Secretariat paper concerning the DPBAC (he was not shown the whole document), he pointed out that the imminent extension of the Security Service role might provide the opportunity to review the DA-Notice wording. He criticised the MoD paper's inconsistent 'disaffection' with the D-Notice System, adding that Ministers, not generally being aware of its day-to-day work, would not fully appreciate its effectiveness. He also criticised some phraseology as being likely to cause difficulties with the Media, for example 'the use of military units in resolution of civil law and order problems'. What eventually emerged was better balanced on the role of the DPBAC, but, because it did not alter the MoD's policy of not commenting on SF matters, it did not reduce the Media's appetite for SF stories.[105]

Within the MoD in late 1995, a long-running internal SF study on disclosure was in fact leading towards tightening up on regulation of publication by serving and ex-soldiers and marines, work of which the Secretary was aware (but had not been asked for advice as to likely media reaction).[106] The then broad aim was to ensure MoD control of material and of 'pecuniary advantage, without unacceptably hindering the author'. Two official histories of the Territorial Army SAS which had been commissioned were put on ice while contractual arrangements for SF personnel were considered. This study coincided with similar studies in the secret Agencies designed further to constrain disclosure by insiders.[107]

In mid-December 1995 the *Mail on Sunday* reported that the (named) CO of the SAS had banned from visiting the Regiment's Hereford base five former NCOs (including 'McNab' and Ryan) and seven others who had supported them, because of their books. The CO's SF connection had not been publicised before, and Pulvertaft gained agreement from the paper that they would not repeat it nor name others without prior consultation. Privately, however, he noted 'Looks to me as though the MoD/Hereford are losing the PR campaign, and it will presumably get rather worse' when other Media plans which he knew were in the pipeline came to fruition. Such matters are of course about more than a PR campaign, as lives and covert operations are potentially at risk; but Pulvertaft was right that this was an area in which the UKSF have since had to endure even more of the kind of publicity which they wish to avoid.[108]

The *Daily Mail* and the *Sun* of 1 January 1996 each carried a short article naming the new Director Special Forces, linking him both with covert operations in Northern Ireland and as the target of the thwarted IRA Gibraltar attack. The Brigadier's 90-year-old uncle had reported to the MoD that the Press had approached him two days before, but this had not been passed on to the D-Notice Secretary, so he had not been able to remind on non-publication of details. The initial approach, as so often happens, had come from an unknown freelance reporter, but was quickly picked up by the *Eastern Daily Press*, whose geographical area included the Brigadier's parent regiment. It also acquired and published a photograph, an error for which the editor apologised when contacted afterwards by Pulvertaft, as did others. Reviewing the case afterwards, the Secretary highlighted the difficulty of protecting identities of senior UKSF officers who alternated between covert and overt appointments, something which those in the secret Agencies do not normally do. He (and the *Daily Mail*) suggested therefore that when such personal security sensitivities were involved, the Press should be forewarned if and when an appointment was announced.[109]

The drawback is that this highlights such information, and the MoD has not normally done it since then, so the problem has remained. Unsurprisingly, a steady proportion of Army/Royal Marines SF officers reach the higher ranks, and become increasingly 'visible' to the outside world; their background is normally widely known within the wider Services community (and they normally continue to wear the SF insignia on their uniform). Subsequent advice therefore has been that it has not normally been realistic to expect the Media not to mention the SF past of a General Officer, that publicity and risk were some of the consequences of seniority, and that, where there was a specific High Threat risk, other security measures should be taken for that individual. Reminders have however been given not to publish details such as participation in specific covert operations, address and domestic status.

Even within the wider military community (and even within the wider SF community), there were and are differing views about the degree to which *all* information about the UKSF should be protected. From August 1995 to July 1996, the Secretary was involved in giving advice on each stage of a Carlton TV series 'SAS; the Soldiers' Story', which covered many post-WWII operations up to the present, and which could not have been made without considerable co-operation from ex-members of the Regiment of all ranks.[110] In 1994, the Managing Director of the Services Sound and Vision Corporation,[111] a retired Air Vice-Marshal, had written to several serving and retired senior SAS officers about making a commercial official Regimental history video. Official rejection was instant, and concerns about excessive publicity voiced (one senior officer wrote 'Too many of the boys at Hereford are seeing just how much money can be made 'selling' the Regiment'). SSVC therefore withdrew, but was surprised to learn a few months later that another commercial company was receiving support with the same plan from some ex-SAS soldiers. Pulvertaft was consulted in November 1995, but at the late stage he was informed, there was little he could do. When the video 'The Story of the SAS' emerged publicly a few days later, the eight ex-SF (including three generals) involved in its making had ensured that there was nothing seriously damaging in it.[112] Before the SBS became fully under command of the Director Special Forces, it had a somewhat more open attitude to publication of its history, and in 1996–7 co-operated on a book; when the MoD discovered this, it ordered cuts in the manuscript.[113]

In January 1996 it was announced in the press that the former Head of the SIS Sir Colin McColl was taking up a public post on the Board of an investment trust specialising in foreign markets, and his photograph was published. This took Pulvertaft (and his SIS point-of-contact) by surprise, since they had not been forewarned of this variation in policy on photographing 'C's. The clarification which followed was that the policy still applied to those serving, for reasons earlier given by McColl, namely that publication would send the wrong message to his own organisation and to its agents; but that, once retired, this argument no longer applied.[114] In all walks of British life, principles are shaped pragmatically, by 'events'.

As examples of routine business, the Secretary was tangentially involved in discussions with publishers of books about the late Robert Maxwell, because of allegations of links with the SIS, but did not feel it necessary to intervene. Pulvertaft contacted the *Sun* in early March about a planned story on secret documents left in a cupboard auctioned off at RAF Northolt; these included security arrangements at RAF stations, and details of IRA bomb-making. Discussion showed the newspaper was well aware of the advice in Notices, the article concentrated on the cock-up rather than the secrets, and the documents were returned to the MoD.[115]

Records for spring 1996 show an unusually high number of books about GCHQ-related activities (but mostly about WWII or before, and most authors in this cerebral field seem attuned to what might still be damaging). There was also an increasing number of books and articles about Special Forces, varying from 'glossies' such as the CollinsGem 'SAS and Special Forces', to individual efforts such as 'SAS Wife'. The Secretary persuaded newspapers who were reporting the rift within SF circles (over measures taken to deter unauthorised publication) not to publish the home address of the Colonel Commandant. Media SF obsessions were fanned by, for example, the front cover and leading article of a special supplement to the February issue of *Combat & Survival*, featuring several serving SF soldiers, including the unignorable bodyguard (known as 'Goose') of General Rose.[116] When Pulvertaft investigated he found that 'Goose' had been shown in close up (and referred to by his General) in a BBC Panorama programme in 1995. An HQ DSF staff officer minuted: 'With the benefit of 20/20 hindsight, the impact of this article might have been reduced had the MoD released a statement about the UKSF involvement in Bosnia'. This would also have enabled the D-Notice Secretary to give pre-emptive guidance to editors.[117]

Because of the volume of such SF works, checking for hitherto unpublished details of operational techniques, weapons and names became a time-consuming task for the MoD, for HQ Special Forces, and for the D-Notice Secretary. Pulvertaft and his PA now started the tedious task of transferring outlines of their files to computer, and a computerised database of detail was initiated by HQ DSF in early 1996; the latter was especially difficult, since meticulous keeping of media references had quite properly not been a key priority of Special Forces.

58

MEDIA DISCOMFORT, NORTHERN IRELAND, EARLY WEBSITE, AND A BOOKS MOUNTAIN

In April 1996 Pulvertaft was forewarned by the SIS that one of its former members, released after his probationary period and refused an industrial tribunal on security grounds, was threatening to tell his story in the *Sunday Times*. While the Secretary was considering how, if at all, DA-Notice No.6 would be applicable, the Treasury Solicitor stepped in, and Pulvertaft dropped out. The newspaper was persuaded initially not to publish his name nor where he had served, for fear of compromising his contacts there. This was the beginning of what later became known as the Tomlinson case.[118]

In May 1996, the Secretary was offered the manuscript of a book about Detective Superintendent Ian Phoenix of the RUC, one of those killed in the Chinook crash in 1994, written by an Irish journalist with the support of his widow, Dr Susan Phoenix. Although police matters were not normally within the D-Notice purview, Pulvertaft accepted the offer in view of the obvious Intelligence cross-over. Because of recent DPBAC discussion about police matters, he also alerted the Chairman and Vice-Chairman, and undertook to consider only counter-terrorist aspects of the book. The publishers agreed also to consult the RUC Deputy Chief Constable, Ronnie Flanagan,[119] and that the RUC would consult Dr Phoenix direct. Pulvertaft's negotiation over detail in the manuscript was interrupted by an article in the Dublin-based *Sunday World*,[120] but a revised manuscript, without most of the endangering detail, was submitted to the Secretary in mid-July. A five-cornered negotiation (Dr Phoenix/RUC/publisher/Pulvertaft/MI5) resolved outstanding points, despite last minute newspaper trailer/serialisation articles based on earlier manuscript versions.[121] A frank and revealing book of considerable public interest, about a very sensitive area, was thus published by negotiation without seriously damaging disclosures or recourse to the heavier hand of governmental litigation.[122]

At the 1 May 1996 DPBAC meeting, the Home Office proposed amendment of DA-Notice No.6, this time concerning the Security Service's new role with law enforcement agencies. The Home Office/MI5 case was principally that the work of the SIS/GCHQ had always de facto overlapped with serious international crime, and that now protection would be needed for MI5 officers, especially those who might have to give evidence in open court.[123] Officials acknowledged it was the early days of this role, but confirmed that, when working with police, MI5 would come under their arrangements [in relations with the Media]. There were however two aspects officials wished to discuss where there might be 'read across' between the serious crime and national security roles, namely the identity and personal safety of Security Officers, and their methods of operation.

Stuart as Vice-Chairman took an uncompromising line, with which the Committee generally agreed: the then lead organisation (the National Criminal Intelligence Service) would have to solve the problem. The DPBAC was concerned only with national security, and although the Media side recognised the interests of those involved both in protecting security and in fighting crime, the Committee and the Secretary had 'no jurisdiction' where crime was concerned. In practice since that meeting this cross-over has very rarely been a problem; despite occasional rivalries and leaks, the police are normally no more prone to compromise their operations by disclosing the identities and methods of those working undercover with them than are, for example, the military. The D-Notice System is de facto consistent with both these aspects of Security Service work, albeit used only for one.

In early May, the BBC's Nine O'Clock News included an item about a video bought in a car boot sale job lot, which contained details of Army pre-deployment anti-terrorist training for Northern Ireland. Pulvertaft contacted the DPBAC's BBC representative Ayre, who had personally and correctly judged what could be included without damage. He said the BBC had decided not also to consult the D-Notice Secretary for fear the Government would hear of the intention to broadcast the programme, and injunct. Pulvertaft countered that, if he had needed to consult the MoD, he would not have had to say which company was involved, but Ayre pointed out the Government's option of a general injunction. He acknowledged the convention that officials could not initiate legislation based solely on information disclosed by the Secretary, but considered that, to be sure, a more specific undertaking was needed than existed in the General Introduction, something he might raise in Committee.

Afterwards, Ayre wrote to Pulvertaft about further unease he felt as a result of their conversation. Firstly, the Secretary had asked for an assurance that no further material from the video would be published, which Ayre took to mean 'irrespective of whether it fell within the terms of a DA-Notice', and he enquired on whose behalf this was asked. Secondly, Pulvertaft had asked what the attitude of the BBC would be if the Military Police requested return of the material, and again he wondered what this had to do with the D-Notice System. He also reminded that recently Pulvertaft had asked the BBC not to publish the name of a deceased intelligence officer, on the grounds that his widow might not be aware of her late husband's role, but when challenged by Ayre on this, he had withdrawn this advice. He ended his letter by implying the Secretary might not have strictly observed the use of the System 'solely for its proper purpose'.

The aggrieved Pulvertaft explained that, in the latter part of their previous discussion, they might have been 'in danger of confusing Committee business with application of a Notice', and that it was Ayre's lack of an immediate reply when asked whether the BBC still retained the video which had prompted him to say, purely as a 'passing remark', that it was something the MoD Police might well ask; Ayre's then assurance that the BBC would not pass the video on nor use it further without consultation with the Secretary had entirely satisfied the DA Notice interest. He took exception to the inference in Ayre's letter that he was acting on behalf of anyone else, and to resurrecting the case of the intelligence officer, where he had admitted his error, a matter he had regarded as closed.

He ended by hoping that the previous relationship of mutual trust could be restored, but it took further exchanges before a modicum of warmth returned. Nevertheless, Ayre retained throughout his DPBAC time some areas of unease, including that officials sometimes asked the Secretary to advise the Media in certain ways, even though this was, if not in accord with the agreed Notices, always refused. He also voiced a more general view that the D-Notice System was inappropriate at the end of the twentieth century, and wondered why such a system was necessary for national security when it was not for the police, customs and excise, tax and other authorities. He thought that the BBC might be more comfortable dealing with each Department as appropriate. Pulvertaft reminded him that this had been the view advanced by Stewart Purvis in 1992, but rejected by the Media side.

This interaction has been recorded in some detail, in part to show that the Media members of the D-Notice Committee are far from being unquestioning stooges of an official-dominated institution, in part to remind that every healthy organisation needs a kernel of insiders who constantly question how and why things are done, and in part to illustrate that the judgements of the D-Notice Secretary and others in the greyer areas of national security benefit from the adversarial nature of the Committee. This strain of healthy scepticism was soon evident in the next stage of the development of DPBAC work.[124]

Books on Intelligence, and Moscow Station

In mid-1996, Pulvertaft was asked if he would approach the publisher about the manuscript of 'New Cloak, Old Dagger' by the *Daily Telegraph* security correspondent Michael Smith (ex-Intelligence Corps), even though the author had consulted the secret Agencies in writing the book. The publisher was reluctant, but the author agreed, and the Secretary did indeed find a few small details on SIS operational procedures, authenticated by direct quotes from a former officer. Smith was initially unhappy to delete these, but accepted Pulvertaft's suggested compromise of replacing the direct quotes with the author's own words. When consulted on some other details, experts in MI5 and DIS also pointed out some factual errors, which the Secretary passed on to the author to amend if he so wished. This relatively harmonious case was, however, briefly complicated meanwhile by an article in the *Telegraph* about Britain's secret support for the Hungarian uprising of 1956, which included details it had been agreed to omit from the book.[125]

A less harmonious negotiation in mid-1996 took place over 'UK Eyes Alpha – Inside British Intelligence' by Mark Urban. Although the publisher was happy to have the manu-script checked, the author, disgruntled over the way his previous book 'Big Boys Rules' had been vetted in 1992, was not. A compromise was eventually reached, albeit regarded as unsatisfactory by Pulvertaft, whereby he and representatives of each of the secret Agencies scrutinised the manuscript in the offices of the publisher's solicitors. Subsequent negotiations removed about half of the changes requested, most of the others proving to be matters already in the public domain. In response to the Secretary's follow-up letter, the publisher did point out that DPBAC involvement in publishing must be described as 'negative', since it required cuts; but he conceded that on the other hand protecting the publisher from prosecution was 'positive'.[126]

That much in the Media touching on the secret Agencies is inaccurate does not mean the Secretary can ignore much of what is published. On 16 June 1996, for example, the *Sunday Times* carried a story entitled 'MI6 stole secrets from French navy'. The French were unlikely to be angered by the story, since they did not have the submarine tracking system in question; nor had MI6 carried out any such operation. Nevertheless the Secretary had to check it out, and then to decide whether to contact the editor to suggest that, had it been true, seeking advice would have been a Good Thing.[127]

A July 1996 event illustrated well the difficulties of advising non-publication where international stories are concerned. The Russians arrested an alleged MI6 informant (Platon Obukhov), and on Moscow Television showed British diplomats waiting at a rendezvous for him; the clip was used in Britain by ITN. Pulvertaft immediately wrote to the 17 editors/controllers who had Moscow correspondents, reminding them of the DA-Notice advice not to identify SIS staff. There were differing responses. None wished to endanger SIS personnel nor to limit their future assignment to covert duties, and some thought the Secretary's message 'clear and proper'. The editor-in-chief of ITN, Richard Tait[128] (a DPBAC Member) was, however, more questioning. He reminded Pulvertaft 200 million Russians had seen the clip shown by ITN. Pulvertaft did not criticise ITN for re-transmitting what was already in the public domain, nor did he argue against ITN then running the same clip on its international service; he had been concerned only that the four should not publicly be described by British media as SIS personnel.

Events however quickly made this an untenable position. The next day the English-language *Moscow Times* announced its intention of naming the Head of Station and his Intelligence role, and this was repeated by *The Times* (of London), albeit following Pulvertaft's advice to make clear this was what the Russians alleged. Other newspapers followed up, and the Head of Station's name and a blurred photograph from a Russian video were used; there was criticism of the 'futile gesture' of using the D-Notice System to attempt to 'salvage' his career. The Secretary did not comment further.[129]

In New Zealand in August 1996, unannounced by its publisher in order to avoid pre-emptive litigation, a book ('Secret Power' by N Hager) appeared which revealed many details of the worldwide listening system operated by US, UK, Canadian, Australian and New Zealand secret Agencies, code-named Echelon. Some details had in fact already been disclosed in previous years by the international media and on the internet, the source usually being disaffected employees. The previous December, for example, the *Baltimore Sun* had run a series of articles about the US NSA and its international partners, including GCHQ. The new book nevertheless caused a flurry of wider dissemination in the UK Press,[130] and Pulvertaft enquired what the official UK line was on this information. It was silence, although since then the USA as the dominant partner has released some information.[131]

Since then too, much more about Echelon has appeared on the internet. The position of successive Secretaries on such speculation or information has been that, although all of it is unwelcome to secret Agencies, because it reminds adversaries they are being listened to, nevertheless in general terms the existence of such collaboration, and areas of interception coverage, can no longer be regarded as other than widely in the public domain, and a legitimate topic of public discussion. It would be astonishing to most adversaries if such interceptions were not at least being attempted. Where publication becomes damaging is in any revelation of new interception techniques, technologies and areas of interest, and in some cases the locations and identities of the listeners/decrypters.

SF Disclosures, and IRA Activity

The *Daily Mail* of 12 September 1996 contained an article on women who had won gallantry awards in Northern Ireland for their undercover work ('Honoured: heroines of the SAS' [not actually badged SAS but working in conjunction with them]). The newspaper had consulted Pulvertaft, and, although the MoD Press Office had helped with the story, the MoD was worried the IRA would be able to identify from the awards list those who had worked undercover, since there were so few women on it.[132] The paper had agreed to delay the article by 24 hours while Pulvertaft did some research in the MoD library (where *London Gazettes* back to 1666 are held); this confirmed that 90% (ten) of the Northern Ireland awards to women in the past 15 years had been for gallantry, as was obvious from the published *Gazettes*. The provider of the information to the *Mail* was threatening to take the story elsewhere, and the paper was therefore determined to publish. A small compromise was agreed, which removed the word 'gallantry', and widened the theatres of operations; but the headline and the opening paragraph ('Women members of the SAS have been secretly honoured for outstanding bravery in undercover operations') made this a somewhat futile intervention.[133]

A fortnight later the *Sun* (26 September) carried an article about the shooting of an IRA suspect in London, alleging agents had spied on him from car boots fitted with see-through number plates. Although not true in this case, it was a then undisclosed counter-terrorism technique (and had recently been removed accordingly from an SAS book); Pulvertaft contacted the apologetic editor.[134] In other secret fields, some relaxation was occasionally perceptible, usually at the behest of the Americans. For example, in the *Sunday Telegraph* of 29 September 1996 ('Code-breakers come clean'), Professor Christopher Andrew publicised a forthcoming Washington conference with the Russians on the 'Venona' papers. These were transcripts of intercepted and decrypted Soviet intelligence communications between Moscow and its 'residences' in the West. Pulvertaft questioned the Agencies on this apparent change of policy, and learned Venona was a one-off exception to the rule that nothing after VJ Day should be released (but that this rule was being reviewed as increasingly difficult to sustain); 'sensitive' names had been edited out of what was being released outside Russia. Another indicator of change was the establishment in January 1997 of a Corporate Communications Unit at GCHQ.

In October 1996, Channel 4 News transmitted an item about the recent bombing of Thiepval Barracks in Lisburn, which included a map of the site and showed the location of one of the damaged buildings, described (reasonably accurately by a former soldier on the programme) as a 'Covert Operations Building: one of the most sensitive buildings in Northern Ireland in which much of the secret signals surveillance work is controlled'. Pulvertaft contacted Channel 4, to suggest that if broadcasting any more on the story they should discuss it with him first. It transpired Channel 4 had considered the security implications, decided they would not be telling the IRA anything it did not already know, and considered the damage was anyway such that new arrangements would immediately have to be made. Pulvertaft agreed the logic, but pointed out not all the several terrorist groups had equally good intelligence.[135]

In late October, Pulvertaft heard that a freelance journalist was offering the *Sunday Telegraph* a story about a recent meeting of the SAS Association Hereford Branch, at which the CO (name already published twice in the past year) had briefed on the new disclosure rules and contractual requirements on duty of confidence. The article was to include that 40 veterans had been banned from the Hereford base and from reunions, and that General de la Billiere[136] was being replaced as President of the Association, because he had himself written a book about his service. The Secretary rang the editor of the paper, Dominic Lawson,[137] who agreed not to give even wider publicity to the CO's name. A few months later the same paper acquired a copy of the Hereford Branch's newsletter, which included the names of some current and former members of the SAS; Lawson again accepted advice not to publish these names, and Regiment and Association tightened up on such documents as newsletters.[138] The flood of SF leaks, books, serialisations and broadcasts nevertheless continued.

Litigation Avoidance, and the Crown Jewels

Before the 6 November 1996 DPBAC meeting, the Vice-Chairman wrote to Ayre about the latter's wish to strengthen the convention that media information disclosed to officials solely by the D-Notice Secretary in the course of consultation could not be used as the basis for governmental litigation. Stuart reminded that 'The question raises the situation that we are damned if we do and damned if we don't'; and that the last time officials had said they could not guarantee never to litigate in these circumstances, the Media had said that, if it happened, it would be the end of the Committee. 'From that stand-off both sides then withdrew and the matter went away – for the time being.'[139] When the DPBAC met, Stuart himself raised this convention; 'As confidentiality was the rock on which the system was based, it should be recognised that, if such action were ever taken, it could well wreck the ship'. After discussion, Mottram summed up as Chairman that it was 'not for the Committee to make judgements in such matters. The Official side could never give a guarantee not to take legal action but the report had resulted in a useful exchange on these important principles'. And there once again it rested. And the convention has yet (2008) to be breached.

Pulvertaft then introduced a short paper on whether to set up a DPBAC internet site, assessing the pros and cons: whether the public accessibility would outweigh 'the potential for misunderstandings or misrepresentation on an international scale'; whether to include a whole set of Notices or some abbreviated information; and whether to list it on the MoD's existing new site or separately. The Media side was enthusiastic about taking advantage of this developing channel of communication as a demonstration of the DPBAC's openness, with the full Notices included, but with only a reduced version of the Introduction, and with a 'cordon sanitaire' around the Secretary's telephone numbers. Mottram preferred it to be 'detached from the MoD if that did not incur too many costs'; it was agreed Pulvertaft should proceed accordingly, with review after a year.[140]

In early December 1996, 'Nigel West' passed to Pulvertaft the first draft manuscript of his new book 'The Crown Jewels: The British Secret Agents at the Heart of the KGB Archives'. This was based almost entirely on Soviet files recently released by the Russians to selected Western historians under contract to Random House, and was to include copies of manuscripts and photographs of original documents. Pulvertaft, who had recently cleared West's 'The Secret War for the Falklands', organised scrutiny by SIS and Security Service experts, who were understandably nervous about unwelcome exposure of much old washing. He and his contacts (including in the Treasury Solicitor's Department) did an enormous amount of work checking names and operations, to see what details might still require protection, not from the Russians, but possibly from others. Of great concern was the impact which publication might have on the confidence of current and future agents that their identity would not eventually be compromised. Officials even considered whether Crown Copyright (of which Allason believed wrongly there was a 50-year cut-off) could be claimed on British documents passed by spies over the years to the Soviets. Also considered was some senior official such as the Cabinet Secretary intervening with West, something which Pulvertaft felt not only unlikely to be effective, but would also send confusing messages about the role of the DPBAC.

After several meetings co-ordinated by the Cabinet Office, which Pulvertaft or Ponsonby attended in an advisory capacity (fortunately, because it enabled them to restrain officials from making impractical decisions vis-à-vis the DPBAC), it was concluded that the only course likely not to be counterproductive, was to continue to use the D-Notice System. The Secretary saw that application of DA-Notice No.6 to material in the possession of the Russians was going to be problematical, but, as was customary, he provided Allason with a list of names and other details believed by the experts not to have previously been published; he acknowledged that deletion of some of them could only be requested to meet the preferences of the secret Agencies, rather than because they were covered by the DA-Notice.

In this he was right, because when he briefed the DPBAC at its spring meeting about the ongoing negotiations, the Media side firmly decided that disclosure of names known to the Russians and now to historians could not be said to damage national security, and that any recruiting difficulties thus caused were an administrative matter for the secret Agencies and not a DPBAC responsibility. They added that these Agencies could not be blamed for (indeed had resisted) revealing the names. The Official side agreed, and Pulvertaft was directed to amend his advice to Allason accordingly, although they had no objection to his continuing to pass on the Agencies' concerns to the author. After the meeting, moreover, the Secretary learned that the deal between the Russians and Random House included that, once the four contracted historians had published their respective books, the material would be available openly to all other historians [the deal then fell apart, but was replaced by an arrangement even more open to other historians].

This left Pulvertaft only to advise omission of the very few names in West's manuscript which did not appear in the Russian material. West accepted this, and requested agreement to mention in the book this co-operation with the D-Notice System, as a demonstration of his responsible attitude as an author. There had been many interesting aspects in this case, including the active role of the Committee as the provider of agreed guidance, the international dimension of secrecy and the public domain, and, of course, the extent of the treachery revealed. The book was duly published in spring 1998, the Secretary also being involved in serialisation by the *Daily Telegraph*; West warned Pulvertaft he was already working on his next tome, 'Venona'.[141]

In mid-December 1996, the *Evening Standard* sought advice about reporting publication in the latest *Lobster* magazine (editor Stephen Dorril) of a Confidential page from the SIS telephone directory. Pulvertaft advised the paper not to re-publish it, especially as some of those named were now in vulnerable posts abroad, and this advice was accepted. At least one of those so vulnerable was himself a subscriber to *Lobster*, and it is a matter of whimsical conjecture as to what degree the circulation of the magazine was sustained by members of its target institutions.[142]

In late January 1997, UK counter-terrorism authorities raised with their American counterparts British concerns about disclosure, 'outside the jurisdiction', of information useful to terrorists; they suggested a multilateral convention or bilateral agreements as a possible way forward. The Americans at the time, while acknowledging the problem, did not favour either of these courses, as they could not be effective, would probably offend against the US First Amendment on freedom of speech, and be against the more liberal US approach to freedom of information in general. The D-Notice Secretary was informed afterwards of these talks, because UK officials concluded that therefore the only course was to maximise efforts to persuade publishers and authors 'to refrain from publishing material which we can convincingly argue would be of significant value to terrorists. We have, of course, had some success on this front [through the D-Notice System] though, if persuasion fails, we have no ultimate sanction.'[143]

When Pulvertaft took stock of books or programmes about Special Forces in the pipeline in early 1997, he found 25. An upward trend was novels by ex-SF soldiers, of varying literary quality, but nevertheless requiring at least an enquiry as to the inclusion of still current techniques. Conversely, there was a dwindling number of books about the secret Agencies.[144] The British Board of Film Classification has not been a frequent recipient of D-Notice advice, but in February 1997 Pulvertaft did remind them of his availability. This followed the Board's clearance of a commercial production video 'SAS Weapons and Training' made with the help of members of the Regiment and its Reserves, and including how a sniper stalks and kills a target, and how to kill in unarmed combat. There was in fact no security implication, but when the MoD saw the video it passed it smartly to the Home Office to check whether it contravened any guidelines on violence (by civilians).[145]

In March 1997, the press carried a number of stories about SF operations in Albania, for example the rescues of a British aid worker and of 29 children from an orphanage. In these cases the soldiers concerned had been entirely open about their being SF, and content for their benevolent actions to be reported on (and in one case assisted by) the UK Media in theatre. HQ DSF did not seem averse to this publicity, and, because no identities or techniques were compromised, Pulvertaft did not need in any way to intervene, except to tease MoD officials about apparent inconsistencies in its SF Information Policy. Although the secret Agencies and Special Forces have continued normally to deal themselves with ex-members who wished to publish something, there have been occasions when they have asked the D-Notice Secretary to lead, sometimes to maintain distance in lesser but potentially difficult cases, sometimes because believing he will be more effective with a particular publisher/author/editor.[146]

The Secretaryship

As an endpiece to the History so far, it is worth recording the system by which D-Notice Secretaries are selected. This was then and is still that, on behalf of the Chairman, the MoD Personnel Department carries out a trawl of senior people at around retirement from the Armed Services and Civil Service, by advertisement and by approach to their appointing authorities. The attributes sought, rather than a background in Intelligence or experience of working with the Media are: possession of the necessary high security clearances (no more Lohans), wide experience of the governmental machine, the stature (ie rank) to gain rapid access at all levels, some evidence however faint of intellect and good judgement, an independent nature, being retired and therefore having no ambition for further promotion or award, and having the ability to get on with all kinds of people.

The Media side have always resisted the suggestion that a candidate might be found from within the Media, partly on the basis that, even when security cleared, an ex-journalist would not have the full trust of officials (this has not stopped a trickle of media poachers becoming gamekeepers in the MoD and other Press organisations), but mainly on the basis that nobody in the Media would trust him or her to be impartial with all parts of the Media other than former employers. The Media side also harbour instincts that an ex-civil servant as Secretary, for reasons of different residual loyalty, would suffer from a similar defect.

From the few volunteers to continue to live in or close to London and to work mainly in Whitehall, for a more modest salary than that to which they had become accustomed, and to be accessible to officials and media 24/365, a (very) short list is produced. The Chairman and Vice-Chairman then interview each aspirant, and recommend their choice to the Committee, who unanimously agree it. He (so far no shes) is then employed for three years as a temporary civil servant, with the option of a further two (Pulvertaft and Ponsonby did longer for reasons connected with the timing of the FoI Act and the D-Notice Review). The Secretary is possibly the only middle-ranking full-time civil servant not answerable ultimately to any Minister, although he is of course somewhat and sometimes constrained by his terms of temporary employment by the Civil Service, and by the OSA. Through the Chairman and Vice-Chairman, he is responsible equally to both sides of the Committee.[147]

59

QUO VADIT?

The D-Notice System 'works because it works'.
BBC Written evidence to House of Commons
Defence Committee, June 1980[148]

For the past century, the D-Notice System has emerged, evolved and survived in response to the symbiotic and vigorous activities of the UK governmental machine and of the Media, in the field of national security. In this field, it remains the only forum in which senior officials and senior media representatives regularly and robustly eyeball each other, and, usually, come to some agreement over the conflicting aspects of the public interest. The context has been shaped by international events, and by political perception of the country's place in the world, and national priorities; the latter two categories have changed through the century, and continue to do so, as does the media context.

Although this History must end pro tem in 1997, the years since have seen major changes which continue to affect how the D-Notice System evolves and is used. These include, in the security context for example, the probable end of terrorism related to Northern Ireland, the operations in Bosnia, East Timor and Sierra Leone, '9/11', Islamist terrorism, Afghanistan and the second Iraq war. In the media context, there has been the exponential use of the internet and the surges in the electronic media and in international rolling news. The DPBAC has revised its Notices post-Cold War and is adapting them further to the current national security and media environments. Since 2000, its website has given it too an openness quite unlike its practices of even twenty years ago.

As late as the mid-60s, 'the Press was generally British with British readers, news agencies were PA and Reuters with their bases in London, TV and radio meant the BBC and the latecomer ITV, and communication was mostly by cable and teleprinter. Now the British Press has a greater circulation worldwide through its websites than it has readers at home, overseas titles are easily read here, the agencies are worldwide in every sense, the broadcasting media have exploded, and global communication is just about instantaneous for live broadcast or immediate print. It is certain that the old Notices, with all their multiplicity of detail, could not have survived in this climate. References to information 'already in the public domain' take on a different meaning.'[149]

Despite its imperfections, the D-Notice System has survived through all the changes because it is flexible, intelligent, and suited to the needs of both sides. Despite the many reviews, neither side has so far favoured abolition, nor had any credible suggestion for any other alternative. Indeed both sides have feared any alternative would in practice be worse.

It is hard, but not impossible, to envisage a future time when the dangers to national interests, and to those of the UK's then allies, will be perceived to be dominated mainly by international social, economic and environmental threats, rather than by national security threats as customarily understood. In such circumstances, the traditional prominence of armed forces, secret intelligence organisations and linked diplomacy might reduce in the Media interest to the point where the D-Notice System would wither away.

Conversely, it is not impossible to envisage the struggle against terrorism, at home and abroad, continuing for many decades; nor is it hard to envisage some future interruption by force majeure of the flow of natural resources and trade on which Britain's life and livelihood depend. The higher possibility therefore is that, at least for some decades, a context will continue in which the D-Notice System is considered by the governmental machine and the Media as valid, useful, and preferable to greater use of litigation.

Certain common threads reflected in this History are likely to remain relevant, one being that, in such a delicately balanced grey area, things will occasionally go less than easily if the calibre/performance of the Official or Media Committee Members, or of the D-Notice Secretary, is inadequate. The principal thread of continuity, however, will remain the conflict between the two aspects of the public interest: the right and duty of the Media to report what is being done in the public's name, against the right and duty of an elected Government to conceal pro tem certain details of activities being undertaken for the protection of the public.

This conflict translates into practical matters for the two sides of the DPBAC to resolve by negotiation. At the time of writing these seem likely to continue to include:

- Refinement of the standing DA-Notices, in order better to alert editors/publishers to details potentially damaging to national security, in times of changing threats, without making the guidance so all-embracing as to hinder legitimate information and debate;
- Disagreements over where the line should be drawn on publicising borderline areas such as the intelligence/security/police interface and UKSF matters;
- Adaptation on restrictions on endangering disclosure in the UK Media, in the light of the impact of 'globalisation' and of rapidly changing international communications technology and culture;
- Reflecting concerns of the Media and public (and indirectly Parliament) over the surveillance and wider legal and other restrictions, imposed by governments primarily to counter terrorism or other threats, but with spin-offs into other aspects of day-to-day life.

Such D-Notice Committee trends have their roots in the past, and their newer branches in the mists of the future. This History has attempted to give wider understanding to the public of 'their' uniquely British and pragmatically useful institution; to give those involved in using the System, officials and media, currently and in the future, better understanding of why and how the System works; and to give historians and aficionados of history more pointers to the clanking, grinding interfaces between and within the Governmental and Media machines.

APPENDICES

Appendix 1

EXAMPLES OF WWI D-NOTICES AND SECRET LETTERS TO EDITORS

Issued through the AWOPC from start of First
World War until closure of Press Bureau 30/4/19

Notes: Author's categorisation below thus grouped in order to give an idea of the range of the different areas of governmental concern (many could be listed under more than one heading). SL = Secret/Confidential Letter/Memorandum to editors (TNA:PRO HO 139/39 (SL) and HO 139/43 et seq (Notices)).

The 'D' before the serial number did not then denote 'Defence'; it was merely an alphabetical category adopted by the Press Bureau/Ministry of Information for this particular type of communication; there were also, for example, far more numerous B&C serials covering detailed government communications to the public on administrative, safety, and technical matters amongst many others. The first reference to D serials as 'D Notices' occurs in PA Manager's Memoranda Vol 9 (late January 1915).

D-Notices 1–58 appear to have been numbered retrospectively, perhaps as the realisation dawned this was going to be a longer war than first anticipated, and that there would be a greater profusion of Notices than the (unnumbered) peacetime system had hitherto had to contend with. The date of issue of some Notices is uncertain. There was a separate series of Irish D-Notices, some shown below, which continued well into 1919 (TNA:PRO HO 139/47). Many Notices *not* listed below were cancellations/amendments of previous Notices, or repetitions of previous prohibitions. Press Bureau (PB) communications were usually marked with the security warning: 'Notice to the Press. Private and Confidential. Not for Publication or Communication.'

Administrative/PB/AWOPC

D12(?) – 28/8/14 – Rules for cable censorship: outgoing processed by Central Telegraph Office (CTO), incoming rerouted by Cable Companies through CTO.

D26 – 8/9/14 – New regulations for handling of cables because of delays caused by 120 inexperienced staff: Press and public cables separated, former handled by extra Press Cable Censorship Committee at PB.

D27 – 9/9/14 – Beware repeating (often false) information from German sources.

D37 – 16/9/14 – Do not publish contents of Defence Notices.

D40 – 16/9/14 – Take care publishing reports of German atrocities, in case unfounded, which would weaken force of other adverse reports about German activities.

D95 – 10/11/14 – Letter from CinC BEF (French), to Buckmaster of PB, complaining about reports (via Denmark) of use by Germany of British Press reports of operations/intentions.

D153 – 11/2/15 – For captions to photographs, Press to use only those already approved by Censors. [Year later, C-serial notice forbade publication all new 'picture postcards and cigarette stiffeners of a naval or military nature', caused immediate query from Newcastle retailer as to whether postcards of (now partially fortified) City were forbidden].

D187 – 16/3/15 – New arrangements for issuing casualty lists –delay of 24 hours imposed in order Provincial Press receive their copy by post, 'so saving postal telegraphists much unnecessary work'.

D190 – 26/3/15 – Because of overload on General Post Office and distribution problems at Front, caused by the public response to 'Lonely Soldier' advertisements in Press by sending letters/parcels, do not publish such advertisements.

D202 – 17/4/15 – Do not publish advertisements asking soldiers on active service to state Brigade/Division when ordering products.

D279 – 24/9/15 – Reminder about publication of indiscreet articles, letters and pictures/ photographs. Comment on difficulties of system of voluntary censorship, and failure by some provincial papers always to submit material to censors. Potential damaging effects on security and morale in particular of publication of Order of Battle [details of British formations], narratives of incidents, and results of enemy action.

D292 – 19/10/15 – Do not publish secret information being offered by disaffected dismissed South African employee of War Office.

SL – 17/12/15 – From 20 December 1915 censorship by PB on behalf of Foreign Office suspended. Reminder to refrain from publishing anything 'prejudicial to His Majesty's relations with Foreign Powers or to the public interest'; to exercise caution over Greece and Rumania; to mention nothing about China's alleged intention to ally herself to Entente Powers and break with Germany; care to be taken over Monarchical question in China, and policy of Chinese and Japanese Governments in this respect; no currency to unfounded reports of Japanese offer to send troops to Europe; and nothing about Caliphate.

D420 – 3/7/16 – Warning to Press to differentiate in articles between information from official communiqués and information from correspondents in theatre, with threat of curtailment of those offending against this distinction.

D422 – 8/7/16 – Extract from Army Orders about prohibition on Army personnel and others subject to military law (including war correspondents) on sending back photographs or films, and on possessing a camera without authorisation, with warning not to advertise for such photographs.

D486 – 13/11/16 – Do not publish letters or advertisements inviting officers/men to correspond with 'strangers'.

SL – 22/2/17 – Complaint about publication in mainstream British Press of extracts from journal *Labour Leader*, which have afforded material for enemy propaganda. Export of the journal now prohibited, no quotations from it should be made.

D542 – 23/2/17 – Do not, in publication, anticipate Royal Commission Reports, for example on Dardanelles Expedition.

SL – 31/5/17 – Report by Swettenham and Cook to Government Departments. To date 564 Notices issued, with few leaks except to Members of Parliament. However, on 26 May, Admiralty and FO warned Press about not publishing details of movements of Balfour and his mission, yet next day *Star* disclosed the details of Notice in leading article. Swettenham and Cook therefore consider it undesirable in future to issue similar 'instructions' unless without danger should details be revealed.

D578 – 6/8/17 – Referring to US Government concerns about reports in UK Press about US troop and ship movements, reminder same rules apply as to British forces.

D584 – 30/8/17 – Referring to new US Government regulations for voluntary censorship issued 30 July, 'it is hoped that Editors of British journals and American correspondents in the United Kingdom will observe these instructions in dealing with all the matters covered by the Regulations' [American regulations were very similar to British regulations].

SL – 17/11/17 – Request not to publish extracts from foreign publications with passages blanked out for censorship reasons, because Germans will buy the foreign publications to see what has been censored.

Military

D3/4 – 17/8/14 – SofS for War, Kitchener, wishes Press within PB to be given complete statement of BEF, but requests no public identification of units, nor anything about post-disembarkation movements, nor those of its CinC after his initial reception in Paris.

D7 – 20/8/14 – No mention of operations around Brussels nor of enemy entry into city (D8 withdrew this Notice same day, presumably because such publication would not tell the Germans anything they did not already know!).

D15 – 28/8/14 – Permissible now to mention regimental unit names in reports on individuals, but not to identify Brigades or above (i.e. Divisions, Corps, Armies, Army Groups).

D28 – 9/9/14 – Do not mention arrival of colonial or Indian troops in Europe.

D36 – 15/9/14 – Admonition of newspapers who have published photographs of Grenadier Guards marching 'on their way to the Front'.

D48 – 24/9/14 – Imposes restrictions on reporting operations within five days, and from within 20 miles of the Front, or reports which suggest that correspondent has been at Front, in breach of current rules.

D108 – 3/12/14 – Do not publish anything about experiments with incendiary bombs at mouth of River Ore, Suffolk.

D110 – 4/12/14 – Relaxations on reporting, e.g. composition of BEF now in public domain, exploits of individual units may be reported after 14 days, individual gallantry may be reported immediately (but not details such as location), but still nothing to be published on movements, strengths, etc.

D137 – 22/1/15 – Publish nothing about the strength and date of deployment of New Armies.

D149 – 3/2/15 – Publish nothing about movements etc of troops to Egypt now it has become 'part of the British theatre of war'.

D158 – 20/2/15 – Avoid publishing any parts of statements by returning British prisoners of war which include adverse criticism of their treatment by the Germans, even if true, because of possible effect on remaining prisoners of war in their hands; 'their lot would almost certainly be made more uncomfortable'.

D163 – 24/2/15 – Refrain from publishing descriptions of enemy fire against Allied aircraft or its results, because this information useful to enemy; similarly do not describe effects of shellfire on British positions.

D169 – 26/2/15 – Do not mention stoppage of all leave in the British Expeditionary Force from 1 March.

D212 – 20/5/15 – Advice against publishing details of British soldiers escaping from captivity in Belgium.

D215 – 29/5/15 – In obituaries, do not report place of death in action until at least 30 days afterwards.

SL – 14/6/15 – Request to exercise restraint in reporting operations in the Dardanelles.

D231 – 15/6/15 – Reiteration of avoiding adverse comment on treatment of British soldiers in German prisoner of war camps, sparked by letter forwarded by Private Secretary to King from Mr Harte, American YMCA representative in Germany [not named in D-Notice, for fear he would not be allowed to return by Germans to his POW camp-visiting duties].

SL – 24/8/15 – Private and confidential information to Press about strengths and casualties of German Army.

D268 – 2/9/15 – Do not mention new Royal Engineers units of Miners/Tunnellers being formed, nor German 'Fire Squirters', and do not publish aerial photographs of either side of Front Line.

SL – 8/9/15 – Explanation of reasons for delays in transporting sandbags to France, i.e. mainly shelling by Germans (62 million sandbags have already been sent, and further five million a week en route).

D330 – 15/12/15 – Reminder not to mention details of higher military formations in such places as Rolls of Honour [another recurring type of Notice].

D356 – 7/2/16 – Publish nothing about 'any novel kind of fighting machine' [first operational test of a tank had taken place in September 1915].

SL – 6/3/16 – Request not to be over-optimistic in reporting siege of Kut (Iraq), to avoid holding out undue hopes to public. [Siege by Turks of British and Indian troops started 7/12/15, ended in surrender of latter on 29/4/16].

D419 – 26/6/16 – Reiteration of D158, sparked by letter written 8/2/16 by Captain Beckett of E Surrey Regiment, himself prisoner of war held in camp near Cologne, in which he corrected report in *Sketch* about German maltreatment of prisoners, including untrue allegation that Private of his Regiment had been used as shield above German trench; the letter had reached Britain via US Embassy in Berlin.

SL – 4/10/16 – Request not to refer to Therapeutic Radio treatment now being used in the British Army.

D546 – 27/2/17 – No mention of Royal Engineers' work on Inland Water Transport at Richborough, Sandwich, 'operations of considerable military importance'.

D556 – 15/4/17 – Do not report Haig's Special Order of Day of 12 April praising troops who took part in Arras victory (because Order mentions units involved).

D567 – 11/6/17 – When publishing photographs of regimental groups in France, omit names of officers (because useful to enemy intelligence). [This Notice led to many queries from 'illustrated papers', and War Office issued supplementary guidance, including: 'In groups taken in hospitals, the names of Officers may be mentioned'; and 'The case of theatrical parties generally, including "pierrots" is more difficult,' because 'a theatrical group might include so many Officers as to become almost a regimental group', so such photographs must be submitted to PB (TNA: PRO HO 139/42).]

D614 – 11/1/18 – Do not mention names of officers involved in unofficial gallantry stories, because this creates resentment amongst others, and often omits those involved in equally important and dangerous work, e.g. artillery spotting, aerial/photographic reconnaissance, etc.

D620 – 2/2/18 – Because document containing British Order of Battle fallen into enemy hands, rules relaxed on publishing unit names etc; now acceptable to mention Battalion numbers and higher tactical units [i.e. Brigades, Divisions, Corps] operating up to 30 November 1917 on Western Front.

D719 – 8/10/18 – Relaxations on reporting Battalion Numbers and In Memoriams on the 'Western Front (France and Flanders only)'.

D722 – 22/10/18 – Relaxations on reporting as in D719 above extended to the Middle East, Italy, Greece, and East Africa.

D742 – 13/2/19 – Restrictions lifted on non-official photographs on the Western Front.

Naval

D2 & D6 – ?/8/14 – No details without the Censors' permission of stopping or searching of British merchant vessels by enemy armed merchant cruisers: gives useful information to enemy about position of his own ships, causes unnecessary alarm amongst shippers/ passengers.

D10 – 25/8/14 – No mention of Admiralty-imposed restrictions on movements of fishing vessels ('especially by East Coast and Scotch newspapers').

D11 – 26/8/14 – No details of departures of British vessels from home/foreign ports, unless advertised by owners.

D13 – 27/8/14 – No mention of sinking of British merchant vessels or trawlers, nor of use of some trawlers for minesweeping.

D14 – 28/8/14 – Publish nothing about the latest HM Ships [sparked by patriotic but over-informative article in *The Engineer*, and led to tightening up on distribution of 'Parkers' to magazines, from *Aeroplane* through numerous other military and technical journals such as *Inventors' Journal*, but also others like *Ladies Field and Country Life* and *Windsor*.]

D25 – 7/9/14 – No mention the position of any naval 'occurrence', e.g. as previously reported, recent loss of *HMS PATHFINDER* off St Abb's Head. And later, no mention *HMS PATHFINDER* sunk by submarine (cancelled next day, when learned that German submarine concerned had returned safely to base).

D38 – 16/9/14 – Until further notice no mention of activities of German cruiser *EMDEN* [then pursuing successful campaign against Allied commerce in Indian Ocean and SE Asian waters, but destroyed by Australian cruiser *HMAS SYDNEY* two months later].

D59 – 2/10/14 – [The first Notice numbered ab initio] No mention of new Notices to Mariners, buoys, lights, etc.

D71 – 11/10/14 – No mention operations of our submarines or destruction of enemy submarines.

D109 – 3/12/14 – Request from Churchill not to report, after naval actions, whether *HMS AUDACIOUS*, or other damaged ships, were subsequently lost or were under repair.

D116 – 9/12/14 – No mention of Admiralty Armoured Cars [this referred to equipment of Naval Brigade fighting as infantry and in particular those guarding Royal Naval Air Service airfields in Belgium, rather than to official cars of Admirals; use of these armoured vehicles led in due course to the interest taken by Churchill, Hankey and Lloyd George in ideas of Colonel Swinton concerning introduction of early tanks].

D117 – 16/12/14 – In reporting gunnery attack by German naval raiding force that morning on East Coast towns (in particular Scarborough and Hartlepool), no details of enemy, nor of damage to own forces, nor of panic locally.

D128 – 11/1/15 – No mention of the escape by certain interned naval officers from Holland, to avoid embarrassment to relations with Dutch Government.

D131 – 14/1/15 – Do not refer to Neutral vessels detained by Royal Navy as 'Prizes' or 'Captures'.

D150 – 3/2/15 – No mention of sighting of enemy submarines in British waters, nor articles speculating how best to deal with them 'as if correct they will give valuable information to the enemy' [German submarine blockade of Britain and her trade routes started in earnest at about this time].

D156 – 18/2/15 – Admiralty requests no mention of any temporary suspension of cross-Channel shipping/ferry services nor any alterations in sailing times.

D161 – 23/2/15 – No mention British merchant ships using neutral flags.

D168 – 25/2/15 – Admiralty gives additional reason for publishing only official reports of losses of British merchant ships to mines and submarines in English and Irish Channels and other coastal waters: owners will hesitate to risk vessels, and 'seamen will almost certainly demand greatly increased rates of pay . . . no doubt one of the principal objects aimed at by the enemy'.

D170 – 28/2/15 – Prohibition in D150 withdrawn, but Admiralty reminds Press 'obviously undesirable to create an impression that the waters round our coasts are swarming with submarines'.

D179 – 10/3/15 – No reference to be made to movements of Allied Cable Ships, nor to cable landing places, routes or breakdowns.

D185 – 16/3/15 – One of several Admiralty requests to avoid highlighting German successes against British and Allied merchant ships.

D223 – 6/6/15 – No mention of use of British 'mercantile auxiliaries' [unarmed merchant ships disguised to look like battle cruisers].

SL – ?/7/15 – No details of HM Ships in *Jane's* and similar publications, and sales of second-hand volumes forbidden, until end of the War.

D276 – 18/9/15 – Relaxation of prohibition on publishing Notices to Mariners, but no comment to be made on them, and not to be collected/published en bloc.

D297 – 25/10/15 – Advance warning and Admiralty explanation of imminent abrogation by Britain of Article 57 of the Declaration of London (by which flag flown by merchant ship was sole test of nationality); this because Germans sometimes using flags of Neutral countries on their ships.

D313 – 19/11/15 – No publication of statements by survivors of ships sunk by enemy unless cleared by PB.

D332 – 21/12/15 – Do not reveal how troops successfully evacuated from ANZAC Beach and Sulva Bay previous day.

D337 – 3/1/16 – No mention of civilians (including women and children) onboard *HMS NATAL* at time of explosion [30/12/15 in Cromarty harbour; fire caused an explosion in magazine, sank almost immediately, with loss of well over 400 lives, including family visitors].

D394 – 28/4/16 – No mention of fishing areas newly prohibited by the Admiralty.

D400 – 11/5/16 – Do give prominence to attacks by German/Austrian submarines on merchant ships sunk without warning [issued after Exchange of Notes with still neutral US Government].

D418 – 29/6/16 – Temporary restriction on reporting movements of Admiral Jellicoe 'or any officers of the Grand Fleet'.

SL – 6/7/16 – No publication of 'anything which would give the enemy ground for inferring that differences of opinion exist amongst Naval officers in regard to the conduct of the battle' [of Jutland].

D488 – 17/11/16 – Publish nothing about landing of fish (where, by whom, whether by neutrals, quantities, etc).

D531A – 2/2/17 – Reminder no publication of holding neutral ships in British ports, or any other measure taken in UK in consequence German submarine blockade (Germans started unrestricted submarine warfare previous day, sank about 230 merchant ships this month).

SL – 14/2/17 – No emphasis of losses of German submarines, as neutrals may believe danger greater than it is, causing 'blockade by terror' of UK.

D538 – 18/2/17 – No mention of distribution of Prize Money from destruction of German cruiser *DRESDEN.*

D539 – 18/2/17 – Nothing more on *News of the World* story 'purporting to describe the destruction of an enemy submarine by a trawler patrol boat'. [Headlines and straplines of the eight page 1d issue give flavour of times: 'PATROL DESTROYS U-BOAT. PIRATE CAUGHT AT ITS DASTARD WORK. GALLANT SEA FIGHT. THRILLING STORY OF ACTION IN THE DAWN'].

SL – 20/2/17 – Warning of Order-in-Council to be issued 21 February, laying down that neutral ships carrying goods of enemy origin or destination would be 'liable to condemnation' unless they called at appointed British or Allied port for examination. Concern that neutrals, especially the USA, might regard this as 'British Navalism'. Hope therefore Press treat this change as 'a matter of everyday work' and refrain from giving it 'undue prominence'.

D557 – 1/5/17 – No mention yet of possible presence of US Navy ships in British waters [USA had declared war on Germany 6 April 1917].

D572 – 7/7/17 – Publish nothing about experimental painting of merchant ships to make attacks by enemy submarines more difficult.

D625 – 12/2/18 – No reference requisition by Admiralty of Liverpool ferry boats 'for a very special and secret purpose'[cancelled by D665 (24/4/18), with thanks from the Admiralty for Press co-operation in not mentioning; although PB did not mention where the ferries had been used, Admiralty request for Notice clearly for raid on Zeebrugge 22/23 April].

D628 – 12/2/18 – Amendment to earlier Notice issued that day on last and heroic/foolhardy action by Torpedo Boat Destroyer *HMS MARY ROSE*, deleting intemperate comment by censor on 'the Naval critics [in the Press], with whose assistance we are wont to belittle the achievements of our Navy'.

D629 – 13/2/18 – Acceptable now to submit U-boat stories to PB, if over six months old.

D664 – 24/4/18 – Acceptable now to mention that US Navy ships are in European waters, but not to say which nor where.

D684 – 21/6/18 – Request not to exaggerate the German Submarine Cruiser threat, because of the impact on Merchant Navy morale.

Air

D51 – 25/9/14 – Publish nothing about 'alleged dropping of a bomb on [neutral] Dutch territory by an English aviator'.

D252 – 30/7/15 – No mention of confidential details from inquest into two deaths at the Airship Shed.

D346 – 18/1/16 – No mention of names of naval and military officers who obtain Aero Club certificates, so Germans cannot calculate number of pilots in pipeline.

D570 – 28/6/17 – No mention of impending reorganisation of Royal Flying Corps.

D592 – 14/9/17 – Refer to PB any German reports of British aircraft going down behind German lines, because not always accurate and sometimes first that relatives hear about it.

D606 – 21/11/17 – No unnecessary prominence to flying accidents, because detrimental to recruiting to Royal Flying Corps; percentage of flying accidents not increased perceptibly despite great increase in number of pilots training. '1/1/17 to 8/11/17 . . . 298 fatal accidents during training; the distance flown was 37,270,000 miles; that is one death for each 125,067 miles flown, which is equivalent to five flights around the world'.

D616 – 17/1/18 – No reports of German pilots dropping messages to our Forces about wellbeing of captured Allied airmen, because this unauthorised (by Germans), so source of information might be closed off.

D627 – 12/2/18 – Amending recent Notice (609) which reminded about not publishing details of new Air equipment: for 'bombing machines' read 'aircraft'.

D649 – 30/3/18 – No mention that a Squadron Commander escaped from German prisoner of war camp was previously prisoner of Turks.

D669 – 13/5/18 – Do not report or speculate on precise duties now assigned to General Tranchard [sic]. [He (Trenchard) had become first head of the Royal Air Force, which had been established on 1 April 1918, as announced in House of Commons 13 May].

SL – 17/5/18 – Air Ministry request no reproduction of 15 April article on new aircraft in American journal *Aerial Age Weekly*.

Spies, Security & Intelligence

D70 – 11/10/14 – Reference reports of 'hostile aircraft operating in Scotland', military authorities offering reward of £100 for information leading to discovery of any places in Scotland being used to store oil or petrol. Poster to be published locally, but do not mention it in Press.

D92 – 6/11/14 – Until further notice no mention of spy Lody shot this morning. 'The sentence of the Court Martial was duly and properly executed'. [This restriction lifted four days later. Karl Lody a German Naval Reserve Lieutenant, entered Britain on false American passport, did some low-level intelligence-gathering in Edinburgh and Liverpool areas, was first wartime spy to be detected (by interception of his mail), arrested in early October en route to Naval Base at Queenstown, Ireland, tried and, having gained admiration of his captors by his patriotic, brave and gentlemanly demeanour, executed by firing squad in Tower of London.]

D119 – 18/12/14 – No publication of interception of German signal traffic.

D167 – 25/2/15 – No mention arrest of Muller. [D197 of 9/4/15 lifted three such spy story prohibitions, but still forbade reporting dates of arrests. Further reminder Notices followed through 1915 about publishing nothing about suspected or arrested spies.]

D204 – 24/4/15 – Clarification of DoRA Clause 18 concerning the collection of sensitive naval and military information: even 'innocent' collection an offence [This draconian interpretation caused such instant consternation it was withdrawn same day, all copies recalled by the PB, even from Government Departments].

D324 – 6/12/15 – No mention of Mrs Lizzie Wertheim, recently convicted for espionage, in connection with imminent Bow Street trial of Dr Bassie, accused of having made false declaration in order for her to obtain British passport [Wertheim, reputedly Berlin prostitute before her marriage to a Briton, died in Broadmoor 1920; her co-conspirator shot in the Tower of London 26 October 1915. TNA: PRO KV 4/112].

SL – 30/6/15 – Name/address of all advertisers to be recorded; advertising managers to consult police confidentially if they suspect advertisements being used by spies or enemy agents; examples given, including 'For sale, a bargain, bankrupt stock of 100,000 boxes cigars now at Tonbridge. Address G957 care of this paper' meaning '100,000 men of specified branch (infantry, cavalry, etc) are quartered at Tonbridge'.

D476 – 11/10/16 – No mention anyone in 'the Secret Service of the Allies'.

D480 – 19/10/16 – Guidance on reporting DoRA prosecution of Joseph King MP; no details to be given of position of depot, nor value or extent of property destroyed.

SL – 25/11/16 – No reference to certain cafes and restaurants considered to be 'German resorts' – Military Authorities intend to take action within next few days.

SL – 13/12/16 – Not for publication, copy of 9-page German questionnaire used by its agents as aide memoire as to what information to seek, circulated by Admiralty as indication to Press of kind of thing that should not be published, for example descriptions of military locations, units, preparations for action, etc, plus advice to agents such as to send small gifts to British troops and claim cost of these out of 'business expenses'.

D532 – 5/2/17 – No publication of 'photographs of Government Agents Booth and Gordon or of any Government Secret Service Official who may give evidence or be present in Court during the hearing of the Conspiracy charge at Derby.'

D571 – 28/6/17 – Refrain from drawing special attention to Commander Gordon Campbell VC in promotions list in *London Gazette* tomorrow (because of secrecy of work on which employed).

D645 – 26/3/18 – No references to Japanese newspaper *Nichi Nichi Shimbun* report of movements of German agents en route Siberia.

Not a D-Notice but filed with them – 11/3/18 – Public Order from Colonel (General Staff) London District, instructing that, without his permission, no photographs to be taken, nor photographic apparatus to be possessed (except in private premises) anywhere in Metropolitan Police District (except Erith, Bexley and Crayford) nor in large areas of Kent, Essex and Surrey contiguous to London.

D670 – 21/5/18 – Request (from 'Admiralty', presumably Secret Intelligence section) not to link USA with information received in UK connecting Sinn Fein with Germany.

D710 – 17/9/18 – Due to 'doubtful authenticity' of some documents issued by the US Department of Information concerning Bolshevik leaders being in pay of German Government, no reference to them at present [Notice withdrawn 17 October, when intelligence confirmed].

Air Raids

D72 – 14/10/14 – Do not mention experimental extinction of lights in various parts of London tonight, scheme connected with Air Department of Admiralty [responsible for UK Air Defence].

D198 – 10/4/15 – Referring to Orders by Home Secretary 10 April under DoRA, concerning reduction in lighting along coast from Northumberland to Dorset, extinction of lights visible from sea along rest of South and West coast, and in certain inland towns, no mention which inland towns.

D205 – 30/4/15 – No mention of details of recent Zeppelin raid over Harwich/Ipswich.

D206 – 5/5/15 – Reiteration detailed prohibitions on reporting details of exact positions and impacts of air raids [one of many such Notices].

D236 – 25/6/15 – No publication of advertisements for commercial anti-Zeppelin 'preventive devices' [i.e. protective equipment] so worded that they increase public panic.

D286 – 16/10/15 – In reporting Zeppelin raids, no mention of names, locations, nor places of London inquests (but official photographs would be available for sale).

D300 – 26/10/15 – No mention part of War Office about to occupy National Portrait Gallery, for fear of becoming Zeppelin target.

D301 – 27/11/15 – No mention of public meeting at Leytonstone to advocate reprisals for recent Zeppelin raids there, because indicate to Germans where bombs fell.

D322 – 6/12/15 – No mention of half National Gallery being put at disposal of Admiralty.

D352 – 2/2/16 – Revised [and slightly more realistic] rules about reporting Air Raids, allowing some unofficial locally-obtained information.

D479 – 18/10/16 – Repromulgation of regulations on reporting Air Raids; more latitude now given but still requiring prior submission to censors and prior issue of official report on raid concerned.

D512 – 5/1/17 – Publish nothing about changes in lighting regulations for London, because be useful to enemy and would 'alarm public opinion'.

D595 – 19/9/17 – No mention if any of those killed in air raids are sailors or soldiers.

D597 – 28/9/17 – Referring to view that public fear of air raids recently increased by reports of overcrowding in underground railways being used as shelters, Commissioner of Police requests Press 'refrain from publishing further articles which may add to the feeling of apprehension which is already prevalent, especially amongst the poorest and most ignorant classes of the people of London'.

D601 – 26/10/17 – 'Whilst reminding the Press of the various instructions which have from time to time been issued in regard to descriptions of air raids, the following explanation of the reasons why restraint is necessary is forwarded to the Press in order to give effect to a resolution passed at a recent meeting of the Admiralty, War Office, and Press Committee' . . . three pages included explanation of difficulties facing a German aviator (who, 'flying by moonlight at a height of over 10,000 feet under heavy gunfire, must always be in some doubt as to his exact whereabouts'), help given to Germans by casualty reports (report of 'night aeroplane raid on Chatham on 3rd/4th August, 1917, [in which] one bomb had killed over one hundred sailors and injured a like number, must have given great encouragement to the enemy'), and: 'Long reports, especially in local papers, should be avoided . . . Nothing should be published to shew either directly or indirectly where bombs were dropped . . . Statements of panic caused by raids, or their bad moral effect on the people, will only encourage the enemy to repeat the raids'.

D637 – 1/3/18 – Referring to Officer Prisoner of War camps about to be established in London and suburbs 'in places specially liable to air raid bombardment', guidance that precise localities should not be known to enemy.

National Morale/Recruiting

D18 – 1/9/14 – In reporting first official Casualty Lists, do not exaggerate British proportion of total Allied casualties ('which are small in relation to the severity of the fighting and to the nature of the operations').

D22 – 4/9/14 – Explanation to Press of what lay behind Lord Kitchener's public appeal for board and lodgings for families of British Expeditionary Force now being removed from Married Quarters at Aldershot and other garrison towns, because of immense influx of recruits into local barracks; considered by Army this made Married Quarters 'no longer suitable' for now unaccompanied wives.

D40 – 18/9/14 – Background to Lord Kitchener's public appeal for 1½ million pairs of blankets for new armies being recruited.

D45 – 18/9/14 – Similar on his appeal for belts and socks too.

D106 – 28/11/14 – No speculation on recommendations for Victoria Cross and other distinctions; can cause needless disappointments and annoyance to individuals, and 'embarrassing enquiries to the Staff of the War Office'.

D135 – 19/1/15 – No publication of advertisement of British Anti-Vivisection Society because 'calculated to deter men from offering to serve in the Nation's Armed Forces at a time when every fit man is needed'.

D183 – 12/3/15 – No exaggeration of British or Allied successes [This Notice caused great offence to Press, who pointed to similar over-optimistic official statements].

D255 – 6/8/15 – Do publish reports of convictions of dependents of soldiers for making false Separation Allowance claims, in order to discourage this increasing practice.

D282 – 30/9/15 – Background to action by Metropolitan Police in attempting to suppress a 'pernicious book', *Socialists and the War*, published in America, and request to Press not to publicise in reviews.

SL – 8/10/15 – Letter from PB to Sir George Riddell (Conference of Newspaper Proprietors, and member of AWOPC) asking Press not to republish pro-German reports by certain American correspondents.

SL – 15/10/15 – Request not to publish contents of Director of Recruiting Lord Derby's letter to every non-starred man of military age [Request withdrawn 21/10/15].

D473 – 9/10/16 – Information about traffic in exemptions by dishonest recruiters.

SL – 25/1/17 – Complaint about publication in Press of justificatory letters from 'gentlemen who have had short periods of service as officers in the Royal Army Medical Corps, and who are, for private reasons, unwilling to serve further ... create the wrong impression amongst the civil community ... the requirements of the civil population for medical attendance have been carefully considered'.

D530 – 1/2/17 – Encouragement to mention Volunteer Forces, including units, because they are not being sent overseas and 'the more the Force is mentioned in the Press the better'.

D537 – 16/2/17 – No reference to additional exemptions being granted by Director General of National Service (Mr Chamberlain) to 'another class of persons'.

D541 – 20/2/17 – No mention of new uses of 'man and woman power of the nation', because premature publication of any plan gives valuable information to enemy (this Notice caused by *Daily Express* story that day: 'Women for the Army in France', for clerical and other departments).

D599 – 4/10/17 – No mention of report by Advisory Committee to Board of Agriculture about growing hostility to farmers amongst urban populations, and about warnings of shortages of beef and milk in 1918, because of low prices fixed for meat, the bad weather and scarcity of labour.

D617 – 20/1/18 – 'The shortage of food supplies is leading to trouble and in some cases to raids on shops. Exaggeration, or even over-zeal, in reporting such cases might easily lead to, or extend the area of, food riots'. Request therefore not to give too much space to such stories, which also encourage the enemy.

D735 – 3/1/19 – Refusal at Folkestone of many troops to return overseas, in particular to France, already reported in evening papers, Press now requested 'to refrain from further reference to the matter', because of impact on morale of those overseas still waiting to come home after being relieved by troops now mutinying.

D742 – 13/2/19 – Restrictions on reporting 'unrest' amongst Royal Army Service Corps mechanised transport repair personnel, because of danger of 'fomenting the general feeling of unrest' (during the 'general strike movement in the country').

Munitions

D258 – 16/8/15 – No mention of anything other than official information about explosions/accidents in munitions factories.

D281 – 24/9/15 – No mention of details of new munitions factories.

D315 – 23/11/15 – No mention of location of power stations increasing their output in order to supply local munitions factories.

D380 – 8/4/16 – Caution about reporting breakdowns in utilities (e.g. because of severe weather) and serious industrial accidents, especially in munitions factories [many Notices along these lines].

D424 – 13/7/16 – Request not to make hostile comment on Belgian refugees working in British munitions factories.

D483 – 1/11/16 – Submit any reports of TNT poisoning in Munitions Factories to PB.

D658 – 15/4/18 – No mention of names and places involved in trials of Hanks Range Finding and Predicting Apparatus.

Economic

D264 – 27/8/15 – Publish nothing other than official announcement about 'financial mission to America' [at request of new Chancellor, Mr McKenna].

D298 – 25/10/15 – Do not repeat false [German inspired?] rumours British bank notes in circulation are forgeries.

SL – 21/1/16 – No mention of purchase of Russian wheat crop.

D382 – 12/4/16 – No mention of Foreign Loans unless HM Treasury authorises publication [similar Notices issued periodically about investment from abroad, dealing in securities at prices below the official minima, etc].

D427 – 22/7/16 – No mention of shipment of bullion and securities.

D452 – 4/9/16 – Reports of Company General Meetings to be cleared with the PB before publication.

SL – 16/10/16 – Plea from Charity Commissioner not to publish appeals for voluntary funds by those individuals/organisations not yet registered under War Charities Act.

D514 – 9/1/17 – Temporary embargo on announcement of Allied agreement on chartering shipping, because international competition pushing up freight prices.

D522 – 23/1/17 – Chancellor of Exchequer 'does not consider it is the national interest for discussion to take place in the Press with reference to proposals for the formation of trust companies or syndicates for the special purpose of investing in the war loan'.

D525 – 27/1/17 – No details of 'stocks of Grain and Flour' unless approved by the Royal Commission.

D526 – 29/1/17 – No 'unauthorised allusions to the subject of rationing of Food', because would cause 'speculative buying on the market and attempts on the part of consumers to accumulate stocks which disturbs prices and prevents even distribution'.

D531 – 1/2/17 – No mention raising of Municipal Loans in the USA (by London, Edinburgh, Glasgow, Manchester, Liverpool and Birmingham).

D535 – 16/2/17 – Guidance on 'gambling operations in produce and other essential commodities' contrary to public interest at present time; Press 'invited' 'to exclude rigorously anything which offers inducements or facilities for such gambling operations'.

D543 – 23/2/17 – No speculation about actual amount subscribed to War Loan.

SL – 1/8/17 – Request to publicise appointment of Belgian Trade Committee, set up to prevent Belgium ever again becoming dependent on German trade and finance, and to assist in development of Belgian commerce with British Empire after the War, 'to their mutual benefit'.

SL – 22/12/17 – Because of reluctance of many neutral ship owners to sail to British and Allied ports, Government decided to requisition forthwith certain neutral ships in British ports, believing that owners/governments concerned unlikely to have 'any great objection to this course'; to be done gradually, so no mention until published in foreign countries.

D629 – 13/2/18 – Reports of tonight's meeting at Institute of Petroleum Technologists to be submitted to PB.

D659 – 15/4/18 – Referring to advertisement for sale of 'Norfolk Farm Lands', guidance that HM Treasury wished to approve such advertisements before issue.

D666 – 24/4/18 – HM Treasury requests no mention of price of Bank of England or Treasury Notes in foreign countries.

D676 – 26/5/18 – Do not publish unauthorised reports about movements and stocks of commodities such as oilseeds, nuts, oils and fat, etc [several similar Notices].

D704 – 4/9/18 – Board of Trade request no mention of [high] shipping insurance rates.

Political/Foreign/Industrial Relations

D33 – 11/9/14 – Avoid reporting anything likely to produce unfavourable impression in Turkey [at that stage of War, British Government still hoped that, despite strong German influence in Turkey, it would remain neutral – remembering perhaps that in 1911 Ottoman Government had secretly proposed alliance with Britain (or that Turkey should become fourth partner to the Triple Entente), turned down then pro tem by Britain on grounds Turkey was at that time at war with Italy, a conflict in which Britain was neutral (TNA: PRO CAB 41/33)].

D34 – 12/9/14 – Request to extol Russian operations in advance on East Prussia and Austria.

D49 – 24/9/14 – Request from Prime Minister not to comment on French generals in command, nor on specific French units.

D83 – 28/10/14 – Request not to publish immediately loss of battleship sunk by a mine previous day because 'it might so seriously affect our foreign relations' [Turkey on brink of deciding whether to join the War on Germany's side, which it did next day].

SL – 30/10/14 – Letter from Foreign Secretary, Sir Edward Grey, complaining about Press articles damaging Britain's relations with neutral countries, e.g. urging Italy to abandon her neutrality, suggesting Holland should lease Zeeland to Belgium, imperilling FO efforts to stop Turkey aligning herself with Germany, and criticising slowness of Russian advance (latter not neutral but Ally).

SL – 17/11/14 – Letter from Buckmaster of PB, encouraging Press to be supportive of France, and to avoid upsetting French sensitivities, especially by saying War will last '2, 3 or more years', that British Army has 'saved France', and of speculating on whether Peace Settlement might restore Alsace and Lorraine to France.

D99 – 19/11/14 – No mention of trouble in the aliens' concentration camp at Douglas, Isle of Man.

D122 – 24/12/14 – No adverse comment on the Caliphate [deleted from D-Notice was the rationale, i.e. that Foreign Office requested great care in discussing questions affecting 'Mohammedan opinion']

SL – FO complaints about damage to Mohammedan opinion, especially in India and Egypt, of Press suggestions that Sultan of Turkey should be deposed as spiritual head of Mohammedan world; and about resentment of all Muslims at non-Muslim suggestions as to his most suitable successor.

D126 – 6/1/15 – Publish nothing about advance by Turks and Kurds on Tabriz (N. Persia).

D143 – 25/1/15 – Make no reference to date of imminent Allied 'Conference on France' in Paris.

SL – 21/2/15 – Foreign Secretary (Sir Edward Grey) refers to 'feeling' between the [still neutral] USA and Great Britain, defends US positions, and makes plea not unduly to offend American opinion.

D186 – 16/3/15 – India Office request to avoid implying Dardanelles operations in any way war of Christians against Moslems, reminding that 'Great Britain has an enormous number of Muhammadan subjects', and asking for restraint not only in articles but also in 'pictures'.

D191 – 27/3/15 – No mention transporting of 'war materials' from the USA.

D201 – 15/4/15 – Because of 'friendly attitude of the Chilean Government' towards Britain and the Allies during the War, use friendly tone in commenting on sinking of German cruiser *DRESDEN* in Chilean coastal waters [The raider-cruiser had sunk much Allied shipping, was cornered by HM Ships *KENT* and *GLASGOW* in March off Robinson Crusoe Island, and, rather than surrender, blew herself up].

D209 – 17/5/15 – No reference to 'any contemplated action of the Allies in regard to the use of gases for offensive or defensive purposes'.

D228 – 10/6/15 – No reference to document entitled 'Acceleration of the Supply of Munitions' circulated at meeting between Lloyd George and Trades Union representatives.

D245 – 9/7/15 – No publication of articles by C H Norman, accusing Government of responsibility for War and calling for immediate stoppage; publication would cause 'anxiety to our Allies, satisfaction to our enemies, and danger to our national cause'.

D246 – 12/7/15 – No mention of employment of chemists or production or use of gas by British Forces, and 'no further descriptions . . . of the effects of German gases on our soldiers'.

D253 – 30/7/15 – No mention of 'want of munitions in the Russian Army' [request via War Office from Russian Ambassador in London].

SL – 10/8/15 – Background to US complaints about Britain preventing imports of US cotton into Germany.

D257 – 16/8/15 – Make no further reference to recent article in *Standard* about 'Labour Plot' against Munitions of War Act.

D267 – 2/9/15 – Publish nothing except official information about strikes/lockouts at 'Munitions Works'.

D273 – 19/9/15 – Reminder of content of DoRA Clause 27, concerning 'causing disaffection' etc; in particular Press in South Wales, both 'in the public interest and for their own protection, should refrain from seeking interviews with or giving publicity to the views of leaders in strike or lockout movements', as this could 'interfere with the success of HM Forces by land or sea'.

D285 – 16/10/15 – No reference to serious strike by shipbuilding and engineering trades on Clyde next week.

D319 – 27/11/15 – No mention of China discreetly assisting Allies.

SL – 4/12/15 – FO briefing that Japanese Government anxious nothing published about document in which Allies engage not to conclude any separate peace (until document published).

D332 – 22/12/15 – Do not reveal names of German prisoners of war and deserters, for fear of reprisals.

SL – 3/1/16 – 'The Secretary of State for Foreign Affairs feels sure that Editors will appreciate the importance of avoiding, in any comments they may publish on the past career of Rasputin, any reference to the highest personage in Russia' [Rasputin then at height of influence on Tsarina and Russian politics, Tsar having left capital to command Russian Army; Rasputin murdered by Prince Felix Youssoupov and co-conspirators 16/12/16].

SL – 10/2/16 – Restraint requested in criticism of President Wilson over the USA/Germany settlement of *Lusitania* controversy, because of impact on American opinion; 'they prefer to do their own criticism'. [British liner sunk off Ireland 7/5/15, with loss of 1195 lives, including 123 American passengers; had marked impact on US public opinion towards Germany]

D363 – 21/2/16 – Do not publish anything likely to offend Muhammedans, including anything which 'appears to shew that Germans and Austrians are more concerned for the comfort, the feelings and the prejudices of Muhammedans than are the Allies' [Concern for the attitude towards the British of Muslims, including the large number in the Empire, recurs in official documents from at least 1880, e.g. 'Attitudes of Musselmans', TNA: PRO CAB 37/1/8].

SL – 10–12/3/16 – Background briefings on the military situation from the French (in French).

D374 – 3/4/16 – Restrictions on reporting the Russian Brigade now in Egypt.

D380 – 8/4/16 – No mention mutinies/disturbances in prisoner-of-war and aliens' camps.

SL – 20/4/16 – Avoid giving any excuse for anti-Allied views among Americans at a time when possibility of rupture in relations between the USA and Germany.

D385 – 22/4/16 – No mention of Secret Sessions of Parliament; threat of seizure of all copies and of printing plant, and prosecution of those responsible.

SL – 27/4/16 – Advice to Editors on how to report imminent surrender to Turks of British forces besieged in Kut; 'The fall of Kut cannot be very long delayed. Although from a purely military point of view it is a matter of minor importance, the effect in the Mohommedan world may be very great. We shall endeavour to make the announcement before the enemy can do so, in order that the enemy's announcement may fall flat and have less effect ... Any short notice which the Press might publish might put the operations of the Kut Force in the light of an heroic band of some 14,000 fighting men which originally advanced to attempt a difficult task'; other 'spin' was suggested on this major military reverse.

SL – 27/5/16 – Lord Grey asked for no comment on confused state of affairs in Greece and Balkans (and again on 25/6, 4/9 and 6/10).

SL – 29/5/16 – Encouragement to mention the strict censorship now being imposed in Greece by government [Former Liberal Prime Minister Venizelos in favour of supporting the Allies, but dismissed by pro-neutrality King (brother-in-law of the Kaiser), had become focus for anti-monarchist forces, supported by the Allies; the King abdicated in June 1917].

SL – 9/6/16 – Royal Navy patrols in Greek waters not to be referred to as a 'blockade'.

D413 – 17/6/16 – No mention of employment in this country of German prisoners of war [withdrawn 2 months later, but still with restrictions as to where].

SL – 23/6/16 – No criticism of Swiss Parliament.

SL – 29/6/16 – FO warning about letters from 'persons in this country professing to represent orthodox Moslem views' and to be in contact with co-religionists in India and the Empire, denouncing Grand Sherif of Mecca and Arabs for taking action against Turks.

SL – 4/7/16 – Because of impact on Britain's 'Arab policy', not to 'write up our enemies the Turks ... The Turks have committed against the Armenians the vilest atrocities and are now deliberately starving Christians of Lebanon'.

SL – 12/8/16 – No discussion of confiscating German property in Dominions as reprisal for murder of Captain Fryatt and other German outrages, because French fear German retaliation against French financial interests in occupied France and Belgium [Captain Charles Fryatt was Master of SS Brussels, Great Eastern Railways ship on Rotterdam route, awarded two gold watches for thwarting U-boat attacks on his ship; however, eventually intercepted by Germans, tried and executed 27/7/16, causing particular revulsion in Britain. Additional unpublished concern was when Germans captured Brussels, they found onboard secret despatches to Commander Cummings of MI6, which enabled mopping up secret British network in Belgium].

D461 – 18/9/16 – Background to threatened railwaymen's strike over war bonus.

D462 – 19/9/16 – Reminder DoRA Regulation 27 about spreading reports 'likely to cause disaffection to His Majesty or to interfere with the success of His Majesty's Forces', with footnote referring to 'all reports of threatened strikes by munitions workers, railwaymen, dockers, miners, etc'.

SL – 5/10/16 – Guidance on commenting on forthcoming US Presidential election (Hughes v Wilson), there being (according to FO) no significant differences between them on foreign policy; if commenting adversely, should be only on trade issues.

D471 – 6/10/16 – Avoid criticising Belgian workers in Britain in order to 'promote good relations between Belgian refugees and the working classes in this country'.

D477 – 11/10/16 – No mention of return of Muhammedan pilgrims to North Africa en route to Holy Places [at the request of the French Government].

SL – 17/10/16 – Background note about influence in Spain of pro-German Basque and other nationalists.

SL – 29/10/16 – Avoid giving impression Britain anxious to bring Norway into War.

SL – 7/11/16 – Do not to refer to Sherif of Mecca as 'King', because this causes 'undesirable complications in the "Peninsula"'.

D485 – 8/11/16 – No mention of presence in UK of any officer 'on parole from an Internment Camp in Germany' (because of threat of Court Martial on return there).

D487 – 16/11/16 – Publish nothing about strike in Sheffield Munitions Factories.

SL – 18/11/16 – No mention diversion of Dutch agricultural produce from Germany to UK.

D494 – 26/11/16 – Publish nothing about military operations in Persia and events in Afghanistan.

D497 – 3/12/16 – No mention of possibility of engineering strike in Manchester.

D500 – 11/12/16 – No mention of boilermakers' strike in Liverpool.

SL – 21/12/16 – No personal attacks on President Wilson [repeated on 1/2/17].

D510 – 2/1/17 – Publish nothing about 'arrangements for Allied propaganda'.

D511 – 3/1/17 – No mention of Chinese labour with British Armies in France (because German agents in China interfering with recruitment).

D513 – 6/1/17 – No mention of Conference of Allied Statesmen in Rome.

SL – 1/2/17 – Refrain from being offensive to President Wilson or the USA in commenting on situation arising from 'last German Note and Memorandum' [Germany started unrestricted submarine warfare 1 February 1917, USA severed diplomatic relations with Germany two days later, declared war on her 6 April 1917 (and on Austria 7 December 1917)].

D533 – 6/2/17 – No reference to Prime Minister and Minister of Labour addressing Delegates of Trades Unions at Central Hall, Westminster.

SL – 13/3/17 – Do not overdo criticism of Russia's internal affairs, because enemy will use this to create dissension between UK and Russia.

D551 – 16/3/17 – No mention of 'strikes of persons being employed on Admiralty work'.

SL – 16/3/17 – Avoid anything to increase anger in Allied countries caused by the UK's restriction of imports (in order to conserve shipping tonnage).

SL – ?16/3/17 – Information from report from HM Ambassador in St Petersburg (was complimentary about discipline and low level of violence of Revolution at that stage), including abdication of Tsar on 15 March and refusal of Grand Duke Michael to accept succession; FO request to avoid speculation.

SL – 20/3/17 – Exercise caution in publishing foreign reports about events in Russia, especially those from Germany (Tsar imprisoned next day).

D552 – 20/3/17 – Great caution to be exercised on (a) terms of compensation to coal owners, (b) recruiting of miners, (c) 'general adjustment of miners' wages as result of Government control'.

D561 – 8/5/17 – Exercise restraint in reporting 'unrest in the Engineering and some other trades in different parts of the country' [to avoid encouraging copycat stoppages elsewhere].

D568 – 14/6/17 – Publish nothing about passage through England 'of Commandant Loyson or of his propaganda [this word was omitted from the Notice] mission to Russia' (at the request of France).

D580 – 10/8/17 – Referring to intention that US troops should march through London following week, no reference to ceremony before official announcement [in deference to American wishes; in fact march was cancelled two days later] [American fighting troops had begun arriving in France in late June].

D582 – 17/8/17 – No mention of parties of Russians going back to Russia for military service, because of enemy submarine threat.

D588 – 10/9/17 – No mention of cable censorship as this 'can only embarrass the United States and our own Administration'.

D591 – 13/9/17 – Reference D588, explanation of abuse by Sweden of privilege of communicating in cipher via British cables, accorded at the outbreak of war to neutral Governments, and therefore not censored by UK. Press therefore free to comment on Allied refusal now of cable facilities to firms doing business with the Central Powers [Germany, Austria etc].

SL – 26/9/17 – Refrain from using term 'Yellow Peril', because offends our Far Eastern Allies.

D602 – 28/10/17 – Referring to 'delicacy of the situation' on Italian Front, publish nothing 'likely to wound the feelings of our Italian ally'.

D607 – 15/11/17 – Reminder to avoid 'suggesting that the military operations against Turkey are in any sense a Holy War, a modern Crusade or have anything to do with religious questions. The British Empire is said to contain a hundred million Muhammedan subjects of the King and it is obviously mischievous to suggest that our quarrel with Turkey is one between Christianity and Islam'.

SL – 8/12/17 – Board of Trade reassurance talks between Unions and Employers going well.

D612 – 3/1/18 – No mention beyond Official Report of today's meeting of Ministers and Labour Representatives at Central Hall, Westminster, especially anything about 'War Aims' and numbers of men now and in future on military service.

SL – 31/1/18 – Request not to express satisfaction at news of strikes in Germany, in order to encourage them to go on widening.

D639 – 4/3/18 – No reference to be made (other than in Court Circular) to audience granted today by King to Dr Weizman [unpromulgated reason given by Foreign Office was that latter was about to go on 'an important mission to Palestine . . . but Arab-Zionist relations are already in a delicate condition, and are apt to become strained if too much stress is laid on the relations of the British Government with one party rather than the other'].

D641 – 12/3/18 – No mention of 'a certain number of Officers are proceeding to the United States and will give lectures about the War'.

D650 – 4/4/18 – 'At the instance of the French Government', no mention of evacuation of civilians from Amiens and environs.

D661 – 16/4/18 – Again at the request of French, when reporting German bombardment of Paris, no mention on which localities shells fell nor 'bad effect upon the morale of the population'.

D670 – 14/5/18 – No reference to Belgian refugees as 'aliens'.

D681 – 6/6/18 – No reporting of occupation by British troops of certain Russian ports on White Sea.

D684 – 21/6/18 – No reporting of visit of Russian politician, Mr Kerensky.

SL – 7/6/18 – Exercise caution in reporting Japanese and Allied intervention against Bolsheviks in Siberia.

SL – 12/6/18 – Warning to be cautious, while negotiations between Britain and Germany under way at The Hague, in referring to maltreatment of British prisoners of war in Germany.

SL – 14/6/18 – Publish nothing, unless USA announces it, about some American troops going to Ireland for training.

D691 – 10/7/18 – No mention strike at aircraft factory of the Alliance Aeroplane Company Ltd, London.

SL – 20/7/18 – Background to labour troubles in Munitions industry.

SL – 21/7/18 – Confidential information about Unions' moves towards an 'Embargo Strike' [updated next day].

D701 – 28/8/18 – No disclosure of details of US aircraft production output.

SL – 9/8/18 – Foreign Office explanation of why no mention should be made of discredited (in Russian eyes) Kerensky.

SL – 14/8/18 – Foreign Office explanation as to why inadvisable to refer in Press to 'Spanish affairs during the next few days'.

D706 – 5/9/18 – No mention of Norway's anti-submarine mining of her waters.

D707 – 5/9/18 – Home Office statement on the Police Strike.

D708 – 11/9/18 – Reminder of prohibitions on reporting the movements etc of US Forces.

D709 – 17/9/18 – Shipping Controller's guidance on reporting meeting of Merchant Seamen at Southampton.

SL – 21/9/18 – No reporting of any trouble at next day's Italian Demonstration in Hyde Park.

D724 – 29/10/18 – During visit to Britain of 'Mr B. G. Tilak of Poona' (as plaintiff in High Court libel case), he would be unable to 'engage in controversy'. [Bal Gangadhar Tilak, Lawyer, Editor (*Poona Journal* etc), Sanskrit Scholar, anti-Imperial educationist and political leader (of the Indian Freedom Movement) who prepared the way for Ghandi (who had returned to India in 1915, supporting the War against Germany) in advocating non-violent rebellion, twice accused of treason by British authorities in India and imprisoned, had been released in 1914. Press subsequently allowed by D736 of 18 November to talk to him on political matters].

D725 – 31/10/18 – No speculation about terms of Armistice under discussion with Germany and Austria.

D727 – 5/11/18 – 'The India Office has noticed references in the Press to the future disposal or use of S. Sophia at Constantinople and desires to remind those responsible for publication of the importance of avoiding references likely to wound the susceptibilities of our own Muhammadan fellow subjects many of whom have, by service in the Indian Army, materially assisted in the overthrow of Turkey'.

D730 – 11/11/18 – 'It is very desirable in the national interest that nothing should be published during the progress of the Peace Congress which might embarrass the representatives of the Allied and Associate Governments or interfere with the unity of their demands. The importance of avoiding the publication of anything which might, directly or indirectly, lead to differences between the Allied and Associated peoples during the peace negotiations is so great that the Prime Minister and the War Cabinet make a special appeal to the Press to refrain from speculations as to, and discussions of, the probable terms of peace. Arrangements will be made to issue to the Press official reports of the progress of negotiations whenever, and so far as, it is possible to do so' [Issued to the Press at 1145 GMT; the General Armistice had been signed on the Western Front at 0500 that morning, and hostilities had come to an end at 1100].

D747 – 16/4/19 – Caution about reporting 'outrages on white women' in Egypt; these not only untrue, but had 'undesirability of giving insurrectionary elements in Egypt any justification'.

Ireland

D387 – 25/4/16 – No mention of 'disturbances in Ireland' except official communiqué [the 'Easter Rising': previous day, large Sinn Fein force had seized Dublin Post Office, in subsequent battle over 30 police/military (and an unknown number of Sinn Fein) casualties].

D388 – 25/4/16 – Deletion from communiqué of words 'A considerable body of troops left this morning from England to Ireland'.

D482 – 31/10/16 – Use 'discrimination' in reporting 'action of members of the Dublin Police Force . . . only likely to increase any trouble that exists'.

D508 – 23/12/16 – No mention in English, Scottish and Welsh newspapers of matters Irish Government considered should not be made public in Ireland 'in cases of urgency'; requests in this category would be passed on by PB marked 'Irish Censor'.

Ireland D1 – 11/1/17 – No mention of visit to Ireland of Canadian Rangers.

D517 – 12/1/17 – Do not publish letters/articles from Mrs Sheehy-Skeffington (then in the USA) about Ireland [Hanna Sheehy-Skeffington (1877–1946), Irish feminist and nationalist, widow of Irish socialist, pacifist, feminist and nationalist, Francis Sheehy-Skeffington (1878–1916), whose ultra-idealism was mocked by his contemporary James Joyce in *The Portrait of the Artist as a Young Man* (as MacCann), and who from 1914 campaigned against recruiting into British Forces, was sentenced to hard labour for 'seditious acts', was released after a hunger strike and went to the USA to campaign for Irish freedom (he wished this to be achieved non-violently). Attempting to stop looting during Easter Rising, was arrested, and having witnessed killing of an unarmed youth by an Irish-born British Army Captain, was himself executed by him, on 25/4/16. Hanna went to USA in 1917, carrried on his campaign for freedom, wrote anti-British Military book (banned until end of World War I), was arrested and put in Holloway jail on her return. Her father David Sheehy meanwhile remained an MP loyal to Britain].

Ireland D4 – 22/1/17 – Allowed to mention 'certain arrests' but nothing 'likely to inflame public opinion in Ireland'.

D618 – 22/1/18 – Reminder of prohibition under DoRA of reference to proceedings of Irish Convention, 'which is now passing through a most critical stage . . . vital importance that its deliberations should be conducted in privacy and that the issues which divide it should not be confessed in the Press'. Irish newspapers generally complied and British Press should too therefore [The Irish Convention was established in July 1917, in an attempt by Lloyd George to introduce some form of self-government in Dublin. Boycotted by Sinn Fein and the Munster Party, but sat until March 1918 and discussed various options. German offensive that month caused British Government to consider for first time conscription in Ireland, opposed by all parties there, and Convention ceased to function].

Ireland D7 – 25/2/18 – Until further notice, nothing about 'any occurrences that may take place in County Clare'.

D655 – 10/4/18 – Permitted to publish and comment on content of Irish Convention Report on future government of Ireland, but not on proceedings of Convention, which continue to be protected by Article 27A of DoRA.

Ireland D9 – 26/5/18 – Nothing in Irish or British Press about speech by Father O'Flanagan today at Ballyjamesduff.

Ireland D15 – 21/1/19 – No mention of Sinn Fein Declaration of Freedom at Mansion House, Dublin, which starts 'Whereas the Irish People is by right a Free People . . .'

Ireland D18 – 30/1/19 – No reporting of Sinn Fein orders to public.

Ireland D20 – 25/3/19 – No mention of Lord Mayor of Dublin's proclamation about military authorities' prevention of meetings.

Movements of Royalty/Politicians/Senior Officers

D16 – 30/8/14 – No mention of three Belgian vessels arriving at Dover next day carrying 'special passengers and cargo' from Belgium.

D19 – 1/9/14 – No reporting of Kitchener's imminent movements (short visit to France – cancelled next day on his return, as usual with these VIP movement abroad Notices, and often as in this case with added request for no retrospective reporting either).

D24 – 7/9/14 – Do not report departure from England of Queen of The Belgians.

D31 – 10/9/14 – Do not report movements of Mr Churchill (cancelled later the same day).

D105 – 27/11/14 – Until further notice, publish nothing about future movements of King.

D123 – 25/12/14 – Publish nothing about movements of Prime Minister during Christmas recess.

D159 – 20/2/15 – No reference to inspection by King on Salisbury Plain of 'Canadian Contingent', nor to whole or part of it now being in France, nor to any other reinforcement by British or Colonial troops.

D442 – 25/8/16 – Do not mention past or future movements of King or other members of Royal Family until published in Court Circular, but if King makes public appearance in UK, it may be reported in normal way afterwards, unless a visit to naval/military location or unit, or otherwise involves some prohibited matter, in which case report must be cleared with PB before publication.

D558 – 4/5/17 – Information on changes to reporting the King's planned movements; letters from Windsor Castle to PB: 'the onus will now devolve on us to tell you when Their Majesties' movements can be given to the Press. As a start I would suggest your giving permission for an announcement that the King and Queen hope shortly to visit some Factories and Industries in Cheshire, Lancashire and Cumberland. I am quite sure that the Public ought to know more of what the King and Queen are doing'. [This well-intentioned Notice, in the context of the preceding one, caused Press confusion].

D563 – 1/5/17 – After King's visits to Munitions Factories in North next week any photographs taken to be submitted to PB.

D686 – 24/6/18 – No mention to be made of holiday whereabouts of the Prime Minister (at his home in Sussex).

D734 – 18/11/18 – Withdrawal of restrictions on reporting planned movements of members of Royal Family.

Weather

D80 – 21/10/14 – Announcing that there would be no more detailed 'Wind and Weather' reports, only 'very general inferences as to the weather' [This was because of the perceived Zeppelin threat. In fact reports were reinstated next day, albeit thereafter in much abbreviated form].

D378 – 7/4/16 – Referring to severe blizzards in UK 27–29 March, which caused almost total collapse of postal, telegraph and telephone systems, request [from Field Marshal

French, CinC in UK] that in future Press might refrain from publishing breakdowns in utilities, and also serious industrial accidents, especially in munitions factories.

D657 – 13/4/18 – Publication of all weather reports prohibited.

D663 – 19/4/18 – No photographs/illustrations to be published showing results of weather (mentioning that German Press do not publish anything about German weather).

D715 – 27/9/18 – After complaints from Press, further lengthy definition of what should be 'rigidly excluded', i.e. everything from 'Atmospheric Pressure, Temperature . . . [to] . . . Thunder and Lightning, Snowfall (Very Important)'.

D732 – 14/11/18 – Restrictions on reporting weather withdrawn.

Curiosities

D1 – 11/8/14 – Reference to certain firms 'declining to sell revolvers to officers of HM Forces except at prices considerably above those usually charged', with a warning that Army Council might use its powers under Army Act unless there was reduction to 'reasonable amount' ('10% over the usual price' was suggested). Hope that Press would 'comment severely on practice of these firms without Council being drawn in directly'.

D21 – 3/9/14 – Do not report serious illness of Captain Jellicoe (father of Admiral Sir John Jellicoe, CinC of the British Grand Fleet).

D114 – 9/12/14 – No mention to be made of Government carrier pigeon service.

D132 – 15/1/15 – Request to publicise certain 'designing persons' who were approaching relatives of men missing in action offering to search for them in return for payment.

D225 – 8/6/15 – It is 'very desirable that no pictures of European nurses attending on [the letter to the Press Bureau said merely "with" rather than "attending on"] wounded native soldiers should be published in the Press'; War Office considered such pictures would 'have a bad effect on discipline'.

D288 – 18/10/15 – Publish no information that might increase the danger to fellow-prisoners of Miss Edith Cavell [the British nurse accused by the Germans in Belgium of helping Allied soldiers to escape (she admitted it), and shot on 12 October. This Notice was published before it was certain she had been executed, and was updated on 22 October].

D291 – 19/10/15 – Request to publicise the potential dangers of dry powder chemical used in fire extinguishers.

D375 – 3/4/16 – Do not publish chess problems unless certain that the senders are 'of British nationality and perfectly reliable' [There was MI5 concern that coded information was being thus passed to the Germans; this Notice led to *Times* pointing out its principal and long-time contributor of chess problems was Dutch; to Editor of *Sussex and Essex Free Press* (perhaps with tongue in cheek) suggesting game of draughts could also be used in this way (with which MI5 solemnly concurred), but also to letter from Editor of *Field* pointing out it took many months to perfect chess problems and that date of publication would always therefore be uncertain, that problems based on military information would be nonsensical as chess problems, and that problems were anyway often copied from foreign journals – MI5 replied that its intelligence was nevertheless 'very definite'; final response to this Notice in July 1918, in letter from Royal Army Medical Corps Captain, asking censors whether he should submit to them draughts problems intended for new Journal of Royal Army Temperance Association].

D414 – 19/6/16 – Restrictions on use of three authorised articles written by Rudyard Kipling on operations on Western Front [his subaltern son John had been killed the previous year fighting in Irish Guards at Battle of Loos].

D472 – 6/10/16 – No reference 'to a new scientific discovery dealing with the delineation of internal organs by an electrical method' [X-rays?], because of the possible applications in engineering (referring to article in British Medical Journal 30 September).

SL – 25/10/16 – Encourage public to write sender's name and address on letters to Germany and neutral countries, to avoid overload on Post Office checking system.

SL – 29/3/17 – Request to impress upon public to avoid travel on railways at Easter, because of current strain on railway system.

D566 – 7/6/17 – Do not mention training or use of dogs as messengers with Armies in the field.

D610 – 7/12/17 – 'The first Commissioner of Works makes an urgent appeal that the Press will make no reference to the removal of National Art Treasures from the public museums and galleries to places of greater safety'.

D611 – 12/12/17 – 'The Director of the National Gallery reports today that a soldier wilfully damaged nine pictures in the Gallery and will be charged tomorrow; if the "outrage" is made public it could lead to copycat attacks in London and the Provinces, and it is therefore in the public interest that no reference to be made to the incident'.

D714 – 26/9/18 – 'The Press are earnestly requested not to publish any photograph of Lieutenant Colonel T. E. Lawrence, C.B., D.S.O. This Officer is not known by sight to the Turks, who have put a price upon his head, and any photograph or personal description of him may endanger his safety' [The Arab uprising against the Turks in which Lawrence was involved had started in June 1916].

D743 – 19/2/19 – Request not to publish 'rumours originating from Paris or elsewhere about His Royal Highness the Prince of Wales [having] become engaged to one of the daughters of the King of Italy, who are also staying in Paris. The rumours are entirely without any vestige of foundation'.

Appendix 2

OUTLINE OF WWII DEFENCE NOTICES

Preface and Observations

Notices:
 Air
 Air Raids
 Defence of the United Kingdom
 Finance
 Government
 Military
 Naval and Shipping
 Neutrals and Foreign Affairs
 Prisoners of War and Internees
 Spies
 Trade and Supply
 Transport

Appendices:
 Press Censorship Directory
 Scope of censorship
 Methods of Submission [of material for publication]
 Defence Regulations, Regulation 3

Appendix 3

EXAMPLES OF D-NOTICES AND LETTERS TO EDITORS AND PUBLISHERS 1945–67[1]

Notice Number/ Letter	Date	Caution/Request Not to Publish
1	28/11/45	UK Secret Intelligence and Counter-Intelligence methods and activities worldwide, identities of those involved, British and Foreign, and training methods.
2	19/1/46	Escape and Evasion systems, equipment and communications, identities of 1939–45 helpers in occupied countries.
3	21/1/46	Codes, cyphers, linked establishments.
5	23/3/46	Until announced, weapons and equipment.
7	13/9/46	Movement of large stocks of toxic gas from Germany to existing RAF storage depots in Wales.
8		New large tank (Centurion) details and trials.
9	1/10/46	Aircraft and Aero-Engines on Secret and Initial Publication Lists (first of post-war Quarterly Notices – routine such Notices not recorded hereafter in this Appendix).
10	26/3/47	Trials, details and tactics of new Anti-Submarine detection devices being developed for use in aircraft (including helicopters).
12	14/4/47	Import, export, movements within UK, of uranium, thorium, and respective ores pitchblende and monazite.
25		Location and progress of work in UK on development and production of atomic weapons, their design, size and other details, materials used, storage locations, identification of individuals with work on atomic weapons.
25A		Import and stockpiling of atomic weapons in UK.
25B		Transfers of staff from Armament Research Departments to Atomic Energy Departments.
31	4/10/48	Until announced, no details (dimensions, tonnage, performance, armament, drawings, etc as in its appendix) of New Ship Building Programme.
33	29/11/48	Without consultation, aerial photographs of listed RAF/RN air stations, Air Defences, Permanent Service Storage Depots, Defence Radio and Radar installations on land, Research Establishments, Industrial Establishments important to Defence with own airfield, Oil Refineries/Depots under construction or new (Notice became known as 'War Potential').

513

Notice Number/ Letter	Date	Caution/Request Not to Publish
42	11/5/49	Further to No.2, no details of the new escape and evasion methods, equipment and clothing.
Letter	20/1/50	Assistant Chief of Air Staff (Intelligence) to Aerial Photography Companies: request for help in reporting any deliberate attempt to photograph locations listed in No.33.
53		Any reference to the existence of the tank referred to in No.8.
Letter	24/8/50	Thomson to book publishers: request to consult on escape and evasion story manuscripts.
59		Certain details of Service aircraft, transferred to the Part Publication List, previously authorised for publication.
71		UK Korea Land Contingent movements.
75	14/12/50	Strengths of various parts of RAF, command and control arrangements, tactics.
Letter	28/12/50	Thomson to national press editors only: As little publicity as possible 'in present circumstances' [Korean War] on No.1 matters.
Letter	3/5/51	Thomson to editors: The desirability of not publishing information about declassified equipment which potential enemies could not otherwise find out without expending a considerable amount of time and trouble.
82	21/5/51	Admiralty use of television for Naval purposes 'other than domestic'.
Letter	17/9/51	Thomson to editors, explaining why, despite No.82, Admiralty had publicised use of underwater TV to identify hull of sunk submarine *HMS AFFRAY* (existence overseas of certain amount of information on such use, and public interest); adding 'for your own info' the current TV capability 'extremely limited' but advances likely, and therefore No.82 applied even more strongly to developments.
Letter	29/9/51	Thomson to editors: 'Not a D.Notice', but trying again to explain thinking behind War Potential Notices; aerial photos reveal potential outputs and stocks, and sources of supply, useful to enemy intelligence; adding always available for advice, 'except when travelling' between 9–10 am and 6–7 pm.
98	10/12/51	Reiteration of No.5, fillings of shells/missiles, protective clothing, special types of operational vehicles, even sometimes those in current use.
Letter	1/5/52	First summary of post-war Notices still in force [these summaries of 'live' Notices appeared thereafter at irregular intervals, not recorded further in this Appendix].
104	11/7/52	New Civil Defence Regional Commissioners Operational Headquarters; nothing beyond which Borough/County District.
Letter	31/7/52	ACAS (Intelligence) to aerial photography firms, tightening up on War Potential locations, now including marshalling yards, docks and public utility centres.
106	14/8/52	Midlands Emergency National Grid Control Centre [normal and known Control Centre was in London].
112	29/9/53	Underground oil storage locations being built.

Notice Number/ Letter	Date	Caution/Request Not to Publish
Notice	5/5/53	(Notices now not numbered because of *Daily Worker* security considerations) Modification of previous Notices on atomic matters after Minister of Supply reply to PQ previous day.
Notice	25/5/53	Revised guidance on atomic weapons, locations and production details, stocks, movements, adding guidance about the results of atomic tests, and the adaptation of particular types of aircraft to carry such weapons and the linked training.
Notice	11/6/53	Underground oil storage depots near coast for civil use in war.
Letter	31/7/53	Thomson to all newspaper editors: no mention of name of incoming DG Security Service or his background [Dick White].
Notice	24/6/53	Follow up to 11/6/53: nothing on their pipelines either.
Letter	13/1/54	(Secret) Thomson to editors: ref OSA offence of Crown employees giving info and others publishing it, this applies equally to information from an agent if it comes from overseas, even if it has already been published in foreign press; Media side of DPBC agree same principle applies to Notice No.1 coverage.
Notice	8/3/54	Government underground cables and communications in London, Birmingham, Manchester, Glasgow and Dover.
Notice	3/9/54	(Following request from Australian authorities) Whereabouts of Soviet defectors Mr & Mrs Vladimar [sic] Petrov [then in Australia].
Notice	29/9/54	New details of gas turbine powered tracked vehicle.
Letter	20/10/54	Thomson to editors: War Potential Notices, further clarification: factories making products essential to conduct of war, other locations as before, but aerial photographs of towns acceptable if not too site-specific or clear.
Letter	16/12/54	Thomson to book publishers ref two recent books giving technical details of British aircraft; request to seek advice in future.
Notice	10/2/55	Ref No.3, reminder about British and foreign methods/systems of ciphering/decyphering, nature of work in Government Communications Establishments, named persons therein.
Letter	21/6/55	Thomson to editors ref War Potential Notices: Statement on Defence 1955 wording, that 'new form of threat to security [H-Bomb] calls for a complete overhaul of our Home Defence plans', does not mean existing prohibitions no longer apply. However, some difficulties in interpreting 20/10/54 letter require revised guidance (included recategorising locations into 2 groups: I. Military and Research installations, and war production factories, II. Iron and Steel, Oil, and Utilities locations).
Notice	30/6/55	Similar to previous Aircraft and Aero-Engines Quarterly Notices, but includes editors to seek advice about unofficial photographs of new aircraft at Initial Publication stage, if believing secret aspects revealed.
Notice	11/10/55	New buildings for control of railway systems.
Notice	16/12/55	Flood protection for London Transport Railways.
Notice	30/12/55	Unannounced movements of units to/from Cyprus.

Notice Number/ Letter	Date	Caution/Request Not to Publish
Notice	18/1/56	Quarterly Aircraft List now increased to 11 pages because of number under development.
Notice	13/2/56	Details of guided weapons now about to start being issued to Services.
Notice	25/2/56	Revision of No.75 with additional specifics on restrictions referring to squadron strengths, command and control systems, air defences, tactics and bases.
Letter	25/2/56	Thomson to editors: ref 25/2/56 Notice, applies too to ground-launched guided weapons [RAF was developing Bloodhound Missile system, initially to protect V-Bomber (nuclear deterrent) air stations].
Notice	27/4/56	More detailed guidance on matters related to MI5 and MI6, including now numbers and organisation, and clues to addresses from which they operate; text started 'In view of the publicity given by recent events to the operations of our Security Organisation', a reference to the Commander Crabbe affair; this Notice later featured prominently in the 1967 Lohan episode – see Section 7.
Notice	21/6/56	Ref No.42, can now mention evasion exercises, but no details of procedures, equipment, resistance to interrogation training methods.
Notices	4&15/8/56	Details of formations, strengths, stores, etc, being moved to Mediterranean [for potential Suez Operation].
Letter	9/8/56	Reminder about what should not be reported following Press visits to aircraft factories.
Notice	1/11/56	'In view of the new situation which has arisen in the Suez Canal, a military censorship has been imposed in Malta, Cyprus and the operational area'; request not publish (without consulting Department concerned) information about that area on: location of units and air defence, command appointments, VIP movements, casualty figures; and nothing on plans and operations, actual or rumoured, effects of enemy action, details of projected attacks, plans for other 'disturbed' Middle East areas [this unusually draconian Notice, although generally followed, was not well received by the media].
Notice	12/11/56	Because of ceasefire, previous Notice withdrawn.
Letter	21/1/57	(Secret) Thomson to 'very limited circulation' of Editors on Soviet 'secret technical devices' for intelligence gathering.
Letter	11/4/57	Thomson to Editors yet again on now agreed revised War Potential guidance.
Notice	26/4/57	Acceptable to reveal RAF North Coates only as a new missile [Bloodhound] station, because the first.
Notice	13/5/57	Ref Cairo trial of British subjects accused of spying, request not to elaborate on nor add to allegations.
Letter	20/5/57	Thomson to SPBC Members: even the Media reception of War Potential letter going well, therefore suggest postpone next meeting until late summer.

Notice Number/ Letter	Date	Caution/Request Not to Publish
Notice	31/10/57	(Secret) Ref Privy Counsellors' Report on phone-tapping, and Notice of 27/4/56, media no longer asked not to mention this practice, but still not who targets are (unless nothing to do with national security), nor techniques and technology.
Letter	25/11/57	(Secret) Secret technical devices used by 'potential enemies' to gain information for counter-intelligence purposes; no mention of how conversations were listened to (issued after Privy Counsellors' Report revealed some details of interception).
Letter	31/1/58	Need to request authority before publishing photographs taken of or inside prohibited places.
Notice	22/2/58	Details of plans for ballistic weapon defence, ie numbers of missiles and sites, precise localities, detailed layouts, and operational relationship between sites.
Letter	7/3/58	Definition of 'precise locality' in previous Notice.
Letter	22/4/58	No further details of new powered guided bomb [the nuclear Blue Steel, carried by the V-Bomber force 1961–69, after which submarine-launched Polaris came into operation].
Letter	28/8/58	Thomson to editors: Powered guided bomb, 'after it has flown, may be treated as an aircraft on the Initial Publications List [ie may be referred to, but still without secret details].
Notice	17/9/58	Ballistic missiles: reminder ref locations of linked guided weapons and radar sites (the accompanying letter acknowledged sites could not be kept secret for ever, but asked editors to make it difficult for the Soviets).
Letter	10/10/58	Thomson to SPBC, referring to two ex-National Servicemen undergraduates imprisoned for three months for article in *Isis* about their secret communications experience, explaining *Guardian* had republished the article not having been told that they should not; new D-.Notice therefore in preparation.
Notice	15/10/58	Further to the above, revised issue of 10/2/55 Notice, adding request: 'whilst you appreciate that on occasions it is necessary in the interest of national defence for the Services to intercept such communications, you will not refer to this fact'.
Notice	14/11/58	Cancelling Notice No.12 on atomic material.
Letter	6/3/59	Reminder regarding secret details of TSR 2 aircraft [multi-role supersonic aircraft, of very advanced technology, cancelled because of technical and cost considerations in April 1965].
Letter	26/3/59	Thomson to Lincolnshire editors: Lincolnshire County Council about to discuss matters that could affect the Air Defence of Great Britain, therefore reminder ref Notices on radar, guided and ballistic weapons [Blue Streak was still being developed as a ballistic weapon, although development as such subsequently discontinued].
Notice	8/8/59	Ref Notice of 17/9/58, prohibition relaxed to include just command, control and communications details, but including any *complete* list of locations.

Notice Number/ Letter	Date	Caution/Request Not to Publish
Notice	2/9/59	Reminder on UK Atomic Energy establishments, including design, materials and output of atomic weapons, air photographs of all AE Establishments and ground photographs of those named in the Notice.
Letter	19/10/59	Thomson to 'Very Limited Distribution' of editors: although D-Notices do not normally refer to Police work, new links between Security Service and Police on secret counter-espionage work are covered by Notice procedure.
Notice	14/1/60	Details of underground operations centres outside London (e.g. location, size, depth, communications).
Letter	19/5/60	Thomson informs editors that, whereas summary of 'Live' D-Notices until now issued annually, to assist busy newsrooms, in future to be issued quarterly and with additional copies (still to be treated as Confidential).
Notice	29/6/60	Re-issue of escape and evasion publication guidance, with removal of prohibition on how special equipment had been smuggled to prisoners of war [Following previous clearance of book by ex-officer on wartime escape and evasion, SIS/Air Ministry had forgotten to tell Thomson to amend Notice].
Notice	4/2/61	Ref espionage case (Lonsdale/Houghton/Gee) due in court 7/2/61, Security Service wished as *little* as possible to be in camera, but nevertheless no publication of MI5 identities, methods and activities, including those of their technical experts giving evidence.
Letter	15/2/61	Thomson to editors: revised interpretation of Notices on UK Atomic Energy establishments; only five were involved with major weapons work (Aldermaston, Woolwich, Foulness, Orfordness, and Capenhurst Works Cheshire), and eight to a lesser extent (Harwell, Risley, Culceth, Calder hall, Chapelcross, Dounreay, Springfield, Windscale).
Letter	21/3/61	Thomson to editors: ref Lonsdale/Houghton/Gee espionage case, court had accepted contents of Secret and Top Secret documents referred to during trial should not be published.
Notice	1/5/61	Request not to mention George Blake was an employee of MI6, and not to connect MI6 with Foreign Office, because lives of some agents were still in danger.
Letter	21/7/61	Reminder that, desired publicity having been allowed in Portland Espionage case, normal reporting restrictions applied to other trials involving MI5.
Notice	27/7/61	Revised Notice on any mention without prior advice of new weapons/equipment, or of aerial photography of 'War Potential' establishments; immediately seen by Media as increasing restrictions on publication.
Letter	12/10/61	Thomson to editors, referring to above Notice: refuting interpretation by media they should now consult Departments rather than Thomson.

Notice Number/ Letter	Date	Caution/Request Not to Publish
Letter	27/10/61	Thomson to editors: referring to 'our potential enemies' not just bugging telephones but allegedly using other secret interception/ listening devices, request to consult him if information received suggested conversations involving national security were being thus listened to.
Notice	30/10/61	Deletion from previous guidance on cyphers of 'methods or systems of official ciphering used by our Government or by any foreign Government'; this Notice later featured prominently in the 1967 Lohan episode – see Chapter 7.
Letter	26/2/62	Revised advice (mostly encapsulating that in several previous Notices) on 'National Defence': whereabouts, depth, size, etc, of oil storage and underground installations, underground headquarters and communications facilities, 'London Tube Railways' underground flood gates, and linked control buildings.
Notice	30/4/62	Lohan starts to stand in for Thomson (ill), issues Quarterly Service Aircraft and Aero Engines Notice, prefacing it: 'It is requested that Admiral Thomson is not disturbed in any way at his home'.
Letter	5/3/63	Lohan to editors: ref MI5 lease on 26/28 Mount Row W1, thanks to those who have already not published.
Letter	25/4/63	Lohan to editors: reminder about reporting Secret Intelligence and Security Services matters, after CND Easter March.
Notice	11/7/63	Name and whereabouts of Soviet defector, 'Dolnytsin'.
Letter	13/7/63	Letter refining request on 'Dolnytsin', in particular about photographs of him.
Letter	19/8/63	Lohan to editors: further reminder on Secret Intelligence and Security Services Notice of 27/4/56, after *Private Eye* named Heads of Services.
Notice	31/1/64	In view of reduced number of aircraft being developed, Aircraft and Aero-Engine Lists reduced from Quarterly to Annual.
Letter	15/5/64	Lohan to editors: referring to operations in Borneo against Indonesia.
1/64	24/6/64	(Lohan restarted the numbering of Notices) Radio and radar transmissions of interest to Soviet intelligence.
Letter	2/10/64	Lohan to editors: referring to aftermath of Greville Wynne case.
Letter	15/12/64	Lohan to editors: ref letter of 15/5/64, further guidance on overflying and troop movements to East of Suez.
Letter	9/3/65	Lohan to editors: Queen due to launch a giant tanker at Barrow-in-Furness on 17/3, but two nuclear submarines visibly in build nearby; request co-operation in observing guidance in previous Notices on Warship building, weapons and photography.
Letter	21/9/65	Lohan to editors: Prime Minister's wife, Mary Wilson, shortly to launch first UK nuclear-powered submarine, *HMS DREADNOUGHT*; similar request to above.
Letter	24/9/65	Lohan to editors: thanks from outgoing DGSS.

Notice Number/ Letter	Date	Caution/Request Not to Publish
Letter	2/2/66	Announcing future loose-leaf booklet for Notices, and similar instructions to those in force, plus a questionnaire updating the addressee list.
Letter	6/66	General information on operation of 'Defence (D) Notice System'.
Letter	12/9/66	Queen Mother due 15/9 to launch Polaris submarine *HMS RESOLUTION*; similar request to above.
Letter	311/7/67	Mr T Cochrane to editors ref his acting as D-Notice Secretary.

Appendix 4

D-NOTICES 1971, 1982, 1993

1971 D-Notices

1   Defence Plans, Operational Capability and State of Readiness.
2   Classified Military Weapons, Weapon Systems and Equipment.
3   Royal Navy – Warship Construction and Naval Equipment.
4   Aircraft and Aero-Engines.
5   Nuclear Weapons and Equipment.
6   Photography.
7   Prisoners of War and Evaders.
8   National Defence – War Precautions and Civil Defence.
9   Radio and Radar Transmissions.
10 British Intelligence Services.
11 Cyphers and Communications.
12 Whereabouts of Mr and Mrs Vladimir Petrov.

1982 D-Notices

1   Defence Plans, Operational Capability, State of Readiness and Training.
2   Defence Equipment.
3   Nuclear Weapons and Equipment.
4   Radio and Radar Transmission.
5   Cyphers and Communications.
6   British Security and Intelligence Services.
7   War Precautions and Civil Defence.
8   Photography.

1993 D-Notices

1   Operations, Plans and Capabilities.
2   Non-Nuclear Weapons and Operational Equipment.
3   Nuclear Weapons and Equipment.
4   Cyphers and Secure Communications.
5   Identification of Specific Installations.
6   UK Security and Intelligence Services.

The full text of 1971, 1982, and 1993 Notices is available to the public from the DA-Notice Secretary's Office on request, prior to being placed in the National Archives. The full text of current (post-2000) Notices can be seen at www.dnotice.org.uk.

Appendix 5

EXAMPLES OF PARLIAMENTARY QUESTIONS

Most of these PQs are not otherwise mentioned in the text, but listed to give an idea of the spread of more routine queries, constitutionally handled through the MoD as the Sponsoring Government Department, but in practice dealt with by the D-Notice Secretary. Some display a lack of understanding of how the D-Notice System works; for example, a Question as to how many D-Notices have been issued in the past x months, invariably gains the answer 'none', as there have for many years been a set of standing Notices. If the Secretary knows what is behind the Question, he is able to add some relevant information, but he deliberately does not normally have direct contact with politicians.

How Many D-Notices in a Past Period?: 30/7/64 (Col 416), 12/3/70 (Col 371), 3/12/71 (Col 359), 14/5/81 (Col 339), 16/5/84 (Col 173), 20/2/91 (Col 191), Lords 25/3/91 (Cols WA 53–4), 27/11/00 (Cols 419–20), 6/12/05 (Cols 1100–1).
How Many Meetings?: 3/3/80 (Col 53/54), 16/5/84 (Col 173).
Cost?: 2/4/80 (Col 277), 31/7/84 (Col 173).
Reviews?: 7/7/81 (Col 122), 31/3/82 (Col 107), 4/2/83 (Col 228), 26/10/92 (Col 510), 14/6/93 (Col 478).
Books/Publishers?: 2/3/55 (Col 103–4), 16/5/84 (Col 173), 31/7/84 (Col 172), 21/11/86 (Col 357).
Committee Membership?: 30/1/68 (Col 285), 20/7/88 (Cols 711–2), 21/4/93 (Cols 132–3).
BBC programmes?: 18/2/88 (Col 730), 11/10/88 (Cols 719–21).
Prevention/Breaches?: 2/3/55 (Cols 103–4), 11/1/88 (Col 270), 19/1/88 (Cols 819–20), 20/12/90 (Cols 298+300), 14/2/96 (Col 608), 20/1/98 (Cols 504+510), 16/12/99 (Col 255), 29/10/04 (Cols 1390–1).

Appendix 6

LISTS OF D-NOTICE COMMITTEE CHAIRMEN, VICE-CHAIRMEN AND SECRETARIES

D-Notice Committee Chairmen

Sir Graham Greene	1912–17
Sir Reginald Brade	1917–20
Sir Oswyn Murray	1920–36
Sir Herbert Creedy	1936–9
Sir Arthur Street	1945
Sir Henry Markham	1945–6
Sir Eric Speed	1946–8
Sir James Barnes	1949–55
Sir John Lang	1955–61
Sir Richard Way	1961–6
Sir Henry Hardman	1966
Sir James Dunnett	1966–74
Sir Michael Cary	1974–6
Sir Frank Cooper	1976–82
Sir Clive Whitmore	1982–8
Sir Michael Quinlan	1988–92
Sir Christopher France	1992–5
Sir Richard Mottram	1995–8

D-Notice Committee Vice-Chairmen/Chairmen of Media Side

No formal Vice-Chairman	1912–67
LJ Dicker	1967–8
WL Clarke	1968–81
JM Ramsden	1981–9
ACD Stuart	1989–97
R Hutchinson	1997–2007

D-Notice Committee Secretaries

Sir Reginald Brade and Edmond Robbins (jointly)	1912–17
Sir Edmond Robbins	1917–23
HC Robbins	1923–39

Rear Admiral Sir George Thomson	1945–63
Colonel LG Lohan	1963–7
T Cochrane	1967
Vice Admiral Sir Norman Denning	1967–72
Rear Admiral KH Farnhill	1972–9
Rear Admiral WN Ash	1979–84
Major General PR Kay	1984–6
Rear Admiral WA Higgins	1986–92
Rear Admiral DM Pulvertaft	1992–9

NOTES

PREFACE

1   AWOPC 1912, AWOAMPC 1919, SPBC 1954, DPBC 1968, DPBAC 1993; the term 'D-Notice' has over the years been written in many ways, even within the same document; for example "D" Notice, D.Notice, D Notice, etc; when referring to the Notices in this book, I have in quotes copied what was printed, but otherwise enjoyed an inconsistency normally impermissible in an Official History.

SECTION 1
PRE-FORMATION: THE LONG DEBATE,
1880s–1912

1   *'Living on a Deadline'*, Chris Moncrieff, Virgin, 2001.
2   It spent £257.15s.3d. on newspapers in 1887, and filed some cuttings, the residue being considered as 'perquisites for the officials'. NS Circular August 1888.
3   Later Field Marshal Sir Evelyn Wood, VC, GCB, GCMG (1838–1919), Midshipman in Naval Brigade Crimea, transferred to Army, served India, West and South Africa, Egypt, Adjutant-General 1897–1901, CinC 2nd Army Corps 1901–5.
4   Later Admiral Lord Beresford, GCB, GCVO (1846–1919), served Nile Expedition 1884–5 in command Naval Brigade, resigned from Admiralty Board 1888 over strength of Fleet, MP four times (interspersed with naval appointments), CinC Mediterranean then Channel Fleets.
5   St Bride's, NS Circulars May 1895 and 1896.
6   Admiral of the Fleet Lord Fisher, GCB, OM, GCVO (1841–1920), action Crimea, China and Egypt, CinC Mediterranean, Second Sea Lord (personnel matters), CinC Portsmouth, First Sea Lord 1904–10 and 1914–15.
7   Field Marshal Earl Roberts, VC, KG, KP, GCB, OM, GCSI, GCIE, PC (1832–1914), Indian Mutiny VC, action Afghanistan, Abyssinia and Burma, later Commander Forces in Ireland, CinC South Africa 1899–1900, CinC of Army 1901–4; Who's Who entry recorded not only his wounds but those of his horses, and his religion, 'Protestant'.
8   St Bride's, NS Circular January 1898.
9   St Bride's, NS Circular January 1911.
10 Notably WH Russell – later Sir William Russell (1820–1907), Irish journalist, also covered Indian Mutiny, American Civil, Austro-Prussian, Franco-Prussian, South African and Egyptian Wars; accompanied Prince of Wales on overseas visits, 'charged by Nubar Pasha with selection of guests at opening of Suez Canal'.
11 See *'The First Casualty'*, Phillip Knightley, Deutsch, 1975.
12 *'Secret Service'*, Christopher Andrew, Sceptre, 1985.
13 *'Power without Responsibility'*, Curran and Seaton, Routledge, 2003.
14 Later Lieutenant General Lord Baden Powell, GCMG, GCVO, KCB, OM, KCVO (1857–1941), action Afghanistan, West and South Africa, organised Defence of Mafeking and later South

African Constabulary, founded Boy Scouts and Girl Guides 1907, wrote books thereon, on pig-sticking and 'spying'.

15 See *'The Great Game'*, Peter Hopkirk, Murray, 1990.

16 Duke of Cambridge, KG, KT, KP, GCB, GCMG, GCIE, GCVO, PC (1819–1904), cousin of Queen Victoria, Colonel Hanoverian Guards as boy, commanded Division Crimean War, CinC of Army 1856–95; long morganatic marriage to actress 'Mrs Fitzgeorge', by whom two Colonel and one Admiral Fitzgeorge sons.

17 Later Captain Sir John Colomb, KCMG, Royal Marines (1838–69), writer on naval/military strategy and imperial defence, Conservative MP.

18 Marquess of Salisbury, KG, GCVO, PC (1830–1903), Prime Minister (1885–6, 1886–92, 1895–1902).

19 Major General Charles Gordon (1833–85), religious Royal Engineers officer, action Crimea, China during Taipei Rebellion 1885, Governor-General Sudan 1876–80, returning 1884, killed in besieged Khartoum January 1885.

20 Sir Robert Anderson (1841–1918), Irish lawyer, Home Office advisor on 'political crime' from 1868, Assistant Commissioner/Head Criminal Investigation Department Metropolitan Police until 1901; wrote books on millenarian Christian theology, and 'Sidelights on the Home Rule Movement' (1906) – principal stimulant to Joseph Conrad's 'Secret Agent' 1907 – see Author's Note 1920 edition.

21 Earl Spencer, KG (1835–1910), known as 'Foxy' or 'the Red Earl' because of luxuriant red beard, First Lord of Admiralty and twice Lord Lieutenant of Ireland, where his staff included several homosexuals, inspiring a local MP to refer to Dublin Castle as 'Sodom and Begorrah'.

22 Sir Edward Jenkinson (1835–1919), Indian Civil Service 1856–80, raised cavalry regiment during the 'Indian Mutiny' 1857, District Commissioner Oudh, Ireland 1882–4.

23 *'Fenian Fire'*, Christy Campbell, Harper Collins, 2002.

24 James Monro (1838–1920), Bengal Civil Service, Inspector-General Police and Commissioner of Presidency Division, Assistant Commissioner of Metropolitan Police/Head of Special Branch 1887, Chief Commissioner 1888, resigned 1890 to return to Bengal to found Abode of Mercy Medical Mission.

25 *'The Rise and Fall of Government Telegraphy in Britain'* by CR Perry, Business and Economic History, Vol 26, 1997.

26 Devised by the American Samuel Morse (1791–1872) in 1837.

27 In particular the work of the US Navy's Lieutenants Matthew Maury and OH Berryman.

28 Later Marchese Marconi, GCVO (1874–1937), established first wireless telegraphy system between England and France 1899, gained Admiralty contract 1903, Nobel Prize for Physics 1909.

29 Which became the Cable and Wireless Company in 1934.

30 St Bride's, NS Circular September 1884.

31 Formal links were made by Reuter's in 1865 with similar agencies in other countries, including Associated Press (USA), Havas (France) and Wolff (Germany).

32 *'Living on a Deadline'*.

33 St Bride's, NS Circular August 1891.

34 NS and PA shared offices and staff from 1868 until 1909 (St Bride's, NS Circular August 1909). First NPA Secretary was George Riddell (see below), also first PPA Chairman.

35 Later Sir George Toulmin (1857–1923), proprietor *Lancashire Daily Post* and *Preston Guardian*, Liberal MP 1902–18; brother of another Lancashire newspaper proprietor; the Director, Press Complaints Commission from 2004 is a descendant.

36 Later Viscount Samuel, GCB, OM, GBE, PC (1870–1963), Liberal MP 1902–18 and 1929–35, Postmaster-General 1910–16, High Commissioner Palestine 1920–5, Home Secretary 1931–2.

37 St Bride's, NS Circular September 1910.

38 *'Newspapers in Victorian Britain'* by Mark Hampton, History Compass, Blackwell Publishing Ltd, 2004.

39 Later Lord Northcliffe (1865–1922), bought *Times* 1908, Chairman British War Mission 1917–18, Director of Propaganda in Enemy Countries 1918.

40   Later Sir Arthur Pearson, GBE (1866–1921); went blind before WWI, later Chairman Blinded Soldiers and Sailors Care Committee, and President National Institute for the Blind.

41   Later Sir Winston Churchill, KG, PC, OM, CH (1874–1965), wrote for *Daily Telegraph* whilst attached to Punjab Infantry in Malakand 1897 and wrote first book afterwards, war correspondent *Morning Post* South Africa 1899–1900, MP 1900–64, inter alia Home Secretary 1910–11, First Lord of the Admiralty 1911–15, Minister of Munitions 1917, Secretary of State for War and Air 1919–21, Chancellor of Exchequer 1924–9, First Lord of Admiralty 1939–40, Prime Minister 1940–5 and 1951–5.

42   St Bride's, NS Circular December 1904.

43   The National Archives of the UK (TNA): Public Record Office (PRO) WO 32/6347.

44   Robert Hanbury (1845–1903), Conservative MP, President of Board of Agriculture 1900–3.

45   The growing importance of the Press was reflected in society and in Parliament; between 1880 and 1908, 31 newspapermen were given peerages and/or knighthoods, and many more were to follow; 21 newspapermen of various kinds were elected as MPs in 1892, and the Parliamentary Press Committee was formed in 1895, chaired by Sir John Leng, MP. St Bride's, NS Circular December 1908.

46   The concern about the wide interpretation of libel being used to prevent fair comment in the Press led in mid-1889 to the London Press, including even *The Times*, joining the Newspaper Society (which then dropped 'Provincial' from its title).

47   *'Official Secrets'*, David Hooper, Secker and Warburg, 1987.

48   TNA:PRO WO 32/6347.

49   TNA:PRO CAB 4/1.

50   Later Field Marshal Viscount Wolseley, KP, GCB, OM, GCMG (1833–1913), action Burma, Crimea, Indian Mutiny, China, Ashanti War, Egypt (CinC), Relief of Khartoum, Adjutant-General 1885–90, CinC Ireland 1890–95, CinC Army (relieving the Duke of Cambridge, and seen as an intelligent moderniser) 1895–1900; allegedly the inspiration for Gilbert and Sullivan's 'very model of a modern major general'.

51   St Bride's, NS Circular September 1898.

52   TNA:PRO WO 32/7138.

53   Later Earl Kitchener, KG, KP, GCB, OM, GCSI, GCMG, GCIE, PC (1850–1916), Sirdar Egyptian Army 1890, relieved Khartoum 1898, Chief of Staff South Africa 1899–1900, CinC there 1900–2, CinC India 1902–09, CID 1910, Agent and Consul-General Egypt 1911–14, SofS for War 14–16, died in sinking of *HMS HAMPSHIRE*.

54   The British and French military axes of advance in Africa came into confrontation there (Sudan), July to November 1898; the crisis ended with French withdrawal in face of Britain's superior worldwide military strength.

55   Later Major General Sir John Ardagh, KCMG, KCIE, CB (1840–1907), topographer of disputed international boundaries, thus in intelligence, including Egypt and Sudan campaigns, DMI 1896–1901; thereafter Arbitration Tribunal between Argentina and Chile, and Permanent International Court of Arbitration at the Hague, Director of Suez Canal Company.

56   Spenser Wilkinson, Chichele Professor of War Oxford University 1909–23, journalist *Manchester Guardian* and *Morning Post*. *'Secret Service'*, Andrew.

57   Member of Army Council responsible for personnel matters.

58   Sir Ralph Knox, KCB, PC (1836–1913), PUS War Office 1897–1901.

59   George Wyndham (1863–1913), Conservative MP, ex-Coldstream Guards, USofS 1898–1900, Chief Secretary Ireland 1900–1905.

60   Marquess of Lansdowne, KG, GCSI, GCMG, GCIE (1845–1927), Governor-General of Canada 1883–8 and of India 1888–93, SofS for War 1895–1900, Foreign Secretary 1900–05.

61   TNA:PRO WO 32/6381.

62   General Sir Redvers Buller, VC, GCB, GCMG, PC (1839–1908), action China, Ashanti, Kaffir and Zulu Wars, Egypt, and Sudan, Adjutant-General 1890–7, GOC Aldershot 1898–1906 including deployment to South Africa.

63   TNA:PRO WO 32/7137.

64   Also one lady amongst accredited journalists, the first female war correspondent, Lady Sarah Wilson (1865–1929) of *Daily Mail*; daughter of Duke of Marlborough, Lieutenant Colonel's wife, captured by Boers outside Mafeking during siege, later exchanged for a Boer prisoner.

65 TNA:PRO WO 32/7138.
66 NS Circular 1899.
67 *'Living on a Deadline'*.
68 St Bride's, NS Circular December 1900. An instructive insight into the self-perception of the British Press is contained in the next section of the Circular, commenting on censorship in France, and ending: 'The Havas Agency occupies a very different position in relation to the French Press to that of the agencies which supply news in this country. In France Havas, at any rate in the departments outside Paris, controls the Press, whilst here the Press undoubtedly controls the agencies'.
69 The telephone installed in the PA offices in 1893, but largely ignored, first came into regular use in 1899, as the link to Johannesburg.
70 Later Lieutenant Colonel W D Jones, CMG, CID Secretariat during WWI.
71 TNA:PRO WO 32/7141.
72 Now back in Aldershot, having been relieved as CinC in South Africa by Lord Roberts after the British defeats in 'Black Week', December 1899.
73 Later Earl of Derby, KG, PC, GCB, GCVO (1865–1948), Chief Press Censor South Africa 1899–1900, War Office 1900–3, Director-General Recruiting 1915–16, SofS for War 1916–18 and 1922–4.
74 Later Earl of Midleton, KP, PC (1856–1942), SofS for War 1900–3 and for India 1903–5, Irish Convention 1917–18.
75 Edgar Wallace (1875–1932), private in Royal West Kent Regiment/Royal Army Medical Corps before becoming Reuter's war correspondent, *Daily News*, *Daily Mail* 1901–2, founder editor of *Rand Daily Mail*; prolific author, later Chairman of British Lion Film Corporation.
76 NS Circular August 1901.
77 Edgar Wallace, much to the fury this time of the rest of the Press, managed to send back *Daily Mail* scoops of these secret negotiations. Censorship in South Africa ended in September 1902, when the NS Circular looked back with dissatisfaction on the military's handling of the Press since 1899.
78 WT Stead (1849–1912), editor *Darlington Northern Echo* 1871–80 and *Pall Mall Gazette* 1883–9, collaborated with Fisher on 'Truth about the Navy' (calling for increased spending) 1884, imprisoned for three months over exposé on child prostitution, founder *Review of Reviews* and Masterpiece Library, campaigned against Boer War.
79 WT Le Queux (1864–1927), foreign editor *Globe* 1891–3, *Daily Mail* correspondent Balkan War, listed 'revolver practice' amongst recreations, early radio ham and President Wireless Experimental Association.
80 Lieutenant Commander RE Childers, DSC, RNVR (1870–1922), Royal Naval Air Service WWI.
81 Earl of Selborne, KG, PC, GCMG (1859–1942), First Lord 1900–5, Governor Transvaal/High Commissioner South Africa 1905–10.
82 The German Naval Staff, with habitual thoroughness, *had* in 1896 considered a contingency plan for invasion of East Britain, but had also rejected it as not feasible. *'Secret Service'*.
83 TNA:PRO WO 32/7139/7140.
84 Rt Hon HO Arnold-Forster (1855–1909), SofS for War 1903–6.
85 TNA:PRO WO 32/7140.
86 TNA:PRO CAB 3/1.
87 Later Earl of Balfour, KG, OM (1848–1930), Conservative MP 1874–1922, SofS for Scotland 1886–7, Chief Secretary for Ireland 1887–91, Prime Minister 1902–5, 1st Lord of Admiralty 1915–16, Foreign Secretary 1916–19.
88 TNA:PRO CAB 2/1 and CAB 3/1.
89 TNA:PRO CAB 2/1.
90 Later Marquess of Milford Haven, GCB, GCVO, KCMG, PC (1854–1921), Egyptian War, DNI 1902–5, CinC Atlantic Fleet 1908–10, Second Sea Lord 1911–12, First Sea Lord 1912–14, forced by media pressure to resign because of his German origins.
91 TNA:PRO CAB 3/1.
92 TNA:PRO CAB 4/1.
93 TNA:PRO CAB 2/1 and CAB 38/6/100&119.

94 Later Lord Sydenham, GCMG, GCIE, GBE (1848–1933), ex-Army, action in Egypt, Sudan and China, various War Office reorganisation studies 1900–4, Governor of Victoria 1901–4, Secretary CID 1904–7, Governor Bombay 1907–13, President National Council for Combating Venereal Disease 1915–20.

95 'strategic build-up'. TNA:PRO CAB 17/91.

96 Unlike shops, station bookstalls were exempt from paying not only Poor Law Rates but also therefore General District Rates; Smith's, then as later, declined to stock titles of which they disapproved for moral or business reasons, and were criticised in the House of Commons (16 March 1885) for having 'established a practical and irresponsible censorship of the Press'; this was given added piquancy by the position of the austere head of the Company, William Henry Smith (1825–91), prominent MP and friend of Lord Salisbury, and First Lord of Admiralty 1877–80 (model for 'The Ruler of the Queen's Navee' in Gilbert and Sullivan's 'HMS Pinafore'), SofS for War 1885–6.

97 TNA:PRO CAB 38/8/12.

98 CinC of Army until post abolished 1904, resigned from CID November 1905 to become President of National Service League, whose membership increased from 2,000 in 1905 to 222,000 by 1914. He continued to issue memoranda on other subjects, including 'Method of Carrying the Rifle by Cavalry', which argued the weapon should be attached to the soldier not to the horse, and opined 'the divergence of practice between the army in India and at home, in regard to a matter so important, is a very serious evil'. TNA:PRO CAB 38/8.

99 TNA:PRO CAB 2/1. In the event, as Asquith told the King when War started in August 1914, there were then about '900 India Officers now here on furlough', a number of whom were rapidly transferred to duties in Europe. TNA:PRO CAB 41/35/24.

100 These imaginative articles showed each day (with maps) those towns which the Germans would reach next day, assisted by their spies and saboteurs, many already in Britain before the invasion; Harmsworth had previously commissioned Le Queux in 1896 to write serialised magazine articles about a possible Franco-Russian invasion, championing a larger British Fleet.

101 NS Circular April 1906.

102 S Brooks (1872–1937), contributor to British and American journals, editor *Saturday Review* and *Sperling's Journal*.

103 TNA:PRO CAB 17/91.

104 TNA:PRO CAB 17/91.

105 Joseph Soames, of 58 Lincoln's Inn, also legal advisor to *The Times*, on whose behalf he had been prominent in an 1888–89 Special Commission investigating allegations of complicity of Parnell's (Irish) Nationalist Party in acts of terrorism, including the 'Jubilee Plot' against the Queen (see *'Fenian Fire'*); the somewhat easy decryption by Dr Walsh, Archbishop of Dublin, of coded telegrams between Soames and an American private investigator is reputed to have led indirectly to improvements in codes used by the Royal Irish Constabulary, the Royal Navy and the Army.

106 AF Walter (1846–1910), great grandson of the founder of *The Times*.

107 Sir John Leng (1828–1906), proprietor *Dundee Advertiser* and founder of other titles, Liberal MP 1889–1906; Yorkshireman by origin, whose elder brother Sir William Leng (1825–1902) was proprietor *Sheffield Telegraph*, recording in Who's Who that he 'Broke down the Trades Union tyranny at Sheffield'.

108 NS Circular July 1906.

109 Lord Tweedmouth, KT, PC (1849–1909), First Lord of Admiralty 1905–8.

110 TNA:PRO CAB 4/2.

111 This exchange ended because Leng died in December 1906.

112 President-elect IoJ, later Sir Alfred Robbins (1856–1931), from a remarkable family of journalists originating in the small Cornish town, Launceston; London/parliamentary correspondent *Birmingham Post* 1888–1923, Chairman Press Lobby Committee 1914–15; brother of E Robbins, future D-Notice Committee Secretary; married to sister of WE Pitt (*The Times*), first Parliamentary lobby correspondent under system introduced 1892, five children, three sons working for *The Times* (one of whom AP Robbins later on D-Notice Committee), one son on *Daily Mail*, one daughter-in-law reporter *Northampton Echo*, another the daughter of Edgar Pardon, Head of the Cricket Reporting Agency.

113 TNA:PRO CAB 17/91.
114 What in modern parlance would be included in 'information already widely in the public domain'.
115 TNA:PRO CAB 38/12/55. This was the meeting at which Admiral Fisher, referring to possible war with Turkey, said he 'hoped no attack on the Dardanelles would ever be undertaken in any form'; because of German influence there, Britain could 'no longer hope to bribe the defenders into allowing us to pass unharmed through the Straits'.
116 NS Circular May 1907.
117 Baron (of the Duchy of Saxe-Coburg-Gotha) Julius de Reuter (1852–1915), whose father had transferred the Company from Berlin to London in 1851 when the telegraphic cable was laid between England and France.
118 Brother of IoJ President, and later to feature prominently in this History.
119 See Section 2; the London Proprietors resented being regarded by officials as equals with the NS and IoJ.
120 Later Earl of Loreburn, GCMG (1846–1923), Oxford Cricket Blue/Racquets Half-Blue 1865–8, Solicitor-General then Attorney-General 1894, Lord Chancellor 1905–1912.
121 St Bride's, NS Circular October 1907.
122 Viscount Haldane, OM, PC (1856–1928), SofS for War 1905–12, Chancellor of Exchequer 1912–15, dropped by Asquith after *Daily Mail* campaign against Haldane for alleged pro-German sympathies, Chancellor again 1924.
123 Earl of Granard, KP, PC, GCVO (1874–1948), Army Boer War, Assistant Postmaster-General 1906–9, commanded Royal Irish Regiment WWI, Royal Household (Master of the Horse), Member Irish Senate 1921–34, Comptroller Ascot Racecourse 1936–45.
124 NS Circular July 1908.
125 NS Circulars September and November 1908.
126 In 1909 the RN had 82 armoured cruisers and battleships to Germany/Japan's 54; by 1912 it was 95 to 75.
127 TNA:PRO CAB 2/2. Remarkably rapid advances were made after the Wright brothers' first petrol-driven flight in 1903, with the first cross-Channel flight in 1908, warplanes by 1914, and a rudimentary international aircraft control regime under discussion in 1919.
128 Lieutenant Colonel CA'C Repington, CMG (1858–1925), served Afghanistan, Burma, Sudan, South Africa, journalist with *The Times*, *Morning Post*, and *Army Review*, military correspondent of *The Times*; HW Wilson (1866–1940), naval correspondent *Daily Mail*.
129 Later Brigadier-General Sir James Edmonds, CB, CMG (1861–1956), served South Africa and WWI British Expeditionary Force, in charge Military History Branch of Committee of Imperial Defence/Cabinet Office 1919–1949, Official Military Historian World War I.
130 By Major (later Lieutenant Colonel) Guy du Maurier, DSO (1865–1915), served Burma and Boer War, killed in Belgium March 1915, playwright and novelist, brother of actor Sir Gerald and uncle of novelist Dame Daphne.
131 FT Jane (1870–1916), journalist and author of naval books, started the annual *Jane's Fighting Ships* series in 1898.
132 Later Admiral Sir Edmond Slade, KCIE, KCVO (1859–1928), served Egypt, CinC East Indies 1909–12, later Vice-Chairman, Anglo-Persian Oil Company.
133 Later Lieutenant General Sir John Ewart, KCB (1861–1930), served Egypt, Sudan, and South Africa, War Office 1904–10, Adjutant-General 1910–14, GOC Scotland 1914–18.
134 Rt Hon Reginald McKenna, PC (1863–1943), Cambridge Rowing Blue 1887, winner Grand and Steward's Cups Henley, First Lord 1908–11, Home Secretary 1911–15, Chancellor of Exchequer 1915–16.
135 TNA:PRO CAB 16/8.
136 Later Major General Sir Vernon Kell, KBE, CB (1873–1942), served Boxer Rebellion (a Chinese linguist), CID secretariat, DMI 1909; and later Captain Sir Mansfield Cumming, KCMG, CB, RN (1859–1923), joined Navy 1872, served in Malacca and Egypt campaigns, invalided 1885.
137 *'Secret Service'*.

138 TNA:PRO CAB 4/3. Linked with these war preparations were many such much-staffed papers as that on 'the control and disposal of aliens'.

139 Rear Admiral Sir Charles Ottley, KCMG, CB, MVO (1858–1932), unusual succession of attaché appointments in Egypt, Turkey, USA, Japan, Italy, Russia and France 1897–1904, DNI 1905–7, Secretary CID 1907–11.

140 Later Field Marshal Sir Henry Wilson, GCB, DSO (1864–1922), action Burma and South Africa, DMO 1910–14, BEF Corps Commander, British Military Representative Versailles 1917, Chief of Imperial General Staff 1918–22, assassinated by Irish Republican Army June 1922.

141 Later Admiral the Hon Sir Alexander Bethell, GCMG, KCB (1855–1932), DNI 1909–12, CinC East Indies 1912, Director RN War College 1913–14, commanded battleships of 3rd Fleet 1914, Commander Channel Fleet 1915, CinC Plymouth 1916–18.

142 Later Viscount Grey, KG, PC (1862–1933), winner Queen's Club and MCC Tennis Championships 1896, Foreign Secretary 1905–16.

143 TNA:PRO CAB 17/91 and DEFE 53/1.

144 The Prime Minister Asquith explained this in a note to the new King George V as 'Bismarckian doctrine: "beati possidentes"' [blessed are the possessors]. TNA:PRO CAB 41/33.

145 *Morning Post* 2 September 1911, on fortifications guarding ports/key points.

146 Sir William Byles (1839–1917), son of founder of *Bradford Observer*, social reformer, Radical MP 1892–5 and 1906–17.

147 Later Major General Lord Mottistone, PC, CB, CMG, DSO, KStJ (1868–1947), French Gold Medal for saving life at sea, action South Africa 1900–1, USofS for War 1911 and SofS 1912–14, rejoined Army 1914–18, returning to Government 1918–19, Chairman National Savings Committee 1926–43.

148 *'Adventure'*, JEB Seely, 1930.

149 Later Marquess of Reading, GCB, GCSI, GCIE, GCVO (1860–1935), Liberal MP 1904–13, Attorney-General 1910–13, Lord Chief Justice of England 1913–21, Viceroy/Governor-General of India 1921–6, Foreign Secretary in National Government 1931.

150 St Bride's, NS Circulars September/October 1911.

151 Later Sir Reginald Brade, GCB (1864–1933), joined War Office 1884, Assistant Secretary 1904–14, PUS War Office 1914–20 (resigned, ill-health), Chairman Special Grants Committee 1920–6.

152 TNA:PRO CAB 17/91.

153 AP Nicholson (1869–1940), *Times* lobby correspondent 1908–13, then for *Daily Chronicle* 1914–23, Chairman Lobby Committee 1921–22.

154 TNA:PRO CAB 16/27.

155 Rt Hon Leopold Amery, PC, CH (1873–1955), *The Times* 1899–1909, served Flanders and Near East 1914–16, First Lord of Admiralty 1922–4, SofS for Colonies 1924–9 and for India/Burma 1940–5.

156 R Nicholson, MBE (1869–1946), son of Senior Master in Lunacy, Assistant Traffic Manager Bengal Nagpur Railway, *Times* 1911–15, Coalition Liberal MP 1918–22.

157 True not all newspapers were NS members, but this opinion reflected more the London Proprietors' view of their provincial cousins; Brade exploited this division, later commenting 'One should never take by force what one can get by fraud'; TNA:PRO CAB 4/5.

158 Founded by Harry Brittain 1909; later Sir Harry Brittain, KBE, CMG (1873–1974), Unionist MP 1918–29.

159 NS Circular February 1912.

160 *Pall Mall Gazette*, 27 July 1912.

161 Later Colonel Lord Hankey, GCB, GCMG, GCVO (1877–1963), Anglo-Australian, Royal Marine Artillery, NID 1902–6, CID Secretary 1912–38, establisher of Cabinet Office Secretariat, War Cabinet Minister 1938–42.

162 Brooks reappears in an aside in Lord Riddell's *'Diaries 1908–1923'*, where in a description of a May 1915 call on Lord Northcliffe, he says 'His tame leader writer was waiting to take his instructions. Poor creature. Name Sydney Brooks. He has sold himself, body and soul, for £1,500 a year, or thereabouts, so I am told.' An unkind comment on an apparently sensible and public-spirited journalist.

163 St Bride's. NS Memoranda, October 1912.
164 He was however now on record as having opined that the 'apparent caress' of a voluntary system would prove more effective than the 'clumsy club' of statutory control; TNA:PRO ADM 17/91.
165 St Bride's, NS Circular January 1912.

SECTION 2
FORMATION AND EARLY MODUS OPERANDI OF THE COMMITTEE, 1912–14

1 Sir Graham Greene, KCB (1857–1950), PUS Admiralty 1911–17 and Munitions Ministry 1917–20; Greene King Brewery family, wealthy uncle of novelist Graham Greene and DG BBC Sir Hugh Carleton Greene.
2 Later Lieutenant General Sir George Macdonogh, GBE, KCB, KCMG, KStJ (1865–1942), Director Intelligence/Chief Censor BEF 1914–16, DMI 1916–18, Adjutant-General 1918–22, later Imperial War Graves Commissioner, President Federation British Industries, Central Committee for Regulation of Prices 1939–41.
3 JSR Phillips (1850–1919), Editor *Kendal Mercury, Manchester Examiner, Yorkshire Post* (1903–19), Chairman PA 1912, President NS 1914.
4 Later Sir David Duncan (1847–1923), Liberal editor *South Wales Daily News*.
5 Later Sir Robert Baird, KBE (1855–1934), proprietor *Belfast Telegraph* and many other Irish titles, President Master Printers' Federation 1910, and Irish Newspaper Society 1913–25, Life Governor Masonic Orphan Boys and Girls Schools Dublin, friend of leading Unionist politicians such as Carson.
6 Ernest Parke (1860–1944), managing editor *Star*, later director Northern Newspaper Company Darlington; previously involved in notorious libel case brought by Lord Euston.
7 TNA:PRO DEFE 53/1; Guildhall Library, PA Manager's Memoranda, Ms 35362/4.
8 Later Sir Edmund Robbins, KBE (1847–1922), apprentice *Launceston Weekly News*, Central Press Agency, sub-editor Press Association on formation 1870, Secretary Provincial Newspaper Society 1870–81, Manager PA 1880–1917; conservative, paternalist, with walrus moustache considered luxuriant even in an era of notable moustaches, elder brother of Sir Alfred Robbins (see Chapter 1), father of six daughters and six sons, four of whom worked for the PA, including his successor HC (see Chapter 3), CE (Head of London Service), and CJ (Head of the Parliamentary Service).
9 10 September, and again on 12 September in response to Phillips' reply – impressive testimony to the speed/reliability of the then postal service.
10 Recorded at length in the PA Manager's Memoranda; Guildhall Library Ms 35362/4.
11 As a young Royal Marines Lieutenant in *HMS RAMILLIES*, Hankey did low-level intelligence work for Fisher, who took him into Admiralty Intelligence, thence to the CID in 1908 with former DNI Admiral Ottley (as his Assistant); promoted to Secretary, with Haldane's support, in 1912.
12 JR Scott (1879–1949), director later Chairman *Manchester Guardian*, son of CP Scott, who edited the paper 1872–1929 and established its national Liberal credentials.
13 5 November 1912. TNA:PRO DEFE 53/1.
14 Brade added a footnote after 'spy class' [in itself a somewhat Gilbertian description of spies]: 'The marginal note to the first section is "penalties for spying", but I believe that such notes do not limit in any way the provisions of a Statute.'
15 Later Sir John Le Sage (1837–1926), former foreign/war correspondent in Egypt, Franco-Prussian War, Paris Commune uprising.
16 Alexander Kenealy (1864–1915), worked in USA, covered Pearey's first Arctic Expedition, embedded with US Navy during Spanish-American War, *Daily Express* 1901–4, Editor *Daily Mirror* 1904–15.
17 Tension had recently increased when many nations sent warships to Constantinople as a demonstration of force, intended to bring an early end to the First Balkan War by putting pressure on Turkey, already weakened by concurrent war against Italy in Ottoman-ruled Libya. Germany sent her newest battleship, the *Goeben*, which outmatched the largest ship the Royal Navy had

in the area at the time. The unintended effect, not only in Turkey but amongst countries across Europe, was that the air of crisis was *increased* by this show of international naval muscle.

18   In his brief for Seely, Hankey suggested the staff might also raise what action should be taken 'in the event of some enterprising newspaper fitting out a fast vessel to accompany the fleet on the outbreak of War'; this novel possibility appears neither to have been discussed by the CID, nor ever effected by the Press.

19   Paper 167-B, dated 22 January 1913. TNA:PRO CAB 17/91.

20   The first documented occasion when the Committee was given a formal title: 'Standing Joint Committee of Admiralty, War Office, and Press Representatives'. The title varied slightly from document to document until 14 January 1913, whence, without apparent formal discussion, it became simply the 'Admiralty, War Office, and Press Committee' – usually AWOPC in this book, although the modern liking for acronyms/initials was not then prevalent.

21   These secret telegrams were given the codename 'Parkers' by the Post Office (see Chapter 4 for the reason). Oral tradition has suggested that the phrase 'nosy Parker' stemmed from this codeword/use; pleasing though this idea is, it is false; the Oxford English Dictionary records that the term was already in use before 1912 in saucy seaside postcards.

22   In addition to the London newspapers, there were on the provincial lists 60 morning papers, 99 evening papers and 150 weekly papers, from the *Aberdeen Journal* to the *Swindon Herald* to the *Dublin Sinn Fein*. TNA:PRO DEFE 53/1.

23   *Army and Navy Gazette, Broad Arrow, Naval and Military Record, The Regiment, Territorial Service Gazette, Military Mail*, and *United Service Gazette*.

24   TNA:PRO DEFE 53/1; letter dated 7 January 1913.

25   While continuing to monitor progress on censorship, the CID produced many other papers on matters pertinent to a possible European War; for example, an Air Committee was established 'As a consequence of the remarkable developments in aerial navigation during the last five years', including the airship threat. TNA:PRO CAB 39/10/90.

26   9 January 1913. TNA:PRO DEFE 53/1.

27   Although it was Robbins who sent it direct to most editors, Baird felt the Irish best approached by a short covering note from himself.

28   Prime Minister (Asquith) in the Chair; as some idea of the place of Press Censorship amongst current concerns, the agenda also covered Naval Policy in Pacific, Aerial Navigation, Control of Aircraft, Postal Censorship, Maintenance of Overseas Trade in Time of War, Grant of Clearance in Time of War to Neutral Shipping Entering British Ports with Arms for Foreign Destination, and Attack on British Isles from Oversea [sic].

29   Churchill had made the first allusion to the new Committee in Parliament, in veiled terms, on 22 January 1913; Hansard Cols 388–9.

30   TNA:PRO CAB 4/5 and CAB 38/23/9.

31   An eclectic collection of hulks moored in Portchester Creek, which together formed the Royal Navy's early torpedo and wireless telegraphy workshop, trials unit and school.

32   Guildhall Library. PA Manager's Memoranda Ms 35362/5, and TNA:PRO DEFE 53/1.

33   Guildhall, PA Manager's Memoranda Ms 35362/5.

34   Thomas Marlowe (1868–1935), joined *Daily Mail* when founded, editor 1899–1926, Chairman Associated Newspapers 1918–26; Northcliffe had absolute trust in his innovations/judgement.

35   Later Colonel Sir Arthur Holbrook, KBE (1850–1946); his mini-bio is typically vivid of many others more abbreviated in this book: founded *Southern Daily Mail*, Commandant Volunteer Battalion Hampshire Regiment (joined as drummer-boy aged 10), Chairman Portsmouth Conservative Association 1885–98, President NS 1913–14, commanded Royal Army Service Corps Salisbury Plain 1914–19, one of his 10 offspring won VC as submarine CO Dardanelles 1915, Unionist MP 1920–29, Provincial Grand Master of Mark Freemasons Hampshire/Isle of Wight from 1921.

36   Robbins had harried Greene previously; reasons for not allowing correspondents onboard during manoeuvres were: any statements on the progress of opposing forces 'of interest to the public' would also give 'information of direct value' to the opposing [British] Admirals; and reports would reveal information of use to 'a possible enemy as to the course which in certain eventualities hostilities might take' (adding that naval manoeuvres were not like army ones 'near

Aldershot' but took place 'in areas of ocean which would be expected to be used in actual war'. Guildhall, PA Manager's Memoranda Ms 35362/5.

37   28 July. TNA:PRO DEFE 53/1.

38   Guildhall, PA Managers' Memoranda, Ms 35417/5.

39   TNA:PRO CAB 16/25 and CAB 16/27.

40   Later Sir Oswyn Murray, GCB (1873–1936), PUS Admiralty 1917–36, Chairman AWOAMPC 1920–36.

41   Baird also described how, when the *Irish Independent* had asked all other Irish newspapers not to take advantage of a strike of its Dublin workers, only the Nationalist *Irish News* had refused to co-operate, despite a personal appeal by Baird to its Chairman. Guildhall, PA Manager's Memoranda Ms 35417/5.

42   TNA:PRO DEFE 53/1.

43   TNA:PRO CAB 38/25/39; but they were not so 'framed', until much later Australia and New Zealand experimented.

44   Parke's last meeting; in April he fell ill; replaced as NPA representative, significantly as it turned out, by NPA Vice-Chairman Sir George Riddell, later Lord Riddell (1865–1934), son of a Brixton photographer, legal adviser to *News of the World*, its Chairman from 1903; with formula 'We're just like the Old Testament – we report crime and punishment', took circulation to 7 1/2 million; also founded *Country Life*, active in NPA and PPA (Chairman of both), golfing/social friend of Lloyd George and other leading figures, first divorced peer appointed to House of Lords (opposed therefore by King George V), author/diarist (not always completely accurate), considerable benefactor, especially of medical institutions, including St Thomas' and Royal Free Hospitals.

45   Guildhall, PA Manager's Memoranda Ms 35362/6.

46   *'Lord Riddell's War Diary 1914–18'*, Riddell, Nicholson and Watson, 1933.

47   TNA:PRO DEFE 53/1.

48   TNA:PRO DEFE 53/1.

SECTION 3
WORLD WAR I, 1914–18

1   Later Earl Lloyd George, PC, OM (1863–1945), Chancellor of Exchequer 1908–15, Minister of Munitions 1915–16, SofS for War 1916, Prime Minister 1916–22.

2   *'Secret Service'*.

3   Later Admiral of the Fleet Sir Henry Oliver, GCB, KCMG, MVO (1865–1965), DNI 1913–14, Chief of Admiralty War Staff 1914–17, commanded Battle Cruiser Squadron then Home Fleet 1918–19, Reserve Fleet 1919–20, 2nd Sea Lord 1920–24, CinC Atlantic Fleet 1924–7.

4   Professor Sir Alfred Ewing, KCB (1855–1935), Professor Mechanical Engineering Imperial University, Tokyo 1878–83, then University College Dundee 1883–90, of Mechanism and Applied Mechanics Cambridge University 1890–1903, DNE 1903–16, Principal/Vice-Chancellor Edinburgh University and President Royal Society of Edinburgh 1924–9.

5   Including the later Commander Alastair Denniston, CMG, CBE, RNVR (1881–1961), WWII the Head of Bletchley Park.

6   Later Rear Admiral (S) CJE Rotter, CB (1871–1948), action Naval Brigade Pekin, NID 1911–19, Director of Statistics, Admiralty 1919–32.

7   Later Admiral Sir Reginald Hall, KCMG, CB (1870–1943), DNI 1914–18, Unionist MP 1919–29, known as 'Blinker' Hall because of habitual rapid blinking, son of 1st DNI Captain William Hall.

8   *'Secret Service'*.

9   When this author worked more prosaically in ex-Room 40 in the 1970s, an autographed copy of the decoded Zimmermann Telegram still hung on the wall.

10   Later Brigadier-General Sir Francis Anderson, KBE, CB (1860–1920), War Office 1914–18, Chairman Army Sanitary Committee 1918–20.

11   Former AWOPC member, appointed BEF Head of Intelligence (and Censorship) at GHQ in Belgium; returned to War Office January 1916 as DMI.

12   Later Temporary Lieut-Col TGJ Torrie ((1880–1917), Light Cavalry.

13   Early in the War, it was safer to be a courier-pigeon in Belgium than a non-combatant pigeon in Britain; spy hysteria included the rumour that pigeons were being used by Germans in UK for carrying messages to enemy spymasters; a temporary pigeon cull ensued.

14   JdeV Loder, Conservative MP 1924–36, succeeded father as Lord Wakehurst 1936, Governor New South Wales 1937–46, and Northern Ireland 1952–64, Boards of Royal Opera House/Royal Ballet 1949–70; *'Tales of Empire'*, Derek Hopwood, Tauris,1989.

15   WWI MI5 Central Registry eventually included over 250K index cards of suspects, coded from AA (Absolutely Anglicised/Allied – undoubtedly friendly) through A, AB, BA, B, to BB (Bad Boche – undoubtedly hostile).

16   Later Sir Basil Thomson, KCB (1861–1939), son of Archbishop of York, Colonial Service (including Acting Prime Minister of Tonga), Governor Dartmoor then Wormwood Scrubs Prisons, Assistant Commissioner Metropolitan Police 1914–1919, Director of Intelligence 1919–21.

17   Sir Roger Casement (1864–1916), Colonial Service until 1912, resigned to pursue Irish Nationalist ambitions, attempted to persuade Germany to provide men and arms to assist uprising in Ireland, hanged Pentonville after trial for treason.

18   TNA:PRO KV 4/112 and 4/113. Details of their 87 cases are contained in MI5's ghoulishly named 'Game Books'; many also mentioned in Sir Basil Thomson's 'Queer People', Hodder and Stoughton, 1922.

19   *'Secret Service'*.

20   TNA:PRO INF 4, Notes.

21   Buckingham Gate, London; CFG Masterman (1874–1927), journalist/author on social conditions, Liberal politician; Chancellor of Duchy of Lancaster, Head WPB from August 1914.

22   Including Conan Doyle, GK Chesterton, Rudyard Kipling, Hilaire Belloc, Arnold Bennett, John Masefield, HG Wells, John Galsworthy, Ford Madox Ford.

23   J Buchan (1875–1940), popular author (*Prester John* 1910, *39 Steps* 1915 etc), one of five war correspondents allowed on Western Front from 1915; wrote communiqués for General Haig 1916; Scottish Unionist MP 1927–1935, Lord Tweedsmuir 1935, Governor-General Canada 1935–1940.

24   Later Lord Carson (1854–1935), Solicitor-General Ireland 1892, led for Lord Queensberry in libel trial against Oscar Wilde 1895; Solicitor-General England 1900; Leader Unionist Party from 1910, founded Ulster Volunteer Force 1913, campaigned unsuccessfully against Home Rule for Ireland (but outbreak of War caused its suspension); in Coalition Government as Attorney-General May 1915, resigned October over Balkans policy (and to manoeuvre for Asquith's replacement as Prime Minister), returning 1916 as First Lord of Admiralty, Minister without Portfolio 1917; resigned January 1918 over introduction of conscription in Ireland.

25   WM Aitken (1879–1964), Canadian stockbroker and journalist, Unionist MP 1910–16, gained control *Daily Express* 1915, created Lord Beaverbrook 1917 by his friend Lloyd George, Chancellor of Duchy of Lancaster and Minister of Information 1918, founded *Sunday Express* 1921, bought *Evening Standard* 1929; in World War II, appointed by Churchill as Minister for Aircraft Production 1940–1, Minister of Supply/War Production 1941–2.

26   EA Bennett (1867–1931), lawyer and journalist, editor of *Woman*, prolific author from 1898.

27   Still owner of *The Times* and *Daily Mail*, had sold *Daily Mirror* 1914 to younger brother Lord Rothermere (1868–1940), who was Director-General Army Clothing 1916–17, Air Minister 1917–18.

28   *'Northcliffe'*, Pound and Harmsworth, Cassell, 1959.

29   Later Sir Robert Donald, GBE (1860–1933), editor left-wing Liberal *Daily Chronicle* 1902–18, reduced price to halfpenny, subsequently achieving circulation greater than *The Times*, *Daily Telegraph*, *Morning Post*, *Evening Standard, and Daily Graphic* combined; later Chairman Committee on Imperial Wireless Telegraphy; commissioned by Home Secretary 1914 to recommend how to improve circulation of pro-British news in neutral Holland, his report is one of small eclectic selection of papers retained in Churchill's personal Admiralty file, along with those by FE Smith on legality of forming battalions of US volunteers in early years of WWI, and by Herbert Samuel recommending formation after War of a Jewish State in Palestine as part of British Empire. TNA:PRO ADM 116/3486.

30 Major General Sir Frederick Maurice, KCMG, CB (1871–1951), later historian and Principal of Queen Mary College 1933–44.

31 The *Chronicle*, founded 1872, merged with the *Daily News* 1930, as the *News Chronicle*, but, with sister evening paper *The Star*, ceased publication 1960.

32 Lieutenant Colonel Lord Decies, DSO (1866–1944), action Matabeleland and Boer War (commanded Imperial Yeomanry) and Somaliland (commanded Tribal Horse), commanded South Irish Horse 1911–16, Chief Press Censor Ireland 1916–19, Director Income Tax Payers' Society.

33 In October 1916, Decies forbade sale of illicitly distributed photographs of Casement (and 'others connected with the late rebellion'), and even of verses about him, eg 'Resplendent knight! Thy vision clear O'er Erin saw the dawn appear – Resurgent shall thy spirit bright Young hearts inspire for Freedom's light'. TNA:PRO CO 904/166.

34 TNA:PRO NATS 1/107.

35 Rt Hon J Hodge (1855–1937), founder British Steel Smelters' Mill, Iron, Tinplate, and Kindred Trades Association, President TU Congress 1892, Labour MP 1906–23, Chairman Parliamentary Labour Party 1915, Minister for Labour 1916–17, Minister of Pensions 1917–19.

36 TNA:PRO HO 45/10765/271164.

37 Rt Hon A Henderson (1863–1935), Labour MP 1903–35, President Board of Education 1915–16, Paymaster-General and Labour Adviser to the Government 1916, Government Mission to Russia 1917, Home Secretary 1924, Foreign Secretary 1929–31, President World Disarmament Conference 1932–33.

38 *'Domestic Censorship in the First World War'*, Deian Hopkin, 'Conflict and Stability in Europe', edited Emsley, OUP, 1979.

39 TNA:PRO FO 395/256.

40 In 1933, MI5's Guy Liddell was told the Germans acknowledged that on 20 August 1914 they 'knew neither when nor where our troops were landed, nor their strength', an indication of the level of Press co-operation early in the War; *'The Guy Liddell Diaries'*, Vol 1, ed Nigel West, Cass, 2005.

41 Later Viscount Simon, PC, GCSI, GCVO, OBE (1873–1954), Liberal MP 1906–31, Solicitor-General then Attorney-General 1910–15, Home Secretary 1915–16, Royal Flying Corps/Royal Air Force in France 1917–18, Foreign Secretary 1931–35, Home Secretary 1935–37, Chancellor of the Exchequer 1937–40, Lord Chancellor 1940–5, Leader National Liberal Party, interrogator of Hess.

42 TNA:PRO CAB 21/93.

43 *'The Riddell Diaries, 1908–1923'*, ed McEwen, Athlone Press, 1986.

44 Later Earl of Birkenhead, GCSI, PC (1872–1930), acerbically witty barrister, Unionist MP 1906–19, Indian Corps France 1914, Solicitor-General 1915, Attorney-General 1915–19, Lord Chancellor 1919–22, Secretary for India 1924–8.

45 Later Viscount Buckmaster, GCVO (1861–1934), Liberal MP 1906–14, Solicitor-General 1913–15, Lord Chancellor 1915–16, Chairman Political Honours Review Committee 1924 and 1929.

46 Sir Frank Swettenham, GCMG, CH (1850–1946), Colonial Service including Resident-General of Federated Malay States 1896–1901, Governor the Straits Settlements 1901–4, still remembered with respect in Malaysia; Sir Edward Cook, KBE (1857–1919), journalist *Pall Mall Gazette*, succeeded WT Stead as editor 1890–2, Editor *Westminster Gazette* 1893–6 and *Daily News* 1896–1901.

47 By late 1916 the Bureau was handling annually about 344,000 telegrams to and from UK, over 50,000 proofs of press articles, over 140,000 press pictures/photographs. By 1917, it employed four Directors/Assistant Directors, 45 Censors, 93 support staff, costing £34,273 per annum.

48 Later Viscount Cecil (1864–1958), Conservative MP 1906–23, Under/Assistant-Secretary for Foreign Affairs 1915–18, also Minister of Blockade 1916–18, Lord Privy Seal 1923–24, President League of Nations Union 1923–45, Chancellor Duchy of Lancaster 1924–7, Nobel Peace Prize 1937.

49 TNA:PRO CAB 21/93.

50 TNA:PRO HO 139/5&9.

51   St Bride's, NS Circular January 1915.
52   *'The Power of News: the History of Reuters'*, Donald Read, OUP, 1992.
53   Later Viscount Burnham, GCMG, CBE, TD (1862–1933), Unionist MP 1885–1916, President Empire Press Union 1916–28, Indian Statutory Commission 1927–39.
54   Guildhall, PA Manager's Memoranda, Vol 9.
55   Riddell had a (now amusingly) egocentric view of his role in many matters, and was certainly not the only person agitating for a better system.
56   Colonel ED Swinton, later Major General Sir Edward Swinton, KBE, CB, DSO (1868–1951), served South Africa, proponent of early tanks, Assistant Secretary CID, Chichele Professor of Military History Oxford 1925–39.
57   But he did not, and no Minister has ever attended a D-Notice Committee meeting.
58   Later Brigadier-General Sir George Cockerill, CB (1867–1957), action NW Frontier and Afghanistan, Intelligence Branch Simla, mapped Hindu Kush and 'discovered' Mt Dasht-i-gul, served South Africa, retired 1910–14, recalled to command Royal Fusiliers, Director of Special Intelligence War Office 1915–19, Unionist MP 1918–31, sculptor and bronze medal skater.
59   Football leagues were subsequently suspended at end of 1914–15 season (Everton Division 1 champions, Oldham Athletic runners-up); not restarted until 1919, when surviving players returned from the Services.
60   Later Field Marshal Earl of Ypres, KP, GCB, OM, GCVO, KCMG (1852–1924), RN then Army, action Sudan, South Africa, CIGS 1911–14, CinC BEF 1914–15, CinC UK 1915–18, Lord Lieutenant Ireland 1918–21.
61   *'The Riddell Diaries, 1908–1923'*.
62   HA Gwynne, CH (1865–1950), *The Times* and Reuter's war correspondent in Balkans, Rumania, Egypt, Sudan, Aegean, Morocco, China and the Boer War (Reuter's chief war correspondent), Foreign Director of Reuter's 1904, editor *Standard* 1904–11, and *Morning Post* 1911–37, active on *British Gazette* during General Strike, banned Churchill from its office.
63   The sinking on 22 September 1914 of three slow old cruisers (*HM Ships HOGUE, CRESSY* and *ABOUKIR*) by German submarine U9, two as they stopped to pick up survivors of the first; afterwards, such patrols were discontinued, and new orders given about not stopping, speeds, zigzagging.
64   After the War, Buckmaster asked to see the file (TNA:PRO HO 139/5), presumably in case he had to prove for posterity his side of something which had occurred at a time when he, his Bureau and the AWOPC system (and of course the First Lord) were all under considerable strain. Asquith told the King that Churchill had offered to resign from the Admiralty to go and take command in Antwerp, but this 'patriotic offer' had been declined, as his services were needed at home. TNA:PRO CAB 41/35/24.
65   Robbins had second thoughts about the distribution, and sent the Notice out to the provincial press by post rather than risking the 'country telegraph offices'; see App 2.
66   TNA:PRO CAB 41/35/24.
67   Rt Hon Sir William Bull, Bt, PC (1863–1931), Conservative MP 1900–29.
68   Later Colonel Sir Edward Yate, Bt, CSI, CMG (1849–1940), Indian Army, Political Agent/Consul Arabia and India, latterly at Quetta ('where a clock tower was erected to his memory by the chiefs and people of the Province on his departure'), Conservative MP 1910–24, served with Ambulance Flotilla River Seine 1915.
69   Arthur Sherwell (1863–1942), author (especially on temperance matters), Liberal MP 1906–18.
70   Rt Hon Andrew Bonar Law, PC (1858–1923), Unionist MP 1900–23, Colonial Secretary 1915–16, Chancellor of Exchequer 1916–18, Lord Privy Seal 1919–21, Prime Minister 1922–3, died in office.
71   *Daily Mail*, 'The Paper That Persistently Warned The Public About The War', 19 November 1914.
72   Buckmaster did not hand over to his two Assistants (Swettenham and Cook) as Joint Directors until May 1915, when he became Lord Chancellor, but from late 1914 one of his Assistant Directors usually attended AWOPC meetings, and dealt with day-to-day AWOPC matters.
73   The following March, Riddell reported that when the revised Act had its second reading, the Attorney-General accepted his amendments. *'Riddell Diaries 1908–1923'*.

74   TNA:PRO HO 45/11007/271672.
75   Later Commander Sir Edward Chichester, Bt (1883–1940), Naval Brigade in Boer War, landowner, director maritime companies.
76   Hansard, Cols 1292–4.
77   Robbins had a personal aversion to the telephone; although the PA had very early installed one in his office, until his retirement many years later he reputedly never used it proactively – if it rang, he summoned an underling to answer it and to relay live both what the caller was saying and also his own side of the conversation; *'Living on a Deadline'*.
78   Regulation 18: communicating naval and military information; Regulation 27: spreading prejudicial reports.
79   TNA:PRO DEFE 53/1, and PA Manager's Memoranda.
80   Later Major General Sir Charles Callwell, KCB (1859–1928), served Afghan and Boer Wars, retired as Colonel 1909, recalled as Acting Major General 1914, military-diplomatic liaison duties 1916–18, historian, recorded his war in 'The Experiences of a Dug-Out'.
81   *Times, Daily Telegraph, Morning Post, Standard, Daily Chronicle, Daily Express, Daily Graphic, Daily Mail, Daily Mirror, Daily News and Leader, Daily Sketch.*
82   Another Australian journalist present was Rupert Murdoch's father; the NPA representative was Ellis Ashmead-Bartlett; together they publicised the ANZAC contribution and the higher command shortcomings.
83   V Williams, MC (1883–1946), son of Chief Editor of Reuter's, war correspondent 1902–13, first accredited correspondent British GHQ March 1915, then joined Irish Guards, wounded twice, won Military Cross, rejoined *Daily Mail*, became author and broadcaster in UK and USA, Foreign Office 1939–41 and in British Embassy Washington 1941–2, screenplay writer for 20th Century Fox and MGM 1942–5.
84   In April 1915, however, in conversation with Riddell, Kitchener blamed France for restrictions on correspondents, and undertook, if General Joffre could be persuaded by the British Press to change his attitude (without however quoting Kitchener), to change the British policy too.
85   The cost of posting 1,400 copies was then £1.11.6d. for clerical labour, and £5.15.6d. for postage.
86   Such flooding (and fires and bombs) in this and other early press premises, with files destroyed or damaged, is one reason why press archives are incomplete; another is that few parts of the media have the clerical habits of a bureaucracy (although all parts share with bureaucracies an inherent furtiveness about their internal workings.)
87   *'Lord Riddell's War Diary 1914–1918'.*
88   The minutes record its existence but not its contents, and no copy apparently survives elsewhere; Riddell refers to it in his 'War Diary', explaining it followed an hour spent by him with Churchill five days earlier.
89   *'Lord Riddell's War Diary, 1914–1918'.*
90   His demotion was demanded by Conservative coalition partners; he became briefly Chancellor of the Duchy of Lancaster, before rejoining the Army and serving for some months on the Western Front.
91   Pre-*DREADNOUGHT* battleship sunk by U-boat torpedo 27 May, with loss of 49 lives.
92   Robbins issued this 30 June 1915; see App 1.
93   At eight shillings a week, with 'a neat respectable uniform consisting of a dark blue serge coat and skirt with brass buttons, black straw hat with black ribbon inscribed "Press Association Limited", boots and mackintosh'.
94   *'Reporter Anonymous'*, George Scott, Hutchinson, 1968.
95   TNA:PRO HO 144/1667/300707.
96   *'The Power of News'.*
97   *'Living on a Deadline'.*
98   *'A History of the NPA'*, Dennis Griffiths, NPA, 2006.
99   Lord Curzon, KG, GCSI, GCIE (1859–1925), Conservative MP 1886–98, Viceroy of India 1899–1905, Lord Privy Seal 1915–16, Lord President of Council 1916–19, Foreign Secretary 1919–24.
100 The final straw for the Government had been such a *Globe* story on 5 November that Kitchener had been to see the King in order to resign.

101 Viscount Morley, OM (1838–1923), Liberal MP 1883–1908, twice Chief Secretary for Ireland, SofS for India 1905–10, Lord President of the Council 1910–14; Viscount Milner, KG, GCB, GCMG (1854–1925), journalist (*Pall Mall Gazette*, etc), Chairman Inland Revenue, Governor and High Commissioner South Africa 1897–1905, SofS for War 1918–19, Colonial Secretary 1919–21; Lord Courtney (1832–1918), Professor of Political Economy University College London, Liberal MP 1876–85, Unionist MP 1885–1900, Deputy Speaker House of Commons 1886–92; Lord Parmoor, KCVO (1852–1941), Oxford Soccer Blue, Attorney-General to Prince of Wales 1895, Conservative MP 1895–1914, Vicar-General of Canterbury 1902–24, Lord President of Council 1924 and 1929–31, British Representative Council of League of Nations 1924, Leader House of Lords 1929–31.

102 TNA:PRO DEFE 53/1 and Guildhall PA Manager's Memoranda Vol 9.

103 The *Mail* was particularly active in its use of photographs, so also more active than most in its (sometimes ironic) interchanges with the censors about them; on 13 December 1915 its Art Editor wrote: 'Dear Sir, I regret that through inadvertence, the small photograph we used of "a man shaving himself in a trench" was not described as an official picture. Yours faithfully . . .'. TNA:PRO HO 139/29.

104 TNA:PRO HO 144/1667/300707.

105 St Bride's, NS Circulars March and July 1916.

106 Robert replaced by George Wilson (1875–1938), proprietor/manager *Edinburgh Evening News*, early aviator, later President SDNS; this was the first time a representative of the Scottish Daily Newspaper Society attended as a full member of the AWOPC.

107 Later Field-Marshal Sir William Robertson, GCB, GCMG, KCVO, DSO (1860–1933), served in ranks 1877–88, commissioned 1888, Intelligence Branch Simla, wounded at Relief of Chitral 1895, Intelligence Officer Boer War, Quartermaster-General then Chief of General Staff BEF 1914–15, CIGS 1915–18, GOC Great Britain 1918–19, C-in-C British Army on the Rhine 1919–20.

108 There was some general antipathy to parts of the American Press at this time, particularly the Hearst Press, who had reported Jutland as a heavy British defeat, and had selectively misused articles on the War written by HG Wells and Jerome K Jerome. TNA:PRO HO139/28.

109 Later Vice Admiral Sir Douglas Brownrigg, Bt, CB (1867–1939), action Soudan, Naval Attaché Tokyo and Pekin, retired 1913, recalled as Chief Naval Censor during WWI, inspiring his breezy 1919 book 'Indiscretions of the Naval Censor'.

110 In addition to the gloomy operational situation at sea and on land, where heavy losses on the Somme were fresh in mind, Prime Minster Asquith had been ousted the previous week, and Lloyd George was in the process of forming a new Government.

111 Passenger liner converted into armed merchant cruiser, struck a mine off Lough Swilly 23 January 1917, whilst carrying £5M worth of gold bullion to Canada, almost all of which was recovered by divers at then extreme depths in the following months.

112 Later Field Marshal Earl Haig, KT, GCB, OM, GCVO, KCIE (1861–1928), action Soudan, South Africa, GOC 1st Army 1914–15, CinC BEF 1915–19, CinC UK 1919–20.

113 'Strictly . . . Confidential', 1917 Pamphlet in Reuters archive.

114 The USA had declared war on Germany on 6 April 1917, and the first American troops were due to arrive in France in June.

115 HC Robbins (1873–1968), thick-spectacled, modest, more modestly-moustachioed than his father, joined PA 1894, Deputy Manager 1904, succeeded his father 1917, retired from PA 1938, but remained Secretary AWOAMPC until start of WWII, then briefly Press Secretary of new Ministry of Information.

116 Apparently a scheme for prioritising available merchant shipping.

117 Cockerill had previously written to the Home Office suggesting Britain should adopt the French practice, whereby police checked all advertisements before publication, but this was not a duty the British police sought to acquire. TNA:PRO HO 144/1667/300707.

118 Lieutenant Colonel Lord Stamfordham, GCB, GCVO, GCIE, KCSI, KCMG (1849–1931), served in Zulu War, Groom-in-Waiting to Queen Victoria, Private Secretary to Queen 1895–1901 and to Prince of Wales 1901–10, Private Secretary to the King 1910–31.

119 Later Field-Marshal Viscount Plumer, GCB, GCMG, GBE, GCVO (1857–1932), served Sudan and South Africa, Quartermaster-General 1904–5, GOC Ireland and Northern Command 1906–14, Corps and Army Commands BEF 1915–17, GOC Italian Expeditionary Force 1917–18 and Army of the Rhine 1918–19, Governor Malta 1919–24, High Commissioner Palestine 1925–8.

120 He recovered, rejoined his regiment, and in October 1918 was invalided back to England with a leg wound sustained whilst leading his men in a charge on a German position; several other ex-PA employees were wounded and many more decorated during the War; amazingly only two were killed.

121 Brownrigg was far from universally disliked; the PA History refers to him as 'the popular and understanding chief naval censor, who appreciated the situation far better than most of his colleagues'; *'Living on a Deadline'*.

122 Sir Eric Geddes, GCB, GBE (1875–1937), lumber/railway manager USA, India and North-Eastern Railway, Deputy DG Munitions Supply 1915–16, DG Transportation of BEF and of Military Railways worldwide 1916–17, Controller of Navy [equipment] 1917, Unionist MP 1917–22, First Lord of Admiralty 1917–18, Minister of Transport 1919–21, later Chairman Dunlop Rubber Companies and Imperial Airways.

123 Riddell and Brownrigg did eventually make it up, mutually praising each other in their respective War memoirs.

124 Sir Edward Henry, GCVO, KCB, CSI (1850–1931), Indian Civil Servant, Inspector-General Bengal Police, 'special duty South Africa 1900–1, Assistant Commissioner then Commissioner Metropolitan Police 1901–18.

125 Captain Sir William Nott-Bower, KCVO (1849–1939), ex-Army, Royal Irish Constabulary 1872–8, Chief Constable Leeds then Liverpool 1878–1902, Commissioner City of London Police 1902–25; father of Sir John Nott-Bower, Commissioner Metropolitan Police 1953–8.

126 CR Buxton (1875–1942), Principal of Morley College (for working men and women) 1902–10, first President South London branch of Workers' Educational Association, Editor *Albany Review*, Liberal MP 1910; in 1914–15 while on mission to Bulgaria (with his brother) to attempt to secure that country's neutrality, he was wounded by a Turkish assassin; (with his wife) peace activist, including calling for recognition of Soviet Union, Labour MP 1922–23 and 1929–31, Treasurer Independent Labour Party 1924–27.

127 Nevertheless, Brade had forewarned Riddell of this agenda item in mid-November, telling him he had got it referred to the AWOPC, where he expected strong opposition, as the Government's proposals involved censorship of all articles advocating peace; Riddell agreed with his assessment of the likely Press position.

128 Elihu Root (1845–1937), American Statesman and Administrator, Ambassador Extraordinary heading mission to Russia 1917.

129 Later Viscount Cave, GCMG, PC (1856–1928), Unionist MP 1906–18, Solicitor-General 1915–16, Home Secretary 1916–19, Lord of Appeal 1919–22, Lord Chancellor 1922–8.

130 When the Newspaper Society dined him out at the Savoy in late 1917, he praised not only the AWOPC, but also the wartime 'Weekly Conference', chaired by Burnham and still dominated by Riddell; NS Circular December 1917.

131 Possibly to do with situation in Belgium, where the Germans had launched their Georgette offensive and were making steady gains.

132 SJ Pryor (1865–1924), editorial appointments in Jamaica and USA 1889–96, managing editor *Daily Mail* 1896–1900 and *Daily Express* 1900–1904, editor *St James Gazette* and *Evening Standard* 1904–5, and *Tribune* 1907, director of *Times* Publishing Company 1909–18, first Press Secretary Buckingham Palace 1918–20.

133 Sir Roderick Jones, KBE (1877–1962), Reuter's correspondent 1895–1905, succeeded Herbert de Reuter on his death in 1915, Assistant Director of Propaganda 1916–18, Chairman/MD Reuter's 1919–41, Advisory Council to Ministry of Information 1939.

134 HW Nevinson (1856–1941), war correspondent *Daily Chronicle, Manchester Guardian,* and *Daily News* 1897–1914, accredited Dardanelles (wounded), Salonika, Egypt, France and Germany, on staff *Nation* and *Herald*, President of PEN Club 1938 and of Council for the Defence of Civil Liberties 1939.

135 Later Admiral Sir Guy Gaunt, KCMG, CB (1870–1953), action Philippines, Samoa (where he raised Gaunt's Brigade), Naval Attaché Washington 1914–18, convoy Commodore 1918, DNP 1918–19, Conservative MP 1922–6.

136 A mail steamer sunk without warning by a German submarine 10 October 1918, with the loss of over 400 lives, the largest number lost in Irish waters during the War.

137 *Daily Mail* leader 3 September 1918.

138 *'Living on a Deadline'*.

139 Riddell phoned the Peace Terms through to Reuters as soon as they were signed on 28 June; he had manoeuvred with Lloyd George and Burnham to be sent to the Peace Conference as Liaison Officer between the British Delegation and the Press; this caused two-fold irritation: firstly the Press had to pay his considerable expenses, and secondly their access to delegates was solely through him. Guildhall, PA Manager's Memoranda, Ms 35362/12.

140 TNA:PRO CAB 24/5.

141 Although the Air Ministry had been established in April 1918, the Committee had yet to include it in its title, or to invite an Air Ministry representative to participate.

142 But not to many in the world at large, since the existence of the Committee remained shadowy, and its deliberations and Notices remained secret, in theory at least, for another half century or so.

SECTION 4
BETWEEN THE WORLD WARS, 1918–39

1 Later Brigadier-General Sir Joseph Byrne, GCMG, KBE, CB (1874–1942), wounded at siege of Ladysmith, Inspector-General RIC 1916–20, Governor Seychelles 1922–7, Sierra Leone 1927–31, Kenya 1931–7.

2 TNA:PRO WO 32/10776.

3 This included advice on recruiting spies: 'In a friendly country, agents should therefore be looked for amongst the most patriotic, brave, intelligent and sporting elements of the population'. TNA:PRO WO 33/1024.

4 TNA:PRO HW 3/37.

5 Later Admiral Sir Hugh Sinclair, KCB (1873–1939), bon viveur known as 'Quex' after the Pinero character, DNI 1919–21, Flag Officer Submarines 1921–3, Head of SIS 1923–39, his latter secretiveness somewhat betrayed by fondness for his large easily-recognised Lancia car.

6 *'Secret Service'*.

7 Later Brigadier-General Sir William Horwood, GBE, KCB, DSO (1868–1943), Chief of Police London and North-Eastern Railway 1911–14, Provost-Marshal BEF 1916–18, Assistant Commissioner Metropolitan Police 1918–20, Commissioner 1920–8.

8 That for cable censorship had grown from a Chief Cable Censor plus one assistant in August 1914 to a Press Bureau department of 802 by 1919, having handled over 80 million cables. TNA:PRO DEFE 1/130.

9 TNA:PRO DEFE 1/131.

10 TNA:PRO NATS 1/107.

11 Later Viscount Hewart, PC (1870–1943), Conservative Liberal MP 1913–22, Solicitor-General 1916–19, Attorney-General 1919–22, President of War Compensation Court 1922–9.

12 Rt Hon Edward Shortt, PC (1862–1935), Liberal MP 1910–22, Chief Secretary for Ireland 1918–19, Home Secretary 1919–22, President British Board of Film Censors 1929–35.

13 Sir Donald Maclean, KBE (1864–1932), Liberal MP 1906–32, Chairman Parliamentary Liberal Party 1919–22, President Board of Education 1931–2, father of spy Donald Maclean (1913–1983), see Section 6.

14 *'Official Secrets'*.

15 TNA:PRO HO 45/11007/271672.

16 Later Viscount Templewood, GCSI, GBE, CMG (1880–1959), Conservative MP for Chelsea 1910–44, SofS for Air 1922–9, SofS for India 1931–5, Foreign Secretary 1935, First Lord of Admiralty 1936–7, Home Secretary 1937–9, Ambassador to Spain 1940–4.

17 Later Viscount Duncannon, CH (1908–1987), diplomat, Territorial Army, political columnist *Daily Chronicle* 1937–9, Conservative MP 1939–74, invalided from Army as Lieutenant Colonel 1941, Ministerial posts 1942–57, Minister Defence 1957–9, Aviation 1959–60, Commonwealth Secretary 1960–4, son-in-law of Winston Churchill.

18 *'Official Secrets'*.

19 Later Earl Atlee, KG, OM, CH (1883–1967), wounded WWI , Labour MP 1922–56, Leader Labour Party 1935–55, Deputy Prime Minister 1942–5, Prime Minister 1945–51.

20 E Wilkinson (1891–1947), 'Red Ellen', suffragette, trade unionist, Labour MP 1924–47, co-founder of *Tribune*, organiser Jarrow March 1936.

21 Air Vice-Marshal Sir Philip Game, GCB, GCVO, GBE, KCMG, DSO (1876–1961), served in Army Boer War, BEF, Air Ministry 1919–22, commanded RAF India 1923, Air Member for Personnel 1923–8, Governor New South Wales 1930–1, Commissioner of Metropolitan Police 1935–45.

22 TNA:PRO MEPO 3/732.

23 See Part II (3) of the June 1923 draft, TNA:PRO T 161/1055.

24 TNA:PRO DEFE 1/132, subsequently amended several times up to 1942.

25 George Lansbury (1859–1940), Labour MP 1910–12 and 1922–40, resigned 1912 to pursue independent radical policies, co-founded and edited *Daily Herald* 1912–22, Commissioner of Works 1929–31, Leader Labour Party 1931–5.

26 Guildhall, PA Managers' Memoranda, Ms 35362/14.

27 Rt Hon JR MacDonald (1866–1937), Labour MP 1906–37, Leader Labour Party 1911–14, Prime Minister and Foreign Secretary 1924 and 1929–35, Lord President of Council 1935–7, died onboard holiday liner en route South America; body brought back to Britain in *HMS APOLLO*; this author's Dartmouth Divisional Chief Petty Officer remembered the Watch-on-Deck affectionately using MacDonald's coffin, stowed in a torpedo compartment, as a card table.

28 Urged on in particular by the Home Secretary Joynson-Hicks, the Chancellor of the Exchequer Winston Churchill, and the Secretary for India Lord Birkenhead.

29 Later Earl Baldwin, KG (1867–1947), Unionist MP 1908–37, Financial Secretary Treasury 1917–21, President Board of Trade 1921–2, Chancellor of Exchequer 1922–3, Prime Minister 1923–4, 1924–9, 1935–7.

30 Later General Lord Ismay, KG, GCB, CH, DSO (1887–1965), served NW Frontier, CID 1926–30, Secretary 1938, Deputy Secretary (Military) War Cabinet and Chief of Staff to Churchill 1940–5, Chief of Staff to Mountbatten as last Viceroy of India 1947, Chairman of Festival of Britain Council 1948–51, Commonwealth Relations Secretary 1951–2, NATO Secretary-General 1952–7.

31 Major General Lord Lovat, KT, GCVO, KCMG, CB, DSO (1871–1933), served Boer War and BEF, PUS Dominions Office 1927–8.

32 TNA:PRO DO 117/112.

33 £735 for 21 weeks, an increase of 40% over the pre-war contract.

34 Guildhall, Managers' Memoranda, Ms 35362/13.

35 *Daily Mail* 6 October 1919.

36 St Bride's, NPA Box 2.

37 Guildhall, PA Managers' memoranda, Ms 35362/14 and /15.

38 AN Chamberlain (1869–1940), Conservative MP 1918–1940, Chancellor of Exchequer 1923–4 and (in National Government) 1931–7, Prime Minister 1937–40.

39 *'Living on a Deadline'*.

40 Sir Leicester Harmsworth (1870–1937), Liberal MP for Caithness 1900–18.

41 *'My Trade'*, Andrew Marr, Macmillan, 2004. The first regular crossword in a British newspaper appeared in 1924 in the *Sunday Express*, *The Times* not following suit until 1930.

42 Later Viscount Southwood (1873–1946), Press business entrepreneur rather than newspaperman, already owner of the *People*.

43 Later Lord Cudlipp, OBE (1913–1998), military service 1940–6 (including commanding British Army Newspaper Unit producer of Forces' paper *Union Jack*), editorial then joint managing director *Daily Mirror and Sunday Pictorial* 1952–63, director Associated Television 1956–73, Chairman *Daily Mirror*/IPC 1963–73.

44 *'Power without Responsibility'*, Curran and Seaton, Routledge, 2003, the title quoting from Prime Minister Stanley Baldwin's 1930 successful counter-attack on the Press Barons.

45 Later Captain Lord Reith, KT, GCVO, GBE, CB, RNVR (1889–1971), Calvinist engineer, Army 1914–15, Munitions Ministry and Admiralty 1916–19, DG BBC 1922–38, Chairman Imperial Airways/British Overseas Airways Corporation 1938–40, National MP 1940, successively Minister of Information, Transport, Works 1940–2, Coastal Forces with Royal Naval Volunteer Reserve 1942, Admiralty/Combined Operations 1943–5, Lord High Commissioner General Assembly of Church of Scotland 1967–8.

46 *'Power without Responsibility'*.

47 Guildhall, PA Managers' Memoranda, Ms 35362/18.

48 *'Power without Responsibility'*.

49 JL Baird (1888–1946), inventor, technical adviser to Cable and Wireless Ltd 1941–6.

50 St Bride's, NPA Box 28.

51 *'A Social History of the Media'*, Briggs and Burke, Polity, 2005.

52 Later Viscount Camrose (1879–1954), founded *Advertising World* 1901, editor-in-chief *Sunday Times* 1915–36 and *Daily Telegraph* 1928–54, Principal Adviser Ministry of Information 1939.

53 Later Viscount Kemsley, GBE (1883–1968), Chairman Kemsley Newspapers and Editor-in-Chief *Sunday Times* 1937–59, Chairman Reuters 1951–9.

54 Sir Herbert Russell, KBE (1869–1944), *Newcastle Chronicle* and *Daily Express*, war correspondent 1915–18.

55 TNA:PRO HO 144/1667/300707.

56 Guildhall. PA Managers Memoranda Ms 35362/12.

57 D625, referring to the Admiralty's requisition of Liverpool ferries for the Zeebrugge Raid.

58 Robbins no longer worked for the PA, the usual conduit of such information, whereas Riddell was still actively involved in the NPA; although Robbins was still nominally the Committee's Secretary, minutes and other paperwork were now handled by a War Office clerk. TNA:PRO DEFE 53/1.

59 Later General Lord Rawlinson, GCB, GCSI, GCVO, KCMG (1864–1925), served India, Burma, Sudan and South Africa, Corps and Army Commander BEF 1914–18, Commander British Forces North Russia 1919, C-in-C India 1920–5.

60 TNA:PRO DEFE 53/1.

61 Sir Arthur Robinson, GCB, GBE (1874–1950), ex-Colonial Office, PUS Air Ministry 1917–20, Ministry of Health 1920–35, Ministry of Supply 1939–40.

62 GJ Maddick (1849–1942), art editor *Illustrated Sporting and Dramatic News*, of which Chairman 57 years and of *Illustrated London News and Sketch* 36 years, and other publishing/paper-mill businesses.

63 AR Kidner, remembered by philatelists as Keeper of Stamps at Somerset House in 1930s.

64 Although this explanation is in part a 'recollection', this author has found no better explanation elsewhere; use of the word for Notices themselves (as opposed to their transmission by telegram) died out in the 1920s, replaced by the already current colloquial 'D-Notice'.

65 TNA: PRO DEFE 53/1. Having waded through many boxes/files/volumes containing Committee remnants, this author pays tribute to the clerkly Boulter; he earned every penny of meagre overtime paid by the War Office 1914–18, and of his annual ten guineas thereafter. Unfortunately, much of the fruits of his labours was destroyed during interwar and WWII years by flood, bombing and fire in PA offices, a further reason why many detailed records of the interwar Committee/Notices are apparently not extant.

66 Guildhall, PA Manager's Memoranda, Ms 35362/13.

67 Guildhall, PA Managers' Memoranda, Ms 35362/13.

68 Later Sir Herbert Creedy, GCB, KCVO (1878–1973), PUS War Office 1920–39, Security Executive 1940–5.

69 Later Sir Walter Nicholson, KCB (1876–1946), ex-Admiralty, PUS Air Ministry 1920–30, Government-nominated Director Imperial Airways 1931–7.

70 Nicholson had not expected to be asked to outline the Air Ministry arrangements, about which he knew little, and at the next meeting he corrected this, confirming the work was done mainly by written communiqués. TNA:PRO AIR 2/151.

71   TNA:PRO DEFE 53/1.
72   Later Viscount Greenwood, PC (1870–1948), ex-Canadian Militia, Liberal MP 1906–22, commanded South Wales Borderers in BEF, Chief Secretary for Ireland 1920–2, Conservative MP 1924–9.
73   TNA:PRO DEFE 53/1.
74   £25 for press travelling expenses, £25 for clerical expenses, and £50 for postage to editors; the Press Association de facto paid the Secretary's wage; although in modern times the Crown pays for the whole system, the Media side pay their own expenses. TNA:PRO T161/149 and AIR 2/151.
75   Edmund Robbins was again too unwell to attend, so was again represented by his son.
76   TNA:PRO DEFE 53/1.
77   TNA:PRO CAB 4/8.
78   At this stage of thinking on Air Power, it was not yet officially conceivable doctrinally that air operations might not be intrinsic to naval and/or military operations.
79   TNA:PRO DEFE 53/1.
80   TNA:PRO DEFE 53/1.
81   TNA:PRO DEFE 53/1. Long lists of secret air equipment did subsequently become the most common type of D-Notices in the interwar years – see below.
82   Guildhall, PA Managers' Memoranda, Ms 35362/16,17,18&19.
83   Later Viscount Brentford, PC (1865–1932), Unionist MP 1908–29, WWI with Belgian Field Ambulance Service and raised two Service Battalions of Middlesex Regiment ('1st and 2nd Football'), Postmaster-General then Minister of Health 1923–4, Home Secretary 1924–9, Chairman Automobile Association, author on Highway Traction, Command of the Air, and The Prayer-Book Crisis.
84   Guildhall, PA Manager's Memoranda, Ms 35362/19.
85   TNA:PRO CAB 4/15; this folder also contains a paper on concerns about the revival amongst Muslims of 'Mahdism' against Colonial regimes in Africa.
86   Its members were however active in other fields; Riddell's many interests included sterilisation of 'mental defectives', suggesting in April 1929 to the Medico-Legal Society 'an operation to prevent the breeding of undesirables . . . subject to proper consents' [not clear whose]; his correspondence with Neville Chamberlain (Minister of Health) ended when Chamberlain announced he could not legislate at present, prompting one MP to table a Question: when he did legislate, 'will he consider making it retrospective?'; TNA:PRO MH 58/103.
87   Later Air Chief Marshal Sir Charles Burnett, KCB, CBE, DSO (1882–1945), ex-Army, served South Africa and Nigeria, with RFC/RAF in BEF and after WWI in Iraq and Persia, DAO&I 1931–3, AOC Iraq 1933–5, Chief of Air Staff RAAF 1940–2, Commandant Air Training Corps 1943–5.
88   Later Vice Admiral CV Usborne, CB, CMG (1880–1951), gunnery officer who became mines expert, commanded Naval Brigade Danube 1918–19, DNI 1930–2, returned to active service as Director of Censorship Division Press and Censorship Bureau 1939–40 (see below), special technical projects service Admiralty 1941–5.
89   TNA:PRO ADM 116/4082.
90   Sir Christopher Bullock, KCB, CBE (1891–1972), ex-Indian Civil Service, Rifle Brigade/Royal Flying Corps/Royal Air Force 1915–19, PUS 1931–6.
91   'The Game of Foxes', Ladislas Farago, Hodder and Stoughton, 1972.
92   Later Admiral Sir Gerald Dickens, KCVO, CB, CMG (1879–1962), grandson of author Charles Dickens, WWI Dardanelles and NID, DNI 1932–5, commanded Reserve Fleet 1935–7, returned to active service WWII as Flag Officer Tunisia then Netherlands.
93   TNA:PRO ADM 116/4082.
94   TNA:PRO ADM 116/4082.
95   TNA:PRO ADM 116/4082, 1/8777/164, 1/11307.
96   Later Vice Admiral Sir James Troup, KBE, CB (1883–1975), Naval Brigade Boer and Boxer Wars, DNI 1935–9, WWII recalled as Flag Officer Glasgow.
97   TNA:PRO ADM 1/8776/153.
98   Anticipating the cable-vetting affair of Section 7 by 33 years.

99   Colonel VPT Vivian, CMG, CBE.
100 Sir James Owen (1869–1939), editor/MD *Western Times* and *Express and Echo*, President Newspaper Society 1922.
101 Sir Robert Baird died 8 October 1934, a considerable Ulster figure, not only the dominant newspaper proprietor, but prominent on Bench, Harbour Board, hospital/charitable trusts, freemasonry, Orange Order; his funeral brought Belfast to standstill, crowds four deep, the Northern Ireland Prime Minister, Cabinet, and notables from Great Britain in attendance.
102 D800 – the WWI numbering system had continued unbroken.
103 TNA:PRO DEFE 53/1.
104 TNA:PRO WO 33/1369.
105 Later Lord Clydesmuir, GCIE (1894–1954), served BEF (wounded), Unionist MP 1929–43, Parliamentary USofS Scotland 1938–40, General Staff 1940–2, Governor Bombay 1943–8, BBC Governor 1950–4.
106 TNA:PRO CAB 16/127.
107 Sir Stephen Tallents, KCMG, CB, CBE (1884–1958), Irish Guards 1914–15, wounded and rejoined Civil Service, British Commissioner Baltic Provinces 1919–20, Imperial Secretary Northern Ireland 1922–6, PRO GPO 1933–5, Controller (Public Relations) BBC 1935–40 and (Overseas Services) 1940–1, First President Institute of Public Relations.
108 Rear Admiral HE Dannreuther, DSO (1880–1977), Battles of Heligoland Bight and Falklands, latterly commanded RN Barracks Portsmouth.
109 TNA:PRO HO 45/23627.
110 Respectively December 1935–6 (the 1st War had been won by the Abyssinians 1895–6) and July 1936-April 1939; the latter attracted much Press and newsreel coverage because of the high foreign involvement, individual and governmental, the Left/Right nature of the War, the use of modern tanks and aircraft, and exceptional brutality on both sides.
111 Guildhall, PA Manager's Memoranda Ms 35362/23–25.
112 The three Press Officers, chaired by CP Robertson OBE, long-serving Air Ministry Press and Publicity Officer; journalist, joined Department with Flying Officer rank 1919, stayed as 'temporary' civil servant until 1943.
113 Later Viscount Rothermere (1898–1978), Royal Marine Artillery 1917, Unionist MP 1919–29, Chairman *Daily Mail* Group and Associated Newspapers, Chairman NPA 1934–61, Advisory Council Ministry of Information from 1939.
114 Discussion by author with Sir Geoffrey Cox 10 July 2006.
115 TNA:PRO DEFE 53/2.
116 GM Liddell, CB, CBE, MC (1892–1958), Army 1914–19, subsequently Metropolitan Police Special Branch, Security Service 1931–52, Head Counter-Espionage Division 1940–5, Deputy Director-General 1946–52, Atomic Energy Commission 1952–7.
117 TNA:PRO AIR 2/1974.
118 TNA:PRO CAB 16/127, CID Paper 1422-B.
119 TNA:PRO INF 1/15.
120 TNA:PRO HO 45/23627 and CAB 16/127.
121 Later Major General Lord Burnham, CB, DSO, MC (1890–1963), Army WWI, TA Officer, served France and Belgium 1940, Commanded Yorkshire Division 1941, Director Public Relations War Office and Senior Military Adviser Ministry of Information 1942–5, MD *Daily Telegraph* 1945–61.
122 Later Sir Geoffrey Mander (1882–1962), Liberal MP 1929–45.
123 TNA:PRO MEPO 3/732.
124 TNA:PRO MIC 16 of 31 October 1938.
125 Sir Horace Wilson, GCB, GCMG, CBE (1882–1972), PUS Ministry of Labour 1921–30, PUS Treasury 1939–42.
126 TNA:PRO HO 45/23627.
127 TNA:PRO HO 45/23627.
128 Sir Ernest Fass, KCMG, CB, OBE (1881–1969), Financial Secretary Sudan 1931–4, Public Trustee 1934–44, Custodian of Enemy Property England and Wales 1939–44.
129 TNA:PRO HO 45/23627.

130 TNA:PRO HO 45/23627.

131 St Bride's. NPA Box 29.

132 Later Admiral of the Fleet Earl Mountbatten, KG, PC, GCB, OM, GCSI, GCIE, GCVO, DSO (1900–1979), Chief of Combined Operations 1941–2, Supreme Allied Commander South East Asia 1943–6, Viceroy/Governor-General India 1947–8, Flag Officer Cruiser Squadron Mediterranean 1948–9, CinC Mediterranean 1952–4, 1st Sea Lord 1955–9, Chief of Defence Staff 1959–65, assassinated by IRA on holiday in Ireland 1979.

133 Earl Stanhope, KG, PC, DSO, MC (1880–1967), ex-Grenadier Guards, served South Africa, Lieutenant Colonel Reserves 1909–35, First Lord of Admiralty 1938–9, Leader of House of Lords 1938–40.

134 H Martin (1889–1964), London News Agency 1908–19, *Daily Sketch* and *Evening Standard* 1919–28, editor-in-chief PA 1928–54, author *'The Place of Religion in the Post-War Press'*.

135 Later Sir Dingle Foot, PC (1905–78), Liberal MP 1931–45, Labour MP 1957–70, Solicitor-General 1964–7, elder brother of future Labour leader Michael Foot, uncle of journalist Paul Foot.

136 Later Lord Rowley, PC (1893–1968), Army 1914–18 and 1939–42, Labour MP 1923–66, Commonwealth Minister 1947, SofS for Air 1947–51.

137 Hoare, Foreign Secretary in 1935, made a secret plan with his French equivalent Laval to bring the 2nd Italo-Abyssinian War to an end, leaked by French Press before implementation, seen to be favourable to Italian invaders, and leading to both Foreign Ministers resigning.

138 W Gallacher (1881–1965), Chairman Clyde Workers Committee 1914–18, Communist Party of Great Britain (President 1956–63) and Communist International from 1920, Communist MP 1935–50.

139 But not the first – see the more limited *Daily Herald* incident referred to at the AWOAMPC meeting of 27 July 1934.

140 Major General JH Beith, CBE, MC (1876–1952), Argyll and Sutherland Highlanders WWI, novelist and playwright (pen name Ian Hay), President Dramatists Club, Director Public Relations War Office 1938–41.

141 *World's Press News* 20 April 1939.

142 Sir Arthur Street, GCB, KBE, CMG, CIE, MC (1892–1951), served WWI Egypt, Sinai and Palestine (wounded and MC), PUS Air Ministry 1939–45, Control Office for Germany and Austria 1945–6.

143 This has never since been done however.

SECTION 5
WORLD WAR II: SUSPENDED ANIMATION, 1939–45

1 The fullest collection found of WWII Defence Notices and Letters is in BBC Written Archive R64/41/1&2.

2 Major-General Sir Stewart Menzies, KCB, KCMG, DSO, MC (1890–1968), BEF 1914–18 (GHQ Intelligence from 1915), thereafter SIS, Head 1939–52.

3 Sir David Petrie, KCMG, CIE, CVO, CBE (1879–1961), Indian CID 1909–24, Director Delhi Intelligence Bureau 1924–31, Chairman 1932–36 Public Service Commission India and Indian Red Cross/St John's Ambulance, Palestine Police 1937–8, DG Security Service 1940–6.

4 Later Professor RV Jones, CH, CB, CBE (1911–97), Clarendon Laboratory with Lindemann, 1932–43, Air Ministry and Admiralty 1936–9, Intelligence Adviser SIS 1939–45, Professor Natural Philosophy Aberdeen University 1946–81, Director Scientific Intelligence MOD 1952–3, 1994 CH belated recognition; *'Most Secret War'*, RV Jones, Wordsworth, 1978.

5 Known as Station X (the Roman numeral), 10th SIS acquired wartime site, where ultimately 12,000 people worked; it was also where most of SIS Head Office was located during the War.

6 Later Commander Sir Edward Travis, KCMG, CBE, RN (1888–1956), Staff of Jellicoe 1914–16, Admiralty Signal Division 1916–18, Director-General GC&CS/GCHQ 1944–52.

7 National Services (Armed Forces) Act was passed the day war declared; more than 1million men were under arms by end 1939.

8 Guildhall, PA Manager's Memoranda, Ms 35362/25.

9 Memorandum by Rear Admiral George Thomson, 1945; TNA:PRO DEFE 53/3.
10 Earl of Perth, GCMG, CB (1876–1951), Secretary-General League of Nations 1919–33, Ambassador to Italy 1933–9, Chief Foreign Affairs Adviser to Ministry of Information 1939–40, Deputy Leader Liberal Party in House of Lords 1946–51.
11 Later Sir William Haley, KCMG (1901–87), *Manchester Evening News*, director 1930–43, director Reuters/Press Association 1939–43, editor-in-chief BBC 1943–44, Director-General BBC 1944–52, editor *Times* 1952–66, editor-in-chief Encyclopaedia Britannica 1968–9.
12 Later Viscount Bracken, PC (1901–1958), journalist, Unionist/Conservative MP 1929–51, Minister of Information 1941–5, First Lord of Admiralty 1945.
13 *'Living on a Deadline'*.
14 *'The Power of News'*.
15 *'Blue Pencil Admiral'*, George Thomson, Samson Low Marston, 1946.
16 Memorandum by Admiral Thomson, 1945. It includes subsequent Reuters progress through the War, to a position where Government paid approximately for specific services to the State; TNA:PRO DEFE 53/3.
17 Such unexpected wartime togetherness extended to other fields too; the Dublin Fire Service went up to help fight fires in Belfast, authorised discreetly by de Valera.
18 The censors had been called up 26 August, to establish themselves in London University's Senate Building; on the first day of the War, when *SS Athenia* en route to the USA was sunk by U-boat with heavy loss of civilian passengers, inadequacies of planning of the Ministry immediately became apparent.
19 TNA:PRO INF 1/852.
20 TNA:PRO INF 1/852.
21 Sir Findlater Stewart, GCB, GCIE, CSI (1879–1960), ex-India Office, PUS for India 1930–42, Director-General Ministry of Information 1939, and of secret Home Defence Executive 1940–5, wrote Report on Security and Secret Intelligence Services 1945.
22 TNA:PRO CAB 67/1/23. WP(G)(39)23.
23 Owner of the *Daily Telegraph* and briefly Principal Press Advisor to the Ministry.
24 HJ Staines, (1882–1958), Managing Director *Sheffield Telegraph and Star*, Director PA from 1934 (Chairman 1939).
25 *'Living on a Deadline'*.
26 TNA:PRO T161/1056. Hansard 2 Dec 42.
27 Later Viscount Monckton, GCVO, KCMG, MC (1891–1965), Attorney-General to Prince of Wales 1932–6, Attorney-General to Duchy of Cornwall 1936–51 (played prominent part in Edward VIII's abdication), Director-General P&C Bureau 1939–40, Deputy then Director-General Ministry of Information 1940–1, Director-General British Propaganda and Information Services in Cairo 1941–2, Solicitor-General 1945, Conservative MP 1951–7, Minister of Labour and National Service 1951–5, Minister of Defence 1955–6.
28 TNA:PRO KV 4/17.
29 TNA:PRO INF 1/495.
30 Later Viscount Radcliffe, GBE (1899–1977), Deputy then Director-General Press and Censorship Bureau 1939–41, Director-General Ministry of Information 1941–5, Lord of Appeal in Ordinary 1949–64, BBC General Advisory Council 1952–5, many Inquiries, including Security Procedures and Practices 1961, Vassall Case Inquiry 1962, *Daily Express* and D-Notices 1967, Committee on ex-Ministers' Memoirs 1975.
31 TNA:PRO KV 4/317.
32 TNA:PRO KV 4/317.
33 W Will, CBE (1867–1958), Director Allied Newspapers, Chairman PA 1931–2, Deputy Chairman Reuters, Chairman NPEC 1939–45, leader Media side AWOAMPC 1945–53, President London Caledonian Society.
34 St Bride's, NS Circulars October and December 1939, and October 1941.
35 TNA:PRO T162/522, undated letter but probably 9 October 1939.
36 Later Viscount Waverley, GCB, OM, GCSI, GCIE (1882–1958), Chairman Board of Inland Revenue 1919–22, PUS Office 1922–32, Governor Bengal 1932–7, National MP 1938–50, Home Secretary/Minister of Home Security 1939–40, Lord President of Council 1940–3, Chancellor of Exchequer 1943–5.

37   TNA:PRO CAB 67/1/40. WP(G)(39)40.
38   *Blue Pencil Admiral'*.
39   TNA:PRO INF 1/854.
40   TNA:PRO ADM 1/20123.
41   *Times* 18 and 27 December 1939.
42   TNA:PRO DO 130/6. And *'MI5 and Ireland, 1939–45, The Official History'*, Eunan O'Halpin, IAP, 2003.
43   The Irish High Commissioner in London. TNA:PRO KV 4/317.
44   TNA:PRO INF 1/528.
45   TNA:PRO KV 4/318.
46   TNA:PRO ADM 1/20123.
47   Later Rear Admiral Sir George Thomson, CB, CBE (1887–1965), submariner, Chief of Staff China Station, Captain *HMS DEVONSHIRE*, Second Member Naval Board Australia 1937–9, appointed Ministry of Information 1939, Chief Press Censor 1940–5, Secretary D-Notice Committee 1945–63.
48   TNA:PRO KV 4/317.
49   Against the advice of Kell and the Defence Departments, who considered only they could judge whether damage was being done. TNA:PRO DEFE 1/3.
50   This booklet was based on 'The very few "D" Notices still in force on 3rd September 1939'; until revised in consultation with the media in early 1940, 'the censorship was not properly speaking voluntary'. Memorandum by Thomson dated 1 September 1961, TNA:PRO DEFE 53/2.
51   TNA:PRO DEFE 53/4.
52   *Blue Pencil Admiral'*.
53   TNA:PRO DEFE 53/3.
54   BBC broadcast by Admiral Thomson. 1945.
55   TNA:PRO KV 4/318.
56   TNA:PRO KV 4/37.
57   TNA:PRO KV 4/17.
58   *Blue Pencil Admiral'*.
59   Later Viscount Norwich, PC, GCMG, DSO (1890–1954), Army WWI, Unionist/Conservative MP 1924–45, SofS for War 1935–7, First Lord of Admiralty 1937–8, Minister of Information 1940–1, HMG Representative with French Committee of National Liberation 1943–4, Ambassador to France 1944–7.
60   TNA:PRO HO 45/23627.
61   TNA:PRO HO 45/23627.
62   Later Earl of Avon, KG, MC (1897–1977), Army 1915–19, Conservative MP 1923–57, Minister for League of Nations Affairs 1935, Foreign Secretary 1935–8, Dominion Affairs Secretary 1939–40, War Minister 1940, son in RAF killed Burma 1945, Foreign Secretary and Deputy Prime Minister 1951–5, Prime Minister 1955–7.
63   Later Lord Morrison, CH (1888–1965), started as newspaper errand boy, London County Council 1922–45, Labour MP 1923–24, 1929–31 and 1935–59, Minister of Supply 1940, Home Secretary and Minister of Home Security 1940–5, Deputy Prime Minister 1945–51, Foreign Secretary 1951.
64   TNA:PRO, HO 45/23627, W.P.(41)269.
65   TNA:PRO KV 4/354.
66   TNA:PRO KV 4/31.
67   TNA:PRO DEFE 1/185.
68   *Blue Pencil Admiral'*.
69   TNA:PRO HO 45/23627.
70   Cecil King (1901–87), grandson of Alfred Harmsworth, Director *Daily Mirror* from 1929, Chairman *Mirror/Pictorial* Newspapers 1951–63 and International Publishing Corporation 1963–8.
71   Restrictions had actually been placed even earlier; Morrison had written to Departments on 11 June 1940: 'The policy of the *Daily Worker* as the organ of the British Communist Party is

dictated by the Comintern which is an instrument of the Soviet Government'; he said the newspaper should not be included in tours, conferences, news distribution, advertisements, or issue of permits. TNA: PRO KV 4/317. Retaliating, in August a '*Workers' Gazette*' was published using the presses of the *Dorset County Chronicle*, in the exact format of the *Daily Worker*, but the Government decided it could not prosecute unless further issues appeared; they considered instead limiting the rustic printer's supplies of paper; TNA:PRO HO 45/25581.

72   Sir Percy Hurd (1864–1950), co-founder/editor *The Outlook*, London editor *Montreal Star*, Editor *Canadian Gazette* and *Canada's Weekly*, Allied Relief Committee of Royal Agricultural Society 'in devastated regions of France' 1915–18, Unionist/Conservative MP 1918–45.

73   TNA:PRO HO 45/23627.

74   TNA:PRO HO 45/23627.

75   Private letter dated 28 May 1942.

76   TNA:PRO HO 45/23627.

77   Later Sir Alan Herbert, CH (1890–1971), Royal Naval Division 1914–17 Gallipoli and France, Independent MP 1935–50.

78   TNA:PRO HO 45/23627.

79   Minute of 30 April, 1943, FCO Secret Archives.

80   Professor NHD Bohr (1885–1962), Royal Society (UK) Gold Medal 1908, Professor in Theoretical Physics Copenhagen University 1916–62, Nobel Prize for Physics 1922 for work on structure of atoms, escaped to Sweden after German occupation of Denmark, Atomic Energy Project UK/USA 1943–5.

81   Later Professor Viscount Cherwell, CH (1886–1957), born Frederick Lindemann of Anglo-Franco-German antecedents, leading physicist, played Wimbledon tennis championships, failed to gain commission in WWI so instead became Director Physical Laboratory RAF Farnborough, qualified as pilot, developed theory and practice of aircraft spin-recovery, Professor Experimental Philosophy/Head Clarendon Laboratory Oxford University from 1919, long collaboration with Churchill, appointed by him Government Scientific Adviser 1940 and Paymaster-General 1942–5 and 1951–3.

82   TNA:PRO AB 1/564.

83   IJC Brown, CBE (1891–1974), drama critic *Manchester Guardian* 1919–35, *Saturday Review* 1923–30, *Observer* 1929–54, *Week End Review* 1930–4, *Sketch* 1935–9, *Punch* 1940–2, Professor of Drama Royal Society of Literature 1939, editor *Observer* 1942–8, Chairman British Drama League 1954–65.

84   TNA:PRO HO 45/23627.

85   *Daily Express* headline 7 January 1944.

86   TNA:PRO AB 1/564.

87   Sir Geoffrey Cox/Wilkinson, 10 July 2006; SIS Officers were clearly more willing in those days to be privately identifiable by British journalists.

88   78: No mention, without prior submission, of the activities of enemy agents, counter-espionage methods, pursuit, arrest and trial of spies, and sabotage; 80: No mention, without prior submission, of arrests, charges or proceedings under the OSA, Trading with the Enemy Act, any War Legislation dealing with many of the Defence Regulation offences, and Treason.

89   TNA:PRO KV 4/319.

90   Later Judge EJP Cussen, Civil Assistant to General Staff in War Office 1940, 'Intelligence Corps' 1941–6, Senior Prosecuting Counsel to Crown 1964–71.

91   TNA:PRO KV 4/17.

92   This referred in particular to the powers of search, arrest and interrogation provided by Sections 6 and 9 of OSA 1911, and Section 6 of OSA 1920 as amended in 1939.

93   Later Sir Frank Newsam, GCB, KBE, CVO, MC (1893–1964), 1914–19, DUS Home Office 1941–8, Chairman Governors Police College 1947–64.

94   Later Lord Francis-Williams, CBE (1903–1970), editor *Daily Herald* 1936–40, Controller News and Censorship MoI 1941–5, PR Adviser to Prime Minister 1945–7.

95   TNA:PRO HO 45/23627 and KV 4/319.

96   Security Service Archives.

97 The War with Japan was now over, although the Surrender was not formally signed until 2 September; the Press meanwhile was champing publicly for censorship to end, for example the *Daily Express* asking in its columns on 17 August 'Why maintain the censorship?', pointing out the USA had already ended its own; the UK criteria in both theatres was three weeks after the ceasefire, when all possibility of action by enemy submarines was over, i.e. by when they must all have surfaced and resumed communication with their base.

98 TNA:PRO HO 45/23627.

99 *'Blue Pencil Admiral'*; even Clement Atlee prior to becoming Prime Minister had not known what Churchill had already agreed with the USA.

100 TNA:PRO DEFE 53/4.

101 *Daily Express* 3 September 1945; Thomson received many personal letters of thanks from editors, and even from American correspondents in UK; TNA:PRO DEFE 53/5.

SECTION 6
EARLY YEARS OF THE COLD WAR, 1945–67

1 *'Cabinets and the Bomb'*, Peter Hennessy, British Academy, 2007.

2 The approach of the test had been leaked in the *New York Herald Tribune* in mid-1951, but Churchill had decided to make no announcement then; TNA:PRO PREM 8/1551.

3 This did not happen until 1983; nevertheless, when the author attended school in Cheltenham in the 1950s, GCHQ's secret role was quite common knowledge locally.

4 Later Major-General Sir John Sinclair, KCMG, CB, OBE (1897–1977), Royal Navy then Royal Artillery, DMI 1944–5, Deputy Chief SIS, Chief 1951–6.

5 When the author worked on First Sea Lord's Staff in 1989, he found one of only two complete remaining Top Secret files on the affair in his (unlocked) bottom drawer, detailing continuous errors of judgement, co-ordination and operational technique made by several agencies, the material for an Ealing comedy were it not for the accidental death of 'Buster' Crabb; when dealing with a 1972 BBC programme on the incident, the then Secretary revealed that Naval Divers from nearby *HMS VERNON* had carried out an unauthorised dive of their own on the cruiser; TNA:PRO ADM 1/29240 and CAB 163/207.

6 Sir Dick White, KCMG, KBE (1906–93), Oxford, Michigan and California Uiversities, DGSS 1953–6, Head SIS 1956–72.

7 Sir Percy Sillitoe, KBE (1888–1962), ex-South African Police and Rhodesia Police, served German East Africa campaign 1914–18, Chief Constable successively Chesterfield, East Riding of Yorkshire, Sheffield, Glasgow, Kent, DGSS 1946–53; after retirement published memoirs, *'Cloak without Dagger'*, 1955.

8 'Lonsdale' was Konon Molody, exchanged in 1964 for the British businessman Greville Wynne, who had been convicted in the USSR in 1963 for spying for Britain; the Krogers (aka the Cohens) were exchanged in 1969 for Gerald Brooke, a British lecturer convicted in the USSR in 1965 for distributing anti-Soviet pamphlets.

9 Later Professor Lord Blackett, OM, CH (1897–1974), ex-Royal Navy, Professor of Physics Birkbeck, Manchester, Imperial College, Nobel Prize for Physics 1948, President Royal Society 1965–70.

10 *'Most Secret War'*.

11 Burgess and Maclean. Cmd.9577.

12 The Radcliffe Report of 1962 later disagreed with this view, considering the threat lay 'further back' than the CPGB; it therefore took a much wider view of security measures needed.

13 Cmd.9715.

14 TNA:PRO PREM 8/5524.

15 Sir Frederick Brundrett, KCB, KBE (1894–1974), 1st Division hockey player, RNVR 1914–18, RN/MoD Scientific Adviser (Chief 1954–9), Chairman Air Traffic Control Board 1959–74, Civil Service Commissioner 1960–7.

16 Later Earl of Stockton, OM (1894–1986), Army 1914–18 (thrice wounded), Unionist/Conservative MP 1924–9 and 1931–64, Minister Resident Allied HQ North-West Africa 1942–5, Minister of

Defence 1954–5, Foreign Secretary 1955, Chancellor of Exchequer 1955–7, Prime Minister 1957–63, Chairman/President Macmillan & Co Publishers 1963–86.

17   Later Lord Birkett (1883–1962), High Court of Justice 1941–50, Lord Justice of Appeal 1950–7, Liberal who disagreed with Lord Chancellor over 'political' length of Blake's espionage sentence.

18   Cmnd. 283.

19   Ministry of Food, Treasury, Crown Office in Scotland, Post Office, Port of London Authority Police, various Chief Constables, Director of Public Prosecutions, City of London Police, one of HM Judges, Home Office, Customs and Excise, Scottish Home Department ('for lotteries only'), and the Security Service. Totals were 2,600 telephones monitored and about 10,600 cases of letter-interception.

20   Later Lord Gordon-Walker, PC, CH (1907–80), BBC German Service 1940–5, Labour MP 1945–74, Foreign Secretary 1964–5, Education and Science Secretary 1967–8, Member of European Parliament 1975–6.

21   Later Lord George-Brown (1914–85), Labour MP 1945–70, Deputy Leader Labour Party 1960–70, SofS Economic Affairs 1964–6, Foreign Secretary 1966–8, President Social Democratic Alliance 1981–5.

22   Cmnd.1681. See below for the SPBC involvement and its prior discussion of the draft Report.

23   They were not the only members of the Press who brought legal representation to the Tribunal; 13 barristers appeared for various journals, and there was lengthy and learned discussion of the law, precedent, and journalistic principle and courage. *Daily Telegraph* 17–25 January 1963.

24   Captain Sir Rodger Winn, CB, OBE, RNVR (1903–72), NID 1939–45 (Head of the Submarine Tracking Room), High Court 1959–65, Chairman Permanent Security Commission 1964–71, Lord Justice of Appeal 1965–71, brother of flamboyant journalist Godfrey Winn.

25   Cmnd.2722, July 1965.

26   Cmnd.3121, November 1966.

27   From 1945, broadcasters were also represented on the Committee; but the term 'the Press' was still used for many years thereafter to cover all 'Media', a term which had begun to emerge in 1920s, and which is normally used (other than in quotes) in this History hereafter, when both printed and electronic institutions are referred to.

28   St Bride's, NS Circular November 1945.

29   St Bride's Library, NPA Box 18. Letter of 23 September 1954.

30   Lord Beveridge KCB (1879–1963), Leader-writer *Morning Post* 1906–8, PUS Ministry of Food 1919, Director London School of Economics and Political Science 1919–37, Vice-Chancellor London University 1926–8, Master University College Oxford 1937–45, author of the Beveridge Report 1942 on which the post-War Attlee Government based the 'Welfare State', Liberal MP 1944–5, Chairman Broadcasting Committee 1949–50.

31   Later Lord Pilkington (1905–83), director family glass business, Bank of England, Chairman Broadcasting Committee 1960–2.

32   St Bride's, NPA Box 4.

33   Later Lord Shawcross, GBE, PC (1902–2003), British prosecutor at Nuremberg Trials, Labour MP 1945–58, Attorney-General 1945–51, co-founder and Chairman 1957–72 of Justice.

34   Cmnd.1811, September 1962.

35   KR Murdoch AC (1931–), Chairman/Chief Executive News Corporation Ltd Australia, News International plc UK, News America Publishing Inc, Times Newspaper Holdings Ltd, Twentieth Century Fox, Fox Entertainment Gp Inc, British Sky Broadcasting.

36   Lord Thomson, GBE (1894–1976), Chairman Thomson Org Ltd.

37   IR Maxwell, MC (1923–1991), born Czech as JL Hoch, British Army WWII, 'Foreign Office' 1945–7, publisher (especially Pergamon Press), Labour MP 1964–70, owner Oxford United then Derby County Football Clubs 1982–91, Chairman Mirror Group Newspapers from 1984, disappeared at sea from his yacht.

38   TNA:PRO DEFE 13/169 and PREM 11/1165.

39   Later Lord Jay (1907–96), financial journalist, *Times*, *Economist*, *Daily Herald*, WWII civil servant, Labour MP 1946–83, President Board of Trade 1964–7.

40   Hansard 7 February 1967, Cols 1663–1785.

41   Until March 1946, when its residual functions were transferred to the Central Office of Information.
42   BBC Written Archive, R28/5/1.
43   St Bride's NS Circular October 1945.
44   TNA:PRO HO 45/23627.
45   HC 'Harry' Pincher (1914–), scientist, Royal Armoured Corps and Ministry of Supply 1940–6, Defence, Science and Medical Editor *Daily Express* 1946–73, Chief Defence Correspondent Beaverbrook Newspapers 1972–9, still active as freelance journalist 2007.
46   TNA:PRO AB 1/564; his source was actually American; discussion Pincher/Wilkinson September 2007.
47   AP Robbins, CBE (1887–1967), son of Sir Alfred Robbin; *Times* political correspondent 1923–38, home news editor 1938–53 (similar progression to his elder brother, also following an uncle WE Pitt who was first *Times* political correspondent when the lobby system was established in 1892), member of the AWOAMPC 1945–57, Secretary newly formed Press Council 1954–60; Thomson regarded him as 'the most reasonable as well as the most influential of the Press Members'; TNA:PRO AB 16/716.
48   The absence of the BBC from the Committee pre-WWII was unsurprising as news and current affairs were not then a major part of BBC's own output; discussion John Wilson/Wilkinson 10 December 2007.
49   *'Understanding Journalism: a Guide to Issues'*, J Wilson, Routledge, 1996.
50   Sir Henry Markham, KCB, MC (1897–1946), Royal Garrison (Heavy) Artillery BEF WWI, PUS Admiralty 1940–6 – died in office.
51   TNA:PRO DEFE 53/6 and BBC Written Archive R28/5/1. The deputising practice has varied over the years – currently (2007) stand-ins are not the custom unless an agenda item necessitates representation for that discussion; nor do non-members, official or media, routinely sit in at meetings, as officials did before and immediately after WWII.
52   TNA:PRO HO 45/23627.
53   AP Ryan, CBE (1900–72), *Manchester Guardian, Daily Telegraph*, publicity manager Gas, Light and Coke Co, Squadron Leader RAFVR 1939–40, editor BBC News Services 1940–47, literary editor *Times* 1947–68, author of updated Official History of *The Times*.
54   HE Turner, later Sir Henry Turner, CBE (1891–1961), Army 1914–19, General Secretary Commonwealth (formerly Empire) Press Union 1919–56.
55   Sir Eric Speed, KCB, KBE, MC (1895–1971), Army 1914–18 (MC and Croix de Guerre), PUS War Office 1942–8.
56   TNA:PRO DEFE 53/6. See Appendix 4.
57   TNA:PRO DEFE 53/6, ADM 1/18689, BBC Written Archive R28/5/1.
58   Later Brigadier Sir Owen Wansbrough-Jones, KBE, CB (1905–1982), Colloid Science Department Cambridge 1932–40, Army 1940–6, Director Special Weapons/Vehicles War Office, Chief Scientific Adviser Army Council, then Ministry of Supply.
59   Later Professor Sir Charles Ellis (1895–1980), Professor Physics King's College London, Scientific Adviser Army Council 1943–6, Senior Scientific Adviser Civil Defence London 1947–65.
60   TNA:PRO DEFE 53/6, BBC Written Archive R28/5/1.
61   Sir Stafford Cripps (1889–52), ambulance driver France WWI, Labour MP 1931–50, Solicitor General 1931, founder Socialist League and *Tribune*, expelled from Labour Party 1939 for anti-appeasement views, Ambassador Soviet Union 1940–2, Minister Aircraft Production 1942–5, President Board of Trade 1945–7, Chancellor of Exchequer 1947–50.
62   TNA:PRO DEFE 53/6.
63   Later Sir Martin Furnival Jones, CBE (1912–1997), solicitor, Army 1939–45, DG Security Service 1965–72.
64   Security Service Archives.
65   Sir William Brown, KCB, KCMG, CBE (1893–1947), Army 1914–17, PUS Board of Trade 1937–40, Ministry of Supply 1940–3, Ministry of Home Security 1943–5, Air Ministry 1945–7, died in office.
66   TNA:PRO DEFE 53/6.

67   See Appendix 3.

68   TNA:PRO DEFE 53/6.

69   Lord Rothschild, GBE, GM (1910–90), academic zoologist, WWII MI5 and explosives expert, Head Central Policy Review Staff 1971–4.

70   TNA:PRO KV 4/354.

71   TNA:PRO KV 4/355.

72   TNA:PRO KV 4/356 and 4/355.

73   TNA:PRO ADM 1/20905.

74   Security Service Archives.

75   Later Sir John Cockroft, GCB (1897–67), Artillery WWI, nuclear physicist, Cavendish Laboratory, Ministry of Supply WWII, Director AERE Harwell, Nobel Prize for Physics 1951, Master Churchill College Cambridge 1958–67.

76   TNA:PRO AB 16/716.

77   The Centurion tank.

78   Later Sir John Lang, GCB (1896–1984), Royal Marine Artillery WWI, PUS Admiralty 1964–71, Government's Principal Adviser on Sport 1964–71.

79   TNA:PRO DEFE 53/6.

80   BBC Written Archive R28/5/1.

81   Thomson's correspondence in these months is handwritten from his Putney home, once even 'greatly assisted' by the *Daily Mail*'s editor in summarising the extant 11 Notices, because 'the Government have kicked me out of Cable and Wireless [and out of Electra House] because I'm over 55'; he pushed rather demeanedly (and in vain) for any Ministry of Supply post; later that year, however, he found work as Public Relations Officer to the Hispanic and Luso-Brazilian Councils in Canning House, initially in Upper Berkley Street, then (1953) Belgrave Square; his D-Notice work was conducted from its offices, rather more civilised surroundings than his successors have enjoyed; BBC Written Archive R28/5/1.

82   TNA:PRO AB 16/716.

83   TNA:PRO DEFE 53/6.

84   BA Hill (1904–78), Security Service Legal Adviser 1940–64.

85   Security Service Archives.

86   Sir James Barnes, KCB, KBE (1891–1969), PUS for Air 1947–55.

87   The names of the two resourceful young editors are not recorded, nor whether they went on to distinguished careers in aviation journalism. A supervised outlet for young aviation enthusiasts already existed: the Air Training Corps, founded 1941 from the Air Defence Cadet Corps, still active today.

88   Air Ministry and Board of Trade had discussed in June 1945 what might replace the Air Navigation (Restriction in Time of War) Order, used inter alia to control aerial photography; BoT lawyers advised an amendment to the Air Navigation Act 1920 should quickly be pushed through; the BoT file was then lost, and a year later 'when found among the papers of an officer now left the Service', it was decided no further action would be taken in that Department. TNA:PRO BT 217/111.

89   *AMPHION* Class submarine which had been in the Arctic Ocean for six weeks, conducting tests of physiological problems connected with prolonged 'snorting', and trials of optimum economical speeds/fuel consumption.

90   This was during the period of worsening relations with the USSR in Europe which led inter alia to the Berlin Airlift a few months later. TNA:PRO DEFE 53/6, Pt II.

91   TNA:PRO AB 16/614.

92   TNA:PRO DEFE 53/6, Pt II.

93   BBC Written Archive, R28/5/1.

94   Security Service Archives.

95   TNA:PRO ADM 1/20905.

96   TNA:PRO DEFE 53/6 Pt II.

97   TNA:PRO AB 16/716.

98   The Royal and US Navies had both trialled rubber matting to assist in recovering aircraft landing on carriers; the consequent Pythonesque bounce factor caused the experiments quickly to be abandoned.

99   BBC Written Archive R28/5/1.
100   Sir George Turner, KCB, KBE (1896–1974), served in ranks BEF 1916–19, rejoined War Office, PUS 1949–56.
101   Thomson later recorded (April 1951) that, from the time of the Korean War, US correspondents in UK had been more conscious of British security concerns; he informally gave them all D-Notice No.71 (embarkation of military units for Korea), with which they had complied; several had said they would be willing to comply more generally so long as they could send copies of Notices to their editors in New York; however, senior UK officials had vetoed this; Security Service Archives.
102   TNA:PRO DEFE 53/6 Pt II.
103   Bruno Pontecorvo (1913–1993), Italian-born (elder brother of film-maker Gillo Pontecorvo) naturalised British physicist, whose background, career, and socialist beliefs took him from Italy to Paris, Spain, Oklahoma, Canada and Britain (where he was a Liverpool University Professor, and asked to assist the British atomic bomb project); in September 1950 the Soviets smuggled him and his family from Sweden into the USSR; he allegedly had had no access to British atomic secrets.
104   Arthur Christiansen (1904–63), editor *Daily Express* 1933–57, director Beaverbrook Newspapers 1941–59, director ITN 1960–2. Letters dated 30 October 1950, in Personal Archive of HC Pincher.
105   TNA:PRO AVIA 65/2340.
106   Officials would have remembered that pre-war Notices sent to Reuters quickly found their way via foreign employees to German Intelligence.
107   TNA:PRO DEFE 53/6 Pt II, BBC Written Archive R28/5/3.
108   A later check showed in fact six had been withheld: No.s 25 (atomic weapons, 1948), 33 (aerial photography, 1948), 42 (escape and evasion, 1949), 65 (British Army contribution to Korea, 1950), 71 (departure of forces for Korea, 1950), and 75 (air defence, 1950); TNA:PRO WO 258/124, ADM 1/27276; the staff of the *Daily Worker* had also been infiltrated by MI5 – see TNA:PRO KV 2/601 and 2/2028.
109   TNA:PRO DEFE 53/6 Pt II.
110   TRP Hole, CBE (1908–85), New Zealand-born, London correspondent *Melbourne Herald* 1937–41, BBC wartime broadcaster frequently attacked in Nazi propaganda, editor-controller BBC News Division 1948–58, D-Notice Committee same period, the BBC also representing Independent TV interests until ITN joined Committee mid-60s.
111   BBC Written Archive R28/5/3.
112   Later Lord Penney, OM, KBE (1909–91), mathematician, nuclear physicist, US Manhattan Project 1945, Head British Nuclear Weapons Programme CSAR Fort Halstead and AWRE Aldermaston, Rector Imperial College 1967–73.
113   Sir Archibald Rowlands, GCB, MBE (1892–1953), Army 1914–18, Military Finance Adviser India 1937–9, Air Ministry 1939–40, PUS Ministry of Aircraft Production 1940–3, Governor-General's Executive Council India 1945–6, PUS Ministry of Supply 1946–53, Financial Adviser to Mr Jinnah in Pakistan 1947, Member Economic Planning Board 1947–53.
114   TNA:PRO AB 16/614.
115   Major TM Muggeridge (1903–90), *Manchester Guardian*, *Calcutta Statesman*, *Evening Standard*, Intelligence Corps 1939–45, *Daily Telegraph* (deputy editor 50–2), editor *Punch* 1953–7, television personality.
116   Off NW Australia, where subsequently Britain exploded test bombs in October 1953 and May 1956, Macmillan also having announced in 1955 that an 'All-British H-Bomb' was being developed; *Daily Mail* 18 February 1955.
117   Later Sir Roger Hollis, KBE, CB (1905–73), businessman, joined Security Service 1938, DGSS 1956–65.
118   Security Service Archives.
119   TNA:PRO DEFE 53/6 Pt II.
120   TNA:PRO AB 16/614.
121   TNA:PRO TS 28/566 and AIR 2/12362.
122   The former journal the *Week*, edited by Claud Cockburn, was also still sometimes the non-recipient of Notices.

123 A wartime R Class destroyer, converted to a Type 15 frigate.

124 Presumably because of the confined conditions in ships; this was not altogether justified: ship's companies were well used to putting canvas covers over secret equipment in parts of their ship occasionally open not just to the Press, but to foreign VIPs, and to other visitors.

125 JL Palmer, OBE (1883–1961), editor *Western Morning News and Mercury* 1923–48, Chief SW Regional Officer Ministry of Information 1939–42, Director the *Cornishman*, President Guild of British Newspaper Editors 1949.

126 TNA:PRO ADM 1/23250.

127 American journals *Aviation Weeks* and *American Aviation*, and *Interavia* (published in Geneva in four languages); all were resistant to Thomson's subsequent approaches (the secret Agencies would not let him actually show the Notice to the Editors), but *Aviation Weeks* agreed to be more careful after being reminded of possible legal consequences in UK, *American Aviation* agreed to vet articles more carefully (but emphasised its New York staff would not co-operate 'as it was quite foreign to US practice to have news censored in peace time' [not entirely true; the US authorities had and have ruthless ways of preserving secrecy in key areas]), and *Interavia* passed the request to the Swiss owner, who however imposed unacceptable conditions in discussion with Thomson.

128 AP Chalkley (1886–1959), editor of the *Motor Ship*, PTPWNPA.

129 TNA:PRO DEFE 53/6 Pt II.

130 The author has found no direct documentary evidence of Thomson's 'unofficial' activity, but it has been confirmed by press and civil service sources active at that time; Pincher confirmed the Press Barons' agreement.

131 Readers unfamiliar with warship bridges should understand that then as now a copy of *Jane's Fighting Ships* is kept to hand, so that on sighting a foreign warship her characteristics are immediately understood, if not already known; there is no comparably reliable/comprehensive such reference book provided from official sources, except intelligence documents about potential adversaries.

132 TNA:PRO DEFE 53/6 Pt II.

133 BBC Written Archive R58/5/4.

134 Both had been established in 1952, but, as Hill foresaw, because of the 'disparate nature' of the local press they have not remained active; Security Service Archives; BBC Written Archive R28/5/4.

135 TNA:PRO KV 4/358.

136 BBC Written Archive R28/5/4.

137 It covered Security in peacetime, OSAs, Intelligence as seen by a Foreign Power, Intelligence as seen through British Eyes, each Armed Service, Scientific Intelligence, and War Potential; BBC Written Archive R28/5/3.

138 MoD was still separate from the Services' Departments and not represented on the Committee; the Australian D-Notice Committee had however recently been renamed *Defence*, Press and Broadcasting.

139 TNA:PRO DEFE 53/6 Pt II. Such unusual magnanimity on Martin's part towards officials reflects perhaps that this was his last meeting; he was equally well-known for habitual robustness within his own Association and the Media generally. It is not clear why the Admiralty had not foreseen such problems arising from a submarine launch, which is normally preceded by weeks of preparation, invitations to VIPs and the media, etc.

140 The 'Flying Bedstead', as it was dubbed, was reported widely next day in the media, but what especially irked the Press was that many journalists had known about this prototype VSTOL aircraft for some time, and had obediently not reported it, for security reasons.

141 N Robson, OBE (1897–1969), London editor *Westminster Press* 1948–62, President Institute of Journalists 1950, NS representative on SPBC.

142 Later Sir Cyril Musgrave, KCB (1900–86), Ministry of Supply 1946–59, Permanent Secretary 1956–9, Chairman Iron and Steel Board 1959–67.

143 TNA:PRO DEFE 53/6 Pt II.

144 The administrative support of the Committee had recently been put on a marginally more formal basis, the Secretary being provided with a Personal Assistant/typist, and Notices now being despatched by Departments rather than he himself sticking down envelopes.

145   Representation continued when the Ministry of Supply later became the Ministry of Aviation.
146   TNA:PRO DEFE 53/6 Pt II.
147   BBC Written Archive R28/5/4.
148   Security Service Archives.
149   TNA:PRO KV 4/358.
150   For the full hilarious sequence of cock-ups, see *'Inside Story'*, Chapman Pincher, Sidgwick and Jackson, 1978.
151   Security Service Archives.
152   TNA:PRO DEFE 53/8.
153   Later Lord Roche (1871–1956), Chairman Oxon Quarter Sessions 1932–47, Lord Justice of Appeal 1934–35, Lord of Appeal-in-Ordinary 1935–38.
154   Security Service Archives.
155   TNA:PRO AIR 8/2086; this was written by Frank Cooper (see Chapter 8), who in his private papers later recalled problems caused by Departments not being able to talk to each other because of the closed nature of the Politics.
156   TNA:PRO DEFE 53/8.
157   TNA:PRO FCO 12/180.
158   TNA:PRO DEFE 53/8.
159   TNA:PRO DEFE 53/8.
160   AJ Newling, CB, CBE, MVO, TD (1896–1957), BEF 1916–19, War Office from 1921, rejoined Army 1939–45 inter alia commanding TA Light Anti-Aircraft Regiment, Under-Secretary MoD 1946–57.
161   There was not in reality much purely military action to report; a ship and two Army battalions were deployed, with some acts of personal bravery and initiative by junior Servicemen facing rioters; the author unheroically led a Naval Landing Party, armed with pick-axe handles and adorned with dustbin lid shields and WWII helmets, to be interposed between rival political mobs of African and of Asian ethnic origins.
162   St Bride's Library, NPA Box 15, Minutes of meeting.
163   TNA:PRO DEFE 53/7 and INF 12/300 and 12/630 amongst many others.
164   DS 'Tom' Delmer (1904–79), German-speaking journalist, Black Propagandist for Political Warfare Executive WWII, chief foreign reporter *Express* until 1959, fired by Beaverbrook for having become obese.
165   TNA:PRO DEFE 53/8.
166   TNA:PRO DEFE 53/8.
167   F Allaun (1913–2002), journalist *Manchester Evening News*, *Daily Herald*, editor *Labour's Northern Voice* 1951–67, Labour MP 1955–83, Vice-President CND 1983–2002.
168   Security Service Archives.
169   Lieutenant Colonel SR Pawley, OBE, foreign editor *Daily Telegraph*, who had succeeded Pitt Robbins on the Committee.
170   TNA:PRO DEFE 53/9.
171   CE Jervis, OBE (1907–99), *Liverpool Express*, *Westmoreland Gazette*, then *Croydon Times* 1921–37, PA from 1947, editor-in-chief 1954–65, President Guild of British Newspaper Editors 1964–5, Press Council 1960–5.
172   TNA:PRO DEFE 53/9.
173   TNA:PRO DEFE 53/9.
174   TNA:PRO DEFE 53/9.
175   Hansard, 2 July 1959 and TNA:PRO PREM 11/2852.
176   TNA:PRO DEFE 53/9.
177   The US Department of Defense also asked about the D-Notice system the following year during the Cuban Missile Crisis.
178   No full record has apparently survived of this meeting (nor of one on 12 May 1959), but this dispute was referred to by the DPBC Chairman to Sir Norman Brook in the wake of the Blake case, adding that there was no advantage in having 'a stand up fight with the Press on this issue'. TNA:PRO CAB 21/5163.
179   Security Service Archives, seemingly the only copy of the minutes to survive.

180 Sentenced 1961 to 42 years imprisonment, escaped 5 years later aided by 3 members of 'Committee of 100', fled to the Soviet Union.

181 Hon DFL Astor, CH (1912–2001), *Yorkshire Post* and *Observer* (owned by his father), Army 1939–45, editor *Observer* 1948–75.

182 TNA:PRO CAB 21/5163.

183 Sir Richard 'Sam' Way, KCB, CBE (1914–98), non-graduate, PUS War Office 1960–3, PUS Ministry of Aviation 1963–6, Principal King's College London 1975–80.

184 Later Lord Normanbrook, PC, GCB (1902–67), Deputy Secretary to War Cabinet (Civil) 1942, PUS Ministry of Reconstruction 1943–5, Cabinet Secretary 1945–62, Joint Secretary Treasury and Head of Home Civil Service 1956–62, Chairman of BBC Governors 1964–7.

185 TNA:PRO CAB 21/5163. The mixed feelings of Philby, in the Lebanon at the time, may be imagined. It later transpired that *The Observer*, with which Philby had a journalistic link, had received 'a report dealing with the effect of Blake's activities' at least two days before the D-Notice was issued; 'The first accounts published in foreign papers suggest that they were based on similar information.' War Office to Brook, 16 May 1961. TNA:PRO WO 32/19632.

186 Security Service Archives.

187 TNA:PRO DEFE 13/169.

188 Security Service Archives.

189 Lieutenant Colonel M Lipton, CBE, MP (1900–1978), Territorial Army WWII, Labour MP 1945–78; in 1955 he had named Philby in Parliament as a suspected spy.

190 HTN Gaitskell, CBE (1906–63), civil service 1939–45, Labour MP 1945–63, Chancellor of Exchequer 1950–1, Leader of Labour party 1955–63.

191 Later Lord Marsh (1928–), Labour MP 1959–71, Minister of Transport 1968–9, Chairman British Railways 1971–6 and of Newspaper Publishers' Association 1976–90.

192 Hansard Cols 636–8 and 643–6, 11 May 2006.

193 TNA:PRO CAB 21/5163.

194 Later Lord Trend, PC, GCB, CVO (1914–1987), Deputy Secretary Cabinet 1956–9, Second Secretary Treasury 1959–62, Cabinet Secretary 1963–73.

195 TNA:PRO CAB 21/5163.

196 TNA:PRO CAB 21/5163.

197 Sir Edward Playfair, KCB (1909–99), Inland Revenue/Treasury 1931–56, PUS for War 1956–9, PUS MoD 1960–1.

198 The strain of recent events on the health of the already frail Secretary is indicated by his doctor's and wife's orders in mid-June to take a fortnight's 'lay-off' – in a Worthing Hotel – so much for never having had it so good.

199 TNA:PRO WO 32/19632.

200 TNA:PRO CAB 21/5163.

201 In 1963 he was removed in a coup by Iraqi Army officers, including Saddam Hussein; he was publicly tortured and killed.

202 Later Viscount Watkinson, CH. PC (1910–95), technical/engineering journalist 1935–9, Royal Naval Volunteer Reserve 1939–45, Conservative MP 1950–64, Minister of Defence 1959–62, Falklands Islands Review Committee 1982–3.

203 TNA:PRO PREM 13/1641.

204 For non-cricketers, that is from a first line of stoppage to a second; not an ideal analogy, since the use of a longstop implies exceptionally low-grade standards.

205 TNA:PRO CAB 21/5163.

206 *Sunday Times* 'Portrait Gallery', 14 May 1961.

207 TNA:PRO CAB 21/5163.

208 TNA:PRO CAB 21/5163.

209 TNA:PRO DEFE 53/9.

210 Later Lord Caccia, GCMG, GCVO (1905–1990), Oxford Rugby Blue, seconded to Resident Minister North Africa (Macmillan) 1943, Political Adviser Italy then Greece 1943–4, British Ambassador Washington 1956–61, PUS Foreign Office 1962–5.

211 TNA:PRO CAB 21/5163.

212 Limited War was the terminology used for full-scale war short of escalation to use of 'battlefield' nuclear weapons.

213   Thomson letter 27 July 1961/memo 1 September 1961; TNA:PRO DEFE 53/2.

214   'Press gag: Premier to be quizzed'. 2 August 1961.

215   TNA:PRO CAB 21/5163.

216   Hansard, 2 August 1961, Cols 1473–5, and 3 August Cols 1649–50.

217   Hansard, 2 August 1961, Cols 1473–5, and 3 August Cols 1649–50.

218   Memorandum by Thomson, TNA:PRO DEFE 53/2. Thomson also gave similar oral evidence to the Committee in September 1961. Many aspects of his modus operandi survive to this day, differences being recorded in later chapters.

219   Later published as 'Security Procedures in the Public Service', Chapter 9, April 1962. Cmnd 1681.

220   Sir Robert Scott, GCMG, CBE (1905–82), UK Commissioner-General South-East Asia 1955–9, Commandant Imperial Defence College 1960–1, PUS MoD 1961–3.

221   Later Sir Geoffrey Cox, CNZM, CBE (1910–2008), New Zealand-born Foreign Correspondent *News Chronicle* 1935–7 covering inter alia Spanish Civil War, *Daily Express* 1937–40 in Austria and Russo-Finnish War, commissioned in NZ Army 1940, Intelligence Officer with Freyberg's NZ Division, NZ Legation Washington, BBC Radio/TV 1945–56, editor and chief executive ITN 1956–68, including founding News at Ten 1967.

222   Sir Maurice Dean, KCB, KCMG (1906–78), PUS Air Ministry 1955–63, PUS Ministry of Technology 1964–6, RAF Historian. Hill records Radcliffe did not want the Report published, but Macmillan insisted.

223   As recorded elsewhere, the Secretary's role, then and now, equally involved arguing with Departments *against* (unjustifiable) censorship.

224   This view came from Way's evidence, which he did not reveal was in turn derived from Chapman Pincher, disappointed at not having himself been asked for evidence; TNA:PRO CAB 21/6015.

225   Security Service Archives.

226   TNA:PRO PRO 56/352.

227   However, the National Archives' holdings in this field peter out at about the 1970 mark; hopefully one side effect of writing this History will be to hasten transfer of more records from MoD archives to Kew.

228   Major (Honorary Colonel) LG Lohan (pronounced Lawn), MBE, TD (1910–1979), publisher, Territorial Army then Short Service Commission in Middlesex Regiment, DDPR (Army) 1958, requesting Honorary rank of Colonel for reasons of status in post, granted exceptionally by Army Board.

229   TNA:PRO CAB 21/5163.

230   TNA:PRO CAB 21/5163.

231   For history of these secret headquarters, in particular TURNSTILE, and of plans for government during a nuclear war, see *'The Secret State'* by Professor Peter Hennessy, Allen Lane/Penguin, 2002.

232   Hansard 29 April 1963, and NS Circular June 1963.

233   TNA:PRO DEFE 53/10.

234   Security Service Archives; the file does not record who agreed this arrangement, nor what conditions were attached to it.

235   The Chairmanship, and Lohan, did subsequently transfer to MoD, by a process of 'natural rotation', on 1 June 1966.

236   Discussion Pincher/Wilkinson, 16 October 2006.

237   The 'confirmation' by the Security Service of the wrong name was in order to give further protection to Golitsin, but the media later suspected it was to add further damage to the *Telegraph*'s scoop.

238   Indeed the Home Office PUS had specifically advised Hollis there was no need to advise Ministers immediately.

239   Later Lord Harlech, KCMG (1918–1985), Conservative MP 1950–61, Minister of State for Foreign Affairs 1957–61, British Ambassador in Washington 1961–5, President British Board of Film Censors 1965–85, Chairman National Committee for Electoral Reform 1976–84.

240   TNA:PRO CAB 21/5163.

241   Hansard, 18 July 1963 Cols 722–3.

242   Hansard, 22 July 1963 Cols 445–8.
243   Security Service Archives.
244   TNA:PRO CAB 21/5163.
245   TNA:PRO CAB 21/5163.
246   Commander JS Kerans, DSO (1915–85), Assistant Naval Attaché Nanking 1949 whence he joined *HMS AMETHYST*, took command after CO killed, led escape under fire down Yangtze, Conservative MP 1959–64.
247   Hansard, 1 August 1963, Col 640.
248   TNA:PRO CAB 21/5163 and DEFE 11/376.
249   HJG Grisewood, CBE (1906–97), BBC European (propaganda) Division 1941–5, Controller Third Programme 1947–52, Director of the Spoken Word 1952–5, Chief Assistant to DG 1955–64.
250   TNA:PRO CAB 21/6077.
251   Sir Bernard Burrows, GCMG (1910–2002), Chairman JIC, Ambassador to NATO.
252   Trend did not take this idea further, quite rightly in view of the necessary separation of the Secretary from direct dealing with Politicians. Security Service Archives.
253   *Private Eye*, 22 August 1963.
254   TNA:PRO DEFE 53/10 and CAB 21/6077. Lohan invited the Editor of *Private Eye* to lunch at the Savoy, who explained he was not then on the distribution of D-Notices, and, well fed, undertook to seek advice in future; Lohan had a similar gastronomic interview with the Editor of the CND magazine *Sanity* a few days later, after unthinking publication of the address of 'C's country home; such guests' arrival without a tie was swiftly remedied by the Head Waiter.
255   Sir Denis Hamilton, DSO (1918–88), Montgomery's staff WWII, Editor *Sunday Times* 1961–6.
256   Sir Philip de Zulueta, KCB (1925–89), PS to Prime Ministers Eden, Macmillan and Douglas-Home 1955–64, Hill Samuel and HSBC 1973–89.
257   TNA:PRO CAB 21/6077.
258   For example, the *Radnor Express* of 5 March 1964.
259   G Wynne (1919–90), businessman who assisted the secret Agencies, arrested by KGB at Budapest trade fair 1962, transferred to Russia, sentenced to imprisonment 1963, exchanged for 'Lonsdale' April 1964, subsequently (without SIS permission) wrote *'The Man from Odessa'* about his experiences.
260   TNA:PRO PREM 13/1814. Also confirmed to the author in discussion with Pincher 6 Nov 2006.
261   TNA:PRO CAB 21/6077.
262   As surviving records for this period are so thin, it is unclear whether this resulted from something discussed in Committee; because most contemporary topics were by now already covered by Notice or Letter, and because it suited Lohan's sociable modus operandi with the media, there were apparently even fewer formal meetings and documents.
263   TNA:PRO DEFE 53/11 and 18.
264   Security Service Archives.
265   Lieutenant Colonel O Penkovsky (1919–63), member of GRU (Soviet Military Intelligence), one of the most prolific providers of high-grade intelligence on the USSR to UK/USA, arrested by KGB after tip-off from an American traitor 1962, shot 1963.
266   TNA:PRO DEFE 53/11.
267   Later Lord Wilson. KG, OBE (1916–95), Oxford Lecturer 1937–45, Civil Service 1943–4, Labour MP 1945–83, President BoT 1947–51, Prime Minister 1964–70 and 1974–6.
268   Later Lord Healey, CH, MBE (1917–), Labour MP 1952–92, SofS for Defence 1964–70, Chancellor of Exchequer 1974–9, Deputy Leader Labour Party 1980–3.
269   Later Sir Edward Pickering (1912–2003), Royal Artillery 1940–5, managing editor *Daily Mail* 1947–9 and *Daily Express* 1951–7, editor *Daily Express* 1957–62, director then chairman International Publishing Corporation 1966–75, director *Times* Newspapers Holdings from 1981, Press Council 1964–82, Press Complaints Commission 1991–2003, mentor/friend of Rupert Murdoch.
270   Later Lord Wigg, PC (1900–83), Army 1919–37 and 1940–6, Labour MP 1945–67, Racecourse Betting Control/Totalisator Boards 1957–64, Paymaster-General 1964–7, Chairman Horserace Betting Levy Board 1967–72, President Betting Office Licensees' Association 1973–83; 'his

face ... with the large ears and that bruised jutting beak, is one of Nature's hastiest feats of improvisation ... behind it lives his ceaseless mind: a landscape of bent trees in a driving wind', *Sunday Telegraph* 12 November 1967.

271 TNA:PRO DEFE 53/11.
272 TNA:PRO PREM 13/1501.
273 TNA:PRO PREM 13/576.
274 *Daily Telegraph* 25 June 1965.
275 TNA:PRO DEFE 53/19.
276 TNA:PRO PREM 13/1182.
277 TNA:PRO PREM 13/3072, PREM 13/1195, and CAB 164/847.
278 Cmnd 3309, June 1967, Enclosure A(iii).
279 *'Good Times, Bad Times'*, Harold Evans, Weidenfeld and Nicolson, 1983.
280 TNA:PRO CAB 21/4164/1. A similar document still in the D-Notice Secretary's inner safe in 2000 appeared particularly uninformative, and was returned to the Cabinet Office, who did not demur.
281 TNA:PRO PREM 13/1814.
282 Sir Henry Hardman, KCB (1905–2001), PUS MoD 1963–6.
283 Sir James 'Ned' Dunnett, GCB, CMG (1914–97), PUS Ministry of Transport then of Labour 1959–66, PUS MoD 1966–74.
284 It is ironic that at the same time Lohan was conspiring successfully with the Newspaper Society to remove long-serving, dominant and prickly Robson from the Committee, and to replace him by fellow-conspirator Windsor Clarke, who had replaced Robson at the *Westminster Press*; Security Service Archives.
285 £500 was a not inconsiderable addition to Lohan's annual salary of about £2,000. Thomson too had apparently been paid by MI5 for information picked up in the course of his work; this supplement had presumably been allowed because neither was considered to be in full-time employment as the Secretary; Lohan was the last D-Notice Secretary to receive such a hidden bonus, or indeed to be expected to pass on information about his non-official contacts; the author has found no evidence to support the anecdotal belief that Lohan also received some similar recompense from the Press, apart from regular hospitality.
286 TNA:PRO PREM 13/1814.

SECTION 7
THE 'LOHAN' AFFAIR 1967

1 *'The Labour Government 1964–70: A Personal Record'*, Harold Wilson, Penguin, 1974.
2 25-year-old telegraph clerk/mechanic, worked at *People*, *Manchester Guardian* and *Manchester Evening News*, Associated Press and Reuters, joined RAF 1962, invalided on psychiatric grounds 1964, clerk at cable offices, GPO, Tass and GEC; later wrote to Prime Minister and Lord Radcliffe saying his motivation had been anger with MoD (thrice refused jobs by MoD after RAF discharge) and need for money to support his infant son. LSE British Library of Political and Economic Science (BLPES), WIGG 4/130. *Evening News* 14 June 1967.
3 TA O'Brien, CBE (1907–97), President Institute of Public Relations 1965, DPR GPO 1966–8, PR Manager Bank of London and South America 1968–72.
4 CR Morris (1926–), Army 1945–8, Labour MP 1963–83, Assistant Whip 1966–7, Vice-Chamberlain/Treasurer HM Household 1967–70, PPS to Harold Wilson 1970–4, Minister Civil Service Department 1974–9.
5 TNA:PRO PREM 13/1809. The file referred to must have been returned to the Whips' Office, and is not copied in the National Archives.
6 Discussion Charles Morris/Wilkinson, 18 October 2006.
7 Assessment of Wigg in *'The Time of My Life'* by Denis Healey. Michael Joseph, 1989. Years later, Wigg and Pincher regained their cordial relationship, the former admitting: 'I enjoy inflicting wounds but don't like to see them fester'; Pincher/Wilkinson 10 May 2005.
8 *'The D-Notice Affair'*, Hedley and Aynsley, Michael Joseph, 1967.

9   CTE Ewart-Biggs, CMG, CBE (1921–1976), Army 1942, at El Alamein lost an eye (over which he subsequently wore a smoked monocle), FO Defence and Security Department 1965–69, Ambassador to Republic of Ireland 1976, assassinated by IRA 21 July 1976 by a roadside bomb, which also killed a junior official and injured two others in the car.

10 Recorded later in Radcliffe Committee Report.

11 Pincher always booked the same table, even though he suspected bugging; later Rafael Calzada, long-serving Spanish manager of L'Ecu (closed in 1980s) told him bugging devices under tables had first been installed by MI5 during WWII to listen to foreign officials, especially the Free French; devices had remained there (with suitable upgrading) until closure; Pincher alleged Soviet bugs had also then been found; *Spectator* 22 August 1998, and discussion Pincher/Wilkinson 10 May 2005.

12 Cmnd 3309, Appendix III, B(i).

13 ibid C(i).

14 CA Brittenden (1924–), Reconnaissance Corps 1943–46, *Sunday* and *Daily Express* 1955–64, executive editor then editor *Daily Mail* 1964–71, deputy editor *Sun* 1972–81.

15 Lohan also had other things on his mind that day, as later described to the Radcliffe Committee; Greville Wynne was pestering him about his delayed book, then being vetted by Lohan and others, a publisher was asking for early advice on an ex-agent's book from Australia, and he had a problem from a provincial paper.

16 Later Lord Greenhill, GCMG, OBE (1913–2000), Army 1939–45, FO DUS 1966–69, PUS 1969–73.

17 Group Captain Sir Max Aitken, DSO, DFC (1910–1985), eldest son of Lord Beaverbrook, RAF 1939–45, Conservative MP 1945–50.

18 DJ Marks (1921–75), RAF 1940–6, editor *Daily Express* 1965–71, special adviser Beaverbrook Newspapers 1971–5.

19 *Daily Express*, 21 February 1967. The Bill was, in part, a reaction to the relatively recent furore over the tapping of the phones of some members of the Labour Party, at the request of its own leadership whilst still in Opposition; phone-tapping was thus a sensitive subject for the Labour Government; the sponsor of the Bill was PJ Bessell, MP (1921–85), Ministry of Information Lecturer to Forces 1943–5, Liberal MP 1964–70, Congregational Lay Preacher 1939–70, discredited witness 1979 Jeremy Thorpe murder conspiracy trial (about which Bessell wrote 1981 book), emigrated to California.

20 'Inside Number 10' by Marcia Williams (later Baroness Falkender), Weidenfeld and Nicolson, 1972; she described the affair as the 'real watershed' in bad press coverage of Wilson's first Government.

21 None, as it happened; 16 earlier Notices remained in force; Lieutenant Commander Sir John Langford-Holt, RN (1916–93), Fleet Air Arm 1939–45, Conservative MP 1945–83.

22 Later Sir Edward Heath, KG, MBE, PC (1916–2005), Army 1939–46, Lieutenant Colonel Honourable Artillery Company 1947–54, Conservative MP 1950–2001, SofS for Industry, Trade and Regional Development 1963–4, Leader of Opposition 1965–70 and 1974–5, Prime Minister 1970–4, Father of House of Commons 1992–2001, winner Sydney to Hobart Ocean race 1969.

23 Hansard 21 February 1967, Cols 1432–3.

24 TNA:PRO DEFE 23/22.

25 B Sheldon, CB (1924–2008), RNVR 1943–6, barrister, Colonial Service 1951–9, Security Service 1959–87, Legal Adviser 1967–87.

26 TNA:PRO DEFE 53/6 Pt II. Where not stated otherwise, much information in this section is culled from personal papers of Lord Wigg in the London School of Economics Library, and those of Chapman Pincher loaned to the author.

27 Lord Devlin (1905–92), High Court Judge, Law Lord, moral philosopher, Chairman Press Council 1964–9.

28 Hansard 23 February 1967, Cols 1975–80.

29 CC Douglas-Home (1937–85), Army 1956–7, military then political/diplomatic correspondent *Daily Express* 1961–64, defence correspondent etc *Times* 1965–82, editor *Times* 1982–5.

30 The Labour Government had cancelled the Royal Navy's intended new carrier CVA 01, causing allegations that the RAF had fudged air route distances to support Healey's contention that sea-based air support was no longer essential.

31 Sir George Coldstream, KCB, KCVO, QC (1907–2004), Lord Chancellor's Office from 1939, Permanent Secretary to Lord Chancellor 1954–68 (intermediary between his Minister, the Lords, Commons and Whitehall).

32 AN Halls, MBE (1915–1970), Army 1939–46, Board of Trade from 1947, PPS Prime Minister 1966–70; died of heart attack attributed by his widow to tensions within Wilson's personal staff, for which she later sought compensation.

33 LA Lee Howard, DFC (1914–78), Coastal Command RAF 1940–3, RAF Film Unit 1943–5, editor *Woman's Sunday Mirror* 1955–9, *Sunday Pictorial* 1959–61, *Daily Mirror* 1961–71.

34 LJ 'Jack' Dicker, MBE (1907–68), journalist, foreign editor *News of the World* until 1961, chief sub-editor *Daily Telegraph* 1961–68, spin bowler Ealing Dean Cricket Club.

35 Later Lord Selwyn-Lloyd, CH, CBE (1904–78), Army 1939–45, Conservative MP 1945–76, Minister of Defence 1955, SofS for Foreign Affairs 1955–60, Chancellor of Exchequer 1960–2, Speaker House of Commons1970–6.

36 Lord Shinwell, CH (1884–1986), Labour MP 1922–70, SofS for War 1947–50, Minister of Defence 1950–1, Chairman Labour Party 1964–7.

37 JJ Thorpe, PC (1929–), Liberal MP 1959–79, Leader Liberal Party 1967–76, resigned 1979 in wake of allegations of involvement in a homosexual murder conspiracy.

38 AR Watkins (1933–), RAF Education Branch 1955–7, *Sunday Express* 1959–64 as New York then political correspondent, thereafter political columnist inter alia *Spectator*, *New Statesman*, *Sunday Mirror*, *Observer*, *Evening Standard*, *Independent on Sunday*.

39 Later Lord Lawson, PC (1932–), RNVR 1954–6, *Financial Times*, city editor *Sunday Telegraph*, special assistant to Prime Minister (Douglas-Home) 1963–64, editor *Spectator* 1966–70, *Times* 1971–72, Conservative MP 1974–92, SofS for Energy 1981–3, Chancellor of Exchequer 1983–9.

40 John Drew, see note 74; this idea was subsequently vetoed by amongst others MI5 and MI6; neither wanted an MoD functionary, however well known to them as in Drew's case, being interposed between them and the Secretary.

41 Security Service Archives.

42 TNA:PRO DEFE 53/19; this group of middle-ranking officials anticipated most reforms which eventually emerged from the subsequent political storm.

43 Cmnd 3309, A(iii).

44 DJ Trevelyan, CB (1929–) of the Home Office, Northern Ireland Office 1972–6, Director General Prison Service 1978–83, First Civil Service Commissioner Cabinet Office 1983–9, Principal Mansfield College Oxford 1989–96.

45 TNA:PRO PREM 13/1815.

46 TNA:PRO PREM 13/1816.

47 Sir Patrick Dean, GCMG (1909–94), DUS FO 1956–60, UK Permanent Representative United Nations 1960–4, Ambassador Washington 1965–9.

48 Chaired the 'Telephone-tapping' Inquiry of Privy Counsellors, 1957; see section 6.

49 TNA:PRO PREM 13/1815.

50 This sensitivity was all the greater because the US authorities themselves operated a similar system (codenamed SHAMROCK) then unknown to the American public, with similar 'watch lists' (codified in 1969 as Project MINARET), not revealed (and ostensibly stopped) until the mid-1970s, with a system of sharing information on request between the US, British, Canadian, Australian and New Zealand interception organisations; US Senate Final Report, 'NSA Surveillance Affecting Americans', April 23, 1976.

51 Security Service Archives.

52 Security Service Archives.

53 Security Service Archives; that Lohan's report is recorded only there indicates only that the MI5 Archive is more complete for this period than those of Whitehall/media.

54 Verbatim reports of the evidence given to the Committee (by all except those from the secret Agencies), and the texts of documents provided, are in the Appendices to the Report (Cmnd 3309 of May 1967); some witnesses were accompanied by lawyers.

55 TNA:PRO PREM 13/1817.

56 According to a civil servant present; interview with Wilkinson 11 December 2006.

57 The background and contents of these private papers are discussed later in this section; they were at this stage known only to a very small number of Ministers and senior officials.

58 TNA:PRO PREM 13/1817.
59 TNA:PRO PREM 13/1817.
60 Wigg had initially suggested the Inquiry should be headed not by Radcliffe but by someone with Defence knowledge such as Lord Head; but he was nevertheless an admirer of Shinwell, whose PPS he had been at the War Office in 1947; *'George Wigg'* by Lord Wigg, Michael Joseph, 1972.
61 BLPES, WIGG/4/127. TNA:PRO PREM 13/1818.
62 TNA:PRO PREM 13/1818.
63 TNA:PRO PREM 13/1817.
64 Discussion by Wilkinson with senior civil servant directly involved, 11 December 2006. The full description of the cable-vetting mechanics is in a still Top Secret Special Annex in the Cabinet Office Archive, the 'retained' portion of PREM 13/1817.
65 TNA:PRO PREM 13/1818.
66 TNA:PRO PREM 13/1818.
67 Trend's own record of this meeting differs in a few details, and records that Wigg agreed with him that officials were doing their duty in pointing out the implications as they saw them.
68 Described in some detail in Trend's own note for the record of this meeting; he had not seen Lohan 'for a good many years' and had found him 'a rather brash individual; but he seemed to know his job, and I had no reason to suspect him'. TNA:PRO PREM 13/1819.
69 Brown had already suggested a compromise of partial publication, and warned against making a scapegoat of Lohan. TNA:PRO PREM 13/1818.
70 Respectively *'Diaries of Cabinet Minister'*, Vol II, Richard Crossman, Hamilton and Cape, 1976, and *'The Castle Diaries, 1964–70'*, Barbara Castle, Weidenfeld and Nicolson 1984; Radcliffe was in 1976 asked to lead a Privy Counsellor inquiry into Ministerial Memoirs, Report in Cmnd 6386.
71 On 30 May, Wilson had told Dunnett that, without breaching the propriety of a Civil Service disciplinary investigation, he should surreptitiously try to winkle out of Lohan incriminating facts about his Press contacts, especially Pincher, and if Lohan asked whether such additional information would be considered as 'privileged', Dunnett had 'the Prime Minister's authority to give such an assurance'; TNA:PRO PREM 13/1817.
72 BLPES, WIGG/4/135.
73 Later Lord Deedes, KBE, MC (1913–2007), *Morning Post* 1931–7 (including covering Abyssinian War, with Evelyn Waugh), Army 1939–45, Conservative MP 1950–74, junior ministerial posts 1954–64, editor *Daily Telegraph* 1974–86, commentator 1986–2007.
74 JA Drew, CB (1907–1995), 'Special Duties' 1940–5, Cabinet Office 1945–8, MoD 1951–67.
75 Deedes confirmed this in the Commons during the D-Notice Debate of 22 June, explaining the informant had been affronted by the treatment of Lohan. TNA:PRO PREM 13/1814, /1815 and /1819.
76 TNA:PRO PREM 13/1819.
77 Cmnd 3312, June 1967.
78 Hansard, 13 June 1967, Cols 309–16.
79 As explained in the previous section, he had not yet been fully positively vetted under new procedures, nor given necessary additional subject-specific high 'codeword' clearances.
80 Later Lord Helsby, GCB, KBE (1908–78), First Civil Service Commissioner 1954–9, PUS Ministry of Labour 1959–62, Joint PUS Treasury and Head of Home Civil Service 1963–8. His seven-page report was duly delivered the next day. TNA:PRO PREM 13/1814.
81 Queen's Messengers are completely trustworthy officials employed to carry highly classified information around the world, chained to their person, reliably and with discretion; with his now notorious personality, it might be that, had Colonel Lohan so applied, selection would have been even harder to achieve than full Positive Vetting; TNA:PRO PREM 13/1814.
82 TNA:PRO PREM 13/1814.
83 TNA:PRO FCO 26/122.
84 TNA:PRO PREM 13/1820.
85 All this was happening in the immediate aftermath of the Arab-Israeli Six-Day War (effectively ended the previous week), which had important implications inter alia for long term international relations in the Middle East, and more immediately for oil supplies and sterling; the Government

also had other major problems, including Smith's Rhodesia, de Gaulle over entry into the Common Market, and dock strikes in London and Liverpool; since April there had also been a series of leaks about Cabinet dissent over Defence policy, especially withdrawal from East of Suez, about which Wilson set up an internal inquiry under the Lord Chancellor; TNA:PRO PREM 13/1796 and 13/1800.

86　Peter Le Cheminant, CB (1926–2007), RNVR 1944–7, PS to Prime Minister 1965–8, Second Permanent Secretary Cabinet Office 1983–4.

87　TNA:PRO PREM 13/1809.

88　TNA:PRO PREM 13/1809.

89　For example, Lord Chalfont had told Wigg he had recently lunched with Wintour, who was 'almost pathologically hostile to the Prime Minister', while Rees-Mogg had said he would listen to Wilson but would not speak; the more moderate of the spectrum of Press views about the meeting was reflected in the previous day's *Sunday Telegraph* editorial, headed 'Long Spoon Needed'.

90　TNA:PRO PREM 13/1813.

91　Who was this mole? It is probable, from remarks reported as made at the NPA meeting, which Editor it was not: the *Daily* nor *Sunday Mirror*, *News of the World*, *Daily Sketch*, *Daily* nor *Sunday Express*, *Daily* nor *Sunday Telegraph*, *Financial Times*, *Sunday Times*, *Evening Standard*; of the others, it was clearly someone who knew the *Express* group well; but it would now be unfair to finger the prime suspect by name here.

92　Later Sir Harold Evans (1928–), RAF 1946–9, *Manchester Evening News* 1952 and 1958–61, editor-in-chief Northern Newspaper Company 1961–66, editor *Sunday Times* 1967–81, editor *Times* 1981–82, editor-in-chief *Atlantic Monthly Press* New York 1984–86.

93　The NPA meeting was followed by many articles critical of the Government, eg 'Fears over D-Notice Appeals' (*Daily Telegraph* 16 June), 'Lord Shawcross: D Notices, Secrets and the Press' (*News of the World*), 'D-Notice Farce' (*Observer*), 'Wilson Putting Foot in It' (*Sunday Times*), all 18 June.

94　JML Green, MBE (1906–87), editor *Financial News* 1934–8, Army 1939–44, deputy editor then editor *Daily Telegraph* 1961–74, President Institute of Journalists 1976–7.

95　TNA:PRO PREM 13/1813; the intimate tone of these briefs indicates the close relationship until then between the two; when Wilson's Private Office perceived he was weary, they would summon Wigg, provide a bottle of whisky, and leave them to chat until Wilson had regained his buoyancy of mind; discussion former Civil Servant/Wilkinson 11 December 2006.

96　TNA:PRO PREM 13/1814.

97　Most of the national newspaper editors, and representatives of editorial associations, agencies, Scottish Press, London evening papers, BBC and ITN.

98　DH McLachlan, OBE (1908–1971), editor *Times Educational Supplement* 1938–40, NID 1940–5, editor *Sunday Telegraph* 1961–6, General Advisory Council BBC 1961–5); he had a wartime intelligence background, but was not present at this meeting, nor is there any record of his having been consulted.

99　WL Clarke, CBE (1916–97), *S Wales Argus*, Army 1939–45, London editor then Group editorial consultant *Westminster Press*, Chairman Newspaper Conference 1965 and 1980, Vice-Chairman S/DPBC 1968–81.

100　Whether Dunnett, sitting beside him, had been aware of this feeling is not clear; it is not mentioned anywhere else in surviving documentation.

101　MR Christiansen (1927–84), Royal Navy 1945–7, editor *Sunday Mirror* 1964–72, deputy editor *Daily Mirror* 1972–74, editor 1975.

102　Sir Gordon Newton (1907–1998), editor *Financial Times* 1950–72, chairman London Broadcasting Company 1974–7.

103　Later Sir John Junor (1919–97), Fleet Air Arm pilot 1939–45, editor *Sunday Express* 1954–86, director Beaverbrook/Express Newspapers 1960–86, columnist *Sunday Express* 1973–89 and *Mail on Sunday* 1990–97.

104　It must be said that such a view of the inclinations of Editors does not accord with this author's experience.

105 RL Dinsdale (1907–95), Army 1942–6, deputy editor *Daily Herald* 1961–2, deputy editor *Sun* 1964, editor 1965–9.

106 TNA:PRO PREM 13/1813.

107 Later Lord Elwyn-Jones, PC, CH (1909–1989), Member of British War Crimes Executive Nuremburg 1945, Labour MP 1945–74, Attorney-General 1964–70, Lord Chancellor 1974–9, Lord of Appeal 1979–89.

108 Later Lord Barber, PC (1920–), pilot 1940–2, POW of Germans then Russians 1942–5, Conservative MP 1951–74, Chancellor of Exchequer 1970–4, Chairman Conservative Party 1970–4.

109 Next day Lohan challenged Shinwell, and another Labour MP who reported rumours of Lohan/Pincher links, to make their remarks outside the House, saying 'it was like being clouted with his hands tied behind his back'. *Daily Telegraph* 24 June 1967.

110 LR Fletcher (1921–91), Army 1941–8, defence correspondent, Labour MP 1964–83.

111 Hansard, 22 June 1967, Cols 1972/2090.

112 Castle and Crossman Diaries, see note 70 above.

113 TNA:PRO PREM 13/1820.

114 Katherine Lohan's father had many years previously sold Lord Beaverbrook their large family home, Cherkley; its Victorian visitors' book contained many famous signatures, including those of Cobden and Bright; Pincher acquired it from her to give to Beaverbrook as an 85th Birthday present.

115 If there were minutes of this meeting, they have not apparently survived.

116 Thomas Cochrane (b.1909), originally journalist *Middlesex County Times*, Air Ministry Chief Press Officer 1941, war correspondent North Africa and Europe, Deputy DPR RAF then MoD, Acting Secretary SPBC June-October 1967, Deputy Secretary 1967–71.

117 Colonel Sir Richard Glyn, OBE, MP (1907–80), commanded Dorset Yeomanry Light Field Royal Artillery Regiments 1944–5 and 1952–5, Conservative MP 1957–70, Commissioner Commonwealth War Graves 1965–70, Chairman Kennel Club 1973–6.

118 *Daily Telegraph* and other papers 28 June 1967. Crossman reported that Wilson was particularly upset by the attack on him in the *Daily Mirror*, attributing it to Cecil King as revenge for having been offered only a Life not a Hereditary Peerage.

119 Under these Thorpe could not pass the information on to colleagues, even to his predecessor as Leader, although 'he would be free to ask [Mr Grimond's] advice on the conclusions which he [Thorpe] formed as a result of his discussion with the Prime Minister' – advice somewhat difficult to give in the absence of facts. Wilson gave Thorpe an even more explicit briefing on 6 July.

120 TNA:PRO PREM 13/1814.

121 William McCall (1929–), Civil Service 1946–52, TUC 1954–8, General Secretary IPCS 1963–89 (youngest ever TU Secretary when appointed), Police Complaints Authority 1991–4.

122 McCall letter to *Times* 12 July 1967, PRO PREM 13/1814, discussion McCall/Wilkinson 10 July 2007.

123 TNA:PRO PREM 13/1814.

124 Formerly the Earl of Home (title renounced 1963) and later Lord Home, KT, PC (1903–1995), Unionist MP 1931–51 and 1963–74, SofS for Commonwealth Relations 1955–60, SofS for Foreign Affairs 1960–3 and 1970–4, Prime Minister 1963–4.

125 TNA:PRO PREM 13/1814.

126 TNA:PRO PREM 13/1814.

127 TNA:PRO PREM 13/1814.

128 Sir William Druitt, KCB (1910–73), Treasury Solicitor 1964–71.

129 TNA:PRO PREM 13/1814. Crossman records in his Diaries (5 July) that Wilson wanted Helsby to head the Inquiry 'because he knew in advance what his report on Lohan would be'.

130 Lord Gardiner, PC, CH (1900–1990), Friends Ambulance Unit 1943–5, Lord Chancellor 1964–70).

131 Lord Francis-Williams, CBE (1903–70), Editor *Daily Herald* 1936–40, Ministry of Information 1941–5, BBC Governor 1951–2)

132 Lord Carrington, KG, GCMG, CH, MC, PC (1919–), Army1939–45, High Commissioner Australia 1956–9, First Lord of Admiralty 1959–63, SofS for Defence 1970–4 and for

Commonwealth Affairs 1979–82, Chairman Conservative Party 1972–4, Director *Telegraph* 1990–.

133   Lord Chalfont, PC, OBE, MC (1919–), Army from 1940, resigned 1961 to become defence correspondent of *Times*; although a Liberal, created Life Peer by Wilson 1964, Minister FCO 1964–70, UK Permanent Representative to WEU 1969–70.

134   Hansard 6 July 1967, Cols 767–845.

135   TNA:PRO PREM 13/1815.

136   Lord Goodman, CH (1913–95, Army 1939–45, solicitor to the Great, Trustee of many media, arts and Jewish organisations, used much by Wilson as advisor and envoy.

137   TNA:PRO PREM 13/1820.

138   TNA:PRO PREM 13/1815 and /1328.

139   Discussion McCall/Wilkinson 10 July 2007.

140   TNA:PRO PREM 13/1328. But Wigg's 'judgement' in these matters was now becoming less often sought, and in November he resigned from the Government in order to become the Chairman of the Horserace Betting Levy Board; significantly perhaps, Wilson did not mention the Helsby Enquiry in his own memoirs.

141   Brigadier W F K ('Sheriff') Thompson, OBE (1909–79), served NW Frontier 1932–6, commanded Airlanding Light Regiment Royal Artillery at Arnhem, during Korean War also collected rare plants for Kew Gardens, defence correspondent *Daily Telegraph* 1960–76, covering inter alia Vietnam and Yom Kippur Wars.

142   Vice Admiral Sir Norman Denning, KBE, CB (1904–79), NID 1937–45, Director Naval Intelligence 1960–4, Deputy Chief of Defence Staff (Intelligence) 1964–5, Secretary DPBC 1967–72; from a Hampshire draper's family, his brothers were Lord Denning, Master of the Rolls, and Lieutenant General Sir Richard Denning.

143   Viscount Head, PC, GCMG, CBE, MC (1906–83), Army 1924–45, Conservative MP 1945–60, SofS for War 1951–6, Minister of Defence 1956–7, High Commissioner in Nigeria 1960–3 and Malaysia 1963–6, Colonel Commandant SAS 1968–76.

144   TNA:PRO PREM 13/1813.

145   This is true, although his Press Office staff had received inputs from the Scottish Daily Newspapers Society, the Newspaper Society and the Guild of British Editors, all of whom were 'emphatically' against any substantial change in the D-Notice system, other than improvements such as the Secretary's clearances; they were firmly against either the Chairman or the Secretary coming from within the Media; TNA:PRO PREM 13/1813.

146   Lord Head's name is not mentioned in the official record of the meeting, but it is in the leaked report in the *Press Gazette* of 11 September headed 'Minor D Notice rejig as editors see Wilson'.

147   TNA:PRO PREM 13/1318.

148   Later Sir Maurice Oldfield, GCMG, CBE (1915–81), Intelligence Corps WWII, 'C' 1973–8, Security Co-ordinator Northern Ireland 1979–80.

149   Security Service Archives; TNA:PRO PREM 13/1815.

150   Later Lord Allen, GCB (1912–), Second Secretary Treasury 1963–6, PUS Home Office 1966–72.

151   Thompson, who had already been in detailed negotiation with Dunnett over his pay, office and new staff, was furious at this perceived slight on his probity, and threatened to (but did not) get his professional institute involved.

152   D-Notice Secretaries have very occasionally since 1967 been accused accordingly, by the semi-informed, of being ipso facto not wholly impartial, being a temporary civil servant accommodated in a government building; however, the Media themselves (and officials) judge the Secretary's impartiality by his deeds and independence of mind, not by his pay-slip.

153   JM Ramsden (1928–), editor-in-chief *Flight International* 1964–89, editor Royal Aeronautical Society Publications 1989–93.

154   TNA:PRO DEFE 53/6.

155   TNA:PRO PREM 13/1318. Prime Ministerial involvement in such selection has not occurred since.

156   PRO PREM 13/1813.

157   Denning started on £3,500 a year, but the MoD civilian personnel department stipulated that, should civil service pay increase as expected in the New Year, his would not. Halls minuted the

Prime Minister 'this [salary] was a bit on the low side' as Wilson had had in mind the pay of an Assistant Secretary [then up to £4,500 a year]; but on this matter the Prime Minister, doubtless in his other hat as First Lord of the Treasury, chose not to intervene in D-Notice Committee business; successive Secretaries ever since have continued in this tradition of genteel under-remuneration.

158   For the first time the D-Notice Secretary was allocated a place in the principal MoD building; although the office has since migrated several times during refurbishments, the Secretary still has the original telephone extension allocated to Denning in 1967 – a token of stability (or inertia) in a changing world.

159   TNA:PRO DEFE 53/11.

160   Security Service Archives.

161   Security Service Archives.

162   *Spectator's Notebook*, 22 September 1967.

163   Pincher acknowledged this friendship, but claimed much later Drew was 'useless' as a source of information; discussion Pincher/Wilkinson 6 November 2006.

164   TNA:PRO PREM 13/1815.

165   'Lohan and No.10', front page *Daily Express*, 30 September 1967. Lohan had taken a part-time job in August as public relations consultant to an Irish commercial aircraft company, and wrote occasional restaurant reviews for the *Evening Standard*.

166   Captain HB Kerby, MP (1914–1971), Army 1933–7, consular posts in Baltic area 1939–40, SOE 1941–5, Conservative MP 1954–71; Kerby had good contacts in Moscow (when Pincher needed local contacts during a visit to a Russian satellite launch, Kerby rapidly put him in touch with a KGB Press Officer) (discussion Pincher/Wilkinson 16 January 2006); the archived *Telegraph* cuttings on Kerby being named as Wigg's informant are inscribed: 'Captain Kerby's name not to be quoted in connection with this case without first consulting the Editor'; whether this was for reasons of friendship, libel, or something more sensitive, is not revealed; it is perhaps pure coincidence that the paper's then recent managing editor, Captain Sir Colin Coote, was a golfing partner of Sir Roger Hollis.

167   All this is recorded in heavy pressure manuscript, with much underlining, in several files of notes from Kerby to Wigg in the latter's archives, now in the London Library of Political and Economic Science.

168   Hansard, Col 203.

169   Later Lord Zuckerman, OM, KCB (1904–93), South-African born zoologist and scientific adviser to many Ministries from 1939, including on Special Operations, Chief Scientific Adviser MoD 1960–6 and to Government 1964–71, friend of Mountbatten.

170   Some 10 years later a private meeting between Wilson and Pincher was arranged by their mutual friend George Weidenfeld (Lord Weidenfeld (1919–), publisher) over tea in his flat; the ex-Prime Minister conceded he had been at fault, and said 'it was not you, it was that b***** Lohan I was after'; discussion Pincher/Wilkinson, 6 November 2006.

171   BLPES, WIGG/4/130.

172   This was either Sir Solly Zuckerman, or Sir Frederick Brundrett; the latter met Pincher soon after WWII through mutual interest in agricultural biogenetics, and was indeed one of Pincher's best sources, feeling the public ought to be accurately informed about non-endangering matters; neither Pincher nor Brundrett is/was Jewish.

173   BLPES WIGG/4/119.

174   M Foot (1913–), journalist *Tribune*, *Evening Standard*, *Daily Herald*, Labour MP 1945–92, Leader of Opposition 1980–3.

175   *New Statesman*, 21 February 1997.

176   Baroness Falkender in discussion with the author 24 January 2007.

177   Wilson, looking back, conceded 'I was wrong to make an issue of it in the first instance'; *'The Labour Government 1964–70'*; Lohan, looking back, attributed his unpopularity with the Government to having been asked by the Rhodesian regime to advise on setting up a D-Notice System there (he declined), and to Press rumours (denied) that he had been the anonymous author of an *Evening Standard* article critical of the future Lady Falkender; *Evening Standard* 5 October 1978.

178   A previous (Conservative) Prime Minister (Macmillan) had also been greatly upset by revelations of Cabinet discussions, asking his staff in May 1959 whether action could be taken to stop the leaks 'or get rid of Mr Chapman Pincher'; TNA:PRO PREM 11/2800.

SECTION 8
LATTER YEARS OF THE COLD WAR, AND
N IRELAND, 1967–90

1   Later Baroness Thatcher, LG, OM (1925–), Conservative MP 1959–92, Leader of Opposition 1975–79, Prime Minister 1979–90.

2   Even at the time there were numerous inquiries and White Papers, eg Cmnds 4823. (1971), 4901 (1972), 5367 (1973), covering some aspects of security operations in the Province.

3   Later Lord Black (1944–), Canadian-born businessman, Chairman *Telegraph* Group 1987–2005, imprisoned in USA 2008.

4   S 'Eddy' Shah (1944–), former owner Messenger Group, founder *Today* and *Post*, author, property entrepreneur.

5   Later Sir David Calcutt (1930–2004), Editor *Times* law reports, Chairman of Bar 1984, Chairman Committee on Privacy 1989, on the Colin Wallace dismissal 1990, and on Review of Press Self-regulation 1993.

6   *'The Downing Street Years'*, Margaret Thatcher, Harper Collins, 1993.

7   *'The Espionage Establishment'*, Wise and Ross, Random House 1967.

8   *The Times*, 20 October 1967; internally, the BBC decided to mention that the names had been published elsewhere, but not to do so itself (accordingly warning participants in unscripted programmes such as 'Any Questions'), also reaffirming that, while the D-Notice System was not perfect, it was better than risking prosecution and/or outright censorship; BBC Written Archive D211–4.

9   Hansard, 26 October 1967, and NS Circular December 1967.

10   TNA:PRO DEFE 53/15; Sir Clive Whitmore later recalled that drafting Notices was not Denning's forte, and that he, as the SPBC Chairman's young Private Secretary, frequently had to draft them himself; discussion Whitmore/Wilkinson 28 June 2007.

11   TNA:PRO CAB 196/31.

12   Publishers' Association record of May 1968.

13   BLEPS, WIGG 4/154.

14   *Times*, 21 November 1967.

15   'Danger . . . we have no satellite spies', *Daily Express* 16 May 1968; Pincher later denied this, saying it must have been a 'fluke'; discussion Pincher/Wilkinson September 2007.

16   TNA:PRO PREM 13/2367.

17   St Bride's, NPA Archive, Box 27.

18   MoD Archive DN/1800/DPBC.

19   Annual Report of the Press Council, March, 1968.

20   T Dalyell (1932–), Army 1950–2, Labour MP 1962–2005, columnist *New Scientist* 1967–2005, Member European Parliament 1975–9, 'Father' of House of Commons 2001–5.

21   BBC Written Archive D211–4; TNA:PRO DEFE 53/17.

22   *Daily Telegraph*, 24 July 1968.

23   Security Service Archives.

24   Sir Ronald Melville KCB (1912–2001), Captain Great Britain Rifle Team, PUS Ministry of Aviation 1966–71, Civil Service Department 1971–3, translator (with twin brother) of Lucretius's *De Rerum Natura* into English verse.

25   Viz a speech by Lord Francis-Williams: 'Intolerable use of D-Notices', being used to protect not security but the reputations of Ministers and civil servants; St Bride's NS Circular April 1970.

26   TNA:PRO DEFE 53/15.

27   TNA:PRO DEFE 24/432.

28   BR Roberts (1906–88, President Institute of Journalists 1954–5, managing editor then editor *Sunday Telegraph* 1961–76.

29 JWP Aitken (1942–), alumnus (he records) of Eton, Oxford and HM Prisons Belmarsh and Standford, Conservative MP 1974–97, director TV-am 1981–8, Minister Defence Procurement 1992–4, Chief Secretary Treasury 1994–5.

30 *Daily Telegraph*, 9 January 1971.

31 *Daily Express* 19 August 1970.

32 Later Lord Rawlinson, PC (1919–), Army 1940–6, Conservative MP 1955–78, Attorney-General 1970–4.

33 Rt Hon JEH Davies, PC, MBE (1916–79), Army 1939–46, Managing Director Shell Mex/BP 1961–5, Director-General Confederation of British Industries 1965–9, Conservative MP 1970–8, SofS for Trade and Industry 1970–2, Chancellor of Duchy of Lancaster 1972–4.

34 Although agreed in 1968, this was the first meeting at which the title '*Defence*, Press and Broadcasting Committee' was used in the minutes.

35 TNA:PRO DEFE 53/20.

36 ACD Stuart, CBE (1927–), RAF 1945–7, editor *Mombasa Times* 1951–5, assistant editor *Scotsman* 1956–60, MD Associated Press of Nigeria 1961–5, London editor *Scotsman* and editor-in-chief Thomson Regional Newspapers 1966–89, launched *Scotland on Sunday* 1989, on DPBC twice, Vice-Chairman 1989–97.

37 TNA:PRO DEFE 23/65.

38 TNA:PRO HO 292/22.

39 TNA:PRO DEFE 23/65.

40 BBC Written Archive B651–008.

41 Later Lord Armstrong, GCB, CVO (1927–), PPS to Prime Minister 1970–5, PUS Home Office 1977–9, Cabinet Secretary 1979–87.

42 TNA:PRO PREM 15/1191.

43 TNA:PRO CAB 176/2, Pt 2; such Prime Ministerial pressure must have been unknown to the Media side, has not happened since, and would now be regarded as unacceptable.

44 Rear Admiral KH Farnhill, CB, OBE (1913–83), Captain RN Supply School 1958–9, Director Management and Support of Intelligence 1966–9, D-Notice Secretary 1973–80.

45 Security Service Archives.

46 Later Lord Carr (1916–), Conservative MP 1950–74, SofS for Employment 1970–2, Home Secretary 1972–4.

47 *Daily Telegraph*, 31 July 1973.

48 Sir John Rennie, KCMG (1914–81), 'C' 1967–73.

49 Windsor Clarke had written a two-column letter in *The Times* of 10 August 1973, explaining and defending the DPBC system.

50 Sir Michael Cary, GCB (1917–76), son of novelist Joyce Cary, RNVR 1940–5, last PUS Admiralty 1964–7, PUS Public Buildings and Works/Housing and Construction 1968–71, Chief Executive Procurement Executive 1972–4, PUS MoD 74–6, died in office.

51 Sir Geoffrey Archer, KCMG (1920–84), Army 1940–5, DUS FCO 1973–5, PUS 1975–9.

52 FCO Archives, WLD/ZCZ11/7/74.

53 FCO Archives, WLD/ZCZ11/7/74.

54 'Getting in on secrets Act', *Observer*, 14 May 1974.

55 MoD Archives, DN/1800/DPBC, Vol III.

56 MoD Archives, DN/1300/DPBC.

57 FCO Archives, WLD/ZCZ11/7/74.

58 Later Lord Jenkins, OM (1920–2003), Army WWII, Labour MP 1948–76, Home Secretary 1965–7 and 1974–6, Chancellor 1967–70, President European Commission 1977–81, SDP MP 1982–7.

59 Although there was no such general antipathy in UK, the level of Committee activity in these years was low compared with the next three decades; discussion 23 October 2007 Wilkinson/James Bishop, a D-Notice Committee Media member for over 30 years.

60 On a recent flight to Nigeria, Oldfield had seen passengers looking at his photograph in the *Daily Express*; captured IRA bombers also had copies.

61 MoD Archives, DN/1800/DPBC.

62   Sir Frank Cooper, GCB, CMG (1922–2002), RAF 1941–6, DUS MoD 1968–70, Deputy Secretary Civil Service Department 1970–3, PUS Northern Ireland Office 1973–6, PUS MoD 1976–82.

63   Sir Arthur Peterson, KCB, LVO (1916–1986), PUS Home Office 1972–7, Chairman British Refugee Council 1981–6.

64   MoD Archives, DN/1800/DPBC.

65   TNA:PRO DEFE 68/23; in this case, the leak had come from a well-placed white Kenyan; discussion Pincher/Wilkinson September 2007.

66   Later Sir Simon Jenkins (1943–), editor *Evening Standard* 1976–78, political editor *Economist* 1979–86, Historic Buildings and Monuments Commission 1985–90, *Sunday Times* 1986–90, Calcutt Committee on Privacy 1989–90, editor *Times* 1990–2, Chairman Buildings Books Trust 1994–, Chairman, National Trust 2008–.

67   MoD Archives, DN/1800/DPBC, Vol III.

68   Ray Tindle of the Newspaper Society, *Press Gazette* 7 May 1979.

69   When Colonel B was named in April 1978 in the House of Commons during the trial, ITN approached Farnhill for comment; he said that as the trial concerned contempt of court, it was not a DPBC matter; ITN misquoted him as saying that the trial did not concern national security, drawing from him a sharp rebuke.

70   Sir Antony Duff, GCMG, CVO, DSO, DSC (1920–2000), Royal Navy 1937–46 (including submarine command), High Commissioner Kenya 1972–5, DUS FCO 1975–80, Deputy Governor Southern Rhodesia 1979–80, DUS Cabinet Office 1980–4, DGSS 1985–7.

71   An unnamed NPA member had told MI5's Legal Adviser the Press now tried stories out on Farnhill, to judge from his reaction whether they were on to something; Security Service Archives.

72   *Daily Telegraph*, 17 June 1978.

73   Later Sir Clement Freud (1924–), Army WWII, writer and broadcaster, Liberal MP 1973–87; his Bill subsequently foundered under opposition from the next Government.

74   Later Lord Hunt, GCB (1919–2008), RNVR 1940–6, Dominions and Cabinet Offices and Treasury 1946–73, Cabinet Secretary 1973–9, Chairman Inquiry into Cable Expansion and Broadcasting Policy 1982.

75   MoD Archives, DN/1800/DPBC, Pt V.

76   MoD Archives, DN/1800/DPBC, Vol V.

77   Sir Brian Cubbon, GCB (1928–), PUS Northern Ireland Office 1976–9 (severely injured in the roadside explosion which killed Ambassador Ewart-Biggs in 1976), PUS Home Office 1979–88, Press Complaints Commission 1995–2009.

78   MoD Archives, DN/1713/DPBC.

79   Admiral Farnhill handed over as Secretary to Admiral Ash at this meeting; in his initial call on MI5's Legal Adviser, Ash said he 'intended to be less inviting of use as a source than his predecessor'; Security Service Archives.

80   Privately Cubbon sensed the Conservative Government had not focused much on the OSAs before coming to power, the concerns having been 'more of a *Guardian* interest', and they did not initially give this high priority; discussion Cubbon/Wilkinson 18 July 2007.

81   MoD Archives, DN/1800/DPBC, Pt V.

82   MoD Archives, DN 1800/DPBC, Pt V.

83   Rear Admiral WM Ash, CB, LVO (1921–), New Zealander, Cabinet Office 1969–71, Captain *HMS GANGES* 1971–3, Director Service Intelligence 1974–7, Sec/DPBC 1980–4.

84   B Page (1936–), Australian, *Melbourne Herald*, *Evening Standard*, *Daily Herald*, *Sunday Times* Insight Team, *Daily Express*, editor *New Statesman* 1978–82.

85   *New Statesman*, 4 April 1980; MoD Archives DN/1633/DPBC, which covers the long fractious interaction with the magazine up to 1986.

86   MoD Archives, 2PUS 55/3, Pt3.

87   DA Chipp (1927–2008), Australian-educated, Merchant Navy gunner 1943, British Army 1944–7, 1st non-communist resident correspondent (Reuters) China 1956–58, editor Reuters 1968–69, editor-in-chief PA 1969–86, Press Complaints Commission 1991–3, Chairman *News World* 1994–6.

88 MoD Archives, 2PUS 55/3, Pt3; discussion Wilkinson/Chipp 5 November 2007.
89 Later Professor PJ Hennessy (1947–), *Times*, *Financial Times*, *Economist*, *New Statesman*, *Independent*, *Tablet*, British Constitutional Historian, Professor Contemporary History Queen Mary University of London 1992–.
90 Later Lord Gilbert, PC (1927–), Labour MP 1970–97, Minister of State MoD 1976–9 and 1997–9, Select Committee on Defence 1979–87, Intelligence and Security Committee 1994–7.
91 MoD Archives, DN/2401/DPBC.
92 *Times* 16 May 1980.
93 Despite his downbeat view, his briefers before he gave evidence could only think of one breach in the previous four years beyond the *New Statesman* case, the naming of the DGSS by the *Economist* in 1979; there had however been leakages originating abroad, and some on intelligence and security matters in the 'fringe press' not belonging to media organisations represented on the DPBC.
94 Cabinet Office Archive, 176/2 Pt 3.
95 MoD Archives, DN/2401/DPBC; discussion Wilkinson/Chipp 5 November 2007.
96 Only New Zealand (very briefly) and Australia have had a comparable system, albeit chaired in the latter by a Minister; Australian Notices were declassified in the early 1970s, and are now (2007) effectively dormant; see *'National Security and the D-Notice System'*, Pauline Sadler, 2001.
97 *Times*, 23 July 1980; BBC Written Archive B651–008.
98 LP Heren (1919–1995), Army 1939–46, *Times* foreign editor 1970–8, deputy editor 1978–81.
99 MoD Archives DN/2401/DPBC.
100 It is ironic that a previous deputy editor of the *New Statesman*, Tom Baistow, had been a leading Media Member of the DPBC a few years previously, and had approved the D-Notices about which the journal was now complaining; but this was not revealed to the HCDC! MoD Archives, 2PUS 55/3,Pt4.
101 MoD Archives, DN/2401/DPBC.
102 Cooper also wrote afterwards to Cubbon at the Home Office (as guardians of Security), warning him public discussion was anyway probable; he opposed however the suggested publication of an annual DPBC Report, as being 'wholly unnecessary and inappropriate', an opposition shared by Clarke on grounds of the impracticability in so doing of not breaching security.
103 Almost as amazingly as over Bletchley Park, nothing had leaked about Chevaline through the late 1960s/1970s before the Thatcher Government made it public; the author in the mid-70s was one of the few Naval Officers and officials privy to the highly complex and costly project (upgrading Polaris warheads with penetration aids/decoys, in order to defeat upgraded Soviet anti-ballistic missile defences around Moscow); Chevaline was kept from their colleagues by tight inner circles of Ministers in the Wilson, Heath, Callaghan and (initially) Thatcher Governments, despite fierce disagreements between ambitious Nuclear Scientists and cautious Admirals over technology, ranges and costs involved; it does show that genuinely vital national security matters can be kept secret, as long as everybody involved is convinced such secrecy is still justified.
104 HC773, Session 1979–80, and reports on 12 June 1980 in most newspapers including *The Times*, *Daily Telegraph*, *Guardian*, *Financial Times*, *Daily Mail*, and *Morning Star*.
105 Northern Ireland Training and Advisory Teams provided training to troops about to deploy, and covert surveillance in theatre.
106 MoD Archives, DN/2401/DBPC.
107 The P&B side of the Committee had met at the beginning of May, so his evidence incorporated their views.
108 BT George, PC (1942–), Labour MP 1974–, Select Committee on Defence 1979– (Chairman 1997–2005), Chairman All-Party Parliamentary Maritime Group North Atlantic Assembly 1981–, editor *Jane's NATO Handbook* 1988–91, Chairman OSCE Parliamentary Assembly 1992–.
109 Having been Vice-Chairman/Media Spokesman for about 12 years, Clarke decided a few weeks later to stand down from the DPBC at the end of 1980, because of his wife's health; his proposal of Mike Ramsden of *Flight* and the PPA as his successor was soon agreed by the Media side;

Cooper later commented to Armstrong that Ramsden was a good deal younger than his predecessor and likely to take a tougher line with the Official side, but that this was what was needed if ultimately the media were to be carried on any changes negotiated with them.

110   MoD Archives, DN/2401/DPBC)
111   Later Viscount Whitelaw, KT, CH, MC (1918–99), Scots Guards WWII, Conservative MP for Penrith and the Border 1955–83, SofS for Northern Ireland 1972–3, Home Secretary 1979–83, Deputy Prime Minister 1979–88; at a meeting of officials next day, the Home Office representatives were unanimously against the continuation of the D-Notice System, but these pro-litigation views were robustly demolished by the Security Service, MoD and other experts, who also pointed out that the Media too liked the System; Security Service Archives.
112   MoD Archives, DN/1706/DPBC. Thatcher's view early in her Premiership was that litigation against the Media was less likely to be effective than other means, according to Sir Bernard Ingham; Sir Brian Cubbon also recalled her reluctance 'to let lawyers loose on National Security' – discussions with Wilkinson 24 and 18 July 2007 respectively.
113   MoD Archives, DN/1300/DPBC.
114   MoD Archives, DN/5301/DPBC.
115   Published in October as HC773.
116   Sir Arthur Hockaday, KCB, CMG (1926–2004), 'Bevin Boy' in Welsh mines 1944–5, 2nd PUS MoD 1976–82, DG Commonwealth War Graves Commission 1982–9.
117   MoD Archives, 2PUS 55/3, Pt4.
118   MoD Archives, 2PUS 55/3,Pt4.
119   Security Service Archives.
120   MoD Archives, 2PUS 55/3, Pt4.
121   MoD Archives, 2PUS 55/3, Pt4; and amongst others *Times* of 13 October 1980.
122   Later Sir John Jones, KCB, CMG (1923–98), Army 1942–6, Sudan Government 1947–55, joined Security Service 1955, DGSS 1981–5.
123   MoD Archives, 2PUS 55/3, Pt4.
124   Cmnd.8129.
125   *'Living on a Deadline'*; his talk was entitled 'Not the Freedom of the Press [to comment] but the Freedom to Report' [uncensored].
126   Colonel AH Protheroe, CBE, TD (1934–), Army 1954–6, BBC Wales 1957–70, BBC TV News 1970–80, Lieut-Col Royal Regt of Wales (TA) 1979–84 and Colonel 1984–90, Assistant Director BBC News and Current Affairs 1980–2, Assistant DG BBC 1982–7, Hon Colonel TA Information Officers 1991–6.
127   MoD Archives, 2PUS 55/3, Pt4; the Private and Confidential marking at the time on D-Notices themselves was not a security classification, but a handling restriction marking recommended by the Security Service (to Colonel Lohan in December 1963) as being that commonly used by solicitors, auditors, bankers, etc.
128   MoD archives, 2PUS 55/3, Pt5.
129   Sir Ian Trethowan (1922–90), Royal Navy 1941–6, MD BBC Radio 1969–75, MD BBC TV 1976–7, DG BBC 1977–82, Chairman Thames TV 1987–90.
130   *Daily Telegraph*, 24 February 1981.
131   Pen name of RWS Allason (1951–), BBC TV 1978–82, European editor *World Intelligence Review* 1985–, Conservative MP 1987–97, author since 1980 of many books/articles on intelligence and security.
132   Sir Frank Cooper (PUS MoD, Chairman), Sir Brian Cubbon (Home Office), Sir Antony Acland (FCO) and Sir Arthur Hockaday (2nd PUS MoD).
133   Discussion Cubbon/Wilkinson 18 July 2007; Security Service Archives.
134   The PA seat was still vacant following Chipp's resignation.
135   MOD archive, 2PUS 55/3. Pt5. Media interest was also active, viz 'Streamlined D-notices come under scrutiny', P Hennessy, *Times*, 1 June 1981.
136   JD Bishop (1929–), *Times* from 1954, features editor 1966–70, editor *Illustrated London News* 1971–87, D-Notice Committee 1977–, editor-in-chief ILN Publications 1987–94, Chairman Association of British Editors 1987–96; in discussion with Wilkinson 23 October 2007, he explained it was concern that previously frank officials would feel more constrained if there was such a degree of openness, but he acknowledged his fears had not subsequently been borne out.

137　Later Sir Richard Francis, KCMG (1934–1992), Army 1957, Panorama/current affairs 1963–72, Controller BBC Northern Ireland 1973–7, Director News BBC 1977–82, MD BBC Radio 1982–6, DG British Council 1987–92, Press Complaints Commission 1991–2.

138　See Appendix 4; Security Service Archives.

139　The answer to a written PQ on 3 March 1980 (Hansard Cols 53–4) revealed the Committee met only 12 times 1971–80, in six of those years only once and in 1972 not at all; another written PQ answer on 2 April (Hansard Col 277) showed the cost of the D-Notice System rising from £12,732 in 1975 to £16,954 in 1979, almost all in the salaries of the Secretary and his PA.

140　The deputy Secretary was at this time called the 'Associate Secretary' and was normally a member of the MoD PR staff.

141　MoD Archives, 2PUS 55/3, Pt5, and DN/2401.DPBC.

142　Security Service Archives; Cooper wrote to Armstrong afterwards that as the D-Notices were not now classified, the HCDC was 'perfectly free' to publish them, and the Media would quickly follow suit.

143　By 2008 however, the (Book) Publishers' Association, the Society of Editors, and an internet organisation (Google) were all represented on the Committee.

144　MoD Archives, DN/1800/DPBC and DN/2401/DPBC.

145　WG Welchman (1906–85), Bletchley Park code-breaker responsible for breaking German Army and Air Force ciphers, emigrated to the USA post-War, worked on secure US Army communications; in 1982 published (initially in USA, soon afterwards in UK) 'The Hut Six Story', Penguin; 'Ultra' was the codename for secret intelligence derived from the 'cracked' German cypher system.

146　The DPBC file about this publication appears to have been destroyed, but the case is covered in the 25 Nov 85 DPBC minutes.

147　TNA:PRO CAB 128/58, 128/60/42 and 129/188/8.

148　'Living on a Deadline'. The 'Regulations for Correspondents Accompanying an Operational Force', and the undertakings to be signed by a journalist and his editor, were recognisably derived from those of the first half of the 20th Century, and still 'Not to be Published', albeit now lacking references to correspondents' horses and servants.

149　'The Power of News'.

150　Later Sir David English (1931–98), editor Daily Sketch 1969–71 and Daily Mail 1971–92, Chairman Associated Newspapers 1992–8 and Teletext UK 1993–8, Press Complaints Commission 1993–8, President Commonwealth Press union 1994–8, Chairman ITN 1997–8.

151　MoD Archives DN/1800/DPBC, Vol VI.

152　MoD Archives, DN/1716/DPBC.

153　Later Admiral of the Fleet Lord Lewin of Greenwich, KG, GCB, LVO, DSC (1920–99), CinC Fleet 1973–5 and Naval Home Command 1975–7, First Sea Lord 1977–9, Chief of Defence Staff 1979–82.

154　MoD Archives, DN/1716/DPBC.

155　A generalist civil servant who, in conducting daily press conferences, had unusually become a public figure, in part because of his notably solemn and cautious manner.

156　Later Sir John Nott, KCB (1932–), Army 1952–6, Conservative MP 1966–83, SofS for Trade 1979–81 and for Defence 1981–3.

157　MoD Archives, DN/5300/DPBC.

158　Later Sir Max Hastings (1945–), Evening Standard, Daily Express, Sunday Times, editor Daily Telegraph 1986–95 and Evening Standard 1996–2002.

159　MoD Archives, DN/1716/DPBC.

160　The Government/BBC relationship had been consistently prickly: Mrs Thatcher's dislike of the publicly-funded Corporation was increased by its refusal to refer to British troops as 'our' forces; Protheroe considered 'the Thatcherites fondly believed the D-Notice system was a system of censorship rather than a forum for logical discussion of crucial wartime events, and failed dismally to understand that we were all 'on the same side' and striving for a satisfying and rapid total victory'; letter Protheroe/Wilkinson 21 June 2007.

161　MoD Archives, DN/1716/DPBC.

162   ADG Milne (1930–), Army 1949–50, Controller BBC Scotland 1968–72, Director Programmes 1973–7, MD BBC TV 1977–82, DG BBC 1982–7, Chairman Gaelic Broadcasting Task Force 1999–2000.

163   *Listener* 24 June 1982; Ash conceded however much was based on US official sources.

164   MoD Archives, DN/1716/DPBC.

165   Later General Lord Ramsbotham, GCB, CBE (1934–), DPR (Army) 1982–4, Commander 3 Armoured Division 1984–7 and UK Field Army 1987–90, Adjutant General 1990–3, HM Inspector of Prisons 1995–2001.

166   St Bride's, NS *Newstime* January 1983.

167   The principal Falklands Island Review, Cmnd.8787, January 1983, by Privy Counsellors chaired by Lord Franks, did not specifically deal with media or censorship aspects.

168   General Sir Hugh Beach, GBE, KCB, MC (1923–), Master General of the Ordnance 1977–81, Warden St George's House Windsor Castle 1981–6, Director Council for Arms Control 1986–9, Council for Christian Approaches to Defence and Disarmament 1988–, Society for Propagation of Christian Knowledge 1994–9.

169   Pincher was also subsequently selected to join the Beach Study Group.

170   MoD Archives, DN/2401/DPBC.

171   BBC Written Archive B651–008.

172   HCDC Report, Session 1982–83, 17-I, para 66.

173   MoD Archives, DN/1800/DPBC; Security Service Archives.

174   Sir Clive Whitmore, GCB, CVO (1935–), PPS to Prime Minister 1979–82, PUS MoD 1983–8, PUS Home Office 1988–94, Security Commission 1998–.

175   MoD Archives, DN/2212/DPBC.

176   Cmnd.8758, December 1982.

177   Cmnd.8820, March 1983.

178   Discussion 29 August 2007 Wilkinson/Beach Group member John Thompson, CBE (Director of Radio IBA 1973–87); the written background paper by Ash is in MoD Archives, DN/2212/DPBC; his subsequent minute to the Beach Group explained the overlap problems of introducing a two-tier system of unclassified and specific classified D-Notices; this 'kite-flyer' idea was dropped.

179   Cmnd.9112, December 1983.

180   King's College Liddell Hart Centre, Cooper 23rd Accession, Institute of Historical Research, August 1998.

181   *Daily Telegraph*, 19 October 1982.

182   *Observer*, 22 May 1983.

183   Ex-Deputy Editor *Times*.

184   MoD Archives, DN/2212/DPBC.

185   As tends to happen with studies contracted out to academics/consultants but whose conclusions are not entirely consistent with official received wisdom, this very competent study had when submitted little influence on ongoing work in Whitehall; text in MoD Archives DN/2212/DPBC.

186   The full record has disappeared, as have full records of several other meetings 1967–84.

187   He referred too to a February dispute with the editor of the *Guardian*, Peter Preston.

188   Security Service Archives.

189   MoD Archives, DN/2212/DPBC.

190   When Ash completed his term of office as D-Notice Secretary in December 1984, no suitable permanent replacement could immediately be found, and the Associate Secretary General Pat Kay therefore acted as full-time Acting Secretary, until early June 1986, when the new D-Notice Secretary appointed was Admiral Bill Higgins – see notes 195 and 211.

191   Cmnd.9499, April 1985.

192   Later Professor DG Trelford (1937–), RAF 1956–58, editor *Observer* 1975–93, DPBC 1986–93, Professor Journalism Studies Sheffield University 1994–2004.

193   Sir Denis Forman, OBE (1917–), Army 1940–5, COI Films 1947, Director British Film Institute 1948–55 (Chairman 1971–3), Granada TV 1955–87 (MD 1965–81, Chairman 1974–87), Chairman Scottish Film Production Fund 1990–3.

194   MoD Archives, DN/1716/DPBC.

195 Major General PR Kay, CB, MBE, RM (1921–), Chief of Staff to Commandant General Royal Marines 1970–4, Director Naval Security 1974–81, D-Notice Secretary 1984–6.
196 Tam Dalyell also asked a PQ about this (Hansard, 7 February 1985, Col 679). But Lord Lewin was not sent to the Tower.
197 Security Service Archives.
198 MoD Archives, DN/1801/DPBC, Vol II.
199 It is not recorded from whom the information came; the Secretary (then and since) keeps in regular touch with many officials and journalists, both categories being equally given to gossip; on other occasions a journalist or official rings the Secretary with specific information on which (s)he hopes to convince him to take some action.
200 A useful and sometimes amusing part of the 'knowledge' to a D-Notice Secretary is the various 'House Styles' of journals and broadcasting companies, usually transmitted seamlessly from one editorial regime to the next irrespective of the editor's personality; in the case of the *Sunday Times*, although the head knows what is happening, individual fingers often do not; in any media organisation, overlaps in journalistic activity frequently lead not to internal co-operation but to internecine competition, sometimes to beneficial overall editorial effect.
201 Later Sir Christopher Curwen, KCMG (1929–), Army 1948–9, Chief of SIS 1985–8, DUS Cabinet Office 1989–91, Security Commission 1991–8.
202 As a Royal Marines Officer, Kay argued this despite the still fresh memory that the former Commandant-General Royal Marines, Lieutenant General Sir Steuart Pringle, had been severely injured by a car bomb outside his home in October 1981.
203 MoD Archives, DN/1801/DPBC, Vol II.
204 NK Whetstone, OBE (1930–2002), Royal Navy 1949–52, Lt Cdr RNR to 1965, editor *Cambridge Evening News* 1964–70, *Coventry Evening Telegraph* 1970–80, President Guild of British Newspaper Editors 1976–77, DPBC 1976–92, editor-in-chief *Birmingham Post* and *Evening Mail* 1980–6, Press Council 1980–6.
205 His successor Admiral Higgins sat in on this and the next meeting; subsequently the arrangement whereby an MoD Press Officer was ex-officio 'Associate Secretary' was discontinued, Kay agreeing to stay on part-time after the succession; the title of his new post was changed by the Committee to 'Deputy Secretary', the arrangement which exists to this day.
206 MoD Archives, DN/1633/DPBC.
207 Later Lord Ashdown, GCMG, KBE (1941–), ex-Royal Marines SBS, FCO 1971–6, Liberal MP 1983–8, Liberal Democrat MP 1988–2001, Leader Liberal Democrats 1988–99, High Representative of the International Community/EU Special Representative Bosnia and Herzegovina 2002–6.
208 PB Johnson (1928–), editor *New Statesman* 1965–70, author and columnist.
209 *Spectator*, 17 May 1986.
210 CT Webb (1939–), Army 1960–4, editor *Cambridge Evening News* 1974–82, deputy editor *Times* 1982–6, editor-in-chief/General Manager Press Association 1986–96.
211 Rear Admiral WA Higgins, CB, CBE (1928–2007), last Flag Officer Medway 1982–3, DG Naval Personal Services and Chief Naval Supply and Secretariat Officer 1983–6, D-Notice Secretary 1986–92, mountaineer.
212 A Whittam-Smith, CBE (1937–), editor *Investors Chronicle* 1970–7, first editor *Independent* 1986–94, editor-in-chief *Independent on Sunday* 1991–94.
213 Security Service Archives.
214 Later Sir John Blelloch, KCB (1930–), Army 1949–51, 2nd PUS MoD 1984–8, PUS Northern Ireland Office 1988–90, Security Commission 1991–2000.
215 MoD Archives, DN/2212/DPBC.
216 Later Lord Campbell-Savours (1943–), Labour MP 1979–2001, Public Accounts Committee 1979–2001, Intelligence and Security Committee 1997–2001.
217 PQ 6252, December 1986.
218 Pincher made no secret he did not submit his books, relying on his own encyclopaedic knowledge of what was already widely in the public domain; Sir Dick White (ex-DGSS then 'C') quickly realised his main source on this book was Peter Wright.
219 Later Baroness Park, CMG, OBE (1921–), FANY 1943–7, 'FO' 1948–79, Principal Somerville College Oxford 1980–9, Governor BBC 1982–7.

NOTES

220 Professor Sir Ronald Mason, KCB (1930–), Professor Inorganic Chemistry Sheffield University 1963–71, Professor Chemistry Sussex University 1971–88, Chief Scientific Adviser MoD 1977–83.

221 Later Lord Sheldon (1923–), Labour MP 1964–2001, Financial Secretary Treasury 1975–9, Chairman Public Accounts Committee 1983–97.

222 Sir Gordon Downey, KCB (1928–), Army 1946–8, Comptroller and Auditor General 1981–7, Complaints Commissioner Securities Association 1989–90, Parliamentary Commissioner for Standards 1995–8.

223 Lord Barnett (1923–), Army WWII, Labour MP 1964–83, Chief Secretary Treasury 1974–9, Vice Chairman BBC Governors 1986–93, Chairman Public Accounts Committee 1979–83.

224 *Guardian* and *Daily Mail*, 25 October 1986.

225 Sir Peter Middleton, GCB (1934–), Army 1958–60, Press Secretary Treasury 1972–5, PUS Treasury 1983–91, Director/Chairman Barclays Bank 1991–2004.

226 MoD Archives, DN/1328/DPBC.

227 Whitmore recalled the enormous shock to Government and officials that this most secret of deterrent-related intelligence projects had apparently been leaked; hence the very strong governmental reaction; discussion Whitmore/Wilkinson 28 June 2007.

228 Sir Peter Marychurch, KCMG (1927–), RAF 1945–8, Director GCHQ 1983–9.

229 Done with the help of the future Foreign Secretary Robin Cook; *New Statesman*, 22 August 2005.

230 Many Press reports, and letter Protheroe/Wilkinson 21 June 2007.

231 Letter Stuart/Wilkinson, 21 September 2007.

232 MoD Archives, DN/1328/DPBC.

233 'The journalist as patriot', *Observer* 8 February 1987.

234 The Whitehall oversight system for secret intelligence and security was exposed in some detail by Peter Hennessy in *Independent* of 3 December 1986.

235 Later Sir Christopher Mallaby, GCMG, GCVO (1936–), Deputy Secretary Cabinet Office 1985–8, Ambassador to Germany 1988–92 and to France 1993–6, Trustee Reuters 1998–.

236 Discussion Ingham/Wilkinson, 24 July 2007; and *'The Downing Street Years'*.

237 Later Sir John Bailey, KCB (1928–), Procurator General and Treasury Solicitor 1984–8.

238 Later Lord Hurd, CH, CBE (1930–), diplomat, Conservative MP 1974–97, SofS for Northern Ireland 1984–5, Home Secretary 1985–89, Foreign Secretary 1989–95.

239 MoD Archives, DN/1900/DPBC.

240 A temporary frisson between them had already occurred when Higgins returned one day to his office to find the unannounced diplomat reading some files on his desk; in the short conversation which followed, Higgins reminded that DPBC files were not for official eyes; discussion Higgins/Wilkinson, November 2004.

241 Later Sir Nigel Wicks, GCB, CVO, CBE (1940–), PS to Prime Minister 1975–8, Treasury 1978–83, Economic Minister Washington Embassy and UK Executive Director IMF 1983–5, PPS to Prime Minister 1985–8, 2nd PUS Treasury 1989–2000.

242 Security Service Archives; discussion Higgins/Wilkinson, November 2004.

243 MoD Archives, DN/1328/DPBC.

244 MoD Archives, DN/1900/DPBC.

245 MoD Archives, DN/1328/DPBC.

246 Rear Admiral AJ Whetstone, CB (1927–), submariner, Flag Officer Sea Training 1978–80, Assistant Chief of Naval Staff (Operations) 1981–3, DG Cable TV Association 1983–6, Deputy Secretary DPBC 1987–92.

247 His pre-meeting suggested conciliatory line to take on *'Spycatcher'*, if raised by the Media side, had been displaced by the Cabinet Office with the Government's line on lifelong duty of confidentiality; Higgins thought it unlikely the Media side 'elder statesmen' would accept being 'fobbed off' with 'PQ type of answers', and so neither line was taken at the meeting; Security Service Archives.

248 At the Media side pre-meeting, not all his colleagues agreed with him that some acceptable backdoor approach to the BBC could have been made by the Government; subsequently Ramsden (whom Higgins thought now no longer fully supported by all colleagues) lunched with Whitmore and Higgins to discuss his own view that there was indeed a relationship between D-Notices and the OSAs; in retrospect, semantics were involved.

249 A General Election had now been called and discussion was therefore postponed; Blelloch had already wound up his Steering Group on the Beach Report follow-up; life had moved on from Falklands matters.

250 MoD Archives, DN/1801/DPBC, Vol II, and DN/1800/C/DPBC.

251 Later Sir John Boyd, KCMG (1936–), DUS FCO 1987–9, Chief Clerk 1989–92, Ambassador to Japan 1992–6, Master Churchill College Cambridge 1996–2006.

252 Later Lord Butler, KG, GCB, CVO (1938–), PPS to Prime Minister (Mrs Thatcher) 1982–5, Cabinet Secretary 1988–98.

253 MoD Archives, DN/2212/DPBC.

254 Later Lord Hussey (1923–), Army 1939–45, MD Harmsworth Publications 1967–70, CEO *Times* Newspapers 1971–82, Chairman BBC Governors 1986–96.

255 MoD Archives, DN/1328/DPBC.

256 'Campbell secrets ban confusion', *Observer* 13 December 1987. MoD Archives, DN/2202/DPBC.

257 'Press could quit D-notice committee over BBC ban', *Independent*, 19 December 1987; the paper had also 10 days previously carried a long article about Higgins – 'a tall, spare man with a ready sense of humour, capable of saying "no comment" firmly but with a smile', in a 'spartan, box-sized office'; such was the extent of official displeasure, however, that a very senior (non-MoD) official told a BBC contact of similar standing that Higgins 'wouldn't recognise a secret if it bit him on the nose' (letter John Wilson/Wilkinson, 8 November 2007); it is sometimes difficult for those immured inside the governmental fortress to accept that sensitive details which have been widely disclosed can only be labelled 'secret' in a historic sense.

258 Later Viscount Younger (1931–2003), 'Gentleman George', Army (Regular and TA) 1950–65, Conservative MP 1964–92, SofS for Scotland 1979–86, and for Defence 1986–9.

259 TNA:PRO CAB 176/2, Pt4.

260 MoD Archives, DN/2212/DPBC.

261 St Bride's, NS *Newstime* January 1988.

262 MD Linklater (1942–), editor *London Daily News* 1987 and *Scotsman* 1988–94.

263 Later Sir Patrick Walker, KCB (1932–), Colonial Service, Security Service 1963–92, DGSS 1987–92.

264 Later Sir Bernard Ingham (1932–), Director of Information Departments of Employment then Energy 1973–7, Under-Secretary Energy Conservation 1978–9, Chief Press Secretary to Prime Minister 1979–90.

265 MoD Archives, DN/2202/DPBC.

266 TNA:PRO CAB 176/2, Pt4.

267 The correspondence was subsequently published in full in response to a further Tam Dalyell PQ, in Hansard 12 February 1988, Cols 387–8; see also press reports, eg *Guardian*, 6 February 1988.

268 MoD Archives, DN/1712/DPBC.

269 Allason however assured Wilkinson (21 June 2007) that, apart from 'some disparaging remarks [by the Solicitor General] about the wisdom of detailing SIS's post-war operations', he was unaware of any other Political pressure.

270 Later Sir Nicolas Bevan, CB (1942–), AUS MoD 1985–92, Cabinet Office 1992–3, Speaker's Secretary House of Commons 1993–2003.

271 MoD Archives, DN/1900/DPBC.

272 MoD Archives, DN/1800/C/DPBC.

273 J Wilson (1936–), reporter/broadcaster N Rhodesia/Zambia 1964–6, BBC 1966, editor BBC News and Current Affairs 1981–6, first BBC Controller Editorial Policy 1987–93.

274 Sir Michael Quinlan, GCB (1930–), RAF 1952–4, PUS Department of Employment 1983–8, PUS MoD 1988–92, author nuclear and ethical publications.

275 Later Sir Kenneth Macdonald, KCB (1930–), RAF 1952–4, 2nd PUS MoD 1988–90.

276 Discussion Cubbon/Wilkinson 18 July 2007.

277 MoD Archives, DN/1706/DPBC, Vol IV.

278 MoD Archives, DN/2212/DPBC, Vols II – IV, for the whole protracted and largely nugatory process.

279 Cmnd. 408, June 1988.
280 MoD Archives, DN/1706/DPBC, Vol IV.
281 *Press Gazette* 3 October 1988.
282 MoD Archives, DN/1706/DPBC, Vol IV.
283 MoD Archives, DN/1706/DPBC.
284 Hansard Col 1464.
285 Discussion BBC's Wilson (who had been prominent in setting up a national agreement with police forces on kidnapping/hostages) with Wilkinson, 10 December 2007.
286 MoD Archives, DN/1801/DPBC.
287 Letter Stuart/Wilkinson, 21 September 2007.
288 MoD Archives, DN/1706/DPBC.
289 The Security Services Act was also passed in 1989, and the Intelligence Services Act in 1994; seen by the Government as a quid pro quo – discussion Cubbon/Wilkinson 18 July 2007.
290 eg *Times* 16 June 1988, 'Book names 13 ex-MI6 officers'.
291 Hansard, 23 June.
292 MoD Archives, DN/0300/13/DPBC.
293 Later Sir Colin McColl (1932–), Chief of SIS 1988–94.
294 Discussions Higgins/Wilkinson and Pulvertaft/Wilkinson, since November 2004; MoD Archives, DN/1801/DPBC.
295 Later Lord Birt (1944–), Deputy DG BBC 1987–92, DG 1992–2000, Strategy Adviser to Prime Minister 2001–7.
296 MoD Archives, DN/5301/DPBC.
297 MoD Archives, DN/5301/DPBC.
298 Later Sir John Adye, KCMG (1939–), Director GCHQ 1989–96, Director National Biometric Security Project Washington 2003–.
299 BBC's John Wilson later enlarged: there was 'journalistic concern that the System could conveniently be made to suit the times . . . Terrorism deriving from Northern Ireland did not . . . threaten the existence of the British State and menace all of its people. To apply the Notices to it seemed to conflate two concepts – national security and the national interest. The former is part of the latter, not the same as it'; letter Wilson/Wilkinson 8 November 2007.
300 MoD Archives, DN/5301/DPBC.

SECTION 9

POST COLD WAR, 1990–97

1 For the information of non-cricketers, this means (in much simplified terms) not only an unprepared playing area, but a surface favouring the other side.
2 MoD Archives, DN/2212/DPBC, Vol V.
3 MoD Archives, DN/1801/DPBC; letter Stuart/Wilkinson 21 September 2007.
4 MoD Archives, DN/5301/DPBC.
5 Submitted to DPBC member Bob Hutchinson by its author Dr Alastair MacWillson, who had formerly worked with but not for the secret Agencies.
6 Later Sir John Major, KG, CH (1943–), Conservative MP 1979–2001, SofS FCO 1989, Chancellor of Exchequer 1989–90, Prime Minister 1990–7.
7 MoD Archives, DN/5301/1/DPBC.
8 Cabinet Office Archive, 176/2 Pt4.
9 These and many other media comments received in the following months led in due course to the amendment of the MoD's 'Green Book' (Working Arrangements for the Media in Time of Tension and War).
10 MoD Archives, DN/0300/21/DPBC.
11 MoD Archives, DN/1801/DPBC.
12 TC Grove (1945–), editor *Sunday Telegraph* 1989–92, group exec editor *Telegraph* 1992–94, editor El *Periodico de Tucuman* 1994, and *Inside Time (the Prisoners' Newspaper)* 2004.
13 Known as the 'trouser-legs problem', because of the configuration of overlapping pipes of different metals.

14   MoD Archives, DN/0300/26/DPBC.
15   DR Hutchinson (1948–), defence correspondent PA 1977–83, deputy editor *Jane's Defence Weekly* 1983–7, publishing director *Jane's* 1987–97, editorial policy adviser *Jane's* 1997–2007, D-Notice Committee 1988–2007, Vice-Chairman 1997–2007.
16   Later Sir Moray Stewart, KCB (1938–), Asst Sec Gen NATO 198486, 2nd PUS MoD 1990–6.
17   MoD Archives, DN/1801/DPBC.
18   MoD Archives, DN/5301/DPBC.
19   Security Service Archives.
20   Later Dame Stella Rimington, DCB (1935–), DGSS 1992–6.
21   MoD Archives, DN/5301/DPBC; Security Service Archives.
22   Sir Christopher France, GCB (1934–), PUS MoD 1992–95, Staff Counsellor Security and Intelligence Services 1995–99.
23   AF Neil (1949–), editor *Sunday Times* 1983–94, Sky TV 1988–90, editor-in-chief Press Holdings 1996–, chief exec *Spectator* and *Apollo* 2004–.
24   MoD Archives, DN/1801/DPBC.
25   MoD Archives, DN/5301/DPBC.
26   MoD Archives, DN/5301/DPBC. *The Times* Diary of 11 August also pointed out McColl's full address was published in the Old Boys' List of his school (Shrewsbury), as were those of founders of the satirical *Private Eye*.
27   MoD Archives, DN/5301/DPBC.
28   An agent of the Army's Force Requirements Unit until arrested on charges of conspiracy to murder, sentenced February 1992.
29   MoD Archives, B/3/6/2/DPBC.
30   Later Dame Pauline Neville-Jones, DCMG (1939–), Deputy Secretary Cabinet Office and Chairman Joint Intelligence Committee 1991–4, DUS FCO 1994–6.
31   Cabinet Office Archive, R6/3.
32   PJ Preston (1938–), editor *Guardian* 1975–95, Chairman Association of British Editors 1996–9, British Chairman IPI 1988– (World Chairman 1995–7), co-Director *Guardian* Foundation 1997–.
33   Later Professor SP Purvis (1947–), editor-in-chief ITN 1991–5, Chief Executive 1995–2003, Professor of TV Journalism City University from 2003. His first-hand view of the DPBC was that it had become dominated by an establishment 'looking for a new threat' post-Cold War, concerned with suppressing information about Northern Ireland and intelligence memoirs, supported by long-serving Media administrators rather than hands-on editors (discussion Purvis/Wilkinson 20 July 2007); his speech was foreshadowed in the *Guardian* two days before: 'A peculiarly British practice', Richard Norton-Taylor.
34   The *Press Gazette* of 28 September 1992, for example, carried the Purvis view and the opposing view of his DPBAC BBC colleague Wilson.
35   Letter Stuart/Wilkinson, 21 September 2007.
36   MoD Archives, DN/1901/DPBC.
37   Rear Admiral DM Pulvertaft, CB (1938–), nuclear submarine engineer but DG *Aircraft* (Navy) 1987–90, DG Procurement and Support Organisation (Navy) 1990–2, D-Notice Secretary 1992–9, expert on British warship figureheads; the Deputy Secretary had recently been replaced by another submariner, Commander Francis Ponsonby, LVO, OBE, RN.
38   MoD Archives, DN/1300/DPBC.
39   Later Lord Lang (1940–), Conservative MP 1979–97, SofS for Scotland 1990–95, President Board of Trade 1995–97.
40   The High Threat List included some Ministers involved with past Northern Ireland security and/or current anti-terrorist measures, some similar senior officials and officers, and a few other named special operations servicemen; some had guards, and all were on local police lists for rapid response protection.
41   MoD Archives, DN/5301/DPBC.
42   MoD Archives, B/2/3/DPBAC.
43   *Guardian*, 9 April 1993.
44   MoD Archives, B/2/3/4/DPBAC.

45 *Sunday Express*, 24 January 1993.
46 MoD Archives, DN/5302/DPBC.
47 He reiterated his views in the spring issue of *British Editor*.
48 MoD Archives, DN/5201/6/DPBC.
49 GP Samuel (1945–), DTI/Dept of Transport 1975–92, MoD 1992–7, Director Corporate Communications P&O 1998–2005.
50 By 2004 this was still true; nevertheless, the Secretary dealt almost invariably, initially at least, with the specialist or even sometimes novice journalist working on a story, on the basis that by the time it became an editor-level matter (as occasionally it did), the ditch had been dug and the testosterone level raised, and it was somewhat harder to negotiate a solution reflecting both sides of the public interest.
51 MoD Archives, DN/5201/6.
52 MoD Archives, D/DPBAC/1/2/1.
53 The general pattern of media consultation has remained more or less constant through to the early years of the 21st century, so most 'routine' cases are not further recorded individually in this History; nor are most of the occasions on which the Secretary has declined official requests to intervene, because he has not considered that national security is likely to be damaged; nor are most of the routine reports of briefings of incoming editors and officials, lectures, seminars, conferences, etc, undertaken by the Secretary in order to spread understanding of the D-Notice System; similarly only a handful of the books vetted are mentioned individually, fuller details being found in MoD Archives, B/2/3/DPBAC series.
54 Letter Stuart/Wilkinson, 21 September 2007.
55 MoD Archives, DN/5201/6/DPBC.
56 Three days previously, under the Open Government Document initiative, the Security Service information booklet had been published, including photographs of Rimington.
57 MoD Archives, DN/1801/DPBC; Hansard 23 July 1993, Col 454.
58 See Appendix 5.
59 Stewart Purvis remained not entirely comfortable with the System; he felt in 1993 his input had achieved little, but now sees it did lead to the significantly greater openness currently achieved in operation and information (the post-1999 website being the 'single most important' factor); discussion Purvis/Wilkinson 20 July 2007.
60 'A sleeper penetrates British intelligence', 27 May 1993.
61 These included Britain and the IRA, Israel and the PLO, Spain and ETA, and 'America and Islamic fundamentalism', a reminder that modern history did not start in 2001.
62 MoD Archives, DN/1300/DPBC.
63 'Sssh! MI5 Chief just sold home: Stella blunder', 18 August 1993.
64 MoD Archives, B/3/5/DPBAC.
65 Not mentioned was the creation of the scrutinising Intelligence and Security Committee in August 1993; being a Political committee, it has had no direct impact on the DPBAC, although the D-Notice Secretary did brief it about the System in 2004, when it was reviewing the relationship between the secret Agencies and the Media.
66 M Howard (1941–), Conservative MP 1983–, Home Secretary 1993–7, Leader of Opposition 2003–5. MoD Archives, B/3/6/DPBAC.
67 MoD Archives, DN/5302/DPBC.
68 *Daily Telegraph*, 1 November 1993. There was nothing sensitive in the book, although Pincher many years later laughingly conceded to Wilkinson that some of his best scoops had derived from indiscretions by his political and official fishing/shooting companions.
69 MoD Archives, B/2/3/6/DPBAC.
70 MoD Archives, B/3/6/DPBAC.
71 MoD Archives, B/3/6/DPBAC.
72 Later Sir John Scarlett, KCMG, OBE (1948–), Moscow 1976–7 and 1991–4, Director Security and Public Affairs SIS 1999–2001, Chmn JIC and Head I&S Cabinet Office 2001–4, Head SIS 2004–).
73 MoD Archives, B/3/6/DPBAC and D/DPBAC/3/2/2).
74 Later Sir David Spedding, KCMG, CVO, OBE (1943–2001), Head SIS 1994–9).

75 Experience shows this was a vain hope; the only marking not normally abused is 'Top Secret', which, quite apart from there not being many topics meriting it, involves especially tedious clerical handling; it is this which has the most effective deterrent effect – except possibly on the SIS.

76 Strangely, this massive list, which included all 158 HM Prisons (detailed maps allegedly available at a reasonable price from former inmates), did not until 1993 include the large Anglo-US Menwith Hill listening post, even though its security measures had been challenged many times in the courts – this omission turned out to be pure bureaucratic mix-up, the assets of GCHQ not having been listed by the Department responsible for the site (MoD) as it was not the parent Department (FCO) of GCHQ! For similar reasons, nor was the SIS training establishment included.

77 MoD Archives, D/DPBAC/3/2/2.

78 Sir Timothy Daunt, KCMG (1935–), Army 1954–6, Ambassador to Turkey 1986–92, DUS(D) FCO 1992–5, Lieut-Governor Isle of Man 1995–2000.

79 Hansard, 20 April 1994, Col 542.

80 MoD Archives, B/3/6/3/DPBAC.

81 Since that time, organisation of commercial radio having stabilised/concentrated, proliferation of stations has not in fact caused the Secretary undue problems.

82 MoD Archives, B/3/6/DPBAC.

83 D-Notice Secretaries have since believed themselves to be more familiar with nooks and crannies of the national/international 'secret' information diaspora, thanks to the internet.

84 MoD Archives, B/1/1/DPBAC.

85 MoD Archives, B/1/1/DPBAC.

86 Later Sir Stephen Lander, KCB (1947–), DGSS 1996–2002, Chairman Serious Organised Crime Agency 2004–.

87 But a Muslim name did once attract attention to a junior Security Service member; the editor of the *Harrow Observer* accepted advice not to run the story. MoD Archives, B/3/6/DPBAC.

88 Sir John Masterman, OBE (1891–1977), represented England at tennis and hockey, interned in Germany 1914–18, Intelligence Corps 1940, 'specially employed' 1941–5, Provost Worcester College Oxford 1946–61.

89 MoD Archives, B/2/3/12/DPBAC.

90 Later Sir Richard Mottram, KCB (1946–), PUS Office of Public Service and Science 1992–5, PUS MoD 1995–8, PUS DETR/DTLR 1998–2002, PUS Dept for Work and Pensions 2002–6, I&S Co-ordinator Cabinet Office 2006–7.

91 MoD Archives, D/DPBAC/3/2/1.

92 For example, *Daily Express*, 29 May 1995.

93 MoD Archives, B/1/1/DPBAC.

94 For example, *Mail on Sunday*, 25 June 1995, 'Anne's husband wanted protest rig stormed'.

95 His first, *'Bravo Two Zero'*, had been dealt with by MoD as a book by an insider in October 1993; MoD had misgivings about a trend being started, but had accepted that, after agreed deletions, there was not enough damaging material to sustain litigation.

96 MoD Archives, B/2/3/20/DPBAC; and *Guardian* 10 November 1995.

97 'SAS knives out for film debunking Gulf heroes', 7 January 1996; the journalist had followed Pulvertaft's advice about non-identification of those not already in the public domain.

98 MoD Archives, B/2/2/DPBAC.

99 MoD Archives, B/3/6/DPBAC.

100 MoD Archives, D/DPBAC/4/3/1.

101 MoD Archives, B/2/2/DPBAC.

102 Later Lord Wilson, GCB (1942–), PUS DoE 1992-, PUS Home Office 1994–7, Cabinet Secretary 1998–2002, Master Emmanuel College 2002–.

103 MoD Archives, D/DPBAC/3/2/1. Pulvertaft's initiative on archiving had been sparked by a University of California student, who in his doctoral dissertation research had found to his (and the Secretary's) surprise there were then no relevant DPBC papers at Kew; the 'Registered' files are now indeed in the National Archives, mostly in the DEFE 53 series. The spirit of the Media side guidance above has been liberally interpreted in writing this History, so that much

media/Secretary interaction is referred to, albeit with a degree of confidentiality on detail, the greater degree the more recent the event. Many more files are now (2008) overdue for release to TNA; it is mainly manpower constraints which make this a slow process. MoD Archives D/DPBAC/5/2/2/1.

104 MoD Archives B/2/3/4/DPBAC.

105 MoD Archives B/1/1/DPBAC.

106 This initiative had first been made public by the *Daily Express* on 20 November 1994, 'SAS plan to gag ex-soldiers', following the success of 'Andy McNab' and others.

107 MoD Archives, B/2/3/DPBAC.

108 MoD Archives, B/3/6/DPBAC.

109 MoD Archives, B/3/6/DPBAC.

110 MoD Archives, B/2/2/1/DPBAC.

111 The SSVC is an independently funded organisation providing broadcasting and audio-visual facilities and training to the Armed Forces at home and abroad; to help fund itself, it also makes some commercial productions about the Forces, profits being distributed to Services charities.

112 MoD Archives, B/2/2/DPBAC.

113 MoD Archives, 2nd PUS/10/5/1.

114 MoD Archives, B/3/6/DPBAC.

115 'RAF Sell Filing Cabinet Full of IRA Bomb Plans', *Sun* 11 March 1996. MoD Archives, B/1/1/DPBAC.

116 General Sir Michael Rose, KCB, CBE, DSO, QGM (1940–), CO 22 SAS 1979–82, Director Special Forces 1988–9, Adjutant General 1995–7.

117 MoD Archives, B/2/3/DPBAC.

118 MoD Archives, B/3/6/DPBAC; *Sunday Times*, 17 November 1996, 'MI6 seizes agent's book in new Spycatcher row'.

119 Later Sir Ronald Flanagan, GBE (1949–), Deputy Chief Constable RUC 1995–6, Chief Constable 1996–2002, HM Inspector of Constabulary 2002–5, Chief Inspector 2005–.

120 'RUC Fears Crisis if Book Comes Out; Government considers banning revelations', 30 June 1996.

121 For example, Liam Clarke in *Sunday Times* of 4 August 1996.

122 MoD Archives, B/2/3/31.

123 MoD Archives, 2nd PUS/10/5/1.

124 MoD Archives, B/1/1/DPBAC.

125 MoD Archives, B/2/3/36/DPBAC.

126 MoD Archives, D/DPBAC/3/2/2 and B/2/3/18/DPBAC.

127 MoD Archives, B/3/6/DPBAC.

128 Later Professor RG Tait, CBE (1947–), Editor-in-Chief ITN 1995–2002, International Board IPI 1998–, Director Centre for Journalism Studies Cardiff University 2003–.

129 MoD Archives, B/3/6/DPBAC.

130 eg *Independent* and *Guardian* 14 and 15 August 1996 respectively.

131 MoD Archives, D/DPBAC/2/2/1.

132 Names of SAS personnel given gallantry awards after the 1987 Loughgall ambush had been worked out and published by the IRA, based on the official announcement of non-attributed awards in the *London Gazette*.

133 MoD Archives, B/3/6/DPBAC.

134 MoD Archives, B/3/6/DPBAC.

135 MoD Archives, D/DPBAC/2/2/1.

136 General Sir Peter de la Billiere, KCB, KBE, DSO, MC* (1934–), CO 22 SAS 1972–4, Director SAS 1978–83, Commander British Forces Middle East for Op TELIC 1990–1.

137 Hon DRC Lawson (1956–), deputy editor then editor *Spectator* 1987–95, editor *Sunday Telegraph* 1995–2005.

138 MoD Archives, B/3/6/DPBAC.

139 MoD Archives, B/1/1/DPBC.

140 MoD Archives, D/DPBAC/3/2/1; the Secretary had also reissued the DA-Notices in July 1996, as Open Government Document No.93/06.

141 MoD Archives, B/2/3/38/DPBAC.
142 MoD Archives, B/3/6/DPBAC.
143 MoD Archives, B/2/1/3/DPBAC.
144 MoD Archives, B/2/3/DPBAC.
145 MoD Archives, D/DPBAC/2/1/3; and *Sunday Times* 9 February 1997.
146 MoD Archives, B/3/6/4/DPBAC.
147 MoD Archives, D/DPBAC/3/1/3.
148 BBC Written Archive B651–008.
149 Former Vice-Chairman Alastair Stuart/Wilkinson, 21 September 2007.

APPENDIX 3

1 TNA:PRO DEFE 53/8–11, BBC Written Archive R34/272/1 and D211–4. Very few Notices/ Letters went to the whole distribution list, book publishers receiving very little, and London suburban and provincial newspapers also often omitted. Many Notices and some Letters also in BLPES WIGG/2/11. Not all dates are clear.

BIBLIOGRAPHY

Excludes books perused formally by D-Notice Secretary or by officials (those are listed in the Index).

Includes:
'The Debate on Wartime Censorship in Britain 1902–14' by P Towle, in 'War and Society' Vol I, ed Bond and Roy, Croom Helm, 1975.
'Blue Pencil Admiral' by George Thomson, Samson Low Marston, 1946.
'The D-Notice Affair' by Hedley and Aynsley, Michael Joseph,1967.
'Lord Riddell's War Diary, 1914–18', by Lord Riddell, Nicholson & Watson, 1933.
'The Riddell Diaries, 1908–23', ed McEwen, Athlone, 1986.
'Adventure' by J Seely, 1930.
'George Wigg' by Lord Wigg, Michael Joseph, 1972.
'Inside Number 10' by Marcia Williams, Weidenfeld and Nicolson, 1972.
'I've Lived Through It All' by Emmanuel Shinwell, Gollancz, 1973.
'The Labour Government 1964–70: A Personal Record' by Harold Wilson, Penguin, 1974.
'Diaries of a Cabinet Minister', Vol II, by Richard Crossman, Hamilton and Cape, 1976.
'The Castle Diaries, 1964–70' by Barbara Castle, Weidenfeld and Nicolson, 1984.
'The Time of my Life' by Denis Healey, Michael Joseph, 1989.
'The Downing Street Years' by Margaret Thatcher, Harper Collins, 1993.
'March of Journalism' by Harold Herd, Allen and Unwin, 1952.
'Northcliffe' by Pound and Harmsworth, Cassell, 1959.
'Reporter Anonymous' by George Scott, Hutchinson, 1968.
'The First Casualty' by Phillip Knightley, Andre Deutsch, 1975.
'Newspaper History from the 17th Century to the Present Day', Boyle, Curran and Wingate, Constable, 1978.
'Good Times, Bad Times' by Harold Evans, Weidenfeld and Nicolson, 1983.
'The Rise and Fall of Fleet Street' by Charles Wintour, Hutchinson, 1989.
'The Power of News: the History of Reuters', Donald Read, OUP, 1992.
'Encyclopaedia of the British Press', ed Dennis Griffiths, Macmillan, 1992.
'Understanding Journalism: a Guide to Issues', J Wilson, Routledge, 1996.
'The Rise and fall of Government Telegraphy in Britain', CR Perry, Business and Economic History, Vol 26, 1997.
'Victorian Internet' by Tom Standage, Weidenfeld and Nicolson, 1999.
'Living on a Deadline' by Chris Moncrieff, Virgin, 2001.
'Press Gang' by Roy Greenslade, Pan, 2003.
'Power without Responsibility' by Curran and Seaton, Routledge, 6th edition, 2003.
'Newspapers in Victorian Britain' by Mark Hampton, History Compass, Blackwell, 2004.
'My Trade: a Short history of British Journalism' by Andrew Marr, Macmillan, 2004.
'A Social History of the Media' by Briggs and Burke, Polity, 2nd edition, 2005.

'A History of the NPA' by Dennis Griffiths, NPA, 2006.

'Queer People' by Basil Thomson, Hodder and Stoughton, 1922.

'The Espionage Establishment' by Wise and Ross, Random House, 1967.

'The Game of Foxes' by Ladislas Farago, Hodder and Stoughton, 1972.

'Most Secret War' by RV Jones, Wordsworth, 1978.

'Inside Story' by Chapman Pincher, Sidgwick and Jackson, 1978.

'Conflict and Security in Europe', ed Emsley, OUP, 1979.

'Their Trade is Treachery' by Chapman Pincher, Sidgwick and Jackson, 1981.

'Secret Service' by Christopher Andrew, Sceptre, 1985.

'Official Secrets' by David Hooper, Secker and Warburg, 1987.

'Tales of Empire' by Derek Hopwood, Tauris, 1989.

'The Great Game' by Peter Hopkirk, Murray, 1990.

'Secrecy and Power in the British State' by Ann Rogers, Pluto, 1997.

'The Culture of Secrecy' by David Vincent, OUP, 1998.

'MI6' by Stephen Dorril, Fourth Estate, 2000.

'Fenian Fire' by Christy Campbell, Harper Collins, 2002.

'The Secret State' by Peter Hennessy, Allen Lane/Penguin, 2002.

'MI5 and Ireland, 1939–45, The Official History' by Eunan O'Halpin, Irish Academic Press, 2003.

The Pursuit of Victory' by Roger Knight, Penguin, 2005.

'The Guy Liddell Diaries', ed Nigel West, Frank Cass, 2005.

'Cabinets and the Bomb', by Peter Hennessy, British Academy, 2007.

And to balance the strongly pro-self-regulation views of the author of this History, two less pro-D-Notice System books (unfortunately written without full access to archives):

'The History of the D-Notice Committee' by Alasdair Palmer, in 'The Missing Dimension', ed Andrew and Dilks, Macmillan 1984.

'National Security and the D-Notice System' by Pauline Sadler, Ashgate 2001.

INDEX

Introduction

i) Subheading references to Chairman, Notices, Committee, Secretary and System refer to D-Notice Committee and related aspects.

ii) Subdivisions of D-Notice Committee heading cover a) Principle Officers, b) History of Committee, and c) System. All subheadings in index are in chronological order

iii) Officers are given their final rank.